Leach Library
276 Mammoth Road
Londonderry, NH 03053
Adult Services 432-1132
Children's Services 432-1127

GAYLORD

THE COLUMBIA HISTORY OF
AMERICAN TELEVISION

Columbia Histories of Modern American Life

COLUMBIA HISTORIES OF MODERN AMERICAN LIFE

The books in this new series are concise interpretive histories focusing on major aspects of the American experience since World War II. Written by leading historians, the books draw on recent scholarship to create a lively and interesting account of the subject at hand. The books are written accessibly with a general reader/student audience in mind. Each volume includes an excellent bibliography and a detailed index.

Religion in America Since 1945: A History, Patrick Allitt
More Than Just a Game: Sports in America Since World War II, Kathryn Jay

THE COLUMBIA HISTORY OF
AMERICAN
TELEVISION

Gary R. Edgerton

COLUMBIA UNIVERSITY PRESS NEW YORK

09 april 13
B+T
24.50 (2450)

Columbia University Press
Publishers Since 1893
New York   Chichester, West Sussex

Library of Congress Cataloging-in-Publication Data
Edgerton, Gary R. (Gary Richard), 1952–
The Columbia history of American television / Gary R. Edgerton.
    p.   cm. — (Columbia histories of modern American life)
Includes bibliographical references and index.
ISBN 978-0-231-12164-4 (cloth : alk. paper)
1. Television broadcasting—United States—History. 2. Television broadcasting—Social
aspects—United States. I. Title. II. Series.
PN1992.3.U5E34 2007
791.450973—dc22

2007012701

Columbia University Press books are printed on permanent and durable acid-free paper.
Printed in the United States of America
c 10 9 8 7 6 5 4 3 2 1

CONTENTS

ACKNOWLEDGMENTS

Researching and writing a history of American television has been an all-consuming activity for me. Despite the enjoyment I have derived from the experience, it has sometimes been a daunting project as well, given the topic's enormous size and scope. Early on I adopted as my own personal mantra the old children's joke—how do you eat an elephant?—and just kept on chewing away, one bite at a time. For readers interested in an overview reference to this vast subject area, a number of serviceable timelines already exist. For example, Erik Barnouw's *Tube of Plenty: The Evolution of American Television*, 2nd Revised Edition (New York: Oxford University Press, 1990), pp. 549–560, includes an extremely concise chronology, as does David E. Fisher and Marshall Jon Fisher, *Tube: The Invention of Television* (San Diego: Harvest, 1996), pp. 357–366. In contrast, Robert Hilliard and Michael Keith's *The Broadcast Century and Beyond: A Biography of American Television* (Oxford: Butterworth-Heinemann, 1992) is basically a 340-page chronology of radio, TV, and the newer web-related electronic media.

One of the genuine pleasures of preparing this *Columbia History of American Television* was meeting for the first time or reconnecting with a wide assortment of professional colleagues and friends. Literally dozens of individuals were invaluable to me at all stages of producing this book. James Warren at Columbia University Press (CUP) was instrumental in getting this whole project off the ground. Later, Juree Sondker became my primary editorial contact, and she and her colleagues at CUP were most helpful in shepherding this volume to completion. A particularly heartfelt thank you goes to the very talented handful of scholars who contributed cameo chapters to the *Columbia History of American Television*. It was a delight to once again collaborate with Kathryn Fuller-Seeley of Georgia State University, Mary Ann Watson of Eastern Michigan University, and my former colleague at Old Dominion University, Timothy Havens, who is now at the University of Iowa. I also enjoyed my initial working experience with Jimmie Reeves of Texas Tech University and Michael Epstein of Southwestern Law School in Los Angeles. All five of these authors added an indispensable dimension to the book from their own special perspectives and areas of expertise that simply wouldn't have been part of this history without them.

Many other people helped me in both researching the *Columbia History of American Television* and securing the wide array of accompanying images that are included inside this volume. Overall, I want to acknowledge the generous assistance of Bernard Finn, Charles McGovern, and Elliot Sivowitch at the National Museum of American History, Smithsonian Institution Archives in Washington, D.C.; Karen Fishman and Michael Henry of the Library of American Broadcasting at the University of Maryland, College Park; Alexander Magoun, executive director of the David Sarnoff Library in Princeton, New Jersey; Colleen Cooney of the John Fitzgerald Kennedy Library in Boston, Massachusetts; Kathy Struss of the Dwight D. Eisenhower Library in Abilene, Kansas; Dorinda Hartmann of the Wisconsin Center for Film and Television Research at the Wisconsin Historical Society in Madison; Susanne Belovari of the Murrow Center in the Fletcher School of Law and Diplomacy at Tufts University in Medford, Massachusetts; Ron Simon of the Museum of Television and Radio in New York; Robert Spindler, university archivist, and Marilyn Wurzburger, special collections librarian of the Department of Archives and Special Collections at Arizona State University Libraries in Tempe, Arizona; Camille Ruggiero of Landov (an image rights management agency) in New York; and John Rockwell of the Norman Rockwell Family Agency in Antrim, New Hampshire.

Thanks, too, to the many helpful colleagues and friends who have aided me over the years in either researching or thinking through much of the material covered in *Columbia History of American Television*, including Carolyn Anderson, Erik Barnouw, Larry Bonko, Ray Browne, Gary Burns, Glen Creeber, Chris Geist, Donald Godfrey, Douglas Gomery, Bill Hart, Fran Hassencahl, Kathy Merlock Jackson, Jeff Jones, Bill Jones, Terry Lindvall, Michael Marsden, Michael Murray, Jack Nachbar, Kyle Nicholas, Marty Norden, George Plasketes, Peter Rollins, Brian Rose, Maury Shelby, Chris Sterling, and Rick Vincent, among many others too numerous to list but whose conversations with me were all greatly appreciated and essential in shaping my own developing ideas concerning the history of American television. I acknowledge the support of Dean Chandra de Silva and Provost Tom Isenhour at Old Dominion University for enabling me to take a sabbatical leave during which I wrote most of this manuscript. All of my colleagues in the Communication and Theatre Arts Department at Old Dominion University have helped me immeasurably during the time when I was working on this book, and I thank them for their friendship and support.

My deepest gratitude goes to my family for their seemingly boundless reservoirs of love and understanding. Nan, Katherine, and Mary Ellen's many enthusiasms and insights are a source of continuing inspiration, expanding my horizons in countless ways each and every day. This book is dedicated to them with all my love.

INTRODUCTION

Anyone who does not watch television cannot possibly understand main-stream American culture.
CARYN JAMES, *New York Times*, 2000[1]

The idea of television existed long before its realization as a technology. The dream of transmitting images and sounds over great distances ac-tually dates back to the nineteenth century, becoming an increasingly common aspiration of scientists and inventors in the United States and Europe after the first telegraph line opened up the modern communi-cation era in 1844. Just over a century and a half ago, mediated infor-mation and imagery moved only as far and as fast as men and women could carry them. Today, in contrast, we see the new digital language of instantaneous communication everywhere, mostly as a result of our televisions and computers, which together number almost one billion units in North America alone. Many social theorists have written about how Americans and members of other Western societies have radically transformed themselves and their cultures since World War II. They describe these various changes and the resulting new era by a number of fashionable terms, such as "postindustrial," "postmodern," and "the information age." Whatever we choose to call this period, America has profoundly changed since 1946, redefining the way people conduct their home life, work, and leisure time; participate as citizens and con-sumers; and understand the image-saturated world that envelops us all—largely as a result of the unprecedented reach and influence of television.

No technology before TV ever integrated faster into American life. Television took only ten years to reach a penetration of thirty-five mil-lion households, while the telephone required eighty years, the auto-mobile took fifty, and even radio needed twenty-five. By 1983, moreover, the representative U.S. household was then keeping the TV set turned on for more than seven hours a day on average; two decades later, this mean was up to eight hours a day and counting. Despite the "couch potato" stereotype, virtually all Americans from every walk of life watch lots of television. There are slight variations depending on age, sex, race, socioeconomic background, and educational level, but, by and large, the typical person in the United States watches approximately four hours of TV each and every day. For the first generation that grew up on television, the characteristic baby boomer will spend nine full years in front of a TV set by the time he or she turns sixty-five. The comparable numbers for his or her children—whether they be Gen Xers or Millennials—are already destined to be higher, and these basic figures don't even include the hours that they will be consuming other old and new media as well. The central paradox of the past sixty years is that the flow of television images and sounds has been torrential, while our historical-critical understanding of TV as a technology, an industry, an art form, and an institutional force has largely been a peripheral concern for most people.

The earliest exception to this longstanding tendency was Erik Barnouw's groundbreaking and highly influential three-volume history of broadcasting in the United States—*A Tower of Babel* (1966), *The Golden Web* (1968), and *The Image Empire* (1970).[2] The seminal impact of this trilogy cannot be underestimated. In a 1991 special issue of *Film and History* devoted to "The Future of Media Historical Research," Christopher H. Sterling wrote a heartfelt personal appreciation of Barnouw's pioneering work:

> It's now been a quarter of a century—almost to the day—since I walked into the old University Co-op bookstore near the University of Wisconsin in Madison, to find a book called *A Tower of Babel*, about the rise of American radio to 1933. I shelled out $8.50 for a copy in days when I could rarely afford a book at its retail price (I was just in my first year of graduate work), took it home and devoured every word in two or three days, hungrily reviewing its bibliography of riches I barely knew about. I was especially excited to see that a serious author and a university press were issuing a scholarly series (two more volumes were promised) about a topic I found exciting—but figured few other people cared about. Maybe this *was* [emphasis in text] a legitimate field of study after all![3]

Barnouw's trilogy was clearly something of an anomaly at the time. A handful of American radio histories did exist,[4] although none was as broadly conceived or as well researched and readable as *A Tower of Babel* and its two successive companion volumes. Barnouw was also familiar with the first two installments of Asa Briggs's monumental chronicle of radio and television in Britain, coming as these books did from his own publisher, Oxford University Press.[5] Still, he actually found more numerous and seasoned models for planning his general history of broadcasting by reviewing the existing film and journalism literature.[6] Even then, the sheer quantity and quality of historical research that existed about movies and newspapers far outstripped anything on radio and television in comparison. To fill a gaping hole in the literature, Barnouw condensed the material on television from his trilogy into the first edition of *Tube of Plenty* in 1975 (later revising this one-volume history of TV in 1982 and again in 1990).[7] Furthermore, in contrast to Barnouw's work, Sterling's aforementioned reference to broadcasting as a "field of study" alluded to a nascent discipline that at the outset was heavily social scientific, mostly producing public opinion surveys, experimental studies on media effects, and quantitative content analyses. This is the scholarly context into which Chris Sterling and John Kittross published their first edition of *Stay Tuned: A Concise History of American Broadcasting* in 1978.

Many of us who were young graduate students at the time welcomed *Stay Tuned* with nearly the same level of enthusiasm that Sterling greeted *A Tower of Babel* more than a dozen years before. Barnouw, too, was our first point of reference, but *Stay Tuned* was even more meticulous and comprehensive in telling the interrelated stories of radio and television as industries and institutions, sketching out the broad parameters of "what happened" with unmatched depth and skill. Barnouw employed a multidimensional approach to the material in his wide-ranging three-volume narrative. Sterling and Kittross learned from Barnouw's model and even expanded on his holistic design, as the historiographic choices that they made in the original edition of *Stay Tuned*—and have continued in their two subsequent revisions and updates (1990, 2002)—reflect more the dominant social scientific perspective of the broadcasting field over the last two generations, a time when this subject became an increasingly "legitimate" discipline.[8] The late Erik Barnouw was indeed a pioneer on many fronts. His memoir describes the dizzying array of positions that he held in his long and varied career—actor, stage manager, lyricist, translator, journalist, broadcast writer, director, and producer—before becoming a university professor, curator, archivist, and the preeminent historian of broadcasting with the publication of his trilogy.[9] He created the benchmark that Sterling and Kittross were to build on in researching and writing *Stay Tuned*.

Where Barnouw's historical narrative was always informed first and foremost by his personal experiences of having worked in the broadcasting and advertising industries, Sterling and Kittross were far more scholarly in the way that they self-consciously crafted a historiographic approach that is probably best described as developmental and empiricist in outlook. By adopting a developmental view of radio and television history, Sterling and Kittross perfectly exemplify a second wave of historical consciousness, mapping out this newly emerging field of broadcasting (and later television studies). Their principal goal in writing, revising, and updating *Stay Tuned* for a second time remained to thoroughly delineate in one manageable volume the specific contours and traditions of this young discipline for their academic peers and students. "In order to affect the future wisely," wrote the authors toward the end of the first chapter of the third edition, "we *must* [emphasis in text] become aware of past principles, trends, decisions, and events."[10] In this way, developmental history on any topic always attempts the dual functions of informing and socializing those who are drawn to a particular field of study. This practical dimension of *Stay Tuned* also infuses this history of radio and television with a much clearer purpose, thus dovetailing nicely with the more vocational disposition of the broadcasting discipline when the book was first published.

In practice, a developmental perspective is frequently combined with one or more other outlooks in constructing a more fully realized historiographic approach. In the case of *Stay Tuned*, Sterling and Kittross reflect their social scientific roots by designing and executing a classic example of an empiricist history of broadcasting. Job one for historians from an empiricist standpoint is to exhaustively assemble the "facts" of history into identifiable patterns that largely reflect the field's (and their own) commonsense view of the subject. In managing this research agenda, Sterling and Kittross are always striving—as much as possible—for a posture of impartiality and neutrality. "We try to provide data that may help you [make decisions]," disclosed the authors in their preface, "but we are not egotistical enough to act as 'the' judge. Although both of us are trivia buffs, we also are well aware that trivia of person, time, place, and gadget is much less important than are trends."[11] As a result, Sterling and Kittross became researchers par excellence in *Stay Tuned*, collecting and arranging together in one volume a reasonable facsimile of what is currently known and accepted as the standard version of American broadcasting history. This single volume has understandably grown in size by more than 85 percent over its three editions (from 562 to 705 to 975 pages), reflecting a comparable expanse in the supporting literature on the subject.

Stay Tuned is a tour de force of developmental and empiricist history, remaining an invaluable benchmark to check on any one of the myriad of specifics that are now understood to be part of the history of radio and television in the United States. No better single source presently exists, even as the next generation of electronic media historians is already rethinking and rewriting the established approach and agenda of television history (and its close relationship to radio and now the Internet) as best exemplified by the third edition of *Stay Tuned*. In being empiricists, therefore, Sterling and Kittross occupy one end of the historiographic continuum, while a younger generation of critical and postmodernist historians of electronic media have started to rein-terpret this subject area from a much different set of assumptions. Where empiricists strive for a certain degree of objectivity, postmod-ernists are decidedly subjective in their theoretical outlooks. Empiri-cists perceive facts as being outside themselves to be gathered and categorized; postmodernists regard all facts as reflecting the relative position of the historian-critic. Empiricists value comprehensiveness, reliability, and validity in their work; postmodernists assume partiality, uniqueness, and contingency. The social science perspective no longer monopolizes the field of broadcasting and its descendant—television studies—as it did a generation ago.

Instead, more humanities-based approaches to TV have resulted in a marked upswing of scholarly work in history, theory, criticism, styles and genres, authorship, political economy, institutional structures, and other cultural matters, such as gender, race, ethnicity, nationality, and class. Besides *Stay Tuned*, a handful of other general histories of broad-casting, radio, and television have been published so far.[12] In *Only Connect: A Cultural History of Broadcasting in the United States*, for in-stance, Michele Hilmes admits her "great debt" to Sterling and Kit-tross in her preface, noting that *Stay Tuned* "has provided a basic reference point and remains one of the most comprehensive sources for U.S. broadcasting history." *Only Connect* is neither developmental nor empiricist, though, displaying an approach to the subject that the author describes as "interventionist history, seeking to generate ques-tions as much as provide answers." Unlike Sterling and Kittross, her goal was less to document and describe the evolution of an institution, an industry, and a profession. Rather, her stated intention was to "de-flect or diminish the effects of certain counterprogressive events that would set back the cause of diversity and democracy."[13] Hilmes wrote *Only Connect* from a politically engaged perspective, where history is best understood as an instrument of social change rather than merely a record of the past, no matter how thoroughly rendered.

A third wave of historical consciousness has clearly emerged among electronic media historians, flush on the heels of scores of more tar-geted historical-critical studies that have all been published since the 1978 debut of *Stay Tuned*. Selected examples include aesthetic, bio-graphical, cultural, industrial, intellectual, international, political, so-cial, and technological histories of television[14] (mostly without radio these days), as well as literally hundreds of like-minded books and articles that comprise an ever-expanding scholarly literature. As Michele Hilmes asks in chapter 1 of *Only Connect*, "Where can we possibly begin such a history? How could we draw lines around it sufficient to contain it within the covers of a single book? In short, we can't. And part of the intellectual heritage of 20th-century postmodernism is acknowledgment of this fact."[15] Within that now widely held spirit, *Only Connect* is the first textbook survey of broadcasting to emerge from the second generation of scholars who were formally educated in electronic media studies. Given the continuing maturation of the field, more histories of television (addressing its close relationship to the Internet as well as radio) are bound to follow from a variety of perspectives and written for very different kinds of audiences.

The *Columbia History of American Television*, in particular, was the brainchild of a former executive editor at Columbia University Press, James Warren. His idea was to commission a concise one-volume narrative history of TV in the United States that was designed for the literate generalist. The assumption we shared was that television is the main preoccupation of most Americans, and therefore the reader we most wanted to reach is the nonspecialist. Nevertheless, the intention was always to write a historical narrative that is fully informed by the scholarly record and, at the same time, to keep this inherently dramatic story of television appealing and accessible to a broader educated readership. In that way, my approach to the *Columbia History of American Television* as it developed was to construct a narrative that is interpretive rather than exhaustive. My intention was never to write a history as all-inclusive and detailed as *Stay Tuned* or a textbook survey like *Only Connect*. Probably the closest models that came immediately to mind are Erik Barnouw's *Tube of Plenty*, Susan Douglas's *Listening In* (on radio), and Robert Sklar's *Movie-Made America*.[16] The great value of these narrative histories is the fact that they are resolutely holistic, skillfully integrating a number of historiographic approaches, primarily biographical, technological, economic, social-political, and cultural.

Similarly, my approach is above all holistic, preferring to make connections and chart continuities, rather than list each important innovator and document every first occurrence (although this volume certainly is filled with enough seminal events and figures to render a thorough history of television). *Tube of Plenty*, *Listening In*, and *Movie-Made America* have long served general educated readers as well as students and scholars by highlighting select examples to illustrate significant developments and trends. Like these books, the *Columbia History of American Television* is intended to be a history of its subject, but not the one and only definitive history. Moreover, this historical narrative is organized chronologically with the intention of interweaving fundamental cultural concerns, such as changing tastes, values, and lifestyle issues, while always stressing their many interrelations rather than exploring each one of these agenda items in relative isolation. The glue that holds this large cultural agenda together is narrative, as I adhere to a story line that relays how TV ultimately evolves into a convergent technology, a global industry, a viable art form, a social catalyst, and a complex and dynamic reflection of the American mind and character.

In addition, the *Columbia History of American Television* is admittedly partial and selective. Given the enormous scope of this subject, I chose representative examples throughout where I was always aware of the many other events, programs, and individuals that I simply was unable to include because of space limitations. Each chapter alone could have easily served as the basis for its own book-length study. I therefore had to make choices (such as emphasizing prime-time programming more than the content in other parts of the day) with the hopeful understanding that other television scholars will eventually fill in many of the existing gaps in the historical literature. In a field this young, it almost goes without saying that much work still needs to be done.

This particular history is also being told from the point of view of television in the United States, even though international trends and developments are regularly assessed in relationship to American TV and thus make up a significant part of the narrative. Furthermore, the book follows the growth of U.S. TV from a local, to a regional, to a national, to an international, and finally to a global medium. During its international phase, American television was selective and partial in its emergence beyond its national borders. In the current era, however, it is now a global presence along with the American economy, culture, and political power. Today, American TV reaches into virtually every country on Earth.

Last, television in this book is always perceived as being part of a larger communication revolution; in many ways, it operated as the bellwether for half a century before it was forced to share this position with the ever-growing presence of the Internet after the mid 1990s. For the time being, at least, television remains the centerpiece of American culture in the first decade of the twenty-first century. Television is now adapting to the enormous power and influence of the Internet, just as radio, motion pictures, magazines, newspapers, and books likewise adjusted to the arrival of TV during the late 1940s and early 1950s, thus ushering in a complete transformation in the country's mass-mediated habits and preferences.

Commentators spent the last half of the twentieth century specu-lating about an atomic age, when the single, most important techno-logical development resulting from the efforts surrounding World War II is arguably the computer, more so than the bomb. The per-sonal computer in tandem with television—which existed in experi-mental form during the 1920s and was unveiled to the general public in two succeeding exhibits at Philadelphia's Franklin Institute in 1934 and then a half decade later at the New York World's Fair in 1939—has eclipsed our nuclear obsession with a more fundamental (though less tangible) preoccupation, especially as we move further away from the urgencies of the Cold War. A global communication revolution is cur-rently assuming far greater proportions in the twenty-first century. The *Columbia History of American Television* underscores the ascen-dancy of this revolution from the standpoint of its most instrumental catalyst so far. It chronicles TV's emergence as an idea whose time had come at the end of World War II through its eventual growth and matu-ration into the most influential social force in American civilization during the second half of the twentieth century. We routinely summon into our homes with our remote controls the most extensive rendering of a national culture ever available. This ephemeral stream of pictures and sounds also contains many clues about who we are, what we value, and where we might be headed in the future. The *Columbia History of American Television* is a one-volume starting point on which to explore these fundamental questions. Moreover, it includes dozens of addi-tional references to other historical works that I hope will encourage readers to continue thinking about the profound and transformative effect that TV has had on all of us as individuals, as well as on the life of our nation over the last seven decades.

PART I

GOING PUBLIC

AN IDEA WHOSE TIME HAD COME
Imagining Television—Before 1940

PREEMPTING THE WORLD OF TOMORROW

> Today we are on the eve of launching a new industry, based on imagina-
> tion, on scientific research, and accomplishment. We are now ready to
> fulfill the promise made to the public.
> DAVID SARNOFF, "The Birth of an Industry," 1939[1]

The coming of television involved the most extensive and ballyhooed
series of public relations events ever staged around any mass medium in American history. Throughout the 1920s and most of the
1930s, no new communication form had ever been more anticipated
in the press—then postponed time and again for a variety of legitimate technological, economic, and cultural reasons—than TV. In the
spring of 1939, David Sarnoff, the ever driven and increasingly powerful forty-eight-year-old president of the Radio Corporation of America (RCA), had arranged his share of press conferences on television,
often thinly disguised as scientific demonstrations. In the previous
year alone, RCA conducted 134 such TV exhibitions "for audiences
largely made up of important representatives of industry, advertising,
engineering, and the press."[2] His belief in the life-transforming possibilities of the medium was as genuine as his interest in its eventual
windfall earnings potential for his corporation. More than anyone
else in the United States, Sarnoff had become the public face of TV's
future promise as he relentlessly championed the nation's next great
social and consumer product innovation with near missionary zeal.
The trade papers even started calling him a "televisionary."

Through his leadership, RCA had been setting the agenda for television as an emerging technology and forthcoming commercial service
for well over a decade. Other competing parties were also contributing
mightily to this ongoing process. Some, such as inventor Philo T. Farnsworth with his groundbreaking all-electronic TV system, were even
responsible for breakthroughs that were far more fundamental and
consequential than anything ever achieved at RCA's first research laboratory in Camden, New Jersey. Still, Sarnoff's innate public relations
skills and his lifelong obsession for self-promotion were legendary,
having been honed when he was a young man making the improbable

climb out of abject poverty on the lower east side of New York. He had once been a nine-year-old Russian immigrant boy who couldn't even speak the language; now, less than four decades later, he was one of the most powerful industrialists in America. His rise to the top was truly amazing by any reasonable standard.

Way back in April 1912, for example, he exaggerated his role as the sole telegraph operator coordinating rescue efforts and tirelessly relaying word of survivors on the ill-fated ocean liner *Titanic*. As the story goes, he supposedly manned his post for seventy-two straight hours on the roof of the Marconi-owned Wanamaker's department store in midtown Manhattan. Such embellishments were evidently pivotal in advancing Sarnoff's skyrocketing career, particularly in the face of regular mistreatment by fellow employees who even referred to him derisively as "Jew boy" on occasion: "One story has it that Sarnoff's co-workers would harass him by putting every bit of extra busywork on his desk. They stopped only when they realized he was doing all of it without complaint . . . developing a better grasp of the company . . . than anyone else at Marconi, including its president."[3]

As a result, Sarnoff quickly became a personal favorite of Guglielmo Marconi, the company head and famed inventor of wireless telegraphy, who, in turn, served as an early mentor for the young man and a life-long friend. Sarnoff rapidly ascended the corporate ladder from office boy to personal assistant to Marconi, eventually becoming commercial manager for the entire American Marconi Company. When in 1919 the United States government forced British Marconi to sell its American subsidiary to General Electric (GE), fearing that too many of the world-wide rights for wireless communication were falling into the hands of a foreign-held corporation, Sarnoff was swept in on the ground floor during the initial formation of RCA.

After considering and rejecting on philosophical grounds the prospects of establishing a public monopoly, the U.S. Navy created a privately owned trust under the auspices of RCA by pooling all of the wireless patents that it had developed during World War I. At first, RCA was comprised of only GE and all of the newly acquired resources that General Electric had absorbed from American Marconi. Within months, however, three other U.S. companies—Westinghouse, the American Telephone and Telegraph Company (AT&T), and United Fruit (an early developer of ship-to-shore communication for importing produce)—joined GE in a cross-licensing arrangement that enabled the four American partners to share more than two thousand electronic patents under the corporate umbrella of RCA.

In one bold and decisive move, the U.S. government produced a home-grown private monopoly that instantly became the American leader in wireless communication. This decision also secured RCA's insider position and formidable financial standing to profoundly influence the nature and development of radio and television in America from that point onward. Thirty-year-old David Sarnoff was chosen commercial manager at RCA, the title he held earlier with the American Marconi Company. "While later described by others as the founder of both the Radio Corporation of America and the National Broadcasting Corporation [NBC, RCA's broadcasting subsidiary created in 1926], Sarnoff was neither," confirms media historian, Louise Benjamin. "These misconceptions were perpetuated because Sarnoff's later accomplishments were so plentiful that any myth was believable. Indeed, his foresight and corporate savvy led to many communication developments, especially television."[4]

By the fall of 1937, David Sarnoff was intensely pursuing a fast track to affect NBC's transition from experimental TV to launching the first commercial television system in the United States. In August, he had traveled to Europe to see for himself what the current state of the medium was. His experience in London, specifically— where the British Broadcasting Corporation (BBC) inaugurated regularly scheduled telecasting to the general public some ten months before, on November 2, 1936—convinced him that America was now as ready as England to begin the long and arduous process of bringing television into homes across the nation.

On arriving back in New York on September 25, 1937, a spirited Sarnoff disembarked from the S.S. *Paris* and approached a bevy of reporters. The first question he fielded was the one on everybody's mind: "Is England ahead of the United States in television?" His answer was that RCA was essentially at a point of technological parity with its British counterpart because of cross-licensing agreements where both corporations shared the same electronic television patents. More to the point, though, Sarnoff recognized that commercial TV in the United States ultimately required the creation of a workable distribution network, not merely the development of a technical infrastructure. "I firmly believe in the American system of private enterprise, rather than government subsidy," he continued, contrasting RCA/NBC's support structure with that of the BBC, while adding that he was also certain that "in due time we shall find practical answers to practical problems that now beset the difficult road of the pioneer in television."[5] Here Sarnoff was implying that he was TV's principal trailblazer. That was the corporate image that he had been carefully cultivating for years, and few people watching him speak on that cool Saturday afternoon doubted his steely resolve.

Within a month, David Sarnoff had organized a promotional tele-cast from studio 3H in Radio City at Rockefeller Center over NBC's experimental TV station, W2XBS, where he was to sign a contract en-suring RCA's participation in the 1939 World's Fair, although such corporate involvement was always a foregone conclusion. This inter-national exposition, dubbed "The World of Tomorrow," was the brain-child of an elite group of New York City businessmen, including the top executives at Chase Manhattan Bank, Consolidated Edison, the Manufacturers Trust Company, the New York Trust Company, and Macy's, along with Mayor Fiorella La Guardia. They initially conceived of the fair in 1935 at the height of the Depression as a daring and in-spired civic initiative that would both jump-start the local and national economies and stimulate increased investment in the future.

For his part, Sarnoff was invited to join the executive planning committee of the World's Fair in his capacity as president of the Radio Corporation of America. He was already preparing an expanded role for television at the exposition well beyond its coming-out party at the RCA exhibit. He knew that, in December 1937, NBC was about to un-veil the first mobile television station in the United States. Comprised of two large buses, this transportable TV unit would soon be available for remote telecasts—leading to similar kinds of on-the-spot report-ing once the fair opened. Sarnoff "had studied the massive impact of Alexander Graham Bell's telephonic demonstration at the opening of the Philadelphia exposition in 1876 and he was counting on igniting a similar brushfire of popular interest" with television.[6]

Sarnoff held court before an oversized RCA TV camera in studio 3H, sitting behind a large wooden desk and flanked on his right by Major Lenox R. Lohr, a military engineer who was then the newly in-stalled president of NBC, and on his left by Grover Walen, president of the World's Fair Corporation. In a telltale sign of the fair's growing importance to Sarnoff, he had originally hired Lohr in 1936 because the former army officer had successfully organized and directed the 1933–1934 Chicago Century of Progress Exposition. Only a year later, however, Sarnoff was already growing disenchanted, "confid[ing] to public relations counsel Edward L. Bernays that Lohr showed little *sa-ichel*, or shrewdness."[7]

Once again, Sarnoff took charge, occupying center stage between the two men with a map of the proposed fair in the background, as well as miniatures of the three-sided obelisk, the Trylon, and its com-panion globe, the Persiphere, before him on the desk. Turning to Walen, he asked the one-time New York City police commissioner and recent head of Roosevelt's New Recovery Administration (NRA) to comment on the models before them. The elegantly dressed and mustachioed Walen smiled broadly and explained that the actual seven-hundred-foot Trylon and the two-hundred-foot Perisphere, connected by a giant ramp called a Helicline, would serve as the focal point for the entire World's Fair. He noted that these futuristic monuments sat at the place where most visitors would enter The World of Tomorrow. Painted fully white, he added, the Trylon and the Perisphere were already becoming the most recognizable symbols of the upcoming exposition, conveying the bright and optimistic future that lay ahead for the country, as well as the power of technology to solve many current problems and improve the daily lives of most Americans. Walen ended his remarks by calling the World's Fair a blueprint for progress. The portly Sarnoff beamed approvingly at his guest, feeling that his own vision of television dovetailed perfectly with Walen's upbeat and hopeful message about The World of Tomorrow.

As was the case with all of these experimental NBC telecasts, the audience was relatively small, composed mainly of two hundred to three hundred news people and public officials, along with several dozen other NBC executives and engineers watching on company sets throughout the New York metropolitan area. NBC's studio 3H was originally designed for radio, but Sarnoff had ordered it remodeled for television back in 1935. It "was a two-story room measuring about 20-by-40 feet, with a control booth elevated on the second story level, and featuring a glass window."[8] Because of the cramped surroundings, the attending members of the press were escorted to various meeting rooms and halls inside the RCA building to comfortably view this early promotional telecast on an assortment of newly tested RCA model TVs sporting either five-inch, nine-inch, or twelve-inch screens.

The overall picture quality of RCA's electronic television system was now getting better than ever, having increased in definition from 343 to 441 lines at thirty frames per second in just the last two years alone. The reporters present were duly impressed by the technical demonstration they were witnessing, although most were highly skeptical about the prospects of commercial TV actually being made available to average Americans by the opening of the World's Fair. They had heard similar claims too many times before. Sarnoff clearly understood the legal and economic obstacles that still stood before his corporation. Nevertheless, he had given his senior staff their marching orders, and Sarnoff fully expected to be introducing television to the general public on April 30, 1939, no matter what challenges were being posed by a reluctant Federal Communications Commission (FCC) in Washington, as well as by RCA's main industrial competitors in the field.

Sarnoff and his executive team had been intently working behind the scenes for well over a year, lobbying to have their own electronic television system adopted as the industry standard. Achieving this kind of acceptance was crucial in both getting the upper hand on RCA's principal rivals—specifically, Farnsworth, Philco, DuMont, Zenith, and CBS (Columbia Broadcasting System)—and minimizing the inevitable consumer confusion that would hurt all parties involved if several incompatible systems ended up canceling each other out in the marketplace. Ultimately, too, the FCC had to formally approve the start of commercial service in America before TV advertising of any kind could officially begin.

Back in 1931, the Radio Manufacturers Association (RMA) had established its first nonbinding but generally accepted standard for television—forty-one lines at fifteen frames per second—as a way of bringing order to what was then a chaotic technical environment. Now, five years later, the RMA was urged by RCA and others to step in and once again evaluate the various existing TV systems and attempt to determine the best available format. The FCC would eventually have to review any RMA recommendation and make its own judgment. Still, the FCC tacitly welcomed the RMA's engineering expertise and counsel at this stage of the review process.

Since its creation in 1927 as the Federal Radio Commission (becoming the Federal Communications Commission with the passing of the Federal Communication Act of 1934), the FCC had always been subject to all sorts of outside pressures from special interests residing in both the public and private sectors. In the case of television, in particular, the extraordinary amounts of time and money already invested made for an unusually competitive and contentious situation. The RMA's engineering subcommittee finally recommended the standard of 441 lines at thirty frames per second, which was largely advocated by RCA and the Farnsworth Television and Radio Corporation in September 1938. These higher-resolution images proved to be "forty to fifty times as clear as those of 1931 . . . [being] equivalent to that of 16 mm. home movies."[9] The 441-line electronic TV system was indeed state of the art, and at first the FCC informally hinted that it might allow commercial TV operations to commence in the United States.

For various reasons, Philco, Zenith, CBS, and inventor Edward Howard Armstrong all protested vigorously to the regulatory agency about the RMA recommendation. Philco and Zenith accused the engineering subcommittee of being unduly influenced by and prejudicial toward RCA; CBS warned against upsetting the delicate balance of power that currently existed in network radio by arguing that NBC

would become all the more dominant if it was accorded the opportunity to begin a commercial TV system on its own terms; and Armstrong charged that the spectrum allocation that was now attached to
the proposed standard would ultimately impede his development of
FM (frequency modulation) radio across the United States.

All of the aggrieved parties had their own legitimate points to
make. The bottom line was that any agreed-upon standard would
help some companies experimenting with television and hurt others. With so little consensus and so much at stake, the FCC typically
gravitated toward a middle position. They praised the technical progress achieved so far but called for additional field testing based on
the standard just recommended by the RMA. Furthermore, the FCC
saw no need to rush into commercial TV, warning that "television is
not yet ready for public service on a national scale. . . . There does
not appear to be any immediate outlook for the recognition of television service on a commercial basis."[10] The introduction of TV into
American homes was basically put on hold because of the fierce
competition that existed in the private sector over which technical
standard to approve, coupled with the unwillingness of the FCC to
take a controversial stand. This jockeying for position stood in stark
contrast to the current conditions in England, where the BBC was
then completing its second full year of providing public service television to British citizens.

The executive staff at RCA/NBC was understandably disappointed
by the FCC's inaction. Sarnoff responded in characteristic fashion
by going on the offensive, telling the RMA at its annual meeting on
October 20, 1938, that "television in the home is now technically
feasible. . . . We believe that the problems confronting this difficult
and complicated art can be solved only by operating experience gained
from actually serving the public in their homes. Therefore, RCA pro-
poses to take a[nother] step in the solution of these problems [beyond
laboratory research and conducting experimental telecasts] by beginning a limited program service to the public."[11] In essence, "Sarnoff
was taking a risk of make-or-break proportions. Sans FCC adoption of
commercial standards, operating only with the experimental authority of a test license, which did not permit the sale of commercial time,
he was gambling that public enthusiasm would stampede the industry and the commission behind the RCA system."[12]

The reason behind Sarnoff's decision to sidestep the FCC was largely
due to the economic conundrum now facing RCA. In January of 1938,
broad estimates ranged "between $10,000,000 and $20,000,000 [on
what had already] been spent in this country on television work."[13] Sarnoff was claiming that RCA had expended $20 million all by itself, but

most impartial industry observers placed the electronic giant's costs at somewhere just below $10 million. Even with this amended figure, RCA's cumulative investment in television was staggering when seen within the context of a lackluster Depression economy. For its part, RCA was in the enviable position of being able to raid its considerable NBC radio profits to underwrite its experiments in television. None of its competitors could come close to marshaling the kinds of resources that RCA possessed in this regard. Still, Sarnoff felt impelled to force a transition into commercial television since no foreseeable end was in sight to this continuing drain on RCA/NBC's finances.

In an October 1939 issue of *Public Opinion Quarterly*, an industry analyst succinctly pinpointed an obvious solution for RCA and all of its principal business competitors who manufactured televisions:

> The problem is a circular one. The costs of sponsoring television programs are ten to fifteen times as great as radio. . . . If such entertainment is not forthcoming, sets will not be sold; if sets are not sold, business will not advertise via television; if business does not advertise, programs comparable to radio's will not be forthcoming. A way to break that circle must be found. Will it be found in a successful campaign for the sale of receivers?[14]

Sarnoff certainly thought so. In early 1939, he "declared that by the end of the year, RCA would sell a hundred thousand sets."[15] *Forbes* reported in its May 1939 issue, which coincided with the opening of the 1939 World's Fair, that "after years of research, television is about to become a commercial reality in the U.S. About $13,000,000 has already been sunk in it and a dozen manufacturers will be making receivers this year. Revenue for the manufacturers depends on volume sales, and these, in turn, depend on entertainment value."[16]

RCA/NBC had literally been preparing for this moment for years. In yet another display of managerial bravado, Sarnoff next decided to preempt the fair with another promotional telecast. A week and a half before the actual April 30th inauguration of the 1939 World's Fair, David Sarnoff officially dedicated the Radio Corporation of America exhibit. Rather than compete with the pageantry of the fair's grand opening, which would be attended by the president of the United States and literally dozens of other visiting dignitaries and celebrities, Sarnoff and public relations pioneer, Edward Bernays, astutely decided to maximize RCA's press coverage by hosting a preview event of their own, featuring only Sarnoff and the wondrous new spectacle of NBC television in action. The plan worked to perfection. "The crowning moment of the new RCA service was supposed to have come ten

RCA president David Sarnoff's televised visage at the 1939 World's Fair would survive as the defining image of the beginning of TV in America. Courtesy of The David Sarnoff Library.

days later with the telecast of President Roosevelt's opening ceremony speech," conclude David Fisher and Marshall Fisher in *Tube: The Invention of Television*, "but once again Sarnoff had grabbed the spotlight. It would not be FDR's visage but his own . . . that would survive through the decades as the defining image of the beginning of regular television broadcasting in America."[17]

RCA engineers had been field testing all of the interrelated TV technologies that would be needed for this day since first introducing its mobile television station sixteen months before. This remote production unit was basically composed of two linked buses—one serving as a working studio out on location and the other functioning as a large and powerful transmitter, relaying TV signals to an aerial antenna perched high atop the Empire State Building some eight miles away. For example, "on February 26, 1939, a test pickup from the unfinished fair grounds featured a telecast of *Amos 'n' Andy* in blackface make-up."[18] This dry run of what was basically an on-screen performance of a radio program was designed both to generate publicity and to see how well NBC could produce a television show from the World of Tomorrow. Subsequent in-house reactions were all positive to this experimental production, so preparations were set in motion for covering the formal dedication ceremony of the RCA exhibit on April 20, 1939.

NBC's second telecast from the fair actually began with a medium shot of celebrated sports announcer Graham McNamee welcoming the viewing audience as he sat comfortably behind a desk from studio 4H at Radio City in Rockefeller Center. The scene then cut to the fairground at Flushing Meadow Park in Queens, where a remote camera crew provided a long, establishing shot of the Trylon and the Perisphere to orient the estimated three hundred invited guests from the press, city government, and industry who were watching on television sets at the fair, at Radio City, and in homes throughout the metropolitan area.[19] The whole affair was being simulcast on NBC radio, where news correspondent George Hicks provided a running commentary for both the TV and radio audiences. The bulky TV camera and its accompanying operator were perched on top of a wheeled dolly, which was pushed up the Avenue of Patriots—capturing many festive sights of the fairground for viewers—before finally stopping in front of the RCA Pavilion, which was an impressively designed structure shaped like a giant radio tube.

NBC president Lohr began the official proceedings with a greeting before a makeshift podium comprised of two vintage NBC carbon microphones perched high on tripods and draped with a darkened banner emblazoned with a bright RCA insignia. Within moments, he introduced David Sarnoff, who strode confidently into the picture, pausing briefly to smile at the camera. The RCA president then launched into his formal remarks from a prepared text. Framed in a tight, medium shot, the slightly balding and compactly built Sarnoff looked every inch the industrial tycoon in his charcoal gray business suit. He spoke slowly and clearly, with only a faint hint of his foreign-born accent, eventually concluding a talk that lasted approximately ten minutes by observing that "now we add radio sight to sound. It is with a feeling of humbleness that I come to this moment of announcing the birth in this country of a new art so important in its implications that it is bound to affect all society. It is an art which shines like a torch of hope in a troubled world."[20]

Despite the booster rhetoric, Sarnoff's belief in the transformative power of television was more than realized in the years to follow. No one in the audience on that sunny afternoon could have possibly imagined that TV would soon emerge as the centerpiece of American culture—becoming a vital fixture in over 90 percent of all U.S. homes over the next generation. Most people in the spring of 1939 were more aware of television as an amazing technological novelty, if they spent any time thinking about the medium at all. There simply were far more pressing matters to consider, both at home and abroad.

The American economy remained stubbornly tepid some ten years after the great stock market crash of 1929. Appeasement had not worked with Hitler in Europe, as Germany continued to move aggressively

David Sarnoff announces "now we add radio sight to sound," as he dedicates the RCA exhibit at the 1939 World's Fair on April 20, 1939. Courtesy of The David Sarnoff Library.

against its neighbors. Italy was similarly bellicose, having just invaded Albania, and Mussolini stood on the verge of signing a military alliance with Germany. Japan, too, was well into a second year of its brutal, undeclared war on China. "The sense of gathering crisis cast an atmosphere of doom around the anticipated coming of television," remembers broadcast historian Erik Barnouw, "but [TV] went forward on schedule, and generated some of the hoped-for excitement."[21]

Coverage of the opening ceremony of the 1939 World's Fair began at 12:30 P.M. on a bright, chilly Sunday, April 30, 1939. The NBC mobile unit started the telecast by relaying what had now become the fair's obligatory establishing shot of the Trylon and Perisphere before the camera swept across the majestic reflecting pool to reveal high, vaulting fountains, flags flapping vigorously in the breeze, and crowds of milling spectators numbering in the thousands. America's first television special commenced with an hour-long parade, featuring representatives from various fair exhibits. The camera panned across scores of recognizable personalities, who were either marching or watching the festivities from the grandstands. For example, "Mayor La Guardia walked directly up to the camera as he led the procession, and New Yorkers who were watching at Radio City had no difficulty spotting him. . . . Mr. La Guardia was rated by the engineers on the mobile van as 'the most telegenic man in New York.' "[22]

The high point of the nearly three-hour program was the first ever televised appearance by a sitting president of the United States.

At 2 P.M., Mrs. Roosevelt took her place in the presidential box, dressed in a matching outfit that was discretely decorated with small Trylons and Perispheres. Approximately two minutes later, Franklin Roosevelt arrived by automobile in dramatic fashion with a police escort, causing everyone at the "Court of Peace" to rise to their feet. The U.S. Army Band played a rousing version of "The Star Spangled Banner," followed by World's Fair Corporation president Grover Whalen, approaching the microphone and ably serving as master of ceremonies for the remainder of the event.

Whalen welcomed the president to the podium, and FDR officially inaugurated the 1939 World's Fair, touching on themes of progress and world peace in his remarks. Whalen then called on a number of local officials to speak, including New York Governor Herbert Lehman and Mayor La Guardia. David Sarnoff was also asked to say a few words, as Whalen retold the fabled story of how the RCA president had "relayed wireless messages from the sinking Titanic" as a young man, before introducing him as the "father of American radio."[23] As recorded by the New York Times: "Reports from receiving outposts scattered throughout a fifty-mile radius of New York indicated that the spectacle by television was highly successful and that a new industry had been launched into the World of Tomorrow. It was estimated that from 100 to 200 receivers were in tune and that possibly 1,000 persons looked in on the pageant" to complement the projected six-hundred thousand spectators at the fair and the millions of others who listened intently to live coverage of the event by radio.[24]

Inside the RCA Pavilion, four different kinds of TV sets were on display in the "Hall of Television" exhibit. They ranged in screen size from twelve-inch to nine-inch to five-inch consoles, as well as a much smaller five-inch tabletop model. A recent nationwide survey conducted by the American Institute of Public Opinion confirmed Sarnoff's earlier projection that "a large potential customer audience await[ed] the new television industry." While acknowledging that TV was "likely to be confined to the larger metropolitan areas for some time, the institute estimated that approximately 4,000,000 families throughout the United States—or about one family in eight—consider themselves good prospects for home television sets."[25]

To stimulate sales, RCA hosted TV's "first night" of sponsored programming by the NBC network. Over the previous few years, in-house producers had been busy probing the boundaries of TV production in their experimental telecasts, adapting styles and genres from radio whenever possible. When "first night" began at 8 P.M. on that Wednesday, May 3, 1939, mistress of ceremonies Helen Lewis introduced "stars of radio, motion pictures and stage" as part of that inaugural show. Guests included "Fred Waring and his Pennsylvanians, Richard Rodgers and Marcy Wescott, composer and featured singer, respectively, of 'The Boys of Syracuse,' and Walt Disney's new creation, 'Donald's Cousin Gus.' "[26]

TV news, too, had its official debut that evening, with the widely acclaimed commentator Lowell Thomas reading the "tele-topics" of the day, much as he did most nights from 6:45 to 7 P.M. on the NBC-Blue radio network. On-the-spot interviews were also conducted outside the RCA exhibit in what was to become an enduring feature of those early telecasts. A female moderator gently prompted visitors to speak about their general impressions of the World's Fair, as each guest was given a card signed by RCA Pavilion director Joe D'Agostino, certifying that they "ha[d] been Televised at the RCA Exhibit Building, New York World's Fair."[27] This segment quickly became one of the more popular offerings on the NBC lineup.

Despite such auspicious beginnings, television sales were flat from the outset. NBC's regular scheduled programming continued on Wednesday and Friday evenings from 8 to 9 P.M., and remote telecasts originating from the fairground were shown every Wednesday, Thursday, and Friday afternoon. Still, the limited amount of available program material ran counter to the relative expense of a new television set for consumers. RCA models ranged in price from $600 for the twelve-inch console to $199.50 for the five-inch tabletop model. These costs were simply prohibitive for most Americans in 1939, when the average annual salary was $1,850:[28] "The RCA sets were offered for sale in Macy's, Bloomingdale's and Wanamaker's department stores in the New York Metropolitan area. Although shoppers were curious, television sales right up to the beginning of World War II were disappointing."[29] Only an estimated three thousand TVs were sold to the public in 1939, a far cry from the one-hundred thousand predicted by Sarnoff at the start of the year.[30]

The high hopes and excitement surrounding television at the 1939 World's Fair were eventually justified, although the long-term significance of the medium was only recognized by a few at the time. For one, Orrin E. Dunlap Jr., the *New York Times* radio columnist since 1922, concluded that "as the radio men studied the results of their day's work and many weeks of planning they put April 30, 1939, down as holding the same significance as Nov. 2, 1920, holds for broadcasting [referring to the inaugural election night newscast by KDKA in Pittsburgh], for that was when the 'radio craze' started."[31]

The RCA exhibit remained one of the most well attended sites at the World's Fair through the entire run of the exposition ending on October 27, 1940. RCA had even designed a "Television Laboratory"

inside its pavilion to promote the most significant discoveries of its world-class research team, especially head engineer Dr. Vladimir Zworykin, who was being touted as the inventor of television. To be sure, Zworykin and his colleagues had achieved important innovations over the years with their incremental improvements of the iconoscope (camera tube) and kinescope (picture tube). Nevertheless, the man most responsible for developing the first all-electronic TV system in the world was never even mentioned. Philo T. Farnsworth's name was conspicuously absent from any of the television exhibits and demonstrations at the World of Tomorrow.[32] Without a doubt, this omission of Farnsworth was intentional, reflecting the fierce competition that marked the race for television from its very beginning.

A Dream in the Making

So far I have dealt in probability. Let me now ask the reader's indulgence [with] . . . a dream of possible scientific achievement. . . . The child born to-day in New York city, when in middle age he shall visit China, may see reproduced upon a screen, with all its movement and color, light and shade, a procession at that moment passing along his own Broadway. A telephone line will bring to his ear music and the tramp of marching men. While the American pageantry passes in full glare of the morning sun its transmitted rays will scintillate upon the screen amid the darkness of the Asian night. Sight and sound will have unlimited reach through terrestrial space.

CHARLES H. SEWALL, *Harper's Weekly*, 1900[33]

Columnist Charles H. Sewall was characteristic of many Americans who imagined television long before it became a workable experimental technology in the 1920s and 1930s. Writing for *Harper's Weekly*, America's leading illustrated newspaper in the nineteenth century, Sewall published an article on December 29, 1900, titled "The Future of Long-Distance Communication," complete with companion lithographs, to illustrate his vision of TV. The first print, titled "A Procession in New York," depicted a marching band parading in front of a series of soaring brownstones with the American flag flying prominently from a windowsill high in the upper right-hand corner of the picture. The second image showed a much smaller, though luminous, representation of the original scene, emanating as if from a picture tube that was embedded in a tall, dark frame. This print was accompanied by the caption "Visible on a Screen in Peking." To a New Yorker such as Sewall, televising a live event around the world to China seemed a distinct possibility in the not too distant future after having just witnessed the arrival of one wondrous communication invention after another over the last half century. In his essay, Sewall tellingly dubbed his dream machine the "optograph," in an allusion to the telegraph, thus illustrating how the conceptual foundation of each "new technology typically emerges from modifications to and combinations of existing technology."[34]

Television was always envisioned by scientists, inventors, and lay people as a direct descendent of earlier forms of electronic communication, dating back to the opening of the nation's first telegraph line between Baltimore and Washington, D.C., on May 24, 1844, when Samuel Morse typed in his fateful question—"What hath God wrought?" Well covered by the press at the time, Morse's demonstration functioned much like the introduction of TV at the 1939 World's Fair in that his well-staged presentation of the telegraph marked the end of an initial experimental phase where the medium was now largely out of the laboratory and into the public arena for good. This event launched "the era of modern communication in America," explains historian Daniel J. Czitrom: "Before the telegraph there existed no separation between transportation and communication. Information traveled only as fast as the messenger who carried it. The telegraph dissolved that unity and quickly spread across the land to form the first of the great communication networks."[35]

Samuel Morse was publicly recognized from 1844 onward as the inventor of the "first practical electromagnetic telegraph," although "Ampère in France; Schilling in Russia; Steinheil in Germany; Davy, Cooke, and Wheatstone in England," all made important contributions in realizing the full potential of this technology.[36] Likewise, most people who learned about television while visiting the 1939 World's Fair—or more likely followed the accompanying media coverage of the various TV displays at the RCA exhibit—were left with the distinct impression that David Sarnoff was the "father of television" and Vladimir Zworykin was its inventor. Thanks to the effectiveness and sophistication of RCA's crack publicity team, these vague public perceptions held fast for most of the next fifty years.

The actual history of all the various people who had a hand in inventing television is a far more complicated and nuanced tale than the one fashioned by RCA during the immediate prewar era. The explosive growth and diffusion of the medium throughout the United States after World War II further clouds the fact that the development of TV was always international in scope and "probably [was] the first invention by committee."[37] A case can be made that Samuel Morse did create the telegraph, although the work of earlier scientists and engineers certainly aided in producing this particular medium. Alexander Graham Bell is similarly remembered as the inventor of the telephone—and Marconi the wireless—but these celebrated figures also came at the end of a long line of earlier innovators who paved the way for them.

The coming of television, too, was profoundly influenced by the history and development of the electronic media that preceded it. TV technology relies on the same basic theories of electricity that served as the foundation for the telegraph and the telephone. "The first steps towards *instant* communication," recounts television historian Albert Abramson, "were really taken by seventeenth and eighteenth century scientists such as Luigi Galvani, Allesandro Volta, Hans C. Oersted, André Ampère, George S. Ohm, Michael Faraday, and James Clerk Maxwell, who found that electrical currents could flow through certain materials as well as interact with magnetic forces."[38] These basic principles were the same ones applied by Morse in sending coded messages at the speed of light from Baltimore to Washington on that historic day in 1844.

The origins of TV are sufficiently complex enough that the myth of the lone inventor never fit neatly over the sprawling web of associations that were eventually needed to bring about the birth of this revolutionary new medium of communication. Advocates from several countries have laid claim to their own "father of television" over the years—including John Logie Baird in Britain, Karl Braun in Germany, Boris Rosing in Russia, and Kenjiro Takayanagi in Japan—as well as David Sarnoff, Vladimir Zworykin, and Philo T. Farnsworth in the United States. The idea of television was an international conception from the beginning, due mainly to the ever-expanding reach and influence of a growing, transnational scientific community. Still, the dream of TV was particularly compelling in the United States, supported largely by the same four institutional forces that were fundamentally reshaping American life and culture throughout the nineteenth century.

The first and probably most formidable of those forces was the industrial revolution. Well under way in England by the mid-eighteenth century, this unprecedented development gradually took hold in the United States after 1790 when Samuel Slater introduced the first American-made, steam-powered cotton-processing machine, followed closely eight years later by Eli Whitney's invention of a mechanized cutter that produced muskets with standards and interchangeable parts. Fueled by a belief in mechanized progress, the beginning phase of the industrial revolution replaced the cottage industry emphasis on handmade goods and services with a factory-styled system based primarily on methods of mass production, ever-higher forms of mechanical technology, and an emerging culture subsidized mainly by mass consumption.

"With rapid industrialization," observes Leo Marx in his classic study *The Machine in the Garden* (1964), "the notion of progress became palpable; 'improvements' were visible to everyone. During the 19th century, accordingly, the awe and reverence once reserved for the Deity and later bestowed upon the visible landscape is directed toward technology."[39] Slowly but surely, a rising ambivalence also surfaced in some quarters about the growing costs of the industrial revolution. Social critics, such as Henry David Thoreau in *Walden* (1854), warned against the "illusion" that results from "a hundred 'modern improvements.' . . . Our inventions are wont to be pretty toys, which distract our attention from serious things."[40] Among those more important matters alluded to by Thoreau were the stifling living conditions in America's cities and the wanton misuse of the environment by certain unregulated commercial interests. The industrial revolution had indeed improved the quality of life for many upper-class and middle-class Americans. Still, the working class and the poor, in particular, endured long hours in monotonous jobs for little pay, along with the mounting pressures resulting from the second major force that was then transforming the country—the urban revolution.

From 1870 to 1890, the total population of the United States doubled. Villages became towns, and towns became cities. From 1860 to 1910, the size of Philadelphia tripled, New York quadrupled, and Chicago increased twentyfold to two million inhabitants. Immigration was the key factor in accounting for these extraordinary gains in population. Although the number of immigrants actually declined in the decade immediately after the Civil War, it exploded quickly in the later decades. Only 1 percent of all Americans were foreign born in 1860, but this proportion skyrocketed to 38 percent by 1910. One million immigrants a year poured into the United States from 1900 to 1910 alone. The nation's farmers also began their wholesale move to the cities in this period. They comprised half of the population in 1880; by 1922, their ranks had shrunk to 10 percent. Overall, millions of people were now centralized in an ever-expanding urban America; eventually, they became the mass consumers who eagerly supported the widespread adoption of the telephone, the proliferation of big-city newspapers, the emergence of Hollywood, the birth of radio, and the imminent arrival of television.

The coming of TV, moreover, was contingent on an enormous amount of investment capital. As late as 1926, inventor Lee de Forest, the self-styled "father of radio" and "grandfather of television," proclaimed, "while theoretically and technically television may be feasible, yet commercially and financially I consider it an impossibility."[41] In contrast, industrialists such as David Sarnoff and his peer competitors in broadcasting and set manufacturing were willing to risk considerable sums of money on the prospects of developing TV. As Kenneth Bilby, former executive vice president of RCA and close associate and biographer of Sarnoff, summarizes:

> Sarnoff's career offers various constructive insights into the evolution of American business management. He was perhaps the last of that remarkable strain of individualistic entrepreneurs—Rockefeller, Ford, Carnegie, Frick, Harriman were among them—whose autocratic governance of industrial oligarchies bruised the precepts of free competitive enterprise but spurred the tumultuous growth of the late nineteenth and early twentieth centuries in America.[42]

Sarnoff and his business contemporaries were themselves molded by the third major sea change that was then redesigning the social fabric of the United States in the nineteenth century—the economic

revolution. This particular metamorphosis occurred in large part because of the powerful commercial stimulus brought about by the industrial buildup during the Civil War. There were fewer than one
thousand millionaires in all of the United States before 1860; by
1865, there were more than ten thousand. Henry James wrote years
later that Americans came out of the Civil War having "eaten of the
tree of knowledge, and the taste will forever be in [their] mouth[s]"[43]
What he was referring to, besides a growing materialism in the country, was a loss of innocence and a metaphoric fall from grace, both of
which were byproducts of the two new philosophies that were then
motivating the behavior of many of the country's most influential
business and political leaders.

Social Darwinism was a theory brought to the United States in the
late 1860s by Englishman Herbert Spencer. According to this outlook,
the marketplace was a Darwinian jungle in which the strong and talented self-made man prevailed as the fittest survivor in this highly
competitive commercial environment. The proponents of industrial
capitalism enthusiastically embraced this rationale of how things
worked because it afforded their success an almost preordained justification, while those who failed became walking symbols of their own
moral and personal inadequacies. In addition, this perspective was
soon popularized and widely disseminated in such publications as
steel tycoon Andrew Carnegie's *Gospel of Wealth* and the many rags-
to-riches stories written by Horatio Alger.

Social Darwinism, specifically, provided Americans with a clear if
distorted yardstick by which to measure their business acumen since
those who came up short in the marketplace had no one to blame but
themselves. With so much at stake, therefore, Charles C. Peirce and
William James, Henry's older brother, introduced a second complementary philosophy named American Pragmatism. This viewpoint
held that truth and virtue were relative to their time and place. It later
was encapsulated and overly simplified in the common cliché, "the
ends justify the means." Together Social Darwinism and American
Pragmatism were responsible for unleashing a tidal wave of entrepreneurial energy into the domestic marketplace that accounted for much
of the economic success and licentiousness of the last quarter of the
nineteenth century.

Never before or since have politics and culture been so dwarfed by
economics in the United States. No longer was the prototypical American a Lincoln, a Grant, a Thoreau, or a Whitman. A new ideal emerged
along the lines of a Morgan, a Vanderbilt, a Carnegie, and a Rockefeller. In an 1873 satiric novel, Mark Twain christened the era *The Gilded
Age* in which he and his co-author, Charles Dudley Warner, presented

a modern-day portrait of America filled with high living and corrupt businessmen, class conflict and inner-city slums, and an ever-widening gap between rich and poor.[44] Just in the nick of time, a second phase of the industrial revolution arrived in which electrical energy took precedence over machines that were once powered by coal or water and steam-driven engines. "As the dreams of a mechanical utopia gave way to the realities of industrialization," declares cultural critic James Carey, "a new school of thought [arose] dedicated to the notion that there was a qualitative difference between mechanics and electronics, between machines and electricity, between mechanization and electrification. In electricity was suddenly seen the power to redeem all the dreams betrayed by the machine."[45]

The youngest and most invisible of the four forces that were forever changing the face of America was the communication revolution. The first great electrical advance had been the telegraph, but a fresh enthusiasm was rekindled with the successful completion of a transatlantic telegraph cable in 1866. A rising nationalist pride was gaining even more momentum in the United States throughout the 1870s in response to such technological breakthroughs as Thomas Edison's incandescent light bulb and phonograph. Many Americans were starting to believe anew, as their forebearers had at the beginning of the century, that technology still had the power to change their lives for the better, only this time through the wonders of electricity.

Alexander Graham Bell devised his telephone in 1876, moving well beyond dots and dashes to relay voices and music from one point to another through distant wires. "The first public showing of a projected motion picture in the United States is difficult to fix," admit film historians Gerald Mast and Bruce Kawin in *A Short History of the Movies*, although cinematic demonstrations were being staged before "limited audiences as early as 1891."[46] Guglielmo Marconi used Morse code to enact the first transatlantic communication by wireless telegraphy in 1901. Thus having conveyed sound through the air on radio waves, scientists and inventors around the world subsequently turned to the next great challenge of transmitting moving images in a similar fashion through a yet-to-be-realized communication technology that had no agreed upon name at the time.

Even though the idea of television existed long before it was ever created as a workable apparatus, the notion that a device could actually transmit motion pictures from one distant location to another was not seriously considered until the arrival of the telegraph. After this "first application of electricity to communication, the last quarter of the nineteenth century has a special importance," as "five proto-mass media of the twentieth century were invented during this period: the telephone, phonograph, electric light, wireless, and cinema."[47] Together, the conceptual and electro-mechanical foundations of these new communication technologies inspired a groundswell of creative thought and activity that eventually culminated more than a half century later in the coming of television.

Some of this thinking turned out to be fanciful, and many of the claims hyperbolic. Bell, for example, reported in the June 5, 1880, issue of *Scientific American* that he "had filed at the Franklin Institute a 'sealed description of a method of seeing by telegraph.'" This announcement sparked a published reply by two British scientists, John Ayrton and William Perry, in the September 23, 1880, issue of *Nature*: "While we are still quite in ignorance of the nature of this invention, it may well be to intimate that a complete means for seeing by telegraphy have been known for some time by scientific men." Similar boasts and even reports of working models came from various inventors and entrepreneurs in the United States, "Portugal, France, Russia, England, and Italy," but at this early stage of television's prehistory, "it was all illusions and imaginings."[48]

The dream of seeing faraway events as they unfold became ever more common in the late nineteenth century, finding a wide array of artistic and scientific expressions both inside America and abroad. For instance, the French illustrator (and occasional science fiction writer) Albert Robida produced a series of prints in 1882 depicting a "telephonoscope." These images featured an upper-middle-class family at home in their parlor, breathlessly watching a large rectangular screen on which two armies attack each other on camels and horses in some exotic desert location; a middle-aged man reclining comfortably on a chaise lounge in his living room as he smokes a cigar and enjoys a "televised" performance of *Faust*; his wife "shopping for silks" at her vanity while a clerk appears in the mirror before her, displaying an assortment of samples for her to choose from; and a "debutante of the '80's" attentively taking notes as a professor of mathematics stands at a blackboard lecturing from an oval screen perched high in her study.[49] These stylish and playful illustrations by Robida are amazingly prescient in retrospect, prefiguring a broad spectrum of programming choices for the entire family that includes news, entertainment, advertising, and even educational TV.

What is also telling in hindsight are the various names that these artists and scientists gave to this newly emerging technology during its prehistory, underscoring TV's indebtedness to earlier forms of electronic communication. One important example is the "electric telescope," devised by Paul Nipkow in 1883, then a twenty-three-year-old engineering student living in Berlin. He developed his idea for television into a patent application named *Elektrisches Teleskop*, which was approved by the German government the following year, serving as the theoretical basis for mechanical television from that point onward. The key to Nipkow's design was a rotating apertured disk, reminiscent of the one used in the old phenakistiscope (Greek for "deceptive view"), invented simultaneously by Joseph Plateau in Belgium and Simon Stampfer in Austria more than fifty years before. This optical toy enabled a viewer to look through a series of slots that were cut into the circumference of a turning cardboard wheel, thus creating the illusion that a sequence of mirrored pictures were actually blending together as one moving image.

Nipkow's conception of his "electric telescope" was far in advance of the phenakistiscope in comparison. He theorized that light from a subject would pass through a spinning perforated disk onto a photoconductive cell made of selenium. The "Nipkow disk" mechanically scanned whatever was in front of it, turning the incoming light rays into electrical impulses. This electricity was then transmitted to an identically synchronized receiver disk that transformed these onrushing electrical particles back into an image of the original subject on a small picture tube. As sophisticated as this design was for its time, Nipkow's proposal remained largely speculative since he never built a working model of the "electric telescope" himself. He had nevertheless created a viable theory for the eventual development of mechanical TV, inspiring a new generation of scientists, inventors, and dreamers of all sorts who came to believe that "seeing-by-telegraph" or "telephonography" or "audiovision" would soon be possible.[50]

The first recorded use of the word "television" came in a paper titled "Télévision au moyen de l'électricité" ("Television by means of electricity") which was written and delivered by Russian physicist Constantin Perskyi on August 25, 1900, at the International Electricity Congress in Paris, France. This weeklong conference was convened under the auspices of the 1900 Paris Exhibition, the third such gathering of its kind and magnitude in the French capital in less than a quarter century. At Paris's 1878 world's fair, the first outdoor electric lighting display was unveiled; at its 1889 exposition, the first gas-powered automobile. The 1900 Paris Exhibition was especially designed to herald the dawning of a new century, particularly in an increasingly electrified and modernizing Europe and America. Tens of thousands of curious visitors saw many of the latest technologies in transportation and communication, including exhibits on the forthcoming airplane, the breathtaking spectacle of the movies, and a series of the most extravagant electric light shows ever staged on the continent. All in all, those attending the 1900 Paris Exhibition were primed to expect the arrival of even more wondrous inventions in the not too distant future.[51]

Life in the United States was rapidly changing at the turn of the century in unprecedented ways. Americans were already beginning to discover a fuller appreciation of the nation as a whole because of advances in transportation—beginning with the completion of the first transcontinental railroad in 1869—as well as with all the new media technologies that had emerged in quick succession over the past half century. These many innovations in travel and communication were together bridging the vast distances and the seemingly inescapable time lags that had once divided the country into mostly separate and distinct regions. In addition, the importance of recreation and entertainment in people's lives was on the rise. Labor was now organizing for improved job conditions, resulting in a shorter workweek for many Americans. Leisure time was, thus, becoming far more widespread and democratized than ever before.

Many modern inventions were also being adapted for personal and public consumption. The telephone and the motorcar are two prime examples. At the turn of the century, there were only 1.4 million telephones for a population of more than seventy-six million Americans, even though the medium had been commercially introduced some twenty-three years earlier.[52] By 1920, the telephone reached "something resembling true ubiquity" when it finally became an integral part of the average U.S. household, advancing well beyond the more restricted and specialized realms of business and government.[53] Likewise, the number of registered automobiles grew from 8,000 in 1900 to 194,000 in 1910 to 8 million in 1920, as road trips became commonplace and even fashionable for many middle-class families in the United States.

The telephone and the motorcar were henceforth two of the defining harbingers of change in the United States at the start of the twentieth century. Still, modernity arrived slowly for most Americans as they fitfully considered which inventions to adopt and how to eventually put these new and unfamiliar technologies to best use in their daily lives. The telephone, for example, took nearly sixty years to find its way into 19.5 million U.S. homes; similarly, the automobile needed forty years to become the standard means of transportation for twenty-five million American families.[54] "The tendency of every age [is] to read history backward from the present," explains Carolyn Marvin in *When Old Technologies Were New.* "We often see it as the process by which our ancestors looked for and gradually discovered us, rather than a succession of distinct social visions, each with its own integrity and concerns."[55]

A classic case in point is the electric light, which was first used as a communication medium meant to captivate and charm audiences of all sizes at various official and commercial illuminations across the United States and Europe during the last quarter of the nineteenth century. Marvin reminds us that "the electric light was a public spectacle before it was anything else, certainly before it was a common furnishing in private residences."[56] "In modern television," she continues, "the element of the spectacle recalls the electric light show, the most dramatic tradition of electrical experimentation in the late nineteenth century."[57] Marshall McLuhan fully corroborates this observation in *Understanding Media*, where he points out that the electric light was initially "a medium without a message, as it were, unless it [was] used to spell out some verbal ad or name." He further contends that "the electric light escapes attention as a communication medium just because it has no 'content' . . . yet [it] eliminates time and space factors in human association exactly as do radio, telegraph, telephone, and TV."[58]

The conceptual linkages between television and previous forms of electronic communication became increasingly evident during the early decades of the twentieth century. The first time the word "television" appeared in print was in a 1907 *Scientific American* article that featured German physics professor Arthur Korn's invention of the photo-telegraph through which he successfully transmitted photographic images by wire from Munich to Nuremberg in 1904. This report, titled "The Problem of Television," described the current state of TV research, suggesting possible "solution[s]" that might involve either wire or "real aerial image[s]."[59] Also in 1907, Russian Boris Rosing applied for a television patent "for a system using a mechanical scanner at the pickup end and a cold cathode tube as a receiver."[60] Rosing's main contribution to the future development of TV was incorporating the earlier discovery of another German scientist, Karl Braun, who in 1897 had "found a way to shoot an electron beam [or cathode ray] through a [vacuum] tube to a screen on the other end."[61] Rosing worked feverishly to improve Braun's cathode ray tube, eventually enabling him to send crude black-and-white silhouettes by mechanical television in 1911. Even more significant in the long run, Rosing was joined in 1910 by a student protégé, Vladimir Zworykin, who instantly discovered his lifelong passion for TV while working in his teacher's laboratory at the Saint Petersburg Technical Institute.

Another singularly influential figure who inspired a generation with his reveries about television was editor, publisher, author, and sometimes inventor Hugo Gernsback. He was a one-of-a-kind dreamer and entrepreneur par excellence. "*Life* magazine once called him the

'Barnum of the space age,' while his 1967 *New York Times* obituary referred to him as the 'father of modern science fiction."[62] Gernsback started more than fifty periodicals, including *Radio News*, *Radio-Craft*, *Electrical Experimenter*, *Science and Invention*, and *Practical Electrics*. He initiated his first publication, *Modern Electrics*, in 1908, writing an article in the December 1909 issue called "Television and the Telephot," which forecasted a combined person-to-person telephone/television communication medium.[63] In 1927 alone, he founded *All about Television* and *Amazing Stories*, one of the most popular science fiction magazines of all time. His obituary stated that "in *Ralph 124C 41+*, a novel he wrote and serialized in 1911, Mr. Gernsback described what he and colleagues subsequently classified as radar, the direction finder, space travel, germicidal rays, micro-film, two-way television, night baseball, tape records, artificial silk and wool, stainless steel, magnesium as a structural material, and fluorescent lighting."[64]

Among his many fans was twelve-year-old farm boy Philo Farnsworth, who found a "treasure trove" of old scientific and technical magazines—many published by Gernsback—when his family moved from Utah to a new homestead in the Snake River Valley of Idaho in 1919. Three years later, he read the "arresting" though premature news that "television has now been perfected" from "the pages of *Science and Invention*." Farnsworth, too, had now found his life's calling while only in his early teens, identifying completely with inventor C. Francis Jenkins's fierce obsession with "radio vision" and curious that "he had [just] succeeded in sending still photographs by radio."[65]

Charles Francis Jenkins had actually been chasing the vague possibility of "seeing at a distance via radio . . . as distinguished from wire television" for more than a quarter century.[66] He first imagined the possibility of "transmitting images . . . by electricity" in 1894, while he was otherwise preoccupied with partner Thomas Armat in producing the first workable motion picture projector out of Thomas Edison and W. L. K. Dickson's kinetoscope or peep show.[67] The next year, they accomplished their goal by inventing what Jenkins called the "phantascope," only to have his one "working model" stolen out of his home "by his financial backer and sold to the Gammon theater chain, which then marketed it all over the world" as Thomas Edison's vitascope. After losing a bitter and costly legal fight in 1896, Jenkins accepted $2,500 in compensation for his phantascope, leaving him philosophical at the ripe old age of twenty-nine: "The inventor gets the experience and the capitalist gets the invention. I'll know better the next time."[68]

Although a generation older than Philo Farnsworth, Jenkins was cut from the same cloth. He, too, was a farm boy who grew up an inveterate technician fascinated with all things mechanical. Jenkins mostly attended country schools in his native Indiana, eventually finishing one year at Earlham College in Richmond. By and large, C. Francis Jenkins was a self-taught inventor and a jack-of-all-trades with no corporate affiliation other than the companies he created himself. Over his long career, he nevertheless obtained over four hundred U.S. patents for a wide assortment of inventions, including a jack for greasing wagon wheels, a bean-shelling machine, a disposable cone-shaped paper milk bottle, a horseless carriage, a bus that was able to transport up to two dozen people, and, on March 22, 1922, a prototypical mechanical television that relayed rudimentary wireless images.[69]

Besides the phantascope, his other breakthrough media-related invention was his prismatic ring, which was a new and improved scanning device composed mainly of two glass prisms spinning in opposite directions that worked much faster and more efficiently than the old Nipkow disk alone. As early as 1920, Jenkins was the only American inventor of consequence working on mechanical TV. In 1921, he opened the Jenkins Laboratory in Washington, D.C., and within a few years, he almost single-handedly ignited a white-hot publicly contested race for television that soon included many of the most formidable electronic communication corporations in the country—namely AT&T, Westinghouse, GE, and RCA. The reason Jenkins was in the eye of this TV firestorm was that he was both a talented inventor and a skilled "promoter of mechanical scanning television," making him "largely responsible for strong and passionate interest in television in the 1920s and early 1930s in the United States."[70]

Being an independent inventor, Jenkins identified most with the thousands of ham operators who were then fueling the radio craze throughout America. These amateurs were his target audience, and his plan for promoting mechanical TV was to reach out to this cohort by staging a series of public demonstrations for the press and then launching regularly scheduled telecasts. The first presentation of "radio vision" by Jenkins that Farnsworth had read about in the pages of Science and Invention took place on May 19, 1922, and involved the wireless transmission of photographs. Jenkins referred to these facsimiles as "radio photos," greatly impressing the reporters who attended the exhibition in his laboratory. The best was yet to come, however, as an even more distinguished group of spectators returned some three years later for what journalists subsequently christened the "windmill broadcast."

On a bright sunny Saturday afternoon, June 13, 1925, Jenkins unveiled his crude mechanical television receiver to Curtis D. Wilbur, the Secretary of the Navy; Dr. George M. Burgess, director of the

Bureau of Standards; Admiral D. W. Taylor of the Naval Research Laboratory; a handful of other public dignitaries; and a room full of newspaper and magazine correspondents. Jenkins engineered an experiment where a ten-minute motion picture of a spinning windmill was broadcast across town from the Navy's Anacostia radio station to the Jenkins Laboratory. The next morning, the spectacle of television was described in detail on the front page of the *Washington Sunday Star*: "What the officials saw yesterday afternoon was the image of a small cross revolving in a beam of light flashed across a light-sensitive cell at Station NOF. . . . The image, while not clear-cut, was easily distinguishable." The *Star* hailed it as "the first time in history that man has literally seen far-away objects in motion through the uncanny agency of wireless."[71] *Scientific American* predicted "the dawn of a new epoch"; Hugo Gernsbeck reported in *Radio News* that he had just seen "the most marvelous invention of the age"; and the *New York Times* crowned Jenkins "the father of television"—the first of several competing inventors who would claim that storied title over the next fifteen years.[72]

Despite the public accolades for Jenkins and his "radiovisor," Scotsman John Logie Baird actually beat the American to the punch with a public demonstration of his own makeshift television apparatus just three months earlier. Baird was another compulsive inventor and starry-eyed mechanic whose career up to this point largely included failed get-rich-quick schemes involving products as diverse as jams and preserves, waterproof socks, and soap. Bedridden for several months in 1922 with an illness, Baird turned his thoughts to TV, obtaining a British patent the next year for a mechanical system he devised, which relied heavily on the Nipkow disk. "He never claimed to have invented television," contends Michael Ritchie in *Please Stand By: A Prehistory of Television*, "but he was the first to take it out of the lab and get publicity for it."[73]

The colorful Baird and his evolving "televisor" easily made good copy because together they were a sight to behold. The inventor had a Gyro Gearless quality about him: rumpled in appearance, round shouldered, and peering intensely at curious onlookers through wire rim glasses framed by a shock of floppy red hair. His large, homemade machine was similarly a one-of-a-kind contraption of "old bicycle sprockets, biscuit tins, cardboard discs, and bulls-eye lenses, all tied together with string and sealing wax," relayed *Radio Broadcast*. Consequently, Baird's initial "demonstration" of television on March 25, 1925, at Selfridges flagship department store on Oxford Street in London, "created [a] considerable stir."[74] This transmission was merely "a fuzzy 16-line rendition of a simple mask."[75] One member of the Radio Society of Great

Britain described it as "very rough and flickering, and mere outlines."[76] Later that year, on October 30, in his Frith Street Soho flat, however, Baird succeeded in telecasting the recognizable face of "a puppet called 'Stooky Bill,'" followed by the flickering visage of one William Taynton, a "solicitor's junior clerk" from an office next door, who, the inventor recalls, "was the first person ever to be seen on television; but I had to bribe him with half a crown to become historical."[77]

John Logie Baird "was not well trained in electronics, and this lack of basic knowledge often limited his thinking and experiments," explains broadcast historian Christopher Sterling. "Beginning in 1923 . . .Baird produced a series of mechanical video systems that could scan (and thus transmit and receive) moving images. These offered a crude picture (about 30 lines of definition from 1929 to 1935)."[78] In contrast, C. Francis Jenkins's "radiovisor" already featured forty-eight parallel lines, thus rendering a much higher quality image. Baird's dogged determination, combined with a fertile imagination, resulted in a series of genuine breakthroughs, though, such as his prototypical phonodisc (a primitive video recording disk), an early color television system, and a large-screen TV. He also continued to improve his "televisor," forcing the British Broadcasting Corporation into a cooperative agreement in 1930 at the behest of the British Post Office (who oversaw wire and wireless activities in the United Kingdom at the time) where Baird was given work and frequency space for his television experiments. Still, the BBC ultimately opted for an all-electronic TV system developed in the laboratories of Marconi-EMI (Electric and Musical Industries Ltd.), as their standard when it started public service telecasting in November 1936.

Meanwhile, back in the United States, a similar fate awaited C. Francis Jenkins and his two main rivals—Dr. Herbert Ives of AT&T and Dr. Ernst F. W. Alexanderson of GE—in the now increasingly competitive race to introduce mechanical television to the general public. According to Donald Godfrey, a historian who specializes in the prehistory of TV, "1926 through 1929 were the pinnacle years for Jenkins Television."[79] The Federal Radio Commission (the forerunner of the FCC) awarded the inventor-turned-entrepreneur the first experimental television station license in the United States, W3XK in Washington, D.C., on February 25, 1928. W3XK began service on July 2 of that year, and, by the end of 1929, the *New York Evening World* reported that "some 25,000 fans [are] looking in regularly on the broadcasts from the Jenkins stations at Washington and Jersey City [N.J.]," just five miles across the Hudson River from Manhattan where Jenkins had subsequently secured a second license with the call letters WZXCR.[80]

The stock market crash, "Black Thursday," on October 24, 1929, spelled the beginning of the end for the Jenkins Television Corporation, as well as for this first exuberant stage in trying to establish a foothold for TV with America's consumers and in the domestic marketplace. The success of W3XK in Washington encouraged Jenkins to take his company public in December 1928, "with a capitalization of ten million dollars in common stock."[81] He basically bet the bank on the belief that there were enough amateur enthusiasts within receiving range of his stations who were willing to purchase affordable "radiovisor kits" and then assemble these receivers themselves. Through aggressive marketing, the Jenkins Television Corporation did enjoy some initial success in building its audience, but the death knell came with the onset of the Great Depression. which rendered TV a prohibitive expense for most prospective adopters. In addition, the Federal Radio Commission (FRC) restricted W3XK and WZXCR from publicizing the "radiovisor," calling such promotional bulletins advertisements instead of public service announcements as Jenkins preferred. Then, "in 1932, the Jenkins Television Corporation collapsed, and its assets became part of the De Forest Radio Company, which was also experimenting with TV transmission. Within a year the De Forest Radio Company folded, too," as all of the corporate holdings, including C. Francis Jenkins's and Lee de Forest's television patents were absorbed by RCA for $500,000, "thereby eliminating two competitors in the broadcast industry."[82]

Just seven years before this takeover, RCA's David Sarnoff was much too preoccupied with launching and expanding NBC's red and blue radio networks to be overly concerned with any early TV experiments from independent upstarts such as Jenkins or corporate competitors such as AT&T. A team of AT&T scientists under the supervision of Dr. Herbert Ives enjoyed their greatest achievement with a public demonstration staged at Bell Laboratories on 55 Bethune Street in downtown Manhattan on April 7, 1927, when Commerce Secretary and presidential candidate Herbert Hoover and company vice president J. J. Carty were telecast via telephone cables from a studio in Washington, D.C., all the way to New York City. "More than 200 miles of space intervening between the speaker and his audience was annihilated by the television apparatus developed by the Bell Laboratories of the American Telephone and Telegraph Companies," recounted the *New York Times*. "When the television pictures were thrown on the screen two by three inches, the likeness was excellent. It was as if a photograph had suddenly come to life and began to talk, smile, nod its head and look this way and that."[83]

Hoover presaged a "new era" in his brief remarks, while Carty congratulated Ives and his professional colleagues on a job well done.

"Next came a vaudeville act" broadcast over the air from a second studio in nearby Whippany, N.J., featuring a comedian named A. Dolan, who "first appeared before the audience as a stage Irishman, with side whiskers and a broken pipe, and did a monologue in brogue. Then he made a quick change and came back in blackface with a new line of quips in negro dialect." The assembled politicians, business executives, bankers, editors, and journalists watching on either small TV screens or a faint two-by-three-foot projection of the proceedings were mostly delighted by all these shenanigans. Such ethnic and racial stereotyping was part and parcel of vaudeville, as it would soon be for broadcasting, especially after the debut of *Amos 'n' Andy* the next year on WMAQ in Chicago, leading to its NBC pickup in August 1929, where it instantly became the most popular radio show in the nation. As for "the commercial future of television, if it has one," concluded the *Times* in its postscript to the AT&T telecast, it "is thought to be in public entertainment [and] super-news reels flashed before audiences at the moment of occurrence."[84]

The success of Dr. Herbert Ives's combined wire and wireless demonstration was quickly superseded by the subsequent experiments of Dr. Ernst Alexanderson, the chief consulting engineer at GE's research and transmission facilities in Schenectady, New York. The center of gravity in the race for television in the United States was now beginning to subtly shift away from smaller entrepreneurs such as Jenkins, de Forest, Ulises Sanabria in Chicago, and Hollis Baird in Boston (no relation to John Logie Baird) to corporately affiliated electrical engineers holding advanced degrees who could easily call on much greater human and financial resources to support their efforts. Alexanderson was a Swedish émigré who came to America in 1902 and worked for General Electric his entire career. Almost immediately he proved his considerable talents as an inventor by producing on assignment a high-frequency generator for long-wave transmissions— the Alexanderson alternator—which enabled Canadian Reginald Fessenden to host the first radio broadcast featuring the human voice (his own reading of the Christmas Story from the Book of Luke) and music (his own violin rendition of "O Holy Night") originating from his coastline station at Brant Rock, Massachusetts, on Christmas Eve, 1906.

Ernst Alexanderson began work on turning the promise of mechanical television into reality in 1923, and within three years, his employer, GE (30 percent), joined forces with RCA (50 percent) and Westinghouse (20 percent) to found the National Broadcasting Company (NBC).[85] These three partners, known as the "radio group," were no longer aligned with AT&T and United Fruit as they once were in the 1919 founding of RCA "because of conflicting interpretations in the alliance agreements" involving commercial rights as to which of these companies was entitled to advertise over the air, mass-produce radio sets, and network. Moreover, all five original firms received the "start[ling] bombshell" in 1924 that they were being jointly charged by the Federal Trade Commission with having "combined and conspired for the purpose of, and with the effect of, restraining competition and creating a monopoly in the manufacture, purchase and sale in interstate commerce of radio devices."[86] The solution to these internal commercial disputes and external legal troubles came with the creation of NBC on November 15, 1926, which freed up RCA president David Sarnoff to buy AT&T out of the business of station ownership and networking, while also agreeing to lease AT&T's phone cables on a long-term basis. Now the lines of enterprise between the "radio group" and the telephone giant AT&T were clearly delineated and agreeable to all parties.

For his part, Alexanderson took immediate advantage of his "radio group" ties by inviting Sarnoff and RCA's foremost engineer, Theodore A. ("Ted") Smith, up to Schenectady in 1927 "to see his mechanical system," with an eye toward collaborating more closely on television in the future. Alexanderson's TV came in two models: a larger home console unit combining radio and television; and a smaller "octagon" that could be placed on top of any three-foot or taller radio receiver. In both cases, Alexander's prototypes used a typical Nipkow disk (a screen that was actually a magnifying lens intended to enlarge the image) and a sound system comprised of a synchronized radio signal transmitted on a different wavelength. Ted Smith remembers, "I went up with [Sarnoff] and saw [Alexanderson's operation]. They had a little studio where they had produced these elementary programs. We weren't that impressed with the system itself. When we were riding home, Sarnoff said, 'It's a great advance, but we can't sell it.' "[87]

Undaunted, Alexanderson pressed forward with only occasional contact and some financial support from Sarnoff and RCA. On May 11, 1928, he and his GE associates began regularly scheduled programming for ninety minutes a day on Tuesdays, Wednesdays, and Thursdays over W2XAD in Schenectady. At the time, his twenty-four lines at sixteen frames per second picture was only half as clear and sharp as the image generated by the Jenkins "televisor." Then, on August 22, 1928, Alexanderson produced the first remote television pickup, having designed a portable camera that captured New York Governor Alfred E. Smith delivering his acceptance of the Democratic Party's nomination for president. The GE field production unit was given permission to set up its equipment only twenty feet to the left of

Dr. Ernst Alexanderson, the chief consulting engineer at GE's research and transmission facilities in Schenectady, New York, watching his large home console unit that combined radio and television in 1928. Courtesy of The David Sarnoff Library.

Smith as he presented his speech on a platform perched in front of the capitol in Albany. A simulcast of television and radio on different frequencies relayed picture and voice fifteen miles to GE's headquarters in Schenectady. The entire experiment was an exhilarating success for everyone involved, as Alexanderson and his colleagues rose to the on-the-spot challenge of being the first broadcasters to demonstrate the news-gathering potential of TV.

Less than a month later, Ernst Alexanderson set his sights on staging a televised drama over W2XAD. "For the first time in history [on September 11, 1928]," announced Russell B. Porter on the front page of the *New York Times,*

a dramatic performance was broadcast simultaneously by radio and television. Voice and action came together through space in perfect synchronization, in a forty-minutes broadcasting of J. Hartley Manners one-act play "The Queen's Messenger," an old spy melodrama, for years a favorite with amateur thespians, which was chosen for the experiment because its cast contains only two actors, who could alternate before the television camera.[88]

Despite employing a three-camera setup, which would eventually become standard operating practice in television studio production, *The Queen's Messenger* was stylistically primitive. This earliest of teleplays relied exclusively on close-ups of the male and female leads, interspersed with simple cutaways showing mostly hand gestures coupled with dramatic manipulations before the camera of various props, including wine glasses, keys, and a revolver. A string of GE-branded octagonal televisions were attached to the tops of cabinet-sized RCA radio sets and positioned one after the other along the corridor outside of the WGY-W2XAD broadcast studio, enabling as many journalists as possible to watch the unfolding drama. Radio columnist and early TV enthusiast Orrin Dunlap described the pictures as "about the size of a postal stamp [three by three inches] and are sometimes blurred and confused."[89] Aesthetics aside, the overall reaction to *The Queen's Messenger* was overwhelmingly positive, as resulting newspaper and magazine coverage was far more extensive than anyone at GE expected.

Public awareness of television continued to rise throughout the late 1920s and into the early 1930s, spurred on by these high-profile

The first televised drama, The Queen's Messenger, *was produced at W2XAD (later WRGB) in Schenectady, New York, on September 11, 1928. Courtesy of The David Sarnoff Library.*

demonstrations. There were also an estimated two dozen experimental station licenses already granted by the FRC at the start of the new decade, mostly in the northeastern states of New York, New Jersey, Pennsylvania, and Massachusetts, as well as in cities as widely dispersed as Washington, D.C., Pittsburgh, Chicago, and Los Angeles. Press commentaries from around the country began weighing in on the coming of TV: for example, the *Philadelphia Public Ledger* forecast "the swift development of 'radio movies' [as a result of] successful demonstrations of vision [before] an amazed and somewhat skeptical world"; the *Utica* [N.Y.] *Observer* predicted that "motion-pictures by radio may become as effective in keeping people home as the automobile has been for taking them away"; and the *Milwaukee Journal* prophesied that "the mechanical age we brought is hustling us. Now it is movies by radio in the home."[90]

Ernst Alexanderson foresaw the future of television as being linked to motion pictures, too, but his vision was of a new and improved form of public entertainment rather than a domestic appliance. He specifically imagined "a chain of [TV] theatres all over the country or the world, without actors, musicians, scene shifters or stage hands, receiving identical broadcasts of theatrical or musical performances by radio television from a central broadcasting station."[91] Eventually he assumed color would be a part of these theatrical spectacles, but, for the time being, he decided to make his own closed-circuit large-screen extravaganza come to life at Proctor's Theatre in Schenectady on May 22, 1930. Alexanderson used his newly developed mechanical TV projection system with forty-eight lines at sixteen frames per second, powered by a high-intensity arc lamp designed by German collaborator August Karolus.[92] The resulting six-by-six-foot image thrilled the assembled spectators that night, including one reviewer who described the whole performance for *Outlook and Independent*:

> With figures life-sized, faces reasonably clear, images not too jumpy, television took a long step forward and bowed to a theatre audience in Schenectady, New York. An orchestra conductor, standing in a television studio a mile away, came onto the theatre's screen and conducted the musicians seated in the orchestra pit. With radio and television assistance, vaudeville performers joked back and forth, one on the stage, the other on the screen. Duets were sung with the soprano and contralto a mile apart. Performers on the screen could hear the applause from the audience and in response to it they smiled and bowed their thanks.[93]

Ernst Alexanderson was delighted by this reception, but it was his "last hurrah" as a television innovator. The "expert evaluators at RCA were a [much] tougher audience" than the people at the Proctor Theatre, who were "understandably impressed by the [mere] demonstration of working television."[94] Alexanderson was not to blame; nor were his competitors Jenkins, Baird, and the other lesser accomplished engineers and technicians who were blindly committed to mechanical television. The format itself "was doomed from the start," explain David Fisher and Marshall Fisher: "The Nipkow disk was simply not fast enough and the holes in it could not possibly be made small enough or spaced closely enough ever to produce a system that would be good enough to make television an integral part of people's lives."[95]

Interestingly, the race for TV was now replaying the pattern that marked the history and development of the industrial revolution. Television similarly began with a mechanical phase in 1920 that inevitably ran into a dead end a decade later during the depths of the Great Depression. After a brief lull, the race for TV ignited again in 1934 through the technological breakthroughs achieved by Philo Farnsworth and Vladimir Zworykin, only this time using the speed-of-light potential of electricity. The future belonged to electronic television and to those inventors who were feverishly developing this higher form of technology. The days of mechanical TV were decidedly over, leaving in their wake a legacy of once high hopes dashed into now-forgotten disappointments in the early 1930s. "The inventors who built mechanical systems, Jenkins, Baird, and Alexanderson," concludes broadcast historian Erik Barnouw, "got people excited about the possibilities of television, getting them to accept the idea that it was inevitable in spite of the fact that it was so obviously unsatisfactory at the time. That was their importance."[96]

No Holds Barred

> There are liars, damn liars, goddamn liars, and patent experts.
> ERNST F. W. ALEXANDERSON, *The Box*, circa 1930[97]

The United States experienced a period of unprecedented economic growth during the 1920s for a variety of reasons. Europe limped out from World War I bruised and battered, while America emerged with its investment and manufacturing sectors working on all cylinders. Correspondingly, the Harding and Coolidge administrations encouraged pro-business policies such as cutting corporate taxes, imposing protective tariffs on foreign goods, and generally following a philosophy of deregulation whenever possible, as well as turning a blind's eye toward homegrown monopolies and oligopolies. Percolating beneath the surface of the Coolidge prosperity (1923–1929) was a sharp increase in electronic innovation, diffusion, and consumption. In general,

> new technology helped propel the boom. Industries such as automobiles, road construction, movies, radio, and home appliances helped create the world's first consumer economy. The U.S. Patent Office had not issued its millionth patent until 1911; by 1925, it had issued another million. One of the most startling developments was the growth of electrical power. In 1912, only 16 percent of American households had electricity; by the mid-1920s, 63 percent of households were electrified and the United States was generating more electric power than all the rest of the world put together.[98]

The family of Philo Taylor Farnsworth was among those early adopters of electricity when they moved to a new homestead owned by an uncle in Bybee, Idaho, in 1919. They were descendants of Philo T. Farnsworth Sr., an Ohioan who converted to the Church of Jesus Christ of Latter-day Saints as a teenager and eventually followed Brigham Young to the valley east of the Great Salt Lake in 1848. His son Lewis E. Farnsworth continued the family's peripatetic ways by relocating his wife and children a half-dozen times throughout south-central Utah before leading them north to greener pastures at the recommendation of relatives living in Idaho. Named after his paternal grandfather, young Philo was literally born in a log cabin on August 19, 1906, in Indian Creek near the small town of Beaver, Utah. His parents barely eked out a living while Philo was a boy because of the dry desert heat, recurring droughts, and wide temperature swings characteristic of the region. By the time Lewis and Serena Bastian Farnsworth decided to leave Utah in search of more promising farmland in the Snake River Valley of Idaho, twelve-year-old Philo was already filled with the dream of "follow[ing] in the path of Thomas Edison and Alexander Graham Bell." Years later he recalled: "I guess I decided it would be nice to be an inventor when I first saw a hand-cranked telephone and gramophone. These things seemed like magic to me."[99]

Growing up to be the next Edison or Bell was a common fantasy that Farnsworth shared with many boys his age; few of his contemporaries, though, had his extraordinary scientific aptitude, along with his relentless single-minded drive to excel. Philo's life story is so improbable that it initially appears to be the stuff of legend. In his specific case, however, the fact that he contributed as much as anyone to the invention of television would hold up under the cold, harsh scrutiny of prolonged litigation during much of the 1930s. Quite simply, Philo Farnsworth first imagined how electronic TV would work while growing up a shy, precocious, Mormon teenager in a small Idaho farming community out in nowhere. His imagination was set free by poring over popular scientific magazines, especially those quasi-technical reports describing the wonders of electricity and the possibility of transmitting pictures by radio. His eureka moment came one spring morning in 1921 at the young age of fourteen while he was plowing a hayfield on the family farm. As usual, he was daydreaming, seated on a single-disk harrow pulled by a team of three horses: "Suddenly the future hit him with a vision so startling he could hardly sit still: a vision of television images formed by an electron beam scanning a picture in horizontal lines. He could create an image line by line just like the hay field in front of him, and the electrons would scan so fast that the human eye would see it as one instantaneous picture."[100]

Later, "Farnsworth . . . wrote that the 'solitude of the open country was most conducive to thought and reflection.' "[101] Moreover, his absent-minded demeanor during this particular hay field incident suggests Philo's uneasy relationship with working on the family farm. A feature article from the *Deseret News* (Salt Lake City) further illustrates this point some twenty-five years later:

> Lew [Philo's father] saw him standing on the harrow, one rein in his hand, the other dragging, the three horses plodding peacefully over the field. Should they become frightened Phil would have no control over them [and he would be pulled headfirst into the rotating blades]. Lew hurried to the scene, grabbed the horses' bits to avoid possible tragedy, ready to give Phil a tongue lashing— but Phil spoke first. "I've got it, dad, I really think it will work!" His father choked back his reproof.[102]

Philo's parents and siblings affectionately referred to him as "the engineer" because he so easily mastered the Delco generator that powered the house and barn, being the only member of the family who could tune up and regularly maintain the entire electrical system of the farm all by himself.[103] Later that fall, Philo started high school in nearby Rigby, a four-mile horseback ride that he made every day of the school year. "Because he was intrigued with the electron and electricity, he persuaded his chemistry teacher, Justin Tolman, to give him special instructions and to allow him to audit a senior course. You could read about great scientists from now until the 22nd century and not find another instance where one of them celebrates a high school teacher," asserts media critic Neil Postman, "but Farnsworth did, crediting Tolman with providing inspiration and essential knowledge." Tolman for his part was always modest about his influence on the development of young Philo, claiming he was more of a sounding board than anything else for the boy. Still, Justin Tolman took the time to provide extra after-school tutoring for him, discussing ideas with Philo and recommending that he read certain chemistry, physics, and electronics books.[104]

One afternoon in the spring of 1922, fifteen-year-old Philo Farnsworth walked into an empty classroom at Rigby High School and began filling the chalkboard with hand-drawn models and equations that he had worked on for weeks in a school notebook; "he covered Tolman's blackboards with drawings, diagrams, [and] mathematical formulae which . . . [represented] the terrific new idea of electronic television."[105] "I told you I wanted to be an inventor, and this is my invention," the teenager blurted out to Tolman, "I got to tell you about it. You're the only person I can make sense to."[106] Justin Tolman was amazed by the boy's presentation. "Looking back," he "realized that nearly every question he asked me had some bearings on the problem of television. I see now that it was all coming together in that head of his."[107] Philo excitedly gave his mentor a piece of paper containing a sketch of what would eventually become his blueprint for the image dissector (or television camera) five years later. Significantly, that rudimentary drawing would prove a godsend to Farnsworth when RCA instigated a patent infringement case and brought the weight of its corporate power against him in 1932.

For the time being, though, experiments in mechanical TV were grabbing all the headlines, while any public consideration of electronic television in the early to mid 1920s was merely an afterthought. Bucking the conventional wisdom, Philo already believed that "nothing mechanical can ever move fast enough . . . to reproduce moving images on a screen." He told Tolman and his "brothers and sisters" as much by the time Lewis Farnsworth moved his family from Bybee, Idaho, to Provo, Utah, in 1923, where he once again hoped to make a better living for his wife and children in yet another new locale.[108] Provo also provided Philo with the opportunity to attend Brigham Young University, where he matriculated after passing six months of remedial work, even though he had only completed two years of high school in Rigby. Then Philo Farnsworth's formal education ended abruptly at age eighteen, when his father died unexpectedly of pneumonia in January 1924, forcing the teenager to withdraw from the university at the end of his sophomore year in order to find a job. Over the next two years, Philo delivered and installed radios for a local furniture store in Provo before moving to Salt Lake City, where he next worked as a radio repairman. While in Salt Lake, however, everything changed for Philo when he met George Everson and Leslie Gorrell, two fundraisers for the Community Chest, dazzling them with his dream of electronic television and assuring them that the invention would make them all rich. They decided to invest $6,000 of their hard-earned savings in this electronics prodigy and his plans for the future. Though he was only nineteen years old, Philo looked older, and when he discussed TV, he obviously knew what he was talking about and spoke with the fervor of a true believer.

Philo left Salt Lake City for Los Angeles by train in May 1926, accompanied by his eighteen-year-old sweetheart and new bride, Elma ("Pem") Gardner Farnsworth, a girl he had met through his sister Agnes when the family first moved to Provo three years earlier. Pem became Philo's research assistant as they lovingly merged their personal and professional lives together. After arriving in southern California, the couple turned their newly rented furnished apartment in Hollywood into a makeshift laboratory, where they made slow progress and realized early on that the task of inventing electronic television would be far more costly and challenging than Philo had ever imagined. In consultation with Everson and Gorrell, Farnsworth purchased a new business suit and started fundraising again, eventually convincing the owners of the Crocker First National Bank of northern California to

Philo Farnsworth flanked by his first two financial investors, Leslie Gorrell (left) and George Everson (right). Courtesy of Arizona State Library Special Collections.

invest $25,000. Philo's passion for television was undeniably conta-
gious as the Farnsworths relocated their operation to the simple and economically outfitted Crocker Research Laboratory on 202 Green Street
in San Francisco during late September and early October of 1926. On
January 7, 1927, Philo applied to the federal government for several patents that covered his current all-electronic television system (and they
were eventually granted on August 16, 1930). He also became the first
inventor to ever transmit moving images—"black lines, a triangle, and
a dollar sign painted on a sheet of glass"—by electronic TV on September 7, 1927.[109] Investor and friend George Everson arrived soon after the
start of this landmark experiment, and he and Farnsworth subsequently
"raced to the telegraph office and sent a wire to Leslie Gorrell, who was
working in Los Angeles. Just four words: *The Damned Thing Works!*"[110]

Over the next twelve months, Farnsworth and his expanding staff
of "seven full-time lab employees" slowly improved the image quality
of his television camera and receiver to the point where Philo and his
investors decided they were ready to host a public demonstration for
the press corps. Farnsworth and his partners knew that the "key to
raising money and interesting buyers was publicity."[111] Consequently,
the inventor unveiled his all-electronic television system to visiting
journalists on September 1, 1928. A reporter for the *San Francisco
Chronicle* described what he saw as

> a system of television basically different from any system yet in
> operation. . . . All television systems now in use [are mechanical]. . . .
> Farnsworth's [electronic] system employs no moving parts what-
> ever. Instead of moving the machine, he varies the electric current
> that plays over the image and thus gets the necessary scanning. The
> system is thus simple in the extreme, and one of the major mechani-
> cal obstacles to the perfection of television is thereby removed.[112]

When news of Farnsworth's accomplishment spread across the
country during the remainder of 1928, Jenkins, Baird, Alexanderson, and all of the other proponents of mechanical television still believed they had each invented the best system. Nevertheless, the
"publicity attracted a good deal of national and [even] international
attention to the Green Street Laboratories," including the growing
curiosity of then acting RCA president David Sarnoff and the watchful attention of a struggling electronics researcher at Westinghouse
named Vladimir Zworykin.[113] All of these various mechanical and
electronic television pioneers were emblematic of a more fundamental cultural shift that was just now surfacing after more than a generation of intense scientific activity. "In the late 19th century, as the

nation's physical frontier closed," declares historian Daniel Kevles, "inventors, entrepreneurs, and, then, corporations turned increasingly to a new frontier—the laboratory."[114]

The year 1893 is when Frederick Jackson Turner introduced his seminal "frontier thesis" in a presentation to the American Historical Association at the World Columbian Exposition in Chicago. His paper "The Significance of the Frontier in American History" argued that the "primal American experience was over." He pointed out how the 1890 census announced that the frontier region of the United States was now officially closed, leading him to claim that American history up to that point had been largely created by "the European continually confront[ing] the land on an imaginary line between frontier and civilization." Moreover, Turner contended that the source of the nation's exceptionalism—America's uniqueness, vitality, resourcefulness, and ingenuity—sprang from this collision of the wilderness with society. Frederick Jackson Turner's thesis "did not define American history so much as [it] defined for European Americans the central myth of their history," concludes cultural critic Jack Nachbar.[115]

An increasingly diverse, urban-oriented, technologically sophisticated America was then taking shape at the turn of the twentieth century. As a result of this growing modernity, the "story of science and technology" emerged as an essential component of the "American narrative." The Wizard of Menlo Park, Thomas Edison, "had shown the way by what he called his 'invention factory.'" By 1910, "several of the nation's new high-technology companies—notably AT&T, General Electric, and DuPont—established industrial research laboratories."[116] Even lone and uncredentialed mechanics and engineers such as C. Francis Jenkins and Philo Farnsworth were inspired to create their own do-it-yourself work facilities by tapping into a widespread mythos that idealized the research laboratory as America's next frontier. "Farnsworth [specifically] was an independent experimenter, a charismatic scientist, and [an] idea person who was able to initiate ideas and convince investors. However, his primary focus was always in the laboratory."[117] What "was less obvious to the general public . . . was a change in the nature of the inventive process," summarizes Daniel Stashower, the dual biographer of Farnsworth and Sarnoff. "As the English philosopher Alfred North Whitehead observed, 'The greatest invention of the nineteenth century was the invention of the method of invention,' meaning a shift away from the solitary inventor in his isolated lab to the well-funded, well-organized efforts of large research centers."[118]

Vladimir Kosma Zworykin's life story is as improbable as Philo Farnsworth's in its own way. He arrived in America on New Year's Day 1919 aboard the S.S. *Carmania*. Unlike millions of other immigrants before him, however, the twenty-nine-year-old Vladimir was traveling first class when he entered New York Harbor in full view of the Statue of Liberty. Such exclusive accommodations reflected his privileged background as the son of a one-time well-to-do businessman during the days of Tsarist Russia. At age twenty-three, Zworykin had earned a degree in electrical engineering under the tutelage of television pioneer Boris Rosing at St. Petersburg Institute of Technology. Rosing's hybrid TV experiments were more electronic than mechanical because he incorporated a primitive version of Karl Braun's newly invented cathode ray display tube. Rosing introduced young Vladimir to the possibilities of television, and soon after his arrival in the United States in the early 1920s, he read the work of Scotsman Alan Archibald Campbell Swinton, which dated back to 1908 "describ[ing] in great detail what would be needed to build an all-electrical television system that used cathode rays at both the transmitter and the receiver."[119] All of these influences, as well as his advanced studies in X-ray technology at the Collège de France in Paris from 1912 until World War I broke out in 1914, convinced Zworykin of the electron's wondrous potential and the future promise of electronic TV.

Following the Bolshevik Revolution in 1917, Zworykin was a man without a country. His passage to America via Copenhagen and London left him jobless in a Brooklyn boardinghouse trying to improve his English as quickly as possible. He worked temporarily "at the Russian Purchasing Commission in New York as a mechanical adding-machine operator" before receiving "an offer of an engineering job [for half his current salary] at the Westinghouse Research Laboratory in Pittsburgh," where he eagerly relocated in 1920, "determined to make his living as an engineer" and "begin, finally, his true career at the age of thirty."[120] At the outset, Zworykin developed radio tubes and photocells for Westinghouse rather than for television, but he was given the opportunity to concentrate on TV two years later when he submitted his first rudimentary plans for an all-electronic system to the U.S. Patent Office in December 1923. This preliminary application featured his iconoscope (camera tube) but was merely conceptual in design. Zworykin's blueprint also had a number of similarities with other patent proposals and existing technologies, thus his submission was subject to continual review or litigation over the next fifteen years.

Still, Vladimir Zworykin was adjusting well to life in America. He became a naturalized citizen in 1924, as well as a doctoral candidate in physics at the University of Pittsburgh. By the fall of 1925, he created working prototypes of his iconoscope and kinescope (picture tube), hosting an in-house demonstration for Harry P. Davis, the vice president and general manager of the Westinghouse Electric and

Manufacturing Company; Samuel Kintner, his immediate supervisor and head of the research laboratory in Pittsburgh; and other key members of the corporation, including its patent lawyers. Zworykin succeeded in transmitting a faint, two-inch-square stationary image of a Greek cross (+) which he "took as a great achievement." In contrast, Davis "had expected something more worthy of his attention." In the ensuing discussion, Zworykin "naively 'scotched his own case' by giving a vivid description of the technical difficulties which remained to be solved, how long it would take, and how much more it would cost." Davis discreetly told Kintner that "it was better to get this 'guy' to work on something more useful," suggesting that the company's entire television initiative be turned over to his most favored engineer, Frank Conrad, who had jump-started radio broadcasting in the United States with coverage of the November 2, 1920, presidential election returns over Westinghouse's experimental station 8XK (later KDKA).[121]

Zworykin dutifully worked on other projects for Westinghouse, completed his Ph.D. at Pittsburgh in 1926, and watched quietly as the veteran Conrad, fifteen years his senior, developed a far more conventional mechanical television apparatus that was subsequently displayed to the top "radio group" brass (including David Sarnoff) and the working press on August 8, 1928. The exhibition of "radio movies" produced an image of sixty lines at sixteen frames per second, sent by wire from the Westinghouse research laboratory to KDKA two miles away in East Pittsburgh where it was broadcast back "as clear as the usual newspaper half-tone illustration."[122] Although the demonstration was a success, "considering the state of the art of the time, . . . eventually Westinghouse's mechanical work faded out of history."[123]

When it was clear that his colleagues at Westinghouse were not going to change their minds about electronic television, Zworykin finally made an appointment to meet with David Sarnoff during the first week of January 1929, while he was already in New York delivering a paper at the annual meeting of the Institute of Radio Engineers. Vladimir Zworykin had only been in the country for a little more than a decade when he strode into Sarnoff's office and outlined to the newly appointed RCA president his vision of electronic television, explaining why it was superior to mechanical TV and describing how television receivers would one day be as ubiquitous as radios in homes across America: "When Sarnoff asked how much a workable television system would cost, Zworykin told him that he needed a few additional engineers and facilities, but that he hoped to complete the development in about two years, at an estimated cost of about a hundred thousand dollars. Sarnoff replied, 'All right, it's worth it.'"[124] RCA insider Kenneth Bilby reveals that "this proved to be one of the classic cost underestimates of technological history—by about $50 million—but Sarnoff did not quibble with it then or later." Furthermore, Bilby believes that the "Sarnoff-Zworykin encounter proved to be one of the most decisive in industrial annals. It brought together television's leading inventor and the executive who would guide its development."[125]

All of the pieces were now falling into place for David Sarnoff. As a world-class industrialist, he had all the requisite talents. Sarnoff was hard driving, socially adept, and able to grasp the larger implication of things. He also was a venture capitalist who was willing to take intuitive as well as calculated risks. Both he and Zworykin were Russian émigrés and self-made men, but what Sarnoff most identified with in his visitor was "the intensity of the slight sandy-haired inventor whose blue eyes sparkled behind thick-lensed glasses." He had "discovered someone on his [own] wavelength."[126] Sarnoff was also a highly skilled and efficient manager, even to the point of being ruthless whenever necessary. For example, when he and Ted Smith visited Alexanderson at GE's Schenectady lab in 1927, he not only invested token research dollars in the inventor and "publicly declare[ed]" that he was the "Marconi of television," he simultaneously ordered Smith "to build a television station in New York" because "he realized that sooner or later RCA and GE might not be following the same path."[127] As usual, Sarnoff was covering all of his bases, investing in GE despite the fact that he was lukewarm about Alexanderson's system, then furtively leading RCA into TV development in the belief that you always "had to be first" if you wanted to "make all kinds of money."[128]

In the spring of 1928, Ted Smith and his crew built RCA and NBC's first experimental television station, W2XBS, which commenced operation on June 30, 1930, from the New Amsterdam Theatre in New York City. By this time, Zworykin had made noticeable headway in perfecting his iconoscope, and he was now appointed director of electronics research at RCA's newly acquired research facility in Camden, New Jersey. Despite the success of Alexanderson's Proctor Theatre telecast on May 22, 1930, Sarnoff and his engineering staff were now convinced that electronic television was the wave of the future. Zworykin had replaced Alexanderson as the main recipient of RCA's financial support. That year "90 percent" of the corporation's television research budget went to him "and his cathode-ray work. . . . It was only the insistence of GE management that their system was still worthwhile, as well as Alexanderson's preeminence, that garnered them 10 percent."[129]

David Sarnoff was additionally a top-drawer negotiator. Never was this talent more on display than during the two years in which he navigated the Justice Department's 1930 antitrust suit against the original RCA partners demanding the "termination of the 1919–21 patents agreements" and that RCA, GE, Westinghouse, and AT&T "disentangle themselves from each other," including any "interlocking directorates."[130] Sarnoff was literally handed the summons by a U.S. marshal on the evening of May 30, 1930, just as he was about to enter a dinner honoring his ascendancy to the presidency of RCA five months before.[131] All of the partners felt blindsided, but the antitrust action was a direct result of the laissez-faire excesses of the Coolidge years, followed by the recent stock market crash and the worldwide financial crisis.

When it became clear to all of the defendants that the government would not compromise on its demand to break up the RCA trust, AT&T became the first partner to enter into a consent decree in late 1931. Soon afterward, Sarnoff seized control as the central figure behind the scenes, crafting a plan of divorcement where GE and Westinghouse were handsomely compensated for withdrawing from RCA. Final consent decrees were signed by all of the remaining parties on November 21, 1932. "Miraculously, RCA emerged as a strong and self-sufficient entity. No longer owned by other corporations, it had its destiny in hand," affirms Erik Barnouw in *Tube of Plenty*: "It had substantial new obligations in the form of debentures, but it owned two networks [NBC was now its wholly owned subsidiary], broadcast stations, manufacturing facilities," and numerous other holdings, including its "experimental laboratories. At its apex sat David Sarnoff."[132] David and Marshall Fisher fully concur: "David Sarnoff would never again share power at RCA."[133]

Sarnoff's greatest assertion of RCA's arrival into the highest echelons of American business, industry, and culture was moving his corporate headquarters to the sixty-five-story Rockefeller Center complex in June 1933 during one of the Great Depression's darkest periods. The U.S. unemployment rate had skyrocketed from 3 percent in 1929 to more than 25 percent by the spring of 1933. Over thirteen million people were then out of work, and more than half of the entire population was living below the poverty line. Ten thousand banks, or 40 percent of the nation's total, had already closed their doors between 1929 and 1933. Sarnoff nevertheless relocated NBC to Radio City, the state-of-the-art centerpiece of Rockefeller Center. He moreover "had seen enough of Zworykin's progress to arrive at perhaps the most significant decision in television history. He decided to jettison the accumulated knowledge of a half century, cut loose from the spinning disc that underpinned TV's first boomlet, and lead the industry in the development of a new, all-electronic" system.[134] David Sarnoff had now committed himself fully to winning the race for TV, and, as usual, he would be a force to be reckoned with.

Vladimir Zworykin already knew that his main competitor in creating electronic television was Philo Farnsworth, who he had been reading about in the trade and popular presses since 1928. Only three
months after forging his momentous relationship with Sarnoff,
Zworykin decided to travel to San Francisco to see the young inventor
and his image dissector. Farnsworth was in "a most jubilant mood"
over the prospects of meeting Zworykin, reports George Everson;
"there was no engineer in the country that he would rather have view
his results."[135] Farnsworth, Everson, and their partners knew that
Zworykin had major corporate connections, and they hoped that his
visit would result in additional financial investment in their ongoing
efforts. Zworykin arrived at the modest Crocker Research Laboratory
in San Francisco on April 16, 1930. He was escorted around what was
essentially a factory loft at 202 Green Street while the inventor and his
associates held back nothing in presenting their electronic television
system to Zworykin. Farnsworth's wife, Pem, later admitted that their
unguarded demonstration was a mistake: "Philo good-naturedly talked
too much to one whom he considered a scientific colleague."[136] At one
point, "Zworykin paid Farnsworth high praise by picking up a dissector tube and saying, 'This is a beautiful instrument. I wish that I might
have invented it,'" details Albert Abramson in *Zworykin, Pioneer of Television*. Upon returning to RCA's Camden laboratory, Zworykin "wrote
a report" to his superiors, "prais[ing] the image dissector [camera]
tube," while commenting "that Farnsworth's picture tube was quite
deficient." Zworykin also went right to work on a new camera tube of
his own. "On May 1, 1930, Zworykin filed for a patent. . . . It was his
first application for a camera tube since July 1925, and was completely
different from the earlier proposal."[137]

An indication of RCA's interest in Philo Farnsworth came a little
more than a year later when David Sarnoff traveled to San Francisco to
see the then twenty-four-year-old inventor's television setup during May
of 1931. Farnsworth was out of town at the time, discussing a possible
business arrangement with the Philadelphia Storage Battery Company
(Philco), so "Everson was left to conduct the tour. Sarnoff was shown a
demonstration and seemed particularly impressed with the seven-inch
picture." Afterward he offered $100,000 for Farnsworth's "services and
patents."[138] Much to Sarnoff's surprise, Philo and his partners declined
his business proposition. From Sarnoff's perspective, Farnsworth was
running a mom-and-pop operation and his financial offer to the young
inventor was generous, especially considering the state of the economy.
Philo Farnsworth wanted to control his own patents, however, while
RCA conversely followed an unwritten policy of never paying royalties
to anyone under any circumstances. The inventor and the corporation

were thus at odds with each other, holding fast on a course destined to collide. Pem Farnsworth later characterized the situation as a " 'David and Goliath' confrontation."[139]

"Sarnoff respected Farnsworth—even liked him, he later claimed—but business was business and he set out to teach the young Mormon a lesson. He moved quickly on two fronts," recaps Jeff Kisseloff in *The Box: An Oral History of Television, 1920–1961*. "First, he pushed RCA's own television research ahead at full speed. Second, he instructed his lawyers to do whatever was necessary to stop Farnsworth," intending to bog down the inventor in protracted litigation and grind him into submission under the weight of costly legal fees that he simply couldn't afford.[140] Zworykin achieved his first all-electronic television system in early 1933 as RCA essentially put their TV research project under wraps by curtailing all public demonstrations for the foreseeable future. At the same time, its legal team hoped to "goad Farnsworth into filing an expensive patent clarification suit . . . by claiming that Zworykin should be credited with inventing all-electronic television, due to his 1923 patent application."[141] "In March 1932," Zworykin also "applied for a patent for an improved dissector tube."[142] Farnsworth took the bait, submitting an interference suit that argued RCA's latest TV system infringed on his earlier television patents. Overall, "patents are widely supposed to protect the lone inventor, the pioneering genius in a garage, against the predation of big companies. Historically the opposite has been true," contends James Gleick in *What Just Happened: A Chronicle from the Information Frontier*. "As basic industries like electricity, telephony, and broadcasting developed in the twentieth century, the great corporations learned to create arsenals of interrelated patents to use as sword and shield."[143]

Philo Farnsworth decided to take matters into his own hands by signing a two-year renewable contract with Philco, which was the largest manufacturer of radios in the country. Farnsworth, his wife Pem, and a cadre of five engineers moved their small television operation east to Philadelphia in June 1931. Philco provided them with much-needed capital and a working space to conduct their research at the company's downtown manufacturing plant. In return, Farnsworth granted Philco nonexclusive rights to his television patents so it could mass produce TV sets as well as radios. Philco was eager to get out from underneath the yoke of RCA, to whom it was already paying steep royalties for each radio it manufactured. Restarting their television research efforts again in July, Farnsworth and his staff soon picked up test telecasts from RCA's laboratory less than ten miles away across the Delaware River in Camden, New Jersey. Philco next acquired experimental station W3XE for Farnsworth's use, and Zworykin and his team of more than sixty engineers likewise began to monitor their rival's progress. Pem Farnsworth later recalls that "RCA tried to get information from our secretaries by plying them with drinks." Occasionally "RCA employees" also "harassed" Philo when he was invited to deliver "public lectures" in the area.[144] Finally Philco did not renew the inventor's contract in 1933. Farnsworth "later learned that when Sarnoff found out about the Philo-Philco plan to commercialize television, he threatened to rescind the Philadelphia company's license to produce radios under RCA's patents, which would effectively put Philco out of business."[145] Philo Farnsworth and his small band of associates responded by creating the Farnsworth Television Corporation in December 1933, relocating their modest laboratory to suburban Philadelphia, and resolving to carry on together in the face of mounting RCA pressure.

Eight months later, Farnsworth enjoyed his "greatest triumph," maintains Donald Godfrey in *Philo T. Farnsworth: The Father of Television*. "It was not in amassing his constantly growing list of patents, the sophistication of the picture, the cabinetry or laboratory experiments, but rather the world's first general public demonstration of an all-electronic television system."[146] In the early summer of 1934, Philo was asked to be one of the inaugural speakers at the newly opened Science Museum at the venerable Franklin Institute in Philadelphia. The program was designed to stimulate public interest and understanding of scientific matters, and Farnsworth fit the bill. His subsequent appearance was so well received, in fact, that institute president Nathan Howard invited the inventor back later that summer for an extended stay to demonstrate his television apparatus. Farnsworth saw the proposed exhibition as a unique promotional opportunity, so he agreed to return for ten days beginning on Monday, August 24, and continuing nonstop through Wednesday, September 2. Especially for the event, Philo dreamed up an entertaining gimmick to grab people's attention from the outset. He greeted visitors with a live portable TV camera at the entrance and, in turn, these individuals immediately saw themselves televised on a nearby screen inside the institute's archway. This simple yet effective display of television in action caused a great deal of excitement, enticing patrons to pay 75 cents apiece to attend a rotating twenty-minute exhibition of electronic TV inside the fifty-seat museum auditorium from 2 P.M. to 10 P.M. daily, except for Saturday, August 29, when the performances continued from 10 A.M. to 10 P.M.

Almost five years before RCA introduced Zworykin's iconoscope and kinescope at the 1939 World's Fair, Philo T. Farnsworth and his all-electronic television system were smash hits at the Franklin Institute. The twenty-eight-year-old inventor and his close-knit crew of family and friends needed to fill lots of time during their ten-day run, so they anticipated the choices that network programmers would make ten to twenty years into the future: Farnsworth and his staff scheduled mostly vaudevillian-styled acts leavened with an occasional high-cultural set piece or sports-oriented segment; Philo even improvised a variety of outdoor reality shots when all else failed. Specifically, the standing-room-only audiences watched chorus girls, comics, ventriloquists, trained dogs, and dancing bears; they were serenaded by popular and classical singers and amused by a music professor from nearby Swarthmore College, who broke two strings while playing his cello; they were introduced to two star members of the U.S. Davis Cup Team who "talked, swung tennis rackets and demonstrated their favorite grips"; Farnsworth also took his portable camera up to the rooftop at well-timed intervals to telecast the cityscape and the night sky, earning a rave review from the *Christian Science Monitor*: "Reproduction of the moon's likeness is just another sensational achievement by the young inventor."[147] All of this trial-and-error TV programming was captured on a one-foot-square television screen featuring 240 lines at thirty frames per second. In response to Farnsworth's advanced image quality, the *New York Times* proclaimed that "some of the scientists who watched declared it the most sensitive apparatus yet invented."[148] Philo was both elated and exhausted by the ten-day experience. Characteristically, he had never thought of asking for a performance fee or a percentage of the ticket revenues from the administrators at the Franklin Institute. Unfortunately, Farnsworth would never again enjoy a comparable level of public recognition and appreciation for all that he had accomplished over the years against seemingly impossible odds.

The future of electronic television instead belonged to RCA. The corporation commandeered by the hard-driving entrepreneur David Sarnoff possessed deep pockets because of its popular NBC red and blue networks and its owned and operated radio stations. Now it employed a world-class electronics innovator in Vladimir Zworykin, surrounding him with all the manpower and equipment he needed to succeed. As a result, Zworykin made rapid strides forward in a relatively short amount of time. In 1930, he inherited an RCA system that was fully mechanical and produced a blurry two-inch-square picture of only sixty lines at twenty-four frames per second. Rather than being known for its image quality, RCA's claim to fame up to this point was its test figure—a thirteen-inch Felix the Cat doll made of papier-mâché that rotated continuously on a record player turntable. By early 1931, RCA engineers were combining their existing mechanical scanner with an electronic cathode ray receiver, suggesting Zworykin's growing influence. The subsequent image of 120 lines at twenty-four frames per second was better than RCA had realized before but still deficient when compared with what Farnsworth had already achieved.

Zworykin began asserting himself more at RCA by 1933, convincing his associates to completely abandon mechanical scanning in favor of an all-electronic system that greatly improved the picture quality to 240 lines at twenty-four frames per second. His next important breakthrough came late in 1934, when he succeeded in increasing the number of scanning lines to 343 at thirty frames per second. The key feature in this new and improved TV system was a refinement called "interlacing"—"a process of scanning all of the odd numbered lines, then returning to the top of the plate and scanning all of the even numbered lines to make the complete image."[149] This procedure resulted in a much clearer picture and virtually eliminated any flicker. Sarnoff was so encouraged with the headway that Zworykin and his colleagues were making at RCA's Camden research laboratory that he decided in May 1935 to invest "$1,000,000 . . . in field tests" throughout the New York metropolitan area. The *New York Times* reported on its front page that he was inviting his "research experts to emerge from the seclusion of their scientific dens and use the great open spaces as a proving ground." Sarnoff basically announced a three-point plan that plots out the necessary foundation for commercial television:

1. Establish the first modern television transmitting station in the United States . . . located in a suitable center of population [near] RCA's research laboratories, manufacturing facilities, and its broadcasting centre in Radio City.
2. Manufacture a limited number of television receiving sets [and place them] at strategic points of observation in order that the television system may be tested, modified and improved under actual service conditions.
3. Develop an experimental program service with the necessary studio technique to determine the most acceptable form of television programs.[150]

In short order, a brand-new transmitter "incorporating the highest standards of the art" was installed 1,285 feet above the ground at the top of the Empire State Building, then the tallest skyscraper in the world. Approximately one hundred receivers were built and "placed in homes and offices of RCA engineers and executives" within a fifty-mile radius of the transmitter, including the five boroughs of New York, as well as localities as widespread as Tarrytown in Westchester County, New York; Farmingdale, West Orange, and Ridgewood, New Jersey; and Westport, Connecticut, among dozens of other communities.[151] Intensive field testing began in earnest on June 10, 1936, and proved so promising that the press was invited to a public telecast on November 6 from studio 3H in Radio City. Betty Goodwin hosted this historic program with guest stars including the singer Hildegarde, the Ink Spots, comedian Ed Wynn, and actors Eddie Albert and Grace Brandt performing in the first original teleplay, *The Love Nest*, written by Albert. Over the next eighteen months, "RCA scientists [led by Zworykin] 'ironed out the kinks' with "practical usage," thereby increasing the "number of scanning lines per frame to 441" and "greatly sharpening the detail of the image."[152]

Farnsworth's ability to position his television operation so it would one day be a profitable enterprise was far more limited in comparison. Significantly, he won his patent interference suit against Zworykin on June 22, 1935, which allowed him to keep complete control over his image dissector "and the low velocity scanning method to be used in RCA's Orthicon tube."[153] Ever since Sarnoff had tried to buy the young inventor out in 1931, "the intense rivalry between Farnsworth and RCA shifted [primarily] to the U.S. Patents Office, where RCA [tried] everything, especially patent interferences, to get control of the dissector tube."[154] What turned the case in Farnsworth's favor was a combination of direct and circumstantial evidence. In particular, Philo and Pem meticulously recorded each day's progress, complete with illustrative diagrams, in a series of notebooks, which supported Farnsworth's claims that he had invented the image dissector in 1927. Moreover, Farnsworth's lawyers secured a deposition from the inventor's high school teacher, Justin Tolman, who described how the boy outlined on the blackboard his system of electronic television for him in 1922, even submitting to the court the original sketch Philo made of the dissector tube. In addition, several eyewitnesses testified that Zworykin exclaimed, "This is a beautiful instrument. I wish that I might have invented it," after first inspecting the image dissector in 1930. Most important, Philo produced initial versions of his invention, whereas Zworykin relied "entirely [on] oral" evidence; he also "did not hold up well under cross-examination from Farnsworth's lawyers."[155] Still, RCA appealed the decision, but the ultimate outcome was a foregone conclusion for most reasonable observers.

The pressures of this drawn-out litigation, however, along with the usual demands of the job and constant money worries, took their accumulated toll on Philo Farnsworth. "After ten years of working almost around the clock, at times with a complete lack of concern for food and sleep," his health began to deteriorate.[156] His sister Agnes remembers, "It was around 1935 that I saw the beginning of a change in my brother. . . . He [grew increasingly] withdrawn. . . . He would be working on a problem and he couldn't turn it off."[157] Despite being a Mormon, Farnsworth began to drink heavily as his only release from his constant conflicts with RCA and his single-minded focus on work: "He sought help from doctors and psychiatrists who urged him to slow down and regenerate his body. They even recommended alcohol and tobacco, and finally gave him a prescription for chloral hydrate [a sedative for insomnia], but these drugs [became] addictive" to him over the long run.[158]

In December 1936, Farnsworth and his engineering staff launched W3XPF in Wyndmoor, Pennsylvania, the sixteenth experimental TV station to actually get on the air in America.[159] The Farnsworth Television Corporation operated W3XPF in suburban Philadelphia for two years, while the inventor-turned-businessman applied to the FCC for a commercial license. RCA lobbied hard against him, and his request was eventually denied. Philo Farnsworth and his associates then decided that the next best thing to do was restructure the company, refocusing it on manufacturing, as well as researching and telecasting. He also began to think for the first time that he might be losing his competitive edge over Zworykin and his associates; the quality of RCA's electronic TV system had now reached a kind of parity with his. He also felt that time was running out on his television patents which had been originally issued in 1930. "The problem was patents go into public domain after seventeen years," explains Pem Farnsworth, and Philo "worried that we wouldn't have commercial television until his patents were about to expire."[160] With all of this weighing on his mind, Farnsworth and his family moved away from Philadelphia in 1938 to the peace and quiet of rural Maine, providing him with a modicum of breathing room to relax. His immediate concerns were renewing his waning strength and attending to his growing bouts of depression and alcoholism.

Executives from RCA and the newly reorganized Farnsworth Television and Radio Corporation signed a patent licensing agreement on October 2, 1939, where RCA consented to pay $1 million to Farnsworth over a ten-year period, along with any and all royalties for the use of his patents. Formal talks began the week after the gala opening of the 1939 World's Fair in New York, and tough negotiations continued for four grueling months. David Sarnoff was not there, but he directed Otto Schairer, his close confidant and vice president in charge of patents, to cut a deal. Sarnoff had always boasted, "It's our job to collect royalties; we don't *pay* royalties," but there was no getting around the fact that Farnsworth "held six basic patents for television" and without them, no satisfactory all-electronic TV system could operate at peak efficiency or comparable sets be manufactured.[161] Sarnoff was humbled, but he was also a realist. He "had tried everything to outmaneuver his smaller and supposedly weaker rival—buyout offers, legal challenges, patent avoidance, and smear campaigns. In each case, Farnsworth had demonstrated an astonishing resilience."[162] Philo Farnsworth was seriously wounded, but he was not dead and gone forever.

Like Sarnoff, Farnsworth also did not attend the signing. He had suffered a nervous breakdown in June, and after a brief stint in a Boston hospital, he was back recovering at his home in Maine. Bargaining on his behalf was his longtime friend and lawyer, Donald Lippincott, and the new president of Farnsworth Television and Radio, Edwin ("Nick") Nicholas, who had previously headed the patents division at RCA. Nicholas had joined Farnsworth a year earlier, after being chosen to lead the corporation at the end of an extended national search, and his insider knowledge of RCA's personnel and procedures made him invaluable during the complex and prolonged negotiations.[163] Pem Farnsworth later disclosed that the "agreement was pretty close to what we were asking, and Phil was pleased."[164] The Farnsworths were eager to start all over again with their new corporation, despite having already weathered a lifetime of experiences chasing Philo's dream of an all-electronic television system. After all, he was still a young man of thirty-three. The fact was that many individuals had similarly put their hearts and souls into the race for TV—inventors and their supporting engineers, industrialists and their lawyers. RCA's chief negotiator, Otto Schairer, for example, felt deep down in his bones that there was "more at stake than royalties," recounts Daniel Stashower in *The Boy Genius and the Mogul*. He had been "instrumental in bringing Zworykin to Westinghouse in 1923," and other than the inventor whom he had known for years and his old ally David Sarnoff, no one had "a more personal investment in RCA's television program" than Schairer. After his former colleague Nick Nicholas signed the contract and "pushed [it] across the conference table," Otto Schairer "was overwhelmed by a devastating sense of loss. Bending down to sign, the lawyer's eyes filled with tears."[165]

For his part, David Sarnoff "shrugged off the humiliation of signing a patent royalty agreement and gone full steam ahead with NBC's broadcasts." Since boyhood, his modus operandi was to find ways to turn temporary setbacks into even greater victories down the road. He was fully "aware that Farnsworth's percentage [of all essential TV patents] was invisible to the public whose television sets carried the NBC logo."[166] From his point of view, the silver lining in the agreement was that he was now free to develop the commercial potential of the NBC television network. After predicting in his opening April 20th remarks at the 1939 World's Fair that the "miracle of . . . television will one day . . . bring into the home the visual images of scenes and events which up to now have come there as mind pictures conjured up by the human voice," he directed the NBC mobile unit to produce a series of televised "firsts" for airing on WNBT-TV (later WNBC-TV) housed at Radio City in Rockefeller Center.[167] In rapid succession, the NBC field team captured the first baseball game between Princeton and Columbia Universities at Baker Field in New York on May 17; the first championship boxing match between Lou Nova and Max Baer at Yankee Stadium on June 1; the first network transmission to WRGB-TV in Schenectady of King George VI and Queen Elizabeth's visit to the 1939 World's Fair in New York on June 10; the first major league baseball game between the Cincinnati Reds and the Brooklyn Dodgers at Ebbets Field on August 26; and the first pro football game between the Philadelphia Eagles and the Brooklyn Dodgers at Ebbets Field on October 22, among other special events.

Farnsworth was likewise concentrating on the future as he moved his wife and children out to Fort Wayne, Indiana, soon after the patents agreement was signed, while still keeping his Maine residence as a family retreat. Farnsworth Television and Radio had purchased the Capehart Corporation phonograph plant in Fort Wayne during February 1939 and used it to manufacture record players and radios, as well as televisions. Philo's new title was vice president in charge of research; he was now thankful and relieved to be spending more time in the laboratory than in the boardroom. Nevertheless "the foundation of the Farnsworth organization had always been the man [and] his patent portfolio" and so it remained.[168] *Time* magazine declared that Farnsworth Television and Radio was in the "strongest patent position in television outside of RCA"; furthermore "no television sender or receiver can be made without using some of his patents."[169] "The reverse was also true," reminds Donald Godfrey; "Farnsworth needed access to RCA's Zworykin patents" as well.[170]

For all intents and purposes, electronic television had arrived in the United States by the end of 1939. Philo T. Farnsworth had first introduced it to the general public in a fifty-seat museum at Philadelphia's Franklin Institute during the dog days of August 1934. Less than five years later, David Sarnoff mobilized the full resources of RCA and NBC to reintroduce the medium to an audience of international proportions at the 1939 World's Fair in New York. Sarnoff produced a coming-out party of such historic magnitude that Farnsworth's earlier achievement paled by comparison and quickly faded away. This collective amnesia did not occur by accident. It "was mainly due to the treatment that Farnsworth received at the hands of the RCA patents and publicity departments, who claimed that RCA had virtually single-handedly invented television and refused to give any other inventor or company the slightest credit." Over the next half-century, David Sarnoff, Vladimir Zworykin, and RCA earned the lion's share of the money and the glory, while "Farnsworth has largely been relegated to the dustbin of history."[171]

Today, a reclamation project is well under way. A growing number of articles and books, along with an hour-long documentary, have emerged over the last generation, weighing the relative merits of Philo T. Farnsworth versus Vladimir Zworykin and debating who of the two inventors most deserves to be called "father of television."[172] Despite the fact that both made pivotal and indispensable contributions to the invention of TV, Farnsworth usually emerges victorious in these new scholarly and popular sources, largely out of sympathy for the teen-aged prodigy whose story is almost too good to be true, as well as a backlash against the harsh and shameful treatment he received at the hands of RCA during the 1930s. "It is absolutely mind-boggling what Farnsworth accomplished," marvels Erik Barnouw: "This kid out there put together the first electronic television. And it came just at the time that everyone was assuming that from now on inventions are going to be something in corporate laboratories."[173]

In retrospect, the race for television was simultaneously wondrous and ignominious. The current state of TV technology probably reveals more of Zworykin's imprint than anyone else's. His "camera tube (the iconoscope) and picture tube (the kinescope) are clearly the forerunners of modern camera and picture tube technology," testifies current historian and former television engineer Albert Abramson, while "Farnsworth's camera tube (the image dissector) had no storage capacity [and thus] bore the seeds of its own destruction."[174] However, Zworykin's research and development was far better funded, supported over a longer period of time by an immense corporate infrastructure, and less impeded by outside pressures and harassment than Philo Farnsworth's work. To be sure, no one person "fathered" television; instead, many people are responsible for bringing TV into being. Television as a technology is much more than a camera and a receiver; it is a process of conception, invention, commercialization, program production, and nonstop innovation. Television's birth involved one-of-a-kind inventors and workaday engineers, farsighted industrialists and bottom-line corporate executives, creative personnel and consumers adventurous enough to embrace this astonishing new technology and make it their own.

In the end, the coming of television does not just reach well back into the nineteenth century; its periodic reinvention is an ongoing process that continues today. In addition, TV's history and development is always subject to the push and pull of American culture. As

Despite creating the first all-electronic television system, Philo Farnsworth's camera tube (the image dissector) was limited by its lack of storage capacity. Courtesy of Library of American Broadcasting at the University of Maryland.

RCA's money and man-power support of Vladimir Zworykin's research led to the creation of the image orthicon in 1939—the next-generation camera tube. Courtesy of Library of American Broadcasting at the University of Maryland.

representatives for RCA and Farnsworth Television and Radio were hammering out their new patent agreement during the fall of 1939, for instance, the U.S. economy was steadily recovering from the 1938 recession. Business prospects were looking up, while tensions in Europe suddenly erupted. Without warning, Germany invaded Poland on September 1, bringing about the start of World War II. Britain and France responded by declaring war on Germany on September 3. America was also inching ever closer into this international conflict. On November 4, President Roosevelt signed the Neutrality Act of 1939, permitting the United States to sell arms to Britain, France, and their allies in anticipation of the oncoming German *blitzkrieg* (lightning war). These developments created an ominous if still seemingly faraway backdrop as Farnsworth, Zworykin, Sarnoff, and literally thousands of other people busily worked to realize television as an emerging industry and art form. TV's imminent rising would be a "false dawn" during the early 1940s, according to Christopher Sterling and John Kittross in *Stay Tuned: A History of American Broadcasting*.[175] Like the rest of America, no one in this newly arrived television industry dreamed that in two short years all of their professional energies would be devoted to a wartime buildup and mobilization. Television technology would be rethought and reinvented throughout the 1940s to accommodate the life-and-death struggle of World War II and the eventual commercial fulfillment of an industry, just as it would when facing similar crises and challenges time and again in the decades to come.

2

NOT GOING ACCORDING TO PLAN
Remodeling the Tube in a Time of Crisis—1940–1947

JUST AROUND THE CORNER

> Television is one of the few sciences which, from its earliest beginnings, has been developed out in the open and in full view of the questioning public.
> *New York Evening World*, 15 December 1929[1]

When the New York World's Fair closed its doors for the winter on October 31, 1939, the number of visitors had slowly been declining over the late summer and early fall months, and overall attendance stood well below projected expectations. A similar pattern was evident in the reception that TV was receiving from the general public. "Television has suffered from its own prophets," charged the *Saturday Evening Post*; "too much prophecy has made the magic box something of an anticlimax."[2] Indeed, the arrival of TV had been promised so often from so many different quarters since the earliest demonstrations of Jenkins's "radiovisor" and Baird's "televisor" in the mid 1920s that much of the country and its press corps had long ago grown weary of all the unrealized expectations. For example, *Newsweek* cautioned in February 1935 that "television has been 'just around the corner' for the past seven or eight years."[3] This same newsweekly reflected three years later that "the mushrooming of radio stations and networks in the early 1920s gave a miracle-minded public its first faith in the imminence of television . . . but nothing happened. . . . Hopes [have] been dashed so many times since 1925."[4]

In December 1934, analysts at the Market Research Corporation of America (MRCA) took the pulse of domestic consumers throughout the East Coast and Midwest in an extensive month-long survey to gauge the public's awareness of television and its interest in adopting this new technology. In a report published in February 1935, the MRCA researchers found that 91 percent of the population had already heard of TV and that 50 percent "expect[ed] television to be in the home in 4¾ years or sooner."[5] In that same year, *Collier's* associate editor Owen P. White asked: "Television is an accomplished fact in the laboratory. Why haven't we it in our homes?"[6] On January 9, 1936, the *New York World-Telegram* revealed that "the Federal Trade

Commission told Congress in a rather startling statement yesterday, television is practically ready for popular use," while *Variety* proclaimed a week later that "commercial television is a definite possibility in 1937 and more than a probability in 1938."[7]

When January 1938 rolled around, however, the *New York World-Telegram* was again lamenting the fact that "television, the problem child of twentieth century creative genius, is still eluding its masters with a perplexing game of hide and seek."[8] Corporate researchers and independent inventors alike were attempting to tiptoe along a thin line where, on one hand, they were heralding the coming of TV with their public pronouncements, while, on the other, they were trying not to overstate when exactly the medium would be available to consumers. More often than not, though, booster rhetoric got the best of them, as they typically fell victim to their own enthusiasm when describing the impending arrival of television throughout the 1930s.

A case in point was a widely circulated scenario devised by journalist Don Wharton after "gathering information from dozens of sources, sifting, checking, discarding, and piecing [it all] together." The "following Five-Year Calendar for commercial television" appeared in the February 1937 issue of *Scribner's Magazine* and was reprised a month later in the trade journal, *Radio Jobber News*. Wharton predicted that by "January 1938," TV is possible in New York and Philadelphia, which is "getting a jump on more populous Chicago through the fact that Philco, RCA, and Farnsworth research have been centered in the Philadelphia-Camden area and that Philco and RCA receiving sets will be manufactured there." "By January 1939," television is "fairly probable" in New York and Philadelphia, "with Chicago and Los Angeles a little if any behind." These four cities will together reach nearly twenty million viewers. "By January 1940," TV will also be "on the air" in "Boston, San Francisco, Cleveland, Detroit, Baltimore (transmitter so as to cover Washington too), Pittsburgh, St. Louis, and possibly . . . Milwaukee, Buffalo, Minneapolis, Cincinnati, [and] Kansas City."[9]

"By January 1941," moreover, one or more "networks on the Eastern Seaboard are not unthinkable." And finally, "by January 1942, the potential networks" on the East Coast "could hardly fail to be paralleled by ones in the Great Lakes section," linking Chicago, Milwaukee, Detroit, Toledo, Cleveland, Pittsburgh, and Buffalo.[10] Despite being five to seven years premature in his plan of action, Wharton's blueprint for the commercial development of television was remarkably prescient. He aptly identified that "the larger your city the sooner you will have television"; and he accurately predicted that TV will start out as "a local service."[11] Nevertheless, forecasts by Wharton and others during the 1930s couldn't help but pressure more reluctant broadcasters, such as William S. Paley, president of the Columbia Broadcasting System (CBS) into exploring the possibilities of television, even though it is unlikely that he would ever have taken this step so soon on his own.

On September 26, 1928, William Paley was only two days shy of his twenty-seventh birthday when he assumed the reigns of a small, struggling radio network, the Columbia Phonograph Broadcasting System (CPBS). Paley purchased a majority share of CPBS with the help of his father Samuel, a multimillionaire who had earlier founded the Congress Cigar Company in Philadelphia. Young Bill had originally become interested in radio while experimenting with advertising his family's La Palina cigars (a Spanish neologism of "Paley") on CPBS's Philadelphia affiliate, WCAU. Bill Paley had a natural flair for the broadcasting business, and after selling a minority interest to Paramount in 1929, he acquired the cash reserves and credit rating to rebuild the newly rechristened CBS into a capable and increasingly popular alternative to NBC's red and blue networks. Years later both Paley and RCA president David Sarnoff admitted that their longstanding relationship was cordial but highly competitive. "From the earliest days of radio, when he was the 'grand old man' and I was that 'bright young kid," remembers Bill Paley in his 1979 memoir, "we were friends, confidants, and fierce competitors all at the same time. . . . I always thought his strengths lay in the more technical and physical aspects of radio and television, while mine lay in understanding talent, programming, and what went on the air."[12]

Where Sarnoff dreamed of extending the boundaries of TV as a technology and an industry, Paley was far more interested in producing high-quality entertainment and overtaking NBC in the ratings. CBS reluctantly ventured into television on July 21, 1931, employing a "radiovisor" and other mechanical TV technology that the network purchased from Jenkins. These early experiments over New York station W2XAB ceased in 1933, not resuming again until CBS hired Hungarian inventor Dr. Peter Goldmark in late 1935 to set up an all-electronic TV system. Throughout much of the mid to late 1930s, CBS relied heavily on television cameras, receivers, and accessories acquired from RCA. The network even bought an "experimental transmitter" from its much larger corporate rival, installing it "atop the Chrysler Building," which appropriately was the second tallest skyscraper in New York behind the Empire State Building where NBC already telecast "with much the same equipment."[13] Paley next instructed Goldmark and his staff of four engineers to build the biggest studio in New York, which they did in "the loft above the main waiting room in New York's Grand Central Station."[14] "The urge to beat RCA and its ruler, David

Sarnoff, was such an overriding force at CBS," recalls Peter Goldmark, "that it actually began to shape the direction of my own career."[15]

Vladimir Zworykin and his vast engineering team at the RCA research laboratory in Camden, New Jersey, had a seemingly insurmountable lead over Peter Goldmark and his assistants at CBS in the race for television. Goldmark and his colleagues ardently played catch-up for the rest of the 1930s. In March 1940, however, the inventor experienced an epiphany of sorts while watching *Gone with the Wind*. "It was the first color movie I had seen, and the color was magnificent," confides Goldmark; "I could hardly think of going back to the phosphor images of regular black-and-white television. All through the long, four-hour movie I was obsessed with the thought of applying color to television."[16]

For the next six months, Goldmark worked nonstop on a hybrid TV system that eventually incorporated Philo Farnsworth's (cathode ray) image dissector tube with two mechanical disks containing red, green, and blue filters, which were synchronized at the camera and receiver ends. Together, these spinning disks added rudimentary color to an all-electronic television picture. Goldmark demonstrated his new apparatus to the Federal Communication Commission in September 1940, asking that his color TV process be approved as the industry standard over the existing black-and-white systems that were also under consideration. All of CBS's main competitors—RCA, Farnsworth, Philco, DuMont, and Zenith—argued in response that the mechanical components in Goldmark's hybrid TV system limited its quality and long-term viability. The FCC took the CBS senior engineering executive's request under advisement, as Bill Paley hoped that at least this latest innovation by Goldmark would slow down the RCA juggernaut's aggressive moves toward commercializing television on its own terms.

Ever since the opening of the New York World's Fair on April 30, 1939, David Sarnoff and his colleagues at RCA and NBC were eager to make the transition from experimental to commercial TV as quickly as possible. Sarnoff applied continuing outside pressure on the FCC throughout the fall and early winter until the regulatory agency finally proposed new rules for limited commercial telecasting on December 21, 1939. The FCC followed up this action by holding public hearings in mid January 1940, formally adopting limited commercialization in late February, and authorizing September 1 as the official start date for all interested broadcasters.[17] David Sarnoff was delighted with the FCC's decision in this regard.

Given an inch, though, he took a mile. Instead of slowly easing into commercial TV, RCA issued a nationwide press release on March 12 trumpeting a "new television service" followed on March 20 with full-page advertisements promoting its complete line of console and portable receivers in all of the New York metropolitan newspapers and the major radio trade journals.[18] Sarnoff hoped to sell at least "twenty-five thousand sets at reduced prices."[19] The FCC responded at once by suspending its September 1 approval date and calling for further hearings in April "to determine whether research and experimentation and the achievement of higher standards for television transmission was being unduly retarded by the action of RCA."[20] Sarnoff was stunned by the FCC's sudden assertiveness; he had underestimated the resolve of the agency's new chairman, James Lawrence Fly, who proved straightaway that he would stand toe-to-toe with the RCA president if the situation warranted it.

James Fly was a New Deal liberal from Texas appointed to head the FCC by Franklin D. Roosevelt on September 1, 1939. Just like the Federal Radio Commission before it, the FCC spent its first five years acting in a mostly weak and muddled fashion when faced with the entrepreneurial excesses of the much more powerful broadcasting industry, especially when it came to the brazenness of RCA. In contrast, Fly ushered in a short-lived activist period for the FCC, greatly expanding its regulatory agenda and influence. He believed that broadcasters were trustees licensed "under mandate to serve the public interest," and he saw his job as FCC chairman as one of ensuring that "primary regard" be given to the "rights of the listening public."[21] These ideals are clearly stated in the Federal Communication Act of 1934, but up to this point the FCC had rarely assumed the role of a consumer advocate.

All this changed during James Fly's tenure at the agency. On March 24, 1940, Fly told the *New York Times* that the "current marketing campaign of the Radio Corporation of America" demonstrates an utter "disregard of the commission's findings and recommendations." He called RCA's promotional activities "heedless of advice to go slow," intensifying the "danger" of "crystallizing transmission standards at present levels," and "gaining an unfair advantage over competitors," possibly causing "them to abandon further research and experimentation which is in the public interest."[22] On April 2, he next took to the airwaves over RCA's own NBC blue and the Mutual radio network, "declaring that Congress had placed upon the Commission the duty to issue licenses, to foster research and development, to encourage the achievement of high standards," and to guarantee "that the activities of a single broadcaster" would not make its "own equipment dominant."[23] Finally on April 10, the FCC chairman characterized RCA's marketing foray as a "blitzkrieg" in testimony before the U.S. Senate Committee on Interstate Commerce in Washington, D.C.[24]

Sarnoff got the message and immediately shifted gears. After weeks of being called everything from an untrustworthy and out-of-control captain of industry by his corporate competitors and the FCC to a starry-eyed dreamer by trade journalists (a reporter for *Radio Daily* even christened television "Sarnoff's Folly"), the RCA president mounted a public relations offensive of his own.[25] He fortified his own internal publicity staff with the New York firm of Ames and Norr, flooding the print media with laissez-faire arguments as to why RCA should be allowed to bring TV to the American people as soon as possible. Over the next few weeks, as a result, "the position of the FCC was described by newspapers around the country as 'one of the screwiest examples of federal wet-nursing ever witnessed'; as 'tyrannous restraint'; as 'destructive of the system of free enterprise'; as 'arbitrary and dictatorial'; as 'business baiting'; as the 'ham-stringing of business recovery'; and as 'a new high in bureaucratic stupidity.' "[26]

To no one's surprise, Sarnoff gave as well as he got in his public debate with the FCC, and, in the face of all the outside pressure, the agency backed off a bit. That summer, the FCC called for "yet another committee," the National Television System Committee (NTSC), "comprised of engineering experts from the entire industry, appointed by the Radio Manufacturers Association. The NTSC would develop a final consensus of television standards" and submit their findings to the FCC for final approval. With this action, James Fly and the rest of the FCC commissioners were signaling that if all went well with the work of the NTSC, they would authorize commercial television soon afterward.[27]

Beginning its deliberations in late July 1940, the NTSC worked tirelessly over the next six months to hammer out an acceptable compromise for all of the inventors and broadcasters involved. Chaired by the well-respected GE research engineer, Dr. Walter R. G. Baker (WRGB in Schenectady was later named after him), the NTSC considered a wide range of proposals, including RCA's black-and-white system (441 lines at thirty frames per second with AM [amplitude modulation] sound) at the low end, DuMont's (625 lines at fifteen frames per second with FM sound) at the high end, and CBS's color apparatus somewhere in the middle. Baker and his NTSC associates forged a nearly unanimous industry-wide consensus around 525 lines at thirty frames per second with FM sound, submitting this recommendation to the FCC on March 8, 1941. In addition, they tabled the issue of color TV, pending further refinement. For its part, on May 3, after conducting public hearings on the matter, the FCC announced its acceptance of the NTSC directive. The agency also authorized July 1, 1941, as the debut day for commercial TV in America. "Suddenly the long battle was over," recount David Fisher and Marshall Fisher in *Tube: The Invention of Television.* "Although the standards adopted were not RCA's, David Sarnoff had won again. RCA could easily convert its transmission standards, and commercial television—on which RCA figured to clean up—was finally about to begin."[28]

On May 2, 1941, however, the FCC had one final surprise to deliver to RCA, CBS, and the rest of the industry, in its "Report on Chain Broadcasting." Ever the "antimonopolist of deep conviction," James Fly and his fellow commissioners proposed new rules to eliminate noncompetitive conditions in broadcast networking, such as exerting disproportionate control over affiliate stations and owning "more than one network."[29] According to historian J. Fred MacDonald,

> Fly met formidable resistance. At CBS Paley used his political friendships and company lawyers to resist an FCC order giving local stations greater freedom in their contractual relationships with the national networks; Paley lost. Sarnoff went all the way to the U.S. Supreme Court in seeking to vacate the commission order that NBC sell part of its operation; he also failed. As a result corporate ties with affiliates were made more equitable, and in 1943 NBC blue was sold. Within two years the divested network became the American Broadcasting Company (ABC).[30]

The vague outlines of television as a business and an industry in the United States were slowly taking shape. NBC's W2XBS officially became WNBT at 1:30 P.M. on July 1, 1941, with a USO (United Service Organizations) fundraiser, followed by a series of quiz and game shows, such as "a test video episode of *Truth or Consequences*" hosted by Ralph Edward for Ivory Soap. WNBT's first "commercial rates were $120 for an hour-long sponsored program during the evening and $60 for an hour program during the day."[31] For example, Lowell Thomas's fifteen-minute nightly radio news roundup was simulcast over television and sponsored by Sun Oil for $30. "The absolute first commercial," remembers Lenore Jensen, an actress who also "hosted several early TV women's shows," featured "the face of a Bulova watch. It had a sweep second hand. They would focus on it for one minute while they played the *Minute Waltz.*"[32]

NBC was way ahead of the competition in being in the position to accept advertising from clients during this first full day of commercial service. "CBS had no sponsorship lined up yet," but Bill Paley and company did turn their New York station W2XAB into WCBW (later to become WCBS) on July 1, telecasting "a dance lesson, a newscast, and an art exhibit." DuMont continued its "noncommercial broadcasting of film and live programming" over its "own experimental station, W2XWV," which it opened in "April 1940" at "515 Madison Avenue, a midtown office building."[33] From this point onward, NBC, CBS, and DuMont "dominated television in New York and the rest of the East Coast through the late 1940s."[34] All across the country, in fact, "twenty-three television stations were either on or in the process of construction" during the summer of 1941 at an estimated price tag of "about $500,000 to $750,000" per "station with studio equipment."[35] TV appeared "ready to take off at last," but once again "outside forces intervened to put the medium back in the freezer."[36]

On December 7, 1941, the imperial Japanese air force made a sneak attack on the U.S. naval base at Pearl Harbor, Hawaii, killing nearly 2,500 Americans, wounding more than 1,175 other military and civilian personnel, sinking or damaging 18 warships, and destroying 188 planes. World War II had finally arrived kicking and screaming on the doorstep of the United States as WCBW telecast a "nine-hour report" that day, "providing the first television news instant special" anchored by Dick Hubbel; "at the time the CBS station was the only TV subscriber to the United Press radio wire and had a news staff of two."[37] The next day, the United States declared war on Japan as President Roosevelt addressed a joint session of Congress calling December 7 "a date that will live in infamy." On December 11, four days after the Japanese attack, Germany declared war on the United States, galvanizing American public support behind FDR in an all-out fight for Europe and North Africa as well as for the Pacific Islands and Japan.

When news of the December 7 Pearl Harbor morning attack reached David Sarnoff in New York that afternoon, the RCA president immediately "fire[d] off a telegram" to Roosevelt: "All our facilities are ready and at your instant service. We await your commands." FDR had called Sarnoff to the White House for a private get-together earlier that summer without the usual fanfare of a formal visit in anticipation of America's eventual entry into the war. At that face-to-face meeting, the industrialist had assured the president that "RCA's global communication network could swiftly be integrated with military channels. As the world's largest producer of electronic tubes, RCA was prepared, he told Roosevelt, to convert its plants, machinery, and manpower overnight to war production."[38] For all intents and purposes, World War II put the growth of commercial television on everyone's back burner, although it did greatly stimulate advancements in TV-related research and development. In hindsight, the "cathode-ray tube was one of the secret weapons that played a large part in winning the war."[39] The "intensified research effort" of RCA, GE, AT&T, DuMont, and literally dozens of other smaller electronics firms "produced huge jumps in television technology, which brought TV into the modern era when the war was over."[40]

LONG TIME NO SEE

By the summer of '41, I was convinced we could not avoid war and I knew RCA would be in the thick of it. Our technology would be indispensable for military communications. It was just too late in the game for television.

DAVID SARNOFF, *The General*, 1967[41]

Beginning in 1942, many of the young men who worked in the fledgling TV industry in America either enlisted or were drafted as personnel shortages greatly limited operations in the nation's few existing television stations. On May 12 of that year, the War Production Board prohibited any further expansion of TV across the country. This official ban stayed in effect until hostilities ended more than three years later. Wartime regulations froze the number of authorized stations in the United States at nine (three in New York City, one each in Schenectady and Philadelphia, and two each in Chicago and Los Angeles), of which seven eventually made it on to the air and stayed there.[42] To keep licenses active, the FCC obliged stations to telecast at least a minimum of four hours per week. Still, this modest requirement proved to be a continuing challenge for many outlets because replacement workers and parts were nearly impossible to find. By war's end in 1945, the seven surviving stations were NBC's WNBT, CBS's WCBW, and DuMont's WABD (formerly W2XWV until 1944) in New York City; "the General Electric outlet (WRGB) in Schenectady; the Philco station (WPTZ) in Philadelphia; the Balaban & Katz facility (WBKB) in Chicago; and the Don Lee operation in Los Angeles (W6XAO)."[43]

Despite chronic personnel and equipment shortfalls, television in America was far better off than it was anywhere else in the world just before and during the war. This state of affairs flew in the face of the conventional wisdom when as early as 1935 *Broadcasting* and the rest of the trade press in the United States was reporting that "Europe is alive to television" and well ahead of this nation in making television "a practical entertainment medium operating alongside radio."[44] Mass-circulated magazines, such as *Business Week*, also claimed that "Germany is up front . . . [in] commercializ[ing] television. . . . A network of transmitters is being built, daily programs are already being offered. Five German companies are manufacturing television sets. . . . Experience of Germany and England in this field illustrate one advantage that closely-populated nations have over our own great open spaces."[45]

To be sure, some industry experts were advising against believing these exaggerated assessments, including editor Hugo Gernsback of *Radio-Craft*, who cautioned his readers to "not be deceived by what is going on in Europe today. There is nothing happening in England, Germany or France in television of any great moment."[46] Of course, England, Germany, and France, as well as Russia and Japan, each relied solely on one government-run station that was wholly dependent on state funding for its full support, whereas TV in the United States was currently organized around seven privately owned stations that competed for viewers and sponsors with dozens of more outlets soon to arrive. In addition, "England had "approximately 4,000 to 6,000 television receivers in operation" at the outset of hostilities when set manufacturing virtually ended all over the world because of war-related priorities and resource restrictions. By comparison, "in Germany not more than 500 television receivers [were] in use" at the time; France, Russia, and Japan had even less, while the United States numbered slightly more than eight thousand sets nationwide.[47]

After Pearl Harbor, the American broadcasting industry voluntarily shifted its emphasis away from the commercial development of TV to assisting in the war effort in any way possible. Most of the television programming, for instance, grew increasingly more public service oriented: "Tens of thousands of civil defense volunteers and others were trained via TV sets that were placed in classrooms, firehouses, police stations, and even private homes." Sample lessons telecast included "such topics as blackouts, poison gas attacks, and decontamination procedures."[48] College basketball games and professional boxing matches were also "televised for the benefit of hospitalized GIs" who watched on donated receivers.[49] Moreover, research and development revolved around new applications of television as a means of high-tech surveillance, as a way of extending sight under battlefield conditions, and as the key to certain kinds of precision weaponry.

Radar was one of the most novel innovations that the cathode ray tube was used for during World War II. "By a little different adaptation of the same principles whereby a man in Chicago can watch a ballgame in New York, an observer on a warship can see a plane approaching hundreds of miles away. Or the pilot of the plane can see the ship, even though it is hidden by fog and darkness."[50] Another surveillance device developed from TV-related technology at the start of the war was Loran (long range navigation), a system that accurately pinpoints ship or aircraft positions by timing the arrival of low-frequency radio signals received from two or more strategically placed transmitters. Probably the most versatile use of cathode ray tubing for observational purposes to emerge from World War II was the creation of the oscillograph, which scans everything from machines to rock formations, much the same way as X-rays peer inside the human body. For example, oscillographs regulate watches, time shutter speeds of cameras, test engine ignition at high speed, check "give" in bridges and elevator cables, and measure the effects of radio interference or lightning on power lines, just to name a few of oscillography's many practical applications.

As far as extending sight in other ways, RCA researchers experimented with adapting the infrared imaging tubes that they used in television for purposes as widely different as night viewing and enhancing the accuracy of military sharpshooters. "We put small tubes in binoculars which were attached to a helmet . . . for driving at night with infrared lights," remembers Les Flory, an original member of RCA's electronic TV research group. "We also made something called a Sniperscope. It was a monocular device on an infra-tube with a rifle and also an infrared light. You would illuminate a target with an infrared light and you could see it through your telescope, and whoever you were focusing on couldn't see the light at all."[51] Vladimir Zworykin oversaw the engineering team that developed these top secret image intensifiers, as both the U.S. Army and the U.S. Navy used Snooperscope (for nighttime reconnaissance) and Sniperscope (for high-precision targeting) under battlefield conditions as early as 1943.

Zworykin also provided the initial inspiration for the invention of TV-controlled weaponry. He first proposed this type of application in a 1934 paper titled, "Flying Torpedo with an Electric Eye," but "RCA engineers and scientists" didn't develop and test "the necessary technology, such as relatively lightweight TV cameras that could fly aboard weapons" until World War II finally began in Europe during the fall of 1939. By 1940, "the government started funding RCA's work, now cloaked in secrecy and given such code names as 'Dragon' and 'Pelican.'"[52] "This was Zworykin's idea," confirms Loren Jones, a contemporary and colleague of Les Flory at RCA. "He was the first person to, in effect, propose that you could change the course of a missile after it left the gun barrel." "Loren Jones and I were responsible for that project," adds RCA's engineering vice president Ted Smith. "We persuaded the Navy that TV could be useful to them. One of the contracts we got was to build a small plywood plane without a motor, which could be hooked onto an airplane. There was a television camera that was mounted on this thing that could be controlled from the ground. The point was to put a charge with explosives in it and smash it by remote control into an enemy target."[53]

What enabled this TV-guided weaponry to become practicable and effective up to an estimated 50 percent of the time was the development and refinement of the image orthicon pickup or camera tube. The first-generation orthicon produced in 1939 was ten to twenty times more sensitive than Farnsworth's image dissector or Zworykin's iconoscope. By 1944, however, the image orthicon combined all "the best features" of its predecessor tubes. It was "a hundred times more sensitive than the original orthicon" and thus thousands of times sharper and clearer than the image dissector or iconoscope, even able to produce an acceptable image while relying solely on the light of a match. A younger generation of RCA engineers—Albert Rose, Harold Law, and Paul Wymer—were mostly responsible for the image orthicon. During the war years, Zworykin "was no longer intimately involved. He settled into an administrative position as director of RCA's electronic research laboratory and no longer worked actively as a scientist."[54]

Still, the entire RCA research team, including Zworykin, took great pride in the development of the image orthicon, and all of them began referring to it with droll satisfaction as "Immy." They later feminized their nickname for the tube to "Emmy," which also served as the eponym for the annual creative and production awards given by the Academy of Television Arts and Sciences beginning in 1949. "Al brought Harold Law and me in to work with him," recalls Wymer. "We worked on it continuously throughout the whole war. The objective was the TV-guided torpedo, but the image orthicon ended up being used in television from 1946 until about 1965 or 1970. There aren't many devices that have a useful period of 25 years. They actually called it the 'atomic bomb of television' because it made television a feasible thing."[55]

From 1943 through 1945, though, the image orthicon's main function was providing direction for high-precision weaponry. "TV technology was being used to guide explosives into striking and destroying enemy targets" throughout the European and Pacific theaters. In fact, RCA manufactured about four thousand of these units "for both the Army and the Navy to use in unmanned bombers and other flying weapons."[56] The enemy combatants also developed similar tactics, each in their own way. The Japanese, for instance, launched kamikaze planes loaded with explosives, resulting in the suicide deaths of the pilots involved, as well as killing the victims. The Germans deployed V-1 and V-2 rockets, although these missiles relied on neither humans nor electronic guidance systems so they were relatively inaccurate, despite the terrifying effect they had on civilian populations because of the high-pitched buzzing sound they emitted just before impact.

*TV-related technologies—
such as camera-guided
missiles—served as the basis
for a wide assortment of high-
precision weaponry during
World War II. Courtesy of
The David Sarnoff Library.*

Probably the most celebrated television-guided torpedo mission
was the fatal attempt made by Lieutenant Joseph P. Kennedy Jr. and
his copilot on August 12, 1944, to destroy the Germans' primary V-1
launch site against Britain on the Belgium coast. Kennedy, the older
brother of the future president, volunteered to commandeer a "Navy
PB4Y Liberator bomber loaded with 22,000 pounds of explosives, the
highest concentration of dynamite packed into a plane up to that point
in the war." The plan called for Kennedy and his colleague to bail out
over the English Channel "after activating remote-control guidance
and arming systems, turning the plane into a drone controlled by a
second trailing bomber." While still over Suffolk near the coastline of
southeastern England, a "friendly radio frequency signal" mistakenly
set off an "electrical detonation," blowing up Kennedy's aircraft.[57] No
bodies were ever found, underscoring the high risk associated with
these top secret missions, as well as the experimental nature of this
TV-related technology.

The tide of World War II had clearly shifted in favor of the Allies by
1943. American and Australian forces were finally on the offensive in

the South Pacific, recapturing the Solomon Islands in late August after hard-fought victories at Guadalcanal, Rendova, and New Georgia. Axis troops surrendered in North Africa in May, and the United States and Britain followed up with an amphibious assault on southern Italy in early September. Allied pilots simultaneously began their around-the-clock bombing raids of German cities and munitions factories in the Ruhr Valley, as the Soviet Army broke through the Nazi eastern front with a series of convincing victories at Stalingrad and Kursk, eventually driving Hitler's hungry and exhausted troops westward and out of the Ukraine. By February 1944, General Dwight D. Eisenhower was named Supreme Allied Commander of the Allied Expeditionary Force, thus supervising the planning and carrying out of the long-awaited liberation of Western Europe and the subsequent incursion into Nazi Germany.

In creating the many command centers that he needed to manage for the D-Day invasion, Eisenhower wasted no time in transmitting an "urgent request" to the War Department "in the spring of 1944," soliciting the top brass for their recommendation as to who would be the "best communications expert available to assist him in organizing and coordinating the labyrinthine wireless circuits that would be required for both military and press purposes when the assault on Europe was launched."[58] David Sarnoff was immediately singled out as the ideal choice, and the RCA president accepted the assignment without delay. Twenty-five years earlier, during World War I, he had "applied for a commission in naval communications, only to be turned down, ostensibly because his wireless job was considered essential to the war effort. Sarnoff suspected anti-Semitism."[59]

Nevertheless, David Sarnoff faithfully served as a lieutenant colonel in the Signal Corps reserve beginning in 1924, and in the run up to World War II, he was genuinely "appalled by the menacing anti-Semitism of the Nazis."[60] When Sarnoff was approached "twice in 1942 to help procure equipment and supplies for the military," he was only too glad to oblige.[61] "To satisfy his lifelong craving for acceptance as an American," explains biographer and confidant Kenneth Bilby, "he felt a compelling need to wear the uniform of his adopted land in its time of greatest peril." Consequently, it was a dream come true for Sarnoff when the opportunity arrived for him to serve under General Eisenhower. In turn, he worked hard and carried out his duties with distinction, being promoted to brigadier general "on December 7, 1944, the third anniversary of Pearl Harbor." From that point onward, Sarnoff let it be known "through company echelons" at RCA that "he preferred to be addressed" as "General," adopting the British practice of carrying his military title into civilian life.[62]

David Sarnoff was promoted to brigadier general in 1944. From that point onward, he preferred to be addressed as "General," adopting the British practice of carrying his military title into civilian life. Courtesy of The David Sarnoff Library.

With the outcome of the war looking more promising for the allies, NBC, CBS, and DuMont initiated internal planning sessions during the fall and early winter of 1944 for the imminent restarting of commercial television in America. In retrospect, World War II ushered in an era of windfall profits for literally hundreds of electronics equipment companies throughout the United States, including most of the more prominent names in early TV development such as RCA, GE, AT&T, Westinghouse, Zenith, Philco, and DuMont. RCA, for example, tripled its revenues and more than doubled its profits between 1942 and 1944.[63] "This is not to suggest that RCA behaved in an improper or unpatriotic fashion," clarifies business historian Robert Sobel, "but rather like all the other defense contractors, its profits rose substantially during the war."[64] Even Farnsworth Television and Radio enjoyed a brief respite of growth and prosperity during World War II. Like lots of other smaller firms, though, Farnsworth found it extremely hard to compete against its much bigger and more powerful rivals once the government contracts stopped coming in. As a result, Farnsworth Television and Radio struggled to stay solvent for a few more years after the war before it was eventually absorbed by International Telephone and Telegraph in 1949.[65]

CBS was in a much different position than most of the other large corporations involved in television in that it was primarily a broadcasting network and not a full-fledged electronics giant like RCA. William S. Paley shared David Sarnoff's Russian Jewish heritage, and he was similarly happy and eager to contribute his time, talents, and unique experience as a broadcaster to the allied cause against the Nazis. Beginning in 1943, he first served the U.S. Army in North Africa and Italy "as a civilian consultant to the Office of War Information and wore the uniform of an honorary colonel." Later, he was appointed "chief of radio broadcasting within the psychological division" at General Dwight D. Eisenhower's headquarters, where his principal duty was "producing the broadcasts that would inform the world" about the June 6, 1944, D-Day invasion and it aftermath.[66] "By all accounts," Paley did "excellent work," but he reportedly "complained that he was only a colonel," particularly when Sarnoff received his promotion to brigadier general late in 1944.[67] Eventually, after Eisenhower's European command structure disbanded, Bill Paley returned to New York in August 1945, ready to resume his leadership of CBS as the network renewed its ongoing struggle for broadcast supremacy with NBC.

Challenge number one for Paley in the fall of 1945 was deciding what to do about television. Up to this point, CBS was above all a radio network; it neither manufactured TV receivers nor committed fully to television like its archrival NBC. During May and June of 1945, moreover, the FCC issued its latest decisions concerning what technical standards and frequency allocations would be allowed in resuming commercial TV in America.

On one side, RCA was joined by all the existing set manufacturers (GE, Philco, DuMont, Zenith, and others) who basically favored "immediate establishment of postwar television using prewar standards."[68] This position essentially meant opening up the floodgates of assembly-line TV set production according to the previously approved NTSC guidelines of black-and-white imagery containing 525 lines at thirty frames per second with FM sound.

On the other side, arguing against these 1941 standards, was CBS with only one relatively unseasoned ally, ABC, which had just been purchased in 1943 for $8 million by the self-made candy (Life Savers) magnate, Edward J. Noble. ABC was just finding its footing as a fledgling network and thus provided only token support for CBS's request to slow the scheduled start of commercial television in order to integrate some of the more recent wartime innovations in TV-related technology, as well as to reconsider the newly enhanced CBS color system as the industry standard.

Opponents replied vigorously that they had already invested millions of startup dollars in facilities and equipment based on the NTSC standards. They asserted that commercializing TV sooner rather than later was an important first step in jump-starting the postwar economy. And they added that CBS's color format was incompatible with all the existing receivers, thus penalizing the ordinary American consumers who had already purchased these black-and-white sets. Finally, "as a Philco executive put it, 'There is no good reason why the public should not enjoy our present television while . . . research is going on.' "[69]

Taking this handful of reasons into consideration, the FCC predictably sided with RCA and most of the rest of the industry by reconfirming the status quo in its decision. "It is difficult to see how the FCC could have ruled otherwise," argues Fred MacDonald in retrospect. "To arrest the demand for television when the war ended would have been to thwart a public led to expect TV as soon as possible."[70] Furthermore, the number of entrepreneurs ready and willing to invest in television was skyrocketing between the summer of 1945 and June 1948 when the FCC was inundated with more than 425 television station applications. Over this time frame, the agency authorized 123 new stations (12 licensed, 25 on-air construction permits, and 86 other outstanding construction permits).[71] Still, the FCC's 1945 decision greatly limited the future expansion of both television and radio, and according to Christopher Sterling and John Kittross, "it would be hard to overemphasize the importance of the 1945 decisions that stemmed from these hearings" in determining the eventual shape of broadcasting in America over the next generation.[72]

As far as television was concerned, the agency's allocation of the VHF (very high frequency) band (channels 2 to 13) was wholly inadequate to meet the needs of TV's continued growth because it restricted the number of stations in any one market to only seven. To accommodate its color system, CBS had proposed the selection of the UHF (ultra high frequency) spectrum (channels 14 to 83) instead, which would have also made a larger number of TV channels available for everybody. In effect, the FCC "authorized full-fledged exploitation of television on an inadequate number of channels," thus setting commercial television in the United States on a course that "would endure until the flowering of cable TV in the 1980s. . . . When the commission finally opened UHF channels in 1953, it was already too late for meaningful exploitation of the spectrum." The networks were by then "committed . . . to VHF transmission," and NBC, CBS, ABC, and DuMont "contolled U.S. television" as a functioning oligopoly by the early 1950s.[73]

In the case of radio, moving "FM 'upstairs' to another part" of the VHF spectrum rendered "prewar sets obsolete, antagonized their owners, saddled the industry with huge conversion costs, and delayed FM radio for years," recounts broadcast historian Erik Barnouw, "but the RCA-NBC forces rejoiced. The move tended to protect the status quo in radio while preserving spectrum space for the expansion of television."[74] After his return from military service, David Sarnoff focused primarily on TV. In late December 1944, he called a "staff meeting" for RCA's "top fifteen executives" and gave them their marching orders: "Gentlemen, RCA has one priority—television. Whatever resources are needed will be provided. This time we are going to get the job done. There's a vast market out there and we are going to capture it before anyone else."[75]

To no one's surprise, Sarnoff made good on his corporate directive once the FCC issued its seminal 1945 decision. By the summer of 1946, he and his colleagues unveiled their latest product, "RCA's 630-TS television set, the 'Model T' of television, [which immediately] began rolling off the production line. By the end of the year, the set, with its ten-inch screen, had sold 10,000 units at $385 each. The next year, 250,000 television sets were sold, four-fifths of them RCA." In the interim, Dr. Peter Goldmark demonstrated his ever-improving color television system to the FCC and its new chairman, Charles Denny, in early 1946, and CBS once again asked the agency to adopt it as the industry standard. RCA countered with their own inferior though compatible all-electronic color system, while lawyers for all the set manufacturers argued that CBS's mechanical component was a confining limitation and a reason for denial. At first, the FCC encouraged Goldmark; "then, without warning, the tide seemed to turn against CBS. On January 30, 1947, the FCC declared that the CBS system was 'premature' and required further testing before it could be approved." In the meantime, RCA continued to "saturate the market with black-and-white sets, rendering CBS color more and more impractical every day."[76]

Although "CBS responded dramatically to the FCC ruling: it shut down its WCBS studio, dismissed its production team, and disbanded its research laboratory,"[77] this response was temporary. Less than a year later, Bill Paley and company reopened their Grand Central Station production facility, brandishing a newfound resolve along with talented producer, writer, and director Worthington Minor as studio chief. Television wasn't going away anytime soon, and neither was CBS. Paley had predicted that the postwar years would be a time of relentless competition, but even he was surprised at how cutthroat the atmosphere had gotten in October 1947, when "FCC Chairman Charles Denny, who had presided over these pro-RCA

By the summer of 1946, RCA's 630-TS set, the "Model T" of television, began rolling off the production line, selling more than 200,000 units by the end of 1947. Courtesy of The David Sarnoff Library.

decisions, resigned from the FCC to become NBC vice president and general counsel. The move brought a hue and cry" throughout the industry, but Paley merely girded his network for the long fight ahead.[78] In 1946, he assumed the chairmanship of the CBS board, and thirty-eight-year-old Frank Stanton was elected the new company president; "Stanton concentrated on organizational and policy questions, leaving the entertainment programming and the discovering and nurturing of talent to chair, William S. Paley."[79] Together they made a formidable tandem at CBS for the next twenty-five years, waging all-out war against NBC, ABC, and DuMont inside the survival-of-the-fittest world of network television.

ALL TELEVISION IS LOCAL

Prior to Fall 1948 all television programming was local, with only an occasional special event being carried by more than one station at a time. Even network-owned stations operated as local independents.

CHRISTOPHER STERLING AND JOHN KITTROSS, *Stay Tuned*, 2002[80]

In 1946, thirty-eight-year-old Frank Stanton (shown) was elected the new company president when William S. Paley became chairman of the CBS board. Courtesy of Library of American Broadcasting at the University of Maryland.

World War II officially ended when the Japanese surrendered uncon-ditionally to allied forces on board the U.S.S. *Missouri* in Tokyo Bay on September 2, 1945. American culture was forever changed in the aftermath of this global conflict. In February 1941, Henry Luce, pub-lisher of *Time*, *Fortune*, and *Life*, among other magazines, famously editorialized in *Life* that "the 20th Century is the American Cen-tury."[81] After nearly five years of war, victorious abroad and relatively unscathed at home, the United States was more confident than ever in its position as the ascendant power in the world. Beginning in 1947, the postwar prosperity created new levels of affluence through-out the country. Rationing of shoes, butter, and tires had ended in 1945, but chronic shortages in housing and jobs appeared without much warning as fifteen million veterans returned to the U.S. main-land all at once. To integrate these young soldiers back into society, Congress was prescient enough to pass the G.I. Bill of Rights on June 22, 1944, making the purchase of homes and access to higher educa-tion affordable for literally millions of these ex-servicemen and women through low-interest VA (Department of Veterans Affairs) loans. As a result, America's standard of living soared over the next decade, suburbia flourished, and a wide array of new consumer products—led by television—was introduced into stores throughout the United States.

An evident upsurge in American confidence at having emerged victorious from World War II was nevertheless tempered by a widespread underlying fear that now, with peacetime conditions, the Depression might return. American business and industry converted rapidly from a wartime to a consumer economy, as manufacturers seemingly switched overnight from producing armaments to providing domestic goods. Freed from years of going without, Americans dipped into their accumulated savings to buy all sorts of commodities at an unprecedented rate. Pent-up consumer demand fueled by a decade-long Depression and World War II gave way to an unparalleled economic boom that lasted for nearly a generation. Technological changes also transformed daily life in the United States and promoted the expansion of consumerism. TV especially helped Americans adapt quickly to this ever-changing cultural landscape by reinforcing the era's emphasis on consumption, increasing levels of comfort, and consensus. The last piece in the postwar puzzle was an immense baby boom. There were approximately 2,559,000 births in the United States in 1940, and the number rose dramatically to 3,311,000 in 1946—and this increase was just the beginning. The place reserved for technology in the American imagination noticeably shifted from military to domestic functions and desires. Television had the starring role in this dramatic transformation as CBS, DuMont, and NBC built on their tentative wartime production experiences to lead the way in pioneering commercial TV during the first few years of postwar peace and prosperity, whereas ABC, for the time being, was "badly outdistanced."[82]

When competing against its network rivals, CBS's usual style was to opt for innovative programming strategies. An early example of this creative tendency was when Bill Paley hired critic, editor, playwright, and filmmaker Gilbert Seldes to become CBS's first director of television on September 16, 1937. Paley was greatly impressed by a lengthy speculative article titled "The 'Errors' of Television," which Seldes had published four months earlier in *Atlantic Monthly*, where he skillfully delineated a whole host of technological, aesthetic, and business matters concerning the new medium, demonstrating both his keen understanding of TV and his enthusiastic belief that it might one day "supercede . . . both radio and the movies."[83] Seldes was a bona fide member of America's cultural elite and was best known at the time for his eclectic and strongly democratic tastes—for example, championing Charlie Chaplin and *Krazy Kat* comics, along with Pablo Picasso and Eugene O'Neill. According to biographer Michael Kammen, "CBS clearly felt that it had achieved a coup by hiring Seldes," who was widely known and respected for his many critical commentaries and books, ever since the publication of his 1924 bestseller *The Seven Lively Arts*.[84]

During the next eight years, "Seldes was definitely the man in programming, remembers Carl Beier, a general assistant at CBS." Gilbert Seldes's literate programming tastes ranged from informational (news, art exhibits, a "Women in Wartime" magazine series) to entertainment (original one-act teleplays, sports, quiz shows about books), as "his duties kept Seldes on the go both inside and outside the studio." "When I came on Seldes told me he wanted television to be a window on the world," recalls Jim Leaman, an early CBS producer-director; "he didn't think television was going to get anywhere unless it could get out of the studio." "Seldes was a real visionary," observes CBS cameraman and scriptwriter Edward Anhalt; "I don't think anyone was doing news with his format. Cutting in with film was his concept. He used maps and models." "He would come up with great little aphorisms, which we would repeat like, 'Don't forget you are working in a postage stamp art,'" affirms Rudy Bretz, another CBS producer; "Seldes was a delight."[85]

Gilbert Seldes's strengths as an executive was as a "big picture" creative producer, not a hands-on manager or "true 'company man.'"[86] Veteran Broadway producer and director Worthington Minor was brought in as his assistant in 1939, and although their egos sometimes clashed, together they fostered a cultured atmosphere of freedom and experimentation at CBS that contrasted markedly with NBC's approach of recycling vaudeville via radio onto TV. Certainly, "Minor's achievements in television cannot be overestimated. . . . [He] is credited with establishing the crew positions and production responsibilities for those positions . . . [and he] developed new staging practices and created camera techniques [for example, emphasizing the close-up] that exploited [TV's] limited technical and financial resources."[87] Many of Seldes's and Minor's pioneering producing and directing ideas are seminal and still in use today. But, "despite his successes and growing prominence in the industry, CBS dismissed Seldes as program director in 1945. Working on his memoirs almost twenty-five years later, Seldes correctly surmised: 'I never knew quite why, but I think it was for lack of executive ability, not for lack of imagination in programming.'"[88] Worthington Minor had both of these qualities, and thus he was the individual Paley turned to as the next studio head at CBS.

Before the first fully scheduled television season in 1948–1949, Minor and company busily created a workable programming foundation for CBS in news (by launching the *CBS Television News* with Douglas Edwards), sports (telecasting an assortment of professional

Critic, editor, playwright, and filmmaker Gilbert Seldes was hired as CBS's first program director in 1937. Working on his memoirs more than thirty years later, Seldes admitted that his executive shortcomings, "not [his] lack of imagination in programming," led to his dismissal in 1945. Courtesy of Library of American Broadcasting at the University of Maryland.

and less well known amateur athletic contests throughout the New York metropolitan area, where various CBS field units experimented with new techniques such as the proper use of the zoomar lens), humorous talk (hosting occasional TV appearances by such homegrown radio stars as Arthur Godfrey, who *Newsweek* "labeled in 1947 . . . CBS's most valuable personality property"), and refined drama (nurturing *Studio One* on radio in anticipation of its fall 1948 television debut).[89] Still, CBS's boldest TV programming move to come was still deep under wraps in the recesses of the corporate boardroom. Back in 1936, Bill Paley "had learned that one way to better NBC radio was to raid its pool of talented performers, expending large sums of money and great personal charm to woo to CBS established crowd-pleasers such as Al Jolson, Eddie Cantor, and Major Edward Bowles."[90] Paley and Frank Stanton were now quietly weighing their options, as the CBS chairman considered a similar maneuver as the quickest way to guarantee a comeback for his network in its reenergized effort for television supremacy in America.

In contrast, in the immediate postwar period, Allen B. Du Mont was far more preoccupied with survival for his DuMont Television Network than for supremacy.[91] Du Mont, a talented electrical engineer, who had previously worked for Westinghouse as a production manager and for the De Forest Radio Company as vice president in charge of manufacturing and research, founded DuMont Laboratories in the basement of his Upper Montclair, New Jersey, residence during the depths of the Depression in 1931. From this humble start, Du Mont "and his three assistants were able to produce a picture tube that would last one thousand hours [or] ten times longer than the standard, thus springing television from the laboratories and into the home." As is the case with most independent inventors, Du Mont was chronically strapped for cash, finally forging a partnership with Paramount Pictures in 1938, which initially provided some much-needed working capital for DuMont Laboratories but proved inhibiting over the long run because of meddling by Paramount's representatives on DuMont's board of directors. The Hollywood studio also never followed through on its promise to provide filmed entertainment for DuMont's experimental stations and later its commercial network. "The combination of DuMont and Paramount ought to make a great go in building a network for television," recounts Dr. Thomas T. Goldsmith, DuMont's research supervisor; "I was a scientist. Allen Du Mont was a scientist. We were rookies in Wall Street. We didn't know the jargon. Had I known what was going to happen, I would never have agreed to it."[92]

The DuMont corporation initiated telecasts from its laboratory in New Jersey in early 1938 and from its experimental station in New York City two years later. It was also the first manufacturer to sell all-electronic television receivers to the public when it made its model 180 sets available to various New York and New Jersey department stores in the waning months of 1938. Significantly, DuMont was the only aspiring TV network in the country not being built on the back of an existing radio operation; the company planned instead to fund its expansion into television by manufacturing and selling its receivers and other electronics equipment. In this regard, "military contracts" put DuMont "in a stronger position to finance postwar expansion. Although DuMont was still a small firm, with sales of $176,000 in 1940, business took off during the war years. . . . In 1944, as the company's wartime production peaked, DuMont sales surpassed $9 million." In addition, "DuMont had 120 employees at the end of 1940, and more than ten times that number in June 1945."[93]

Despite the increased financial leverage, DuMont suffered from a lack of available talent and quality programming that radio eventually provided in a steady pipeline to NBC, CBS, and later ABC. DuMont responded to this situation by becoming more aggressive in the chances it took, almost to a fault. "It put more emphasis on formats specifically designed with video in mind. Instead of radio games shows, the network dabbled in travelogue presentations such as *Magic Carpet* and breezy cooking instruction such as *Shopping with Martha Manning*." Most of these makeshift programs were "inexpensive filler," being mainly "cheap, visual, and easy to produce."[94] Nevertheless, DuMont became "the country's first permanent commercial television network" when it began a sustained two-city telecast via coaxial cable from its flagship New York station WABD (named after Allen B. Du Mont) to its new Washington affiliate W3XWT (soon to be rechristened WTTG after Thomas T. Goldsmith) on April 15, 1946. *Newsweek* reviewed the network's debut as having "all the enthusiastic gaucherie of high school productions."[95] Next DuMont premiered *News from Washington* with Walter Compton on June 16, 1947, which was "the first nightly network news show . . . but the program lasted only eleven months."[96] According to its advertising slogan, DuMont was "First with the finest in television" when it came to producing the highest-quality, most expensive TV sets available anywhere throughout the 1940s. Ironically, the network's programming came across as the poor man's alternative, especially when viewed against the innovative and arty appeal of CBS and the many popular stars and programs on NBC.

Not surprisingly, NBC had both the talent and the resources to create the first hit shows on commercial TV. The network initially distinguished itself with the viewing public and Madison Avenue with its sports telecasting, a genre that eventually attracted some of America's top advertisers for NBC. "On Friday, September 29, 1944, the first successful long lasting commercial network television program premiered, *The Gillette Cavalcade of Sports*."[97] That evening, world featherweight champion Willie Pep defeated Chalky Wright in fifteen rounds. The Gillette Razor Company continued its sponsorship of this ratings-friendly series for the next sixteen years. Boxing was an audience favorite at the time, emerging as a major component of local programming through 1948 and afterward becoming a fixture on all four television networks deep into the 1950s. Matches from all weight classes received TV sponsorship and exposure during this era, as all of boxing's greatest names—Joe Louis, Sugar Ray Robinson, and Rocky Marciano—appeared on *The Gillette Cavalcade of Sports*.

On June 16, 1946, for example, NBC and Gillette hosted the Joe Louis–Billy Conn heavyweight title bout from Yankee Stadium in the network's first regional telecast. NBC experimented with a four-city hookup (WNBT in New York, WRGB in Schenectady, and WPTZ in Philadelphia, along with DuMont's W3XWT in Washington, D.C. on a one-time basis). Although Louis badly outclassed Conn, knocking him out in the eighth round, "140,000 Americans watched the fight," spurring the *"Philadelphia Daily News* to declare, 'The winner—Television!"[98] Another contemporaneous review predicted that "this is the kind of event that'll make people buy televisions, not the endless boring cooking shows that seem to turn up on every channel."[99] Boxing became something of "an institution in early television." In fact, in the late 1940s and into the 1950s, "it was common to have as many as five or six network boxing shows on during consecutive evenings of the same week."[100]

From the outset, NBC producers recognized that the specifics of boxing—a small, confined arena with only two participants—lent itself much better to the technical and aesthetic limitations of early television than baseball's broad field, its wide dispersion of players, and its comparatively fast and unpredictable play. Still, baseball was the national pastime, and NBC had been covering the sport ever since its mobile unit produced the first sports telecast, showing a college game between Columbia and Princeton at Baker Field in uptown New York. On the following day, the *New York Times* reviewed the event, concluding that it "was pretty well done," although "the players [looked] like white flies running across the 9-by-12 inch screen."[101] Much of the credit for the relative success of this telecast was accorded to Bill Stern, who was already well known for his radio work. In retrospect, though, this sportscast was poorly framed and hard to follow since only one camera with a fixed lens was used. Two days later, another *New York Times* reporter succinctly analyzed the challenge of televising baseball with only limited technology: "A single camera anchored at one spot does not see the complete field; it leaves too much to the imagination. Baseball by television calls for three or four cameras, the views of which can be blended as the action calls for it."[102]

Through trial and error, NBC had the production talent, the technical ingenuity, and the financial resources to hone its skills by telecasting hundreds of baseball games during the mid to late 1940s. Most televised contests in this period were locally produced, and WNBT's field crews had ready access to the New York Yankees, the New York Giants, and the Brooklyn Dodgers. "The first baseball games we did on television were simulcasts," reveals Mel Allen, pioneering baseball announcer and longtime voice of the Yankees; "you had to adjust by taking a little off your radio report so you wouldn't be overtalking for television." "Put yourself in the stands," continues Harry Doyle, the dean of baseball directors at NBC: "Where are the best seats in the house? Behind home plate, so that's where your main camera should be. Baseball is the toughest sport going . . . you don't know where the ball is going to go. We play percentages."[103] Years later, Burke Crotty, a producer attached to NBC's mobile unit, reminisced about the difficulties surrounding those early telecasts: "In those days, TV was a foul weed in the garden of entertainment. The public gawked at us as a curiosity. Radio people viewed us as a freak. And we had absolutely no prestige at all."[104]

The conventional wisdom about television began to change appreciably after the first televised World Series during late September and early October 1947, when the New York Yankees played their crosstown rivals, the Brooklyn Dodgers, featuring Jackie Robinson in his Rookie of the Year season. Red Barber was at the microphone for NBC, which again transmitted the games along a four-city network, only this time the Washington, D.C. affiliate was its own newly opened WNBW (later renamed WRC).[105] Gillette and the Ford Motor Company cosponsored the 1947 fall classic, paying Major League Baseball $65,000 for the rights, with the hope that at least 500,000 viewers would tune in. The ensuing series was hard fought and frequently exciting, lasting a full seven games with Joe DiMaggio's Yankees prevailing in the end. *Variety* reported that television had "proved conclusively that it's better than radio—and even better than a seat on the first base line—when it comes to dramatic moments."[106] Moreover, "viewer response to the World Series was even greater than the reaction to the Louis-Conn fight of the year before. The TV audience was estimated to be at least 3.8 million, and retailers reported a sharp increase in TV set sales during early October."[107] The aftereffect lingered, as "25,000 more Americans bought TV sets" in November 1947, beginning an extended "television boom."[108] The "total number" of purchased receivers across the country was now "doubling every four months."[109]

NBC was likewise attracting the best sponsors and TV's biggest audiences for its debuts in variety and drama during 1946 and 1947. The roots of the variety show lie in vaudeville, a tradition already successfully translated into radio by such evergreen stars as Fred Allen, Jack Benny, Bob Hope, and Ed Wynn, among others. Network radio was at its height of popularity when NBC and Standard Brands (Chase and Sanborn Coffee, Fleischmann's Yeast, Tender Leaf Tea) hosted the premiere of *Hour Glass* on May 9, 1946. Significantly, the program was booked by the J. Walter Thompson agency, indicating an ever-increasing interest in TV's potential as an advertising medium. *Hour Glass* was a landmark show in several respects: "It was the first hour-long entertainment series of any kind produced for network television, the first show to develop its own star [Helen Parrish], the first big variety series, and the most ambitious production by far ever attempted up to its time."[110] Formerly a child star in Hollywood, Helen Parrish was a high-spirited and eager-to-please "femcee," and veteran NBC director Ed Sobol provided a steady hand for the format, which typically "borrowed a vaudeville bill" that included, for example, "comedy sketches, a ball-room dancing sequence, musical numbers, a film about South American dancing, and a long commercial about coffee."[111]

From May through November 1946, *Hour Glass* was simply telecast to a New York audience over WNBT; after that point until its cancellation in March 1947, the Thursday night 8 P.M. series was also fed to NBC's affiliates in Philadelphia and Schenectady. Over that time, some of NBC radio's first-tier and second-tier stars appeared on the program, such as ventriloquist Edgar Bergen and Charlie McCarthy; comics Bert Lahr, Jerry Colonna, and Doodles Weaver; and singers Dennis Day and Peggy Lee. Standard Brands invested $200,000 in this series over its ten-month tenure at a time when that level of investment just couldn't be supported and sustained, leading to the *Hour Glass*'s abbreviated run; in addition, "James C. Petrillo, president of the American Federation of Musicians . . . issued a rule that a musician could not work for television at any price" until an agreement was reached between his union and the networks. Petrillo exacerbated the situation by being unwilling to even begin negotiations until he could "find out first where TV's going."[112] In the meantime, television directors and singers had to resign themselves to using pre-recorded music. Still, "producers and sponsors knew that they had hit on a successful formula, and had the viewing audience been larger, it might have justified continuing the series. As it was, others would have to pick up where *Hour Glass* started."[113] NBC wasted no time making plans for its next variety show, even as the network was simultaneously branching out into the one-hour drama format.

"The *Hour Glass* was a big deal," confirms veteran TV director Ira Skutch. "It was a network show and it was completely agency produced, and it had commercials. That's why it was so important: it showed that there was money coming in. J. Walter Thompson was happy with the show, and so they brought in the Kraft Theater, which was the first big, live dramatic anthology."[114] Just as television looked to vaudeville by way of radio to develop the variety show, the networks reached out first to Broadway to create its prime-time dramas. CBS's Worthington ("Tony") Minor had worked in New York as a stage actor, director, and producer since 1925. At NBC, producer-director Ed Sobol inaugurated the *NBC Television Theater* on Sunday evening, April 15, 1945, by recruiting and presenting the first installment of "a three-part adaptation of Robert Sherwood's Pulitzer prizewinning *Abe Lincoln in Illinois*." When Sobol left the *NBC Television Theater* a year later to direct *Hour Glass*, his thirty-two-year-old assistant Fred Coe assumed the helm of this live anthology program. By 1947, NBC's drama series had acquired a sponsor, Kraft, and a new night Wednesday, where it was televised weekly for the next eleven years as *Kraft Television Theatre*. The series "alternated between three production teams... using actors and actresses from the New York theater scene just as Tony Minor was doing ten blocks away at WCBW."[115]

Notably, though, NBC was the one TV network with the stability and clout to attract a sponsor for its dramas, despite Minor's prior reputation and innovative approach at CBS. Former J. Walter Thompson advertising executive Al Durante discloses that "they had a new product they were bringing out called Cheeze Whiz. There were discussions about how to introduce it, and the decision was made to try a dramatic show. That's why the *Kraft Theatre* came about."[116] As a result of this routine marketing decision, the live dramatic anthology format was launched commercially as the *Kraft Television Theatre* on May 7, 1947. It was "one of television's most prestigious showcases, winning top ratings and many awards, and becoming a Wednesday night institution;" by the end of its run on October 1, 1958, "more than 650 plays, drama and comedy, both originals and adaptations for TV, had been presented."[117] More important, *Kraft Television Theatre* paved the way for literally dozen of similar dramatic series over the next fifteen years; most of these offerings were one hour in length, although a few also filled either thirty-minute or ninety-minute time slots. As a genre, moreover, the live dramatic anthologies—meaning that their

Pioneering producer, writer, and director Worthington ("Tony") Minor joined CBS in 1939, setting the standard for innovative TV programming throughout the 1940s. Courtesy of Library of American Broadcasting at the University of Maryland.

stories, characters, and themes changed weekly—were "effective barometers of contemporary attitudes and values." In their day, live teleplays "assumed the major responsibility for exploring the social reality and domestic problems of a majority of Americans."[118]

At the beginning of 1948, television was taking an increasingly greater role in people's lives across the country. "It was in the late 1940s that the TV audience was established, not the 1950s as earlier researchers have led us to believe," contends media historian Douglas Gomery; "pioneering TV set owners lived principally in cities or suburbs, were more likely to buy if neither very rich nor very poor, were relatively well educated, young, had two or three children in the household, and were quick to praise the new technology."[119] "Much of what has been written about these early years would make it appear that everything emanated from the network and was passed on to local stations," add Donald Godfrey and Michael Murray; "in reality, however, many programs and personalities were successful at the local level before they were nationally distributed. . . . The programming innovations of local television are legion."[120]

In the spring of 1948, television was on the verge of moving beyond its embryonic roots as a local medium to assert a larger regional profile. The overwhelming majority of TV watchers in those days resided in the eastern corridor; as late as 1950, in fact, "one in five of all viewers" still lived in the New York metropolitan area.[121] On March 20, 1948, the three-year ban on live music was finally lifted when NBC, CBS, DuMont, and ABC came to terms with the American Federation of Musicians. NBC then called again on their go-to producer-director Ed Sobol to restage their hit variety series *Texaco Star Theater* for television. This variety show had originated as a vehicle for Fred Allen on NBC radio in October 1940 and moved to CBS in 1942. Allen wasn't quite ready yet to make the leap to television, so Texaco, in collaboration with the William Morris Talent Agency, optioned the program to NBC with a handful of hosts—Milton Berle, Henny Youngman, Jack Carter, Morey Amsterdam, and Harry Richman—who were meant to rotate from week to week.

The premiere was June 8, 1948: "Texaco budgeted $10,000 . . . , and Sobol used it to hire Pearl Bailey, comedian Al Kelly, ventriloquist Señor Wences, as well as dancers, an orchestra, and even a few circus acts. As with vaudeville, the acts were arranged to create variety and build to several high points."[122] Milton Berle presided over the first few episodes, and he eventually became the permanent emcee on September 21. A little more than a year later, the *New Yorker* announced that Berle had set off "a phenomenon of massive proportions."[123] Appearing on the cover of *Time* on May 16, 1949, Milton Berle and the

Texaco Star Theater drew "approximately 75 percent of the television audience—around 5 million viewers"—on Tuesday nights at 8 P.M. throughout the 1948–1949 TV season.[124] "The American household is on the threshold of a revolution," announced *New York Times* TV critic Jack Gould the previous summer; "the reason is television."[125] By the start of 1950, 9 percent of the nation, or an estimated 3,875,000 television households, now owned TVs.[126] In addition, each of these early adopters kept the set turned on for an average of three hours and twenty-four minutes a day.[127] Millions of pioneer owners were currently finding a place for television in their lives, and, as a result, TV was slowly emerging as the centerpiece of the country's rapidly changing postwar culture.

LEARNING TO LIVE WITH TELEVISION
Technology, Gender, and America's Early TV Audiences

3

Kathryn H. Fuller-Seeley

Television took America by storm during the first decade of the Cold War era, alternately fascinating and consternating its viewers and critics. "It may be a reflection on our sense of values," reported one dazed observer in 1950, "but the sundered atom is far behind the TV tube as the greatest technological influence on the daily lives of millions of Americans."[1] Others characterized commercial broadcast TV's arrival at the end of the World War II as a "home invasion," one claiming that "television began to take over the American living room as a loud-mouthed, sometimes delightful, often shocking, thoroughly unpredictable guest."[2]

The demanding box at the hearthside wreaked havoc on schedules for meals, homework completion, and bedtimes. "Television will take over your way of living and change your children's habits," warned one mother. "At first there will, of course, be great excitement over this new and wonderful thing that has come into your children's lives. You will be excited yourself and perhaps you will have some trouble getting to sleep after your first nights of watching television."[3] As families sat spellbound before their new sets, concerns rose about TV's destruction of traditional family ties. "When the set first came into the house," another mother complained, "I was convinced the opponents were right and conversation in our home was dead. We ate our suppers in silence, spilling food, gaping in awe. We thought nothing of sitting in the dark for hours at a stretch without exchanging a word except 'who's going to answer that confounded telephone?' "[4]

The changes wrought by the intrusive new medium were not unidirectional, however. Television and public discourses about it were also shaped—domesticated—by the families who watched it. As media historians have noted, new technologies do not simply appear like Venus arising on the shore, fully formed and ready to be implemented, nor can their uses be fully predetermined by their producers. Human beings employ the new tools, reacting to them and adapting them to sometimes unexpected purposes. Technologies develop within social, cultural, and historical relationships—in the United States within a profit-seeking capitalist system, as well as within structures of gender, family, social class, and race.[5] These relationships shape and limit the operation and meaning of the technologies. When television appeared on the American scene in the mid 1940s, it was marketed not as a public apparatus but as an appliance for the living room, which would bring a world of entertainment, education, and enlightenment into the private sphere of the family home. To be truly successful in its tasks, however, TV would have to learn to accommodate itself to existing gender practices and family ideology.

How did television's installation in American homes during that initial decade of broadcasting affect family ideology? How, in turn, was TV shaped by social relations? How did that process work as broadcasting and TV sets spread across the nation between 1945 and 1955? Television altered and solidified family gender roles and expectations, brought new public vistas into the private realm, and created new ways in which viewers interacted with media. TV built a nationwide audience, which coalesced sporadically over the course of a decade, in response to changing technologies, expanding consumer culture, programming choices, and product marketing strategies.[6]

The Whole Family's Watching

As with electricity, telephones, radios, computers, and other new technologies that have been introduced into American households, television's arrival was greeted with a mixture of utopian hopes and fearful expectations. Media historian Lynn Spigel has shown that proponents of television (broadcasters, station owners, and manufacturers of television sets) hoped TV would help cement together members of the new postwar, suburban middle-class nuclear family with a sense of renewed domestic values. Members of this new ideal family would stay at home together during their leisure time rather than run their separate ways all over town. Stronger bonds of affection and shared interests would form while everyone gathered around the living room's new "electronic hearth." "Not only was it shown to restore faith in family togetherness," Spigel notes, but TV did it "in the splendors of consumer capitalism."[7]

The transformations brought by television were made possible by profound social changes sweeping across the United States at the end of World War II, especially suburbanization and the Baby Boom. An unprecedented number of people returned from the war, got married, and moved to metropolitan areas from the hinterlands to take the new industrial jobs. They established families and produced children at far greater rates than had families during the Great Depression. The postwar nationwide housing shortage, combined with couples' fervent desires to purchase single-family homes, led to the hurried development of new suburban housing subdivisions, which entrepreneurs like Abra-

Marketed toward the nuclear family, television sets had to be eased into the formal ambiance of most postwar American middle-class homes. Courtesy of The David Sarnoff Library.

ham Levitt constructed on former farmlands located well outside the old urban centers. Media historian Douglas Gomery notes that such demographic, economic, and social factors worked together to attract great numbers of middle-class and working-class families away from the pleasures of the big city's public sphere toward amusements experienced in the privacy of their own suburban homes. These couples' desires to "invest" in a family-focused lifestyle led them to embrace television entertainment as preferable to traveling downtown to attend movie theaters, as they might have done in previous decades.[8]

At the same time that postwar television promoters touted the new "family togetherness" that TV viewing would generate, Spigel writes that social critics worried that television could have an array of "devastating effects on family relationships and the efficient functioning of the household."[9] On the one hand, educators warned that too much viewing might create a generation of passive, pale, "bug-eyed" children who were addicted to TV. On the other hand, they feared young people might become dangerously aggressive from being exposed to too much cowboy shoot-'em-up TV violence. The glowing box in the living room might replace the father's traditional voice of authority. Critics worried that husbands' attention would stray from their wives to the allure of televised sports and scantily clad showgirls seen on TV. They fretted about the disharmony that would result when housewives cooped up all day in the kitchen scrubbing and cooking might long to take their amusements outside the home, while world-weary husbands, just home from work, might want to retreat from the public sphere into the privacy of the TV room. Initially, critics raised the sharpest alarms over TV's influence on children. Reflecting on the situation in the late 1940s, *New York Times* reporter Dorothy Barclay recalled:

> Its advent played hob with daily routines of family living, created a packet of new problems for the then fashionable "permissive" parent and touched off more widespread viewing-with-alarm than any other single event affecting children's development within a generation. Inevitably, it was held, youngsters mesmerized by such early TV attractions as "Howdy Doody" would be turned from active "doers" to passive "viewers," from "irresistible forces" to "immoveable objects." Their vision and physical development would suffer; they would ignore their schoolwork, give up their hobbies and let innate creativity lie dormant; they would forget how to read, and quite likely, never even learn how to converse. They would be stunted physically, mentally, emotionally. It was a sad prospect.[10]

Educators' investigations found that children immensely preferred the new pastime to any other recreation, including radio listening, comic book reading, and movie going. One Illinois teacher reported that children no longer asked for "recess" in school but a "station break."[11] Another complained that her students "always have TV hangovers on Monday, because they stay up so late Sunday nights." Concerned educators decried survey results showing that children were watching as many as thirty hours of TV a week, more than three hours on school nights. A Catholic archbishop warned parents that too much TV caused children to suffer eyestrain, headaches, and "great nervousness and inability to concentrate in the classroom."[12] "Television is twice as compelling as radio!" one critic cried. Another took it even further, claiming that TV's effect was from three to twenty times as powerful as radio's, fretting that, "No Pied Piper ever proved so irresistible."[13] The vivid action of visual media was to blame, they charged. One critic worried that youngsters could listen to radio programs while doing other things, but that TV demanded children's full attention, and it was more difficult to pry them away from the set after a show was over.[14] In response, a TV set manufacturer even advertised a new model that came complete with a lock for parents to forcibly keep their children away from it.[15]

Most educators counseled, however, that rather than take such drastic measures, parents could instead exert more subtle control over their children, rationing TV viewing, making certain that homework and chores were completed, going through the TV schedules together to locate suitable programs, and watching shows as a family group. Lynn Spigel notes that the TV networks "aggressively sought to change those rhythms [of daily family life] by making the activity of TV viewing into a *new* daily habit."[16] In this effort they were ultimately quite successful, for by the mid 1950s, as a majority of families in an area purchased TV sets, its novelty lessened, and the community grew used to it. Although children continued to watch just as many hours of programs, concern about TV's deleterious effect on children abated. Educator Paul Witty observed in Evanston, Illinois, that even teachers, who had been only half as likely to own TV sets as their students' families at the beginning of the decade, had finally become more adjusted to living with the sets. "With increase in ownership," he noted, "reactions to TV changed. Parents and teachers increasingly came to accept TV and to recognize its potentials."[17]

Television affected family dynamics and traditional parental authority. Although in most postwar working-class and middle-class families, fathers still generally took the lead role in choosing leisure-time activities, suburban men were also preoccupied with the business of daily life, doing yard work, starting new hobbies, and commuting to jobs in the big city. Dads had relatively few opportunities to laze in front of the TV set by themselves, and they were usually not at home weekdays to watch daytime programs. While many fathers commandeered the TV tuner in the evenings, members of his democratically organized family might challenge his choices. So while inside the home, fathers might be engaged in a tug-of-war with wives and children to control the TV set, at least in the early years of television, there were important alternative TV viewing sites for men outside their homes. Part of television's success was due to its ability to adapt to existing social practices, such as insinuating itself into the separate sphere of male gatherings. In major cities, which already had strong ethnic, working-class male traditions of congregating in pubs, lodge halls, and barber shops, many men watched their first television programs in taverns that posted prominent signs announcing "We Have TV."[18]

Cleveland, Ohio, was typical of many cities whose first TVs (in 1947, at least three hundred of them) were mostly located in bars and appliance stores. A Cleveland newspaper predicted that "early television tastes would be formed in public places and that sports would be important programming." Even government sought to benefit from the popularity of these gatherings, as in 1948 when northern Kentucky officials asserted their right to collect admission fee taxes at suburban Cincinnati bars that used television to attract crowds.[19] By one estimate, 60 percent of all early TV programming consisted of sporting events, which would be expected to appeal more to adult men than to women and children. All six networked East Coast stations carried the first game of the 1947 World Series, featuring the New York Yankees and the Brooklyn Dodgers, and sports telecasters claimed to have attracted an audience of nearly four million viewers, mostly in taverns.[20] In Hoboken, New Jersey, police clamped down on one generous tavern owner who kicked out the regular sports-watching patrons from 5:00 P.M. to 6:00 P.M. each weeknight so that the neighborhood children could come in to watch *Howdy Doody*.[21] In 1949, sporting events still dominated local TV programming with a mixture of college and professional games, boxing, bowling, and wrestling. New York City's three channels all featured professional wrestling matches, aimed especially at attracting working-class male viewers. Station WABC, on a tight budget and unable to afford the broadcast rights to professional sporting contests, invented roller derby, hiring the players and organizing the teams. Legend has it that the station determined the winners as well.[22]

In the early years of TV broadcasting, there was a decidedly public and participatory element to watching programs. Certainly, the crowded living rooms of the first families in any neighborhood to get a TV set might have seemed as raucous as the taverns. Swarms of curious friends and neighborhood children filled those fortunate houses to view some special show. TV may have reconfigured public entertainment into a private experience, but these impromptu viewing parties turned the private sphere of the home into a kind of "home theater." The era of viewing TV in public settings did influence stations' early programming decisions and civic discourse about the new medium and its audiences, but it was brief. Middle-class and working-class families considered TV sets among their most highly desired consumer products, and by 1949, TVs were featured in the Sears Roebuck "Wish Book" catalog. By 1950, 45 percent of families who lived in those areas in which TV was available had purchased television sets. The camaraderie of watching TV in a bar was out-weighed for many men by the convenience of watching it at home. The rest of the family would no longer complain about being left out of the TV viewing. Harried homeowners who had purchased the first TV sets in their neighborhood were also relieved when they no longer had to play host to a dozen fellow citizens in their living rooms every night.[23]

Unlike the assumed right of men to watch sporting events and chil-dren to be entertained by puppets, the appropriateness of women enjoy-ing television presented a more contentious issue. The question of women's viewing was wrapped up in more social debate than for other members of the home audience. Many social critics feared that wives would quit attending to their domestic duties if they were paying rapt at-tention to TV. Postwar American culture made little distinction be-tween housewives' labor and leisure time, for although housework was not "real" work it was nevertheless a constant endeavor. While critics in the early 1930s had initially worried that radio would distract women from their housework, the new entertainment medium and its female listeners learned to accommodate themselves well to each other. Radio's programs during the daytime were brief, so housewives did not feel guilty tuning in for just a while. Their shows often addressed household issues such as cooking, cleaning, and health and family care, so female listeners could argue that it was time well spent. The continuing serial melodramas that became known as "soap operas" were brief (fifteen minutes long) and repetitive, so the plot never traveled far if the listener missed an episode. The shows (sixty-five different programs at their ra-dio peak) focused on women's and family problems and created fantasy friends and families to keep women company at home. Radio became a vital link for housewives to the outside world.[24]

But could television fulfill the same needs for women? Supporters and critics both initially assumed that television absorbed the view-er's concentration more intensively than radio, and they worried that housewives could not be released from their duties to pay full atten-tion to a TV set. Advertisements for TV sets in the late 1940s re-flected this cultural anxiety by depicting women standing in the kitchen washing dishes while the rest of the family watched the set in the next room. Alternately, the wife remained occupied providing refreshments for her guests while the company was engrossed in the program. Lynn Spigel notes that an ingenious combination TV and stove was marketed in 1952 for women to combine their chores with pleasure. Through a process much like that which had brought radio into the home twenty years earlier, television would be integrated into existing gender practices while also reconfiguring those practices

Television was seamlessly integrated into the country's existing gender attitudes, as in this "I dreamed I starred on television in my Maidenform bra" advertisement in McCall's, November 1951, p. 16. Courtesy of Kathryn Fuller-Seeley's personal collection.

I dreamed I starred on television in my *maidenform bra*

I'm beside myself with joy—that girl on TV is no one but me! I'm the nation's darling, the double image everyone wants to tune in! Bare facts show every other leading lady is out-of-focus with envy! They know my lines are better in my Maidenform bra.

Shown: Maidenform's Chansonette* in white satin. Also available in broadcloth; and nylon marquisette and sheer...from 2.00. Send for free style booklet to Maidenform, New York 16.

There is a *maidenform* for every type of figure!

*Reg. U. S. Pat. Off.   ©1951 Maiden Form Brassiere Co., Inc.   Shoes: Delman   Hat: Mr. John to help ensure that TV became a central part of American domestic life.[25]

Although TV networks and local stations sought female viewers, women were initially courted only through family-oriented programming in the evenings. Due to lack of advertising revenues (another indication of corporate nervousness about women), early network TV programming during the daytime was almost nonexistent and even local shows were scarce. As wary local TV stations expanded their daytime schedules in the late 1940s, they targeted women with inexpensive, live programs produced in their small studios—cooking shows, shopping programs, and talk shows featuring women's issues, public service, and community-oriented themes.[26] The first network television soap opera debuted in December 1950. The *Today* show began broadcasting in January 1952 as a news and home lifestyle magazine format program geared to a female audience. Like their radio forebearers, the TV shows that eventually filled the daytime schedule in the mid 1950s, as national advertising revenues rose, could be watched in a distracted manner. Women could adjust their housekeeping routines to this entertainment by turning the volume up, taking small "breaks" for favorite programs, and performing chores such as ironing and mending within earshot and eyeshot of the TV set. They could still miss a few episodes of "their" soap operas and be able to catch up quickly.[27]

LEARNING TO LIVE WITH TV

The new technology's entrance into American households generated questions of where to install it and how to watch it. The television sets themselves had to be "eased" into the formal spaces of the home. Instead of highlighting the TV's scientific status as high-tech marvel, manufacturers designed early TV sets to mimic expensive furniture and marketed them as home appliances. The screens, tubes, and wires were hidden inside finely crafted wooden cabinets and advertised as elegant decorations. Motorola offered a "hand-rubbed furniture-styled cabinet that complements the functional beauty of the modern home," while Zenith touted a "console of breathtaking beauty in imported mahogany veneers." Larger TV sets had doors to camouflage the screen when the TV set was turned off, which deemphasized how much it intruded into the living space.[28] Despite its tendency to unnerve homeowners who sensed that this new "electronic eye" was staring back at them, the TV screen was a very small eye. Media critic Arthur Asa Berger recalled seeing his first TV at a neighbor's house: "He had one of the first sets—one that could not

have been more than eight inches in diameter but, to us, awestruck by the magic of it all, it seemed gigantic."[29] Entrepreneurs attempted to improve viewability by marketing magnifying lenses to place in front of the tiny screens. Other early viewers recall peering through varicolored gel sheets that were placed on top of the screen surface to simulate "color" television.

Early TVs required relatively complex installation and tuning routines—masculine endeavors that involved securing the large antennae to the rooftop and repositioning the TV set for clearest reception. Somebody had to get up from the couch and cross the room each time to turn the channel selector dial and carefully rearrange the "rabbit ear" antennae atop the set. Viewers were plagued by such continuing problems as fuzzy static interference, flip-flopping images, "ghosts" and "snow" caused by thunderstorms (or someone running the vacuum cleaner), and the difficulty of keeping distant stations in tune. The machinations of adjusting the set could sorely test the patience of anyone trying to operate it.[30]

Just bringing a TV set into the house necessitated rearranging the living room furniture away from previous traditional focal points such as pianos, fireplaces, large radio receivers, and phonographs. Many families, crowded for space, removed their pianos, which had been symbols of middle-class gentility for generations. Builders of new suburban homes incorporated the new technology into their architectural plans, turning the formal living room into a more informal den or "family room." Homebuyers in Levittown had the option of equipping their new Cape Cod homes with a TV set built directly into the family room wall.[31] TV's advent brought about corollary innovations to home life, such as "TV dinners" (originated in 1954) that could be consumed on folding "TV snack trays" set up in the "TV room." Manufacturers marketed "TV chairs," reclining lounges that they claimed were perfect for comfortable viewing. The weekly publication *TV Guide* debuted on 3 April 1953; at least 1.5 million copies were distributed in an initial ten cities, and the magazine soon expanded to twenty city-specific editions. The new occupation of television repairman was a buzzword among high school guidance counselors and in ads in the back pages of hobby magazines. Educators fretted that training was not meeting the escalating demand, for in 1955 there were only 100,000 TV repairmen available to fix the 28.5 million cantankerous boxes. Surveys found that most TV owners were so deeply dependent on their sets that they had malfunctioning ones fixed or replaced within just three days.[32]

As necessary as they began to seem, televisions in the late 1940s were still a luxury purchase item for most families. Early sets cost one quarter of the price of a new automobile. (DuMont's top-of-the-line twenty-inch model cost $2,495 in 1947). Purchase of a TV meant a major commitment to the new entertainment for working-class and middle-class families.[33] If TV was to become a mass medium and not remain the purview of rich families and barkeepers, sets would have to become more affordable. After manufacturers improved electronic technologies and economies of scale to pare down production costs, the price of DuMont's largest set fell to $999 within a year.[34] Rather than compromising their desires with the more economical eight-inch screens, American consumers preferred to indulge in the larger TV sets. Surveys showed that 77 percent of purchasers insisted on sixteen-inch models or larger.[35] The expanding economy of the postwar period enabled manufacturers to sell more sets, as the average worker's salary increased by 60 percent.[36] Consumer spending on appliances and home furnishings jumped 240 percent between 1946 and 1951. The astonishing success of TV manufacturers over the decade can be found in the fact that, while inflation pushed the price of most durable goods up by 40 percent, the price of the average TV fell by 50 percent. Manufacturers triumphed in selling TV to the masses. A 1950 survey showed that the growing "middle income group" had purchased 68 percent of all TVs sold, and the "lower income group" had purchased 17 percent, while the wealthy had bought only 15 percent. Consumers continued to acquire six to seven million sets per year throughout the remainder of the decade, propelling TV manufacturing to become a leading sector of the American electronics industry.[37]

TV Spreads Across the Nation

Television was adopted more quickly into urban American homes than any previous new communication technology had been. In 1946, movies and radio were entertaining their greatest audiences ever, while a small number of TV programs were broadcast a few evening hours per week to just several thousand sets displayed in appliance stores, barrooms, and fortunate big city living rooms. Only nine years later, television dominated popular entertainment—more than four hundred TV stations operated across the nation, and nearly two-thirds of all American homes contained a TV set, while public activities of all kinds (from movie going, juke box playing, and magazine reading to library book borrowing) declined.[38] The installation of those thousands of TV sets nevertheless did not occur simultaneously. TVs early audiences were neither evenly distributed throughout the land nor representative of the whole population. The limited availability of television broadcasting, especially from 1946 to 1953, along with the small size of those influential first American audiences and their geographic concentration in urban areas, shaped the popular understanding of television.

In 1946 there were only six television stations operating in the entire United States—three in New York City and one each in Schenectady (home of General Electric), Chicago, and Philadelphia—and only twenty thousand TV sets altogether. A Philadelphia TV veteran recalled of that year, "My first job at the station was addressing postcards telling what we were going to be showing the next week to the only

500 or so people in the Philadelphia area with television sets. Our entire week's programming fit on a three by five penny postcard."[39]

In 1947, television was still concentrated in eleven of the nation's
largest East Coast, Midwestern, and West Coast cities: New York, Schenectady, Philadelphia, Chicago, Baltimore, Washington, D.C., Cleveland, Detroit, Milwaukee, St. Louis, and Los Angeles. Eighteen stations
beamed signals to fewer than 50,000 sets; by the end of the year, the
total had grown to 250,000. In July 1948, 75 percent of all sets were
still located in East Coast cities, and 50 percent of the total TVs were in
the New York City metropolitan area.[40] By 1949, the number of stations had more than doubled and continued to grow. Nevertheless,
fewer than 10 percent of the nation's population had access to TV before 1950. While New Yorkers had six stations to choose from, and
Washington, D.C., residents had four, most other viewers across the
nation still had quite limited service, receiving only one or two stations
which telecast around three to four hours in the evenings, four to six
nights per week (Table 3.1).[41]

A nationwide network of local TV stations, which would make possible the simultaneous telecasting of programs by NBC, CBS, ABC or
DuMont, grew only in fits and starts. In 1947, AT&T technicians laid
cables that connected Boston through New York to Washington, D.C.,
and another linking San Francisco to Los Angeles. As TV broadcasting

Table 3.1 EARLY TELEVISION GROWTH

	No. of TVs in the United States	Percentage of Households with TV[a]	No. of TV Stations[b]
1946	20,000	0.02	6 in 4 cities
1947	44,000	0.04	18 in 11 cities
1948	350,000	0.66	30 in 29 cities
1949	1 million	2.0	69 in 57 cities
1950	3.9 million	8.1	104 in 65 cities
1951	10.3 million	21.5	107 in 65 cities
1952	15.3 million	32.0	108 in 65 cities
1953	20.4 million	42.5	198 in 241 cities
1954	28.5 million	59.4	380 (not available)
1955	30.5 million	64.0	458 (not available)

[a] Cobbett Steinberg, *TV Facts* (New York: Facts on File, 1985), pp. 86–87; Douglas Gomery, "Finding TV's Pioneering Audiences," *Journal of Popular Film and Television* 29.3 (2001), p. 121.

[b] Steinberg, *TV Facts*, p. 401, 406; Craig Allen, "Tackling the TV Titans in Their Own Backyard: WABC-TV, New York City," in Michael D. Murray and Donald G. Godfrey, eds., *Television in America: Local Station History from Across the Nation* (Ames: Iowa State
University Press, 1997), p. 6; Michael D. Murray and Donald G. Godfrey, eds., introduction to *Television in America: Local Station
History from Across the Nation* (Ames: Iowa State University Press, 1997), p. xx; Gomery, "Finding TV's Pioneering Audiences,"
p. 122. The freeze on new TV stations that was put into place in September 1948 was lifted by the FCC's "Sixth Order and Report"
on April 11, 1952.

expanded outward from its original big city bases, the network cable system extended slowly down along the East Coast. The Deep South's first station, WSB in Atlanta, went on the air in September 1948, beaming signals to between 750 and 1,000 TV sets. To spur public interest that first month, the station broadcast an additional four hours of live programming daily to sixty closed-circuit TVs displayed in the downtown Rich's department store. Florida's first TV station, WTVJ in Miami, reached two thousand sets when it began operation in March 1949, arousing much consumer interest. Most sets were in public places—bars, and on the display floors of Burdines's and appliance dealers—and they were surrounded by crowds "huddling six and seven deep," as an observer noted. In the first two years, ownership jumped from two thousand to thirty-four thousand families, despite the fact that there was only a single station operating and the network cable only reached south Florida in June 1952.[42]

Midwestern cities saw similar patterns of adoption. WEWS in Cleveland started operation in December 1947 with broadcast coverage that reached about three hundred sets in a radius of forty to fifty miles. Cincinnati's WLW began in January 1948, providing twenty hours of weekly programming for one hundred area TV sets. An early employee remembered, "The early—VERY—early days of WLW-T were a mélange of movies, game shows, cooking classes, and shorts. Lots and lots of sports—like college and high school football, bowling, boxing, baseball, softball and of course the staple item, wrestling." WLW signed on with the NBC network in April 1948 (initially receiving programs via filmed kinescopes) and hooked up to the network cable system in September 1949, but, as with other early stations, the bulk of WLW's schedule was not network-provided—in 1950 more than 65 percent of WLW programming was produced locally.[43]

Programming on the local level could establish close connections between stations and its viewing community: from the Boy Scout troops who appeared on Saturday morning programs to the County Extension Agent's demonstrations to members of the garden club or PTA who appeared on talk shows to promote an upcoming event. Teenage viewers might rush home in the afternoons to watch their favorite local high school "stars" perform on the teenage dance music programs. Homegrown versions of *Bandstand* were popular in Washington, D.C., New Haven, Baltimore, Philadelphia, and New York.[44] It is important to note that these "virtual" local communities were overwhelmingly white and middle class. African Americans, immigrants, and the urban poor were seldom addressed or even acknowledged. Douglas Gomery's study of local programming in Washington, D.C., highlights the racial divide: stations promoted country and western

All across America in 1947, there were only forty-four thousand television sets receiving programming from eighteen stations in eleven of the nation's largest cities, including this early receiver in St. Louis, Missouri. Courtesy of The David Sarnoff Library.

music programs that would attract suburban white Maryland and Virginia viewers with Southern roots, but failed to create shows for local black audiences until the late 1960s (even though they made up a majority of residents in the District of Columbia).[45]

Hundreds of new stations were scrambling for licenses in September 1948 when the FCC, concerned about signal interference between stations, imposed a freeze on any further new station allocations. Between 1949 and April 1952 (when the moratorium was lifted), only 107 TV stations were operating in sixty-five cities. While frustrated Americans still without access to stations waited impatiently, audiences in these fortunate areas continued to grow. When WOI in Ames, Iowa, went on the air in 1950, it was greeted by the thirty-five hundred families who already had purchased TV sets. During the subsequent week, fifty-six hundred more sets flew out of appliance and department stores. By the end of the year, thirty thousand families in central Iowa had acquired sets for their homes.[46] Meanwhile, AT&T's network cables linked St. Louis and Milwaukee to Chicago, Cleveland, Pittsburgh, and Buffalo. Just in time for telecasts of President Harry S. Truman's inauguration in January 1949, the East and Midwest became connected between Philadelphia and Pittsburgh. Cables continued to snake across the South and Midwest while they extended on the West Coast down to San Diego and up to Seattle. In mid 1951, the coasts were finally linked as the cables spread from Omaha to Denver, Salt Lake City, and Reno to San Francisco. National hookup had been achieved, and one-third of the nation's households had purchased TVs by the end of 1952.[47]

When the FCC "freeze" on granting new station licenses was rescinded in July 1952, a great surge of openings followed. Lubbock, Texas, with seventy thousand residents of the nation's first "small market" city to get a station, experienced a TV-buying frenzy months before its station even began telecasting. As one resident recalled, "Before KDUB went on the air, we used to just sit around and watch the test pattern. Occasionally we would flip it around and we could get random stations. Once we picked up a football game by accident." Station owner W. D. "Dub" Rogers remembered, "We had been on the air for about two or three hours when we got the word that people were going to the stores, which had stayed open late to sell the sets, to buy televisions just like they would go to the store to buy a dozen eggs. It was unreal." He journeyed downtown to watch the commotion. "One would stay in the car, while the other went in to buy the television. He would come back with the television still in the box and just put it in the trunk and drive off, one car after another. This went on for days." Other preexisting stations grew to be able to reach a larger proportion of their area population. A power boost in 1953 expanded WEWS's coverage across 150 miles of northeastern Ohio, and brought it access to over one million additional potential viewers.[48]

Stronger signals and taller broadcast towers expanded the reach of Miami's station to sixteen counties. By 1954, when a second station opened in central Iowa, the number of TV sets had expanded from 30,000 to 248,000. By October 1953, there were 347 stations on the air. Television manufacturers had shipped 28.5 million TV sets to dealers across the country between 1946 and 1953. Sixty percent of the nation's households were now "television families." These impressive nationwide statistics, however, masked wide regional divergences of TV availability. The urban East Coast states, which had both the highest concentrations of population and most TV stations in late 1953, had TV ownership rates of 84 percent or more. In California and the industrial Midwestern states, 60–72 percent of families had televisions. Their urban areas were well saturated with TV, but the more isolated hinterlands had few sets. Americans who lived in pockets of mountainous terrain or rural areas in late 1953 still weren't part of the TV revolution, due to factors of geography, isolated settlement, lower agricultural incomes, and conservative moral reservations about commercial mass culture.[49]

About 33 percent of Southern families from Texas to North Carolina had acquired TV sets, while only 15 percent of families in Arkansas and Mississippi were "plugged in."[50] In the mountain West, northern prairie states, and northern New England, radio ownership had been nearly universal since the early 1930s, but TV signals were

rare; in the Dakotas, Montana, Idaho, Nevada, and Wyoming, TV ownership ranged only from 7 percent to 18 percent of families. Only one-
third to one-half of the families in the remaining states across the
Upper South, Midwest, and Pacific West had TVs. While these un-
equal rates of ownership evened out by the end of the 1950s, this temporary lack is important to keep in mind when considering the early
American television audience. In those significant first years of telecasting (the era of Milton Berle, Ernie Kovacs, I Love Lucy, and Playhouse 90), the "national" TV audience was much smaller and more
urban than representative of the country as a whole. A great many
Americans continued to await the coming of television to their homes,
with much anticipation and some anxiety.

CONCLUSION

In the three years after the FCC lifted the station freeze, which allowed new stations to begin telecasting, the number of operating television stations quadrupled, so that by 1955 there were more than 450.
The nationwide mass television audience coalesced in the later 1950s,
and its breadth across the land and attachment to the medium is still
astounding to contemplate: the percentage of American families who
owned sets rose from 66 percent to 90 percent. Viewers typically
watched from 3 to 3.5 hours of TV every day. TV broadcasting spread
much more completely across the nation, seeping into the medium
and smaller-sized cities of each state, and larger cities boasted two or
more competing stations. In increasing numbers, small-town and rural residents joined the televisual community of their urban cousins
by installing huge TV antennae atop their homes to attempt to capture
snowy images from the nearest big city's stations.[51]
    In 1955, CBS president Frank Stanton proposed the development
of a thorough study of "the present place of television in the minds
of its public" to be undertaken by scholars associated with the Bureau of Applied Social Research. In the spring of 1960, Gary A.
Steiner and a team of interviewers undertook a national survey of
twenty-five hundred urban men and women. Both network and researchers alike considered the audience a nationwide group stratified only moderately by class and gender (attitudes that were evident
in their programming strategies). Steiner did not investigate questions of differences influenced by region, race, ethnicity, politics, or
urban-rural culture. Rather, Steiner framed his study around the effect of TV on the leisure lives of its viewers. "The focus of discussion
has now shifted, understandably, from initial awe with the technical

scope, growth and potential of the medium, to its content and use,"
he noted.[52] Surveyors asked about the relative value of television
compared with other sources of entertainment and information, the
reasons viewers watched TV, and the satisfactions and frustrations
that TV brought their families.

Steiner opened his resulting study with two responses to surveyor's
questions about audience attitudes toward television:

> TV is wonderful—just wonderful. Why, TV has brought me the
> whole world. I just love it. I love everything. I love to see our Presi-
> dent, that's something I could never do. And I love the stories and
> the westerns I just love every minute. It's the most thrilling thing
> of my life.

> TV engineers are going to roast in hell till eternity as a result of
> what they have done.[53]

Such attitudes, Steiner discovered, were extremes. He found that typical American viewers had so fully integrated television into their lives
that they watched TV for 3.5 hours per day but largely took the medium
for granted. Like a steady diet of bland candy, TV was filling but flavor-
less, and Steiner found that people seemingly consumed it out of habit
more than passion. Although the average viewer "has come to depend
a great deal on routine, daily viewing—or perhaps because he has—
television is not often terribly exciting," Steiner reported. "In the beginning, it was 'really something to talk about'; today, the viewer gives
little evidence of extreme response in either direction. He is not often
overwhelmed by what he sees, nor is he often bored or disgusted."[54]

When asked to rank which one modern "necessity" they would
keep if forced to forsake all others for two to three months, 42 percent
of men deemed their cars to be the most important modern device,
and 56 percent of women claimed that their refrigerators were most
irreplaceable. Only 5 percent of either gender ranked TV as the one
thing they could not live without. So perhaps there was nothing for
cultural critics to worry about after all. And yet, Steiner was disturbed
by respondents' reactions to questions about what had happed the last
time their TV set broke down. In Steiner's view, the answers approached the high melodrama of a "new American tragedy":

> We went crazy. My husband said, 'what did I do before TV?' We're
> sitting here. The children say, 'Please get it fixed.' We couldn't do
> anything. Didn't even try to read a paper. Just walked around
> brooding.

I went from house to house to watch TV, or to the filling station, or went to bed early because I was lost for something to do.

I nearly lost my mind. The days were so long, and I just couldn't stand to miss my continued stories.[55]

In an afterword to the study, eminent communication researcher Paul Lazarsfeld worried that such responses exhibited symptoms of a nationwide dependency: "When television first came upon the American scene we attributed the heavy use to a so-called novelty effect. Surely by now the novelty must have worn off, yet the usage rates show no signs of dropping. Could it be that television has acquired the character of an addiction whereby people hate themselves the next morning but cannot help starting all over again when evening comes?"[56]

Was it a fevered addiction, a dull habit, a scourge, or a blessing? All were aspects of the impressive success of television in the early Cold War era in that it could thoroughly infiltrate American homes; accommodate itself to the differing habits and tastes of men, women, and children; and please the middle class, wealthy, and working class. At the same time, it thoroughly reshaped everyone's patterns of daily life. It was both adaptable and revolutionary, to be both a technological marvel that fascinated and a piece of bulky furniture that talked incessantly. TV became the center of the urban and suburban household, the reliable children's babysitter, the harried housewife's friend, the sports buddy of the exhausted husband.

TV was a fantasy "bomb shelter" kind of escape, featuring showgirls and dancing puppets—a perfect tranquilizer for a nation worried about Commies at the door and subversives under the bed. And yet it brought the reality of war, politics, and the real world into pristine suburban living rooms. Television historian Horace Newcomb, who grew up in small town in Mississippi during the early 1950s, recalled that television "intruded" into his life at age nine and irreversibly altered his experience of what he terms his region's "closed culture": one "heavily circumscribed" by religious ideology, racial attitudes, and localism. Watching African American prizefighters, comedies and dramas, Korean War news broadcasts, atomic bomb detonations, and the whole parade of television programming "offer[ed Newcomb] a perspective on the world at large that [he] rarely found in other media, other forms." He concluded that "I, and others, took up many aspects of that broader perspective and knew that our lives were changed."[57]

TV was hailed as the great facilitator of "togetherness," that highly prized 1950s domestic state of tranquility. "Certainly it has brought back the family circle in the living room," marveled a formerly critical woman, who counseled other parents to move dinnertimes back to accommodate children's TV shows, make them sit eight feet back from the screen, and negotiate with them to complete their homework before the nightly programs began.[58] And yet TV was often charged with killing meaningful living room conversation and stifling creative thought. With the average American in the mid 1950s watching 3.5 hours of TV programming daily, concerned critics knew that they had not "won" any victories over the home invader and that viewer interest in television was not lessening to any foreseeable degree since the tumultuous time of its introduction into the home. Quite the contrary, television and viewers' lives had now forged a permanent relationship in the rapidly changing priorities and habits of American family life.

PART II

BECOMING NATIONAL

VAUDEO DAYS

> When vaudeville died, television was the box they put it in.
> BOB HOPE, *New Yorker*, 1949[1]

Journeyman entertainer Milton Berle was an unlikely candidate to emerge as television's first bona fide superstar during the 1948–1949 season. Born Mendel Berlinger in 1908, he grew up the son of Jewish immigrants in a five-story Harlem walkup on the upper west side of Manhattan. Moe and Sarah Berlinger were desperately poor, struggling to raise five small children. One day Mendel's mother "borrowed 20 cents carfare to take the five-year-old boy to an amateur contest after he had done an impromptu street imitation of Charlie Chaplin." He won straightaway, "and Mom promptly went to work on his career as if it were a sacred mission."[2] From that point on, personal and professional lives merged for mother and son. Sarah changed Mendel's name to Milton and her own to Sandra Berle. She pushed young Milton with a manic fury that he carried over into his performances for the rest of his life. He became a child actor who at six appeared in the *Perils of Pauline* (1914) starring Pearl White. He was subsequently cast in more than fifty silent films, including Mack Sennett's *Tillie's Punctured Romance* (1914) with Charlie Chaplin and Douglas Fairbanks's *The Mark of Zorro* (1920).

Consumed by a self-professed "great want to conquer," Milton Berle matured into a comic jack-of-all-trades on the vaudeville stage, in sound movies, and on the radio, finding his greatest success during the 1940s as a nightclub entertainer. By the time Berle hosted *The Texaco Star Theater*, he was a thirty-five-year show business veteran, who later admitted that the reason he became so successful on television was because of his vaudeville training and his relentless drive to succeed. Then, "on June 8, [when] he stepped out for the first *Texaco Star Theater* . . . it was as if television had been reinvented."[3] Berle himself was christened Mr. Television "by recycling the detritus of his countless nights on a vaudeville road that had vanished years earlier: slam-bang Smith-and-Dale-style sketch comedy, garish drag shenanigans out of 'Charley's Aunt,' smart-alecky insult humor.

Almost none of it was original," but the postwar TV audience still loved it, as did Sandra Berle, who always remained her son's biggest fan.[4] She sat among the live TV audiences in Studio 6B at Rockefeller Center, laughing loudly at Milton's outrageous shtick, even being caught on camera occasionally for the viewers at home. Mrs. Berle faithfully attended every Tuesday night performance of *The Texaco Star Theater* (later renamed the *Buick-Berle Show*) until her passing in 1954. She wouldn't have missed these stage shows for the world. After years of "traveling more than 100,000 miles with him . . . as business manager, cook, claque, straight woman, goad, and inspiration," the improbable dream of stardom she shared with her darling boy had finally come true.[5]

Debuting just as NBC, CBS, ABC, and DuMont were beginning to schedule all seven nights of the week, *The Texaco Star Theater* was the no. 1 program in the country between 1948 and 1951, falling to no. 2 in 1951–1952 and to no. 5 in 1952–1953. "The 'comeback' of vaudeville is television's hottest development," heralded *Variety* on its May 26, 1948, front page, dubbing the new trend "Vaudeo." The "first major indication of vaude's return," continued the industry weekly, "is seen

Milton Berle was a thirty-five-year show business veteran by the time he emerged as TV's first bona fide superstar on The Texaco Star Theater *in the 1948–1949 television season. Courtesy of Library of American Broadcasting at the University of Maryland.*

in *The Texaco Star Theater*'s premiere on NBC."[6] Just like prewar vaudeville, *The Texaco Star Theater* was throwback entertainment from an earlier America, providing viewers with the kind of comforting escape and amusement that they temporarily craved in the immediate wake of World War II. Each sixty-minute episode began with the opening credits framed within a proscenium arch followed by the four "merry Texaco men" (as they called themselves) singing their catchy refrain, "Tonight we may be showman, Tomorrow we'll be servicing your cars." Then Berle burst through the curtains—dressed outlandishly as Brazilian singer Carmen Miranda, or as a June bride escorted by second banana Fatso Marco as Milton's unwitting and much shorter husband—to the howling appreciation of the live studio audience.

After his grand entrance, Berle typically launched into a rapid-fire avalanche of one-liners, grinning from ear to ear through his strongbow-shaped mouth and buck teeth. He was a bug-eyed mass of nervous energy onscreen, flicking his left eyelid from time to time with his right pinky finger, whistling through his teeth, and even slapping his hands together in a kind of do-it-yourself rim shot after a

In true vaudevillian fashion, Milton Berle would do anything for a laugh. Courtesy of Library of American Broadcasting at the University of Maryland.

series of well-worn jokes crested like a wave over the crowd in front of him. In true vaudevillian fashion, Berle and his sidemen would do anything for a laugh. They performed pratfalls, pushed and slapped each other, sprayed seltzer at their guests, and hit one another in the face with whipped cream pies. The audience especially loved it when Berle shouted "Maaakeup!" at some point during the show, and he or Fatso Marco or a guest performer such as Danny Thomas would get a powder puff smacked in the kisser, leaving the victim staggering around in mock affliction on the stage. "If it were possible," wrote critic Richard Corliss years later, Milton Berle "would have stuck his head through the TV screen, jack-in-the-box like, and licked your face."[7] Every Tuesday night, Uncle Miltie served up a heaping helping of comic mayhem with an occasional musical interlude, capturing more than 70 percent of all viewers watching television during the program's first three seasons on the air.

The extraordinary success of *The Texaco Star Theater* set the stage for the creation of other vaudeville-influenced prime-time variety programs over the next few years. CBS was the next network to embrace vaudeo when it debuted *Toast of the Town* on June 20, 1948, with *New York Daily News* gossip columnist and former sportswriter Ed Sullivan as emcee. He had briefly hosted a similar program on radio, showcasing his many show business connections by booking the likes of Jack Benny, Irving Berlin, and Florenz Ziegfeld. CBS studio chief Worthington Minor explained that the reason he chose Sullivan to head up *Toast of the Town* was because he wanted someone in charge with "a proven flair for spotting talent."[8] More candidly, Bill Paley admitted that "Ed Sullivan was hired as temporary master of ceremonies for a variety program I wanted in 1948 because the CBS programming department could not find anyone like Milton Berle." *Toast of the Town* had no sponsor at the time, and Sullivan "knew the world of entertainment and he promised that he could produce a good show cheaply. We planned to replace him as soon as we could afford a professional master of ceremonies."[9] Despite his stiff and awkward presence on stage, Sullivan proved to be a top-notch talent scout and an able executive editor for *Toast of the Town*. As comedian Alan King later quipped, "Ed does nothing, but he does it better than anyone else on television."[10]

A case in point was the very first episode of *Toast of the Town*, which Sullivan "produced on a meager budget of $1,375. Only $375 was allocated for talent, and the two young stars of that show, Dean Martin and Jerry Lewis, split the lion's share of that—$200. But Ed had class. Also on that first telecast was concert pianist Eugene List, Richard Rodgers and Oscar Hammerstein II, and the six original June Taylor Dancers."[11] The critics grew to love the program, but they were baffled by this impeccably dressed, round-shouldered, arm-flaying emcee, who kept reminding his audience that they were in for "a really big shew." For one, Jack Gould of the *New York Times* cautioned two weeks after the premiere of the series that "the choice of Ed Sullivan as master of ceremonies seems ill-advised."[12] Sullivan's wooden and somewhat dour persona made him the anti-Berle. He readily conceded that "I can't sing, dance, tell jokes, tumble, juggle, or train wild animals."[13] Sullivan knew how to book and schedule these kinds of acts into a balanced evening of entertainment, though, enabling *Toast of the Town* (later renamed *The Ed Sullivan Show* in 1955) to last twenty-three years and become a Sunday night institution for CBS.

After *The Texaco Star Theater* and *Toast of the Town* debuted during the summer of 1948, the floodgates soon gave way, and by 1951 vaudeville-styled shows made up nearly one-third of all prime-time programming. That year, a feature story in *Look* touted "TV's Old-New Stars," putting Fred Allen, Jack Benny, Bob Hope, Groucho Marx, Eddie Cantor, Ken Murray, Ed Wynn, Bobby Clark, George Burns, Gracie Allen, and Jimmy Durante in a group shot on the cover. Many of these old-time vaudevillians had also achieved stardom on radio during the 1930s and 1940s, but the transition to television now allowed them to employ their full grab bag of facial expressions, body language, and signature costumes onscreen. A prime example is Red Skelton, the son of a circus clown, who started out in burlesque and vaudeville as a teenager in Indiana, eventually working his way up to the big time in New York before hosting his own eponymous radio show for NBC beginning in 1941. A warm, lovable, often giddy performer, Skelton, became a hit on radio, but he was "essentially a visual comedian all along."[14] On September 30, 1951, *The Red Skelton Show* debuted on NBC-TV and ended its first season as no. 4 in the country, spending twenty more years in prime time (seventeen of them with CBS).

Red Skelton followed a typical comedy-variety format on television, with an opening monologue, performances by guest comedians and singers, and sketches with each week's visiting talent or by himself. Red created a "repertoire of regular characters" in vaudeville and adapted them to radio, but they worked even better on TV, given the added visual dimension. Among the best known were "The Mean Widdle Kid, who left chaos wherever he went (his favorite expression: 'I dood it!'); Clem Kadiddlehopper, the befuddled rustic; Sheriff Deadeye, the scourge of the West; boxer Cauliflower McPugg; Willie Lump-Lump, the drunk"; and his cross-eyed seagulls, Gertrude and Heathcliffe. A "major addition to Red's character list for the TV show was Freddie the Freeloader, a hobo who never spoke." Skelton's routines with Freddie "were always pantomimed, and would, therefore,

Vaudeville-styled shows made up nearly one-third of all prime-time programming in 1951. Here George Burns (left) and his best friend, Jack Benny (right), perform together onscreen. Courtesy of the Wisconsin Center for Film and Theater Research.

have been completely lost on a radio audience."[15] Skelton was also part of "the migration of superstars to CBS . . . which came to be known as the 'Paley Raids,'" starting in September 1948, when Freeman F. Gosden and Charles Correll (*Amos 'n' Andy*) departed from NBC for $2 million.[16] Jack Benny, Edgar Bergen (with his puppet Charlie McCarthy), Ozzie and Harriet Nelson, and Skelton, along with Bing Crosby from ABC, soon followed.

Network radio had "two or three very good years" before it finally succumbed to TV after "a lively knockdown fight over top stars and their shows. Television helped instigate the radio 'talent raids' of 1948 and 1949. CBS started them when it realized it was behind in the race for television affiliates. Headed by Chairman William Paley, who had a bent for showmanship, CBS, realizing that radio stars might also become popular on television, came up with a novel interpretation of the tax laws."[17] Paley convinced several top performers at NBC and ABC to incorporate their own programs, while declaring themselves to be company employees and the main stockholders. Paley then offered to purchase their shows outright, allowing them "to declare their own salaries as capital gains, [thus] lowering their taxes dramatically. . . . With its new roster of popular performers, CBS had armed itself to compete with NBC in network TV as well as radio."[18] Bill Paley had "thus acquired control of a galaxy of leading entertainers for the television age. No one called it statesmanlike," concludes Erik Barnouw, "but it was considered shrewd."[19]

Although CBS assumed "the radio ratings leadership in 1949–1950, 'Paley's Raid' proved to be the last act in the great network radio ratings wars of the 1940s. A TV-set purchase boom, which commenced in 1948, began to eat away at radio's audience."[20] NBC retaliated by luring Bob Hope, Groucho Marx, Kate Smith, and Ed Wynn away from CBS during the 1949–1950 season; "ironically, none of this had a lasting effect on network radio, [which was] all but defunct in five years, but [it] strengthened CBS's financial and programming resources for television."[21] In addition, NBC and CBS signed long-term contracts with many of their top prime-time talents in order to insulate themselves from further defections to other networks. Fearing the loss of its most successful star, NBC negotiated a contract with Milton Berle in 1951, calling for it to pay him $200,000 annually over the next thirty years for his exclusive services as a producer and performer. This deal soon proved premature as Berle's Tuesday night juggernaut ran completely out of gas in 1956, forcing NBC to renegotiate his contract downward from $6 million to $4.8 million in 1965.[22] Vaudeo was no longer king by the mid 1950s. The composition of the American television audience had changed, and along with it came a noticeable shift in the country's programming preferences and tastes.

In retrospect, the demise of *The Texaco Star Theater* was attributable to three interlocking factors. The first reason was simply that, with each successive television season, Milton Berle faced increased competition from entertainers of his own generation, as well as younger talent. Some of radio's biggest stars started making the transition to TV, led by CBS's Arthur Godfrey with his simulcasting of *Talent Scouts* on December 6, 1948. Over the next three years, all of radio's elite followed suit. Other programming genres that competed favorably against variety shows were also introduced to prime time between 1948 and 1950, such as situation comedies (*The Goldbergs, Mama*), live dramas (*Philco Television Playhouse, Studio One*), Westerns (*The Lone Ranger, Hopalong Cassidy*), children's programs (*Kukla, Fran and Ollie; Captain Video*), quiz shows (*Twenty Questions, What's My Line?*), and many other formats. During 1950–1951, moreover, innovations in vaudeo proliferated, including a burgeoning new TV production center on the West Coast (*The Colgate Comedy Hour* was the first commercial series to originate in Hollywood), hybrid formats (for example, *The Jack Benny Show* mixed variety with situation comedy), and more middlebrow content and stylistics (beginning with Max Liebman's *Your Show of Shows*, starring Sid Caesar and Imogene Coca, which instantly raised the bar for the television variety show in terms of production values and sophistication when it premiered on February 25, 1950).

Your Show of Shows actually had a dry run between January and June 1949, as the *Admiral Broadway Revue*, a one-hour Saturday night spectacular, that "was one of the few major programs ever to be carried on two networks simultaneously"[23] NBC and DuMont shared the cost of $15,000 an episode, which was two-and-a-half times higher than the average for a variety show at the time.[24] "The comedy, for perhaps the first time on television," aspired to be smart, sophisticated, and topical. It was the brainchild of Broadway (and former Borscht Belt) producer-director, Max Liebman, who "realized that most of the programs being presented [on TV] really originated in vaudeville and night clubs, or were an extension of radio."[25] "Television's devotion to broad comedy and the straight vaudeville format was toppled by the Admiral show. It dared to satirize modern painting, psychiatry, movie epics, advertising, and other themes" not commonly treated on TV before.[26] Still, the *Admiral Broadway Review* came across much better as a live show in New York's International Theatre than on television for viewers sitting at home. For example, "instead of demanding intimate camera placement, Liebman was content to let the crews shoot the stage from a distance out in the audience." He learned a great deal by trial and error during his first year of producing and directing TV "and had considerably more success the following season when he returned with a re-structured version of the program, retitled *Your Show of Shows*."[27]

Despite being dropped by the Admiral Television Corporation, which "decided that the money allotted to the show could be put to better use manufacturing more television sets," NBC's newly hired programming vice president, Sylvester ("Pat") Weaver, approached Liebman to mount a weekly two-and-a-half hour Saturday evening extravaganza the next season to compete against *Cavalcade of Stars*.[28] This one-hour comedy-variety hit on the DuMont network disproved the conventional wisdom that people wouldn't stay home on Saturday evenings to watch television. Liebman balked at 150 minutes but agreed to mount a 90-minute Broadway-styled revue if Weaver provided a $2 million annual budget so he could bring back Caesar, Coca, head writers Mel Tolkin and Lucille Kallen, choreographer James Starbuck, set designer Frederick Fox, and conductor Charles Sanford, as well as expand his writing staff and ensemble cast (soon adding Carl Reiner and Howard Morris). Weaver not only secured Sarnoff's approval for Liebman's lavish budget request but also hired vaudevillian-turned-TV host Jack Carter away from *Cavalcade of Stars* to emcee a one-hour variety program on NBC to precede *Your Show of Shows*, clearing the way for Jackie Gleason's rise to TV stardom when DuMont eventually hired him to replace Carter in July 1950. *The Jack Carter Show* from Chicago and *Your Show of Shows* from New York debuted live between 8 and 10:30 P.M. in February 1950 under the umbrella *NBC Saturday Night Revue*. Jack Carter only lasted a little more than a year, paling in comparison to *Your Show of Shows*, which modernized the TV variety show for a new generation of viewers over its four-year run.

"*Your Show of Shows* was surely one of the most ambitious undertakings on television, *ever*. It was 90 minutes of live, original comedy, every week."[29] Besides Liebman's inspired direction, the series definitely had the greatest collection of writers ever assembled on one television program up to that point. Led by Tolkin, Kallen, Caesar, and Reiner, newer additions soon included Mel Brooks, Neil Simon, and Larry Gelbart, among others. This core of talent wrote from their own experiences in a way that struck a responsive chord with the new suburban consumers, who were now purchasing a majority of the more than 100,000 television sets being sold in the United States each week. "Remember, all of us had started out very young, making small salaries, but as the show became a hit," recalls Mel Tolkin, "we began to acquire things, we could draw on what happened to us for a good deal of the humor."[30] For example, Sid Caesar and Imogene Coca "often focused on the small crises of everyday life," such as being expectant parents, dropping their children off to their first day of school, buying a family car, or even knowing how much to tip at a fancy restaurant. Physically, Caesar and Coca were a study in contrasts: he was tall, heavyset, a rubbery-faced mime and dialectician; she was petite, pixie-like, gracefully fluttering about him with her large mischievous eyes. Often they played "a mismatched couple, the Hickenloopers. Doris Hickenlooper was the modern, upwardly mobile American woman, married to Charlie, the average American 'slob.' "[31]

Sid Caesar appealed to a much younger-oriented audience than Milton Berle, as he was fourteen years younger and only twenty-eight when *Your Show of Shows* premiered. He was also an ex-GI who lived in the suburbs with his wife and baby, much like the millions of other new parents watching him and Imogene Coca satirize suburban middle-class life every Saturday night on NBC. Likewise, Carl Reiner often portrayed a slick, slightly pompous white-collar professional, while Howard Morris was his diminutive sidekick anxious to prove himself to anybody, anywhere, anytime. Together, the four of them constituted a small-screen repertory company that never played down to the audience, always assuming that the viewers at home were as hip

Physically, Sid Caesar and Imogene Coca of Your Show of Shows *were a study in contrasts: he was tall, heavy-set, a rubbery-faced mime and dialectician; she was petite, pixie-like, gracefully fluttering about him with her large mischievous eyes.*
Courtesy of Library of American Broadcasting at the University of Maryland.

to the jokes as they were. For instance, they lampooned opera ("No No Rigoletto"), foreign films (Mizoguchi's *Ugetsu* became "Ubetchu"; De Sica's *The Bicycle Thief* "La Bicycletta"), and Hollywood epics (*Shane* became "Strange"; *From Here to Eternity* became "From Here to Obscurity"). In addition, "ballet sequences and scenes from grand opera were . . . featured, to give the show an undeniable 'classy' air."[32] These light and serious touches were a far cry from the stock and trade of *The Texaco Star Theater*, and Uncle Miltie and his legion of vaudeo imitators were already seeming out of date by the time Texas Oil and the Kudner Advertising Agency decided not to renew its sponsorship of Berle's show after the 1952–1953 season. Instead, the oil company economized by underwriting two alternating half-hour sitcom-variety hybrids on Saturday evening during 1953–1954—*The Donald O'Connor Texaco Show* and *The Jimmy Durante Show*. NBC and Texas Oil cancelled both of these programs after only one season.

Another reason for the slow enervation of *The Texaco Star Theater* between 1948 and the mid 1950s was the changing economics of television. By 1952–1953, Milton Berle was offering blue-collar entertainment at white-collar prices. Max Liebman introduced a new Broadway-quality variety show on television with *Your Show of Shows*. Competing series in the genre needed to adopt similar production values to keep pace. When *The Texaco Star Theater* premiered in 1948–1949, for example, an average hour of variety on prime time cost $5,900 compared with $10,800 for drama; in 1952–1953, these figures skyrocketed to $35,900 for variety versus $21,100 for drama; and by 1955–1956 (the last year of *The Milton Berle Show*), variety amounted to a whopping $67,700 per episode versus $34,100 for drama, the next most expensive genre.[33] In effect, the variety show was slowly being priced out of the market with each succeeding television season, except for those few top-20 series (such as *The Jackie Gleason Show* and *Toast of the Town* on CBS; *The Martha Raye Show* and *The George Gobel Show* on NBC) and the occasional one-time spectaculars, such as the specials that Max Liebman was now producing for Pat Weaver at NBC.

Before being hired NBC's vice president in charge of television programming in September 1949, Pat Weaver was already a twenty-year veteran in the radio and advertising industries, first with the American Tobacco Company and then at Young and Rubicam. Weaver's primary responsibility at NBC was to expand and schedule the corporation's fledgling TV network, which consisted of only twenty-five affiliates in the fall of 1949, mostly situated up and down the East Coast. He was much like the fox who found himself inside the henhouse looking out. Over time, Weaver planned to shift the center of gravity in television more toward the networks and away from sponsors and their advertising agencies, who were still deeply involved in program development. The way he intended to do that was either to eventually replace full sponsorship (where naming a series after a sponsor was still commonplace) or to alternate arrangements (by which two companies shared expenses week to week, as *Philco TV Playhouse* and *Goodyear TV Playhouse* did on Sunday nights between 1951 and 1955), with participant advertising or what he called the "'magazine concept'—a system under which sponsors would buy only inserts in programs produced by the network, or by independent producers for the network, under network control."[34]

Weaver attempted to first introduce participant advertising in 1950 with *Your Show of Shows* because of the high production costs associated with the series. "From the day I first imagined the show I was worried about selling it," he reveals in his memoir; "I wanted to launch it with rotating commercials, which would guarantee every sponsor at least one exposure during each half-hour segment. The Federal Communication Commission [initially] refused to approve that plan," as did the sponsors and ad agencies involved.[35] Instead, Weaver struck a compromise with them on *Your Show of Shows*, when he pioneered the concept of "shared sponsorship, in which each sponsor dominated a segment of the program. The arrangement involved some diminution of control," where Liebman was basically in charge of producing the series under the auspices of NBC, while the various sponsors were able to provide some input but nothing like the degree of hands-on control they normally exercised when they completely paid for a program themselves.[36] In contrast, *The Texaco Star Theater* was locked into a full sponsorship agreement. When Texas Oil departed in June 1953 because of rising production costs and sagging ratings, the series resurfaced in the same Tuesday evening time slot during 1953–1954 as the *Buick-Berle Show*. When Buick shifted its allegiance to Jackie Gleason after the 1954–1955 season, *The Milton Berle Show* lasted one more year, "alternating variously with Martha Raye, Bob Hope, and Steve Allen."[37] The rest was downhill for Berle's TV career as he hosted the *Kraft Music Hall Presents Milton Berle* (1958–1959) and *Jackpot Bowling Starring Milton Berle* (1959–1961) on NBC, never again regaining the luster of those early days when he reigned as prime-time's no. 1 star.

The most important reason for the inevitable downward spiral of Milton Berle and *The Texaco Star Theater* was the growth of American television beyond its pre-1948 local roots to become an East-Midwest regional telecommunication system by the early 1950s, well on its way to reaching its full potential as a true national medium by the end of the decade. Over the eight years (June 1948 to June 1956) that Berle hosted his Tuesday night comedy-variety show, the number of commercial stations in the United States grew from 16 to 441; the total television households from 940,000 to 34,900,000; and the percentage of all residences owning TVs from 2.3 to 71.8 percent.[38] He "was credited with stimulating more sales of TV sets in that medium's infancy than any other single agency. People would gather at the homes of friends who had sets, or stand outside appliance stores and press their noses against the glass to watch Berle's zany antics—and then would often return to buy a set for themselves."[39] Suburban communities were springing up outside large and medium-sized cities all across the United States. In turn, television and furniture manufacturers alike were benefiting from this coast-to-coast back-to-home movement fueled by the ever-growing baby boom.

"Ironically, Berle's particular type of urban vaudeville comedy was responsible for both his rise and demise," argues historian Arthur Wertheim, whereby "the high ratings really signify the perfect match between Berle's citified comedy style [and] the limited size and scope of the urban audience."[40] "As the new medium spread from the Northeast corridor to the hinterlands," a much larger suburban and rural mix of viewers soon "arrived that had less affection for a comic persona as unabashedly Jewish as Berle's. All too fittingly, one of the first rivals to inflict ratings damage on his time slot was Bishop Fulton Sheen, sermonizing on the DuMont network."[41] The thirty-minute *Life Is Worth Living* debuted on February 12, 1952, reaching its popularity peak in early 1955 at 5.5 million households, during an era when an average three viewers were watching each receiver at a time. "Bishop Fulton J. Sheen remains first and foremost an icon of the 1950s," reminds Mary Ann Watson; he "intuited the void in modern Americans. He sensed their frustration and aimlessness."[42]

Despite all the outward signs of affluence and success, many Americans were searching for new sources of meaning in their lives, even as they pursued a more-contemporary, less-traditional version of the American dream in the suburbs. Likewise, the images they now watched on the tube reflected both their heightened expectations and their hidden insecurities. As the postwar consumer culture grew, viewers looked increasingly to television to help them negotiate the transition they were making away from the customs and values of the previous generation to a more upwardly mobile middle-class view of themselves and the future. On April 3, 1953, *TV Guide* debuted with Lucille Ball and her newborn son, Desi Arnaz Jr., on the cover. Both the magazine and TV's latest no. 1 superstar were harbingers of an America that was becoming a much different place to live in than the country it had been before World War II.

Keeping Up with the Joneses

> Television, in commercial use for a little more than five years, is influencing the social and economic habits of the nation to a degree unparalleled since the advent of the automobile.
> Jack Gould, *New York Times*, 1951[43]

The commercial realization of television in the late 1940s and early 1950s was even more lightning fast and momentous than that of radio during the mid 1920s. Movie attendance plummeted nearly 30 percent nationwide by the end of 1950, according to estimates provided by the major film distributors. The saturation of sets in the New York metropolitan area made it something of a bellwether regarding TV's influence on radio. Television's share of the listening and viewing audience in New York City equaled that of radio's top-10 programs in 1949; by 1951, TV's lead over radio had risen to 80 percent over 20 percent. Prime-time radio listenership in Philadelphia similarly dropped off 25 percent during the same period.[44] Signs of the postwar changeover to television were everywhere. On the November 5, 1949, cover of the *Saturday Evening Post*, for instance, commercial artist Norman Rockwell depicted the raising of a "television dingus" (antenna) on the peak of a rickety old nineteenth-century Victorian gable roof. "In the Adams street neighborhood of Los Angeles, Norman Rockwell found an ancient house which once upon a time was the newest, snazziest design," reveals the caption on the contents page; "that's the way it is in the U.S.A.—today something really new is always being hooked onto what yesterday was the latest thing."[45]

Norman Rockwell, one of America's best-known illustrators, created more than three hundred covers between 1916 and 1963 for the *Saturday Evening Post*, a top-circulated general-interest magazine for well over a century. He specialized in highly evocative though sentimentalized portrayals of small-town life before World War II, focusing more on the country's transition to a new suburban consumer culture after 1945. His painting "New Television Antenna" is a prime example of this latter phase in his career. This image looks like it is set in anytown, U.S.A, not Los Angeles. The eaves of the cedar shake

Norman Rockwell's "New Television Antenna" graced the November 5, 1949, cover of the Saturday Evening Post. *Courtesy of the Rockwell Family Agency. Copyright © 1949 the Norman Rockwell Family Entity.*

gable roof dominate the lower three-fifths of the frame, while a pale hazy overcast sky fills the upper two-thirds. Leaning out of a small window, an older man in his sixties, wearing a white shirt, suspenders, and arm garters, talks animatedly to a younger repairman in his twenties, who is perched on the angled peak fitting the antenna into place. Rockwell is both a master genre painter and storyteller. The elderly gentleman is smiling broadly, pointing to the luminous black-and-white picture on the set inside. The younger workman, sleeves rolled up on his bright red shirt, is more matter-of-fact about the service he's performing. Apparently, he takes for granted that the TV will work, and he's concentrating intently on finishing the task at hand. Off in the distance are two smaller structures. A church steeple, once the tallest sight in the neighborhood, is now just one of several points of interest on the horizon. The corner of a square rectangle skyscraper can also be glimpsed many miles away. This old-frame weather-beaten home is currently the main center of attention. Yet another American household has eagerly joined the onrush to television.

Just like in the "New Television Antenna," TV adopters came from all generations. The old fellow in the image was evidently a member of the lost generation (born between 1889 and 1907), while the TV technician was too young to belong to the GI generation (1908–1926). Instead, *Time* coined his cohort the "silent generation" (1927–1945) in a November 5, 1951, cover story that described those individuals who came of age at the tail end of World War II and currently were fighting in Korea and generating the new baby boom (1946–1964), along with their older brothers and sisters. "The most startling fact about the younger generation is its silence," wrote the editors of *Time*; "it wants to marry, have children, found homes. . . . Today's generation, either through fear, passivity or conviction, is ready to conform."[46] "The silent generation was a phenomenon of the 1950s, as characteristic as its tailfins and white bucks," wrote William Manchester in *The Glory and the Dream* (1973); "never had American youth been so withdrawn, cautious, unimaginative, indifferent, unadventurous—and silent." A member of the GI generation himself, Manchester continued: "They would conform to the dictates of society in their dress, speech, worship, choice of friends, length of hair, and above all, in their thought. In exchange they would receive all the rights and privileges of the good life; *viz.*, economic security."[47]

Probably no one captured the inner workings of postwar mass society at midcentury better than sociologist David Riesman, along with his colleagues Nathan Glazer and Reuel Denney, in their unexpected best seller *The Lonely Crowd* (1950), a title suggested to them by their publisher. "In the now-familiar terminology of *The Lonely Crowd*, there are three dominant types of social character, which correspond to phases of Western, but especially American, societal development, and are correlated with demographic changes: persons who are tradition-directed, inner-directed, and other-directed."[48] The traditionalists resist change and rigorously follow time-honored beliefs and practices; the inner-directeds are far more self-made, stubbornly self-reliant, and goal-oriented; and the other-directeds tend to obsessively seek approval, prefer group over individual action, and freely sublimate their own needs and desires to the will of the crowd. Riesman and his colleagues recognized that the zeitgeist of the 1950s "was different somehow from life in decades past, and that, for all their outward success, many Americans were [now other-directed] leading lives of inner emptiness and desperation."[49] They found a large and sympathetic readership for *The Lonely Crowd* in which they critiqued corporate culture and those people who are "at home everywhere and nowhere." Sloan Wilson's *The Man in the Gray Flannel Suit* (1955) and William Whyte's *The Organization Man* (1956) struck similar chords, but *The Lonely Crowd* went even further in identifying the skyrocketing importance of "words and images" in contemporary America whereby "relations with the outer world and with oneself are increasingly mediated by the flow of mass communication."[50]

Television emerged as the ideal medium for the nuclear family in postwar America. Households consisting of a working dad, a mainly stay-at-home mom, and one or more young children living in the suburbs separated from the traditions of an extended family was now a majority lifestyle throughout the United States. As reported, "the increase in single-family homeownership between 1946 and 1956 outstripped the increase during the entire preceding century and a half. By 1960, 62 percent of American families owned their own homes, in contrast to 43 percent in 1940. Eighty-five percent of the new homes were built in the suburbs, where the nuclear family found new possibilities for privacy and togetherness."[51] Rates of divorce and illegitimacy fell, as Elaine Tyler May reports that "the isolation of the nuclear family sometimes helped keep couples together."[52] Still, "most people understood the 1950s family to be a new invention," contends Stephanie Coontz in *The Way We Were*: "The Great Depression and the Second World War had reinforced extended family ties, but in ways that were experienced by most people as stultifying and oppressive." As a contemporaneous alternative, suburban homeowners in the GI and silent generations currently "hailed" the nuclear family "as the most basic institution in society."[53]

Historian Daniel Boorstin described the changing landscape of postwar America as a land of newly expanding "everywhere communities" spreading out from coast to coast. Beginning in the late 1940s and continuing throughout the remainder of the century, the nation's cities and suburbs started developing similar kinds of interchangeable neighborhoods, shopping malls, franchised retail outlets, and fast-food chain restaurants. And Americans in the suburbs "leaned on one another as they moved rapidly about the country and up the ladder of consumption." In their upwardly mobile quest for a good life marked by mounting levels of comfort, convenience, and predictability, members of the GI and silent generations with their baby boomer children shared a common culture of "repeatable experiences" through photography, phonograph records (LPs and 45s), and movies, as well as "experiences-at-a-distance" through radio and television. Daniel J. Boorstin in *The Americans* stated, "Just as the printing press five centuries before had begun to democratize learning, now the television set would democratize experience." By the early 1950s, "the normal way to enjoy a community experience was at home in your living room at your TV set." Watching television was a "more equal" but a "more separate" use of leisure time and was increasingly available to all Americans as the decade wore on.[54]

The mushrooming presence of TV transformed thousands of suburban neighborhoods composed of millions of mass-produced houses and apartment complexes all across the United States. "There was an odd sense of connection and disconnection in this new suburbia," explains Lynn Spigel in *Make Room for TV*—"an infinite series of separate but identical homes, strung together like Christmas tree lights on a tract with one central switch. And that central switch was the growing communication complex, through which people could keep their distance from the world but at the same time imagine that their domestic spheres were connected to a wider social fabric."[55] By the turn of the new decade, television was already emerging as the hub of the country's nationwide grid of mass media, soon to become the centerpiece of American culture by the end of the 1950s. No pastime was currently preoccupying U.S. consumers like TV, and the more that people tuned in, the more they made sense of the world in terms of what they were seeing on the small screen. "The line between what happened in real life and what people saw on television began to merge," affirms David Halberstam in *The Fifties*; "many Americans were now living far from their families, in brand-new suburbs where they barely knew their neighbors. Sometime they felt closer to the people they watched on television than they did to their neighbors and their distant families."[56]

A prime example of this increased importance of TV in people's lives is evident in the early reception of situation comedies between

1947 and the mid 1950s. Sitcoms began at the inception of network radio in the mid-to-late 1920s, but the initial use of the term "situation
comedy" came much later, in the trade lingo of scribes writing for publications such as *Variety* and *Broadcasting* during World War II. This
genre is based on creating a simple comic premise for each program
(for instance, a wife rebelling against the expectation that she become
a happy homemaker) played out by an ensemble cast of characters (often a family or a quasi-family of neighbors or coworkers) set in a recurring locale (usually the home or a place of employment). The first
television sitcom, *Mary Kay and Johnny*, premiered on November 18,
1947, for DuMont, featuring the misadventures of two young, attractive newlyweds and their baby boy in their Greenwich Village apartment (starring real life husband and wife Mary Kay and Johnny Stearns,
along with their newborn Christopher). The action revolves around
Mary Kay, a good-natured screwball who wreaks havoc on her domestic
surroundings, only to be rescued each week by her much more stable
spouse, thus reflecting a generic formula common to radio sitcoms.

In yet another sitcom variation, many of the most successful pioneering sitcoms depicted urban, ethnic, working-class families struggling to make ends meet, such as CBS's *The Goldbergs* (1949–1954)
and *Mama* (1949–1956), NBC's *Life of Riley* (1949–1950, 1953–1958)
and *Amos 'n' Andy* (1951–1953), and DuMont's "The Honeymooners,"
which began in 1951 as a weekly sketch on *Cavalcade of Stars*, before
Jackie Gleason brought it to CBS when he jumped networks in 1952 to
host his eponymous comedy-variety show there, later turning it into a
thirty-minute series, *The Honeymooners* (1955–1956). These popular
domestic comedies represented a variety of ethnicities and settings
spanning both coasts. The Goldbergs were Jewish living in the Bronx;
Mama's family was Norwegian in San Francisco; the Rileys were Irish
in Los Angeles; Amos and Andy were African American in Harlem;
and the honeymooners were Irish in Brooklyn. Four of these five programs (all but *The Honeymooners*) had antecedents on radio, but as
George Lipsitz points out in *Time Passages*, they "placed more emphasis on nuclear families and less on extended kinship relations and ethnicity" in their adaptations to television.[57]

Overall, Lipsitz argues that millions of postwar TV viewers used
these urban ethnic working-class situation comedies as a way of easing their own transition into a more middle-class suburban lifestyle.
These traditional family-oriented sitcoms invited their audiences back
each week—for example, to Apartment B on Tremont East Avenue as
the Goldbergs slowly upgraded their living conditions by purchasing
new furniture at Macy's; or to the Hansens, gathered around the
kitchen table to discuss Papa's recent promotion to foreman and

DuMont's "The Honey-mooners" began in 1951 as a weekly sketch on Cavalcade of Stars, *before Jackie Gleason brought it to CBS when he jumped networks in 1952 to host his eponymous comedy-variety show, later turning it into a thirty-minute situation comedy in 1955. Courtesy of Library of American Broadcasting at the University of Maryland.*

daughter Katrin's dreams of becoming a writer, while Mama brewed another pot of Maxwell House ("good coffee goes with family moments like this, always good to the last drop"). In stark contrast to the loud, high-pitched humor of vaudeo, these low-key, slice-of-life comedies showed "families struggling for material satisfaction and advancement"; at the same time, the unresolved tensions, inequalities, and prejudices that were part and parcel of working-class life in the United States were all but ignored. Thus, "in the midst of extraordinary social change, television became the most important discursive medium in American culture. As such it was charged with special responsibilities for making new economic and social relations credible and legitimate" to vast audience in the tens of millions who were acclimatizing themselves to "the consumerist present of the 1950s."[58]

The rise of the situation comedy coincides with the gradual ascendancy of CBS in the television ratings throughout the early 1950s. As a result of Paley and Stanton's stable and aggressive leadership, the network finally overtook NBC to become no. 1 during the 1955–1956 season (and remained on top thereafter for the next twenty-one years). The series most responsible for CBS's climb to prime-time supremacy was also the most popular program of the decade—*I Love Lucy* (1951–1957). Lucille Ball's pre-TV career was deeply rooted in both motion pictures and radio. She was a modestly successful Hollywood veteran costarring in over seventy-five films for MGM, RKO, Columbia, and Paramount during the 1930s and 1940s. Like many of her contemporaries,

Lucy was genuinely ambivalent about working in television during those early days, fearing that such a move would damage her long-term marketability in the movies. Even after starring in the CBS radio sit-com, *My Favorite Husband* (1948–1951) alongside Richard Denning, Lucy still lobbied for major film roles in Hollywood through Desilu, the independent production company that she formed in 1948 with her musician and band leader husband, Desi Arnaz. Originally intended to develop big-screen properties for the couple, Desilu shifted its primary focus to TV production and syndication after the remarkable success of *I Love Lucy*, eventually growing in size and stature to rival the largest studios in all of Hollywood by the late 1950s.

Lucy's unique comedic talent on radio was somewhat of a revelation when she first starred in *My Favorite Husband* in July 1948, even though she had the reputation for being a humorous and offbeat big-screen performer. She completely realized her attractive, zany, and irrepressible "Lucy" persona when she began performing live before a studio audience for radio. Her creative team on *My Favorite Husband*—including producer Jess Oppenheimer and head writers Madelyn Pugh and Bob Carroll Jr.—provided her with just the right kind of medium and format to show off the full range of her abilities as a comedienne. This same team, along with underrated straight man Desi Arnaz, who was also president of Desilu Productions, transformed the hit Los Angeles–based radio program into an even bigger television success. Unlike vaudeo, many TV situation comedies revolved around women stars (such as Gertrude Berg as Molly Goldberg; Peggy Wood as Mama; and Gracie Allen as herself in CBS's *The George Burns and Gracie Allen Show*, 1950–1958). Lucy immediately joined this elite group when *I Love Lucy* debuted on Monday October 15, 1951, in the 9–9:30 P.M. slot, piggybacked behind *Arthur Godfrey's Talent Scouts*, then the no. 1 show on TV. Within a month, *I Love Lucy* was attracting fourteen million viewers a week, and by January 1952, the average was up to sixteen million and rising.

Lucille Ball was forty years old when *I Love Lucy* premiered, and her long and varied experiences in film and radio served her well in bringing Lucy Ricardo to life on the small screen. The Lucy persona is multidimensional and elastic, blending the effervescent beauty of a movie star with the verbal expressiveness of a screwball comedienne, the reckless abandon of a silent film pantomimist (one of her closest professional mentors was Buster Keaton) with the everywoman vulnerability that made her irresistible to TV audiences for three decades. The first episode telecast, titled "The Girls Want to Go to a Nightclub," illustrates her appeal. A "battle of the sexes" conflict erupts on Fred and Ethel Mertz's eighteenth wedding anniversary: Ethel wants to

celebrate at a nightclub; Fred, at the fights. Fred and Ethel (played by William Frawley and Vivian Vance) are Ricky and Lucy's landlords and best friends. Predictably, the men and women team up against each other as a two-act structure with a brief coda ensues. In the first act, Ricky and Fred refuse to take their wives to a nightclub, so Lucy and Ethel take matters into their own hands as Lucy hatches a plan where the women will find dates as escorts and go anyway. In reaction, Ricky and Fred decide to get dates themselves and secretively tag along to keep an eye on their wives.

In an Elizabethan plot twist, a mutual friend sets the couples up with each other on blind dates with Lucy and Ethel disguised as hillbillies, resulting in a comedy of errors based on Ricky and Fred's inability to recognize their wives. The second act thus is a grand farce in the tradition of Molière as the men and women parry with each other—singing, dancing, joking, and teasing one another. Throughout the eight-minute sequence, Lucy's extraordinary talents are on full display, including her humorous facial expressions, her vocal dexterity, her physical agility, her unrestrained energy, and her sweet innocence and good intentions. After the husbands finally see through their wives' disguises, the episode culminates with a short scene showing the two couples sitting together at the fights. Lucy and Ethel are huddled side by side, bored and forlorn, all dolled up in fancy evening dresses with nowhere to go. Typical of the series as a whole, the women are finally brought under control after twenty-plus minutes of inspired high jinks. Lucy's ingenious tactics inevitably unravel as she and Ethel find themselves back where they started at the beginning of the episode, reluctantly obeying their husband's wishes. Still, Ricky and Fred's containment of their wives seems more like a temporary truce than a permanent state of affairs. Lucy is such an indomitable life force that the audience senses she is ready and raring to break free once again next Monday night at 9 P.M. Lucy's weekly rebellion was a breath of fresh air for millions of Americans adjusting to the same kinds of restrictive societal expectations in their own daily lives.

In hindsight, *I Love Lucy* and Desilu Productions epitomize the changes occurring in both American culture and the U.S. television industry during the 1950s. From a cultural perspective, "Lucy and Ricky Ricardo prospered in the pattern followed by others in postwar America. The young city couple grew in affluence, bought a television set and a washing machine, had a baby [in the 1952–1953 television season], ventured across the country to Hollywood where they saw big stars [in 1954–1955 because of Ricky's blossoming movie career], and ultimately moved to the suburbs [out of their brownstone apartment on East 68th Street to nearby Connecticut during 1956–1957], always with antic complications of Lucy's devising."[59] The most common dramatic conflict in the series involved Lucy's continuing attempts to break into show business. One of the most famous examples takes place during the first season in episode thirty, "Lucy Does a TV Commercial," where she diverts an actress who Ricky has hired to perform a live "Vitameatavegamin" ad. Lucy turns up in her place and becomes hilariously drunk as she downs spoonfuls of the twenty-four-proof tonic in rehearsal and then later on the air. Her intoxication promptly short-circuits her performing career, as happens time and again throughout the program's six-year run. After finishing no. 3 during its first season, *I Love Lucy* was no. 1 in four out of the next five years, only falling to no. 2 in 1955–1956 behind CBS's *The $64,000 Question*. *I Love Lucy* also holds the highest seasonal rating of all time at 67 in 1952–1953 (translating into an average thirty-one million viewers per episode), topping the previous record of 62 set by Milton Berle's *Texaco Star Theater* in 1950–1951.

I Love Lucy was moreover a transitional program between the urban ethnic working-class sitcoms of the late 1940s and early 1950s (with its mixed marriage between Ricky Ricardo and Lucy MacGillicuddy) to the increasingly unalloyed WASP-oriented, middle-class

Lucy's great ambition was to break into show business, such as in "Lucy Does a TV Commercial," where she diverts an actress who Ricky has hired to perform a live "Vitameatavegamin" ad. Courtesy of CBS/Landov.

domestic comedies that initially emerged on CBS with such shows as *Father Knows Best* (1954–1963) and *Leave It to Beaver* (1957–1963). In these latter two sitcoms, the mothers are placed on an ever-higher pedestal at the same time as they are pushed back to the margins of the action. Lucille Ball was always the center of attention in *I Love Lucy*. She was the first breakout television superstar since the rise of suburbia, and she reflected the ambivalence that millions of Americans—both women and men—felt about the personal satisfaction that they saw in family and children on the one hand, contrasted to the loss of freedom and the added responsibilities on the other. *I Love Lucy* implicitly acknowledges the limited options afforded to women by the happy-homemaker stereotype. Lucy is never sorry to be a wife and mother; she just wants her career as well. In this way, the situation comedy format domesticates Lucy's natural exuberance and professional ambitions as she eventually defers to Ricky and returns to her wifely and motherly duties at the end of every episode, keeping intact the myth of the nuclear family.

Not by accident, the most-watched *I Love Lucy* episode of all time was titled "Lucy Goes to the Hospital," as a frenetic Ricky, Fred, and

Ethel forget Lucy at home, before going back to retrieve her and then rushing pell-mell to the maternity ward so she can deliver "little Ricky." With this January 19, 1953, telecast, which garnered an astonishing 71.1 rating, forty-four million Americans saw the baby boom comically dramatized through the personal misadventures of Lucy and Ricky, literally transforming a national trend into an understandable and entertaining television event for the American viewing public. "The show [even] upstaged" Dwight D. Eisenhower's inauguration "as President of the United States the following day, admittedly not in prime time, [when] only 29 million people tuned in."[60] Lucille Ball now represented "the outstanding figure in popularity for all TV programs," according to *New York Times* critic Jack Gould. In an article highlighting ten prominent female comics on television (CBS's Lucy, Gracie Allen, Eve Arden of *Our Miss Brooks*, Joan Caulfield of *My Favorite Husband*, Ann Sothern of *Private Secretary*, Marie Wilson of *My Friend Irma*; NBC's Imogene Coca, Martha Raye, Joan Davis of *I Married Joan*; and ABC's Jean Carroll of *Take It from Me*), Gould marvels at this new phenomenon spearheaded by Lucille Ball where "the male of the species" previously "outnumbered" women "on the stage and screen. . . . The rise of the comedienne in TV may be attributed to the nature of the medium itself. Since the TV audience is the family at home, the domestic comedy, revolving about the woman of the house, is a natural formula."[61]

The sitcom formula itself is also deeply rooted in sound broadcasting. During its first decade, television grew out of the nurturing environment provided to it by the NBC, CBS, and ABC radio networks' steadfast financial support, their leadership in how to best organize and operate a network, their supply of creative talent and other kinds of personnel, and their programming antecedents. "Contrary to some assertions, it was not advertiser abandonment of radio that motivated the rapid removal of network assets from the old medium to the new," maintains Michele Hilmes in *Radio Voices*. "During the immediate postwar years, still-flourishing radio network profits were taken from that side of the business and applied directly to television's growth." During the transition to television, the aggregate audience for sound broadcasting, described by Hilmes as "the feminine majority," continued to reign at 55 to 60 percent in the evening and was more than 70 percent in the daytime.[62] If anything, the postwar rotation of women out of the workforce and into the rapidly growing domestic sphere increased the relative importance of female viewers in the eyes of industry executives, who saw them as the principal arbiters of what types of programming were most acceptable and which genres were most appropriate for the intimate surroundings of the typical American household.

The adroitness with which CBS tapped into the feminine majority by promoting female stars and female-friendly male performers (such as Arthur Godfrey, Jack Benny, Art Linkletter, and Garry Moore) was a key reason that the network eventually surpassed NBC in the ratings by the mid 1950s, along with its accessible and populist programming strategies and the residual effects of Paley's 1948–1949 talent raids. The quickness with which CBS turned around its fortunes is remarkable. After temporarily shutting down its Grand Central Station production facility in the wake of the 1947 color television foray, CBS was up and running again early the next year. On September 29, 1948, the FCC issued its "freeze" on awarding any new TV station licenses, thus allowing CBS more breathing room to follow through on developing an array of competitive programs for those affiliates that were already on the air or soon to be operational once station construction was completed. The anticipated six-month freeze lasted nearly four years, as the FCC took time out to reduce chronic interference problems, open up more spectrum space (granting access to channels 14 to 83 on the UHF band), settle the color television controversy (ultimately bowing to outside industry and marketplace pressures by reversing itself and approving RCA's all-electronic color TV system in December 1953 after having surprised everyone by authorizing CBS's hybrid color technology in 1950), and reserve a small portion of the broadcast spectrum for the future development of educational television.

In retrospect, "the term 'freeze' is misleading," asserts William Boddy in *Fifties Television*: "Although the commission suspended license approvals from September 1948 through April 1952, the number of VHF stations on the air grew from 50 to 108, the number of television sets rose from 1,200,000 to 15,000,000, the percentage of homes with television increased from .4 percent to 34 percent, and television's share of broadcast advertising leaped from 3 percent to 70 percent."[63] Overall, NBC and CBS benefited greatly from the FCC action, which essentially preserved the status quo, while ABC and especially DuMont fell increasingly behind. For instance, "between 1949 and 1952 network billings for NBC and CBS rose from $9.9 million to $153.3 million, more than 84 percent of all network time sales; figures for ABC and DuMont increased from $2.4 million to $28.5 million."[64] Put another way, fifty-one of the existing sixty-three TV markets at the start of the freeze had only one or two licensees, meaning that these stations formed affiliate relations with either NBC or CBS, or both. ABC and DuMont were left out of all but the twelve remaining markets, allowing NBC and CBS to form a virtual duopoly in television networking during the late 1940s and early 1950s.

From an industrial perspective, *I Love Lucy* and Desilu Productions pioneered a number of significant innovations that soon became standard in the post-freeze TV environment. This series established much of the style and many of the techniques that would characterize the television situation comedy for years to come. Lucy also emerged as TV's top attraction, while the sitcom rode on her coattails to become the foremost programming staple that CBS used in its annual competition with NBC for prime-time dominance. Desilu, moreover, evolved into the prototypical independent television production and syndication company over the course of the decade. None of these developments were preordained when Philip Morris and the Biow Advertising Agency initially expressed interest in sponsoring *I Love Lucy*. They wanted the show produced live in New York and with someone other than Desi Arnaz as Lucy's costar. Lucy held firm for Desi, and together they proposed shooting the series on film, as a way to both stay close to their suburban home northwest of Los Angeles and obviate any problems that arose from the three-hour time delay in telecasting the show all across the country. Lucy and Desi gravitated toward this solution because they already had Desilu developing movie properties for them; they merely expanded the company's purview to include TV. CBS, Biow, and Philip Morris finally agreed to the filming when the couple proposed that they take a much smaller fee upfront in order to produce *I Love Lucy* themselves. The rest as they say is television history.

TV's potential as a national medium slowly came to full fruition after the FCC lifted the freeze in April, effective July 1, 1952. *I Love Lucy* had a key role in getting the ball rolling and moving the situation comedy beyond its roots in radio. From a production standpoint, Desi, Jess Oppenheimer, and their team at Desilu adapted the modest General Services Studio on Los Palmas Avenue in downtown Los Angeles for a live audience, with bleachers seating three hundred people; hired Oscar-winning cameraman, Karl Freund, who Lucy had known years earlier at MGM, to design a revolutionary "flat" lighting setup that worked well for an entire scene, instead of having to reconfigure the lights for every shot as was required in the movies; and adapted Ralph Edwards and his production coordinator Al Simon's "multicam" approach to live television where two or more cameras recorded the action simultaneously from a series of vantage points. Edwards and Simon first employed this technique on the game show *Truth or Consequences*, which debuted on CBS in 1950 and was also sponsored by Philip Morris through the Biow Agency. The multicam approach was later refined at Desilu when RCA perfected a device that could synchronize multiple film strips, thus increasing the editing precision required for fast-paced comic storytelling. Each of these production innovations provided *I Love Lucy* with what was at the time a cutting-edge style; together, these elements worked so well that they constituted a broad set of general guidelines by which TV sitcoms were filmed for the next two decades.

In addition, Desilu unexpectedly grew in size and stature to rival the largest Hollywood studios by the end of the 1950s, thus signaling the growing ascendancy of television over the movies in Hollywood. As late as 1954–1955, 87 percent of all network programming was still shot live, as opposed to filmed, and the shift in television production from the East to the West Coast was just gaining momentum.[65] Following its success with *I Love Lucy*, Desilu was one of a handful of trailblazing companies, along with Hal Roach, Republic, MCA's Revue, Columbia's Screen Gems, and Ziv, that began developing new in-house television programs for the networks. Desilu produced such situation comedies as *Our Miss Brooks* (1952–1956), *My Little Margie* (1952–1955), and *December Bride* (1954–1958), as well as a *Dragnet*-styled clone titled, *The Lineup* (1954–1960). It also rented out its studio space to other independent productions, beginning with Danny Thomas's semiautobiographical sitcom, *Make Room for Daddy* (1953–1964). Most important, though, Desilu started syndicating *I Love Lucy* in April 1955 toward the end of its fourth season, eventually selling all of its 180 episodes of the show to CBS for $4.5 million dollars (along with *December Bride*'s backend rights for an additional $500,000) in October 1956. Syndication proved to be a gold mine for the TV industry as a whole, both domestically and overseas, although neither Desilu nor CBS anticipated the lucrative nature of these ancillary markets when *I Love Lucy* first began filming in the summer of 1951.

For his part, Desi Arnaz channeled much of his and Lucy's profits back into Desilu, enabling them to purchase RKO studios in December 1957 for just under $6.2 million. Their wildest dream had finally come true. They had originally thought of Desilu as a self-styled homage to Pickfair (the contraction that Mary Pickford and Douglas Fairbanks used to name their luxurious Beverly Hills mansion where they held court during the 1920s as Hollywood's reigning power couple). Now three decades later, Lucille Ball and Desi Arnaz were the toast of the town themselves. For Lucy especially, everything had come full circle. Just twenty-five years earlier, she was one of many contract players at RKO; now she and Desi were the resident superstar and mogul of this one-time major movie studio. Their professional triumph with Desilu embodied the rising fortunes of television in general within the rapidly changing Hollywood of the 1950s.

The only serious professional scare that Lucy experienced throughout the entire decade as her career rocketed ever skyward occurred between April 1952 and September 1953, when she was under investigation by the House Un-American Activities Committee (HUAC) for having registered to vote as a communist in 1936 at the behest of her late maternal grandfather, who was a lifelong socialist. The film and television industries endured special scrutiny from HUAC because of their relatively high profiles with the public. Unfortunately for Lucille Ball, she was the biggest star to ever fall under the committee's gaze. Lucy was eventually exonerated, but not before she was attacked by several conservative newspapers across the country, as well as by influential gossip columnist and radio commentator Walter Winchell, who was a staunch anticommunist and a strong supporter of Wisconsin Senator Joseph R. McCarthy. The upshot of this ordeal for Lucy was that she never voted in any election for the rest of her life. The Red Scare left an indelible mark on her, as it did the nascent television industry, where she devoted most of her creative energies for the next quarter century.

A Patron Saint for an Age of Unreason

> Of the incalculable ways that television transformed American life—in family and friendship, leisure and literacy, consumer habits and common memories—the expansion of freedom of expression and embrace of human difference must be counted among its most salutary legacies. During the Cold War, through television, America became a more open and tolerant place.
>
> Thomas Doherty, *Cold War, Cool Medium*, 2003[66]

Former *Washington Post* and *Newsweek* publisher Philip Graham once famously described journalism as the first rough draft of history, and no medium ever provided these types of instant impressions faster and more intimately than television. The earliest TV news and documentary programs could be as compelling as the best prime-time dramas; they could also be bloodless exercises or the stuff of on-air puffery. As early as June 24–28, 1940, NBC and Philco telecast the Republican National Convention from Philadelphia on a three-station hookup (including New York City and Schenectady). An estimated forty thousand people watched at least some part of the five-day event, when Wendell Wilkie finally pulled out an upset win for the GOP presidential nomination well past midnight on the last day of the proceedings. A month later, the Democrats held their own convention in Chicago, but no TV stations yet existed in America's "Second City," so newsreels of FDR's nomination for an unprecedented third term were flown East and transmitted over an embryonic ad hoc Philadelphia–New York–Schenectady network the next day. Both 1944 conventions were also staged in Chicago, so television coverage was again restricted to showing day-old films on a few interconnected East Coast stations.

After World War II ended, however, network radio news organizations slowly expanded their repertoires to include more on-the-spot TV newsgathering, such as NBC's seven-city East Coast hookup (Philadelphia, New York, Schenectady, Boston, Baltimore, Washington, Richmond) of Congress's opening ceremonies on January 2, 1947, followed on October 5 of that year with the first telecast from the White House, when President Truman made an impassioned appeal to his fellow Americans for their support of the newly instituted but costly Marshall Plan that boldly intended to rebuild the noncommunist countries of Western Europe by the early 1950s. The postwar years were turning out to be an anxious time for most Americans. The nation's transition to peace was tempered by a succession of events, beginning with a rapid escalation of tensions between the United States and the Union of Soviet Socialist Republics (USSR). The Soviet Union had seized much of Eastern Europe in the wake of World War II, and now it was exerting its hegemonic control over the region. Anti-Russian fears at home resulted in the reestablishment of HUAC in 1946 as a standing committee. HUAC began investigating possible communist influences and affiliations within the borders of the United States the next year.

A majority of Americans across the political spectrum were now coming together into a loose Cold War consensus based on their shared anticommunism, their faith in economic progress through corporate capitalism, and their belief in the inherent goodness and superiority of the American way of life, even as Democrats and Republicans vied bitterly for power and control over the levers of government. The fait accompli for the nation occurred on August 29, 1949, when the Soviets detonated their first atomic bomb, much to the surprise of official Washington and the American people. In one fell swoop, the Soviet Union joined the United States as the world's nuclear power. The general public was shocked by the realization that America no longer held a monopoly on atomic weaponry; many citizens also resigned themselves to the sobering expectation that nuclear war with the Russians was inevitable at some undetermined time in the future. Next, China, who had been an American ally during World War II, fell to the communists as Mao Zedong formed the People's Republic of China (PRC) on October 1, 1949. As a result of all these developments, HUAC became even more aggressive in its investigative activities, pursuing a string of high-profile espionage cases, such as the one involving Alger Hiss beginning in 1948, which alleged that this former State Department official passed secrets to the Russians. HUAC, moreover, spent a great deal of time and energy conducting exhaustive inquiries into the domestic movie and television industries, pursuing a toxic mixture of evidence and hearsay about possible communist infiltration.

Suddenly things went from bad to worse on June 25, 1950, when ninety thousand regulars from the North Korean People's Army staged a surprise attack on South Korea, which began a three-year proxy war between the East supported by the PRC and the Soviet Union and the West led by the United States. The Korean War ended in a stalemate with a cease-fire on July 27, 1953, symbolizing the start of a protracted superpower standoff abroad, along with an undercurrent of unease and suspicion at home that percolated underneath the surface of daily life. Print and radio newspeople were the acknowledged journalistic leaders covering these stories for the American people in the late 1940s and the early 1950s. NBC was the foremost pioneer in television news, investing the most time and resources in this area as it teamed with Fox Movietone to produce the first continuing nightly news program, *Camel Newsreel Theater*, starting on February 16, 1948. CBS responded on April 28, 1948, by premiering *Douglas Edwards and the News* underwritten by Oldsmobile with filmed inserts supplied by Telenews. Respected radio correspondent John Daly was lured away from CBS to head up a similar early evening newscast for ABC in October 1953 (while remaining as host of CBS's hit prime-time quiz show *What's My Line?* which began in 1950). Each of these fifteen-minute dinnertime newscasts on NBC, CBS, and ABC was basically a news presentation read by an on-air personality and supported by theatrical newsreels edited for TV; actual in-house newsgathering was kept to a minimum because of the added expense.

NBC experimented more than its two major rivals with on-the-spot coverage and establishing overseas filmed exchanges (such as its agreements with the British Broadcasting Corporation, Pathé, and Radio Diffusione Italiano). (DuMont failed to mount a continuing newscast because of financial exigency. The eleven-month *News from Washington* was followed by *Camera Headlines*, which began in January 1948 but lasted for only two years.) NBC's professional superiority was evident in the higher-quality thirty-five-millimeter visual presentation that it made rather than relying on the far more inexpensive and grainy sixteen-millimeter film gauge used by CBS and ABC. Occasionally, the networks worked together, as when they pooled their 1948 coverage of the Republican National Convention (54 hours between June 21 and 25) and the ensuing Democratic National Convention (41.5 hours between July 12 and 14), but NBC clearly dominated these telecasts with its larger number of personnel and its more advanced television technology, such as its seventeen-city hookup along the East Coast, where more than 400,000 TV households tuned in to an aggregate audience exceeding 1,250,000 over the course of these two events. NBC also led the way in pioneering alternative news formats with the debut of *Meet the Press* on November 20, 1947, originating from the Washington studio of affiliate WNBW (now WRC). The program began on NBC radio on October 5, 1945, created by host Martha Rountree and editor-panelist Lawrence Spivak. *Meet the Press* set a high standard from the outset in the interview-news format, as all of the leading politicians and public figures of the day appeared on the show at one time or another, facing questions from a panel of print-trained journalists.

Less serious and weighty in tone, the "NBC early-evening news became the *Camel News Caravan* [on February 16, 1949], featuring the breezy, boutonnièred John Cameron Swayze." This nightly news show named after its sponsor "maintained a brisk tempo. Near the end of each telecast came a moment when Swayze exclaimed with unbounded enthusiasm: 'Now let's go hopscotching the news for headlines!' What followed was a grab-bag of items that had regrettably taken place without benefit of cameras. Each event had to be dispatched, it seemed, in one sentence. Then Swayze would say: 'That's the story, folks. Glad we could get together.' "[67] Despite the glib presentation, NBC was the only network to maintain its own news and documentary film service before 1951, resulting in its first critical and popular miniseries success with the twenty-six-part *Victory at Sea*, which premiered on Sunday afternoon, October 26, 1952. Produced by Henry "Pete" Salomon and his Project 20 unit, this ambitious long-form documentary chronicled the battles fought by the U.S. Navy during World War II and featured nearly thirteen hours of archival footage. Even though NBC pioneered almost all of the earliest techniques and formats in TV news and documentary programming, the network division in charge of these nonfiction genres eventually fell behind its CBS counterpart in the ratings during 1954. "Since NBC was the first network to establish an organization for news-gathering, it experienced a good number of accidents and failed experiments," recounts journalism historian Kristine Brunovska Karnick; "when CBS established its news film organization in the early 1950s it was able to benefit from the lessons NBC had learned, while avoiding many of its mistakes."[68]

No one is more responsible for the rise of CBS television news and documentary programming than Edward R. Murrow. Reluctant at first to make the transition to TV, Murrow was already an international celebrity because of his radio reporting from Europe during World War II. His rich, full, and expressive voice first came to the attention of

America's listening public in his many rooftop radio broadcasts during the Battle of Britain in 1939. Murrow frequently used the airwaves to revivify and popularize many democratic ideals, such as free speech, citizen participation, and the sanctification of individual liberties and rights. Resurrecting these virtues for a mass audience of true believers during the London Blitz was high drama, as the impending threat of totalitarianism, made real by Nazi bombs, was ever present in the background. Murrow's persona was thus established back home, embodying the political traditions of the Western democracies, and offering the American public a heroic model on which to focus their energies. Edward R. Murrow was only one of many heroes to emerge from World War II, but he became the eminent symbol for broadcasting. He was a seminal force in the creation and development of electronic newsgathering as both a craft and a profession in the United States.

Murrow hired a generation of journalists at CBS, such as Eric Sevareid, Charles Collingwood, Howard K. Smith, Larry LeSueur, Winston Burdett, Bill Downs, Marvin Kalb, and many others, for whom he set the example as their charismatic leader. After he made his first tentative moves into television, "Murrow's boys" soon followed. This influx of journalistic talent literally transformed CBS news during the early to mid 1950s. Murrow was on camera as he worked the floor of the 1948 Republican and Democratic National Conventions, though "radio was still king" and "for most of the country" these political events were "still audio conventions."[69] Murrow remained largely a radio news commentator until he assumed the helm of the news and documentary program *See It Now* (1951–1958), after being approached by Alcoa, which wanted to sponsor his first regularly scheduled television series. This weekly show was an adaptation of CBS radio's popular *Hear It Now*, which was also coproduced by Murrow and Fred W. Friendly. *See It Now* premiered on Sunday afternoon, November 18, 1951, opening with Murrow's characteristic restraint and directness: "This is an old team trying to learn a new trade." By April 20, 1952, CBS moved the series to prime time, where it stayed until July 5, 1955, typically averaging a respectable three million viewers and occasionally drawing as many as seven million for its highest-profile episodes.

Murrow additionally hosted television's initial foray into celebrity journalism, *Person to Person* (1953–1961), which he also independently owned and coproduced with John Aaron and Jesse Zousmer. Every Friday evening at 10:30 P.M., Murrow chatted informally with a wide array of well-known politicians, movie stars, writers, musicians, and athletes on this hugely popular series that usually hovered around the edges of

Edward R. Murrow's first words on See It Now (18 November 1951) were "This is an old team trying to learn a new trade." Producer Fred W. Friendly is sitting on the right. Courtesy of Library of American Broadcasting at the University of Maryland.

the top 10, attracting somewhere between eighteen million and twenty-one million people on a regular basis. He remained with *Person to Person* through the 1958–1959 TV season, "visiting" with guests in their homes, including such newsmakers and personalities as Harry Truman, John and Jackie Kennedy, Marlon Brando, Marilyn Monroe, Duke Ellington, Frank Sinatra, John Steinbeck, Roy Campanella, and Rocky Marciano. Edward R. Murrow was so skillful in his role as a conversationalist and raconteur that he won an Emmy for the Most Outstanding Personality in all of television after *Person to Person*'s inaugural season. Still, he made his greatest mark on early TV in *See It Now*, where he received four other individual Emmys for Best News Commentator or Analyst, and the series itself was awarded four Emmys for Best News or Public Service Program. At the time, *New York Herald Tribune* TV critic John Horne coined "the phrases 'high Murrow' and 'low Murrow' to distinguish between the two broadcasts."[70]

In hindsight, the most lasting and vivid memory of America's first great television journalist is much more "high" Murrow than the celebrity interviewer. In *The Powers That Be*, David Halberstam observed that Edward R. Murrow was "one of those rare legendary figures who was as good as his myth."[71] He was apparently driven by the democratic precepts of modern liberalism and the more embracing Weltanschauung of the American Protestant tradition. (Murrow's brother, Dewey, once described the intense religious and moral tutelage of their Quaker parents: "They branded us with their own consciences."[72])

Ed Murrow also hosted television's initial foray into celebrity journalism, Person to Person *(1953–1961). Courtesy of the Murrow Center, Fletcher School of Law and Diplomacy at Tufts University.*

Murrow's imagination and obsession with these secular and spiritual belief systems impelled him to integrate these complementary values into his own personality to such a degree that he became the virtual fulfillment of his industry's public service aspirations—the "patron saint of American broadcasting." Murrow's on-air appearance was unlike anyone else's on television. He was almost always sitting in shadows, dressed formally in a conservative pin-striped suit, and peering skeptically from behind his ubiquitous cigarette as if transfixed on some indeterminate worry. His clothes and posture bespoke sophistication and experience, while his sense of sadness and irony disclosed feelings of incertitude and disillusionment. In the context of TV's lightness, action, and inveterate presentism, Murrow projected a presence ever darker, more trapped, and nearly paralyzed with awareness. For an entertainer, such a countenance would have quickly worn his audience out; for a newscaster and commentator, however, it provided viewers with an element of high drama, no matter how intrinsically dry and prosaic the news topic might be at any given time.

Many of *See It Now*'s telecasts were duly considered breakthroughs for the television medium when they first appeared. For example, the

Ed Murrow drove himself to become the virtual fulfillment of his industry's public-service aspirations—the "patron saint of American broadcasting." Courtesy of Library of American Broadcasting at the University of Maryland.

expanded one-hour *This Is Korea . . . Christmas 1952* (shown on December 28) was produced on location "to try to portray the face of the war and the faces of the men who are fighting it." Unlike Vietnam, Korea was not a living-room war. Before "This Is Korea . . . Christmas 1952," each and every network relied solely on official briefings from Washington and government-supplied footage to cover this conflict. In contrast, *See It Now* not only took the American viewing public to the Korean Peninsula through its film footage but also provided them with a close-up portrait of a largely chaotic open-ended war manned with workaday dedication by the troops on the ground. Murrow in uniform mixed easily with the young GIs as they dug foxholes in the frozen earth or tried to celebrate the holidays as best they could, in between carrying out their mundane tasks and sometimes dangerous duties. He interviewed them about their sweethearts and families back home or the daily orders they received, as one patrol is photographed trudging off into the cold unknown to face the enemy. "There is no conclusion to this report," Murrow closed matter-of-factly, "because there is no end to the war." Jack Gould of the *New York Times* called the episode a "visual poem that caught the poignancy, frustration and resolution of life on the front lines of Korea," concluding that "it was one of the finest programs ever seen on TV."[73]

Over the course of its seven-year run, *See It Now* tackled late-breaking stories (such as hurricane flooding along the Mississippi), controversial subjects (segregated schools in Murrow's native North Carolina), international issues (the extent of Third World poverty), and new scientific findings (the linkage between cigarettes and lung cancer). The series traveled the world as Murrow interviewed foreign leaders as diverse as Marshal Tito of Yugoslavia, Prime Minister David Ben-Gurion of Israel, and Premier Chou En-lai of China. *See It Now*'s most-celebrated episodes were telecast during the 1953–1954 television season, when Murrow, Fred Friendly, and their production team took on Joseph R. McCarthy and the effects of McCarthyism on the body politic. The wave of anticommunist hysteria that gripped America predated McCarthy's rise to national prominence, which occurred almost by accident after he delivered a Lincoln Day speech on February 9, 1950, before the Republican Women's Club of Wheeling, West Virginia, where he held up a piece of paper and claimed to have a list of 205 known subversives who were working in the State Department. The accusation set off a firestorm of press reaction, which McCarthy fueled with a continuing barrage of half-truths, distortions, and outright fabrications over the next two years leading up to the 1952 local, state, and national elections, even though his evidence was often incomplete or just plain nonexistent.

McCarthy soon emerged as the most prominent and vocal anticommunist in the country. An ex-marine bombardier during World War II, "Tail Gunner Joe" (as he was nicknamed by both his supporters and his detractors) was a down-and-dirty political infighter whose crude personal attacks emboldened ultraconservatives across the country and damaged liberal Democrats who were painted as either communist sympathizers or hopelessly naïve and out-of-date New Dealers. His reactionary and polarizing rhetoric provided McCarthy with a national power base by galvanizing what was an indefinite but palpable mood of fear and discontent about the vulnerable state of the country, but now was referred to simply as McCarthyism. Because of his meteoric rise, Republican leaders appointed McCarthy chairman of the powerful Senate Permanent Subcommittee on Investigations in 1952 where he was free to roam and attack communists wherever he and his staff suspected they might be hiding within the U.S. government. He set his sights on the Voice of America, the State Department, the Department of Defense, and finally the Army Signal Corps, where he presumed a clandestine spy ring was operating. McCarthy carried out his committee duties with great relish, often bullying and browbeating witnesses, resorting to innuendo and slander, and regularly delivering windy speeches attacking those who held political and social views different from his own.

Even though television was beyond McCarthy's purview, the industry had been subject to similar kinds of fear and paranoia for years. Encouraged by HUAC's example, three former FBI agents started publishing a four-page weekly newsletter entitled *Counterattack* in 1947, which called for "the blacklisting of 'traitorous' actors, producers, directors, announcers, writers, and others in the entertainment field." Executives at the networks and the movie studios took this rather slapdash publication very seriously: "It mattered little that *Counterattack*'s charges were unsubstantiated, distorted, out of context, based on rumor, or culled from questionable newspaper citations."[74] On June 22, 1950, former FBI agent Theodore Kirkpatrick and TV producer Vincent Harnett compiled an expanded 213-page booklet named *Red Channels: The Report of Communist Influence in Radio and Television* and published it under the auspices of *Counterattack*. The pamphlet listed 151 broadcast talent and personnel who supposedly belonged to or supported organizations with procommunist sympathies. As a result of being cited in *Red Channels*, people were immediately fired or rendered unemployable. CBS ordered all of its workers to sign a loyalty oath in December 1950 to buffer itself against outside pressures and claims that the network was nothing more than the liberal-leaning "Communist Broadcasting System." NBC already required similar pledges of all of its new employees, while ABC opened up an internal security office whose staff collaborated closely with HUAC. The Red Scare was alive and well in the corridors of power at all of the major networks.

Back at CBS's Studio 41 in New York, Murrow and Friendly waited until October 23, 1953, to address the climate of McCarthyism in "The Case of Lt. Milo Radulovich A0589839." He was a twenty-six-year-old Air Force officer from Dexter, Michigan, who was being discharged from the service as a potential security risk because his immigrant father and sister allegedly held communist sympathies. They supposedly were "fellow travelers" because they actively participated in their United Auto Workers local chapter. The *See It Now* team produced a thirty-minute rejoinder contending that Milo Radulovich was being unfairly judged and penalized solely on the grounds of his family ties. A plain-spoken and sympathetic Milo appeared on screen and explained that he was being held accountable for "maintaining a close and continuing relationship with my dad and sister over the years"; the elderly father spoke, too, in an emotion-laden scene where he asserted in a thick Serbian accent that neither he nor his union "want any part of communists." At the end of his remarks, he revealed that he wrote a letter to the president of the United States asking for "justice for my boy." Murrow summarized, "we believe that 'the son shall not bear the iniquity of the father,' even though the iniquity be proved; and in this case it was not." The public reaction to the episode was instantaneous and overwhelming: CBS received "approximately eight thousand letters ... with the bias about 100 to 1 in favor of Radulovich."[75] Fred Friendly recalled: "It was the first time that Ed and all of us understood the power of television."[76]

Five weeks later, the Secretary of the Air Force, Harold E. Talbott, appeared on *See It Now* announcing that after careful review "it is consistent with the interests of national security to retain Lieutenant Radulovich." With the mounting confidence provided by this experience, and at Murrow and Friendly's behest, the *See It Now* staff started collecting and cataloguing film clips of Joseph R. McCarthy in action. On March 9, 1954, *See It Now* presented its examination of Senator McCarthy and his methods "told mainly in his own words and pictures." The episode was expertly constructed and provided a damning indictment of McCarthy's reckless and bullying tactics: "the program's 'working thesis' was that if the fight against communism was made into a fight against the two great political parties, one party soon would be destroyed and the Republic could not long survive. These words were taken from a speech by Senator McCarthy" himself in late 1952.[77] The portrait of Joe McCarthy was not a pretty one; his dark, hulking presence hectored witnesses, twisted their words, and giggled menacingly at his own nasty quips (such as "Alger—I mean Adlai [laughter]" in a film insert taken from an October 27, 1952, campaign speech where McCarthy links Democratic candidate Adlai Stevenson to convicted spy Alger Hiss two weeks before the presidential election). Watching an uncensored McCarthy for half an hour held the same strange fascination for most viewers as peering incredulously at a car wreck. At the conclusion of the episode, Murrow didn't mince words:

> We will not walk in fear, one of another. We will not be driven by fear into an age of unreason. . . . No one familiar with the history of this country can deny that congressional committees are useful . . . but the line between investigation and persecution is a very fine one and the junior Senator from Wisconsin has stepped over it repeatedly. . . . This is no time for men who oppose Senator McCarthy's methods to keep silent, or for those who approve. . . . The actions of the junior Senator from Wisconsin have caused alarm and dismay amongst our allies abroad and given considerable comfort to our enemies, and whose fault is that? Not really his. He didn't create the situation of fear; he merely exploited it and rather

successfully. Cassius was right: "The fault, dear Brutus, is not in our stars but in ourselves."[78]

In the aftermath of this episode, the descriptions of Edward R. Murrow began to transcend the more secular cast that appeared in response to his championing of democratic action and principles in Britain during the London Blitz. Jack Gould, for instance, wrote that "last week may be remembered as the week that broadcasting recaptured its soul."[79] In contrast, McCarthy's supporters simultaneously went on the attack. A case in point was the New York *Journal-American* TV critic, Jack O'Brian, who reported that his newspaper "had been flooded by calls hostile" to the "hate McCarthy telecast" as had "other papers."[80] Twenty-four hours later, however, "CBS and its affiliates had received over 10,000 phone calls and telegrams. Within days hallways were piled high with boxes of letters. The letters, telegrams, and calls eventually totaled over 75,000, the greatest reaction to any single program in the network's history. The count continued ten to one in favor of Murrow."[81] "That night [with the March 9 McCarthy episode] television came of age," remembered Don Hewitt, *See It Now*'s on-air director (and later creator and executive producer of *60 Minutes*); "television was now a real force to be reckoned with in the world."[82]

Murrow, Friendly, and CBS offered Senator McCarthy equal time for rebuttal, and he responded four weeks later on April 6, 1954, probably doing himself more harm than good in the long run by delivering an over-the-top attack on Murrow as "the leader and the cleverest of the jackal pack which is always found at the throat of anyone who dares to expose individual Communists and traitors." For twenty-two minutes, McCarthy ranted and raved about Murrow's past membership in the Industrial Workers of the World ("a terrorist organization") and his work as a young man at the Institute of International Education ("a job that would normally be done by the Russian secret police"). He culminated his harangue by holding aloft the March 9, 1954, issue of the *Daily Worker*, the newspaper of the American Communist Party, pointing out that the publication praised Murrow's March 6 *See It Now* telecast, and supported his contention that McCarthy's behavior offers "comfort to the enemy." In a bravura finish, Joe McCarthy concluded that he "ought not be in the Senate" if Murrow and the *Daily Worker* were correct; "if on the other hand, Mr. Murrow is giving comfort to our enemies, he ought not be brought into the homes of millions of Americans by the Columbia Broadcasting System." The ploy didn't work. Murrow experienced some backlash in the press, but the CBS brass stood by him. More than anything, McCarthy's performance on *See It Now* deepened the public's perception that the senator was a loose cannon operating largely on his own without the usual checks and balances that typically governed federal and state officials.[83]

Murrow always minimized the part that *See It Now* played in arresting the growth of Joseph R. McCarthy's excesses, as he did five years later in a *New York Post* interview when he explained that the "time was right" for these telecasts and the series probably received "too much credit."[84] Murrow was not the first American journalist to criticize Senator McCarthy. He was the most prominent, though, and the one who had the greatest influence because his challenge came on prime-time TV, not newspapers, magazines, or radio. Murrow, Friendly, and the *See It Now* team came to realize the immense power and reach of the television medium as they went along. More than anything, insists broadcast historian Erik Barnouw, "the Murrow-McCarthy conflict prepared the moment."[85] A little more than two weeks after McCarthy's appearance on *See It Now*, the Army-McCarthy hearings began. This investigation was convened to explore conspiracy charges against certain members of the U.S. Army stationed at Fort Monmouth, New Jersey, who allegedly had communist ties. ABC and DuMont carried 187 hours of gavel-to-gavel coverage over seventy-one half-day sessions from April 22 through June 17, 1954, while NBC and CBS mostly telecast filmed highlights on their nightly newscasts or in fringe time slots rather than interrupt their regularly scheduled programming.

From an economic perspective, the fact that the hearings were carried on a sustaining basis without advertising "validated the concerns of CBS and NBC about the cost. ABC lost a reported $600,000 from its coverage; DuMont's costs added to a host of other problems" and pushed the network to the brink of bankruptcy, where it dangled precariously for another year before going completely out of business during the late spring and early summer of 1955.[86] In terms of reception, however, thirty million Americans tuned into the opening session, and the entire proceedings averaged a healthy daytime rating of 10 for an estimated twenty million unduplicated viewers each week. For Senator McCarthy, the hearings turned out to be a personal and professional embarrassment. On June 9, especially, the inquiry reached a crescendo when he was dressed down for his "reckless cruelty" by U.S. Army counsel Joseph N. Welch. McCarthy accused one of Welch's junior attorneys of being "a member of an organization . . . for a number of years" that did "the legal bulwark of the communist party." Welch shot back: "Have you no decency, sir, at long last? Have you left no sense of decency?" After a moment of stunned silence, spectators in the gallery and people throughout the senate caucus room slowly began to applaud. "Joseph McCarthy's personality [was] fully exposed under the glaring eye of television," and his bullying and erratic performance proved to be "an even greater liability to his political future. The senator's favorable ratings in public opinion polls plunged following the conclusion of the Army-McCarthy hearings."[87]

For all intents and purposes, Joseph R. McCarthy's political career took a humiliating about-face on December 2, 1954, when his senate colleagues voted 67 to 22 to censure him for "abuse of senatorial powers" and "conduct that tends to bring the senate into dishonor and disrepute." Shaken deeply by this rebuke, McCarthy never recovered his influence on the hill, and his health seriously declined from that point onward. His quick ascent to national importance and his equally swift descent came to an ignominious end in only seven short years when Joseph R. McCarthy died on May 2, 1957, of a degenerative nerve disorder brought on by his excessive drinking. He was just forty-eight years old. The speed of his rise and fall from grace was truly breathtaking. "Television and McCarthyism are fellow travelers in American history," observes Thomas Doherty, "the rising arc of the medium and the falling arc of the man intersecting at a pivotal moment for each."[88] Moreover, McCarthy and Murrow are forever bound together in America's collective memory of itself in 1954: one sinner, one saint, eternally at odds with each other. Even though "the Murrow documentaries helped make television an indispensable medium," according to Erik Barnouw, and "few people now dared to be without a television set," the future would not be kind to Edward R. Murrow either.[89]

Fred W. Friendly relays an apocryphal anecdote in his memoir *Due to Circumstances Beyond Our Control* that on June 7, 1955, he and his partner watched the debut of *The $64,000 Question*, the new program now scheduled in the 10 P.M. Tuesday time slot just before *See It Now*: "Murrow, who seldom watched any show preceding ours, was riveted and horrified by what he saw. His instincts, accurate as usual, made him realize before the half-hour was over that the carny, midway atmosphere heralded by the big-money quizzes would soon be dominating the airwaves." Revlon was paying CBS $80,000 per episode to telecast *The $64,000 Question*. Alcoa's fee was $50,000 for *See It Now*. "Ed leaned over to me in the control room," remembers Friendly, "and asked, 'Any bets on how long we'll keep this time period now?' "[90] Within a month, *The $64,000 Question* was the no. 1 show on television, spawning a rash of prime-time quiz programs that lasted for three more years until a nationwide scandal put a halt to their spread. Alcoa did decide to invest its advertising dollars elsewhere as CBS cut back *See It Now* to seven one-hour specials scheduled irregularly during the 1956–1957 season. Several TV critics and advertising executives informally redubbed the series *See It Now and Then*.[91]

On October 15, 1958, Edward R. Murrow took the fateful step of publicly excoriating the broadcasting industry for being "fat, comfortable and complacent" and television for "being used to detract, delude, amuse and insulate us" in his plenary address before the Radio and Television News Directors Association's (RTNDA) annual banquet and awards ceremony in Chicago. His remarks landed like a "bombshell both inside and outside the industry. TV, already undergoing investigations that fall for the quiz show scandals, had been exposed, denounced by one of its superstars."[92] The CBS board of directors felt betrayed by Murrow's commentary when they received advance copies of his speech, and several of the journalist's harshest critics in the press began referring to him more and more as the "voice of doom." The network hierarchy at Black Rock on 52nd Street had grown increasingly ambivalent about Murrow. His old friend and boss William S. Paley called him the "conscience of CBS"; still, Fred Friendly reported that the "attitude at CBS was: 'Why does Murrow have to save the world every week?' "[93] The tragedy of Murrow's slow enervation at CBS after this latest controversy was implicit in his apparent need to ascribe higher motives to his own profession. Murrow had long reveled in his role as broadcasting's Jeremiah. His urgent and inspirational style of presentation fit the life-and-death psychological milieu of a world war, as it was later appropriate for the McCarthy crisis. By 1958, though, the viewing public and the television industry were less inclined to accept yet another ethical lambaste, especially since his RTNDA speech was directed at them and their shortcomings. As the business of television grew astronomically throughout the 1950s, Murrow's priorities fell progressively out of step.

A small plaque in the lobby of CBS headquarters in New York City contains the image of Murrow and the inscription: "He set standards of excellence that remain unsurpassed." During his twenty-five-year career, spanning both radio and television, he made more than five thousand broadcasts. More than anyone else, he invented the traditions of television news, moving it with his CBS colleagues beyond its humble roots in radio and the theatrical newsreel. Murrow, Friendly, and the See It Now team essentially created the prototype of the TV documentary. Later, they extended the technological reach of electronic newsgathering in Small World (1958–1959), which employed simultaneous hookups around the globe to facilitate unrehearsed discussions among several international opinion leaders. Most of Murrow's See It Now associates were reassembled to produce CBS Reports beginning in 1959, although Murrow was only an infrequent participant in this series. Over the years, he had simply provoked too many trying situations for CBS, and the network's leadership made a conscious decision to reduce his profile. Murrow finally left CBS in February 1961, accepting President Kennedy's invitation to join his administration as director of the U.S. Information Agency. The apparent irony between Edward R. Murrow and the way that he is subsequently remembered is that the industry that finally had no place for him still holds Murrow up as its model citizen—the "patron saint of American broadcasting."

THE HALCYON YEARS

Beyond Anyone's Wildest Dream—1955–1963

OPERATION FRONTAL LOBES

> I had begun work, shortly after my arrival at NBC, on the development
> of a cultural project, tentatively titled "Operation Frontal Lobes." . . . I
> appealed to our creative people at NBC to conceive of programs that
> would use entertainment to enrich, inspire, and enlighten viewers.
> SYLVESTER ("PAT") WEAVER, *The Best Seat in the House*, 1994[1]

For millions of returning soldiers and their families, the 1944 GI Bill
of Rights helped democratize the American dream of owning a home
and living the good life. This final act of New Deal largesse put higher
education and vocational training, as well as low-interest loans for a
home, farm, or small business, within the reach of many ex-GIs who
would have otherwise been unable to afford such high-priced investments. By 1947, for example, 49 percent of all college enrollees were
World War II veterans. This increased access to all kinds of advanced
educational opportunities not only eased the country's unemployment
problems but also prepared ex-servicemen and -women for better-
paying jobs and improved living conditions once they completed their
coursework. Before World War II, most of the suburbs that existed in
the United States were exclusive enclaves populated by upper-class
and upper-middle-class Americans. Over the course of the first GI Bill
(running from June 22, 1944, through July 25, 1956), millions of
other middle-class, lower-middle-class, and working-class veterans
and their families left their urban apartments and rural homesteads
and joined the nationwide suburban boom in a move that would have
been unthinkable just a generation before.

Overall, more than 7,800,000 out of 15,440,000 ex-GIs received
some sort of educational or job training during this time period. Literally millions of these newly matriculated students adopted cultural
and artistic interests that they were learning about in school—many
for the first time—as 2,230,000 ex-servicemen and -women eventually earned their college degrees. At the same time, most of these veterans also carried some of their more traditional class-bound lifestyle
preferences into the suburbs with them after they graduated and
started their families and careers. As a result, American culture

entered a period of rapid transformation where the old social hierar-
chies grew less clear-cut than ever before, right as television began
expanding by leaps and bounds. TV, in turn, stimulated this growing
tendency toward cultural eclecticism by the ever-increasing array of
programming choices that it offered viewers nationwide during the
late 1940s and continuing throughout the 1950s. One popular mani-
festation of this rising social mobility was a renewed interest in the
notion of taste cultures and what proved to be a widespread preoccupation with trying to figure out where one exactly fit into the American scheme of things.

As early as February 1949, for instance, Russell Lynes wrote a
much-talked-about article for *Harper's Magazine* titled "Highbrow,
Lowbrow, Middlebrow." This mildly satirical essay was a follow-up to
"The Taste-Makers," another of his pieces that appeared soon after he
assumed the managing editorship of *Harper's* in June 1947. "The
Taste-Makers" had incited a partisan row in the art world by claiming
that certain custodians of culture were imposing their high modern-
ist standards on the rest of the population when it came to judging
quality and deciding what to patronize. Now with "Highbrow, Lowbrow, Middlebrow," Lynes "trained his guns on a broader front," arguing that the "old structure" of "American society" based on "wealth or
family" was "on the wane." Lynes contended that class was no longer
the great determinant of position and prestige in the United States; instead, it was "high thinking" or taste that he sardonically pinpointed
as leading to "a social structure in which highbrows are the elite, the
middlebrows are the bourgeoisie, and the lowbrows are the *hoi polloi*."[2]
Beyond these three basic categories, Lynes subdivided middlebrows
into upper and lower strata. The author caused quite a stir with these
classifications, not because they turned out to be wholly accurate in
retrospect, but because they highlighted an area of dramatic change
in postwar America, where culture was actually becoming much less
stratified rather than more so.

Two months later, "*Life* magazine, ever attuned to trends in public
interest, produced a feature . . . that not only summarized Lynes's
bemused conclusions about American taste, but captured a huge
public for his views by doing what *Life* did best: making an event or
an issue into a highly visual and visible phenomenon."[3] Similarly
named "High-brow, Low-brow, Middle-brow," *Life*'s April 11, 1949, article opened with a photograph of three men standing with their backs
to the camera and looking upward, toward a trio of contrasting por-
traits: the tallest is a slim, relaxed highbrow dressed in a Harris tweed
suit gazing intently at a painting by Picasso; the shortest is a stocky,
round-shouldered lowbrow in shirtsleeves and suspenders eyeing a

saucy pinup with her skirt hiked up high above her knees; and the averaged-sized gent is a stiff-postured middlebrow looking straight ahead at his artwork of choice—Grant Wood's instantly recognizable *American Gothic*. Lynes's taxonomy is thus economically rendered in one all-purpose image. On the next two pages, popular artist Tom Funk designs a chart that more precisely illustrates Lynes's taste levels according to highbrow, upper middlebrow, lower middlebrow, and lowbrow preferences in clothes, furniture, entertainment, reading, and a half-dozen other categories.[4] Interestingly, *Life*'s four-page pictorial essay with brief accompanying remarks, by senior writer and self-proclaimed highbrow Winthrop Sargeant, contains no mention whatsoever of television. Even though the TV boom was well under way by the winter of 1949, the medium was only mentioned twice in passing in Lynes's earlier *Harper's* essay as well.

Be that as it may, much had already been written about television's inherent potential to either smarten up or more likely dumb down the diverse cultural landscape of the United States. Author and critic E. B. White presciently captured this ambivalence back in October 1938 when he predicted in *Harper's Magazine* that "television is going to be the test of the modern world, and in this new opportunity to see beyond the range of our vision we shall discover a new and general peace or a saving radiance in the sky. We shall stand or fall by television—of that I am quite sure."[5] Media historian James Baughman recounts that the vast majority of social critics who regularly commented on the promise of American television during the 1930s and 1940s envisioned the medium "to be another instrument of a mass culture funded by advertisers and oblivious to uplift. . . . They saw the TV displays," he concludes, and "were not impressed."[6] The main exception to this majority opinion was the cohort that Russell Lynes referred to as "upper-middlebrow," who "talked about television as potentially a new art form."[7] Few individuals fit that profile better than Pat Weaver, NBC's innovative programming chief. "Television is a miracle," he proclaimed in 1954, and "must be used to upgrade humanity across a broad base." Weaver believed most of all that TV "must be the shining center of the home."[8]

Such idealistic and visionary language came naturally to Weaver, reflecting his privileged background as the son of a millionaire roofer from Los Angeles and his classical liberal arts education at Dartmouth College, where he majored in philosophy, made Phi Beta Kappa, and graduated magna cum laude in 1930. Both brilliant and charming, Weaver was unique to television, being able to move seamlessly between the more button-down, bean-counter executive and the unconventional creative sides of the business. He stood six-foot-four and was lean and energetic, with short-cropped, curly red hair now flecked with gray, bright blue eyes, and large protruding ears. When Weaver entered a room, people usually noticed. He joined NBC in June 1949, when he was forty-one years old, bubbling with ideas; basically, he started from scratch when the number of TV stations in America was fifty-one (with his network owning 49 percent of them) and the total of television households was just shy of one million. RCA president David Sarnoff's ambitious assignment for Weaver was to take NBC national (beyond the East-Midwest axis), create an in-house production service, and expand the network's prime-time schedule into morning, afternoon, and late-night segments like what already existed on radio. Pat Weaver was excited by and fully up to the job. As one executive colleague affirmed at the time: "He's probably the first top guy we've had here who can dream up a big show, sell a sponsor on the idea, figure out the show's dramatic form, and get the right budget for it and the right scriptwriters, as well as the right talent and the right air time against the right competition. A broad-stroke guy in every respect."[9]

As first a vice president, then president, and finally chairman of the board at NBC between 1949 and 1956, Pat Weaver was an inspirational leader and an avid memo writer, thinking out loud to his executive staff, who became known inside and outside the company as "Weaverites." He set a preliminary agenda for them, spurring his team forward to turn their evolving plans into the working reality of network television. On September 10, 1949, for example, he counseled his colleagues to consider how "television, like all realities, will be decided by action. There is no inevitable pattern which it will follow, no inexorable development. Rather, some of us will determine and direct the advance of this medium." Two months later, he followed up with "we will make the future of television more than any other group of men. . . . It is well for America that television be entrusted to the guardians who have served the public with the home entertainment instrument of radio."[10] Weaver's sense of mission was part noblesse oblige and part staunch belief in television's potential "to change social history."[11] "Under the leadership of Weaver and Robert Sarnoff [David's son], NBC hired a group of executives in the early 1950s culled from the brotherhood of the Ivy League–educated American postwar intellectual aristocracy. This group's ideological outlook shaped the television programming of the early 1950s to a great degree."[12]

NBC's executive programming staff was television's best and brightest, who took their cues from Weaver's strategic goal of merging the dictates of commerce with a number of home-grown public service initiatives code-named "Enlightenment Through Entertainment" (where shows such as the children's series *Kukla, Fran and*

Ollie featured episodes on taste cultures, traffic safety, and the Senate, among other educational topics); "Operation Wisdom" (which encouraged the production of TV documentaries, or what Weaver called "telementaries," as well as other kinds of informational programs such as conversations with accomplished men and women, including poet Robert Frost, anthropologist Margaret Mead, and architect Frank Lloyd Wright); and, most important, "Operation Frontal Lobes" (reflecting Weaver's sincere, if paternalistic, "grand design" for television "to create an aristocracy of the people, the proletariat of privilege, the Athenian masses—to make the average man the uncommon man").[13] Pat Weaver embodied the highest aspirations of the GI generation to transform American society and culture for the better, according to the liberal pluralist consensus that was quietly taking shape in the United States. John F. Kennedy would bring a similar kind of pragmatic idealism to the White House ten years later. Above all else, Pat Weaver believed in both the windfall potential of television as a business and industry and its promise to enlighten, improve, and empower tens of millions of American viewers.

Pat Weaver was the preeminent programmer during American television's classical phase of development, when it grew from a local to a regional to a national medium in less than two decades (1948–1963). In particular, Weaver pursued the overarching strategy of providing uplifting entertainment that blended four closely coordinated business and creative tactics. First, he championed the changeover to participation advertising, where multiple sponsors bought sixty-, thirty-, and later fifteen-second spots within the same program ("When I went to NBC in 1949, the networks were no more than facilities that the big advertising agencies used to broadcast shows they created, owned, and controlled. . . . By the time I left, NBC owned most of the shows it put on the air, and the other networks had begun to follow").[14] Second, he promoted a strongly held public-service vision of using television to elevate mass culture in postwar America. Third, he was a vigorous advocate of live programming across all genres (variety, drama, music, comedy, kids' shows, news and public affairs, and talk), which he saw as differentiating TV from film or the Hollywood mode of production.

Using these three precepts, Weaver and his executive team relied heavily on the New York theatrical tradition (Broadway and vaudeville) and the recently emerging "Chicago school" of television production, which was an "imaginative approach . . . born of necessity. Lacking big budgets, elaborate equipment and big-name talent," the Chicago group "specialized in what they called 'simplified realism' and 'ad-lib drama.' By banning studio audiences they used the four walls of every set," employing close, intimate camera shots that effectively created an immediate, personal connection between the on-stage performers and the viewers at home.[15] Although all of Chicago's pioneering TV stations contributed to the school, NBC's WNBQ, "more than any other, was the creative force behind the distinctive style of television production that came from Chicago" during the late 1940s and early 1950s.[16] Between 1949 and 1951, thirteen network programs originated from Chicago, including such NBC series as *Kukla, Fran and Ollie, Garroway at Large* (talk-variety starring Dave Garroway), *Studs' Place* (talk-variety-drama starring writer Studs Terkel as a neighborhood barkeep), *Hawkins Falls* (soap opera-comedy), and *Portrait of America* (interview-documentary).

The beginning of the end for Chicago-based programming "came in December of 1951 when NBC dropped *Garroway at Large* in favor of *The Red Skelton Show*. Garroway moved to New York to take over the *Today* show," and the remainder of Chicago's top performing, producing, directing, and writing talent soon left for "the two coasts to find work in the new shows coming from studios in New York and Hollywood." In hindsight, Chicago's modest if inventive production techniques and offbeat, hybrid "formats were actually more regional than national in character," as NBC, CBS, ABC, and DuMont ended up adapting the Second City's innovations into their more polished and professional network styles.[17] For example, *Garroway at Large* "would become the template for NBC's subsequent development of the *Today* show."[18] By 1958, no network television programs at all were being produced in Chicago, prompting *Saturday Review* TV critic Robert Lewis Shayon to deduce that this development was part of a much larger trend in which "regionalism is increasingly disappearing in the standardization of our mass economy."[19] Providing national coverage for NBC, after all, was one of Pat Weaver's major responsibilities as vice president in charge of television and director of network development. Weaver successfully followed through on this corporate mandate by expanding the number of affiliate stations from 25 to 189 during his seven-year tenure at NBC.

Closely aligned with his advocacy of all kinds of live productions, Weaver championed a fourth and final tactic of encouraging innovation in program format, techniques, and scheduling. Weaver's style of remodeling NBC's programming reflected both a new generational sensibility and a bold attempt to explore the boundaries of what sorts of shows and aesthetic strategies were best suited to the inherent strengths and weaknesses of television as a medium. One of his earliest accomplishments was modernizing the mostly lowbrow TV comedy-variety format with the debut of the more contemporary Broadway-influenced *Your Show of Shows* in February 1950. Like many series that Weaver and his team developed, this popular and critical success was simultaneously inventive and much more expensive than anything else like it on television. This emphasis on continuing innovation supported by lavish budgets became a hallmark of Weaver's modus operandi as a programming executive at NBC.

Pat Weaver's reliance on the combination of inventiveness and high capital investment was once again on display as he pioneered the production and strategic use of prime-time special-events programming beginning in 1952. Averaging more than one a month over the next four years, Weaver scheduled what he called "spectaculars" as a way of attracting millions of new viewers to NBC: "The network offered a range of specials with an eye toward different audience segments: *Peter Pan* for children, *Richard III* for adults interested in prestige programming, *Satin and Spurs* for fans of the Broadway musical tradition, and *Amahl and the Night Visitors* for the holiday family trade."[20] "When the 'spectacular plan,' as Weaver liked to call the promotion, was at its height in the middle 1950s, NBC was spending an average of $250,000 for each 90-minute special when prime-time variety or drama programs of comparable length were costing an average of approximately

$75,000." Over the short term, Weaver wanted as many TV viewers as possible to sample NBC's prime-time schedule. "We get them coming for caviar," a Weaver colleague quipped, "and they stick around . . . for the bread and butter."[21] Most significantly, though, Pat Weaver's longer-term goal was to build an identity for NBC within the industry and with audiences nationwide as the network that provided the highest-quality, most innovative shows anywhere on television.

Probably Weaver's most lasting innovation was his "T-H-T" plan. This initiative was designed specifically to expand NBC's offerings well beyond prime time (7 P.M. to 11 P.M.) into other segments of the broadcast day now serviced only by radio and local television. T-H-T euphemistically referred to Weaver's conception of three signature programs (*Today*, *Home*, and *Tonight*), which would prop up crucial non-prime-time points throughout the weekday schedule. He was the first network executive to think so creatively about developing TV series that complemented what viewers were doing at home during specific times of the day. *Today*, for instance, would be a magazine-styled show starting at 7 A.M. in the early morning (6 A.M. to 9 A.M.), tailored for people waking up and getting ready for work or school. *Home*

Peter Pan *starring Mary Martin was one of Pat Weaver's most successful television "spectaculars" in 1955. Courtesy of The David Sarnoff Library.*

would next hold up the morning (9 A.M. to 12 noon) at 11 A.M., "with public service talk" for women, and *Tonight* "with comedy/variety talk" would "tentpole" the late-fringe (11 P.M. to 11:35 P.M.) and late-night segments (11:35 P.M. to 2 A.M.), which up to this point was filled mostly by local entertainment shows, reruns of old movies, or nothing whatsoever on most stations.[22] Moreover, the economic rationale of Weaver's T-H-T plan was to maximize the largest possible audiences at all times, thus making television a viable advertising medium for the many less-affluent clients, who numbered more than those who were currently turning to television to promote their products. In this way, the Fortune 500 companies would continue to sponsor throughout prime time, but now mid-range and smaller firms could easily afford to buy time wherever they wanted in the less costly early morning, morning, afternoon (12 noon to 4 P.M.), early-fringe (4 to 7 P.M.), and late-fringe/late-night day parts.

Pat Weaver's first T-H-T experiment was the short-lived *Broadway Open House*, which premiered on May 29, 1950, and lasted just fifteen months through August 24, 1951. This late-night series beginning at 11:30 P.M. was a definite throwback, featuring the broad brash comedy of rotating hosts Jerry Lester and Morey Amsterdam (who left the show after several weeks), supported by an ensemble of regular cast members, including announcer Wayne Howell, music director Milton Delugg, and a tall, buxom, blonde bombshell named Dagmar (née Jennie Lewis), who acted dumb and delighted audiences with her nightly string of suggestive one-liners. *Broadway Open House* started out as a live, unscripted, one-hour program that was expanded to ninety minutes after Amsterdam's departure. The effervescent Lester ad-libbed his way through a vaudevillian hodgepodge of wisecracks, sight gags, and slapstick, punctuated by brief conversations with the rest of the cast and the evening's guests. Jerry Lester left the show in midsummer 1951, reportedly because Dagmar had emerged as the program's most popular star. In retrospect, *Broadway Open House* made money, although it was never a major hit nor did it ever fulfill Weaver's original conception of an innovative comedy-variety series custom made for young adults after 11 P.M. "Reluctantly, the network turned the time slot back to the local affiliates. NBC had demonstrated the viability of late-night TV, but had also discovered the importance of finding just the right personality for the slot."[23]

Pat Weaver's second foray into making T-H-T a reality was the premiere of *Today* on January 14, 1952. The show barely survived its first few months until host Dave Garroway was oddly paired with a chimpanzee named J. Fred Muggs as the program's mascot, which immediately increased viewer interest. This pioneering series originated from the tiny Victor Theater on 49th Street, a former remodeled showroom for RCA TV sets, allowing passersby to watch the show in progress from the street. *Today*'s Chicago-styled intimacy contrasted with the more formal proscenium arch–inspired presentation of *Broadway Open House*. For the first time, Weaver and his team were realizing the unique potential of T-H-T. They designed *Today* to be something of a cross between *Garroway at Large* and the freeform nature of morning radio; it blended news, entertainment, interviews, features, and low-key chitchat. Pat Weaver was taking television into uncharted territory. As a result, many critics were highly skeptical of *Today*, labeling it "Weaver's Folly." "For one thing, the show began at 7 A.M., an hour when nobody ever dreamed of looking at television in those days," reported the *New Yorker* in 1954; "for another, it was believed that even if the program did succeed in attracting some sort of audience, seven o'clock in the morning was no time to try to interest people into buying something."[24] Garroway was an amiable salesman, however, tall and willowy, with a wry sense of humor. He kept the highly segmented series on an even keel, turning when needed to the chimp in his turtleneck and rubber pants for comic relief. In a little more than two years, *Today* paid off handsomely. By then, the show's soaring popularity made it the most profitable program on NBC's entire schedule.

Pat Weaver was on a roll. *Home* was launched on March 1, 1954, as an all-purpose electronic magazine for women. Arlene Francis was the hostess and "editor in chief," aided by the able Chicago émigré Hugh Downs (who later became the announcer on *The Tonight Show with Jack Paar* from 1957 to 1962 and then host of *Today* from 1962 to 1971). Competing favorably against CBS's lineup of soap operas, *Home* was a breakthrough series in being "the first major effort by a national network to capture the daytime audience of women [which averaged 70 percent of all viewers during the morning and afternoon hours] with a woman host and a serious informational format."[25] Weaver pulled out all the stops in developing the show, spending $200,000 on a brand-new state-of-the-art studio with a revolving set created specifically for the series. *Home*'s ambiance was chic, modern, and sophisticated; it was much more an upscale New York-style than a modest Chicago-style production. The format was comprised mostly of happy talk, interviews, and an occasional musical interlude as a change of pace. The consumer-oriented segments emphasized food, fashion, beauty, child care, decorating, gardening, and leisure activities. *Home* "was an immediate hit and dominated late morning programming for three and one-half years."[26] The decision to take it off the air on August 9, 1957, "was a shock to the staff and many of its viewers, and the decision is still somewhat shrouded." Arlene Francis

was told the ratings were starting to fall, but others believe David Sarnoff wanted "to clean house and purge the slate of programs promoted
by Pat Weaver," who left NBC in September 1956.[27]

Most of the scholarly and popular literature on Pat Weaver is highly
complimentary, portraying him as NBC's "thinker-in-chief" who "developed programming and business strategies the other networks
would imitate for years to come."[28] A few revisionists, however, have
characterized him as the "consummate huckster" or have adjusted the
focus away from Weaver as "television's bold visionary" to larger con-
textual matters that better explain the maturation of television as a
business and industry on a macro level during the 1950s and into the
early 1960s. "Even the end of Weaver's reign in late 1955 had less to do
with his personal status than with a measurable industry shift," argues media historian Vance Kepley, for example; "by the middle 1950s,
the television market showed signs of leveling off. . . . Policies stressing company stability rather than expansion would dominate the last
half of the decade."[29] Still, biography matters. Personal agency can be
underestimated, just as easily as it can be overestimated, as was often
the case with many of the first generation of TV historians before

1980. Individuals are products of their time and subject to the broader historical currents that engulf them. Nevertheless, they do sometimes help shape events where others in the same situation would have little or no impact whatsoever. In this way, Pat Weaver was more than a "capable manager"; he was a charismatic leader who both worked within and expanded the confines of network television during his years at NBC by the influence that "Operation Frontal Lobes" and his other major initiatives at the network had on his contemporaries, the strategies he and his executive staff chose to advance, and the tactics they eventually enacted.

Similarly, why Pat Weaver was eased out of NBC by the early fall of 1956 actually has more to do with "personal status" than it does with the growing emphasis on "stability" over "expansion" at the network and throughout the TV industry in general. Just as television was transitioning from a period of innovation to one of increased standardization in the mid to late 1950s, Weaver also emerged at the time as a media darling whose heightened profile exceeded the celebrity enjoyed by even David Sarnoff himself. During his short tenure as NBC president (December 4, 1953, through December 7, 1955), for instance, Weaver appeared on the cover of *Newsweek*, he and his family were featured in an extended *Life* photo-text essay, and Ed Murrow interviewed him on a prime-time episode of rival CBS's *Person to Person*. He also served as the public spokesperson for NBC by frequently contributing op-ed pieces to various trade publications, such as *Variety* and *Television*, and making many personal appearances as part of his executive responsibilities, such as his walk-on before tens of millions of viewers on the June 5, 1954, final episode of *Your Show of Shows* to thank the cast and crew for all they had accomplished during their four-and-a-half years on the air.

The fait accompli came "in the summer of 1954 when the *New Yorker* magazine approached our press department about doing one of their famous profiles about me," recounts Weaver in his memoir, "though the magazine had never profiled the real publicity and fame seeker in our organization—General Sarnoff." Sarnoff was a friend of "Raoul Fleischmann, the publisher of the *New Yorker*, and had been trying for years to get the magazine to profile him."[30] Weaver attempted to beg off the assignment, even suggesting that the magazine cover the RCA president instead. He was told by an editor at the *New Yorker* that the piece was going to run whether he cooperated or not, so Weaver finally agreed to be interviewed, resulting in a highly favorable two-part profile that appeared in October 1954. "Weaver's unorthodoxy fascinated the press," reveals Sarnoff's biographer and former RCA insider Kenneth Bilby; "to David Sarnoff, this was not a welcome development.

Suddenly there were two stars in the RCA firmament, where there had long been one. . . . Rather than summarily dismissing the highly visible Weaver, and thus risk another round of stories about executive turmoil at NBC, Sarnoff decided to strip him of his authority under the guise of promoting him."[31] In the end, Pat Weaver's problems at NBC stemmed less from a policy shift away from growth and innovation toward increased stability and standardization (although this transition did indeed occur during the latter half of the 1950s) than because of petty jealousy that caused a breakdown in his professional relationship with Sarnoff. David Sarnoff appointed his son Robert to be NBC president during early December 1955, ostensibly promoting Weaver to network chairman where he remained until September 7, 1956, before resigning from what turned out to be a largely titular post.

Likewise, Pat Weaver's legacy is often misunderstood by scholars. There is little argument that Weaver was the driving force behind the growth of NBC television from a regional to a national network. He is the executive most responsible for the establishment and widespread acceptance of participation advertising, thus strengthening the position of the networks in dealing with advertising agencies and sponsors over the development and scheduling of programming. He successfully expanded the NBC schedule from 7 A.M. to 1 P.M. He encouraged the merging of the New York and Chicago schools of television production in his quest to expand the range and quality of live TV. In this regard, Weaver's influence was evident on many traditional genres, such as comedy (where he nurtured a revolving stock company of stars— Fred Allen, Bob Hope, Dean Martin and Jerry Lewis, among others— into The Colgate Comedy Hour) and drama (where he supported the breakthrough work of Fred Coe at Goodyear/Philco Television Playhouse). Even more important, in hindsight, he and his creative colleagues invented a number of new formats designed specifically for the medium (especially T-H-T and dozens of one-time spectaculars). Beginning in 1953, he also pioneered NBC's changeover to color with The Howdy Doody Show, the no. 1 daytime program at the time, which became the first regularly scheduled series produced and telecast in color; and Gian Carlo Menotti's opera Amahl and the Night Visitors, which was TV's inaugural prime-time colorcast. Weaver continued promoting color over the next two years with a series of high-priced "spectaculars" produced by Max Liebman of Your Show of Shows.

Where the greatest misunderstanding about Pat Weaver occurs is in the longstanding depiction of him as a highbrow or upper-middlebrow working among network philistines, trying to raise the quality of television against almost insurmountable odds. Weaver's lofty and often hyperbolic rhetoric is partly to blame for this misconception, as is the sympathy he rightfully engenders for being marginalized at NBC before he had a full opportunity to realize his high-minded aspiration of molding television into a public service as well as an entertainment medium. What has been lost over the years is the recognition that Pat Weaver's legacy at NBC is as much J. Fred Muggs on *Today* and Mary Martin in *Peter Pan* as it is Pablo Picasso on *Wisdom*. "Quite a few critics and intellectuals" at the time accused him of devoting too much of the NBC schedule "to the lowest common denominator" with some justification.[32] Under his tutelage, for instance, *Your Show of Shows* would shift with ease from vaudeo shtick to Sid Caesar and Imogene Coca as the Hickenloopers to a Verdi aria. For Weaver, the workaday entertainment of TV was a given, and, thus, his major contribution was to widen NBC's range of programming possibilities. He was not a fish out of water in the world of television. Weaver thrived in this culturally diverse atmosphere; TV allowed him to be high, low, and in-between all at once.

Another way of thinking about Pat Weaver is to view him as part of the postwar vanguard of what sociologists Richard Peterson and Roger Kern now classify as "omnivores," or, according to Herbert Gans, people "who have the time, money, and education to choose more culture from several taste levels, making all forms and genres of culture potential hunting grounds for them—and for the culture suppliers serving them."[33] Weaver was one of those early suppliers. The *New Yorker* profile captures the heterogeneity of his interests when it describes his "conversation style" as "a dialectal fugue of parasociological phraseology, Madison Avenue advertising talk, Broadway chatter, merchandising argot, and oblique philosophical references, all flowing together in a brisk counterpoint."[34] Weaver was not alone in his cultural eclecticism. For one, he found a kindred spirit to host *Tonight!* (which contained an exclamation point in its first incarnation)—thus finally completing his T-H-T plan. Steve Allen was quick-witted, inventive, playful, sometimes even silly—but never dumb. He was a humorist, composer, musician, and conversationalist, ideally suited for the ever-fluid comedy/variety talk format. When Allen first took his seat at the piano and began joking with the audience at 11:30 P.M. on September 27, 1954, late-night television would never be the same again.

This Could Be the Start of Something Big

Pat [Weaver] and I have long constituted a mutual admiration society. He was kind enough not only to put me on his network for ninety-minutes-a-night five-nights-a-week but later asked me to do a far more important NBC prime-time weekly comedy series. . . . But it needs to be settled now, once and for all, that he had nothing whatever to do with "creating" *Tonight*.

STEVE ALLEN, *Hi-Ho, Steverino!*, 1992[35]

The roots of *Tonight!* stretch back to a thirty-minute late-night records-and-talk radio program that Steve Allen hosted in 1948 on KNX, the CBS affiliate in Los Angeles. The show was originally titled *Breaking All Records*, until Allen's ad-libbing became the most popular feature on the program and it was eventually renamed *The Steve Allen Show*. Local CBS executives decided to adapt the show to television on KCBS, which shared CBS Columbia Square in the heart of downtown Holly-wood with KNS. *The Steve Allen Show* became a local TV talk program, premiering on Christmas Day 1950. Achieving success in television in those days meant moving from west to east and relocating in New York City, the nation's undisputed TV production center at the time. (Inter-estingly, the migration of talent would turn around and head mainly westward circa 1957.) In 1953, however, Steve Allen accepted an invita-tion from producer Mark Goodson and his partner Bill Todman to re-place humorist Hal Block as a panelist on CBS's *What's My Line?* This Emmy award–winning quiz show provided Allen with a highly visible platform for his ad-libbing (for example, his opening query "Is it bigger than a breadbox?" became a national catchphrase) as he effortlessly shared the stage with Dorothy Kilgallen, Arlene Francis, Bennett Cerf, and moderator John Daly. With this increased exposure on a bona fide prime-time hit, Allen was invited by Ted Cott, general manager of NBC's flagship WNBT-TV (soon to be retitled WNBC), to host a local version of his west coast late-night comedy/variety talk show. Debuting in June 1953, this five-nights-a-week forty-five-minute program begin-ning at 11:15 P.M. became a New York sensation, eventually catching the eye of Pat Weaver who was still looking for a way to establish a presence for his network during the late-night segment.

Because of the long shadow cast by Weaver's truly momentous ca-reer at NBC, his role in creating *Tonight!* has been overstated time and again in both the scholarly and popular literature over the years.[36] This misperception has endured for so long because Weaver was an innovator of the first order. His many accomplishments at NBC in-cluded first recommending the T-H-T plan and then being deeply in-volved in overseeing the productions of both *Today* and *Home*. Still, Weaver never had a hand in shaping *Tonight!* as he had with the other two programs. During the more than three-year absence since *Broad-way Open House* ended, he seriously considered launching "a journal-istically news-oriented magazine" show in late night, much along the lines of *Today* because of its enormous success. Then as Bill Harbach, producer of *Tonight!* recalls, Weaver started watching "that crazy little local show that everybody's flipping over in New York City." Weaver knew what he wanted when he saw it, and he thought *The Steve Allen Show* just might work as a national entry on the NBC schedule. "The day's over," explains Harbach, Steve comes on and "it's insane, it's crazy, it's fun, it's loose—*loose* is the operative word."[37] It was also the chance of a lifetime for Steve Allen, and he knew it. His partner, agent, and the program's executive producer, Jules Green, asked that he and his client retain sole ownership of *The Steve Allen Show*, thus assuring Allen's creative control. In return, Weaver wanted the name changed to *Tonight!* and the show expanded to ninety minutes. Green and Allen happily agreed, and they went straight to work with Harbach, director Dwight Hemion, and comedy writers Stan Burns and Herb Sargent to expand the show to twice its current length.

Furthermore, the frequent claim that *Broadway Open House* was a forerunner to *Tonight!* is mistaken. The former was a prime example of vaudeo—loud, frenetic, almost amateurish in its execution—while *Tonight!* starring Steve Allen was smooth, freeform in tempo, and jazz-oriented in its sensibility and approach to not only the music but also the comedy and the conversation on the program. The only thing *Broadway Open House* and *Tonight!* had in common was their 11:30 P.M. to 1 A.M. national time slot. A new generation of bop-influenced improvisational comedians led by Sid Caesar (who was an accomplished saxophone player) and Allen were now surfacing as big stars on television. Thirty-two-year-old Steve Allen, in particular, was one with the zeitgeist—in style and urbanity. His down-to-earth accessible persona was perfect for TV. Physically, he looked "square": six-foot-three, borderline gangly, and bespectacled with his signature horn-rimmed glasses. He was nevertheless "hip" when he opened his mouth. The format of *Tonight!* developed out of a "personal 'workshop' process" begun on radio but accelerated in Allen's move to television, where he and his production staff "discovered which entertainment forms were most effective for [him] and gradually constructed a new kind of program based on those strengths."[38] In the show's latest version on NBC, Steve Allen was free to intermix the worlds of jazz, Broadway, sports, and serious talk within an atmosphere that simulated a hip, happening New York nightspot with an occasional remote outside the studio or to a different locale as a change of pace.

The format of *Tonight!* evolved by trial and error, beginning with a low-key opening monologue often delivered while Allen was seated comfortably at a piano. He would then chitchat with his announcer and sidekick, Gene Rayburn, and engage in some playful banter with his orchestra leader, Skitch Henderson. He next brought the audience into the format of *Tonight!* in a way unlike any other program before it on TV. To begin, Allen would simply grab a microphone and stroll up the aisle at the 44th Street Hudson Theater, ad-libbing with the regular folks in the seats. For instance, in one of the early episodes when a curious gentleman asked him, "Do they get your program in Philadelphia?" Allen responded, "They see it, but they don't get it." Steve then characteristically broke out laughing with the rest of the audience with his warm, distinctively high-pitched cackle. He also would take random questions from members of the live studio audience, usually written on cards while he sat at his piano; or he played "answer man" with Gene Rayburn, who would provide him with an answer and Allen would reply with a funny question (Johnny Carson resurrected this shtick as the "Great Carnac," and Merv Griffith later adapted it sans humor as the basic hook on his game show *Jeopardy!*). Moreover, music was always a large part of *Tonight!*, as it was for Steve Allen in general, who composed several thousand songs, including the show's themes, "Mister Moon" (1954–1956) and "This Could Be the Start of Something Big" (1956–1957). He often asked the assembled theater audience to call out song titles to see if they could "stump the band," or he would segue to a well-placed musical interlude featuring himself or one of the band's musicians, such as first trumpeter Doc Severinsen, or one of the show's array of up-and-coming vocalists, including Steve Lawrence, Eydie Gorme, Andy Williams, and Pat Kirby.

"Steve Allen's most familiar playground was television," once wrote TV critic Tom Shales, "and he treated it as both a romper room and a

Steve Allen first played "answer man" with Gene Rayburn in 1954. Years later Johnny Carson (right) resurrected this shtick as the "Great Carnac," with sidekick Ed McMahon (left) feeding him the answers as he replied with funny questions. Courtesy of Library of American Broadcasting at the University of Maryland.

laboratory of comedic experimentation."[39] For example, Allen would read funny items from the paper (as all subsequent *Tonight* show hosts would), or he played the enraged newsman wearing a fedora with a "press" card stuck in the brim as he mock-angrily read actual letters to the editor from the New York papers as his sidemen and the band egged him on with choruses of "Yahhh, Yahhh!" He also impersonated a late-night pitchman (who Carson turned into Art Fern), and he took a camera and microphone outside to conduct "man on the street" interviews (as later adopted by David Letterman). Steve soon parodied himself and *Tonight!* by staging faux man on the street interviews with members of his own stock company playing "average" people, such as the stuttering, anxiety-ridden Don Knotts; the slow-witted, easygoing Tom Poston; and the bubbly, slightly effeminate Louis Nye, who delighted audiences with his continuing comic character, Madison Avenue executive Gordon Hathaway, who always greeted Allen with the mock-hip "Hi-ho, Steverino!" In addition, Steve set up elaborate sight gags called "crazy shots" (again appropriated by Letterman) and cultivated on-air relationships with a handful of audience regulars—eccentric amateurs such as Mrs. Miller and Mrs. Sterling—who continued attending the *Tonight!* show well after his departure.

Most of all, though, the heart and soul of *Tonight!* was talk. Steve Allen conducted celebrity interviews with all sorts of entertainers (such as Judy Garland, Bob Hope, Joan Crawford, Sammy Davis Jr., and Jerry Lewis), sports figures (such as Jackie Robinson and Bob Cousy), writers (such as Carl Sandburg and Tennessee Williams), and a wide range of public figures and opinion leaders discussing such topics as organized crime and blacklisting. He devoted entire shows to special talents (such as Fred Allen, Richard Rodgers, and Count Basie, much like Dick Cavett would years later with Orson Welles and Katharine Hepburn). In the spirit of Operation Frontal Lobes, which was encouraged throughout the NBC schedule, Allen would spend entire episodes on the food, music, fashion, décor, and artifacts of different cultures. In this regard, he hosted all-Japanese, all-Italian, all-Israeli, all-Irish, all-Mexican, all-Hawaiian, and all-Chinese evenings. Moreover, Steve occasionally took the show on the road to such diverse locales as Niagara Falls, Cleveland, Miami, and Hollywood; locally, he and his producer would enlist the NBC mobile unit to capture the sights and sounds of the New York metropolitan area. During the September 27, 1954, premiere of *Tonight!*, for instance, the show went on location to Willie Mays's home in Harlem. Just two days before the start of the 1954 World Series between Mays's New York Giants and the Cleveland Indians, Steve Lawrence and Eydie Gorme serenaded the baseball superstar in his "front yard," singing "'Say Hey,' a song based on Mays's greeting to other ballplayers."[40] Steve then amiably chatted with Willie about New York's prospects in the upcoming series (the Giants ended up sweeping the Indians in four games), and *Tonight!* was off and running as a nationwide cult favorite.

On November 3, *New York Times* TV critic Jack Gould strongly praised Allen's work and recommended that his readers sample the program. Despite the late hour, he described the show's "narcotic influence," advising prospective viewers that "you're apt to be up until 1 A.M." Gould also contended that "Steve's alertness of mind and inventive intelligence are needed in full measure on *Tonight!* because his is an assignment to tax the durability of any personality. He is on stage most of the night—interviewing guests, playing the piano, engaging in assorted stunts and rambling around at will." Like Allen's nightly musical improvisations with the band, his ad-libbed jazz-accented patter was similarly a digressive creation, subtle in variation, and smooth in the way that it so genially connected with his fellow performers, his guests for the evening, the live studio audience, and the viewers at home. Gould's one major complaint revolved around the relatively new experience of watching participation advertising in action. "*Tonight!* is broken into segments to allow for a maximum number of commercials. Probably this will move Steve and NBC up a few notches in the eyes of the Internal Revenue Bureau, but it can lead to irritation for the viewer."[41] Commercial clutter aside, *Tonight!* averaged a rating of 4 for the rest of 1954 and into 1955, translating into two million TV households at a time when there were fewer than thirty-one million in the entire country. Allen was also receiving eight hundred fan letters a day.[42] He therefore became the first television star to prove unequivocally that the late-fringe/late-night portions of the television schedule were viable segments for entertaining a national audience.

Just as critics were beginning to refer to Steve Allen as "Mr. Midnight" (implying that he now reigned as the king of late night, much the same way as NBC's Milton Berle had earlier been crowned "Mr. Tuesday Night"), behind-the-scenes negotiations were developing that would eventually cut his tenure short on *Tonight!*[43] Unbeknownst to the public and most of the people within the industry, Pat Weaver had been courting Ed Sullivan throughout much of 1954, trying to lure him away from CBS, where *Toast of the Town* had finally cracked the top 10 at no. 5 during the 1954–1955 season. CBS countered by signing Sullivan to a twenty-year contract in January 1955 and agreeing to rename the program *The Ed Sullivan Show.*[44] Weaver then shifted gears and spent the next nine months looking for someone who could compete against Sullivan on Sunday night at 8 P.M. with a whole new variety show of his or her own making. He felt it was time to replace *The*

Colgate Comedy Hour, which was growing ever more costly while start-ing to fade badly in the ratings after five years on the air. Weaver finally settled on Steve Allen, signing him to a brand-new three-year contract in September 1955, which raised his annual salary from $250,000 to $1,500,000 a year.[45] The NBC brass wanted Allen to host both *Tonight!* and *The Steve Allen Show* during prime time. For four months, Allen was on the air nine hours and forty-five minutes a week. At his insis-tence, however, *Tonight!* was cut back from ninety to sixty minutes on October 29, 1956, with Ernie Kovacs brought in to guest host on Mon-days and Tuesdays.[46] This arrangement continued until January 25, 1957, when Steve Allen finally left *Tonight!* altogether.

In twenty-twenty hindsight, Allen has occasionally been criticized for leaving *Tonight!* too early, but his career had been stuck in over-drive since 1953 and he needed to cut back somewhere on his numer-ous commitments.[47] While hosting *Tonight!,* for example, he also costarred in several Max Liebman–produced NBC color spectaculars as a humorist and musician; played the lead in *The Benny Goodman Story* (1955) for Universal (relocating *Tonight!* to Hollywood for eight weeks in the summer, acting all day long, and then emceeing his talk show during the weeknights); composed several popular songs, most notably the theme for the Columbia hit film *Picnic* (1955), starring William Holden and Kim Novak; and published four books, including *Bop Fables* (a 1955 compilation of his columns for *Down Beat,* the mu-sicians' magazine, where he retold classic fairy tales in the bop idiom), *Fourteen for Tonight* (a 1955 collection of short stories), *The Funny Men* (a 1956 insider's analysis of America's leading comics), and *Wry on the Rocks* (a 1956 book of poetry). Allen couldn't continue indefinitely at this breakneck speed and still succeed with his new prime-time show, so leaving *Tonight!* seemed like the most sensible option available to him. NBC had already increased his salary 600 percent to move to prime time, and despite their growing importance, the late-fringe/late-night segments were still second-tier portions of the overall sched-ule back in 1956–1957.

When Steve Allen finally left the show in January 1957, after two years and four months, NBC replaced him with veteran *Today* an-nouncer Jack Lescoulie as the nominal host of a magazine-styled pro-gram titled *Tonight: America after Dark,* which started off disorganized and quickly went from bad to worse. Lescoulie supposedly directed the proceedings, switching back and forth between a handful of newspaper columnists (including Paul Coates, Bob Considine, Hy Gardner, Irv Kupcinet, and Earl Wilson), who were on location across the country, serving up what turned out to be a confusing mix of news, celebrity in-terviews, and gossip from New York, Chicago, Los Angeles, and other

U.S. cities such as Miami and Las Vegas, depending on the evening. For seven months, the ratings for *Tonight: America after Dark* literally plummeted. During this same time period, NBC tried unsuccessfully to hire Ernie Kovacs to host the show, but he had already committed to star in two upcoming movies. The network next turned to Jack Paar, a former game show host, emcee of *The Morning Show* (CBS's alternative to *Today*), and an occasional guest host on *Tonight!* when Kovacs was unavailable. Paar accepted and debuted on July 29, 1957, experiencing a rocky first few months as he garnered "terrible reviews" and only a 2.6 rating, or 1.1 million TV households by year-end. As one TV critic observed, "Jack Paar is the only bull with his own China Shop."[48] He got better on the job, however, raising the profile of *Tonight* to a 6 rating and nearly three million TV households by early 1959, when the nation's total number of TV households had risen to forty-two million.[49]

In a sense, Jack Paar domesticated the original *Tonight!* for a time by introducing the desk-and-couch arrangement and refocusing it more heavily on talk. Paar was a monologist rather than a traditional entertainer like Allen, Kovacs, or his successor, Johnny Carson. His strength was as a droll conversationalist—excessive in his language and emotions, sometimes temperamental, always wearing his heart on his sleeve. *The Jack Paar Tonight Show* (also sometimes called *The Jack Paar Show*) was known for its urbane talk, as well as its host's occasional missteps and outbursts. Most notoriously, Paar walked off the set during his opening monologue on February 11, 1960, over a dispute with the NBC censor for cutting a rather tepid bathroom joke of his the night before. Sidekick Hugh Downs was as surprised as anyone when Paar suddenly left the stage, leaving the announcer to finish the show as best as he could for the rest of the evening. Jack Paar subsequently returned after a five-week hiatus. Still, a large part of *Tonight*'s appeal during Paar's tenure as host was watching his impulsive and mercurial behavior and the roller-coaster effect it had on the show. Late-night audiences were never quite sure what might happen next; nor were NBC executives. In 1958, the network finally began videotaping *Tonight*, shifting from live production to recording the program in the early evening and playing it later at 11:30 P.M. This practice was followed to ease the pressure of the nightly grind on Paar, as well as to stockpile episodes for future use.

After nearly five years, both Paar and the network were ready for a change, and he stepped down as host on March 30, 1962. "When NBC wanted to replace Jack Paar, whose naked psyche was leaving too many viewers uneasy," remembers announcer Ed McMahon, "the network turned to Johnny [Carson], whose wit was delivered by a cool and composed man of thirty-six."[50] NBC hired Carson early, even though he was unable to begin hosting *Tonight* until October 1, 1962, because of previous contractual obligations. The network simply used an assortment of guest hosts (including Joey Bishop, Hugh Downs, Arlene Francis, Merv Griffin, and Groucho Marx) in the interim. NBC, in turn, developed *The Jack Paar Program*, "a prime-time version of his earlier late-night talk show," which debuted Fridays at 10 P.M. on the new fall 1962 schedule.[51] "By 1962 *Tonight* had become a lucrative profit center and an important cog in the network's relations with its affiliates," notes industry analyst Ed Papazian; "hence NBC's decision" to protect its investment.[52]

Soon *The Tonight Show Starring Johnny Carson* "turned into an even greater bonanza than it had been under Jack Paar."[53] More important, Carson transported viewers back to a hip nightspot on the screen, somewhat evoking the attitude and ambiance of Steve Allen's original *Tonight!*, only this time sixties' style. Johnny restored the smart, swinging, sophisticated edge of New York City, as the show once again personified the Big Apple, just as Allen's original version had done so well a decade earlier. By and large, though, the *Tonight* show's format had now congealed into a predictably entertaining blueprint for Carson to follow. "I was able to be a ripe second banana for Johnny because I had spent years studying the brilliant wit of *The Tonight Show*'s father, Steve Allen," acknowledges Ed McMahon. "I knew that Johnny also loved Steve, and so the format of our show became the one this master had invented."[54] Carson was a talented ad-libber in his own right, and *Tonight*'s conventions provided him with a reliable template on which to display his many talents—from delivering the opening monologue, to kidding with his supporting cast and chatting with members of the studio audience, to enacting a wide assortment of skits and recurring comic characters, to interviewing two to three guest celebrities on every episode. *The Tonight Show Starring Johnny Carson* soon grew to be widely recognized throughout the industry as a television institution, especially after moving to NBC Studios-Burbank in May 1972, where the program became even more boilerplate over time.

Indicative of the industry at large, a brief cycle of freewheeling innovation on *Tonight!* (1954–1957) was followed by a more extended and predictable period of stability and standardization, where modifications appeared from time to time (such as the enhanced living room atmosphere of the desk and couch), while any turbulence that threatened the long-term stability of the *Tonight* show franchise was managed as quickly and efficiently as possible (such as replacing Jack Paar, despite his good ratings, with the far more unflappable and viewer-friendly Johnny Carson). By the early 1960s, NBC and CBS had developed competing lineups of dependable and popular daytime, afternoon, nighttime, and late-night programs. Ironically, NBC and CBS dominated television as a business and industry while following production trends and programming patterns largely pioneered out west over the previous decade by ABC. When *Tonight!* first began in 1954, New York was the TV production capitol of the world. Live programming was still very much in vogue at the networks, where it made up close to 90 percent of all productions. By the time Johnny Carson took over the show in the fall of 1962, live production was becoming an endangered species at 25 percent of all programming, as the center of gravity had decisively shifted toward Hollywood, where new series were almost always shot on film.[55]

By necessity, Leonard Goldenson, chairman and CEO of ABC, and his executive team devised a five-year business plan in early 1953, which brought ABC Television back from the brink of bankruptcy. Previously the president and CEO of United Paramount Theaters, Goldenson had just purchased this struggling second-tier network for $24.5 million on the gamble that television was rapidly transforming into the mass-entertainment medium of the future. ABC's farsighted strategy contained three basic and interrelated agenda items: first, build bridges between the network and the Hollywood film industry; second, schedule alternative kinds of programming rather than competing head to head against NBC and CBS; and third, target an audience that is currently being underserved by these two television giants. As a result, ABC soon became the network of choice for young families and their baby boomer children. By the time ABC's five-year plan had finally run its course, NBC and CBS were also swept up in a period marked by a three-network, rather than a two-network, oligopoly, the widespread standardization of product, and growing profitability for all. By 1962, 90 percent of the country, or almost forty-nine million television households, owned their own sets. Significantly, these family units currently kept their TVs turned on for more than five hours a day on average. In less than a generation, television had emerged as the national pastime for the vast majority of people across the United States. The speed with which TV had penetrated the very fabric of American life was beyond anyone's wildest dream.

TELEVISION'S NEW FRONTIER

The shift to television production in Hollywood—particularly by those producers with the heaviest investment in the Old Hollywood—marked television's emergence as America's principal postwar culture industry,

while it also signaled a growing trend toward the integration of the media industries.

CHRISTOPHER ANDERSON, *Hollywood TV*, 1994[56]

The postwar baby boom reached its midway point in 1955 with
4,097,000 births. Two years later, it rose to its high-water mark of
4,300,000 before slowly receding every year after that point, until the
number of new babies fell to a still impressive 4,027,000 in 1964.
Baby boomers were the largest generational cohort in U.S. history.
From 1946 through 1964, their ranks swelled to seventy-six million.
By 1955, moreover, the birth rate was 30 percent higher than during
the depths of the Depression two decades earlier. Postwar prosperity
was one major reason that fueled this upsurge: people simply felt they
could afford more children than a generation before. This increased affluence also resulted in the emergence of young people as a designated
market unto themselves. Children were similarly targeted from the
outset as a separate audience by pioneering television executives and
producers. For instance, DuMont's *Small Fry Club* debuted on March
11, 1947, from 7 to 7:30 P.M., and NBC's *Kukla, Fran and Ollie* on November 29, 1948, during the same time period (after having already
emerged as a local hit on Chicago TV in 1947). These two shows were
the earliest network successes in children's programming, designed
specifically to jump-start sales of new TV receivers by making the
opening hour of prime time more conducive to younger viewers and
thus more attractive to their parents. Soon the economics of children's
television shifted more toward marketing and retailing ancillary merchandise toward kids, especially with the prime-time premieres of
NBC's *Hopalong Cassidy* and ABC's *The Lone Ranger* in 1949, as well as
CBS's *The Gene Autry Show* in 1950.

William Boyd earned one of the first great fortunes in television. Beginning in 1935, he starred in fifty-four low-budget Westerns based on
the pulp-fictional character, Hopalong Cassidy. He had the foresight to
purchase the TV rights to these motion pictures in early 1948 when all
of the major Hollywood studios were basically ignoring the new medium, acting as if they wished it would just succumb to market pressures and quickly fade away. Television was here to stay, however, and
Boyd had his old cowboy films recut into thirty-minute episodes as he
led the stampede of juvenile Westerns onto the small screen. Silver-
haired Hoppy and his trusted horse Topper were soon joined on prime
time by other B-movie stars, including Gene Autry (who premiered on
CBS in 1950) and Roy Rogers (who debuted on NBC in 1951). These
three shows in particular were "generally held responsible" for "an estimated $150,000,000" retail boom in Western products between 1949

and 1951 aimed primarily at children aged four to fourteen. These items were strategically placed in both toy and children's apparel sections of department stores nationwide, so "chaps, bandannas, spurs, denim Levis, Stetsons," and boots sold, as well as toy guns and plastic lariats. The informality of the West was slowly becoming more an American than a regional lifestyle. For example, blue jeans on youngsters grew as commonplace in cities and suburbs as on ranches and farms all across the United States. The West had "enjoyed a moderate, but fairly steady popularity for several generations," reported John Sharnik in the *New York Times*, but with the arrival of "television after the war," this preoccupation reached new "unbelievable" levels, especially among youngsters. "There has never been anything like this," admitted one major manufacturer of Western gear at the time. "And this is a trend in *children!*"[57]

Children's programming was evolving as rapidly as its target audience during the early to mid 1950s. Several kids' shows were developing into solid hits in a variety of time slots, such as DuMont's *Captain Video and His Video Rangers* (during prime time), NBC's *Ding Dong School* (in the early fringe), and CBS's *Winky Dink and You* (on Saturday mornings). Scholar Leo Bogart conducted the first systematic study of children's viewing patterns in 1952. He found that *The Howdy Doody Show* was by far the most popular program with youngsters under age ten, but, surprisingly, *I Love Lucy* and *The Texaco Star Theater* were the favorites of viewers aged eleven to sixteen.[58] As all of the networks started expanding their programming schedules into non-prime-time segments, children's shows were usually the first to be moved elsewhere. A case in point was the still highly rated *Kukla, Fran and Ollie*, which was shifted to Sunday afternoons in August 1952 by NBC programmers to make room for the ever-growing size of the adult audience during prime time. Busy parents especially appreciated finding wholesome series designed specifically for their toddlers and adolescents in the late afternoons on both weekdays and weekends. They often used TV as a temporary babysitter while they paid more attention to their household chores, especially preparing dinner. Television executives were likewise happy because they were finding virtually no drop-off in prime-time viewing among children, since all of their research suggested that young people were watching kid-friendly adult programs as well as shows targeted directly at them.

Still, no TV character quite captivated youngsters so completely during the late 1940s through the early to mid 1950s as Howdy Doody. Howdy originated in 1946 as a country bumpkin named Elmer, who was merely one of the many voices used by "Big Brother Bob" Smith on his Saturday morning NBC radio program *Triple B Ranch*. At some point in each episode, Smith would greet his live studio audience as

Elmer—"Well, Howdy Doody boys and girls, hyuh, hyuh, hyuh"—and the kids in the "peanut gallery" would go absolutely nuts screeching with delight. NBC adapted the show to television on Saturday, December 27, 1947, during the early fringe as *Puppet Playhouse*, which was comprised mostly of fun and games, musical and animal acts, and the now Buckskin-clad "Buffalo Bob" Smith trying to coax "an extremely shy Howdy Doody out of a desk drawer." NBC commissioned "an artist from Walt Disney Studio" to draw "a friendly red-headed cowboy-like figure," who was then "handcrafted by puppet-maker Velma Dawson in Burbank." Howdy was modeled after his fan base, finally emerging on screen from his hiding place in early 1948 as a smiling, all-American, freckle-faced ten-year-old dressed in a Western shirt with a red bandanna and blue jeans. *Puppet Playhouse* was renamed *The Howdy Doody Show* in 1949 as NBC scheduled the program on Mondays through Fridays from 5:30 to 6 P.M. It grew to be a "money machine generating millions for NBC," while its "frantic commercialism" also upped the ante for all children's series.[59] Besides the show's sponsors (which included Welch's Grape Juice, Wonder Bread, and Hostess Twinkies), the Doodyville Gang also hyped a wide assortment of Howdy Doody merchandise, such as comic books, records, T-shirts, lunch boxes, and Western-style clothing resembling the attire worn by the show's live performers and puppets, along with dozens of other licensed products.[60]

The extraordinary power of television to galvanize the youth market was demonstrated once and for all in 1955 by the unleashing of a

No TV character captivated youngsters so completely during the late 1940s and through the early to mid 1950s as Howdy Doody (far right). His costars were "Buffalo Bob" Smith (left) and Clarabell the Clown (center). Courtesy of Library of American Broadcasting at the University of Maryland.

Davy Crockett craze that generated an estimated $300 million in merchandising in less than a year.[61] This phenomenon resulted from the synergistic coupling of the television and motion picture industries first initiated by ABC's Leonard Goldenson and his network chief, Robert Kintner. Unlike his counterparts at RCA/NBC and CBS—David Sarnoff and William S. Paley—Goldenson was a veteran of the motion picture, not the broadcasting industry. Fresh out of Harvard Business School in 1933, he was "hired to help reorganize the then near bankrupt theater chain of Hollywood's Paramount Pictures." He performed so well in this capacity that he was asked to stay on in 1938 and "manage the entire Paramount chain."[62] Goldenson appeared destined to have a long and distinguished career as a movie executive until the 1948 *Paramount* decision jettisoned the film industry into a period of turbulence and realignment. In this landmark case, the Supreme Court found against Hollywood's five major studios (Paramount, MGM [Metro-Goldwyn-Mayer], RKO [Radio-Keith-Orpheum], Twentieth Century-Fox, and Warner Bros.), as well as its three mini-majors (Universal, United Artists, and Columbia) for essentially operating as an illegal cartel that indulged in a number of longstanding monopolistic practices (such as price-fixing and block booking). One of the key provisions of the ruling was that Paramount and the other four majors were ordered to divest themselves as soon as possible of their exhibition holdings.

As a result, Leonard Goldenson assumed the presidency of the newly independent United Paramount Theater (UPT) chain in 1951. The court ruling prohibited UPT from affiliating or investing in the movies any longer, so Goldenson looked elsewhere to put his corporation's vast capital resources to work. Before long, he set his sights on ABC, whose major asset was its struggling television network that possessed five owned-and-operated stations, along with eight affiliates, reaching approximately 35 percent of the nation's households. "To the merger Paramount could bring substantial working capital—and a business of uncertain future," observed Erik Barnouw; "ABC could bring less working capital—and an apparently glowing future. The merger foreshadowed a more spirited competition among networks."[63] After a protracted review, the FCC finally approved UPT's purchase of ABC on February 9, 1953. Goldenson was now free to exercise his considerable entrepreneurial skills. He assumed that only three networks would survive over the long run, so he next proposed a merger between his corporation and DuMont, where UPT's large capital reserves would subsidize a combined ABC–DuMont network. Fearing further antitrust sanctions, however, DuMont's minority shareholder, Paramount Pictures, nixed UPT's friendly takeover. This action ensured DuMont's downward spiral from that point onward, as it fell ever deeper into fourth place, never to recover. Allen B. DuMont's pioneering network finally ceased telecasting altogether on August 8, 1956.

Characteristically, Goldenson shifted gears after this temporary setback and searched for other ways to move ABC forward. He was not as personally flamboyant as Sarnoff and Paley, but he was every bit as creative and bold as a network mogul—maybe more so because of his relentless drive to prove ABC's worth (and his own). Goldenson first approved the infusion of "$30 million into the network, initiating a five-year plan to boost ABC into full competition. While $7.5 million was used for improvements in network facilities, $22.5 million went directly to purchase programming."[64] He then charged ABC president Robert Kintner with cultivating alliances in Hollywood, leading eventually to film production deals that would differentiate ABC's product from its two larger rivals. Goldenson realized his network was not in a position to compete head on with NBC and CBS for stars, nor was it currently able to produce much original programming on its own; "ABC was tacitly admitting that . . . it was willing to rely on outside sources (even film studios) for major programs, thereby ceding some loss of network control."[65] At the same time, ABC was far more eager to gamble than were NBC and CBS. "Guys in third place are perennially willing to take risks," maintains media analyst Ken Auletta about Goldenson's management style during the 1950s; "they're the guys who throw the hail mary pass on third down."[66]

Under Goldenson's directive, ABC's first initiative was also its boldest. On April 2, 1954, the network announced an agreement with the Walt Disney Co. to produce a one-hour weekly series, titled *Disneyland*, to debut on ABC that fall. Five years later, Leonard Goldenson described the Disney collaboration as the "turning point" for ABC.[67] "The price was high but ultimately worthwhile," concurs film historian J. P. Telotte. After both NBC and CBS passed on similar terms, ABC agreed "to pay Disney $2,000,000 for one season of programs, renewable for a total of seven years, while adding $500,000 for a 35 percent ownership in the theme park, also to be known as Disneyland, and guaranteeing up to $4,500,000 in loans for the park's construction."[68] For its part, Disney started production on its first of twenty original episodes in which each one-hour installment was related to one of the four broadly defined generic subdivisions of its forthcoming theme park: Frontierland (Westerns), Tomorrowland (science fiction), Adventureland (live-action films and nature documentaries), and Fantasyland (animation). All of these twenty episodes would be rerun once, and then twelve of them would be repeated a second time

to constitute the show's fifty-two-week run. Even the name of the series revealed Walt Disney's ulterior motive of using *Disneyland* to promote his upcoming theme park (which opened on July 17, 1955), along with his newest theatrical releases. At the time, he confided that "through television, I can reach my audience. I can talk to my audience."[69] Before long, though, *Disneyland* (renamed *Walt Disney Presents* in 1958) became an end unto itself for him, as well as for ABC Television.

Disneyland was a smash hit from the outset, greeted enthusiastically by audiences and critics alike when it premiered on October 27, 1954. "It's happening and it's wonderful," effused Jack Gould in the *New York Times*; "Walt Disney is on TV!"[70] It's hard to exaggerate the transformative effect that this one series had on ABC's financial well-being and its professional image. For instance, "during its initial season *Disneyland* was responsible for nearly half of ABC's advertising revenues."[71] It ended the 1954–1955 television season at no. 6, the highest-rated ABC program to date; in 1955–1956, it even improved its position to no. 4 in the ratings. *Disneyland* won a prestigious Peabody Award in 1954 for Outstanding Youth and Children's Program, being cited as "a show that changed the bedtime habits of the nation's

children." Network chief Robert Kintner had wisely scheduled the series on Wednesday nights from 7:30 to 8:30 P.M., allowing *Disneyland*
to get a half-hour jump on its competition—CBS's *Arthur Godfrey
and His Friends* (knocking it out of the top 10) and NBC's *I Married
Joan* (causing its cancellation after three years on the air). The program also proved to be an economic powerhouse for ABC, propelling
the network to its first year of profitability in 1955. *Disneyland* also
picked up three Emmys in 1954, for "Best Variety Series," "Best Individual Show" (for "Operation Undersea," a behind-the-scenes look at
the making of Disney's latest theatrical feature, *20,000 Leagues under
the Sea*, starring Kirk Douglas), and "Best Television Film Editing"
(for the same episode, which was nicknamed "The Long, Long
Trailer" within the industry). The following year, Walt Disney won an
Emmy for "Best Producer of a Filmed Series" (for *Disneyland*), and
the program's three Davy Crockett episodes were recognized as the
"Best Action or Adventure Series" of the season.[72]

Disneyland's popularity skyrocketed to frenzied levels after the initial telecasting of "Davy Crockett—Indian Fighter" (on December 15,
1954), "Davy Crockett Goes to Congress" (on January 26, 1955), and
"Davy Crockett at the Alamo" (February 23, 1955). "The modern Crockett craze, appearing in early 1955, is now considered to be one of the
great popular culture events of the decade," declares cultural critic
Margaret King; "it was catapulted into existence by two of America's
most formidable media forces—Walt Disney and television—and
ignited by the catalyst of a new consumer audience: the baby boom
generation."[73] Even Disney was completely surprised by the sheer
magnitude of the phenomenon: "We had no idea what was going to
happen to 'Crockett.' Why, by the time the first show finally got on the
air, we were already shooting the third one and calmly killing Davy off
at the Alamo. It became one of the biggest overnight hits in TV history, and there we were with just three films and a dead hero."[74] An estimated ninety million viewers tuned into the first run of these three
serialized episodes, and then, remarkably, the size of the audience "actually increased for the reruns."[75] The merchandising of ancillary
products also reached record proportions, topping $250,000 in sales
by summer's end. The seemingly insatiable demand for "Davy Crockett coonskin caps, blue jeans, cap pistols, lunch boxes and dozens of
other items" drove *Time* to exclaim, "Why, Davy Crockett is bigger
than Mickey Mouse."[76] Then, all at once, the nationwide craze lost its
momentum in October, slowing down just as ABC was introducing
yet another original Disney series, *The Mickey Mouse Club*, which targeted preteens and grade-schoolers even more precisely than had
Disneyland.

More than anything, the Davy Crockett phenomenon demonstrated that the baby boomer generation was already having an effect on the national culture, only ten short years after its conception. Before TV, children received presents on their birthdays and special holidays, but now, after a decade of postwar prosperity, baby boomers and their teenage counterparts from the silent generation were expressing their collective identities on a regular basis through the merchandise they were buying and the products their parents were purchasing for them. The whole notion of a youth culture is in large part a media and marketing creation. Television, therefore, was either generating new fads and fashions through its own home-grown programming (as was currently the case with *Disneyland's* Davy Crockett) or further enabling the spread of other lifestyle trends that originated elsewhere (such as the nascent subculture then forming around rock 'n' roll music). For its part, the Davy Crockett craze confirmed that America's new emerging postwar culture was increasingly both youth oriented and media centric. The three Davy Crockett telefilms were among the highest-rated episodes of the entire 1954–1955 television season. They, in turn, spawned a hit song, "The Ballad of Davy Crockett," that topped "the *Hit Parade* for 13 weeks and sold 10 million records"; a reedited theatrical film, retitled *Davy Crockett: King of the Wild Frontier*, which "earned a profit of $2.5 million"; and a slew of new books and old reissues about Crockett's life, such as the young adult reader, *The Story of Davy Crockett*, which sold 300,000 copies in 1955, among other medi-

ated spin-offs.[77] By the mid 1950s, television had become indispensable in mobilizing the other mass media around a commonly shared
cultural agenda for most children and teenagers.

This tendency would surface again in 1956, when the medium introduced the country as a whole to Elvis Presley. In retrospect, Elvis's
coming out to a national audience was a slow and fitful process. At
first, the television establishment didn't know what to make of him or
his music. His initial forays into the new medium—on CBS's *Stage
Show* starring the Dorsey Brothers on January 28 and NBC's *The Milton Berle Show* on April 3 with a return engagement on May 6—were
studies in contrast: Elvis looked and sounded like the wave of the future with his sleek physique and his seductive voice, gyrating on stage
while he sang hits like "Hound Dog"; his hosts were phenoms from
an older generation whose prime-time runs were slowly winding
down. Even the red-hot Steve Allen, who on July 1 was only one week
into his Sunday-night face-off with the venerable Ed Sullivan, avoided
appearing passé by dressing poor Elvis in a tuxedo and asking him to
serenade a real basset hound. Needless to say, this masquerade did
soften Presley's rockabilly edges and mute his explosive sexual appeal.
Still, *Newsweek* described the transparency of this prime-time charade
as "trying to embalm a firecracker," as *The Steve Allen Show* did beat
Ed Sullivan's program in the ratings for the first of only three times
that season.[78] Sullivan, who had publicly vowed never to host the suggestive Presley on his variety show, promptly changed his mind, signing the rock 'n' roller to perform three times during the upcoming
season for a record $150,000. Ed Sullivan was already firmly estab-
lished as "the unofficial Minister of Culture in America" after anchoring CBS's Sunday-night lineup for the last seven years. Viewers
expected *The Ed Sullivan Show* to be "the great national variety theater" where the biggest acts in show business were brought before the
American people each week.[79]

Even by Sullivan's standards, Presley's popularity was unprecedented. On September 9, *The Ed Sullivan Show* opened the 1956–1957
season with Elvis as its headliner. Sixty million viewers, or 82.6 percent
of the American viewing public, tuned in, setting a new TV-audience
record at the time.[80] His two subsequent performances in October and
January similarly garnered 80 percent shares for Sullivan.[81] Some sort
of generational shift was evidently taking place in postwar America, but
the newness of what was happening to young people of all ages had
journalists searching for clues to make better sense of the silent and
baby boomer generations. The term "teenager," for example, was gaining some currency by the mid 1950s, having just been coined a decade
earlier in a January 7, 1945, *New York Times Magazine* cover story,

"A 'Teen-Age' Bill of Rights." Describing what would later be called the "silent generation," this article sympathetically observed that each age group "feels that it is the future. To the 'teen-ager' nothing is more important than to find out where he fits in in relation to life around him. It is a serious quest, often a painful one."[82] No one had ever captured that youthful angst more exuberantly than Elvis Presley. With his dyed jet-black hair, loose-fitting shirts unbuttoned to the chest, and transgressive dancing, Elvis's rebellion was more visceral than political. "The Elvis Presley craze will pass," one social commentator reassured parents and grandparents toward the end of 1956; "teenagers are merely having a vicarious fling."[83] Little did the older generation realize that the youth culture's love affair with rock 'n' roll was just getting started.

No network was more in tune with teens and baby boomers throughout the remainder of the decade than ABC. Young people were already coming of age as "a brand-new consuming class" by the mid 1950s. For example, "*Scholastic* magazine's Institute of Student Opinion showed that by early 1956 there were 13 million teenagers in the country, with a total income of $7 billion a year, which was 26% more than only three years earlier. The average teenager, the maga-

Ed Sullivan (left) *booked Elvis Presley* (right) *for three separate appearances during the 1956–1957 television season, with each episode garnering at least an 80 percent share of the audience. For his second guest spot on October 28, 1956, Elvis performed on national TV for the first time with his hair dyed jet black. Courtesy of CBS/Landov.*

zine said, had an income of $10.55 a week."[84] This kind of disposable cash in the hands of thirteen- to nineteen-year-olds was a wholly new phenomenon and a sign of the country's growing affluence. ABC responded by tailoring more of its programming than ever toward teens and preteens. On October 7, 1957, *American Bandstand* made its prime-time debut after starting as a local Philadelphia pop-music program back in 1952. The show joined ABC on August 5, 1957, from 3 to 3:30 and 4 to 5 P.M. Mondays through Fridays and then, two months later, added Monday nights. Host disc jockey Dick Clark was the "new rage" with the after-school set. He was then a boyish twenty-seven, with all-American good looks and an easy rapport with the teenagers on his show, who mostly danced to top-40 hits, pausing occasionally to rate the latest 45-vinyl releases. *American Bandstand* featured "the kind of music that most teenagers love[d] and many adults abhor[ed]. Rock 'n' roll as bellowed by such latter-day idols as Elvis Presley, Fats Domino and Jerry Lee Lewis [was] de rigueur," even though everything else about the program was as wholesome and clean-cut as Dick Clark himself.[85] In February 1958, the prime-time version of *American Bandstand* was renamed *The Dick Clark Show*, and ABC moved it to Friday nights as a way to counterprogram NBC's easy-listening musical-variety series, *The Perry Como Show*, and CBS's powerhouse legal drama, *Perry Mason*.

ABC's policies were gradually changing the entire landscape of network television, despite its perennial third-place position. After the enormous success of *Disneyland*, Leonard Goldenson became even more aggressive in pursuing additional film production agreements in Hollywood, especially with Warner Bros. and MGM. As one scholar notes, "The importance of ABC's telefilm deal with Disney, which was not a major Hollywood studio, was the model it provided for the entrance of the major studios into telefilm production for the networks."[86] What Hollywood learned from *Disneyland* was the windfall potential of producing telefilms. What ABC realized was that the Hollywood mode of production offered it a way to distinguish its programming from NBC and CBS. Certainly, "Hollywood production values would differentiate the series from live television, while Hollywood genres might appeal to an audience dissatisfied with the radio-style fare of variety shows, situation comedies, and anthology dramas."[87] ABC was thus eager to increase the number of reliable studio-made genre-style programs that Disney and Columbia's Screen Gems (with *The Adventures of Rin Tin Tin*) were already producing for the network. The breakthrough came when Jack Warner agreed to kick off ABC's Tuesday night schedule at 7:30 P.M. with three different rotating series— *King's Row*, *Casablanca*, and *Cheyenne*—under the umbrella *Warner*

Bros. Presents. This deal was a significant coup for Leonard Goldenson because it marked the first time that one of Hollywood's major studios expanded its repertoire to include telefilms, as well as theatrical motion pictures. Soon MGM followed Warner Bros. to ABC with *MGM Parade* and Twentieth Century-Fox to CBS with *The Twentieth Century-Fox Hour* during the 1955–1956 season.

Warner Bros., MGM, and Twentieth Century-Fox's transition to television was anything but smooth. Problems arose almost immediately because each one of these studios failed at first to take their TV work as seriously as Disney had the year before. In the first place, they spent far too much on-air time promoting their upcoming theatrical features. They also didn't give much thought to who their respective audiences were and what types of stories would best appeal to them. In the case of *Warner Bros. Presents,* for instance, the quality of execution for *King's Row* and *Casablanca* was well below the original movie versions: the original *King's Row* (1942) had been nominated for three Academy Awards; *Casablanca* (1942) was nominated for eight and won three Oscars, including Best Picture. In addition, the two telefilm adaptations were mature melodramas—heavy on romance and light on action. Still, *King's Row* and *Casablanca* were already earmarked for the 7:30 to 8:30 P.M. hour when ABC's preadult target audience skewed even younger. To make matters worse, ten minutes at the end of each episode was devoted entirely to plugging upcoming Warner Bros.' movies. Consequently, *King's Row*'s ratings were so low that it was canceled in December 1955. *Casablanca* was similarly phased out a few months later for the same reason, as was the use of the weekly ten-minute studio promo. Only *Cheyenne,* one of television's first adult Westerns that also played well with children, caught on with ABC's early evening audience. This program eventually ran for eight seasons, being paired in later years with other original Warner Bros.' series, including *Conflict, Sugarfoot,* and *Bronco.*

Within five years, Warner Bros. boasted the largest telefilm production budget in Hollywood, exceeding $30 million, as it supplied ABC with one-third of its prime-time schedule during the 1959–1960 season.[88] By that time, however, Robert Kintner was long gone from the network. Leonard Goldenson had grown increasingly disenchanted with Kintner's cautiousness as an executive. Kintner had been with ABC since 1944, working his way up the corporate ladder to network president in 1950 under founder and owner Edward J. Noble. When Goldenson's purchase of ABC was finalized in 1953, Noble convinced him to keep Kintner on as network chief. Goldenson soon grew to regret this decision, feeling that Kintner was unwilling to take the kind of calculated risks that he wanted him to try in procuring

programs for ABC. Goldenson also believed that his head programmer reacted far too slowly to the kinds of creative problems that surfaced early on with *Warner Bros. Presents*. Goldenson thus convinced
his board of directors to dismiss Kintner in October 1956, and "immediately afterwards, Goldenson moved from his office at United Paramount into one at ABC and began to oversee the network's day-to-day
operations, inserting Oliver Treyz as vice president in charge of the
network and James Aubrey as vice president in charge of programming."[89] Aubrey especially was the kind of hard-driving executive that
complemented Goldenson's style and aspirations for ABC. Kintner
landed on his feet, accepting an executive vice president position at
NBC in January 1957 as part of the corporate shake-up that eventually
led to Pat Weaver's departure. David and Robert Sarnoff were looking
to Kintner to help standardize NBC's policies and practices along the
lines of the operational changes that were then taking place at ABC.
Kintner did not disappoint the Sarnoffs, and in July 1958 he was
named network president.

For his part, James Aubrey was exactly the kind of entrepreneurial
programmer that Goldenson was looking for when he hired the thirty-
seven year old away from CBS, where he had just developed the soon-
to-be top-10 hit, *Have Gun—Will Travel*. Aubrey's main strength as an
ABC vice president was his unique ability to innovate within a standard genre format while never losing sight of the bottom line. He was
especially adept at working within ABC's tight budgets. Aubrey was totally in sync with Leonard Goldenson's "bread and butter" strategy of
targeting young families, teenagers, and children. "We're after a specific audience," Goldenson explained: "the young housewife—one cut
above the teenager—with two to four kids, who has to buy the clothing,
the food, the soaps, the home remedies."[90] To that end, Aubrey encouraged Warner Bros. and other Hollywood telefilm suppliers to produce
standard formulaic stories, only this time with some sort of added
hook that would appeal specifically to ABC's target audience. For example, Aubrey supported producer Roy Huggins's move to modernize
the adult Western in 1957–1958 with his offbeat parody, *Maverick*, starring James Garner in his breakout role. In 1958–1959, Huggins again
delivered *77 Sunset Strip*, an updating of the classic detective whodunit
by setting the series in Hollywood with two new glamorous stars,
Efrem Zimbalist Jr. and Roger Smith, along with a young, attractive
sidekick named "Kookie" (Edd Byrnes), who spent much of his onscreen time talking jive and combing his ducktail hairdo.

Other programs that Aubrey developed during his two years at ABC
were such top-10 hits as the increasingly violent coming-of-age Western, *The Rifleman*, starring Chuck Connors and Johnny Crawford as

father-and-son ranchers, and TV's first rural sitcom, *The Real McCoys*, a harbinger of things to come. Situation comedies would become Aubrey's special forte as he both developed new series, such as Screen Gems' *The Donna Reed Show* (which featured teenage costars Paul Peterson and Shelley Fabares as a means of reaching out to ABC's core constituency), and renovated evergreen sitcoms, such as the already five-year-old *Adventures of Ozzie and Harriet*, which began spotlighting the rock 'n' roll talents of son Ricky Nelson as a singer-songwriter at the start of the 1956–1957 season. In 1958, Bill Paley lured James Aubrey back to CBS with an especially lucrative offer and the understanding that he was being groomed to take over the top spot at America's no. 1 network. Paley actually promoted him earlier than expected when Louis G. Cowan was let go in December 1959 at the height of a nation-wide quiz show scandal. Aubrey then proceeded to practically double the network's annual profits, from $25 to $49 million, during his five-year stint as CBS's president.[91] By 1960, all three network presidents—Aubrey, Kintner, and now Oliver Treyz as Goldenson's new chief executive—"had a part in the rise of ABC" and "all proceeded to push the successful formula."[92]

The year 1957 was pivotal in television networking, with ABC on the rise, Hollywood acclimating itself to telefilm production, and the blacklist finally on the wane. When Goldenson officially took control of ABC in 1953, NBC led its competitors in the seasonal prime-time ratings 28.1 to CBS's 25.5 to ABC's 11.8; four years later at the end of the 1957–1958 season, ABC had already made up considerable ground with CBS now in first place at 23.5 to NBC's 21.6 with ABC at 16.8.[93] "ABC became the first network to stock the majority of its prime-time schedule with filmed programs," notes Christopher Anderson.[94] Over-all, "63% of ABC programming was filmed" at the start of 1956–1957, "compared to 20% for CBS and 16% for NBC."[95] ABC moved into tele-films in order to differentiate its product from its two larger rivals, and ironically within five years, CBS and NBC followed suit as three-quarters of all prime-time programming was being shot on film or videotape by 1961–1962. The benefits of this changeover far out-weighed the drawback of having to share some control in the produc-tion process with Hollywood's majors, mini-majors, and independent suppliers. The film studios brought much higher production values to prime time; they also shared in some of the financial risk. Telefilm producers also routinized and accelerated the pace of program produc-tion, increasing output while also enabling the first-run and syndica-tion markets to operate more efficiently and to expand exponentially. Over time, too, all of the major and mini-major studios learned from their early mistakes, as television grew to be an even more robust and prosperous business for them than theatrical movies. By the early 1960s, the Hollywood mode of production was the norm at all three networks, virtually replacing the live New York and Chicago styles of a decade before.

Likewise, Hollywood usurped New York as the TV production capitol of the world by the 1957–1958 season. "Though the amount of prime-time programming originating on the West Coast had been increasing slowly" throughout the early to mid 1950s, "in 1957 it jumped from 40% to 71%."[96] NBC was the network that changed most dramatically; under Pat Weaver the emphasis was on New York–based live productions such as *Today, Home,* and *Tonight!,* as well as one-time "spectaculars" by Max Liebman and others and the many dramatic anthologies that drew heavily on Broadway talent. When Robert Kintner joined Robert Sarnoff as the executive tandem in charge of NBC in 1956, the trade press immediately began referring to "Bob and Bob," instead of their earlier "Pat and Bob" shorthand. What Kintner brought to NBC was a philosophy of programming that sounded remarkably like that of Leonard Goldenson's at ABC. He even appropriated a culinary metaphor to spice up his rhetoric when he told *Newsweek* in 1957 that the "theory of NBC is basically to create what we call a schedule of meat-and-potatoes programming, including adventure-mystery, adult Westerns plus live variety of the Perry Como type. A schedule that will appeal to the maximum number of people seven days a week."[97] During his decade-long tenure as president of NBC, Robert Kintner proved that the network didn't need to be innovative to be profitable. Nevertheless, his safe middle-of-the-road approach to prime time also assured that NBC wouldn't catch CBS in the ratings, either. Under Kintner, "the company shifted from live programs to predominantly telefilms." NBC also "abandoned a schedule noted largely for its specials to implement one characterized by the routines of series programming," recounts Vance Kepley, and "established a policy of acquiring its shows from a stable set of outside program suppliers."[98]

As a result, Fred Coe, the creative force behind the *Goodyear/ Philco TV Playhouse,* "quit NBC stating, 'I just wasn't happy doing nothing.' Max Liebman and NBC parted ways. All season, stories about great drama shows being emasculated by fearful sponsors and networks circulated in the press."[99] The prime-time climate was indeed growing more conventional and regimented by 1957–1958; moreover, the "Golden Age" label that is usually applied to the live dramatic anthologies that frequented TV for the better part of fifteen years needs to be reconsidered. By and large, this golden reputation continues, despite the fact that most of the original telecasts are lost forever. From the debut of NBC's *Kraft Television Theatre* in 1947 to the cancellation of CBS's *Playhouse 90* in 1961, an estimated two thousand live dramas were produced, but fewer than one hundred, or 5 percent, are currently available for critical review in various archives around the country. Moreover, many of these surviving telecasts are among the most-celebrated examples on which to judge the entire genre. The notion of a golden age for television, therefore, is best taken with a grain of salt—as is the assumption that the medium's early live dramas were the highest-quality programs of the era. This observation is not meant to demean the many accomplishments of creative producers such as Fred Coe and Worthington Minor; directors such as John Frankenheimer, Sydney Lumet, Delbert Mann, Arthur Penn, and Sidney Pollack; writers such as Paddy Chaeyevsky, Horton Foote, Reginald Rose, Rod Serling, and Gore Vidal; and a whole generation of new, young, talented actors including James Dean, Julie Harris, Grace Kelly, Jack Lemmon, Paul Newman, Sidney Poitier, and Joanne Woodward, among many others. Instead, the point is to give the golden label a more measured historical appraisal.

First, an aura was intentionally created around these programs when they were initially telecast as a way of more effectively selling them to early TV audiences:

> As the nation's economy grew and the population expanded, television and advertising executives turned to dramatic shows as a programming strategy to elevate the status of television and attract the growing and increasingly important suburban family audience. "Golden age" dramas quickly became the ideal marketing vehicle for major U.S. corporations seeking to display their products favorably before a national audience.[100]

Second, part of the golden halo derives from the astonishing artistic legacy left behind by all of the young talent who cut their teeth on these live dramas and continued making their marks afterward on stage, in theatrical films, on series TV, and in other kinds of creative venues. As good as they are in retrospect, live dramas such as *Marty* (from the *Goodyear TV Playhouse*), *Patterns* (from the *Kraft Television Theatre*), *Requiem for a Heavyweight* (from *Playhouse 90*), *The Trip to Bountiful* (from the *Philco Television Playhouse*), and *Twelve Angry Men* (from *Studio One*) are comparable rather than superior to *Your Show of Shows* (variety), *I Love Lucy* (situation comedy), *Tonight!* (talk), *Gunsmoke* (adult Western), and *Perry Mason* (legal drama) as being among the best early representatives of their respective genres.

Actually, live dramas are much more similar to telefilms from a stylistic point of view than is usually acknowledged. The dramatic potential of television that was first realized in these live weekly anthologies crossed over and eventually influenced the development of telefilm aesthetics. Beginning as early as 1948, Worthington Minor's main "concern was with the visual impact of the stories" rather than just the written word. In adapting CBS's *Studio One* from radio to TV, "Minor's major contribution to television drama was more in his experimentation with camera techniques and other innovations in what the viewer saw, rather than in what was heard."[101] He pioneered the kind of intimate shot types, shallow depth of field, higher key lighting strategies, and uncomplicated editing styles that coalesced into a new sort of televisual style for both live and telefilm dramas. For him, characterization also took precedence over plot structure and setting to better adapt these live dramas to the segmentation of prime time and the lower definition and limited aspect ratio of the television screen. As Rod Serling pointed out at the time, "The key to television drama is intimacy. The facial study on a small screen carries with it a meaning and power far beyond its usage in motion pictures."[102] Championing the unvarnished live aesthetics of these dramas was also a way of privileging the New York and Chicago schools over the Hollywood mode of production. Ironically, the unpolished live nature of these dramas was often touted as being more authentic and therefore of better quality than the much higher production values evident in the average theatrical motion picture or telefilm episode of the 1950s and early 1960s.

Accordingly, a program that "followed a predictable, repetitious formula" was "not automatically bad."[103] CBS's *Perry Mason*, for instance, was the longest-running and most popular lawyer program in the history of television, being a top-20 show for most of its prime-time run from 1957 to 1966, even reaching no. 5 in the ratings for the 1961–1962 season. The person who initially conceived of Perry Mason was California attorney and soon-to-be best-selling novelist, Erle Stanley Gardner. He based Perry Mason largely on his own courtroom experiences, merging elements of the pulp whodunit with the hard-boiled detective and lawyer narratives that probed the ins and outs of the American legal system. "The triumph of *Perry Mason*," argues Thomas Leitch, "is a triumph of formula."[104] In this way, the 271 episodes of this series largely repeat a ritualized plot structure, which starts with a crime (usually a murder) that threatens to break up a family or quasi-family unit, followed by an innocent being accused of this transgression; Perry Mason then takes on the case and eventually ensures his client's release by coaxing a confession out of some witness who breaks down under his relentless cross-examination. During its initial prime-time run, the program enacted in this stylized way many of the most cherished ideals underlying the American legal system, bringing them to life onscreen for a whole new generation of postwar viewers. Shot at Twentieth Century-Fox studio a half-century ago, *Perry Mason* still holds up as one of the better-told, most skillfully acted examples of series television from the first generation of prime-time drama.

Similarly, adult Westerns such as *Gunsmoke* worked within familiar story lines with continuing characters but often tackled contemporaneous issues such as corporate greed, political corruption, and deep-seated racism, albeit in formulaic ways. Before 1955–1956, only two Westerns had ever made it into the top 10: *The Lone Ranger* was no. 7 and *Hopalong Cassidy* was no. 9 in 1950–1951. The kids who grew up watching Buffalo Bob Smith and Howdy Doody, the Lone Ranger and Tonto, and Hopalong Cassidy were primed for something a little more sophisticated when a second wave of TV Westerns made it to television beginning in September 1955 with the premieres of *Gunsmoke* on CBS, as well as *Cheyenne* and *The Life and Legend of*

Gunsmoke *was not just the first adult Western to break into the top 10 at no. 8 in 1956–1957; it was also the no. 1 TV program in the whole country for four straight seasons, from 1957 through 1961. James Arness (center) starred as Marshal Matt Dillon, and Dennis Weaver (right) played Chester Goode, as part of a large ensemble cast of characters. Courtesy of Library of American Broadcasting at the University of Maryland.*

Wyatt Earp on ABC. *Gunsmoke* even received the ultimate Western-size stamp of approval when John Wayne briefly introduced the first episode speaking directly to a broad-based audience of adults, teenagers, and children: "I think it's the best thing of its kind that's come along. It's honest and realistic." *Gunsmoke* was not just the first adult Western to break into the top 10 at no. 8 in 1956–1957; it was also the no. 1 TV program in the whole country for four straight seasons, from 1957 through 1961, during the genre's heyday. *Gunsmoke* earned an important institutional recognition when it won the Emmy for "Best Dramatic Series with Continuing Characters" in 1957.

The popularity of the adult Western during the late 1950s and early 1960s was unchallenged at the time and remains unmatched by any other television genre ever since. The number of Westerns on prime time rose from sixteen in 1957–1958, to twenty-four in 1958–1959, to a peak of twenty-eight in 1959–1960, before starting its slow descent to twenty-two in 1960–1961.[105] During this four-year stretch, moreover, there were ten Westerns in the top 30 in 1957–1958, fourteen in 1958–1959, eleven in 1959–1960, and eight in 1960–1961.[106] Just as Westerns had been a staple of the film industry between 1940 and 1960, producing 25 percent of its annual output during these years, the rise of the genre on prime time marked the clear-cut arrival of Hollywood as an important partner in the television business.[107] The major and mini-major studios producing adult Westerns included Warner Bros. (*Cheyenne, Maverick, Sugarfoot*), Twentieth Century-Fox (*Broken Arrow, Daniel Boone, Lancer*), MGM (*Hondo, How the West Was Won, Northwest Passage*), Universal/MCA (*Tales of Wells Fargo, The Virginian, Wagon Train*), United Artists (*Bat Masterson, MacKenzie's Raiders, Stoney Burke*), and Columbia (*Empire, The Iron Horse, The Outcasts*).[108] Even Paramount entered the fray of telefilm production with the September 12, 1959, premiere of *Bonanza*, which ran for fourteen years on NBC, including three seasons as the nation's no. 1 show between 1964 and 1967.

Oliver Treyz was named president of ABC on February 17, 1958, following the departure of James Aubrey. He had always been a successful salesman, bringing "many telefilm sponsors to the network," but now he expanded his purview further into program development. Working closely with Goldenson, he built on the network's momentum of the previous five years by initiating what was later referred to as the "Treyz trend."[109] What this eponymous tendency meant was that ABC was relying more than ever on action-adventure series, especially Westerns and detective shows, which Treyz counterprogrammed against NBC and CBS whenever possible. In addition, the "Treyz trend" alluded to the fact that action at ABC was becoming synonymous with violence. In retrospect, no series illustrated this pattern more clearly than Desilu's *The Untouchables*, which debuted on October 15, 1959, against NBC's *Tennessee Ernie Ford Show* and CBS's *Playhouse 90* (which, in turn, was forced to cut back to twice a month instead of its standard weekly production schedule on January 21, 1960).[110] Even though *The Untouchables* was a police drama, its good-versus-evil scenario was not unlike the Western (and the series was similarly popular with teenage and adolescent viewers). Led by a strong, silent leader, Eliot Ness (Robert Stack), the program's federal agents were incorruptible (thus the anonym "untouchable"). The show featured a lot of tough talk, fast cars with squealing tires, and machine-gun battles as the "untouchables" waged all-out war against a series of notorious crimelords with memorable nicknames such as Al "Scarface" Capone (Neville Brand), Frank "The Enforcer" Nitti (Bruce Gordon), Jake "Greasy Thumb" Guzik (Nehemiah Persoff), "Bugs" Moran (Lloyd Nolan), and "Mad Dog" Coll (Clu Gulager).

The extreme violence of *The Untouchables* brought ABC lots of attention and controversy, and by the program's second season, it had grown into another top-10 hit for the network. ABC, in fact, peaked in 1960–1961, finally achieving a degree of respect if not parity with its larger, more affluent rivals by coming in second for the first time ever that season. CBS still led in the ratings at 20.7, but ABC temporarily slipped ahead of NBC 18.4 to 18.1 for one year.[111] Scholars Harry Castleman and Walter J. Podrazik point out that, "though the number and strength of its affiliates had increased, ABC was [still] far weaker than CBS and NBC. Its news, public affairs, sports, and daytime programming were virtually nonexistent. Even its success in prime time had come almost entirely from one program type, action-adventure, with only occasional hits in other genres."[112] For all intents and purposes, then, ABC remained television's "third network." Nevertheless, its rapid recovery from near bankruptcy to become the most influential programming force in the entire television industry between 1954 and 1961 was nothing short of remarkable. "ABC had been a leader in seeking new program sources and sharply redefining the aims and responsibilities of a network," concludes William Boddy; "by 1960 the programming philosophies and prime-time schedules of the other networks were nearly identical."[113]

Still, the industry as a whole was shaken to its very core by a quiz shows scandal that erupted unexpectedly during the late summer of 1958 and continued to plague NBC and CBS especially for the next two years. Rumors concerning the possible rigging of these immensely popular prime-time programs surfaced soon after CBS's *The $64,000 Question* skyrocketed to the top of the ratings in the summer of 1955.

Producer Louis G. Cowan followed up this smash hit with a spin-off, *The $64,000 Challenge*, before severing all ties with his independent production company in 1956 to join CBS as a vice president in charge of programming and talent. Cowan's rise at the network was meteoric; he was soon promoted to president in 1958. In the meantime, game shows with ever-higher jackpots, such as *The Big Game*, *Dotto*, *The Price Is Right*, *Twenty-One*, *Tic Tac Dough*, and many others, were proliferating on CBS and NBC. The "quiz show meshed perfectly with the materialism of the times. The postwar economy was booming, and wages were rising rapidly. Consumers bought homes, cars, household appliances, novelties, and luxury items. And television advertising both celebrated and fanned the buying image. When quiz show winners marched off with their loot, they were fulfilling an American Dream—a dream defined by television."[114]

All prime-time genres develop through a boom-and-bust cycle, beginning with a white-hot ascent and ending with a slow gradual decline over the course of several years. By the summer of 1958, audiences were already tiring of game shows, when all of a sudden the whole house of cards came crashing down on the networks. Several former contestants went public with charges that they had been given the answers ahead of time; one even made a formal complaint to the FCC. The program in question, NBC's *Dotto*, was abruptly canceled on August 12, 1958, and "within days, some 20 quiz shows left the air in television's first major programming scandal. Network officials claimed ignorance, program producers said that people did not understand commercial television's purposes and practices, and advertisers said nothing."[115] In response, some editorialists went so far as to claim that the whole sordid affair marked "the end of American innocence."[116] At the center of this firestorm stood a tall, soft-spoken thirty-two-year-old English instructor from Columbia University named Charles Lincoln Van Doren. Less than three years earlier, he had emerged as an improbable television star. Van Doren's popularity resulted from his highly dramatic three-and-a-half-month performance on *Twenty-One* (from November 28, 1956, to March 11, 1957), an NBC quiz show based on the card game blackjack. Van Doren eventually won $129,000 on *Twenty-One*, propelling him to both fortune and fame.

Television specializes in odd juxtapositions. Charles Van Doren was someone Russell Lynes would have instantly recognized as a highbrow, starring on a program that belonged to the lowest-brow genre in all of prime time. He was not in the least bit snobbish, though; Van Doren was charming, intelligent, and, most important, telegenic. The American viewing public was taken by him right away. He had all the proper credentials and pedigree, being an Ivy League–educated scion of a

Charles Van Doren (right) *emerged as an improbable television star because of his highly dramatic three-and-a-half-month performance on* Twenty-One *from November 28, 1956, through March 11, 1957.* Twenty-One *was hosted and coproduced by Jack Barry* (center). *Courtesy of Library of American Broadcasting at the University of Maryland.*

famous literary family. (His father Mark was a Pulitzer Prize–winning poet; his mother Dorothy was a celebrated novelist and one-time editor of *Nation*; and his late uncle Carl was a Pulitzer Prize–winning biographer and renowned literary critic.) Charles's life so far was charmed, and his future looked as bright as it could be. A close-up of his face adorned the February 11, 1957, cover of *Time* underneath the headline, "Brains v. Dollars on TV"; in the picture, Van Doren wore headphones and a look of intense concentration as he apparently was just about to give another right answer while cloistered inside his isolation booth on *Twenty-One*. After his three-plus-months on the show, NBC's *Today* quickly snapped him up for "a permanent spot . . . where he discussed non-Euclidean geometry and recited seventeenth-century poetry. He put an all-American face to the university intellectual in an age just getting over its suspicion of subversive 'eggheads.' "[117] In the end, Charles was both a deceiver and a victim of circumstance.

Charles Van Doren's fall from grace came gradually but inevitably. When the scandal first broke, he was asked often about his appearance on *Twenty-One*. His standard response—first to the press, then to a grand jury—was to vehemently deny any wrongdoing. The truth was, however, Van Doren had indeed been coached by *Twenty-One*'s coproducers, Jack Barry and Robert Enright. They had given him answers ahead of time, as well as tips on how best to perform under the pressure of a watchful prime-time audience. Barry and Enright were in the business of making their shows as entertaining as possible, and they had found a natural performer in Van Doren. A number of other former quiz show contestants also perjured themselves when they were called before the grand jury, even though there was no criminal statute at the time against fixing TV quiz shows. Like Van Doren, they wanted to avoid the public embarrassment. Finally, a House Subcommittee on Legislative Oversight was convened in the fall of 1959 to get to the bottom of what had become a front-page story, indicating the growing importance of television in the cultural life of the nation. The star witness at these hearings was the most famous contestant of all—Charles Van Doren—who appeared on November 2 and confessed his guilt before the entire country: "I would give almost anything to reverse the course of my life in the past three years. . . . I have learned a lot about myself. . . . I've learned a lot about good and evil. They are not always what they appear to be." The moment was revelatory for the public and climactic for the industry as a whole.[118]

After his Congressional testimony, Charles Van Doren was summarily dismissed from Columbia and fired from his starring role as the urbane cultural commentator on *Today*. He eventually pled guilty to second-degree perjury and was given a suspended sentence along with nine other codefendants. NBC and CBS disavowed any knowledge whatsoever of the mass deception, blaming it all on the program suppliers. ABC largely got away scot free, having so few game shows on their schedule to begin with. Collectively, though, the networks canceled all of their remaining quiz shows, purging prime time of the now-tainted genre for the foreseeable future. Even though NBC was the main target of criticism, Bill Paley and Frank Stanton felt the need to clean house, replacing Louis Cowan as president of CBS with James Aubrey on December 8, 1959. Likewise, Jack Barry and Robert Enright became personae non gratae at the networks, unable to find work there for more than a decade. All told, the "scandal illuminated some things about television in addition to its growing, addictive power." The seemingly ever-present power of the medium now "*cast* everything it touched" from entertainment to news to commerce, culture, and politics. "Among the first to benefit from that new casting requirement was a young junior senator from Massachusetts, who, like Charles Van Doren, was young, attractive, upper-class, and diffident because he was cool on a medium that was hot."[119]

John F. Kennedy won a razor-thin victory (two-tenths of a percentage point) over Richard M. Nixon to become the thirty-fifth president of the United States on November 8, 1960. At the time, there were almost ninety million television sets in the United States, or nearly one for every two Americans. TV played a decisive role throughout the campaign, allowing the lesser-known Kennedy to speak directly to the American people in an apparently intimate and spontaneous manner. He, too, was a born-natural on camera, and the viewers at home liked what they saw. Kennedy and Nixon squared off in four so-called Great Debates during September and October 1960. They were the first contests of their kind and still remain the highest-rated presidential debates in history. (The first earned a 60 rating, which translated into an estimated viewership of 60.4 million; the second and third garnered 59 ratings, meaning audiences of approximately 59.4 million watched each one; and the last a 66 rating, with 66.5 million viewers.)[120] Inspired by the country's pioneering spirit and its Western mystique, JFK christened his activist administration the New Frontier. On May 9, 1961, the president's thirty-five-year-old FCC chairman, Newton N. Minow, a fervent New Frontiersman, delivered what turned out to be a scorching indictment of the current state of television at the annual National Association of Broadcasters (NAB) convention in Washington, D.C. Minow challenged the industry executives in the audience to "sit down in front of your television set when your station goes on the air and stay there without a book, magazine, newspaper, profit-and-loss sheet or rating book to distract you—and keep your eyes glued to that set until the station signs off. I can assure you that you will observe a vast wasteland."[121] "The young chairman was suddenly a genuine celebrity," recalls television historian Mary Ann Watson: "Never before or since has an FCC chairman been a household name." Moreover, the "phrase 'vast wasteland,' inspired by the T. S. Eliot poem, immediately entered the American vocabulary."[122]

Being put on notice was a new experience for the NAB. Furthermore, the association's membership had never before heard anyone make a literary allusion to T. S. Eliot when discussing television. Minow, like his boss, was probably more upper-middlebrow in taste, but his speech was replete with highbrow criticisms: "You will see a procession of game shows, violence, audience participation shows, formula comedies about totally unbelievable families, blood and thunder, mayhem, violence, sadism, murder, Western badmen, Western good men, private eyes, gangsters, more violence and cartoons. And, endlessly, commercials—many screaming, cajoling and offending. And most of all, boredom."[123] A few called the speech "courageous," but most of the NAB members were merely stunned. "Many broadcasters admitted they were indignant over the speech," reported Jack Gould in the New York Times, but few could argue with the larger point Minow was making. The FCC chairman's position actually echoed Pat Weaver's high-minded vision for the medium from the early 1950s. Broadly speaking, Minow asserted that TV was too important a public resource to just squander away. With nearly fifty million television households comprising over 90 percent of the country's total, he argued that TV should not be "allowed to sink to the least common denominator of the national audience merely because that is where survival and profit come most easily. A rising curve in leadership and accomplishment in entertainment, education and information must be asked of TV if it is to do its part in elevating cultural standards and in helping Americans cope with the urgencies of the 1960s."[124] Like Edward R. Murrow's 1958 RTNDA speech, Newton Minow's NAB jeremiad called attention to the country's underlying fault line "in which the dominant interests of the country were rapidly diverging between those of the intellectual or aristocratic elite and those of the growing forces of corporate capitalism, and the television industry chose the latter route toward economic rather than cultural hegemony."[125]

Interestingly, Charles Van Doren had just made the very same choice in his own personal life, and it tore him apart before he had realized what happened. In hindsight, Van Doren's made-for-TV fall from grace revealed to millions of fellow citizens the broader ideological struggle that was then percolating just beneath the surface of American life. Unfortunately, the New Frontier would not resolve this divide, being abruptly cut short on November 22, 1963, with the midday assassination of President Kennedy in Dallas, Texas. The fissure would widen even further throughout the 1960s between competing liberal and conservative visions of what America should be. In the meantime, television rose to the occasion with grace and resourcefulness during the Kennedy funeral and burial, drawing words of praise and appreciation from nearly every sector of society. TV had always played a major part in JFK's rise to political prominence and power, and now the medium would assume an even greater role in laying him to rest, as well as shaping the nation's memory of him in the years to come. The networks pooled their coverage, providing four days of continuous commercial-free service that was mostly telecast live with the rest rerun on videotape and film from Friday, November 22, through Monday, November 25, costing them an estimated $100 million in lost advertising revenue.[126] Americans across the board were grateful for television's pro bono performance, as nearly three-quarters of the country's nearly 190 million citizens experienced firsthand at some point in the proceedings what TV was fully capable of in a crisis. The television industry's response to this national tragedy did more good for the medium's reputation than all of the extra public affairs, documentary, and New Frontier–style dramatic programs (such as NBC's Dr. Kildare, CBS's The Defenders, and ABC's Ben Casey) that the three networks produced following Newton Minow's 1961 wake-up call.[127]

On the evening of November 25, few Americans were thinking that television was a vast wasteland. Reaching a record-setting 93 rating at peak periods, over 100 million Americans at a time watched

Over 100 million American television viewers watched transfixed on November 25, 1963, as President John F. Kennedy's burial cortege passed the east side of the Capitol. Courtesy of Library of American Broadcasting at the University of Maryland.

transfixed—along with tens of millions of additional viewers in twenty-three other countries around the world—using the medium to process the unthinkable, mourn collectively, and cope with the feelings of shock, sadness, and disbelief that overwhelmed many in the face of this terrible and unexpected tragedy. A series of images would be forever seared into the shared memories of a nation, beginning with CBS's Walter Cronkite tearing up after being the first on-air newscaster to announce that all of the incoming news flashes were "apparently official. President Kennedy died at 1 P.M. Central Standard Time, two o'clock Eastern Standard Time. Some 38-minutes ago"; followed by a shell-shocked Lyndon B. Johnson facing the cameras later that night at Andrews Air Force Base and promising to "do my best. That is all I can do. I ask for your help and God's"; to Jack Ruby gunning down Lee Harvey Oswald at the Dallas city jail on Sunday at 12:21 P.M. EST live on NBC-TV; to thousands of mourners quietly filing past the president's flag-draped coffin in the Capitol rotunda later that afternoon and evening; and finally to three-year-old John Kennedy Jr. saluting his father's casket as it solemnly passes by on the street after the Monday funeral, carried along on a horse-drawn caisson as it slowly makes its way out of the city to Arlington National cemetery for the burial.[128] Television was at the center of a deeply heartfelt personal experience that most viewers would never forget for the rest of their lives. TV had also emerged as the one place where Americans still came together on a daily basis throughout the remainder of the 1960s, even as the nation's social fabric continued to pull apart at the seams.

TELEVISION AND THE PRESIDENCY
Eisenhower and Kennedy

6

Mary Ann Watson

Ike Adapts to the Television Age

On December 7, 1951—ten years after the United States entered World War II—the promise of a better life that motivated Americans to so much sacrifice seemed to have been realized. At the end of the war, optimism for the future was the most fitting tribute that could be paid to those whose lives were given for democratic principles. The booming postwar economy steadily elevated the American standard of living.

As the second half of the twentieth century dawned—and Dwight Eisenhower, the great hero of the D-Day invasion, contemplated a run for the presidency—a culture of abundance was growing rapidly. Suburban areas sprouted, and new single-family homes were brimming not only with children but also with modern marvels: air conditioning, automatic washers and dryers, frozen foods and refrigerators with large freezer compartments to store them, and, the most wondrous of all, television.

A decade after Pearl Harbor, TV was becoming a fixture in American life. Another ten years later, on December 7, 1961, when John Kennedy was in the White House, television had already become the common reference point among Americans, a palpable force in creating national consensus on what mattered most, setting the country's agenda for debate and action. The time span between General Eisenhower's announcement that he was running for president and John Kennedy's burial at Arlington Cemetery is the period of greatest change in the nature of the relationship between the chief executive and the American people, change that was a direct result of the new medium.

Early in 1952, famed CBS newsman Edward R. Murrow went to Paris to film a documentary on the Supreme Headquarters Allied Powers in Europe (SHAPE), which was under Eisenhower's command. The general didn't like to give broadcast interviews, but he held Murrow in high esteem because of his courageous war reporting from Europe. So Ike acquiesced. The interview was a disaster. Eisenhower wouldn't look at the camera, he mumbled with rambling syntax, and he appeared to be totally uncomfortable with the situation.

Skillful editing would be required to salvage the effort. When the film stopped rolling, Murrow spoke frankly to Eisenhower, suggesting that he get some coaching on his television performance because the medium would soon be the dominant means of communication. Refusing to use it was not an option for a modern leader.[1]

A week or so later, Eisenhower called David Schoenbrun, a CBS correspondent he knew well. He asked if Schoenbrun could coach him, confidentially, in on-air skills. Schoenbrun hesitated, wondering if he was crossing a professional line since Eisenhower was a news source and a subject of much of his reporting from Paris. But he agreed because Murrow specifically suggested him as the person Ike should call. It was decided that Army Signal Corps cameramen would be used for the practice sessions. If civilians participated—either a CBS news crew or French technicians—they would not be subject to military discipline and would likely tell their friends and family about the five-star general taking TV lessons.

Eisenhower was not an apt or eager pupil. His coaching usually came at the end of the day when he was more likely to be tired and grumpy. When Schoenbrun explained there was a problem with his baldness, Eisenhower snapped, "I know I'm bald. What do you want me to do, put on a wig?" The solution would be to keep his head at a slightly higher angle and not to look down so much. He also needed a little makeup and powder to reduce the reflection from the lights. "Why don't you just get an actor?" Ike bristled: "Get a double to do my interviews for me."[2] In that pre-video era, the practice sessions were filmed, and it would take up to forty-eight hours for the lab to process the moving pictures. When Eisenhower finally saw himself, he knew he needed to work at the techniques he was resisting. When he did make a good effort, and did permit the application of makeup, he saw great improvement in the image.

Ike's convoluted style of speech, though, was a tougher assignment for Schoenbrun. Sometimes, with a few notes as a guideline, he did well speaking extemporaneously. But just as often, his words snarled together in a confusing tangle of thought. Although Eisenhower had not yet announced his intentions, Schoenbrun knew the man under his tutelage was planning to run for president. "If you don't improve your work on TV," the newsman warned, "you'll never get elected."[3]

Both major political parties wooed Eisenhower to be their candidate, but he decided on a Republican affiliation. According to a Roper poll taken in March 1952, Dwight Eisenhower was the most admired living American.[4] That same month, for the first time, television covered the New Hampshire primary. CBS and NBC film crews went to the small state, which offered few delegates, and viewers got their first glimpse of "I Like Ike" buttons and banners.

Voter turnout was small, but Eisenhower's write-in ballot victory over Robert Taft, the Republican senator from Ohio and son of the twenty-seventh president, William Howard Taft, was big news. From then on, New Hampshire's presidential primary was considered a national bellwether, covered with increasing fanfare every four years. The significance of network television's focus on state primaries couldn't be fully discerned in 1952, but it would ultimately diminish the power of party organizations in selecting candidates.

When President Truman granted Eisenhower's request to be relieved of his duties as supreme commander in Europe, Ike was able to officially begin his campaign. He named James C. Hagerty as his press secretary. Hagerty had been press secretary to Governor Thomas Dewey of New York and then a political reporter for the *New York Times*. Hagerty, like Eisenhower, had close connections in the world of advertising—an industry that was taking hold of postwar American consciousness. In *A Nation of Salesmen*, author Earl Shorris posits that the growth of television advertising at midcentury was having a profound influence on the culture and character of the country, changing the nature of consumerism.[5] Restraint was no longer a virtue; indulgence no longer a vice. So, too, was television advertising beginning to change the nature of political persuasion.

Voters knew very little about Eisenhower's position on issues. As a war hero it didn't matter, but as a presidential candidate, he had to go on the record. The general decided to introduce his political stance from his hometown of Abilene, Kansas. The decision by CBS to carry the event live was good news to Ike's campaign—but not for long. In the stadium of the town's rodeo, softball, and picnic area— recently renamed Eisenhower Park—a crowd estimated to be between fifteen thousand and twenty thousand people gathered long before Eisenhower was to speak. As his car arrived, rain was falling on the faithful. It was suggested that perhaps he should make his address from the storage barn where the television cameras were being kept. There was just enough light to convey his image to the national audience. Ike flatly refused, though, to jilt the good people waiting to see him.

Shortly after the candidate began his speech, a drenching cloudburst drove half the supporters from the stands. The wind whipped the few strands of hair on his head, as well as the pages of his speech, each in a protective cover. He wore a borrowed see-through plastic raincoat, and his pant legs were rolled up above his ankles. Occasional thunderclaps drowned out his words. Eisenhower soldiered on, though, stating his philosophy on foreign policy and outlining his conservative views on domestic matters: government spending should be cut, unnecessary federal agencies should be eliminated, government controls to fight inflation should be removed, and the responsibility for civil rights should be turned over to the states. Whether or not one agreed with his words, the picture was dismal.

The following day, an Eisenhower press conference was scheduled to give reporters the chance to question the candidate more closely on the issues. But that night Hagerty announced that television cameras and lights were not welcome, explaining that the Washington press corps of print journalists resented the intrusive presence of television. David Schoenbrun, though—who was now the CBS correspondent assigned to cover the Eisenhower campaign—suspected it was the general himself who initiated the TV blackout. The stakes were high for all involved. Print journalists wanted to retain their superior position. Television networks wanted parity. The Eisenhower campaign wanted to control the candidate's forum. Voters did not yet fully realize that they, too, had a vested interest in the outcome of this showdown.

The top executives at the three main TV networks—Bill Paley of CBS, David Sarnoff of NBC, and Leonard Goldenson of ABC—knew this was a defining moment for the medium and refused to be denied access. "Wherever a pencil goes, our cameras go," became the slogan in the fight for the fundamental right of television news to cover a presidential candidate.[6] If TV journalism was ever to gain legitimacy as a member of the fourth estate, this battle had to be fought.

Cameras had already been installed in the Plaza Theatre—which had been Abilene's "opry house" when Eisenhower was a boy—but the Republican National Committee was insisting they had to be taken out. Edward R. Murrow remembered that the wrangling "culminated with a heated late-night exchange aboard the campaign train with the Eisenhower coterie led by Press Secretary James Hagerty."[7] Murrow warned that the cameras were expensive and delicate pieces of equipment and if they were moved by anyone other than CBS technicians, the Republicans would be liable for any damages.

The standoff was still not resolved the next morning. David Schoenbrun, selected to be the all-network pool reporter for TV, was in an awkward spot. He entered the theater not knowing whether he would be turned away. His directive from the network was to force his way through any security barrier and to defy any orders to leave. The image of a newsman being carried away would not help the cause of getting Ike elected—and might cause voters to question why they were being prevented from watching the news conference. The Eisenhower campaign, beginning to recognize the inevitability of television's participation in the political process, relented. Television journalists had called the bluff of the Republican National Committee and struck a blow against second-class citizenship.

In the summer of 1952, radio still had a larger overall audience than television. But that was changing fast, especially in the populous Northeast. In the evening hours, though, more TV sets than radios were switched on because Americans were getting acclimated to video entertainment like My Little Margie and I've Got a Secret in prime time.

Although television had covered both of the party nominating conventions in 1948, the 1952 Republican Convention in Chicago was the first at which television news possessed the technical resources and attracted a large-enough audience to have a significant political impact. At the recommendation of the TV networks, the International Amphitheater was chosen as the convention site. Instead of constructing the platform in front of the auditorium, television producers instructed that it be placed in the corner, with the delegates seated diagonally, in order to create a better picture on the small TV screen.[8] The performance of speakers at the podium was enhanced by the use of a TelePrompTer. The introduction of zoom lenses and handheld cameras nicknamed "creepie peepies" gave the coverage much greater range and mobility. Interviews with delegates on the floor and the politicians who were trying to cut deals with them gave viewers a lesson in convention power wielding.

Eisenhower's key rival for the nomination was Senator Robert Taft, known sentimentally as "Mr. Republican." Taft claimed he had 607 committed delegate votes going into the convention—three more than he needed to win the nomination. But his tally included disputed delegates from three Southern states. Delegates chosen by precinct conventions from Texas, Louisiana, and Georgia were more favorable to Ike. The state committees, though, selected an alternative slate of Taft supporters who demanded their place at the convention.

The issue would be decided at a credentials committee hearing. The Taft campaign wanted to keep TV cameras out on the assumption that an open hearing would likely give Ike the edge. So, this time the Eisenhower campaign was insisting on the right of television cameras and the American public to go behind the closed doors. It was an absolute about-face from the Republican position in Abilene. The vote by Taft's allies to hold the deliberations out of public view was a public relations disaster.

Political historian Steve Neal writes, "Walter Cronkite, making his debut as the anchorman for CBS News, stood with a microphone outside the locked doors of the hearing room and made constant reference to the secrecy of the proceedings." TV coverage of the controversy was affecting the opinions of viewers at home, who began telephoning and telegraphing their delegates with complaints about Taft's steamroller approach. "Television was unkind to Taft," Neal observes. He was a skillful debater and was respected for his thoughtful style of argumentation, "but at the Chicago convention, Taft came across on the little screen as defensive and testy."[9] The presence of television cameras was undermining a candidate's support—the first solid evidence that the medium was transforming the nominating process.

Delegates to both party conventions in 1952 were warned that probing TV lenses could capture embarrassing moments. Reading a newspaper in the audience while a speaker was at the podium would translate into a show of boredom, as would a gaping yawn. They were even cautioned to be prudent about what they said to each other on the convention floor for fear of lip-reading viewers. Women were advised against wearing dresses with large floral prints. And ostentatious jewelry brought with it the risk of alienating working-class voters. The reality of presidential politics in the Television Age was that network producers—not party officials—decided what aspect of the convention would be shown.

The former president of NBC News, Reuven Frank, was a news writer covering the nominating conventions for the network in 1952. In his autobiography, Frank pinpoints that year as the one in which television began to dominate political decision making. "Old hands were learning," he said of campaign managers; "new ones were growing up conditioned to know that no decision is judged solely on its merits. First you asked how it will look on television."[10]

Although it must have seemed ridiculous to him, even Speaker of the House Sam Rayburn, the bald, rough-hewn chairman of the 1952 Democratic convention, agreed to wear makeup gavel to gavel. Betty Furness, however, was accustomed to the cosmetic requirements of television. She was the spokeswoman for Westinghouse appliances, which had purchased the CBS television coverage of both political conventions in 1952. At each convention, she performed a cycle of ninety-six live commercials. "I logged more air time than any speaker of either party," Furness recalled; "and because an enormous number of people had bought TV sets just to watch the conventions, I became famous."[11]

The Democrats nominated Adlai Stevenson, the governor of Illinois, who disliked appearing on television as much as his opponent did. Stevenson had different shortcomings, though. Unlike Eisenhower, Stevenson was a man of eloquent words, an intellectual who was loath to simplify and shorten his remarks to meet the demands of the medium. Although Ike was far from a common man, he allowed his media advisors to strategize on how to best convey the common touch. To Stevenson, it all felt like a gimmick, and he rejected the notion of developing a TV technique. Lew Gomavitz, the director of the whimsical TV show, *Kukla, Fran and Ollie,* was one of Stevenson's media advisors. He was given the task of helping the candidate relax in front of the cameras. He recalled, "Adlai was great in small groups where there was no pressure, but he couldn't speak on television. He'd freeze and forget his lines. . . . Adlai was afraid to adlib. I just couldn't get him to loosen up."[12] Republican media strategist Ted Rogers explained the contrast between the two men simply: "Stevenson didn't listen to his people (media advisors). Eisenhower did. That was the difference."[13]

In the presidential election of 1952, television was a totally new element in campaigning, and the Republicans had more than double the money to spend on advertising than the Democrats did. Early in the campaign, Stevenson told his supporters, "I am frank to say without embarrassment or self-consciousness that I think the Democratic national ticket will by no means be able to match the Republican campaign dollar for dollar."[14] They didn't even come close. The Democrats spent $1.2 million on radio and television that year, while the Republicans spent more than $2.5 million.

The powerhouse agency Batten, Barton, Durstine and Osborn (BBD&O) was awarded the accounts of both the Republican National Committee and the Citizens for Eisenhower-Nixon. The goal of the ad agency's campaign, according to its president Ben Duffy, was "merchandising Eisenhower's frankness, honesty and integrity, his sincere and wholesome approach." Bruce Barton suggested that Ike emulate the on-air performance style of Bishop Fulton J. Sheen, the star of the successful program of the era *Life Is Worth Living*. If the candidate just used notes, as Sheen did, instead of a scripted speech, he would give the impression of "talking to people as one frank, unassuming American to his fellow Americans."[15]

While Eisenhower waged an intensive, old-fashioned, whistle-stop campaign on a train dubbed "Look Ahead, Neighbor," his media advisors worked on advertising strategy. Stevenson's PR people came from news media backgrounds or had served in government information posts. Eisenhower's team, in contrast, was skilled in product advertising and understood the landscape of prime time. They placed Ike's campaign spots before and after highly rated programs, like *The Jack Benny Show*, knowing a huge audience would already have been assembled at the expense of the shows' big sponsors.[16]

Stevenson's campaign made the costly mistake of displacing entire programs, instead of piggybacking on their popularity. One evening, viewers tuning in to see America's favorite situation comedy were greeted instead by a Stevenson campaign program. A letter to the candidate from a highly disappointed fan of the series said, "I love Lucy, I like Ike, drop dead."[17]

The famous adman Rosser Reeves was a consultant to the general's media team. After reviewing all the candidate's public remarks, Reeves concluded that Eisenhower was introducing too many themes for any one to have impact. Research conducted by George Gallup indicated the American people were most concerned about three issues: Korea, corruption, and the cost of living. Eisenhower's speeches were combed for his words on those issues, and scripts were prepared for an ad campaign called "Eisenhower Answers America." On September 11, 1952, Eisenhower recorded his "answers" to questions that would be asked and filmed later. The candidate was nearsighted and required eyeglasses to read the cue cards. Reeves decided the glasses had to go, so the scripts were rewritten as headlines on poster boards held close enough for Ike to see without squinting.

The original plan was to send camera crews across the country to find diverse citizens to pose the questions. But another idea turned out to be more efficient. Tourists who stood in line at Radio City Music Hall in New York came from all walks of life and all areas of the country. There were many regional accents and various styles of dress. Those who fit the casting requirements were asked to come to the film studio just a few blocks away. They read the questions from cue cards. Footage of the ordinary citizens was edited with the Eisenhower film to give the impression they were in the same room looking at each other face to face.

If, on the one hand, television news was being admitted to report and to reveal the democratic process, on the other hand, the medium was being used to invent political imagery out of whole cloth. Eisenhower wasn't entirely comfortable with the artificiality of the ad campaign. He complained between film takes, "To think that an old soldier should come to this."[18]

Stevenson expressed great distaste for a presidential candidate being packaged and sold like a breakfast cereal or detergent. The erudite, also baldheaded, Democrat—for whom the term "egghead" was coined—could be off-putting to average voters. Media historian Erik Barnouw explains that Stevenson's "verbal brilliance" actually became a liability during the campaign. The Democrat "became a target for anti-intellectuals," he reports, "who scorned his 'teacup words.'"[19] Eisenhower couldn't resist a little dig to underscore this perception. During one of his campaign speeches, Ike apologized after using the Latin phrase "status quo." It was Stevenson, he said, who was the intellectual candidate. Even though Eisenhower had been the president of Columbia University from 1948 to 1950 and still, in fact, lived in the university president's house at Morningside Heights, he avoided any veneer of intellectualism.

In the 1952 presidential campaign, the image of Ike held by most Americans was shaped, or created, by salespeople. The significance of a candidate's reliance on those skilled in the manipulative arts would become more debatable with each passing quadrennial. A salesperson who works on a campaign, writes advertising analyst Earl Shorris, "can avoid the ethical questions associated with politics by stating his belief in the wisdom of the electorate; it is the moral comfort of the 'invisible hand' brought to politics."[20]

The TV networks hoped for a close race and a dramatic election night. Both CBS and NBC were proud to show off the brand new Univac computers that would rapidly tabulate votes. But there was little tension to be mined. Eisenhower's victory was evident early on in the coverage. Ultimately he received 55 percent of the vote and carried forty-one of the forty-eight states.

About half the population of the United States watched some part of the televised inaugural festivities on January 20, 1953.[21] In appliance stores and classrooms, corner bars and city halls, a new tradition was taking shape—Americans were beginning to use television as a gathering place to view events of consequence to the republic.

During his first year in office, Eisenhower's TV appearances were hardly stellar. In June 1953, for instance, a thirty-minute broadcast titled *Television Report to the American People by the President and Members of the Cabinet* aired on all networks. The meeting of Eisenhower and four cabinet members was ostensibly intended to give the public an inside view of the president in an informal round-table discussion with his team. But it was really an event carefully orchestrated by BBD&O.

The day before the telecast, a rehearsal was held in the White House conference room with strict secrecy precautions. The *Washington Post* reported: "The White House itself took on something of a Radio City appearance. Television technicians and advertising agency officials scurried through the lobby in a bustle of preparations. . . . White House reporters were barred from the conference room, which has been transformed into a TV studio."[22] The purportedly spontaneous chat was actually scripted, and cue cards were provided for the participants, resulting in a stilted dialogue. The awkwardness of the program was well noted in press coverage. The producer of the broadcast acknowledged in his own critique, "The show was not the best in the world."[23]

Helping the president hone a more natural style on TV required more time and effort than press secretary Jim Hagerty could devote. In December 1953, a Hollywood insider volunteered to help. Robert Montgomery had appeared in forty motion pictures, was experienced in film directing, had served four terms as president of the Screen Actors Guild, and was host of the NBC dramatic anthology series *Robert Montgomery Presents*. He understood makeup, lighting, and camera direction. Montgomery came to the White House to prepare Ike for a Christmas telecast and ended up staying on as a special consultant to the president for the next seven years.

Eisenhower was a fan of radio and TV star Arthur Godfrey's down-home style. Montgomery worked to combine that type of folksiness with the aura of Ike's World War II leadership. His concern was never the content of the president's television appearances; it was the tenor of his delivery and the cosmetic dimensions. Montgomery used stand-ins similar to Eisenhower in stature, appearance, and skin tone. Studio tests allowed decisions to be made about makeup and wardrobe without any time demands on the president.

Helping President Eisenhower (center, seated) hone a more natural TV style was former screen actor, director, and media advisor Robert Montgomery (left, pointing) and press secretary John Hagerty (right). Courtesy of the Dwight D. Eisenhower Library.

For the first two years of his presidency, Eisenhower maintained the tightly controlled news conference policy of his predecessor, Harry Truman. No photographs, no film or broadcast, and no direct quotations were allowed without White House authorization. Journalism historians Michael Emery and Edwin Emery observe that such safeguards offered some protection from Truman's tendency to "shoot from the hip." Ike too benefited from a safety net. "Eisenhower made many slips of the tongue," the Emerys explain; he "thought faster than he talked, and skipped parts of sentences so that press-conference transcripts had to be reworded to be intelligible. A penetrating personal question might bring a display of the famed Eisenhower controlled anger." [24]

By the time of the 1954 midterm elections, though, a majority of American voters also owned television sets, and TV news producers were growing more interested in visuals to tell the story. Incrementally, the press conference restrictions were relaxed, and on January 19, 1955, movie cameras were permitted to record the president's news conference for delayed broadcast on television.

This was the beginning of a major shift in presidential communication. No longer were the chief executive's words and ideas always filtered through reporters or subject to political analysis. Press conferences were now a vehicle for the president to talk directly to the American public. In Ike's first TV press conference, for example, a question about his reelection plans gave him the opportunity to spend five minutes telling the viewers in eight million homes about the successes of his administration.

The guessing game about whether Eisenhower would run again took a somber turn on September 24, 1955. While vacationing in Denver, the president suffered a heart attack. Several weeks of convalescence followed, during which time James Hagerty became a familiar presence on American TV screens as he gave frequent updates on the president's progress. The press secretary attempted to guide the public perception of Ike away from that of an elderly, frail patient to that of a strong leader who had a medical setback and was getting better every day.

Though Hagerty was not dishonest with journalists, he was strategically manipulative. Lewis Gould writes in *The Modern American Presidency*, "[Hagerty] made sure that the press had ample amounts of trivia but provided little in the way of real information about the state of the president's health."[25] The flood of medical minutiae—even a report on the chief executive's bowel movement—moved the focus of attention off longer-term health issues. Hagerty wanted to keep open the option of his boss running for reelection. So he didn't offer full disclosure. He told the press about what the president ate, what books he read, what music he listened to, the color of his pajamas, and the décor of his room. But, explains one historian of the Eisenhower health crisis, Hagerty was careful "not to reveal the occasional small medical setbacks, such as the transient pains . . . or worries about arrhythmia."[26]

Months of recuperation followed. The president returned to work in the Oval Office in late December 1955. Although he had made a full recovery, he still pondered the wisdom of embarking on another strenuous campaign. But Ike considered all of the younger Republicans who were likely to be candidates in 1956, including Vice President Nixon, to be deficient in some way. He concluded that duty compelled him to run again to prevent the election of a Democrat. The president told his press secretary, "I just hate to turn this country back into the hands of people like Stevenson, Harriman and Kefauver."[27]

Ike announced his intention on February 29, 1956. He had decided that it would be unbefitting of a sitting president to "barnstorm" the country on a train as he did in his first campaign. Television was the vehicle of choice in 1956. In the quadrennial since his first campaign, the number of TV sets in the country had doubled, and the number of television stations had quadrupled.

The plan was to have the president participate in fewer than a half dozen nationwide broadcasts during the election season. Eisenhower had some concern that voters might interpret his lack of travel as unwillingness to work for reelection. The low-key approach, however, made all the more sense after the president suffered another medical

Ike announced his intention to run for a second term on television on February 29, 1956. Robert Montgomery (center, pointing) gives some last-minute advice to the president (center, seated). Courtesy of the Dwight D. Eisenhower Library.

crisis in June 1956 that involved abdominal surgery for a digestive problem. During his weeks of recovery, Eisenhower had lost weight and was frustrated with the natural fatigue he was experiencing. By the time of the Republican convention in San Francisco in late August, however, he looked and felt much better—like a vigorous sixty-five-year-old man who was ready to work for another four years.

By 1956, both political parties had retooled their convention programs to better fit the demands of television coverage. The pace of the telecasts, party managers understood, was critical to keeping viewers watching. So stricter time limits were imposed on speakers, tedious introductions and seconding speeches for vice-presidential candidates were eliminated, roll-call votes were streamlined, and parliamentary procedures were downplayed. Daytime sessions were dropped so that the conventions were entirely prime-time affairs.[28]

The 1956 Republican convention, the party's centennial gathering, held little in the way of surprises. Since the outcome of the nomination was already known before home viewers tuned in, drama had to be manufactured in other ways. The arrival of the president in San Francisco, for example, was precisely planned for live TV pictures of the first family being met by an enthusiastic crowd at the airport and along the motorcade route to the St. Francis Hotel. Dozens of portable cameras roaming the floor of the Cow Palace could capture the sparkle and spectacle so well planned to convey the feel of spontaneity on the small screen.

During the general election, the media savvy of the GOP steam-
rollered the Democratic ticket of Adlai Stevenson and Estes Kefauver. The Republicans again engaged the services of BBD&O, while
the Democrats had a hard time even finding an agency to take their
account. The Democrats were given the cold shoulder, it was reported in the trade press at the time, because "big agency men don't
want to alienate the Republican businessmen who head many client
companies."[29]

The paid advertising of Eisenhower's campaign focused on personality projection, with a greater emphasis on production values than
had been employed four years earlier. Among the election broadcasts
was one targeted at housewives. The president and his wife Mamie
participated in a televised chat session with seven women, who, in
1956, preferred to be called "ladies." The set looked like a comfortable
living room in a middle-class home. The host and hostess were informal with their guests, who wanted to know not only about weighty
matters like the economy and national security but also about Ike's
childhood. The program aired in the afternoon and gave the feeling of
a block meeting in a pleasant neighborhood.

Another Republican innovation in 1956 was the five-minute
"hitchhike" campaign program. Sponsors of popular thirty-minute
prime-time series were persuaded by the Eisenhower camp to offer a
twenty-five-minute version of the program and allow the Republican
National Committee to purchase the remaining time. Just as with

*The paid advertising of
Eisenhower's 1956 campaign
focused on personality
projection, such as in the
homey "Women Ask the
President" spots. Courtesy of
the Dwight D. Eisenhower
Library.*

the thirty-second "piggybacks" in 1952, the hitchhikes automatically garnered large audiences by virtue of their placement.[30]

On election eve, an hour-long broadcast originating from the White House, featuring the president, the first lady, Vice President Nixon, and his wife Pat, hosted by newsman John Cameron Swayze, appeared on all three networks. Media scholar Craig Allen describes it as "one of early TV's most elaborate displays of film, live broadcasting, and production razzle-dazzle." The telecast included reporters in various cities—most of whom, Allen reveals, were "actually hired actors"—commenting on Eisenhower's groundswell of support "as if returns were already coming in."[31] It was a deceptive technique, but even before the first vote was cast, all indicators pointed to the Eisenhower landslide as a fait accompli.

In the first year of Ike's second term, the country faced several domestic and international crises that prompted the president to request free airtime of the television networks to speak to the American people. In autumn 1957, the integration of Central High School in Little Rock, Arkansas, was the first racial conflict that television covered comprehensively and on location. The situation created a dilemma for the president. Personally, he felt sympathy for Southern whites who wanted to keep schools segregated. But as the commander in chief, he could not allow federal law to be flouted by a recalcitrant governor and mob of violent extremists.

Eisenhower hoped, in vain, that moderation and deliberation would prevail. Finally, though, he ordered the U.S. Army into Little Rock and put authorities and citizens on notice that their resistance was to cease and desist. That night he explained his actions on television, stating "the foundation of the American way of life is our national respect for law." Eisenhower biographer Stephen Ambrose observed about the address to the nation, "Eisenhower had to be pushed to the wall before he would act, but at the critical moment, he lived up to the oath of his office."[32]

The launch of the Soviet satellite *Sputnik*, also in the autumn of 1957, was the subject of four television addresses by President Eisenhower. He attempted to reassure citizens that American defenses had not been jeopardized and to calm the lingering fears about deficiencies in U.S. education and commitment to lead in space exploration.

After so many formal televised appearances from behind his desk in the Oval Office, which seemed to signal crisis and foreboding, the president hoped to add some variety to the format of future broadcasts. He proposed an idea to Robert Montgomery. The media advisor's first instinct was to veto the plan—but, unfortunately, he didn't.

Upon returning from a NATO meeting in Paris, which he attended with John Foster Dulles, Eisenhower suggested a report to the nation in a joint television appearance with his secretary of state. Eisenhower had recently suffered a very mild stroke that caused no lasting effects. He wanted to show the American people that he was fine. Montgomery had no problem with that reasoning. He understood, too, that the president's willingness to share credit and put others in the limelight was a virtue citizens appreciated. But Dulles was more soporific than inspirational in his style of public address, and Montgomery had no time to coach him in any depth.

The compromise between Ike and his media advisor was an interactive format. The president and the secretary of state would engage in give-and-take for a more lively telecast. Montgomery assumed both men understood the plan. But Dulles delivered a twenty-minute monologue. The TV director, expecting an exchange, stayed primarily on a two-shot that revealed Eisenhower fidgeting with his eyeglasses, shifting his weight, and looking generally disengaged. Although it had nothing to do with his mental acuity, the picture sent the image of someone who wasn't able to keep up with an important discussion.

In the following year, Eisenhower's media appearances declined, as 1958 was fraught with difficulties for the White House. The economy was in a mess, with both unemployment and inflation rising. The GOP did poorly in the midterm elections. And in the waning hours of the year, a revolution in Cuba put rebel leader Fidel Castro in a position of unchallenged authority, which the U.S. government correctly assumed would be murderously abused. With a Democratic majority in both houses of Congress, Eisenhower realized he had little chance of accomplishing any significant domestic initiatives in his final two years in office. International affairs and his legacy were paramount now. Two modern technologies—jet air travel and television—combined to set the scene for the last act of the Eisenhower administration.

In the summer of 1959, the first jet plane available to a U.S. chief executive—a Boeing 707 called *Air Force One*—was at Ike's disposal. It made travel easier, faster, and more comfortable. Eisenhower sincerely believed a U.S. president could advance the cause of world peace by personal outreach. He also understood, along with his advisers, the potential such travel carried for cementing his image as an outstanding international leader. During his last eighteen months in office, then, Eisenhower visited Europe, the Far East, and South America. Television cameras followed each leg of the journeys. He met with Pope John XXIII in Rome and with Prime Minister Jawaharlal Nehru in New Delhi, where the president addressed a massive crowd estimated to be in the millions. In Tehran he lunched with Shah Mohammad Reza Pahlovi, and in Madrid Ike had breakfast with Generalissimo Francisco Franco. Little official business was accomplished, nor intended, on Ike's travels. But viewers back home saw their president as a towering statesman.

It was a humbled Eisenhower, though, who held a press conference on May 10, 1960—taking full responsibility for the decision to send a U-2 spy plane over the Soviet Union just weeks before he was to have a summit meeting with Nikita Khrushchev. When the Soviets announced they had shot down the American plane on May 1st, or May Day, the day of communist celebration, the United States claimed it was an unarmed weather plane that had flown off course. The White House assumed the pilot, Francis Gary Powers, who had ejected the aircraft, had not survived and that the plane had been obliterated. The official lies seemed safe. But Powers was not dead and had in fact confessed that he was on a spy mission. Film of Khrushchev giving a tour of the plane wreckage was made available to broadcast systems around the world.

The remaining months of 1960 continued to be depressing for Eisenhower as he watched Richard Nixon make mistakes in elementary media strategy in his presidential contest with John F. Kennedy. The America to which Ike was returning as a private citizen was a vastly different place than the country he headed on the day of his first inauguration. Much of the cultural transformation could be attributed to television and advertising.

In the late 1950s, a debate about American materialism and its glorification on television emerged among scholars and social critics. In the 1957 best seller *The Hidden Persuaders*, author Vance Packard

On May 10, 1960, President Eisenhower faces the cameras to take full responsibility for the U-2 spy plane incident. Courtesy of the Dwight D. Eisenhower Library.

warned, "Marketers are being admonished to reassure consumers that the hedonistic approach to life is the moral one and that frugality and personal austerity are outdated hangovers of Puritanism."[33] The following year, John Kenneth Galbraith's book *The Affluent Society* made the case that advertising was creating synthetic needs and damaging desires in American citizens. He claimed that while Americans were enjoying private prosperity, the public sector was becoming impoverished.[34] Television and advertising, two critical elements in Eisenhower's journey to the White House, were now displacing the World War II–era values of thrift, sacrifice, and discipline.

JFK Masters the Medium

As a rising star on the political scene, young John Kennedy experienced none of the awkwardness with television that had dogged Eisenhower.[35] His appearances in the early 1950s on news panel discussion shows, such as *Meet the Press*, were not flawless, but his ease in front of cameras was apparent. In 1956, he learned firsthand the magnitude of television's impact. Although the senator from Massachusetts lost his bid to be the vice presidential nominee on the Democratic ticket, his consolation prize was to deliver the convention speech nominating Adlai Stevenson. Kennedy's prominent television exposure at the 1956 Democratic convention made the winsome war hero "overnight a nationally acclaimed figure."[36] He was very soon the most sought after speaker in the Democratic Party and clearly a strong contender for 1960.

Kennedy's reelection to the Senate in 1958 was a romp. His 1957 Pulitzer Prize for *Profiles in Courage* elevated his status and made him an especially attractive guest on network public affairs programs. He understood that the medium was his ally. The readers of *TV Guide* spotted John Kennedy's byline in the November 14, 1959, issue. In his article, "A Force That Has Changed the Political Scene," he argued that a candidate's television image should be considered a substantive factor in his capacity to govern and lead. "Honesty, vigor, compassion, intelligence—the presence or lack of these and other qualities make up what is called the candidate's 'image,'" he wrote; "my own conviction is that these images or impressions are likely to be uncannily correct."

Throughout the presidential campaign of 1960, Kennedy displayed far greater astuteness about the process of television production than his opponent did. The most critical example of this gap in attention to details is the first of the televised Great Debates. A week before the broadcast, Kennedy himself joined his broadcast strategist J. Leonard Reinsch, in a meeting with Don Hewitt, the director of the

CBS telecast. Hewitt recalls, "Kennedy was very curious. He wanted to know, 'Where do I stand?' 'How long do I have to answer?' Will I get a warning when I've gone too far?' He really wanted to know the nuts and bolts of what we were going to do."[37] Among the things they discussed were set design and shooting patterns. Nixon was afforded the same opportunity, but declined, thinking his time could be put to better use studying his "campaign bible" of facts and statistics.[38] "I never saw Nixon before they arrived in the studio that night,"[39] Hewitt remembers. "They just didn't think it was that important," the director concluded about Nixon's inner circle.[40]

The image problems the Republican candidate encountered on September 26, 1960, could have been remedied if he had applied the TV lessons Eisenhower had learned the hard way. A skillful application of makeup would have improved Nixon's peaked appearance, but he refused after hearing Kennedy say no to an offer of makeup. A better-fitted shirt collar and a crisper dark suit would have been an easy fix, but appearance didn't register as an important detail at the time. So Nixon, who had recently lost eight pounds during a hospital stay, went on the air with a slightly sagging collar and a light gray suit that blended blandly into the neutral gray set. An understanding that even when he wasn't speaking he might be on camera could have spared Nixon a few embarrassing moments.

President Eisenhower later complained about Nixon's failure to accept his advice or help: "Dick never asked me how the campaign should be run. I offered him [Robert] Montgomery, who would never have let him look as he did in that first television debate."[41]

Another mistake was Nixon's old-fashioned, and exhausting, pledge to visit every state in the Union. The Kennedy campaign knew that tactic was unnecessary in the television age because viewers everywhere in the country would get to know the candidate through the tube. The Democratic travel schedule emphasized swing states instead, allowing JFK to make personal appearances where they were likely to be most helpful.

In 1960, the Democrats made greater use of the five-minute hitchhikes at the end of popular programs, a technique the Eisenhower campaigns had proven effective. Nixon, in contrast, favored thirty-minute programs packed with more information—but they preempted regularly scheduled entertainment and disrupted viewing routines. Not only were they less appealing to viewers, but also they cost considerably more to air.

Kennedy's commercials were an intentional blend of image and substance, while the Republican team made little use of impressionistic ads. Nixon preferred straightforward spots, such as those in which he sat on the edge of a desk in front of a plain background. Talking straight into the camera, the candidate would answer a question from a voice-over announcer: "Mr. Nixon, what is the truth about our defenses? How strong should they be?"[42]

The vice president's failure to appreciate the potency of stylized TV imagery did not wane—even in the home stretch. Nixon's media staff had prepared a film called *Ambassador of Friendship*, meant to evoke a rousing and heroic image, which they planned to be televised nationally following *The Ed Sullivan Show* on the Sunday before election day. But the candidate nixed the presentation and chose instead to go on the air himself to make his positions on the issues perfectly clear.

The Image Candidates provides some insight into Nixon's resistance to campaign advertising that was focused on character and personality rather than policy alone. Author Gene Wyckoff was a television writer and producer who worked on the image-oriented programs that the candidate rebuffed. "It was not that he disagreed with the premise," Wyckoff recalled; "rather he seemed not to understand the premise and therefore relegated such television effort to a low priority in his campaign efforts." Contributing to the problem, Wyckoff adds, was the fact that Nixon's closest advisers were "oriented to newspapers rather than television," which made it difficult for the media advisers "to have any time alone with the candidate."[43]

On election eve, NBC president Robert Kintner told his assembled news staff, "Men you may think this election is a contest between Kennedy and Nixon. It's not. It's a race between NBC and CBS."[44] While NBC would emerge victorious in the ratings race by a wide margin, the political contest came to a close just the way any TV dramatist would have scripted it. It was a horse race with a photo finish. More than 90 percent of the television sets in American homes were tuned in for some part of the coverage. In the following days, the significance of television in the outcome of the election became the subject of wide discussion in classrooms and around office water coolers. Most people came to the same conclusion the president-elect and the defeated candidate did—television was indeed the edge in the razor-thin margin of victory.

A postelection survey by public opinion analyst Elmo Roper found that "57 per cent of the voters said they had been influenced to an extent by the debates." Of those who "decided how to cast their ballots on the basis of television performances . . . their verdict was 3 to 1 for Kennedy, providing him with considerably more votes than the 2/100th of 1 per cent by which he won the popular count."[45]

January 20, 1960, Inauguration Day, was full of striking television imagery: the touching sight of the elderly poet Robert Frost blinded by the sun's glare as he attempted to read his manuscript; the reserve of Kennedy's wife and the exuberance of his sisters; and the gracious and familiar smile of a now former president who suddenly looked very old. TV pictures presented a wonderfully paradoxical portrait of John Kennedy on that first day. It was the new leader of the free world who punctuated the lofty rhetoric of his inaugural address with emphatic finger jabs. But it was a regular kind of guy who got caught running a pocket comb through his generously endowed head of hair when he thought no one was looking.

The New Frontier was off and running, but television would do more than simply follow. An unspoken alliance had been formed, a symbiotic bond between Kennedy and the medium. An unprecedented sense of familiarity and proprietary interest on the part of the American public toward a U.S. president and his family would develop because of television.

Five days after he took the oath of office, Kennedy conducted the first live televised presidential press conference. Though it would not be true for any of his successors in the twentieth century, for the thirty-fifth president of the United States, no more mutually beneficial arrangement between the medium and the man could have been devised. Some argued that live television could be hazardous—a slip of the tongue could be embarrassing to the United States or its allies. But John Kennedy was sure enough of his own rhetorical and intellectual capabilities to take the uncushioned chance.

More than four hundred reporters were present at the live press conference debut, which took place in the spacious State Department auditorium. While many of them were not sitting as close to the president as they would have preferred, the home viewers had ringside seats. They could examine his face and observe his expressions freely.

After the first three live press conferences, *Television Magazine* felt safe in declaring "television has proven about as hazardous for Kennedy as water for a fish."[46] Even early skeptics could not deny that the president's grace under pressure and his capacity to retain information were remarkable. Kennedy also possessed a stylistic virtue essential to the small screen—he was not overexpressive in his bearing. On a medium that magnifies personalities and mannerisms, this reserve translated into a dignified, statesmanlike persona. He also employed an economy of language well suited to television. While he could be charmingly evasive, he could also be uncommonly direct, answering a question with a single word, "No."

After watching rebroadcasts of the first few press conferences, JFK was a bit concerned with the lighting and camera angles. So famed TV and film director Franklin Schaffner was brought to Washington to

JFK was especially adept at using live press conferences to talk directly to the American people. Courtesy of the John F. Kennedy Library.

JFK was especially adept at using live press conferences to talk directly to the American people. Courtesy of the John F. Kennedy Library.

consult on the setup for the telecasts. Kennedy grasped the nuances of television in a way that surprised CBS newsman George Herman. Kennedy opened his press conference on March 23, 1961, with a statement on the advance of communist-backed rebels in Laos. Herman observed that when the president spoke, "he didn't look at any reporter in the auditorium. . . . He was not trying to give the appearance of a news conference; he wasn't looking around the room. He looked right over all our heads, right into the camera with the red tally light on it, the one he knew was on. It was clear to me at that time that this was a man who was extraordinarily professional and that this was something that was carefully planned. This was to go direct to the people."[47]

NBC correspondent Ray Scherer also observed JFK's awareness of picture power. In the spring of 1961, Kennedy, who had just returned from Vienna, the site of a summit with Khrushchev, was about to deliver his first formal national television address. Scherer recalled the president remarking that he didn't think he looked his best in a recent television appearance. Kennedy said, "These lights sometimes give me a double chin." The president asked a *New York Times* photographer to sit in his chair while he checked out the shot. "He squinted through the viewfinder of one of the cameras," Scherer said; "he didn't like what he saw." The technicians suggested that the president go to the remote truck in the White House driveway and look at that monitor while they adjusted the lighting to remove the shadow under the proxy's chin. "As Mr. Kennedy walked to the truck," explained Scherer, "electricians lowered each of seven floodlights in the office six inches. The President peered into the monitor tube and decided this was a vast improvement."[48]

By the end of his first year in the White House, Kennedy had become a familiar face in American homes. Everything about him and his young family fascinated TV viewers, and the networks provided a steady flow of images. This caused an imbalance, though, between the reporting of the presidency and the coverage of Congress and the Supreme Court. During the Kennedy years, because of television, the executive branch psychologically became the center of American government. In *The Twilight of the Presidency*, George Reedy notes that increased television coverage of the president and his family changed the "bully pulpit" into a much more encompassing space—a stage. "A pulpit," he writes, "is a platform for persuasion and exhortation." A stage, in contrast, "can be an instrument for education and leadership or an attention-getting device for entertainment." No other government official enjoyed a venue of such direct connection with citizens. "As a stage," says Reedy, "the White House has no equal in the electronic age."[49]

Arguably the most critical television address of the Kennedy presidency occurred in the autumn of 1962. On the morning of October 22nd, White House press secretary Pierre Salinger requested that the television networks prepare for an address from the president of highest national security. That same morning, Franklin Schaffner arrived at the White House and noticed an unusually high degree of security. Salinger had summoned the film director to help make the president look as relaxed as possible on camera. The medication Kennedy took for his painful back condition resulted in puffiness in his face. Schaffner recommended lighting and lenses that contributed an extra measure of confidence to the president. After giving his hair a final brushstroke, Kennedy took his place at his desk. Viewers at home were hearing announcements like "*Stump the Stars* will not be seen tonight." The president got right to the point: there were missiles in Cuba, they were deliberately provocative, and this was unacceptable. It was the first time television was used as a forum for international diplomacy. Eschewing traditional channels to negotiate with Moscow, Kennedy issued a public ultimatum that left little room for bargaining.

The holiday season of 1962 was a bright one for the thirty-fifth president. His mettle had been tested and proven superior. Because of his frequent press conferences, John Kennedy was cautiously selective about other TV appearances. He understood that the mystique of leadership could not survive unsparing entry. Normally, the numerous requests for TV interviews were turned down. But in the weeks after the successful conclusion of the Cuban Missile Crisis, the networks were clamoring for access, and the president thought the time might be perfect for interviews.

Each network had individually requested a year-end TV discussion with Kennedy. The White House press secretary, Pierre Salinger, offered the president's availability for a sixty-minute program that would include one newsman from each network. It would be less formal than a press conference. But, absolutely mandatory to the plan, was the provision that ninety minutes would be taped and thirty minutes would be edited from the conversation. Salinger explained that this arrangement would allow for slow sections or less-interesting comments to be deleted, resulting in a better program. Only CBS News President Dick Salant protested the stipulation and considered pulling out of the venture. But Salinger reassured all the participants that the White House would in no way interfere with the editing process. One representative of each network would form the committee that would make editing decisions.

On December 16, Bill Lawrence of ABC, Sander Vanocur of NBC, and George Herman of CBS sat in a cozy cluster around the president in his rocking chair in the Oval Office. After about fifty minutes, Kennedy suggested they all take a coffee break. Then they continued the discussion for another half hour. The official title of the broadcast, which aired the following day, was *After Two Years: A Conversation with the President.* But it came to be called "The Rocking Chair Chat." A case could easily be made that it was the most effective TV appearance of Kennedy's presidency. He was clever and funny. He was contemplative and charming. He displayed a graceful command of the English language as he looked back at the first half of his administration. "Success has a hundred fathers and defeat is an orphan," he said in reference to the debacle at the Bay of Pigs. And, in a remarkably perceptive stroke of self-assessment, he claimed, "Appearances contribute to reality."

What viewers couldn't see was the amount of control John Kennedy exercised in this situation. After the program was recorded, George Herman realized, "Every time we asked an unfriendly question, he gave the most magnificently dull answer that I have ever heard in my life with the certain knowledge we were going to cut out one-third of the material. . . . All his dull answers to those unfriendly questions were almost certain to be dropped. It was a fascinating performance of skill."[50]

In 1963, the nonviolent civil rights movement reached its zenith, and television had become an ally to the cause. Network news divisions had come to realize their inescapable role in exposing massive injustice. Not every story had two sides with equal merit. Balance was not a journalistic prerequisite in matters of human decency. Villains deserved excoriation, and good guys rightfully earned sympathetic coverage.

Although President Kennedy was a strong supporter of civil rights, many black leaders felt he could and should do much more. Two days before the integration showdown at the University of Alabama, Martin Luther King Jr. appeared on the syndicated talk show *Open End*, hosted by David Susskind. He was harshly critical of Kennedy, claiming his commitment was "inadequate." He called on the president to speak out and explain to the nation on television that civil rights was not a political but a moral issue. King's remarks were reported the following day on the front page of the *New York Times*.

On June 11, 1963, the governor of Alabama, George Wallace, stood in the "schoolhouse door" in an attempt to block the registration of two black students, Vivian Malone and James Hood. President Kennedy federalized the Alabama National Guard, and ultimately a brigadier general asked Wallace to "please stand aside." The governor had little choice but to comply.

That night, the president made an uncharacteristically sudden decision to go on television. At 6:00 P.M., the White House asked the networks for a fifteen-minute block of time beginning at 8:00 P.M. John Kennedy took twelve minutes to say what black Americans had been waiting three years to hear from this president:

> One hundred years of delay have passed since President Lincoln freed the slaves, yet their heirs, their grandsons are not fully free. We preach freedom around the world and we mean it. And we cherish our freedom here at home. But are we to say to the world— and much more importantly to each other—that this is the land of the free, except for Negroes? . . . Now the time has come for this nation to fulfill its promise.[51]

Martin Luther King heralded the address, soon to be called "The Television Manifesto," as a masterpiece. But there was little time to celebrate Kennedy's willingness to commit the full force of his office to the civil rights struggle. Just hours after the address, Medgar Evers, an NAACP (National Association for the Advancement of Colored People) field secretary in Jackson, Mississippi, was murdered by a gunshot in front of his home. Public opinion polls taken in the following weeks revealed, not surprisingly, that the president had a high

On June 11, 1963, President Kennedy delivers a television address on civil rights. Courtesy of the John F. Kennedy Library, Abbie Rowe, White House photographer.

disapproval rating among southern white voters, while his popularity with black Americans soared.[52]

On September 2, 1963, Labor Day, a historic television event occurred that would further strengthen the impact of the medium on the political process. "Good evening from our CBS newsroom in New York," said Walter Cronkite, "on this, the first broadcast of network television's first daily half-hour news program."[53] For the special occasion, CBS requested and received an exclusive interview with President Kennedy—who understood that doubling the length of fifteen-minute network newscasts would be a significant development for current and future occupants of the Oval Office. The prerecorded discussion with Cronkite took place at Kennedy's Hyannis Port home, where the two men were seated outdoors in wicker chairs.

After a summer of crucial civil rights events, a proposed trip to Dallas in November to do some fence mending with southern Democrats seemed like a good idea. The election was less than a year away, and President Kennedy was thinking about how best to use television. He'd seen an ad for Volkswagen that said "Think Small," and the whimsy impressed him. He instructed his brother-in-law Stephen Smith to look into the advertising agency that created it and talk to them about taking over the Democratic Party account. JFK was convinced that Barry Goldwater was going to be the Republican

On September 2, 1963, CBS anchorman Walter Cronkite interviews the president at the Kennedy compound in Hyannisport, Massachusetts. Courtesy of the John F. Kennedy Library, Cecil Stoughton, White House photographer.

candidate. And the two men, who enjoyed a cordial relationship, had already determined they would engage in televised debates.

The logistical enormity of the television coverage of President Kennedy's assassination and funeral was not something for which the networks were prepared. For four days, however, from November 22 through November 25, the medium provided a monumental service to the republic, providing assurance that the American democracy would stay the course and allowing all citizens to participate in the national ritual of mourning.

THE PRIMARY FACTOR

The time between General Eisenhower's first campaign for the presidency and his return to the White House to pay respect to his successor whose body rested on a catafalque in the East Room—a little more than a decade—coincided with television's ascendancy to the dominant mass medium of American culture. In those years, profound changes occurred in the way candidates campaigned for the office and governed once elected.

Eisenhower's use of short spot commercials in the 1952 presidential campaign broke entirely new ground in the field of political persuasion. In anticipation of the 1956 campaign, the Brookings Institution published *Television and Presidential Politics: The Experience in 1952 and the Problems Ahead*. The report warned:

> When dealing with contemporary politics, advertising agencies tend to stress personal qualities rather than issues. There is also the temptation to stage events, and to make bowdlerized versions of governmental institutions and processes available through mass media, which gives pause to those interested in a serious presentation of genuine political events and institutional operations.[54]

The same concerns have been voiced in every presidential campaign since.

The high cost of running for office in the Television Age, and what effect it had on the democratic process, was an emerging concern in the 1950s and early 1960s. The pitch of that debate continued to rise throughout the remainder of the twentieth century. The large proportion of campaign budgets spent on the purchase of airtime for advertising and other candidate-controlled programming continues to be a prominent issue on the national agenda as the twenty-first century unfolds.

Television's coverage of state primary elections in 1952 began to elevate their importance in the nominating process. A good showing for a presidential hopeful in early primaries became a critical campaign goal. A long-term effect of the increased interest in presidential primaries by TV news organizations has been a lengthening of the campaign season each quadrennial. By the 1990s, it had become routine for candidates to make preliminary visits to key states as early as a year before the primary election.

The growing importance of primaries diminished the significance of nominating conventions. The 1956 Republican convention foreshadowed the future of such gatherings. The likelihood was that the nominee was already known. The convention became primarily a promotional event for the party, designed to accommodate the needs of the TV coverage. Eventually, the television networks would seriously question the newsworthiness of conventions, and the amount of airtime devoted to presidential nominating conventions would be drastically cut.

Each of Eisenhower's successors in the Oval Office relied, as he did, on the advice of advisors whose primary interest was in how well the chief executive appeared on television. Skillful use of the medium was not a counterfeit measure of a statesman's timber; it had become a requirement in effective governance. Gaining as much control as possible of image and message became a presidential imperative.

John Kennedy's live television press conferences were an innovation that became an institution in the American presidency. They allowed a chief executive to make his case to the public unadulterated. President Kennedy once playfully remarked to his friend, journalist Ben Bradlee, "When we don't have to go through you bastards, we can really get our story to the American people."[55]

During the Eisenhower and Kennedy years, as the amount of news and documentary programming steadily increased, the significance of television news rose exponentially. The advancements of video technology and satellite communication enlarged the possibilities of journalistic coverage. The American public came to rely on TV as its primary source of news. As a result, television was the major factor in altering the conduct of the presidency, stylistically as well as structurally. By the time Lyndon Johnson took the oath of office as the thirty-sixth president of the United States, the forcefulness of television in the formation of public opinion had become the foundation of all presidential communication strategies.

BECOMING INTERNATIONAL
PART III

A GREAT AWAKENING

Prime Time for Network Television—1964–1975

The World Turned Upside Down

> America is the impression I get from looking in the television set.
> ALLEN GINSBERG, "America," 1956[1]

The major historical and cultural currents that are typically associated with the 1960s—the civil rights movement, President Lyndon B. Johnson's Great Society, the generation gap, rock 'n' roll music, the Vietnam War, student protests, women's liberation, the rise of the counterculture and the subsequent reaction by the silent majority—all seemed to surface soon after John F. Kennedy's assassination. Surely these events and issues simmered for years beneath the calm exterior of postwar America before finally boiling over with a pent-up fury that took many people in the country by surprise. Daniel Boorstin once observed that the "most popular" method of organizing historical periods is in yearly, decade-long, and "hundred year packages. Historians like to bundle years in ways that make sense, provide continuity and link past to present."[2] More often than not, though, history is not that neat and clean. For all intents and purposes, the era known as the Sixties did not kick into high gear until after JFK was gone and the nation had experienced the shock of his passing. This turbulent and transformative period also extended well into the early to mid 1970s, culminating with Watergate and the withdrawal of American troops from Vietnam. Through it all, television remained the one constant for most Americans, who could turn on their sets for a brief respite or a quick update on what was happening beyond the TV screen.

Most television entertainment during the mid to late 1960s disguised current events in the usual assortment of familiar and comforting formulas, even resorting to far-out fantasies at times, before inching its way toward relevancy by the end of the decade. Electronic newsgathering, too, was slow to illuminate many of the seismic developments that marked the era, gradually coming into its own by its workmanlike coverage of the civil rights movement, the Vietnam War, and the space race. TV news, documentary, and public affairs programming was spotty and tentative at first in addressing America's hot-button issues. During the mid to late 1950s and into the early 1960s, the civil rights movement, in particular, was handled as primarily a regional rather than a national story by network news organizations. After the landmark Supreme Court decision *Brown v. the Board of Education of Topeka* (1954), which essentially outlawed racial segregation in the nation's public schools, the civil rights movement made news with the 1955 Montgomery, Alabama, bus boycott (where Rosa Parks refused to give up her seat to a white man) and the 1957 federal integration of Little Rock (Arkansas) Central High School and the University of Mississippi. CBS's *See It Now* examined the effects of the *Brown* decision on two North Carolina towns in 1955. NBC's *Meet the Press* hosted Roy Wilkins of the National Association for the Advancement of Colored People (NAACP) in 1956. Wilkins was the first black guest ever to appear on the program. A year later, coproducer and moderator Lawrence Spivak invited Martin Luther King Jr. to discuss his nonviolent approach to civil disobedience and the recent founding of the Southern Christian Leadership Conference (SCLC).[3]

By and large, though, TV coverage of civil rights in America throughout the late 1950s was intermittent at best, reporting on events in a characteristically distant and uninvolved manner. Besides the aforementioned appearances by Wilkins and King on *Meet the Press*, "rarely, if ever, did black participants speak for themselves" or directly address the television audience at home; "nevertheless, civil rights leaders understood how central television exposure was becoming to the success of the movement."[4] In the wake of the 1959 quiz show scandal, a small resurgence in documentary programming occurred on all three networks as a way of shoring up television's damaged reputation with both the federal government and the viewing public. Lasting through the Kennedy years, 1961–1962 was the peak season when "the three networks aired more than 250 hours of [nonfictional] programming," including a handful of notable one-hour documentaries on the civil rights movement such as "Sit-In" for the *NBC White Paper* series, as well as "Cast the First Stone" and "Walk in My Shoes" for ABC's *Close-Up!*[5] What made these prime-time offerings so unique was the fact that they "chronicled social problems in America from the perspective of African-Americans."

When the "urgency of the Civil Rights Movement was brought to the nation's consciousness with images on network news of police abuse on passive demonstrators," 1963 proved to be a pivotal year. Starting in April, the SCLC staged a sit-in, protesting the widespread apartheid system that governed nearly every aspect of daily life in Birmingham, Alabama. Soon, Martin Luther King Jr. was jailed for leading the demonstration, and, in a last-ditch effort, he directed that youngsters be recruited to join the sit-ins. Then, "on May 3, Birmingham police used dogs and high-pressure water hoses on the demonstrators. Graphic photographs and television footage resulted in national and international outrage."[6]

The eyes of the world finally opened wide to the civil rights struggle in America because of what audiences were seeing on their television screens. The "children's crusade" included hundreds of six to sixteen year olds, accompanied by their parents and dressed in their Sunday best; they were shown in nightly news reports being brutally manhandled and beaten by Birmingham policemen, led by a ready-made-for-TV villain named "Eugene 'Bull' Connor, a bombastic segregationist of the old, unapologetically bluff sort—a podgy, strutful, middle-aged bossman in a snap-brim straw hat."[7] The time for either ignoring or finessing the situation had ended. President Kennedy publicly chose sides as he and his brother Robert, the attorney general, confronted Governor George Wallace in June, forcing him to comply with federal orders to integrate the University of Alabama, the last all-white public institution of higher learning in the country. Ever conscious of the media, JFK also invited Robert Drew and his production team into the White House to film the intricate negotiations as they unfolded, resulting in the one-hour documentary "Crisis: Behind a Presidential Commitment," which debuted a mere four months later on October 28 as part of ABC's *Close-Up!* series.

In the meantime, President Kennedy delivered a prime-time address to the nation on June 11, 1963, announcing that he was sending far-reaching civil rights legislation to Congress. Then on August 28, JFK and millions of other Americans watched Martin Luther King Jr. live on CBS as he electrified viewers, as well as the 300,000 spectators in front of him on the Washington mall, with his "I Have a Dream" speech.[8] According to a nationwide Roper poll, television was already the most frequently used and most trusted news medium in the country.[9] Seeing was believing in 1963, even though TV newspeople were just beginning to assert themselves as practicing journalists. On September 2, 1963, the *CBS Evening News* with Walter Cronkite (who had only taken over as anchor from Douglas Edwards sixteen months earlier) expanded from fifteen to thirty minutes. NBC's *Huntley-Brinkley Report*, which had quickly become the no. 1 newscast in the country soon after its debut on October 29, 1956, followed suit a week later on September 9. (For its part, *ABC Evening News* lacked the resources to make a similar kind of expansion until 1967.) TV newscasters grew far more aggressive in reporting the events of "Freedom Summer" in 1964, especially after the month-long disappearance of two white Northern civil-rights activists, Michael Schwerner and Andrew Goodman, along with their black Southern coworker, James Chaney, who were all eventually found murdered. "With the death of innocent white volunteers, television was convincing its civilian viewers around the country that the Civil Rights Movement did concern them as well."[10]

Among many other parallel stories, television cameras went to Selma, Alabama, on March 7, 1965, for what turned out to be "Bloody Sunday" when a stream of black marchers demonstrating for voter registration were viciously attacked on camera by a white civilian mob aided by the local police force. Thus, "by 1968, it was clear that television's powerful and visceral images of the civil rights struggle had permeated many levels of American social and political reality." TV's influence was instrumental in garnering support for the Civil Rights Act of 1964, the Voting Rights Act of 1965, and other relevant War on Poverty and Great Society legislation designed to address the chronic and intractable problems related to race in America.[11] For decision-makers at the networks, race was the third rail of TV entertainment throughout the 1950s and into the early 1960s. Since the beginnings of television, the conventional wisdom was to sidestep race-based stories and themes, as well as people of color, whenever and wherever possible. For the most part, this attitude resulted in a near blackout of African Americans, Latinos, Asian Americans, and Native Americans on TV. When racial depictions occurred, most frequently with African Americans, these images were usually highly controlled, nonthreatening, and evocative of traditional stereotypes that harked back to antebellum folktales and minstrelsy involving old-time popular songs and stock racial jokes.

ABC's *Beulah*, for instance, resurrected the good-natured oversized Mammy character, who served the Hendersons, a white, middle-class, suburban family, as their conscientious black maid. Before being spun off as the central character in her own eponymously named television show, Beulah had "a supporting role on radio's *Fibber McGee and Molly* and featured a white male speaking in black dialect."[12] *Beulah* ran from 1950 to 1953, starring Ethel Waters in its first two seasons; Louise Beavers assumed the role during the last year it was on the air.

The most controversial program in TV's initial decade was another radio spin-off, *Amos 'n' Andy*. This wildly popular and long-running radio sitcom was created, produced, and acted by two white men, Freeman Gosden and Charles Correll. When CBS adapted *Amos 'n' Andy* to television with an all-black cast in 1951, the network was deluged with complaints from both sides of the country's racial divide. In the South, a handful of CBS affiliates refused to carry *Amos 'n' Andy* simply because it featured black actors and actresses, even though all of their performances "came complete with baggy pants, plug hats, foul cigars, pushy wives, misfired schemes, and mangled grammar."[13] In contrast, the NAACP mobilized a nationwide protest against the show's widespread use of racial stereotypes, including such familiar throwbacks as "'Sambo' [dim-witted and happy-go-lucky], 'Zip Coon' (the urban dandy version of Sambo), 'Uncle Tom' and others."[14] "World War II had enlarged black goals to include the possibility of full integration into American life," recounts historian Thomas Cripps; "Amos 'n' Andy arrived in full view of the television audience, complete with symbolic baggage from an older time in black history and broadcasting history. Solidly rooted in a segregated world, by its existence, even on television, it seemed to cast doubt on black social goals and to mock the newly powerful, organized black middle class."[15] Under pressure from all directions, especially the NAACP, CBS finally pulled the show after only two and a half seasons.

Overall, TV mirrored the segregated nature of American society in general throughout the 1950s. African Americans were rarely seen on the small screen until the early 1960s, mostly relegated to second-banana status, as in the case of Eddie "Rochester" Anderson on CBS's *The Jack Benny Show*, or doomed to uncommonly short runs even by television standards, as in ABC's musical-variety program, *The Billy Daniels Show* (October–December 1952) and later NBC's *The Nat "King" Cole Show* (November 1956–December 1957). Slowly but surely, Kennedy-era dramas such as *The Defenders* and *The Nurses* on CBS, as well as *Mr. Novak* and *The Lieutenant* on NBC, occasionally tackled racially charged themes and featured black performers on a one-time basis. The first substantive breakthrough came in 1963 on CBS's *East Side/West Side*, starring George C. Scott, where Cicely Tyson had a recurring supporting role as a young black social worker within the slums of New York, who dealt with a wide assortment of problems such as poverty, crime, drugs, and welfare abuse.

Two years later, the "weekly series underwent its most dramatic color change" with the debut of the action-adventure espionage series *I Spy* on NBC. Bill Cosby and Robert Culp starred in this top-20 hit as a pair of U.S. secret agents, who were also best friends, traveling from one exotic locale after another and making the world safe for democracy. Cosby's cover was as a trainer and coach to Culp's tennis pro; he was also young, good-looking, sophisticated, a Rhodes scholar who spoke seven languages, and an expert at his job. Bill Cosby won three straight Emmys between 1966 and 1968 for "Outstanding Continued Performance by an Actor in a Leading Role in a Dramatic Series." His popular and critical success as the costar of *I Spy* made it much easier for other black actors and actresses to subsequently find continuing roles in other television series. For example, Greg Morris soon was cast as an electronics wizard on CBS's *Mission: Impossible*; Diahann Carroll, as a nurse in NBC's *Julia*; and Lloyd Haynes and Denise Nicholas, as teachers in ABC's *Room 222*. "These new characters were signs of social progress," contends media critic Donald Bogle, "no matter how idealized or evasive some of those representations ultimately might be" in hindsight. "In temperament, image, and outlook," continues Bogle, Bill Cosby was "the right actor in the right place at the right time." Jackie Robinson was my "idol," Cosby revealed years later; "he made it happen for blacks in baseball by using his talents, never his rage, to express his blackness. I felt that if in my ballpark I did my job as well as Robinson did his, I would also therefore be moving us down the road a piece."[16]

The fact that Cosby and a whole new generation of black performers were just now integrating prime time in the mid 1960s—more than fifteen years after Jackie Robinson broke the color line in baseball—speaks volumes about the inherently conservative nature of television as an institution and an industry, especially during the

Robert Culp (left) *and Bill Cosby* (right) *portrayed a pair of U.S. secret agents in NBC's* I Spy. *Cosby won three straight Best Actor Emmys between 1966 and 1968 for his starring role in this action-adventure espionage series. Courtesy of Library of American Broadcasting at the University of Maryland.*

dozen years (1964–1975) when the three-network oligopoly was at its peak as a finely tuned, insular, and highly profitable system. Between 1948 and 1963, TV revenues in the United States grew astronomically from $8.7 million to over $2 billion.[17] By 1964, there were 564 television stations in America, and 93 percent of this total were affiliated with either NBC (37 percent), CBS (34 percent), or ABC (22 percent).[18] These three networks were now operating as a close-knit, mature oligopoly that competed against each other for audiences and advertising revenues, while still controlling the television market among themselves when it came to access (deciding what companies to work with), output (determining what programs got made and at what cost), and pricing (knowing what each other's advertising fees were and setting individual rates accordingly). After "combined three-network profits rose from $37 million in 1962 to $56 million in 1963, and reached a record $60 million in 1964," earnings then leveled off somewhat between 1965 and 1968, while still averaging an impressive $63 million annually for the rest of the decade.[19]

The bottom line was that all three networks benefited greatly from TV's oligopolistic market structure during the 1960s. CBS became the first among equals during the network era. Leonard Wallace Robinson in the *New York Times* reported in 1964 that "CBS, Inc., has been—and will remain for the foreseeable future—the largest advertising medium in the world, employing some 13,500 people, including its show business talent. Its corporate achievement according to one leading business commentator is 'almost comparable to what General Motors did in autos or General Electric in electrical equipment.' "[20] This analogy perfectly captures CBS's position in the television industry at the time. Like General Motors and General Electric, CBS was the top network in a mature three-corporation oligopoly that mass produced and distributed standardized, family-oriented entertainment and information to literally tens of millions of consumers domestically and overseas through syndication. Success or failure in television was determined in very simple black-and-white terms: the network (or station) that had the largest audiences could charge the highest advertising rates and make the most money. A. C. Nielsen was then widely recognized as the leading TV audience measurement service in the country, especially after introducing overnight ratings in 1959. Nielsen provided networks and local stations with ratings (the percentage of the total potential audience tuned to a specific program) and shares (the percentage of the total audience with their TVs turned on and watching a particular network or station). CBS won its ninth straight season in 1963–1964; additionally, it had fourteen out of the top fifteen shows on prime time and the twelve leading daytime programs that year. In 1964, the CBS television network also earned twice as much money as its nearest rival, NBC.

In the face of all this success, James Aubrey, president of CBS-TV, emerged as the poster boy for what was both right and wrong with television as a medium during the 1960s. "In the long history of human communications, from tom-tom to Telstar, no one man had a lock on such enormous audiences as James Thomas Aubrey, Jr.," trumpeted Richard Oulahan and William Lambert in *Life* magazine in 1965; "he was the world's number one purveyor of entertainment."[21] In an industry that had become increasingly driven by numbers, no network chief had ever been more relentless in his pursuit of ratings and shares than Aubrey. He was appointed network president at the height of the quiz show scandal, and instead of temporarily moving CBS toward more respectable forms of entertainment programming until the public scrutiny subsided, Aubrey barreled straight ahead with shows that appealed to a wider spectrum of viewers, especially in rural areas where television was still being newly adopted. ABC's Leonard Goldenson had encouraged Aubrey to target young adults, teens, and adolescents during his tenure at that network; now he kept his eye on these key demographics, while also broadening CBS's reach to encompass what he called the "soft underbelly of America."[22] Aubrey's strategy translated into programs that appealed to the lowest common denominator, such as *Mister Ed*, *My Favorite Martian*, and *The Munsters*. Moreover, his perennial success at CBS ensured that NBC and ABC soon moved in similar directions to keep up.

NBC's vice president for audience measurement at the time, Paul L. Klein, even christened this perspective the LOP (least objectionable program) theory in a *New York* magazine article, giving it even wider currency throughout the industry.[23] Basically, this theory posits that viewers watch TV no matter what, usually choosing the least objectionable show available to them. Furthermore, it assumes a limited number of programming choices for audiences to pick from and implies that networks, advertising agencies, and sponsors care little about quality when producing and distributing shows. In a memo early in his presidency, Aubrey famously ordered his executive team to emphasize "broads, bosoms, and fun" on CBS's network schedule.[24] James Aubrey was called the "huckster's huckster" by David Halberstam: "A man so nakedly open about what he was and what he wanted—that is, the greediest side of the network so openly revealed and displayed—that even the other hucksters were embarrassed."[25] Aubrey's effect on CBS's schedule was immediate and profound. Still only forty years old when he was appointed president in December 1959, his growing control

James Aubrey, president of CBS-TV, emerged as the poster boy for what was both right and wrong with television as a medium during the 1960s. Courtesy of Library of American Broadcasting at the University of Maryland.

over network operations grew in direct proportion to his skyrocketing success. "It is difficult for the layman to conceive of the jungle that prevails at the executive level in TV programming," observed Jack Gould of the *New York Times* in 1965; "no man has real security beyond a season or two, yet he must commit hundreds of millions of dollars to dozens of programs that may fail or succeed by reason of their content, star, placement in the schedule, opposition programs at the same hours, [or] shows that come before or after."[26]

Aubrey had no intention of failing, now that he finally had an opportunity to run a network. He therefore acted with a kind of fierce contempt for his competition, the talent who worked for him, and eventually even his bosses at CBS. He nevertheless knew better than any of his contemporaries how to develop programs that appealed to the continually expanding TV market in America that now exceeded 90 percent of all households across the country. CBS had more than its share of 1950s-style series when Aubrey took over as president at the start of the 1960s, including Westerns (*Gunsmoke; Have Gun— Will Travel*), domestic sitcoms (*Father Knows Best, The Danny Thomas Show*), and traditional variety shows (*The Ed Sullivan Show, The Red*

Skelton Show). His plan was to complement these evergreen hits with more baby boomer–oriented series that favorably competed with ABC's lineup, such as *Route 66*, which debuted in October 1960 and followed two attractive, young men driving around the country in a red Corvette convertible searching for adventure. Aubrey also had a special penchant for half-hour comedies: he premiered two new top-10 entries in 1960–1961; reprised *Candid Camera* after nearly a decade since it had last appeared on prime time; and introduced CBS's breakout hit of the year, *The Andy Griffith Show*. This latter program, in particular, reconfirmed the public's seemingly voracious appetite for rural sitcoms, especially as television spread ever deeper into the most provincial parts of the American South, Midwest, and West.

The program that would turn out to be James Aubrey's signature series at CBS was first suggested to him by a writer he got to know while developing Irving Pincus and Norman Pincus's *The Real Mc-Coys* for ABC in 1957. Still rated no. 5 in 1960–1961, *The Real McCoys* involved the misadventures of a West Virginia family who relocates to a ranch in the sunny San Fernando Valley of California. Paul Henning proposed a similar rube-style fish-out-of-water comedy involving an Ozark hillbilly family, who accidentally find oil on their property and move lock, stock, and barrel to Beverly Hills, California. Few series in television history were greeted with the hue and cry that accompanied the September 1962 premiere of *The Beverly Hillbillies*. Despite suffering a critical drubbing, the public immediately tuned into the incongruity of watching the Clampetts live out a farcical, jumbo-size version of the American dream amid the overconsumptive splendor of Southern California. *The Beverly Hillbillies* quickly shot up the Nielsen rankings to no. 1 in only six short weeks; "not since *The $64,000 Question* had a new program risen to the top so fast."[27] The appeal of *The Beverly Hillbillies* was rooted in one of the deepest fault lines of twentieth-century American culture. "A pitched battle [was] fought in each episode between the homespun, right-minded [country] values of the Clampetts," explains TV critic David Marc, "and a cutthroat, money-ruled technocracy, represented by the city people."[28] *The Beverly Hillbillies* averaged a staggering fifty-seven million viewers a week (or 1 out of every 3.3 Americans) between 1962 and 1964, making it the no. 1 show in the nation.

The Beverly Hillbillies spawned a spin-off (*Petticoat Junction*) in 1963–1964 and a clone (*Green Acres*) in 1965–1966. These programs, too, were created and produced by Paul Henning at Filmways, the hottest new independent production company in Hollywood. *The Beverly Hillbillies* became the most popular series of the decade, rivaled only by NBC's *Bonanza*. It propelled CBS way ahead of NBC and ABC in

the ratings. *The Beverly Hillbillies* also delivered millions of extra viewers to the other CBS shows near it on the network's Wednesday-night
lineup. For instance, Carl Reiner's more critically acclaimed autobio-
graphical sitcom, *The Dick Van Dyke Show*, languished in its Tuesday
night at 8 P.M. position behind reruns of *Gunsmoke* in 1961–1962,
ending up a disappointing no. 54 in the ratings that season. James Aubrey believed in the program, however, so he piggybacked it behind
The Beverly Hillbillies the next year, and *The Dick Van Dyke Show*
jumped immediately to no. 9, where it remained a hit on its own
through the end of its run in 1966. Aubrey also used *The Beverly Hillbillies* to revive the situation comedy in general. This genre had experienced a brief period of decline ever since *I Love Lucy* stopped weekly
production and the Western began its rise in 1956–1957. Newton Minow especially singled out "formula comedies about totally unbelievable families" in his 1961 "vast wasteland" speech,[29] but Aubrey
nevertheless loaded the CBS schedule with as many rural and fantasy
sitcoms as he could develop between 1962 and 1965, such as Sherwood Schwartz's *Gilligan's Island*, where the shipwrecked charter boat
was pointedly named the S.S. *Minnow* after the chairman of the Federal Communications Commission.

Overall, the tumult of the 1960s rarely penetrated the facades of
these hugely popular CBS situation comedies and the Aubrey-
influenced clones on ABC (*Bewitched*) and NBC (*I Dream of Jeannie*).
People of color and counterculture types hardly ever appeared on the
literally dozens of prime-time situation comedies that were on the air
during the 1960s. Once in a great while, a couple of stock hippie characters would briefly drift into a scene as a sight gag with their long
hair, unconventional clothing, and loopy behavior. Still, they were presented as being even further beyond the pale than the Clampetts and
the Munsters, who seemed normal in comparison. Throughout the decade, most Americans used TV as a kind of "psychological refuge, a
fortress," argues broadcast historian Erik Barnouw:

> Except for the occasionally disturbing documentaries, evening
> television confirmed the average man's [and woman's] view of the
> world. It presented the America [they] wanted and believed in and
> had labored to be part of. It was alive with handsome men and
> women, and symbols of the good life. It invited and drew [them]
> into its charmed circle.[30]

In developing programs at CBS that appealed to rural as well as urban
and suburban viewers, James Aubrey pushed all of network television
more toward a largely placid consensual middle-of-the-road version of

America that hid the intractable polarization growing daily beyond the screen. Although NBC and ABC eventually innovated in other genres, all three networks initially rode the crest of sitcoms and action-adventure series to record-setting audiences by 1969, as 95 percent of all American households were now watching an average of six hours of TV a day.[31]

Even a decade after *The Beverly Hillbillies* finished its prime-time run in 1971, "nine individual episodes of the series remained among the 50 most watched [shows] in television history with ratings comparable to those of Super Bowls." The program's farcical structure obviously struck a responsive chord among people of all ages and backgrounds from coast to coast. The "consensus narrative" that was *The Beverly Hillbillies* was replayed time and again over 274 episodes for nine straight years. Its essence was succinctly rerun as "a single continuing cultural struggle between the country folk (healthy, good) and the city people (neurotic, bad). The Clampetts will not be corrupted; the Drysdales will not be purified."[32] Consensus narratives such as *The Beverly Hillbillies* operate "at the very center of the life of their culture and are in consequence almost always deeply conservative in their formal structures and their content," discloses David Thorburn; they "desire to speak for and to the whole of [their] culture, or as much of the whole as the governing forces in society permit."[33] In this way, prime-time television during the 1960s was always reflective of what was going on in American society and culture, even when many of the most popular programs were wildly farcical or unrealistic in their depictions. The majority of viewers at home simply preferred to avoid the upheavals of the era for as long as they could, despite being occasionally reminded by news, documentary, and public affairs programming that there were serious cracks in the national consensus over civil rights and Vietnam, especially. TV's "consensus narratives" attempted to hold an increasingly divided country together at a difficult time. The fact that the three networks kept the lid on a more realistic rendering of reality for as long as they did suggests the power and influence that they already wielded over the hearts and minds of most Americans throughout the decade.

CBS stayed mostly on the course set by James Aubrey even after he was fired in 1965. It remained atop the ratings as the no. 1 network in the country for the rest of the 1960s. Aubrey's personal excesses finally caught up with him, despite all of his success against NBC and ABC. He grew to be an increasingly difficult boss, causing a series of high-profile rows with such important CBS stars as Lucille Ball, Garry Moore, and Jack Benny (who even jumped to NBC over his intolerable behavior).[34] Producer John Houseman famously dubbed Aubrey the "smiling cobra," while celebrated director John Frankenheimer publicly called him a "barbarian."[35] James Aubrey even acted contemptuously toward William S. Paley and the "façade of artistic pretense that CBS had so prided itself on." This affront, too, was overlooked "because the profits were so great."[36] Toward the end, Aubrey's personal life spilled over into the tabloids as well—so much so, in fact, that his jet-setting ways later inspired such paperback potboilers as Harold Robbins's *The Inheritors* (1969) and Jacqueline Susann's *The Love Machine* (1969). By the summer of 1964, though, Aubrey's troubles crossed the line into illegality when the FCC began an investigation on charges that he was accepting kickbacks from telefilm producers such as Filmways in return for preferred deals and favorable treatment. Although Aubrey was never formally charged, the accusations panned out, and Paley ordered Frank Stanton to get rid of him immediately. In retrospect, Aubrey's fate was as unforgiving as the dog-eat-dog atmosphere he reveled in at CBS. On February 27, 1965, Stanton's terse thirty-eight-word statement to the press read in part that "James T. Aubrey, Jr. has today resigned as president of the CBS television network division. . . . [His] outstanding accomplishments during his tenure as the head of the CBS television network need no elaboration."[37]

For twenty years, William S. Paley and Frank Stanton had provided the continuity at CBS, and they again guided the network through this period of executive transition and corporate expansion. CBS, Inc., had now bureaucratically grown into seven separate divisions. Besides the CBS Television Network (with 190 affiliates), there was CBS Radio (with 237 affiliates), Columbia Records (with its diverse array of best-selling artists such as Tony Bennett, Bob Dylan, Johnny Mathis, and Mitch Miller, among dozens of others), CBS News, CBS Television Stations (with the legally allowable five owned-and-operated major market stations), CBS Laboratories (for research and development), and CBS International (for worldwide syndication). Characteristic of other highly successful media corporations in the mid 1960s, CBS, Inc., also followed a course of diversification. It reinvested much of its television profits into other premium companies that complemented its corporate emphasis on communication and entertainment. In quick succession, CBS, Inc., purchased the New York Yankees in 1964, the Fender Electric Guitar Company in 1965, Creative Playthings (a manufacturer of educational toys) in 1966, and the book publisher Holt, Rinehart and Winston and Republic Pictures' North Hollywood studio in 1967.

CBS transformed Republic's old movie studio into a new state-of-the-art facility, renaming it CBS Studio Center. It also founded Cinema Center Films for the express purpose of producing in-house telefilm series, made-for-TV movies, and theatrical features. Recently, NBC had closed its ratings gap with CBS by making strategic scheduling use of theatrical motion pictures, as well as innovating in the area of long-form programming (meaning shows that extended beyond a sixty-minute time slot). Hollywood had first flooded the television market with most of its pre-1948 features and shorts in the 1956–1957 season. The reason post-1948 theatrical films were not included in these transactions was because movies made after August 1948 were bound by contractual agreement through which performers had to be paid additional income for subsequent TV showings. The telecasting of motion pictures faded from prime time between the summer of 1957 and the early fall of 1961, however, because of the relative expense incurred by the networks in leasing these theatrical films. It simply was more cost effective for them to fund telefilm series. The networks also labored under the mistaken assumption that Hollywood features would not attract large TV audiences since many people had already seen these pictures before in movie theaters. This misconception all changed on September 23, 1961, when NBC introduced its new series, *Saturday Night at the Movies*, featuring Marilyn Monroe, Lauren Bacall, and Betty Grable in Twentieth Century-Fox's *How to Marry a Millionaire* (1953). This telecast was an astounding success and marked the turning point at which Hollywood's major studios started making their post-1948 films available to TV.

A complete change in thinking took place—first at NBC, then ABC—and these two networks began scheduling Hollywood motion pictures in prime time with much greater frequency after the fall of 1961. *ABC Sunday Night at the Movies* debuted in 1962–1963, and NBC added additional movie nights on Monday (1963–1964), Wednesday (1964–1965), and Tuesday (1965–1966). After the departure of James Aubrey, CBS finally jumped on the bandwagon with *CBS Thursday Night Movies* in 1965–1966. The culmination of this trend occurred on September 25, 1966, when *The Bridge on the River Kwai* (1957) premiered on *ABC Sunday Night at the Movies*. It was reported that "an estimated 60 million viewers in 25 million homes sat down to watch one movie" for which ABC "paid Columbia Pictures $2 million."[38] Even at that price, the network was more than satisfied with the results. NBC, ABC, and CBS entered into a fierce bidding war against each other to lease as many big-budget, star-studded, color extravaganzas as they could. Consequently, the average rental fee for one prime-time showing of a theatrical film jumped dramatically from $180,000 in 1961, to $200,000 in 1964, to $380,000 in 1967, to $750,000 in 1970.[39] To go along with these skyrocketing costs, Hollywood's backlog of old movies was quickly drying up. The stage was now set for the systematic development of feature-length motion pictures made exclusively for the small screen. NBC initially responded to the growing expense and impending shortage of quality theatrical films by nurturing the brainchild of an executive at Universal TV, Jennings Lang. The made-for-TV movie was thus launched at NBC in 1964, where it soon raised the bar for production value, dramatic complexity, and thematic concern on all of prime-time television.

BASED ON A TRUE STORY

> For network-movie watchers, in the beginning there were movies. Then came the nonmovies. And now it's minimovies. For the audience, it's a puzzlement and a frustration. For the networks, it's big business. And where it's all leading no one will guess.
> JUDITH CRIST, *TV Guide*, 1969[40]

Promising conditions for the birth of the television movie began to take shape in the mid 1950s and became imminent during the early 1960s. When Hollywood's major studios entered the fray of TV series production between 1955 and 1958, many of the smaller independent telefilm companies were hurt by the added competition, driven from the business, or absorbed by larger firms. The case of Jennings Lang at MCA's (Music Corporation of America) Revue is instructive in this regard. Lang began promoting longer and more novel programming formats in 1959 as a way of counteracting Warner Bros., Twentieth Century-Fox, MGM, and Paramount's influential move into TV production; his motivation was a desire to create an advantage for Revue in the face of this newly emerging challenge from the major movie studios. Lang was ideally positioned between two merging traditions when he started to innovate on two related programming concepts— the long form and the spectacular. He had already established himself as one of the leading talent agents in the film industry when he joined the MCA agency in 1950. The next year, MCA created Revue, and Lang was placed in charge of television program development. Toward the end of the decade, his dual experiences in both the television and motion picture industries led him to consider feature-length storytelling at a time when CBS's growing success against NBC first motivated that network to fund a telefilm proposal from Lang that extended the usual length of a prime-time program.[41]

Jennings Lang "began his [120-minute or two-parter] experiments with anthology shows like *Alfred Hitchcock Presents* and *Bob Hope Presents the Chrysler Theater*, in the one-hour format, and he had a big hand in the first 90-minute regularly scheduled series, *The Virginian*, which premiered on NBC in September 1962."[42] This was also the year that MCA, the most powerful talent agency in Hollywood at the time, purchased Universal Pictures. As a result, Revue was consolidated as Universal TV in this corporate takeover, and Jennings Lang was selected to direct what immediately became a more expanded and influential operation. Now coming from Universal TV, NBC programmers were simply more receptive to Lang's plan to resurrect the anthology format as a series of "TV epics (or special events), when an entire evening [would] be given over to a single spectacular, made for the occasion."[43] Lang's whole initiative had a back-to-the-future quality about it since it evoked both Pat Weaver's notion of the spectacular and the dramatic tradition of the recently discontinued live anthologies. Significantly, though, Lang now proposed to shoot these teleplays on film. He and his colleagues at Universal TV convinced NBC to invest in what were originally called "minimovies" in 1963. For its part, NBC initially considered Lang's overtures for minimovies because theatrical motion pictures were then doing so well, anchoring two of the network's prime-time evenings (Mondays and Saturdays). Considering the growing scarcity and the escalating cost of these films, TV movies seemed like an economical alternative if audiences would only watch them in large enough numbers to make the investment worthwhile.

The success of *The Virginian* during the 1962–1963 season, telecast on NBC between 7:30 and 9 P.M. on Wednesdays, was the final impetus that motivated the network to contract with Lang and Universal TV to produce self-contained feature-length films that fit into a two-hour time slot to be tentatively scheduled during 1963–1964 under the title *Project 120*, a never fully actualized weekly series whose very name evoked the live dramatic anthologies of the previous decade. NBC allotted $250,000 in 1963 for its first planned telefeature, which was the same amount of money budgeted that season for two one-hour prime-time episodes, as Universal TV hired journeyman Don Siegel to direct "*Johnny North*, an adaptation of Ernest Hemingway's short story, 'The Killers,' starring John Cassavetes, Lee Marvin, Angie Dickinson, and Ronald Reagan" in his last role.[44] The movie that resulted eventually cost $900,000 and was deemed by the network to be "too spicy, expensive, and violent for TV screens. "[45] In early 1964, *Johnny North* was retitled *The Killers* (like its 1946 Hollywood predecessor), and this motion picture was subsequently released that spring to movie theaters nationwide by Universal Pictures. Mort Werner, NBC-TV vice president in charge of programming at the time, reflected on the whole experience: "We've learned to control the budget.

Two new 'movies' will get started soon, and the series (*Project 120*) probably will show up on television in 1965."[46]

The first made-for-TV movie, *See How They Run*, debuted on October 17, 1964, a few months earlier than Werner suggested in his public pronouncement. Appearing under the aegis of MCA-Universal and NBC's *Project 120*, the telefeature *See How They Run* involves the murder of a father by an international crime syndicate and the subsequent pursuit of his three teenaged daughters, who unwittingly stumble on some damaging evidence. This routine crime melodrama was quickly followed six weeks later by the NBC telecast of Don Siegel's next excursion into the made-for-TV movie genre, *The Hanged Man*. Like *The Killers*, Siegel's second assignment for *Project 120* is a remake of a classic film noir, *Ride the Pink Horse* (1947).

ABC began its sponsorship of the made-for-TV movie during the 1965–1966 season with the March 10 telecast of *Scalplock*. The Western, starring Dale Robertson and produced by Columbia's Screen Gems, deals with a gambler who wins a railroad in a poker game and then assumes control over his new enterprise. *Scalplock* was actually characteristic of many subsequent telefeatures in that it was a pilot as well as a TV movie, meaning that it also served as the first episode of a prospective prime-time series (in this case, ABC's *The Iron Horse*) by introducing the original story line and the main continuing characters. This strategy of creating telefeatures as pilots provided prime-time suppliers, such as Screen Gems, with a way of recouping more of their original investment by encouraging greater network participation in financing a property with more than one scheduling purpose. The TV production company then sought additional distribution opportunities through television syndication and theatrical exhibition overseas.

Programming executives at NBC were alerted to the ratings potential of the made-for-TV movie as early as the 1966–1967 season. On the evening of Saturday, November 26, 1966, during the Thanksgiving holiday weekend, NBC hyped its two-hour pilot *Fame Is the Name of the Game* as a "World Premiere" on *NBC Saturday Night at the Movies* rather than as part of *Project 120*. Corporate wisdom had now decided that it was better not to remind TV audiences that stars and story types would not recur on a regular basis, even though a semifrequent series of telefeatures was an obvious reprise of the anthology format. Extensive pretesting had instead convinced NBC to emphasize that these telefeatures were being presented to the public for the very first time. No one at the network would later argue with what turned out to be auspicious results. *Fame Is the Name of the Game*, a series pilot for NBC's *The Name of the Game*, starring Tony Franciosa, Jill St. John, and Susan Saint James, involves an enterprising reporter investigating the murder of a prostitute; it surprised everyone at the network by attracting nearly thirty-five million viewers. More striking is the fact that all nine of the World Premieres that NBC telecast during 1966–1967 had a Nielsen rating over 20 (which meant a minimum of twenty-five million viewers at the time); they also "had, on the average, an audience of 20% more people than the average of all other movies [142 theatricals and two telefeatures] shown on all three networks."[47] The comparative ratings for 1967–1968 were even better when " 'World Premiere' movies attracted 42.2% of the audience, while theatrical films claimed only 38%" in comparison.[48]

The American made-for-TV movie came of age in the 1970s. This maturation process proceeded rapidly on several fronts by the middle of the decade, as the television movie genre was decisively fulfilled as both a viable industrial product and a distinctly televisual form. Theatricals remained the film of choice on prime time until 1972–1973, when the seasonal output of made-for-TV movies first exceeded the number of Hollywood features on television. Theatrical film production by the major movie studios actually plummeted from an average of 180 during the late 1960s to approximately 120 by the mid 1970s.[49] Also, theatricals were more dated for prime-time audiences than were TV movies. In this way, the average age of a theatrical film was more than four years old before its first exposure on the networks between 1970 and 1975.[50] Furthermore, from their inception, movies made for TV were virtual ratings equals to theatricals on TV; their style and content were better shaped to the priorities of television, especially when considering the growing sexual and violent explicitness that was evident in theatrical films during the late 1960s and early 1970s; and these productions supported in-house staffs within the television industry. Many of the better producers, writers, actors, and directors experimented with the telefeature in this period as their way of progressing past the relentless work regimen of series TV. Soon the genre's identity was forged as a feature-length television program that personally dramatizes high-profile concepts and topical themes through continuing advances at NBC with its World Premiere movies, as well as at ABC's *Movie of the Week* (1969–1975) and later *The New CBS Friday Night Movie* (1971–1975).

CBS joined NBC and ABC by starting to seriously invest in made-for-TV movie production during the 1971–1972 season. All three networks had now institutionalized positions for a vice president of television movies within the hierarchy of their entertainment divisions, signaling the newly arrived importance of this genre in planning their prime-time schedules. In retrospect, NBC and ABC were the proven leaders in creating innovations in the TV movie, although each one of the three networks was quick to copy any new prime-time programming breakthrough within a season or two after its introduction. Likewise, made-for-TV movies never varied much in design, practice, or ideology from network to network. The inclination of NBC, ABC, and CBS to follow similar lines of program development is a long-established pattern that results from the high degree of insularity and interdependence within their oligopoly. The networks pioneered the TV movie genre with an identical group of suppliers. They additionally geared their prime-time features toward the same general target audience—women from eighteen to forty-nine—because their current research data supported the contention that this cohort made most of the buying decisions in American households. Like most television genres, therefore, the overall growth of the made-for-TV movie is best understood as a shared experience among the networks, shaped in large part by their mutual priorities, allowing for brief breakout periods for formal experimentation (such as extending plotlines to 90 or 120 minutes) and content innovations (such as addressing relevant and sometimes even controversial subject matter). A case in point is the first major critical success of the genre, Universal TV and NBC's *My Sweet Charlie*, which premiered on January 20, 1970.

My Sweet Charlie is a typical TV movie in that it is a 120-minute social melodrama that concentrates its primary focus on a limited number of characters; in this instance, two principals dominate the entire program. The story is "soft" in that there is no explicit sex, very little violence, and a minimum of action clichés that demand elaborate special effects. The premise, based on a successful novel and Broadway play of the same name, is also decidedly topical for the time this telefeature was made since it deals with race relations, runaways, and unwed motherhood. *My Sweet Charlie* concerns a young white woman, Marlene Chambers (Patty Duke), who is forced by circumstances to share an abandoned summer house in a rural town on the Texas coast for several days with a black lawyer from New York, Charles Roberts (Al Freeman Jr.), who has just killed a white man in self-defense at a nearby civil rights demonstration. Marlene has been cast off by her father because she is pregnant and unwed. Both characters are hiding out, forced by circumstances into being outsiders for very different reasons. One of the most interesting aspects of this TV movie is that the usual stereotypes of the period are reversed as Marlene is presented as a poor, ignorant member of the Southern underclass, whereas Charlie is an accomplished, sophisticated, and intelligent professional. Marlene is portrayed by Patty Duke as a scared and angry bigot; the hostility in her characterization was a television breakthrough, especially considering the climate of prime time before

CBS's *All in the Family* (which debuted nearly a year later on January 12, 1971). Charlie is similarly more than just a noble black prototype; he is racist in his own right. Both Freeman and Duke deliver resilient performances, creating two desperate characters with honesty and compassion.

One way of understanding the fundamental nature of any TV movie is to assess its creative development within the strictures of network television at the time it was made. Independent producer Bob Banner first attempted to package *My Sweet Charlie* as a theatrical film with Sidney Poitier and Mia Farrow in the lead roles. No movie studio was interested, though, because the story is essentially a two-character sketch, however well drawn, with very little happening. This apparent big-screen liability was exactly why the producer-screenwriter team, Richard Levinson and William Link, were attracted to *My Sweet Charlie*. Their joint experiences dictated that "television can usually deal with an intimate personal story better than a large-scale event." They were eight-year veterans of TV (writing for such series as *Alfred Hitchcock Presents*, *Burke's Law*, and *The Fugitive*) when they were hired by Jennings Lang and placed under contract at Universal TV in 1967. After creating the successful program *Mannix*, Levinson and Link were rewarded by Universal TV with an opportunity to "liberate [themselves] from the constraints of series television" by producing their first made-for-TV movie.[51] *My Sweet Charlie* is the project they chose to produce and rewrite for television. They therefore secured its rights for Universal TV from Bob Banner, who retained credit as

Patty Duke (as Marlene Chambers) and Al Freeman Jr. (as Charles Roberts) costarred in My Sweet Charlie. *Courtesy of Universal TV and the National Broadcasting Company/Heldref.*

executive producer. They then proceeded through the budgeting process, cast and crew selection, and determination of shooting schedules, all of which were examples of how the telefeature extended the usual conventions of prime-time television.

For instance, *My Sweet Charlie* was budgeted at $450,000 for a projected 120-minute TV movie that either matched or exceeded the cost-per-minute ratio for two episodes of the most expensive one-hour series on television at the time—these were NBC's *The Wonderful World of Disney* ($450,000), CBS's *Gunsmoke* ($430,000), and CBS's *Mission: Impossible* ($420,000).[52] Levinson and Link also procured their creative talent from within the ranks of the industry's telefilm sector and were provided with in-house technical and blue-collar laborers from Universal TV. They first hired an experienced television director, Lamont Johnson (who had directed for several live anthologies—*Peter Gunn*; *Have Gun—Will Travel*; *The Twilight Zone*; and *The Defenders*, among others). They admired his understated and intimate style, his feeling for character, and his liberal sensibility. Levinson and Link next cast Patty Duke to star in *My Sweet Charlie* because she was an accomplished and bankable TV performer with credits earned on many live anthology dramas and *The Patty Duke Show*. Her television credentials were much more important to them than her Best Supporting Actress Oscar for her performance as Helen Keller in *The Miracle Worker* (1962). In this way, Duke was representative of a new cadre of homegrown TV movie stars (such as Jane Alexander, Ed Asner, Richard Chamberlain, Hal Holbrook, Elizabeth Montgomery, Stephanie Powers, Martin Sheen, Robert Wagner, and Dennis Weaver, among others), who consistently eclipsed comparable theatrical stars in television movie ratings, even in the early 1970s. Finally, the shooting schedule (May 5–27, 1969) turned out to be 50 percent longer than what was usually allotted for the production of 120 minutes of prime-time drama.

As was customary of most made-for-television movies, *My Sweet Charlie* was always envisioned as a first-class, quality production, surpassing in resources any other kind of programming then being developed by the networks. On June 7, 1970, *My Sweet Charlie* became the first made-for-TV movie to be recognized by the Television Academy of Arts and Sciences when it won three Emmys for "Outstanding Single Performance by an Actress in a Leading Role" (Patty Duke), "Outstanding Writing Achievement in Drama" (Richard Levinson and William Link), and "Outstanding Editing Achievement" (Ed Abroms). These awards confirmed the acceptance and position of the TV movie genre within the television industry. *My Sweet Charlie* additionally attracted forty-one million viewers during its debut telecast, which, in turn, encouraged the production of more telefeatures that dramatized cutting-edge social issues. NBC and Universal TV had taken a big step toward establishing a distinctive voice for the TV movie, as well as making it easier in general for topical themes to be openly portrayed on prime time.

Then, on September 23, 1969, ABC inaugurated its Tuesday night *Movie of the Week*, which became the most popular feature-length film series in television history. Barry Diller, a former advertising executive and newly appointed head of prime-time programming, is the man most responsible for devising the "TV movie of the week" concept at ABC. He and his boss, Leonard Goldberg, the vice president in charge of programming, negotiated a deal with Universal TV that in effect doubled the combined output of telefeatures on commercial television in just one year. ABC's *Movie of the Week* "was an innovative 26-week series of original 90-minute 'world premiere' movies specially produced (at an average cost of $375,000 per movie) for television and it became a roaring success." In 1970–1971, *Movie of the Week* was the no. 6 most-watched program in the nation; the next season it climbed to no. 5. "In the early period, we did a lot of junk movies, but we also proved that you could do movies every week," remembers Barry Diller: "Some of what we did was truly landmark for television—the first thing on television about homosexuality [*That Certain Summer* in 1972], about the Vietnam War [*The Ballad of Andy Crocker* in 1969], about drugs [*Go Ask Alice* in 1973]. It gave people in television a way to grow."[53]

Between 1971 and 1973, the *Movie of the Week*'s most significant contribution to the TV movie genre was converting the topicality of the new telefeature into the fact-based formula of the docudrama. The growth of the topical telefeature had indeed changed the entertainment landscape of the made-for-television genre forever. Older narrative types (such as Westerns and crime stories) were soon abandoned in favor of an abundance of present-day stories inspired by social controversies, cultural trends, or whatever was front and center in the nation's headlines. The higher the concept, the better the chance of earning bigger ratings and shares because there is "no word of mouth" for a TV movie. It has "only one shot at an audience."[54] Network programmers therefore were on the prowl for "a strong story premise and a promotable hook—something that [could] be summed up in one line in *TV Guide*."[55] The contemporary nature of the docudrama lent itself perfectly to this requirement.

ABC's first docudrama, *Brian's Song*, premiered on November 30, 1971. Produced by Columbia's Screen Gems, this fact-inspired melodrama is an adaptation of football superstar Gale Sayers's 1970 memoir, *I Am Third*, written with Al Silverman. It is a prime example of how the made-for-TV docudrama sometimes gets compromised in the push and pull between the documentary and narrative conventions that are endemic to the form. *Brian's Song* chronicles the interracial friendship between two professional football players, Brian Piccolo (James Caan) and Gale Sayers (Billy Dee Williams), and the slow, cancerous deterioration and death of Piccolo. This scenario is "based on a true story," meaning that it promises to be an accurate retelling of a historical, socially significant, or controversial tale, but, unfortunately, *Brian's Song* neutralizes the latter criterion by characterizing the racial interaction between Sayers and Piccolo without any of its "real life" rough edges. Piccolo's illness is also presented in the typical "disease of the week" manner, complete with bedside goodbyes and an excess of tears and sentiment. *Brian's Song* was nevertheless the popular (forty-four million viewers) and critical success of the 1971–1972 television season, capturing the "Outstanding Single Program" Emmy that year, as well as being the first made-for-TV movie ever to receive a prestigious Peabody Award for "Outstanding Achievement in Entertainment." These accolades and the overwhelming viewer response encouraged ABC to aggressively pursue more fact-based subjects in 1972–1973 and thereafter. NBC and CBS soon followed suit by commissioning docudramas of their own in 1973–1974. By 1975–1976, more than one-third of all newly produced TV movies were docudramas.

ABC's reasons for sponsoring the first docudramas were threefold. First, the network was proactively targeting the same young, urban, professional audience that all three networks were now trying to appeal to after 1970. Baby boomers were especially attracted to more contemporary and relevant specials and series of all kinds. ABC, in particular, had been appealing to the tastes of this demographic group since the mid 1950s, and it continued to do so by probing America's headlines and popular culture for TV movie topics that were both attention grabbing and up to the minute. Second, the telefeature format was ideally geared to the immediacy of most docudramatic ideas by having a gestation period of only six months to a year; in this way, a television movie could be created and telecast while the newsworthiness of the subject was still fresh on the minds of most Americans. Third, and most important, made-for-television movie production skyrocketed in the 1970s, leaving all three networks desperate for thirty to fifty workable TV movie concepts a season. The yearly output of telefeatures soared from approximately 50 in 1970 to over 120 by 1975. ABC's *Movie of the Week* specifically labored under the relentless demand of producing a television movie a week for thirty-nine weeks over six straight seasons. Under such a grueling schedule, the docudrama was born out of the ongoing necessity for ever more-producible and easily accessible TV movie concepts. From humble beginnings in 1964, the TV movie quickly flourished through cycles that spotlighted a disease of the week, then an issue of the week, and went on to become one of the most resilient and popular prime-time staples, along with situation comedies and crime-oriented action-adventure series.

Born out of the creative interaction between the networks and several of Hollywood's more ambitious and innovative telefilm companies, the telefeature soon became identifiable with a small-screen televisual style and a high-concept approach to subject matter. As early as 1969, the television movie served as a pioneer into bolder and untapped subject areas for all of prime time. The broadcast standards departments at the three networks traditionally allowed this genre more freedom in dealing with controversial topics because of its non-continuous format, as well as the TV movie's higher status within the television industry. Newsworthy events, national issues and controversies, and bits of historical lore and legend promptly became this genre's stock-in-trade. Headline hunting even spawned the docu-drama, a logical extension of the high-concept formula. By the mid 1970s, NBC, ABC, and CBS were attracting more than thirty million viewers on average for a typical prime-time made-for-TV movie. Like the television medium itself, the popularity of these intimate and increasingly relevant "consensus narratives" was truly revolutionary in terms of sheer numbers. In hindsight, the greatest contribution made by the television movie was the influence it had on closing the almost schizophrenic gap between the topicality of TV news and the escapist nature of most entertainment programming throughout the 1960s. By the early 1970s, network television, in general, reflected a greater awareness of the world beyond the screen. American society and culture were rapidly changing during the dozen years between 1964 and 1975. TV grew to be the indispensable medium, as tens of millions of Americans tuned in at home to watch this transformation unfold before their very eyes.

FROM TURMOIL TO TRANQUILITY

For the Man of the Year 1966 is a generation: the man—and woman—of 25 and under. . . . Never have the young been so assertive or so articulate, so well educated or so worldly. Predictably, they are a highly independent breed, and—to adult eyes—their independence has made them highly unpredictable. This is not just a new generation, but a new kind of generation.

Time, 6 January 1967[56]

Less than three months after the Kennedy assassination, the four highest-rated network programs of the 1960s (beside live television events that interrupted regularly scheduled programming, such as JFK's funeral and the 1969 Moon landing) appeared in quick succession over a six-week period between January 8 and February 16, 1964. The second and fourth most watched shows of the decade were the January 8 and 15 installments of *The Beverly Hillbillies*, attracting seventy-two and seventy million viewers, respectively. These two telecasts personified the high-spirited escapist shtick common of most establishment TV. The January 8 episode, for instance, involves a silly string of mishaps resulting from Granny (Irene Ryan) mistaking a kangaroo for an oversized jackrabbit; while the January 15 segment revolves around a freeloading Ozark mountaineer who visits the Clampetts in the hopes of marrying off his roly-poly daughter, Essiebelle, to Jethro (Max Baer Jr.) in order to get his hands on some of Jed's (Buddy Ebsen) money.

In stark relief, the first and third highest-rated programs of the 1960s featured a different kind of entertainment altogether. On February 9 and 16, *The Ed Sullivan Show* presented the Beatles to a mass American television audience for the first time. Network TV's foremost impresario had first spotted the Fab Four while touring England four months earlier, just as Beatlemania was flowering throughout the United Kingdom. Sullivan signed the band for three shows at $75,000, or roughly one-half of what he paid Elvis back in 1956–1957. The amount was still a princely fee for the Beatles and their manager, who eagerly agreed. In turn, John, Paul, George, and Ringo drew nearly seventy-four million viewers for their U.S. television premiere on February 9; a week later, seventy-one million Americans tuned to see what all the fuss was about.[57]

As smartly dressed, well mannered, and benign as the early Beatles looked on coast-to-coast TV, they nevertheless provided a glimpse of an emerging, youthful counterculture that would soon sweep across North America and Western Europe during the rest of the 1960s and into the early 1970s. The excited, grinning Beatles alongside a stiff, round-shouldered Ed Sullivan presented an obvious clash of generational styles and sensibilities. The four mop tops surrounded Sullivan with their slightly deviant hairstyles, Pierre Cardin collarless jackets, and Cuban high-heeled boots. Their personal charm radiated outward, complementing the overpowering sound they had just produced on stage. Predictably, the establishment press panned the band and their performance. The *New York Times* dismissed the Beatles as merely "a fad"; the *New York Herald Tribune* pronounced them "75 percent publicity, 20 percent haircut, and 5 percent lilting lament"; and

the *Washington Post* inexplicably called them "asexual and homely," despite the nonstop screaming evidence to the contrary provided by Sullivan's live studio audience.[58] The intense disapproval expressed by adult critics across the country merely confirmed the fact that the Beatles were a phenomenon that the older generation neither tuned into nor understood. In contrast, younger viewers were completely enthralled by the original music, the thoroughly contemporary look, and the mildly rebellious attitude. Being British, the Beatles also possessed an international cachet that eluded Elvis. Signs of change were everywhere as young people on the tail end of the silent generation, as well as their baby boomer brothers and sisters, embraced this new mod lifestyle.

The Beatles and other countercultural entertainers offered their fans an irresistible alternative to the mostly well worn traditions of establishment television. *The Ed Sullivan Show* had been the only prime-time venue to regularly host African American talent throughout the 1950s and early 1960s. Literally dozens of black performers as varied as Louis Armstrong and Ella Fitzgerald, Nat King Cole and Eartha Kitt, Bo Diddley, and Fats Domino had frequently graced

Sullivan's stage, along with many African American athletes such as Sugar Ray Robinson, Willie Mays, and Wilt Chamberlain, who often showed up to take bows. Now the Beatles opened the floodgates for a new generation of rock and pop acts on Sullivan's show and other musical-variety programs. During the 1964–1965 season, for example, the Dave Clark Five, the Beach Boys, the Animals, the Rolling Stones, and Petula Clark appeared, along with other English and American bands and singers. A few new music programs were also created to capture the under-twenty-five set, such as ABC's *Shindig* and NBC's *Hullabaloo* and *The Monkees*, which was inspired by the Beatles's hit movie *A Hard Day's Night* (1964). An ersatz knockoff of the Fab Four, *The Monkees* used a similar array of "surrealistic film techniques (fast and slow motion, distorted focus, comic film inserts), one-liners, non sequiturs, all delivered at a very fast pace."[59] Beginning in 1965, Beatlemania led to other British imports on TV, such as Patrick McGoohan in *Secret Agent* on CBS, Patrick Macnee and Diana Rigg in *The Avengers* on ABC, and Roger Moore in *The Saint* on NBC. Even American-made series, such as the NBC and MGM-TV spy spoof *The Man from U.N.C.L.E.*, cast British-born actors in prominent roles as a way of appealing directly to young adult and teen audiences. In the case of *The Man from U.N.C.L.E.*, for instance, David McCallum emerged as the breakout star of that show in his role as Ilya Kuryakin.

Any real content changes were slow in coming, however, as the counterculture was used more for its style than its substance by the TV establishment. A prime example was producer Aaron Spelling's *The Mod Squad*, which premiered on ABC in September 1968. Spelling began in television fifteen years earlier as an actor on Jack Webb's *Dragnet*, and now he created a series that updated the police drama for teens as well as adults. "I tried to build up the contrast between our show and the older model of the cop show," recalls Spelling in his 1996 memoir. NBC's *Dragnet* and its *Dragnet '67* update "were right wing, we were liberal. They thought everybody under 25 was a creep, we thought everybody under 25 was misunderstood."[60] *The Mod Squad* was therefore fashioned around three hippie cops ("one black, one white, one blonde," as the branding line noted), whose main purpose was "to infiltrate the counterculture and ferret out the adult criminals who preyed upon the young in Southern California."[61] The program worked with the young because Linc (Clarence Williams III), Pete (Michael Cole), and Julie (Peggy Lipton) never betrayed their peers. Likewise, "the fact that the trio was secretly working for the establishment mollified the oldsters." On the surface, *The Mod Squad* was as hip as Linc's afro and dark sunglasses, Pete's Beatles haircut and denim outfits, and Julie's long, flowing blonde hair and brightly colored flower-child dresses. In this way, "ABC could exploit current issues such as youthful rebellion, drug abuse, and racial tension while making sure legitimate authority always triumphed in the end."[62]

The consequences of appropriating the trappings of the counterculture instead of giving voice to its criticisms of the country's conservative social mores, its ongoing civil rights shortcomings, and its growing military intervention in Vietnam was never more evident than in the differing fates accorded to CBS's *The Smothers Brothers Comedy Hour* and NBC's *Rowan and Martin's Laugh-In*. Both comedy-variety shows were midseason replacements that debuted less than a year apart from each other during a particularly traumatic stretch of the 1960s. *The Smothers Brothers Comedy Hour* premiered on February 5, 1967, and was the latest in a string of sacrificial lambs (*The Judy Garland Show*, *The Garry Moore Show*) that CBS scheduled against NBC's perennial powerhouse, *Bonanza*, the no. 1 series in the nation for three seasons running between 1964 and 1967. To nearly everyone's surprise, *The Smothers Brothers Comedy Hour* became a top-20 hit while also knocking *Bonanza* down to no. 6 in 1967–1968. "We're so college-looking and clean-cut," remarked Tommy Smothers during the summer of 1967; "the American Legion likes us and so does the left wing." The Smothers Brothers additionally appealed to "every wing of the younger generation" at a time when a major demographic shift was taking place across the country in which "citizens 25 and under nearly outnumbered their elders" and "100 million Americans" would be under age thirty by 1970.[63]

At the same time, the Vietnam War was escalating, along with a compulsory draft, which made the conflict a front-burner issue for most baby boomers eligible for military service. For example, "from 184,000 at the end of 1965, U.S. troop strength rose to 385,000 a year later and to 486,000 at the close of 1967. 'Boiled down to its essence,' as one official army historian has observed, 'American strategy was simply to put more U.S. troops into South Vietnam and see what happened.'"[64] *New Yorker* TV critic Michael Arlen christened Vietnam the "living-room war" because it was the "first war brought to the people predominantly by television."[65] "For the first few years of the 'living-room war,'" adds Daniel Hallin, "most of the coverage was upbeat."[66] This attitude took an abrupt about-face on January 30, 1968, when more than 100,000 Vietcong and North Vietnamese troops invaded South Vietnam, attacking all of the major urban areas along with many previously secure high-profile locations such as the presidential palace and the U.S. embassy in Saigon. The Tet Offensive stunned the Johnson administration and the American public. After hearing of the invasion, CBS anchor Walter Cronkite was overheard saying, "What the hell is going on? I thought we were winning the war."[67] Even though the Vietcong and North Vietnamese sustained enormous losses and eventually were beaten back, the fact that they had successfully turned South Vietnam into a bloody, chaotic battlefield had the desired psychological effect on the U.S. government, the world press, and the American population back home. According to the Gallup Organization, the percentage of Americans who thought that U.S. military involvement in Vietnam was a mistake jumped dramatically to 45 percent in February 1968 from just 16 percent two years earlier; likewise, disapproval of LBJ's handling of the war shot up to 50 percent from 22 percent over the same twenty-four-month period.[68]

"Television news came of age during Vietnam," notes historian Charles Pach Jr.: it "showed the war as it was—a confused, fragmented, and questionable endeavor."[69] After Tet, the news in America during the next six months quickly went from bad to worse. On the evening of February 27, 1968, for example, the nation's most-watched and trusted newsman, Walter Cronkite, ended his *Report from Vietnam: Who, What, Where, When, Why?* with the sober conclusion that "we are mired in stalemate . . . it is increasingly clear to this reporter that the only rationale way out will be to negotiate, not as victors, but as honorable people who lived up to their pledge to defend democracy, and did the best they could."[70] "Cronkite's reporting did change the balance," acknowledges David Halberstam in *The Powers That Be*: "It was the first time in American history a war had been declared over by an anchorman. In Washington, Lyndon Johnson watched and told his press secretary, George Christian, that it was a turning point, that if he had lost Walter Cronkite, he had lost Mr. Average Citizen."[71] Then on March 12, LBJ was almost upset (49 to 42 percent) by antiwar candidate Eugene McCarthy in the Democratic primary in New Hampshire. Less than three weeks later, on Sunday, March 31, all three networks carried President Johnson's prime-time progress report on Vietnam, when he concluded with the stunning announcement, "I shall not seek, and I will not accept, the nomination of my party for another term as your President." LBJ's surprising revelation was followed in quick succession by the assassination of Martin Luther King Jr. in Memphis on April 4, triggering race riots in over sixty American cities; the shooting of Robert Kennedy by Sirhan Sirhan in the early morning hours of June 5 after RFK had just won the Democratic presidential primary in California the night before; and the violent clash between police and antiwar demonstrators over four tumultuous days (August 26–29) in the Chicago streets outside the Democratic National Convention.

On the evening of February 27, 1968, the nation's most-watched and trusted newsman, Walter Cronkite, ended his Report from Vietnam: Who, What, Where, When, Why? with the sober conclusion that "we are mired in stalemate." Courtesy of CBS/Landov.

"Few things are more striking, in retrospect," observes cultural critic Josh Ozersky, "than the sheer obliviousness of prime-time television in 1968 to the turmoil surrounding it in the real world."[72] The one obvious exception was *The Smothers Brothers Comedy Hour.* Within the context of American culture between 1967 and 1969, this comedy-variety show was not politically radical. As events spiraled out of control domestically, however, the Smothers Brothers became progressively more outspoken about both the turmoil at home and their opposition to the war in Vietnam. "They were hardly in the vanguard of public opinion when it came to the war, civil rights, or even drug abuse," cautions historian Bert Spector; "instead of leading opinion, they seemed to reflect the views already extant in large segments of the public."[73] In the opening September 29, 1968, episode of their third and final season on the air, for instance, the brothers "looked noticeably different from their clean-cut, short-haired, burgundy-suited previous selves. They both wore longer hair, moustaches, and mod Nehru jackets."[74] Among the many socially informed skits, jokes, and songs, the brothers had invited calypso singer and activist Harry Belafonte to sing the standard "Don't Stop the Carnival" while film clips of the riots outside the Democratic National Convention from a month earlier played in the background. "The 'Carnival' number went through different run-throughs as network representatives and the Smothers negotiated allowable footage," reveals Aniko Bodroghkozy; "ultimately, CBS summarily censored the whole sketch, but the Smothers refused to insert new material to fill the five-minute gap." To add insult to injury, the network then sold the free time to the Republican National Committee for an extended Nixon/Agnew presidential campaign ad.[75] The pitched battles between Tommy and Dick Smothers and the program practices office at the network finally escalated to a point that CBS abruptly canceled the series on April 3, 1969, under the guise that the brothers had reneged on their promise to submit an upcoming show for prescreening.

In contrast, producer George Schlatter of *Rowan and Martin's Laugh-In* never experienced any kind of serious censorship pressures from NBC's standards and practices department. *Laugh-In* premiered as a one-hour special on September 9, 1967, and the response was so enthusiastic that NBC brought it back as a continuing series on January 22, 1968. This comedy-variety show ingeniously borrowed the look and energy of the youth culture while leaving behind all of the controversial subject matter. *Laugh-In* was a nonstop avalanche of one-liners, sketches, and songs delivered at breakneck speed by an ensemble of twenty performers, including such recurring favorites as Ruth Buzzi, Goldie Hawn, Arte Johnson, Henry Gibson, and Lily Tomlin. Essentially, "*Laugh-In* crystallized a kind of contemporary, fast-paced, unstructured comedy 'happening' that was exactly what an agitated America wanted in 1968."[76] It delivered the style of the counterculture without the substance, shooting straight to the top of the TV ratings as the no. 1 show in the nation from 1968 through 1970: "*Laugh-In* demonstrated that 'hippie' or 'countercultural' humor was a controllable commodity, one that could be deployed whenever the network wanted to pull the youthful demographic."[77]

Furthermore, the networks soon discovered that the *Laugh-In* formula was reproducible in other comical and musical styles. For instance, CBS's new rural hit *Hee Haw* adopted "blackouts, nutty running gags, cameos by assorted guest stars, and some of the worst 'corny' one-liners imaginable" as its stock-in-trade.[78] Significantly, CBS first introduced *Hee Haw* as a safe down-home replacement for *The Smothers Brothers Comedy Hour* on June 15, 1969. This stopgap move was only temporary, though, as *Hee Haw*'s "innocent brand of humor soon gave way to a more biting satire" on prime time in the early 1970s "as the Vietnam War mushroomed, then stretched on and on without hope of victory. By twisting this way and that in response to the divergent forces that were emerging," asserts industry analyst Ed Papazian, "television's mass appeal façade was finally rent asunder."[79]

Before the 1960s ended, though, a TV spectacular of epic proportions captured the imagination of audiences worldwide, offering a brief respite from all the international conflict and domestic turmoil found in the United States and elsewhere. The Moon landing was a global television event comprising live feeds and pooled footage provided by the news divisions of CBS, NBC, and ABC. More than anything, the Moon landing functioned as the climactic episode in a kind of continuing miniseries that extended from the telecasting of six Mercury (1961–1963) and ten Gemini (1965–1966) to seven Apollo missions (1967–1969) before culminating on July 20, 1969, with Apollo 11's touchdown on the lunar Sea of Tranquillity approximately 239,000 miles away from planet Earth.

The entire Apollo 11 mission started with the liftoff of a Saturn V rocket at Cape Kennedy in Florida on Wednesday, July 16, and ended with the splashdown and recovery of the command module, *Columbia*, on the following Thursday, July 24, by the aircraft carrier U.S.S. *Hornet* in the Pacific Ocean. Highlights were covered on TV and radio throughout the nine days, but the core telecast took place over thirty-one continuous hours during July 20 and 21 when the much smaller lunar module, *Eagle*, disengaged from *Columbia* and landed on the Moon, carrying mission commander Neil A. Armstrong and *Eagle* pilot Edwin E. ("Buzz") Aldrin Jr. These two men explored the lunar surface for two hours and fourteen minutes, while *Columbia* pilot Michael Collins orbited the Moon, waiting for Armstrong and Aldrin's eventual return. On July 21, *Eagle* blasted off the lunar surface and docked with *Columbia*, and the three Apollo 11 astronauts began their trip home to Earth. An estimated worldwide television viewership of 528 million people watched the Moon landing, the largest audience for any TV program up to that point.[80] The accompanying radio listenership increased the aggregate total to nearly one billion, providing a broadcast audience of an estimated 25 percent of the Earth's population.[81] The Moon landing was clearly a watershed experience for humankind, both fulfilling an ancient dream and signaling the extraterrestrial reach and power of television as never before.

The larger significance of the Moon landing becomes most evident when viewed through the lens of superpower politics and the Cold War. All of the notable early "firsts" in space were achieved by the Russians. They launched Sputnik 1 (meaning "traveler") on October 4, 1957. This artificial satellite was the first to orbit the Earth. One month later, they sent up Sputnik 2 containing a dog named Laika, the first living creature to travel in space. Soviet cosmonaut Yuri Gagarin be-

An estimated worldwide television viewership of 528 million people watched lunar module pilot Buzz Aldrin complete a series of scientific experiments as part of the Moon landing on July 20, 1969. Courtesy of CBS/Landov.

came the first human to journey into orbit and return safely on April 12, 1961. The Americans created the National Aeronautics and Space Administration (NASA) in 1958 but spent the early years of the space program chasing the Russians. On May 25, 1961, newly elected President John F. Kennedy issued a public challenge to his fellow citizens before a joint session of Congress: "I believe this nation should commit itself to achieving the goal, before this decade is out, of landing a man on the moon and returning him safely to earth." Space had emerged as "the new battleground in the Cold War" where the first superpower to reach the Moon would decisively demonstrate its scientific and technological superiority over its political rival for the whole world to see. The space race was also tailor-made for television. The shorter Mercury and Gemini space flights, especially, were covered from start to finish before rapt audiences in the tens of millions, watching on small portable TVs in schools and at work, as well as on bigger screen console models at home.

Each one of these individual space launches was a television news special in its own right, coming as they did on a semiregular basis every

Like tens of millions of other Americans, Jack and Jackie Kennedy watched TV coverage of America's first manned space flight on May 5, 1961. Courtesy of the John F. Kennedy Library, Cecil Stoughton, White House photographer.

three to six months, flush with the inherent drama of a slowly orchestrated countdown, an explosive liftoff, a vicarious journey into space enhanced by cameras positioned outside and later inside the capsules, and usually a traditional happy ending, complete with a stirring splashdown and recovery. What made these telecasts all the more compelling was the palpable sense of danger about them. Occasionally, disasters did happen, as with Apollo 1 on January 27, 1967, when three astronauts were literally burned alive while being trapped inside their space capsule sitting atop a massive Saturn 1B booster rocket on the launchpad at Cape Kennedy. This ever-present sense of danger was a part of every mission. None of the half-billion people watching Apollo 11 could be sure whether the Moon landing would ultimately end in triumph or tragedy. This uncertainty made for an early and unusually compelling brand of reality programming. The climax of the Moon landing occurred at approximately 10:17 P.M. universal time (UTC) (5:17 P.M. eastern standard time) on July 20, when Neil Armstrong slowly descended the ladder attached to the landing platform of the lunar module and stepped ever-closer toward the surface of the Moon. Pausing a third of the way down, he "pulled a D-shaped handle, opening a storage bay and exposing the lens of a black-and-white (RCA) camera," which telecast his movements from that point onward.[82]

The actual landing on the Moon was not captured live on camera. Instead, the Columbia Broadcasting System invested in "full-scale models of the command and lunar modules, manned by CBS reporters and NASA advisers, duplicating the actions of the astronauts in a quarter-acre studio" for TV audiences around the world.[83] Once Armstrong activated *Eagle*'s camera, however, the signal was transmitted to the orbiting command module, *Columbia*, then to three enormous Earth-bound antennae in Australia, Spain, and California, where it was relayed to NASA in Houston, and finally to the networks. Within "1.3 seconds," Armstrong appeared almost luminescent against the dull, gray background, moving as if in slow motion in his shiny, white space suit.[84] He lightly jumped off the last rung of the ladder at the end of his descent, remarking as his boot landed safely on the surface of the Moon: "That's one small step for a man, one giant leap for mankind." Forty million television households in the United States— nearly 70 percent of the total number—were tuned in to the Moon landing at the moment that Armstrong took his first steps on the lunar surface.[85] These Americans were joined by an estimated 425 million more viewers from "49 [other] countries, eyes fixed on TV screens, watching in fascination":[86] "At jet-set parties in Paris, around tribal fires in southern Zambia, in the courtyards of Buddhist temples in Bangkok, on the street corners in Colombo, Ceylon [now Sri Lanka], and in snug Dublin pubs millions huddled close to TV sets and radios as the Apollo voyage was described in dozens of languages."[87]

The drama of the Moon landing was generated more by the extraordinary nature of the event than by its visual aesthetics. The vivid studio transmission of a gray and yellow *Eagle* replica that preceded the actual touchdown greatly contrasted from the somewhat ghostly and indistinct black-and-white images that were first telecast from the lunar surface. Shot with a fixed lens and perspective, these static and hazy pictures harked back to the earliest days of experimental television. Fifteen minutes after Armstrong's initial departure from *Eagle*, Buzz Aldrin became the second human being ever to walk on the Moon. For more than half an hour, these two astronauts tested their mobility according to the Moon's gravity, took pictures of each other, inspected the spacecraft, and set up a second black-and-white RCA camera on a tripod some sixty feet away, pointing it back toward the lunar module. The overall textual quality of the Moon landing noticeably improved with this second, standing TV camera and its closer-angled lens. Armstrong's and Aldrin's movements were now much clearer, even occasionally capturing brief glimpses of their faces, as each astronaut learned to walk anew, negotiating the lighter gravitational pull of the Moon along with the unfamiliar weight and mass of their oversized backpacks. The most elementary tasks obviously took the maximum effort out of them. For instance, Armstrong and Aldrin spent much of the remainder of the Moonwalk collecting twenty pounds of rock samples, before struggling together for over ten minutes to simply hoist these few bags of minerals back into the hatchway of their spacecraft.

Such mundane tasks and their rudimentary black-and-white portrayals were never memorable in and of themselves, but the unprecedented setting and the novelty of live satellite transmissions from outer space made the Moon landing exciting TV. Moreover, the political and propaganda dimension of the Moon landing was never far from the surface of the telecast. In full view of hundreds of millions of spectators worldwide, for instance, Armstrong and Aldrin planted an American flag on the lunar surface, just before a call came during "a two-minute radio hookup" from President Richard M. Nixon offering the entire Apollo 11 crew hearty congratulations from the Oval Office of the White House.[88] Nixon's live image was inserted into the upper left-hand corner of television screens around the globe as he told the astronauts that "because of what you have done, the heavens have become a part of man's world. And as you talk to us from the Sea of Tranquility, it inspires us to redouble our efforts to bring peace and tranquility to earth." Although the Moon landing "took the Vietnam war off the front pages and—at least temporarily—out of the minds" of over a half-billion people all over the world,[89] Nixon's comments provided a subtle reminder that all was not calm and contented at home, despite the unprecedented accomplishments of the Apollo 11 mission. In fact, the widespread reaction to the Moon landing was as complicated and divided as the era itself. "The 1960s had seen the assassination of one president (Kennedy) and the ruining of another through the war in Vietnam (Johnson). Civil strife tore at the nation's colleges, and race riots set fire to its cities," recounts journalism historian Bruce Evensen, "but the moon landing seemed to suggest that a brighter future was still possible."[90]

On July 16, an estimated "1,000,000 earthlings, a record outpouring for a launch, had jammed the beaches near the Cape to give Apollo 11 a lusty, shoulder-to-shoulder send-off."[91] Among the gathered multitude were Vice President Spiro T. Agnew, Lady Bird and former President Lyndon B. Johnson, Senator Barry Goldwater, Jack Benny, Johnny Carson, 200 congressmen, 100 foreign ministers, and 275 leaders of commerce and industry. CBS reporter Charles Kuralt observed that Americans had gone "moon mad."[92] *Time*, in contrast, asked, "Is the moon white?"[93] "On launch day," the magazine continued, "the VIP grandstand was a miniature *Who's Who* of white America; it was disturbing to notice that black faces were scarce."[94] Opposition to the expensive space program was especially strong inside the nation's African American community. "Texas, with its oil wells, large farms, and now space center of the world, symbolizes the affluent America," said Herbert James, the black field director of the National Welfare Rights Organization, "but there exists in this great state a despicable amount of poverty. Starvation and hunger are taking place within miles of the space center."[95] A "mule-cart procession of the Poor People's March, led by Ralph Abernathy," also arrived to protest the Moon launch on July 16. When the civil rights leader saw the Apollo 11 liftoff, however, "he forgot about poverty and prayed for the safety of the men."[96] At least temporarily, the Moon landing generated an unprecedented level of interest in the space program, although some cohorts were clearly more excited by the telecast than others. "If to many the moon seemed white, it also seemed middle-aged," *Time* further surmised; "the young, who have grown up in the TV and space age, seemed the most blasé of all."[97]

Having beaten the Russians to the Moon, the United States government no longer supported NASA's plans for the future, as it once had, which now included a "permanent American base on the moon, manned trips to Mars, and a 100-man space station orbiting the earth," along with a variety of other ambitious goals.[98] Six more Apollo missions (12 to 17) proceeded on schedule, five of which resulted in ten more astronauts walking on the Moon before television cameras. The size of the audiences to these subsequent telecasts waned, however, as worries increased over social problems and the prolonged conflict in Vietnam. Funding was finally rescinded for the last three planned Apollo space fights (18 through 20), causing their ultimate cancellation as the space race came to an abrupt end in December 1972. Thanks to television, though, Apollo 11 provided humans around the world with the opportunity to look at the Earth in a wholly new way. Viewed within the enormity of space, humanity saw its home as one, small, interconnected planet. The *New York Times* carried Archibald MacLeish's poem "Voyage to the Moon" on its front page the morning after the Eagle landed on the lunar surface:

> Over us, more beautiful than the moon . . .
> a wonder to us, unattainable . . .
> the bright earth.[99]

Television was evidently contributing to a growing global self-awareness, even as Cold War tensions were being acted out in the Moon landing for hundreds of millions of people to watch in July 1969 and to quietly reflect on afterward. In addition, the international reach and influence of this extraordinary telecast previewed the future potential of TV beyond the largely self-imposed limits that were already confining the medium in America during the waning years of the network era, which lasted from approximately 1948 through 1975.

END OF AN ERA

> They didn't win the season. They won their season. This is what McLuhan called the "dinosaur effect." CBS has blown to its biggest size just before extinction.
> NBC VICE PRESIDENT, PAUL L. KLEIN, *New York Times*, 1969[100]

Flush from the success of their joint triumph in covering the Moon landing, CBS, NBC, and ABC acted as though their three-network oligopoly would last forever. Sour grapes aside, Paul Klein's assertion about the growing obsolescence of CBS in its present form was remarkably prescient. At the time, however, Klein and many other television insiders had a hard time recognizing that his critique of CBS was just as relevant for NBC, ABC, and their shared three-network stranglehold on the U.S. television industry in general. Klein, who headed NBC's research department, was the first high-ranking TV executive to put so much emphasis on audience demographics with the advertising agencies and the sponsors he interacted with during the late 1960s. ABC had targeted young adults and teens since the mid 1950s, but all three networks had always measured success or failure by the sheer tonnage of viewers they were able to deliver to sponsors. By 1969–1970, however, Klein was arguing that although CBS had marginally won the season with a rating of 20.0 to NBC's 19.9 and ABC's 16.4, his network had actually pulled the better demographics. He provided advertisers with data demonstrating that NBC's audience skewed younger and more urban, while possessing a greater amount of disposable income than CBS's slightly larger but much older, rural, and downscale constituency.[101] Klein's argument was a compelling one. He made a strong case that even though CBS had won the season, NBC was a much smarter buy for sponsors. No insider had ever questioned the underlying logic of TV's mass market model so effectively before. It hinted at the changes taking place beneath the surface of the industry.

Ironically, CBS, not NBC, was the first network to respond strategically to the new emphasis on demographics, despite Klein's innovative reading of the numbers. Under Robert Wood, CBS completely restructured its schedule for demographic reasons. Frank Stanton hired Wood as the network's latest president in 1969. Wood was promoted from within CBS, Inc., where by 1967 he had worked his way up to president of the division of television stations, overseeing the network's five owned-and-operated outlets in New York, Philadelphia, Chicago, St. Louis, and Los Angeles. He knew firsthand what it was like to be affiliated with the no. 1–rated network whose programming was nevertheless too old and rural in orientation to play very well with viewers in five of the largest TV markets in the country. Wood was broadly experienced in sales and marketing, as well as programming, so in making business decisions at the network he understood the increasing importance of demographic variables such as age, sex, household income, educational level, and geographic location. He therefore proposed that CBS radically restructure its schedule to specifically target the young, urban professionals that advertisers were now coveting the most. The problem for Wood as the new president of CBS-TV was that a dozen of his highest-rated prime-time programs simply attracted audiences that were the oldest and most rural in network television. Other than *Gunsmoke,* he wanted to pull the plug on *Mayberry R.F.D., Here's Lucy, The Beverly Hillbillies, The Red Skelton Show, The Jackie Gleason Show, The Ed Sullivan Show, The Glen Campbell Goodtime Hour, Hee Haw, Gomer Pyle, U.S.M.C., Green Acres,* and *Petticoat Junction,* even though the ratings for each of these shows fell within the top 30.

Wood's chief programmer, Michael Dann, was dead set against such a risky all-or-nothing strategy since many of these programs and their stars had defined CBS for most of the decade, if not longer. Wood was convinced, though, that times had changed and simply sticking to the status quo would soon spell disaster for CBS. He thus cultivated Bill Paley's support for his plan, and he eventually prevailed. As a result, Dann left the network in the early summer of 1970 and was replaced by his thirty-two-year-old protégé, Fred Silverman, who, in turn, worked closely with Wood to develop an entirely new generation of younger, edgier, and more topical series at CBS. Together, they green-lighted a situation comedy that had been under consideration at ABC since 1968. Norman Lear and Bud Yorkin of Tandem Productions had originally developed a pilot called *Those Were the Days,* based on a British hit series entitled, *Till Death Us Do Part.* ABC passed on the program twice before Wood and Silverman gambled on bringing a warts-and-all character like Archie Bunker (Carroll O'Connor) to prime time. The Bunkers were a lower-middle-class family from Queens, New York, composed of a loud-mouthed and bigoted patriarch named Archie, his lovable and long-suffering wife Edith (Jean Stapleton), his recently married daughter Gloria (Sally Struthers), and his Polish-American live-in son-in-law Michael Stivic (Rob Reiner). The weekly fireworks were typically set off between Archie and Mike—the old-school, blue-collar, loading dock-worker versus the liberal college student with his long hair and mustache and dressed in tie-dyed t-shirts and jeans. American television had never seen anyone quite like Archie Bunker before or heard the kinds of heated exchanges he had with his son-in-law, who he often referred to as "Meathead." Archie frequently erupted in a nonstop stream of racial and ethnic slurs, calling blacks "jungle-bunnies," Jews "hebes," and Puerto Ricans "spics." He also gave voice to the kinds of deep-seated prejudices that most bigots simply left unsaid except in the privacy of their own homes.

All in the Family premiered on January 12, 1971, behind the soon-to-be-replaced *Hee Haw* on Tuesday nights. To everyone's surprise, the show attracted very little attention at first. Then in early May, after only thirteen episodes, *All in the Family* won Emmys for "Outstanding Comedy Series," "Outstanding New Series," and "Outstanding Continued Performance by a Leading Actress in a Comedy Series" (Jean Stapleton). In 1971–1972, Fred Silverman moved *All in the Family* to 8 P.M. on Saturday night as the anchor of what would become CBS's unbeatable signature evening for the rest of the decade. *All in the Family* quickly shot up to no. 1 in the country and stayed there for the next five seasons. Nothing quite captured the current change at CBS better than the dramatic contrast between this aggressively topical situation comedy and the network's silly and farcical hit of a decade earlier, *The Beverly Hillbillies*. This rural sitcom was still no. 18 in the country when Wood boldly decided to cancel it on March 23, 1971. *All in the Family* was building on the content innovations that had already been pioneered on prime time by the made-for-TV movie during the previous two years. It was, however, the first continuing series to ever tackle issues such as Vietnam, racism, women's rights, homosexuality, impotence, menopause, rape, alcoholism, and many other relevant themes. *All in the Family*'s phenomenal popularity changed the face of television by making it much easier for subsequent prime-time series to incorporate these and other controversial subjects into their story lines. Then, in early 1972, Fred Silverman suggested to Norman Lear that he spin off a series featuring Edith's highly opinionated upper-middle-class liberal cousin Maude (Beatrice Arthur). Thus this strong, outspoken, and assertive female character debuted in her own eponymously named series at no. 4 in the ratings in 1972–1973, remaining a top-10 hit for four straight seasons.

Lear soon emerged as the most influential producer of the 1970s bar none, creating twenty more programs throughout the course of the decade, including *Good Times*, *The Jeffersons*, and *One Day at a Time* for CBS, as well as *Sanford and Son* for NBC. The only other company at the time to approach the success of Lear's Tandem/TAT Communications was MTM Enterprises, another independently owned production company formed in 1970 by Grant Tinker and his then-wife, Mary Tyler Moore. *The Mary Tyler Moore Show* premiered four months earlier than *All in the Family* in September 1970, and it, too, took some time before it found its audience. Grant Tinker invited the producer-screenwriter team of James L. Brooks and Allan Burns, who he had worked with on *Room 222*, to collaborate again on *The Mary Tyler Moore Show*, and they took the character-driven situation comedy to a whole new level of emotional depth and sophistication. *The Mary Tyler Moore Show* was set in the fictional WJM-TV newsroom in Minneapolis, Minnesota, featuring an independent thirty-something career woman, Mary Richards (Mary Tyler Moore), along with a large ensemble of professional colleagues and friends led by her curmudgeonly though caring boss Lou Grant (Ed Asner) and her closest confidante and neighbor Rhoda Morgenstern (Valerie Harper). *The Mary Tyler Moore Show* was certainly not the first TV series to generate a family-oriented atmosphere in the workplace (as early as 1952, in fact, CBS's *Our Miss Brooks* achieved a similar effect at Madison High School, where Eve Arden's Connie Brooks taught). *The Mary Tyler Moore Show* did update and further enrich this familiar trope, however, even innovating story arcs that carried over from episode to episode and eventually season to season. During 1973–1974, for example, Lou's wife Edie left him after nearly twenty years of marriage. In subsequent episodes, these two characters grow and develop through a trial separation, a divorce, and finally, two seasons later, Edie's remarriage to somebody new.

Through the rest of the 1970s, MTM Enterprises produced a handful of other programs for CBS, including two *Mary Tyler Moore Show* spin-offs, *Rhoda* and *Phyllis*, *The Bob Newhart Show*, *WKRP in Cincinnati*, and its first of many one-hour dramas, *The White Shadow*. Once Fred Silverman moved *All in the Family* from Tuesday to Saturday evening in 1971–1972, *The Mary Tyler Moore Show* greatly benefited from its close proximity to the nation's no. 1 show and joined the ranks of the top-10 itself. Furthermore, Silverman hammocked *M*A*S*H* between *All in the Family* and *The Mary Tyler Moore Show* in 1973–1974, facilitating yet another breakout hit for CBS. *M*A*S*H* was a television adaptation of the popular movie of the same name directed by Robert Altman in 1970. The TV series was created by writer Larry Gelbart, who coproduced it with Gene Reynolds. The military sitcom (ABC's *McHale's Navy* and CBS's *Gomer Pyle, U.S.M.C.*) had grown hopelessly out of date during the mid to late 1960s as the news from Vietnam progressively worsened. By 1972 with the war winding down, however, Wood and Silverman believed it was time for an antiwar comedy that captured and expressed the anger, frustration, and resignation that many Americans now felt about Vietnam. The show subsequently became a blockbuster hit for CBS, settling comfortably into the Nielsen top 10 for nine of the next eleven seasons.

M*A*S*H was ostensibly set behind the lines in Korea during the 1950s, following the irreverent exploits of Captain Hawkeye Pierce (Alan Alda) and the rest of the doctors, nurses, and support staff attached to the 4077th Mobile Army Surgical Hospital. Like a lot of the newest sitcoms at CBS during the early to mid 1970s, *M*A*S*H* combined the topicality of *All in the Family* with the character comedy of *The Mary Tyler Moore Show*. By the end of the 1973–1974 season, Robert Wood's strategic gamble at CBS was widely recognized as a bona fide success throughout the industry as his network once again opened up a commanding lead over its competition with a 21.1 rating to NBC's 18.7 and ABC's 17.7.[102] Since each ratings point translated into an estimated $20 million in additional advertising revenue, both Wood and Silverman were riding high at CBS, and, for a time, their approach to program development was copied at the other two networks. In addition to Lear's *Sanford and Son*, for instance, NBC also scheduled other socially relevant sitcoms such as *Chico and the Man*, and ABC likewise added Danny Arnold's *Barney Miller* as well as several one-hour baby boomer–oriented series such as the New Age Western *Kung Fu* and the funky street-smart *Baretta*. All of these shows were targeted at what the three networks now collectively agreed was the ideal demographic—young, urban professionals aged eighteen to forty-nine (especially women). The popularity of CBS, NBC, and ABC would never be greater as their three-network oligopoly reached its peak in 1974–1975, averaging a 93.6 percent share of the prime-time viewing audience that season.[103] Each network was highly profitable, competing solely against each other in what was basically a closed $2.5 billion TV advertising market.[104]

Within ten short years, though, all would be different. The strategy CBS, NBC, and ABC had gravitated toward for short-term success—namely, targeting specific demographics with their programming—also sowed the seeds of change where the TV industry as a whole would eventually move well beyond its mass market model. Over the next decade, a whole host of technological, industrial, and programming innovations would usher in an era predicated on an entirely new niche-market philosophy that essentially turned the vast majority of broadcasters into narrowcasters. In the meantime, however, three tentative moves had just been enacted in the U.S. public sector that reflected a general dissatisfaction with the current state of American television. First, Congress passed the Public Broadcasting Act of 1967. This legislation created the Corporation for Public Broadcasting with the clear intention of jump-starting noncommercial television and radio in this country, which had remained largely unrealized during the past fifteen years. In 1952, the FCC had allocated 242 channels for this purpose when it lifted the four-year freeze on station licenses. Congress's prime motivation was "to fill niches that commercial broadcasters had abandoned or not yet discovered," such as "children's educational programming, especially for preschoolers; 'how-to' programs stressing the pragmatic (cooking, home repair); public affairs programming and documentaries; [and] upscale drama."[105] To this end, National Educational Television (NET) ran the twenty-six-part, BBC-produced *Forsyte Saga* on a weekly basis beginning in October 1969; this introduced American audiences to the prime-time miniseries and paved the way for the eventual development of *Masterpiece Theater* in 1971. In addition, *Sesame Street* debuted in 1969; Julia Child reprised *The French Chef* in 1970; and *The Robert MacNeil Report* premiered in 1975 after veteran newscasters MacNeil and Jim Lehrer worked out so well as a team covering the Senate Watergate Hearings for the newly founded Public Broadcasting Service (PBS) in 1973 and 1974.

Second, the FCC adopted the Prime-Time Access Rule (PTAR) on May 4, 1970, as part of its *Report and Order on Network Television Broadcasting*, which culminated over a dozen years of investigation by the commission. In 1957, the FCC was initially alarmed to find out that 28.7 percent of all prime-time programming was then produced by the networks. By 1969, this figure dropped to 19.6 percent, but the FCC determined that, over these last twelve years, CBS, NBC, and ABC actually increased their overall control over prime time by expanding their joint arrangements with various telefilm producers from 38.5 to 75 percent. During this same time frame, moreover, independently produced prime-time programming dropped from 32.8 to 5.4 percent. Consequently, the PTAR went into effect on September 1, 1971, limiting CBS, NBC, and ABC to only three of the four prime-time hours (usually 8 P.M. to 11 P.M.) Monday through Saturday in the top fifty markets; this reduced them to twenty-two out of the full twenty-eight hours they had previously filled with programming before the rule.[106] The PTAR was adopted "to break the network monopoly over prime time, to open a new market for independent producers who complained of being at the mercy of three customers, to stimulate the creation of new program forms, and to give the stations the opportunity to do their most significant local programming in the choicest viewing hours."[107]

Despite the best of intentions, the PTAR failed in almost every respect when it was implemented in the fall of 1971. The rule did limit network access to prime time by over 20 percent, but practically no local productions or any programming innovations whatsoever were inspired by the PTAR. In addition, any increase in independently produced programming was mainly restricted to the reworking of previously canceled network series, such as Edward Gaylord's *Hee Haw* and Lawrence Welk's *The Lawrence Welk Show*, or the creation of inexpensive thirty-minute "infotainment," or game shows, such as Group W's *PM Magazine* and Mark Goodson and Bill Todman's *Family Feud*. Rather than locally produced programming, these kinds of first-run syndicated shows dominated the 7 to 8 P.M. time slot.

Third and most important, the Financial Interest and Syndication (Fin-Syn) Rule came into being, almost as a sidebar to the PTAR discussions. It, too, was part of the FCC's 1970 *Report and Order on Network Television Broadcasting*, setting severe limits on the amount of original programming that CBS, NBC, and ABC could produce and later syndicate, either at home or overseas. The Fin-Syn Rule was designed to curb "vertical integration" in the television industry, referring to the three-network oligopoly's near total control over manufacturing, wholesaling, and retailing. CBS, NBC, and ABC (the wholesalers) already exercised a contractually advantageous relationship over their affiliates (the retailers); now the FCC had plenty of evidence that they also dominated TV's production sector (the manufacturers). The Fin-Syn Rule (and the future legal actions that gave it added weight and enforceability) greatly curtailed the power of the networks and strictly limited their future involvement as program producers, coproducers, and syndicators. As a consequence, many new independent production companies (such as the aforementioned Tandem/TAT Communications and MTM Enterprises, for example), along with Hollywood's major and mini-major television program producers, flourished under Fin-Syn.

Not surprisingly, CBS, NBC, and ABC dragged their feet at first in abiding by the Fin-Syn Rule, especially after losing 12 percent of their advertising revenue in one fell swoop when Congress banned tobacco ads on television starting January 2, 1971.[108] The networks initially planned to cut their losses in this regard by ignoring the Fin-Syn Rule whenever possible and increasing their influence and participation in program syndication. What stopped them was a Justice Department suit filed on April 14, 1972, claiming antitrust violations against the three-network oligopoly. In fact, these charges were fully justified, but the defendants quickly countercharged that this action was more politically than legally motivated, which was also true.[109] The antagonism that existed between the Nixon administration and the networks over coverage of the Vietnam War is well documented.[110] After the

1968 Tet Offensive, television news, in particular, went from being supportive and upbeat about the progression of events in Vietnam to having an increasingly critical and antiwar perspective. In response, in October 1969, presidential aide Jeb Magruder in the new Nixon administration sent the following written recommendation to White House Chief of Staff H. R. Haldeman:

> The real problem that faces this administration is to get this unfair coverage in such a way that we make major impact on a basis in which the networks . . . begin to look at this somewhat differently. . . . [We can] utilize the antitrust division to investigate various media relating to antitrust violation. Even the possible threat of antitrust action, I think, would be effective in changing their views on the above matter.[111]

Soon thereafter, identical antitrust suits were prepared by the Justice Department as a hedge against future coverage of the administration by the three networks. These briefs could be filed if and when they were ever needed.

The time came in mid-April 1972, two weeks after an especially difficult stretch of bad news following the Eastertide Offensive, when the North Vietnamese launched their largest invasion since Tet across the demilitarized zone into South Vietnam. The directive to file the suits came from Chief Domestic Advisor John Ehrlichman since Attorney General John Mitchell had already left the Justice Department to become chairman of the Committee to Re-elect the President. Whether or not Nixon's Department of Justice would have even paid attention to the Fin-Syn Rule and the networks' oligopolistic control over the production sector of the television industry, especially during a politically sensitive election year, is impossible to determine in hindsight. What is clear is that television coverage of Vietnam was a major factor in the mix of motivations that set these legal proceedings in motion. Once off the ground, moreover, these antitrust suits also outlasted the Nixon administration.[112] They subsequently took on a life of their own, ending in consent decrees signed by NBC (on November 17, 1976), CBS (on July 31, 1980), and ABC (on November 14, 1980), as each network eventually committed to Fin-Syn in a legally binding manner.[113] These concessions weakened the three-network oligopoly even further. The Vietnam War was therefore responsible for all sorts of unintended consequences that reverberated throughout American society and culture, even in sectors that were seemingly unrelated to the conflict in any direct way, such as the U.S. television industry. Ironically, TV's role in the war "was probably more a follower than a leader in the nation's change of course in Vietnam," as it also was in Watergate, which started in 1972 and slowly grew into a national crisis over the next two years.[114]

The Watergate affair was an unfolding series of events that began when five burglars were arrested after breaking into the Democratic National Committee offices at the Watergate Complex in Washington, D.C., on June 17, 1972, and ended with the resignation of President Richard Nixon on August 9, 1974. Even though this Republican dirty-tricks operation occurred only twenty weeks before the 1972 elections, Watergate was still mainly a second-tier concern in comparison with Vietnam during the fall campaign since most of the evidence concerning the affair didn't surface until well after Nixon's landslide victory (60 to 38 percent) over antiwar candidate George McGovern. On January 27, 1973, U.S. involvement in Vietnam came to an official end with the signing of the Paris Peace Accords. After that point, Watergate took center stage with the commencement of Senate Hearings on Presidential Campaign Activities, which began on May 17 and concluded on November 15, 1973, with two extended recesses in between. For the most part, CBS, NBC, and ABC rotated their coverage every third day, for a total of more than three hundred hours. PBS would then telecast each day's proceedings on tape delay in the evening. It was reported that "audience surveys found that 85% of the nation's households watched all or part of at least one of the sessions. CBS estimated that viewers spent 1.6 billion total home-hours watching the daytime coverage on the three networks and an additional 400 million home-hours watching at night on PBS."[115] Watergate became a national obsession for most American viewers who watched in stunned disbelief as the accumulated testimony gradually suggested that an illegal cover-up had indeed taken place—and not only were the president's men involved but also Richard Nixon himself.

A "new phase of Watergate" began on February 6, 1974, "when the U.S. House of Representatives voted 410-to-4 to authorize the House Judiciary Committee to investigate whether sufficient grounds existed to impeach President Nixon."[116] The thirty-eight-member committee began debating in closed-door session on May 9, eventually opening up the final six days of deliberations to television cameras starting on July 24. The climax of these proceedings came on July 30, when the Judiciary Committee voted overwhelming to bring three articles of impeachment against Richard Nixon. The full House next voted to allow TV coverage of the entire impeachment debate, which was scheduled to start on August 18. Sensing the inevitable, President Nixon addressed the country during prime time on the evening of August 8, informing his fellow citizens that he planned to resign

JOHN W. DEAN, III
FORMER WHITE HOUSE COUNSEL

Watergate became a national obsession for most American viewers who watched in stunned disbelief as the accumulated testimony gradually suggested that an illegal cover-up had occurred—and not only were all the President's men involved, such as former White House counsel John Dean, but also Richard Nixon himself. Courtesy of Library of American Broadcasting at the University of Maryland.

the next day at noon. This sixteen-minute speech "was watched by 110 million people, more than had watched any Presidential speech in history and was exceeded only by the TV audience for the first walk on the moon."[117] Americans had been thrown suddenly into this tumultuous era by the assassination of JFK, and now they hoped they were seeing it all come to an end with the resignation of Richard Nixon. Just as the Depression and World War II had left indelible marks on their parents' generation, Vietnam and Watergate would from now on be the two most important formative events in the lives of most baby boomers. "From the tube they first acquired the almost frightening awareness and precocity that so often stuns adults," reported *Time* in 1966.[118] Ten years later, television was still an essential ingredient in shaping a generational perspective that had now grown much less naïve and far more circumspect because of all the traumas and transformations that had occurred during the last decade.

The end of Vietnam and Watergate signaled a new beginning for the nation, as well as the television industry. ABC suddenly emerged as the network to beat in the mid to late 1970s. In November 1974, Leonard Goldenson had promoted Frederick Pierce to the presidency of ABC Television in the hopes of reviving the network's competitive standing within the industry. Pierce was a company man through and through, having served ABC since 1956 in research, sales, promotion, and programming. He was arguably the most well rounded network president in the business at the time. One of his first moves was to lure to ABC the person who the conventional wisdom considered the most talented programmer in television—Fred Silverman. After quietly pursuing Silverman for months, Pierce finally signed him up as ABC's new president of entertainment effective June 16, 1975. The team of Pierce and Silverman quickly proved to be even more dynamic and successful than Wood and Silverman had been during the previous six years. American television was currently in the process of being reinvented, and ABC would be the first major network to catch the wave. In many respects, 1976 was a turnaround year. The United States of America renewed itself through a whole host of Bicentennial celebrations. ABC, too, revitalized its prospects by blazing a trail marked by experimentation, innovation, and risk in the areas of sports, news, entertainment programming, and cable. To begin, "its sports roster in the Bicentennial year [included] the winter and summer Olympic Games and the World Series—which it won over from NBC beginning in 1976."[119] ABC was on the move, both nationally and internationally. Soon it would emerge from the industry's cellar and climb to the pinnacle of network television.

The Wide World of ABC

> There is no parallel in the history of broadcasting—and few in any well-
> established industries—to ABC's sudden rise. It is as if, in the space of
> two years, Chrysler had surged past General Motors and sent Ford reel-
> ing back to Dearborn.
>
> *Time*, September 5, 1977[1]

Sports was second only to news as the programming genre that contributed the most to the growing national and international awareness
of American television audiences. As recently as 1957, even the national pastime—baseball—was for all intents and purposes a regionally played major league sport with only St. Louis located west of the
Mississippi River. In 1958, Major League Baseball (MLB) finally expanded to the West Coast when Walter O'Malley relocated the Brooklyn Dodgers to Los Angeles and Horace Stoneham the New York Giants
to San Francisco. Both owners appeared before a congressional subcommittee investigating antitrust violations in professional sports that
year and testified that the newly renamed Los Angeles Dodgers and
San Francisco Giants were in full support of Skiatron TV's plans to develop a pay-TV system that would telecast baseball by cable throughout
California. Local politicians ultimately nixed this pay-cable venture,
but residents of L.A. and San Francisco enthusiastically embraced their
new teams in no small part because of the extensive broadcast television coverage that the Dodgers and Giants were given from the outset.[2]
TV viewership spurred team interest, which led to increased gate attendance, while the substantial profits that each of these ball clubs eventually enjoyed from selling their local and national telecasting rights
boded well for the windfall potential that television held out for most
MLB franchises, as well as the majority of teams in the National Football League (NFL) and the National Basketball Association (NBA) over
the next two decades. Sports, television, and advertising grew ever
closer together to form a billion-dollar partnership by the mid 1970s,
as the popularity and scope of this kind of programming reached from
coast to coast and throughout the world.

In the United States, specifically, the typical household in 1976 had the TV set turned on for six hours and twenty-six minutes a day on average, and 20 percent of that time was spent watching sports. This figure was even higher for men and boys, who devoted over 25 percent of their total viewing time to this type of programming.[3] Women and girls, too, were starting to pay more attention to sports on television. ABC led the way in this regard by shifting emphasis to the drama and personal dimension of sports, rather than just relying on the usual dry presentation of strategies and statistics, when it reintroduced this genre to prime time after the last regularly scheduled boxing matches were canceled in the early 1960s. Beginning with the 1968 summer Olympic games in Mexico City and culminating with the September 1970 debut of *Monday Night Football*, ABC Sports followed a template created by its president, Roone Arledge, which highlighted the personal lives of athletes as a way of involving more nonsports fans—especially women—in these telecasts. Arledge featured such colorful personalities as Howard Cosell and Don Meredith as commentators, who, along with their play-by-play announcers, Keith Jackson and especially Frank Gifford, emerged as prime-time stars in their own right. At first, sports purists criticized *Monday Night Football* for what they felt was a circus-like soap opera atmosphere; clearly, this program was unlike any of the college and professional football game presentations that they were used to seeing on Saturday and Sunday afternoons. Broadening the appeal of the genre was Roone Arledge's goal, however, and he defended his new series by explaining that "on Monday nights, we are in the entertainment business, competing against other networks for prime-time ratings. Here we work at pontificating less and we also try to document the action in a little more personal manner."[4]

No one at ABC or in the NFL argued with the results. *Monday Night Football* averaged an 18.5 rating and a 35 share in its first season and soon established itself as a perennial top-20 hit by the end of the 1970s.[5] In addition, Roone Arledge was the person most responsible for internationalizing sports on television. He worked briefly for DuMont and several years at NBC before being hired at ABC in 1960 by Edgar Scherick to produce college football games, which was the only major sport that the network had under contract at the time. Arledge was only twenty-nine years old when he and Scherick created *Wide World of Sports* as a way of turning their network's big sports deficit into an advantage for ABC. This series completely redefined the TV viewing experience for the American sports fan. As the show's executive producer, Arledge extended the rela-

ABC Sports followed a template created by its president, Roone Arledge, which highlighted the personal lives of athletes as a way of involving more nonsports fans in these telecasts. Flanked by O. J. Simpson (left), Arledge (right) won thirty-seven Emmys over his long career. Courtesy of Library of American Broadcasting at the University of Maryland.

tively static and colorless stylistics of most sports telecasting at the time, creating a more innovative and compelling style of presenting a wider range of sporting activities. He wrote a memo to Scherick in 1961 describing the kinds of new production techniques that he had in mind for *Wide World of Sports* such as "cameras on jeeps, hand-held cameras, boom microphones for sound, and even the use of heli-copters," concluding, "we are going to use show business to sports."[6] His first major sports events was a United States–Soviet Union track meet in Moscow:

> It was at the height of the Cold War and athletic competition in-volving the world's two superpowers often became bigger than the event and an effective way to attract viewers whose patriotic fervor drew them to sports they normally wouldn't watch. During the first 20 weeks, along with the Moscow track meet, the *Wide World of Sports* schedule included a soccer championship in London, the LeMans auto race from France, and an all-star baseball game in Japan.[7]

By 1965, Roone Arledge and his *Wide World of Sports* team were among "the first users of the Atlantic satellite, enabling [them] to produce live sporting events from around the world."[8] This magazine-style series was the most dynamic, fast-paced weekend afternoon program on any network, and it quickly became a fixture for ABC, revolutionizing the form and content of sports telecasting from that point onward. "What we set out to do was get the audience involved emotionally," explained Arledge in 1966; "if they didn't give a damn about the game, they might still enjoy the program."[9] The two principal ways in which Roone Arledge increased the entertainment value of *Wide World of Sports* was by cultivating star performers and being the first to employ the newest technologies and techniques. He hired journalist Jim McKay (né James McManus) away from CBS to anchor this innovative series. Together, they wrote the program's signature opening spoken by McKay and accompanied by the familiar brassy fanfare that introduced each episode: "Spanning the globe to give you the constant variety of sport, the thrill of victory, the agony of defeat, the human drama of athletic competition, this is ABC's *Wide World of Sports!*" Arledge then paired two consummate showmen—heavyweight champion Muhammad Ali with outspoken, iconoclastic sportscaster Howard Cosell, who kept reminding viewers, "I tell it like it is." Cosell's star rose rapidly because of his association with Ali. He also staunchly defended the boxer when Ali, as a conscientious objector, refused induction into the U.S. Army during the Vietnam War and was stripped of his title by the New York State Boxing Commission (a decision that was later overturned by the U.S. Supreme Court).

Arledge used visually arresting graphics whenever possible, as well as slow motion and instant replay to transform such minor sports as gymnastics, track and field, downhill skiing, figure skating, swimming and diving, rodeo, and auto racing into extremely popular television attractions. *Wide World of Sports* even covered offbeat spectacles such as daredevil Evel Knievel's motorcycle jumps, including his September 8, 1974, attempt over Idaho's Snake River Canyon in his own homemade skycycle, drawing an astonishing 22.3 rating on a Sunday afternoon.[10] Roone Arledge's success with *Wide World of Sports* led to his being named vice president of ABC Sports in 1965 and then president in 1968. He supervised the telecasting of a combined ten summer and winter Olympiads starting in 1964 through 1988.

ABC Sports especially distinguished itself during the 1972 summer games in Munich when Arledge himself went into the control room to direct seventeen straight hours of coverage during September 5 and 6. This was when eight terrorists from the Black September Organization broke into the Olympic compound and, in front of an international audience estimated at 900 million worldwide over the course of the two-day ordeal, took eleven Israeli athletes hostage as a way of publicizing their political cause.[11] The ABC production team adapted quickly to this emergency under Arledge's take-charge leadership and Jim McKay's steady on-air presence, prefiguring the kind of continuing live international coverage that cable news would further pioneer in the 1980s and realize fully during the buildup and start of the 1991 Persian Gulf War. In the case of the Munich hostage crisis, McKay delivered the late-breaking developments just as soon as he heard them from Arledge in his earpiece. When word finally came in about the failed rescue attempt, resulting in a fateful gunfight between the kidnappers and the German police at the Munich airport, an exhausted and visibly shaken McKay turned toward the camera and told the approximately 100 million people watching at that moment (including nearly 45 million in the United States alone) that "our greatest hopes and our worst fears are seldom realized. They now say that there were eleven hostages. Two were killed in their rooms yesterday morning. Nine were killed at the airport tonight. They're all gone."[12]

Even before Munich, ABC was widely recognized as the no. 1 sports network in the industry. Now ABC built on its hard-won prestige and considerable expertise in this area by jump-starting the network's improbable rise to the top of the ratings with its prime-time telecasts of the 1976 winter Olympics in Innsbruck, Austria, and especially the summer games in Montreal five months later. Arledge spent $10 million for the rights to the 1976 winter games, even though NBC had lost money four years earlier after paying $6.5 million when its lackluster coverage resulted in fewer viewers than expected and subpar ratings for the 1972 Olympics in Sapporo, Japan. Arledge, however, had confidence in ABC's experienced and talented *Wide World of Sports* production team, which then "won most of its time slots" against CBS and NBC's prime-time entertainment lineups over twelve straight days in February 1976.[13]

Although the United States won only seven total medals over the entire games, as opposed to the Soviet Union's twenty-seven and East Germany's nineteen, and gold-medal-winning figure skater Dorothy Hamill was America's only breakout star, ABC nevertheless provided plenty of excitement, intimacy, and drama. Veteran producer Don Ohlmeyer remembered years later that he and Roone Arledge started laughing in the control room on the last day of the Innsbruck Olympics after having just completed "six hours at a 40 share without a single event (biathlon and a Swedish-Russia hockey game) they would have even put on *Wide World of Sports*."[14] The people at ABC Sports were justifiably proud of their production and storytelling abilities, as were ABC president Fred Pierce and the network's new entertainment chief, Fred Silverman.

Even though NBC, CBS, and ABC didn't call it branding at the time, each network was already trying out advertising slogans in the mid 1970s as a way of establishing a more distinctive and separate identity from its two main competitors, as well as from the ever-increasing number of newly created cable services. For the first time, NBC, CBS, and ABC enacted large-scale marketing campaigns in order to build up and reinforce a more loyal following among America's young, urban, professional viewers. In this Bicentennial year, for example, NBC started calling itself "the network of America," and CBS promoted its wide array of prime-time performers with "catch the brightest stars."

ABC's marketers, in contrast, devised a two-pronged attack by first appealing directly to audiences with "let us be the one," after the network had just risen to no. 2 in 1975–1976 with a prime-time rating of 19.0 to CBS's 19.6 and with NBC trailing far behind at 17.7.[15] Coupled with this tactic, they also reminded the public that ABC was "the network of the Olympics." Flush from their unexpectedly strong showing in Innsbruck, "when Roone Arledge's consummate showmanship and superb coverage grabbed a nightly 34 share of the audience and blunted the impact of CBS and NBC's new shows," ABC's marketers created a logo based on the five Olympic rings where the top three circles spelled out a-b-c and the lower two pulled the entire iconic image together at the bottom.[16] ABC thus linked its identity as much as possible with the widely recognized symbol of Olympic unity and international sportsmanship. In turn, it intended to go all out in producing a memorable sixteen-day summer spectacle (July 17–August 1) for an even bigger prime-time audience than the one that watched the winter games. While it had these extra viewers, too, ABC planned to relentlessly hype its upcoming fall lineup. ABC was investing more money, people, and resources than ever before in the Montreal Olympics. The television rights for the 1976 summer games cost $25 million in contrast to the almost cut-rate $7.5 million it paid four years earlier for the Munich games.[17] The investment nevertheless paid off handsomely for ABC.

Roone Arledge mobilized "an Olympian team of about 30 commentators, complemented by a crew of 470, including directors, cameramen, technicians, and anchor Jim McKay [who *Time* christened] the Walter Cronkite of TV sports." Arledge set up his command center "from a prefabricated, soundproofed TV headquarters that included two full sized studios" and several "control rooms," where "twelve live signals" were simultaneously fed "to broadcasters from 70 countries . . . via three satellites."[18] For the second summer Olympiad in a row, a diminutive teenage gymnast emerged as the crowd-pleasing favorite, both live at the games and on television screens all around the world. Fourteen-year-old Nadia Comaneci of Romania bested 1972 triple-gold-medal winner Olga Korbut of Russia by dominating three events (individual all-around, balance beam, and uneven bars) with an unprecedented seven perfect 10s. American viewers had even more to cheer about as over two-dozen U.S. athletes won gold medals, including such camera-friendly stars as Bruce Jenner (decathlon) and Sugar Ray Leonard (light welterweight boxing). For nearly two and a half weeks, ABC "won every time-slot every night, with an average 49% share of the audience," translating into more viewers than the combined total watching CBS and NBC. Furthermore, ABC's momentum resulting from this "sports blockbuster" carried well into the fall as it continued to increase its lead over America's other two broadcast networks once the season began.[19] Significantly, ABC's coverage of the 1976 summer games provided a dramatic preview of television's vast potential as an international medium, enhancing the network's reputation with audiences both in the United States and abroad.

Fred Pierce rewarded Roone Arledge for his many accomplishments over the years and especially his recent Olympic triumphs by naming him president of ABC News in May 1977. Pierce allowed Arledge to keep his presidency of ABC Sports and merely expand his purview over the news division. ABC News was then floundering, despite the fact that the network was finally reaching the top spot in entertainment for the first time ever in 1976–1977. Still, the network news division was deeply mired in third place, averaging only 17 percent of the available audience against industry leader CBS's 30 percent and NBC's 26 percent.[20] Morale was low, especially after Barbara Walters was hired away from NBC for a highly publicized $1 million contract to become the first woman to coanchor a nightly newscast. She was paired with longtime veteran Harry Reasoner beginning on October 4, 1976, but he resisted the move from the outset, resulting in a tense and divided news operation. When Arledge took over seven months later to stabilize and improve the situation, the overwhelming in-house and industry-wide reaction "ranged from skepticism to outright scorn."[21] Arledge's critics pointed to his lack of journalistic training and forecast that the *ABC Evening News* would soon devolve into a fun-and-games "Wide World of News." For his part, Arledge guaranteed that he would build "the best news organization with the best people."[22] His prediction was the one that came true over the long run. Arledge did institute a "wide world" approach, but his efforts to further internationalize ABC News actually improved the quality of the programming rather than lowering standards as his detractors had predicted.

Roone Arledge spent a year rethinking the *ABC Evening News* before unveiling the reformatted *World News Tonight* on July 10, 1978, with Frank Reynolds in Washington, D.C., Max Robinson (the nation's first African American coanchor) in Chicago, and Peter Jennings in London. Jennings specialized in international stories, which gave ABC a substantial advantage in this area over CBS and NBC. Within five years, *World News Tonight* had achieved parity with the *CBS Evening News* anchored by Dan Rather, who replaced Walter Cronkite on March 9, 1981, and with the *NBC Nightly News* with Tom Brokaw, who left the *Today* show to coanchor the evening newscast with Roger Mudd in April 1982 before being named sole anchor on September 5, 1983. That was also the day that Peter Jennings first appeared as the lone anchor on *World News Tonight*, after Frank Reynolds had died prematurely of bone cancer several months earlier. Jennings was now the first among equals in the growing galaxy of talent that Roone Arledge was assembling star by star at ABC. Arledge moved the news division forward by creating several new shows with innovative formats, which ABC scheduled in nontraditional segments. Ten days after a group of militant students seized the American Embassy in Tehran, Iran, on November 4, 1979, for instance, Arledge initiated a thirty-minute, five-nights-a-week, hard-news program called *America Held Hostage*. In March 1980, Ted Koppel, a multilingual reporter (English, French, German, and Russian) who specialized in international affairs, became the permanent host of *America Held Hostage* through the remainder of the 444-day ordeal, after which the series converted seamlessly into the popular, long-running, late-night fixture *Nightline*.

In 1981, Arledge lured David Brinkley away from NBC, after he had been there for thirty-eight years, to anchor what would soon become the no. 1 Sunday-morning news program in the country, *This Week*. In 1984, he then paired Hugh Downs with Barbara Walters on the prime-time newsmagazine *20/20*; and in 1989, he hired Diane Sawyer away from CBS to cohost *Primetime Live* with Sam Donaldson. Furthermore, ABC's *World News Tonight* finally overtook the *CBS Evening News* as the nation's no. 1 nightly newscast in 1989–1990. Merging quality journalism with technical wizardry and well-established high-profile stars, Roone Arledge once again transformed an also-ran division at ABC into the industry standard. He also changed the outlook that news was "a loss leader for the networks. With its expanded roster of successful programs," ABC News was generating profits of "70 million a year by 1990."[23]

No one at the network anticipated this level of success when Arledge took over the news division fifteen years earlier. Instead, entertainment was where most of ABC's hopes resided. High expectations abounded once Fred Pierce finally convinced Fred Silverman to accept the presidency of what was still network television's third-place entertainment division. For the twentieth year in a row, CBS handily won the 1974–1975 season, with an overall rating of 20.9 to NBC's 19.8 and ABC's 16.6.[24] After serving as vice president in charge of programs for CBS-TV during the last six years, Silverman joined ABC Entertainment as its new president in mid June 1975. "In hiring away Fred Silverman, we are going to have the shrewdest and most dynamic program leadership in the business," Fred Pierce told the press; "there is no question that he'll give us the shot in the arm that we need."[25] Corporate posturing aside, Pierce's comments captured Silverman's immediate and profound effect on ABC.

Fred Silverman "is probably the first network programmer who grew up laughing—and crying—at TV."[26] Born the son of a middle-class television repairman from Queens, he remembered watching and loving TV from an early age. Still only thirty-eight when he became president of ABC Entertainment, Silverman didn't fit the stereotype of the well-turned-out Ivy League–educated television executive. Fred majored in broadcasting at Syracuse University, then earned a master's degree at Ohio State, where he wrote a 406-page thesis analyzing ABC's programming between 1953 and 1959. "With his shirt billowing over his belt and his unpressed look," however, the tightly wound, hard-driving Silverman was always "regarded as something of an outsider among television's corporate elite."[27] Fred Silverman nevertheless excelled at programming; it seemed to his peers as if he possessed an uncanny ability to predict what viewers wanted to see. "It's not that Freddie understands the audience," one of his rivals once remarked; "he is the audience."[28] Silverman mentored a number of talented associates at ABC, including Michael Eisner and Brandon Tartikoff. Together, they collaborated on program planning and development, but Silverman, along with his boss, Fred Pierce, was ABC-TV's guiding force. Silverman inherited a number of programs with potential, such as *Happy Days* and *The Six Million Dollar Man*, but no top-10 hits. As soon as he arrived at ABC, Silverman characteristically began fine-tuning the creative directions and scheduling positions of these shows, and he started from scratch to develop an entirely new bevy of homegrown series.

For example, Silverman switched the lead focus of the year-and-a-half-old *Happy Days* to the one-time supporting character, Fonzie (Henry Winkler), thus transforming a top-30 program into no. 10 in 1975–1976 and eventually no. 1 in 1976–1977. He additionally moved *The Six Million Dollar Man* to Sunday, rather than keeping it on Friday night where it was pitted against two of NBC's strongest series, *Chico and the Man* and the first thirty minutes of *The Rockford Files*. In its new time slot, *The Six Million Dollar Man* quickly rose to no. 8 in 1975–1976. Fred Silverman also moved the network as a whole in a much different direction than the edgier, more topical programming he had been developing at CBS during the preceding six years. Sensing a change in the public's mood after the end of the Vietnam War and Watergate, he gravitated more toward light, escapist comedy (*Three's Company*), romance (*The Love Boat*), fantasy (*Fantasy Island*), and action-adventure series that emphasized what NBC program chief Paul Klein called "jiggle" over violence (*Charlie's Angels*). Silverman also nurtured spin-offs and clones, most notably *Laverne & Shirley* (from *Happy Days*), which debuted at no. 2 in January 1976 and rose to no. 1 for two straight seasons between 1977 and 1979; and *The Bionic Woman* (from *The Six Million Dollar Man*), which premiered at no. 4 in 1975–1976. By 1976–1977, ABC boasted seven of prime-time's top ten programs as the network took a commanding lead in the overall ratings at 21.6 to CBS's 18.7 and NBC's 18.2.[29] The unthinkable had occurred. ABC was Bicentennial America's no. 1 network, and Fred Silverman was television's latest celebrity programmer (a fitting heir to such high-profile predecessors as NBC's Pat Weaver in the 1950s and CBS's James Aubrey in the 1960s):

Fred Silverman was television's highest-profile celebrity programmer in the 1970s, a fitting heir to NBC's Pat Weaver in the 1950s and CBS's James Aubrey in the 1960s. Courtesy of Library of American Broadcasting at the University of Maryland.

Praised for achieving high ratings, damned for pandering to low tastes, lauded as an innovator, belittled as a caretaker, deified as a program strategist but downgraded as a corporate politician, the heavy-set, rumpled but still boyish-looking Fred Silverman possessed the capacity to unite fans and critics alike on one point— his love for television.[30]

Silverman played by his own rules, mixing retro-style 1950s-flavored series with one-time audience-grabbing spectaculars, such as the Olympics, and applying his unwavering enthusiasm to adapting the English miniseries to American TV. The structural and stylistic roots of the miniseries are directly traceable to programming innovations explored a decade earlier by the British Broadcasting Corporation (BBC) in both its originally scripted productions and its novels-to-television program. Beginning on January 10, 1971, PBS imported the miniseries to the United States for good when it began telecasting one of the network's flagship series, *Masterpiece Theater*, hosted by Alistair Cooke. The first American production to approach the scope and style of the British miniseries was ABC and Universal TV's twelve-hour *Rich Man, Poor Man*, which Silverman scheduled in six two-hour segments over seven weeks between February and March 1976. *Rich Man, Poor Man* captured and translated the British strategy of creating a prime-time soap opera with sociohistorical resonances: the story follows two brothers, Rudy (Peter Strauss) and Tom Jordache (Nick Nolte), and their dual pursuit of professional success and the same woman (Susan Blakely) from World War II through the late 1960s.

The immense popularity of *Rich Man, Poor Man* (forty-one million viewers on average) encouraged Fred Silverman and ABC to proceed with the even more ambitious plan of contracting with David L. Wolper Productions for $6 million to produce a twelve-hour version of Alex Haley's *Roots*.[31] *Roots* ran for eight consecutive evenings—from Sunday, January 23, through Sunday, January 30, 1977—and depicted the odyssey of one black family through several generations of slavery. This miniseries so captivated the imagination of the American viewing public that seven of the eight episodes placed in the top-10 list of most-watched television programs of all time up to that point, while the other segment of *Roots* ranked thirteenth overall. On a nationwide level, "the A. C. Nielsen Co. recorded an average 66 share of the audience—130 million people—more than had watched anything, anytime, anywhere."[32] In covering this cultural phenomenon, *Broadcasting* proclaimed that "television may never be the same again."[33]

Instead of a harbinger of even bigger and better things to come for broadcast TV, however, this miniseries was the last great gasp of the

Network Era. ABC, CBS, and NBC's once-invincible oligopoly was already showing signs of a slow, steady decline in its viewer base. The miniseries and other forms of "event programming," such as the annual Super Bowl, emerged as the primary scheduling strategy by which the three major broadcast networks temporarily countered the incessant erosion of both their nighttime and daytime audiences (from 91 percent of all people watching television in 1976 to 61 percent in 1991). This progressive decline was caused by the ever-increasing number of cable networks (from four in 1974, to twenty-eight in 1980, to seventy-four in 1991).[34] Similarly, CBS's January 15, 1978, telecast of Super Bowl XII between the Dallas Cowboys and the Denver Broncos became the first world championship football game ever to be scheduled during prime time. Before the 1960s, in fact, the NFL was fourth in line behind college football, boxing, and Major League Baseball in television popularity. Nevertheless, TV and professional football enriched each other "between 1961 and 1975" when "the NFL collected a whopping $606 million in television rights," while the pro game prospered as a consistent ratings winner on prime time as well as weekends.[35]

As early as 1963, for example, four of the top-10 rated shows of all-time were then football games that had just been telecast in the previous two years, while the 1967 inauguration of the Super Bowl soon grew beyond anyone's wildest dream as TV's highest-rated yearly homage to "corporate culture, an event that celebrates 30-second spots as sagas and bookmakers as theologians. The Super Bowl evokes a star-spangled yin and yang, all those equal but opposing forces that create a prime-time culture: Coke and Pepsi, Miller and Bud, McDonald's and Burger King."[36] By 1991, nine of the top twenty telecasts to date were Super Bowls, averaging between eighty and ninety million viewers annually. Correspondingly, the cost of a thirty-second Super Bowl advertisement skyrocketed from $185,000 in 1978, to $500,000 in 1985, to $800,000 in 1991. Like every other kind of sports programming, moreover, NFL football games were shown regularly on cable television by the early 1990s, after having first debuted on the Entertainment and Sports Programming Network (ESPN) in 1987. Getty Oil launched ESPN on September 7, 1979; a year later, this first-of-a-kind, all-sports network was telecasting twenty-four hours a day. As cable TV flourished throughout the 1980s, siphoning more viewers and profits away from ABC, CBS, and NBC, the traditional broadcast networks responded by investing in a select few of these new television services as a way of better adapting to their growing popularity with audiences. ABC, for instance, purchased ESPN from Getty on April 30, 1984 (selling 20 percent of its stake to Nabisco later that year). Still, the broadcast networks became targets at "a time of unprecedented mergers, leveraged buyouts, and hostile takeovers as one giant corporation swallowed another" during the hands-off deregulatory climate created by the Reagan administration between 1981 and 1989.[37]

"Never in 39 years of commercial television had there been a season so chaotic, so paradoxical and so marked with convulsive change," declared industry analyst Les Brown in 1978. ABC was just completing its second of three straight years atop the ratings, while the three-network oligopoly "earned an estimated $400 million [in 1977, with ABC garnering $175 million in profits, CBS $110 million, and NBC $105 million] on sales of $3.3 billion." Despite these windfall figures, worrisome signs were evident throughout broadcast TV: the 1977–1978 season saw few new hit programs, the networks were canceling series faster than ever (within weeks instead of giving producers and their shows time to cultivate an audience through the full thirteen-week fall season), and broadcast television's share of the total audience shrank again for the third consecutive year. Most disconcerting of all was "the revolving doors in the network executive suites."[38] For example, Fred Silverman stunned his colleagues at ABC by accepting a $1 million-a-year offer to become the president and chief executive officer (CEO) at NBC effective on June 9, 1978. "Silverman was then an industry *wunderkind* who could do no wrong and who seemed to have a magic touch with programming," recall broadcast historians Christopher Sterling and John Kittross; "but this final shift (Silverman was the only executive to have had senior programming positions with all three networks) was one too many."[39] His stay at NBC lasted only until 1981, when his new network became the first of the big three to lose money over a fiscal year in more than a quarter century.[40] The three-network oligopoly was clearly in a period of retrenchment, and "by 1985, the network locomotives were running low on steam, the advertising economy was entering a deep recession, and competition from cable TV was intensifying. Wall Street had turned predatory, rumors were rampant about network takeovers."[41]

ABC was the first broadcast network involved in a merger when it agreed to be sold to Capital Cities Communication, Inc., on March 18, 1985. "The surprise deal" represented "the first time that ownership of any of the nation's three major networks had changed hands." This transaction also marked "the biggest acquisition outside the oil industry in corporate history." Even though Capital Cities was only one-fourth the size of ABC, Inc., it nevertheless owned seven television stations (four of which were ABC affiliates), twelve radio stations, ten daily newspapers, thirty trade publications, and other communication-related ventures. Capital Cities was cash rich at a time when it was no longer guaranteed that all three broadcast networks would automatically earn a profit every single year. ABC's seventy-nine-year-old chairman and CEO, Leonard Goldenson, was planning to retire soon, so he personally negotiated the friendly takeover with the head of Capital Cities, Thomas S. Murphy, whom he had known for years. Capital Cities paid $3.5 billion for ABC, which was renamed Capital Cities/ABC, Inc. "That is my wish," Goldenson told the press; "I feel that the company I built from scratch is in good hands and that it will be carried on and that's important to me."[42] Exactly one month later, Ted Turner, the Atlanta-based cable entrepreneur, attempted a hostile takeover of CBS. He owned the Turner Broadcasting System made up of the Cable News Network (CNN), CNN Headline News, superstation WTBS (an Atlanta television station transmitted by satellite to cable systems nationwide), the Atlanta Braves MLB team, the Atlanta Hawks NBA team, and other properties. Turner's move signaled the growing strength and stature of cable television, even though CBS short-circuited this leveraged buyout attempt by repurchasing 21 percent of its own stock, which drove the network further into debt.[43]

The TV business was now caught "in the throes of dramatic change. In the march from family ownership to chains and to communication conglomerates, the industry [was] generating mega-mergers that rival[ed] in size the giant mergers of other industries."[44] The television networks were especially attractive takeover targets. ABC, CBS, and NBC still held out great promise for generating hefty profits in the not-too-distant future. They also were highly glamorous acquisitions, since they were part of the entertainment business. The FCC had just relaxed its ownership rules by now allowing corporation's to own up to twelve (instead of only seven) TV stations, making mergers possible with other corporations already in the television business such as Capital Cities Communication. Finally, all of the original network founders were either dead or nearing retirement by the mid 1980s. David Sarnoff, for instance, was succeeded by his son Robert as chairman and CEO of RCA in January 1970; he passed away the following year. Then, after a period of steep decline, RCA's board eventually forced Robert Sarnoff to resign in 1975. A decade later, NBC became the second network to undergo a friendly takeover when General Electric, a broad-based electronics and defense conglomerate, purchased RCA (NBC's parent) for $6.28 billion on December 12, 1985. GE had been instrumental in RCA's founding in 1919, and the two companies were closely aligned until their union was formally dissolved in 1932 by a government-initiated antitrust action. The current regulatory climate was far more relaxed than a half century before, however, so the GE/

RCA merger received easy approval from both the FCC and the U.S. Department of Justice.

GE/RCA, Inc., thus became "the nation's seventh-largest industrial corporation, sandwiched between the International Business Machines Corporation (IBM) and the du Pont Company."[45] Furthermore, this newly created mega-media powerhouse arrived on the international stage as a ready-made, world-class conglomerate, wielding a far greater global influence than either GE or RCA was ever able to do by themselves. The final development that totally transformed the old three-network oligopoly beyond recognition was the ouster of CBS's chairman and CEO, Thomas H. Wyman, on September 10, 1986. He had succeeded founder William S. Paley, who retired in 1983, at eighty-two years old. Wyman was only the second chairman in the whole history of CBS, Inc. He nevertheless lost the confidence of his board of directors during Ted Turner's hostile takeover bid when he initially underestimated the seriousness of this overture, which threw CBS into seventeen months of serious financial turmoil.

As a result, an intense power struggle ensued within the company between Wyman and board member Laurence A. Tisch, chairman and CEO of Loews Corporation, whose holdings included Loews Hotels, Lorillard Tobacco, CNA Financial, and Bulova Watches. A long-time friend of both Bill Paley and Leonard Goldenson, Tisch purchased 25 percent of CBS's stock during 1986 and emerged as the corporation's new CEO in partnership with Paley, who returned at age eighty-five as acting chairman. Paley noted that Tisch "shares the values and principles that have guided CBS throughout the period of its growth. I respect and admire him and look forward to working with him."[46] Indeed, Paley's position was more titular than anything, as he stayed mostly behind the scenes as an advisor to Tisch until his death in 1990. For his part, Laurence Tisch remained in charge of CBS, Inc., for the next ten years, insulating it from other unwanted corporate raiders but also presiding over a period marked by severe cutbacks and the slow, enervating decline of the network's one-time premier news and entertainment divisions.

By the end of 1986, the three networks had lost "their near total dominance of the television market," along with much of "their swagger, their corporate identities and perhaps also their hallowed traditions."[47] The three-network oligopoly was gone forever, as were the annual $100 million-plus profit margins that this top-down, mass-market structure regularly provided for CBS, NBC, and ABC. These broadcast networks had achieved a kind of parity among themselves, following ABC's rise to no. 1 during the mid to late 1970s. Together, they survived the profound technological and economic changes that remodeled TV into a multinetwork niche market industry after 1976. An estimated 70.5 million television households, or 96.4 percent of the nation, owned TV sets in 1976; by 1991, these figures mushroomed to 93.2 million, or 98.2 percent of all residences (which was even five percentage points higher than the number of American homes that had telephones).[48] Significantly, the typical TV household in the United States received, on average, 7.2 channels in 1970, 10.2 in 1980, and 27.2 by 1990.[49]

An increasing number of viewing options was now an essential characteristic of television's second age as the three-network bottleneck was broken beyond repair by the rise of cable and satellite TV. On October 1, 1975, Home Box Office, Inc. (HBO) inaugurated its satellite-cable service with the much-ballyhooed "Thrilla in Manila" heavyweight boxing match between Muhammad Ali and Joe Frazier. This brutal fourteen-round bout won by Ali was a hugely popular success for all concerned, especially the struggling three-year-old pay-TV company that carried the fight live from overseas. In one fell swoop, HBO became a national network, thus ushering in television's Cable Era with its first full year of regularly scheduled satellite-delivered programming in 1976.

THE CABLE ERA

> The Second Age of Television is a new time in which the networks are joined by cable, syndication, VCRs, fourth networks, pay-per-view operators and marketers of backyard dishes in pursuit of the same audiences.
>
> LES BROWN, *Channels*, 1987[50]

HBO signaled that something new and innovative was happening to TV as a technology and an industry during the mid to late 1970s. Cable entrepreneur Charles Dolan first conceived of the network in 1971 as the Green Channel. He was the owner of Sterling Communications, a growing cable concern in the New York metropolitan area, which was largely subsidized by Time, Inc. Dolan began work on the Green Channel with seed money from Time, hiring thirty-three-year-old Wall Street lawyer Gerald Levin as part of his start-up team. Dolan and his associates renamed their channel Home Box Office, reflecting their theater-like conception of a subscription television (STV) service that would primarily offer first-run movies and sports to their paying customers. HBO was based on an entirely different economic model than the one followed by the three broadcast networks, their affiliates, and the country's independent stations, which all sold specific audiences (such as young, urban, professional viewers) to sponsors. Unlike this advertiser-supported system, HBO's subscriber format focused all of the channel's attention on pleasing and retaining its viewing audience. HBO and the other forty-five aspiring local and regional pay-cable channels then trying to survive in America's media marketplace were shifting the center of gravity in this sector of the television industry away from advertisers and more toward serving their target audiences.[51] The FCC, ABC (as the one-time perennial third network), local television stations, and especially movie theater owners long resisted STV. Much of this opposition subsided once the FCC "adopted a 'hands off' approach" with its "1968 *Fourth Report and Order* that opened the door to the creation of permanent subscription TV services."[52] The biggest concern of these recently created STV companies was simply providing programming that was attractive enough for viewers to sign up, pay a monthly fee, and stay connected to the service on a long-term basis.

For its part, HBO debuted on November 8, 1972, telecasting *Sometimes a Great Notion* (1971) starring Paul Newman and a National Hockey League game to a mere 365 cable subscribers in Wilkes-Barre, Pennsylvania. Three months and $1 million in losses later, Time, Inc., fired Dolan and replaced him with Gerald Levin as the new president of HBO. Levin kept HBO afloat for two more years before betting the network's future on signing a six-year, $7.5 million contract that allowed the channel access to RCA's newly launched communication satellite, Satcom 1, during the fall of 1975. HBO's subscriptions grew rapidly from 15,000 to 287,199 over the next year. By the end of 1977, Home Box Office had 600,000 customers, enabling this pay-TV network to turn a profit for the first time. "HBO quickly became an incredible cash cow," reports George Mair in *Inside HBO*, "eventually outstripping" in profitability "the all-important magazine division" at Time, Inc.[53]

As a result, other basic and premium cable networks followed HBO's example of choosing satellite over terrestrial microwave delivery. Ted Turner took WTBS national via Satcom 1 in December 1976, while the Chicago-based Tribune Company similarly converted WGN into a superstation in October 1978. Another movie channel, Showtime, was created by Viacom in July 1976 and began satellite transmission in 1978. Niche channels of all sorts emerged during the late 1970s and early 1980s, including CBN (the Christian Broadcasting Network) and the USA Network (a broad-based entertainment channel) in 1977; ESPN, Nickelodeon (children's programming), and C-SPAN (Cable Satellite Public Affairs Network) in 1979; CNN (Cable News Network), BET (Black Entertainment Television), and TLC (the

Learning Channel) in 1980; MTV (Music Television) and FNN (Financial News Network) in 1981; and CNN Headline News and the Weather Channel in 1982.

"In stimulating the creation of a wide variety of new satellite networks," HBO became "the engine that was pulling cable."[54] The network's own subscriber base skyrocketed to thirteen million by 1983, aiding in the adoption of cable throughout the United States from 15.3 percent of all TV households in 1976, to 21.7 percent in 1980, and to 39.3 percent in 1983.[55] The addition of satellites was transforming the cable business beyond recognition. As early as 1948, community antenna television (CATV), or cable TV, was merely the means by which television signals were brought into hard-to-reach rural and mountainous regions. By the mid 1960s, the number of CATV systems had grown to more than 750 in nearly forty states, so the FCC started regulating cable, mostly to ensure that all local stations were being carried in their respective markets and not being duplicated by any imported signals. In 1972, the FCC also lifted its restrictions on allowing CATV service into the nation's major metropolitan areas. Cable was no longer just the last resort for bringing television into the most out-of-the-way places in the country; instead, it had evolved into a fee-based TV alternative that offered urban, suburban, and rural viewers many more channels than ever before with much better reception. Gerald Levin's plan for HBO to combine cable with satellite delivery was the final innovation needed to usher in the Cable Era. A second television age was officially under way by 1976 as *Channels* magazine dubbed Levin "the man who started the revolution."[56] In turn, the three-network oligopoly was fatally wounded by the rise of cable TV. Cable also gave an unexpected lift to independent stations nationwide, adding even more competition to CBS, NBC, and ABC's long-standing monopoly over the viewing habits of the American public.

Independent stations had long been the second-class citizens of the television industry. Before the 1962 All-Channel Receiver Act, most TVs in the United States even lacked the ability to access the UHF band (channels 14 to 83), which is where the vast majority of the country's thirty-three independent stations resided at the time. This bill required American set manufacturers to include UHF as well as VHF (channels 2 to 13) tuners in all future TV receivers beginning in mid 1964. "The all-channel act was not the whole answer, but it helped immensely," as the number of independent stations slowly increased over the next decade to eighty-six.[57] More than anything, though, the growth of "cable, because it [was] required to carry all local television signals, put UHF independent stations on nearly the same footing as local VHF [network] affiliates, vastly improving their reach and reception."

At the end of 1978, "there were 93 independents in the United States; five years later, 193."[58] Independent stations, in turn (along with the FCC's Prime-Time Access and Financial Interest and Syndication Rules), stimulated the domestic syndication market as never before because they specialized in rerunning off-network series, as well as made-for-TV and theatrical movies. As a kind of broadcast/cable hybrid, independents flourished throughout the late 1980s and into the early 1990s when the prime-time share for these stations plateaued at around 20 percent of all available viewers and then slowly declined thereafter. By 1988, the television landscape became overpopulated with seven superstations that transmitted either nationally (WTBS out of Atlanta and WGN Chicago) or regionally (WWOR and WPIX out of New York; KTLA, Los Angeles; KTVT, Dallas; and WSBK, Boston). By then, the Cable Era was in full swing, providing all kinds of new competition for CBS, NBC, and ABC, including the latest try at creating a viable fourth broadcast network with the Fox Broadcasting Company.

"DuMont tried in the 1950s, United Network in the 1960s, Paramount in the 1970s, [and] Metromedia in the early 1980s," but the dream of starting another broadcast network was not fully realized until the launch of Fox on October 9, 1986.[59] The genesis of the Fox TV network began with Barry Diller, who was head of Paramount Pictures for a decade before becoming board chair and chief executive officer of Twentieth Century-Fox in 1984. Diller had started his career as a programming assistant at ABC in 1966, eventually working his way up to vice president of prime-time television by the time Paramount hired him away in 1974. During his tenure at Paramount, Diller guided both its motion picture division (with such hits as *Saturday Night Fever*, *Raiders of the Lost Ark*, and *Terms of Endearment*) and its television counterpart (with *Laverne & Shirley*, *Taxi*, and *Cheers*) through a highly successful and profitable period. He even flirted with creating a fourth network while at Paramount during the late 1970s and then carried this ambition with him when he moved to the financially troubled Twentieth Century-Fox Corporation (TCF) on October 1, 1984. Within a year, he had revived the film division at that studio and thereupon turned his attention to TV by aggressively pursuing his bold aspiration of starting yet another broadcast network to compete against CBS, NBC, and ABC. The final piece of the puzzle was Rupert Murdoch's arrival during March 1985 when he purchased 50 percent of TCF for $250 million through his News Corporation, later acquiring the other 50 percent six months later for $325 million. After this initial investment of $575 million, Murdoch then bought the highly successful Metromedia chain of six major-market independent TV stations—WNEW in New York (retitled WNYW); KTTV,

Los Angeles; WFLD, Chicago; WTTG, Washington, D.C.; KRLD, Dallas (retitled KDAF); and KRIV, Houston—for $1.4 billion.

The Metromedia television group originally grew out of the failed DuMont network, which was built around its New York flagship WABD (now WNYW) and its second owned-and-operated station WTTG in Washington, D.C. With Rupert Murdoch's acquisition of Metromedia in November 1985, the old DuMont foundation came full circle. These six stations, along with Murdoch's 1987 acquisition of WNXE in Boston (retitled WFXT), provided Fox with the necessary infrastructure to launch a fourth network that after less than two years had ninety-six affiliates and an 80 percent coverage of the nation. At the same time, Barry Diller was deeply involved in the trial-and-error process of developing programming for Fox. The network's first venture was *The Late Show Starring Joan Rivers*, which debuted in October 1986 and was created specifically to compete against *The Tonight Show Starring Johnny Carson* on NBC. After a brief sampling from viewers, however, *The Late Show*'s ratings plummeted and Joan Rivers left the program for good on May 15, 1987. Diller never wavered in his plans to introduce a limited prime-time schedule on weekends, though, beginning on Sundays in April 1987 with the dysfunctional family-from-hell sitcom, *Married . . . with Children*, and the eponymously named comedy-variety show, *The Tracey Ullman Show*, which introduced American audiences to Bart, Homer, Marge, Lisa, and Maggie Simpson via its weekly cartoon vignettes. Matt Groening's *The Simpsons* was soon spun off as its own half-hour animated comedy series on December 17, 1989, emerging as a signature program for Fox, along with its other hip youth-oriented series, such as Stephen J. Cannell's *21 Jump Street* (starring Johnny Depp) and Keenen Ivory Wayans's *In Living Color* (featuring the versatile comedic talents of Damon Wayans, David Alan Grier, Jim Carrey, and Jamie Foxx).

The bread-and-butter programs for Fox were mainly inexpensive reality-based shows, such as the tabloid newsmagazine *A Current Affair*, the self-billed "weekly nationwide criminal manhunt" *America's Most Wanted*, and the "you are there" police documentary *Cops*. After three years of operation, Fox suffered losses of up to $136 million; still, the network was slowly constructing an audience base around the highly coveted urban eighteen- to thirty-four-year-old demographic that advertisers had grown increasingly attached to ever since the late 1970s. Diller and Fox entertainment chief Jamie Kellner introduced the effective scheduling innovation of debuting new programs in August while the other broadcast networks were coasting along on reruns. By the early 1990s, Fox established a younger, edgier, and more multicultural

Matt Groening's The Simpsons *debuted as a half-hour animated comedy series on December 17, 1989, emerging as a signature program for Fox, along with the network's other hip, youth-oriented series. Courtesy of the Fox Broadcasting Company/Heldref.*

identity than the other three broadcast networks. America's fourth broadcast network was clearly here to stay, turning a profit for the first time in 1990–1991 and expanding its programming schedule to five nights a week as it slowly climbed to a 6.4 percent share of the available prime-time audience that season.[60] Just like ABC in the early to mid 1970s and NBC several years later, Fox had discovered that the one saving grace to being last in the overall ratings was that it allowed its programmers to take bigger risks in developing shows and putting their schedules together. During the Silverman years, ABC was still programming for the mass audience, whereas NBC attempted to redefine success in the broadcast sector of the television industry by attracting a smaller, high-end segment of viewers rather than just the most people possible. The network first stumbled onto this strategy almost by accident when Johnny Carson renegotiated his contract in 1974, requiring NBC to move its late-night Saturday reruns of *The Tonight Show* (called *The Best of Carson*) to Fridays so he could cut back from hosting the program five nights a week to four.

The premiere of *Saturday Night Live* (*SNL*) on October 11, 1975, marked a generational shift in television comedy whose breakout success later paved the way for "the show's attitude and approach and collective mindset" to seep into other TV genres on prime time during the early 1980s. This late-night program became an instant "trendsetter in American humor and had a remarkable effect on American mores, manners, music, politics, and even fashion."[61] In August 1974, NBC's new president, Herb Schlosser, recruited twenty-seven-year-old Dick Ebersol away from ABC Sports to head up the network's weekend late-night programming department. Ebersol, in turn, hired twenty-nine-year-old writer-producer Lorne Michaels (né Lorne Lipowitz) to develop a weekly ninety-minute comedy-variety show starting at 11:30 P.M. on Saturdays that primarily appealed to eighteen- to thirty-four-year-old viewers. The challenge of mounting such a series was considerable, not the least of which was attracting this specific target audience at this particular day and time. NBC's research director, Bill Rudin, told Ebersol in April 1975 that "I don't think it'll ever work because the audience for which it is designed will never come home on Saturday night to watch it." Michaels's vision, though, was to create "the first television show to speak the language of the time," blending original cutting-edge comedy with the unpredictability of live TV, which consciously harked back to the most innovative variety series from the medium's first generation—*Your Show of Shows.*[62] A native of Toronto, Canada, Michaels cut his teeth writing and performing radio and television comedy for the Canadian Broadcasting Corporation before immigrating to the United States in the mid 1960s to write for Woody Allen, NBC's short-lived *The Beautiful Phyllis Diller Show*, and NBC's no. 1 end-of-the-decade sensation *Rowan and Martin's Laugh-In.*

Lorne Michaels eventually won two Emmys and established his reputation as an up-and-coming writer-producer with his many creative contributions on three Lily Tomlin specials between 1973 and early 1975 that resulted in NBC offering him a contract "to develop and produce a late-night comedy program," which he signed on April 1, 1975.[63] Six months later, *SNL* debuted, featuring a seven-member cast of mostly baby boomer performers (Dan Aykroyd, John Belushi, Chevy Chase, Jane Curtin, Garrett Morris, Laraine Newman, and Gilda Radner, with Bill Murray replacing Chase in the second season). The style of these so-called rock 'n' roll comics was smart, irreverent, and unique to television at the time, as they were ironically christened the "Not Ready for Prime Time Players." This ensemble specialized in topical humor that demonstrated a keen awareness of the medium and its conventions, as was illustrated in the opening minutes of *SNL*'s premiere episode when "Chevy Chase as the floor manager, wearing a headset and carrying a clipboard, sticks his head in, smiles broadly in that phony-television way, and says—for the first of more than five hundred times that it would be said in years to come—'Live *from* New York, *it's* Saturday Night!' "[64] Michaels, his small repertory company, and his writing team of thirteen men and three women worked out of legendary studio 8H in Rockefeller Center, which was originally built in 1937 for Arturo Toscanini and the NBC Symphony Orchestra. This space had been underutilized ever since *Your Hit Parade* left NBC-TV in June 1958. The *SNL* team reclaimed studio 8H and updated both the New York school of live production and the comedy-variety genre from a whole new generational perspective.

Saturday Night Live's first five years were marked by biting sociopolitical satire (with Chase parodying Gerald Ford; Aykroyd, Jimmy Carter and Richard Nixon; and Belushi, Henry Kissinger), as well as spot-on parodies of television as a medium and its stars (with Chase and Curtin playing the "Weekend Update" anchors; Radner, "Baba Wawa"/Barbara Walters; and Aykroyd, the hyperkinetic "bass-o-matic" pitchman). Lorne Michaels remembers that "we wanted to redefine comedy the way the Beatles redefined" music. In this way, *SNL*'s writers and performers only wanted "to please those people who [were] like us. The assumption was there were a lot of people like us. And that turned out to be so."[65] *SNL* quickly emerged as a popular phenomenon with young adults during the mid to late 1970s, especially eighteen to thirty-four year olds, who became its core constituency. As *SNL*'s target audience aged over the next decade, its lifestyle choices changed, as did the nature of the programs that it watched. Journalist R. C. Longworth was the first writer to label the eighteen to thirty-four cohort "yuppies" in a 1981 *Chicago Tribune* article where he examined the ways in which baby boomers were then entering the workforce en masse and transforming the urban landscape.[66] In general, he noted that yuppies held professional-sector jobs, were solidly middle class to upper middle class, and were growing increasingly materialistic in their lifestyles and long-term aspirations. "Those people are usually college-educated, getting on and even getting up in the world," added author Joseph Epstein in *Commentary* a year later, "but with a bit of hippie-dippie counterculture clinging to them still—yuppies, they have been called [with] the initials YUP standing for young urban professionals."[67]

The independent production company that best captured the yuppie zeitgeist in both the style and content of its representative series during the 1980s was MTM Enterprises. Cofounder and president Grant Tinker aptly described MTM in his 1994 memoir as "a *writers'* company," whose staff included such major writing and producing talents as Steven Bochco, Joshua Brand, James L. Brooks, Allan Burns,

Glenn Gordon Caron, John Falsey, Tom Fontana, Gary David Gold-berg, Michael Kozoll, David Milch, Bruce Paltrow, Gene Reynolds, Jay Tarses, Mark Tinker, Hugh Wilson, and Dick Wolf.[68] For example, Brooks and Burns coproduced CBS's socially relevant one-hour spin-off *Lou Grant* in 1977 with significant writing contributions from Goldberg and Reynolds, while Paltrow created CBS's racially mixed inner-city basketball melodrama *The White Shadow* the next year with similar sorts of help from Brand, Falsey, and Tinker. In addition, NBC president and CEO Fred Silverman initiated program development talks between his executive staff and producers at MTM Enterprises soon after replacing Herb Schlosser as network chief in the summer of 1978. This ongoing relationship was fully supported by Silverman's gifted protégé, Brandon Tartikoff, especially after Tartikoff was ap-pointed in early 1980 to be NBC's president of network entertainment. NBC was already well on its way to finishing dead last in the ratings for the fifth straight season when Fred Silverman offered MTM's Ste-ven Bochco and Michael Kozoll "carte blanche to do what [they] wanted" in following through on his original suggestion of creating a cop show for his network. Silverman was looking for a series that com-bined the interpersonal dynamics of David Gerber's *Police Story* and the ethnically humorous misadventures of Danny Arnold's *Barney Miller* along with the vérité stylistics of the soon-to-be-released theatri-cal film, *Fort Apache, The Bronx* (1981). What resulted was the most innovative, influential, and celebrated prime-time series of the early 1980s—*Hill Street Blues*.

Hill Street Blues premiered as a mid-season replacement on NBC in January of 1981. Viewers at first were unsure of what to make of the program. It was a "new kind of cop show, a total departure from the formulaic style" of recent 1970s successes such as CBS's *Kojak* and ABC's *Starsky and Hutch*.[69] Tim Brooks and Earle Marsh called *Hill Street Blues* "a most unusual mixture of drama and comedy, fast-paced and deliberately choppy, as was life at the station house (each episode began at 7 A.M. role call and ended late at night, with several stories in-terwoven)."[70] The series finished an inauspicious eighty-third out of ninety-seven prime-time programs by the end of the 1980–1981 sea-son as network programmers moved the show three times (from Thursday to Saturday to Tuesday nights) during its first four and a half months on the air. Despite the slow start, Silverman supported Tar-tikoff's recommendation to renew *Hill Street Blues* for 1981–1982 on their shared belief in the program's overall quality, which was likewise confirmed by the overwhelming number of positive reviews from tele-vision critics all over the country. Furthermore, *Hill Street Blues* earned an extraordinary twenty-one Emmy nominations in August, even though the series only totaled seventeen episodes after its initial half-season. On September, 13, 1981, *Hill Street Blues* won eight Emmys in such prestigious categories as Outstanding Drama Series, Outstanding Lead Actor (Daniel J. Travanti as Capt. Frank Furillo), Outstanding Lead Actress (Barbara Babcock as Grace Gardner), Outstanding Supporting Actor (Michael Conrad as Sgt. Phil Esterhaus), Outstanding Writing (Bochco and Kozoll), Outstanding Directing (Robert Butler), Outstanding Cinematography (William H. Cronjager), and Outstanding Achievement in Film Sound Editing (Robert Cornett, Samuel Horta, Denise Horta, and Eileen Horta). Such recognition made *Hill Street Blues* the must-see show on prime time for the "18–49, high-income and well-educated audience that was threatening to defect to cable and pay-TV."[71] "*Hill Street* was the rarest of network birds, a top-20 program [by 1982–1983] with superb demographics," recalls Grant Tinker. The series raised the bar for all of prime-time programming as it emerged as "the standard by which other dramatic work came to be measured."[72]

Media sociologist Todd Gitlin calls TV's style of invention "recombinant," arguing that if "clones are the lowest forms of imitation,

Daniel J. Travanti starred as Captain Frank Furillo in Hill Street Blues, the most innovative, influential, and celebrated prime-time television series of the early 1980s. Courtesy of the National Broadcasting Company/Heldref.

recombinants of elements from proven successes are the most interesting." In this way, *Hill Street Blues* was on the cutting edge of recom-
bination during the early 1980s by being an amalgam of the cop show,
the documentary (with its handheld camera and overlapping sound
techniques), the soap opera (with its multilayered story line and
large cast of continuing characters), and the situation comedy (with its
well-placed scenes of comic relief featuring such offbeat regulars as
trigger-happy right-winger Lt. Howard Hunter/James Sikking and
hot-tempered momma's boy Det. Mick Belker/Bruce Weitz). In addition, *Hill Street Blues* was innovative in the way it quickly shifted tones
(from excitement to anxiety to humor and poignancy), as well as in the
darkly complex nature of its themes. "*Hill Street Blues* was the first
postliberal cop show," asserts Gitlin. Each week the series explored
the limits confronting local law enforcement officials as they tried to
make a positive impact on the lives of their fellow citizens. Unlike the
cop shows that preceded it, *Hill Street Blues* "not only acknowledged
uncertainties but embraced them."[73] In both tackling tough issues
with uncompromising directness and "blurring generic boundaries,"
Hill Street Blues "paved the way" for other "serial hybrids," such as
MTM's *St. Elsewhere*, which debuted in October 1982 on NBC, mixing
the medical drama with the documentary, the soap opera, and the sitcom. Most important, *Hill Street Blues* provided a working model for
network programmers on how to build "audiences comprised of different market segments." As a top-20 show between 1982 and 1985,
this critical hit attracted a niche eighteen- to forty-nine-year-old audience of approximately fifteen to twenty million viewers a week, while
also being no. 1 among all prime-time series with men aged eighteen
to thirty-four.[74]

Despite Fred Silverman's key role in developing *Hill Street Blues*, his
days were numbered at NBC after the network suffered three straight
years of declining ratings and heavy financial losses during his tenure.
When Grant Tinker replaced Silverman as chairman of the board and
CEO of NBC in July 1981, "he brought a significant change to the public face of that network. As former head of the MTM production company, Tinker had built a reputation as a leader in quality television."[75]
During his twelve years at the helm of MTM Enterprises, this company pioneered "the business of exchanging 'quality TV' for 'quality
demographics.'" After asking Tartikoff to stay on as his chief programmer, Tinker led NBC along a similar path "to change its image from
that of the 'losing network' to that of the 'quality network.'"[76] "Based
on the belief that good quality programming makes a strong network,
Tinker worked with programming chief Brandon Tartikoff to revitalize

NBC's prime-time schedule."[77] They relied heavily on series developed by MTM producer-writers, such as *St. Elsewhere* (with Bruce Paltrow, Joshua Brand, John Falsey, Mark Tinker, Tom Fontana, and John Masius) and *Remington Steele* (with Robert Butler, Michael Gleason, and Glenn Gordon Caron) or by MTM alumni, such as *Family Ties* (with Gary David Goldberg) and *Cheers* (with Glen Charles, James Burrow, and Les Charles), in addition to the original programming they invited from select creative personnel from outside of MTM. For instance, Tartikoff recruited Bill Cosby and the producing team of Marcy Carsey and Tom Werner after seeing the comedian on *The Tonight Show* and being convinced that his "family-based banter would make for an excellent sitcom."[78] "NBC's upscale, high-demographic hit" *Miami Vice* was also initiated by Tartikoff.[79] "According to executive producer Michael Mann, the head of entertainment presented him with a short memo which read: 'MTV Cops.'"[80]

Grant Tinker's strategy to turn NBC around was slow, steady, and purposeful. He set in motion a five-year plan to retool the network's image along with its programming philosophy, while at the same time pursuing a specific high-end niche audience that skewed younger, urban, professional, and slightly more male than those for CBS and ABC. Even "*Hill Street Blues* and *St. Elsewhere* went after baby boomer demographics with the iconography of inner-city poverty, not urban affluence," explains Jane Feuer in *Seeing through the Eighties*: "yuppie spectator positions were created indirectly" by appealing "to baby boomer ideals of the 1960s" and "through the commercials."[81] The kinds of luxury items that were advertised on NBC's new generation of quality shows—Mercedes Benzes and BMWs, Rolex watches and Godiva chocolates, Calvin Klein and Ralph Lauren clothing—rarely made an appearance in fifteen-, thirty-, and sixty-second spots anywhere else on TV. By 1982–1983, Tinker and Tartikoff were nurturing a trio of slow-starting, made-to-order MTM programs that anchored Tuesday (*St. Elsewhere*), Thursday (*Hill Street Blues*), and Friday nights (*Remington Steele*) for NBC. These "three series, each of which had a stutter-start, became exactly the kind of double-value successes network sales departments covet: respectable-to-good ratings and demographics [eighteen- to forty-nine-year-old, better-educated, higher-income viewers] that led the league."[82] Under Tinker's leadership, "NBC recovered first the upscale urban audience prized by advertisers, then industry approval with more Emmy awards than CBS and ABC combined, and finally rose to first place in the ratings [for the 1985–1986 season] with blockbusters like the famed Thursday night lineup—*Cosby, Family Ties, Cheers, Night Court,* and *Hill Street Blues*—billed as 'the best night of television *on television.'*"[83] CBS, in contrast, held fast to its old-school mass-appeal programming strategies, as well as the rapidly aging audience that its shows attracted. As a result, no broadcast network fell further and faster during the 1980s than CBS.

The decade started on a high note for CBS. After ABC's brief reign as the no. 1 broadcast network from 1976 to 1979, CBS again asserted its dominance over its two longtime rivals by rising to the top of the ratings for the next six seasons, from 1979 through 1985. CBS's programmers held fast to first place by filling their schedule with holdover hits from the Network Era, including such evergreens as *60 Minutes*, *M*A*S*H*, and *The Jeffersons*. They also introduced several original series every year that fit into the same old familiar genres, while adding a new wrinkle or two to keep its core constituency (women ages eighteen to fifty-four) tuned in, such as redesigning the soap opera for prime time with *Dallas* and *Falcon Crest*, specializing in women-centered sitcoms like *Alice* and *Kate & Allie*, and developing one-hour crime dramas featuring strong women protagonists as in *Cagney & Lacey* and *Murder, She Wrote*. More than any other program, though, CBS's *Dallas* epitomized the mass-audience ideal of an older generation of executive producers, such as Lorimar's Lee Rich (with *The Waltons*, *Dallas*, *Knots Landing*, and *Falcon Crest*) and his contemporary Aaron Spelling (with *The Love Boat*, *Fantasy Island*, *Dynasty*, and *The Colbys*). Although *Dallas* was created by a man (David Jacobs), the evolving two-dozen-deep writing staff for this signature CBS series was always comprised of at least 40 percent women, who had previously earned credits on such daytime soaps as Ted and Betty Corday's *Days of Our Lives* and Agnes Nixon's *All My Children*. For nearly thirty years, the soap opera had been a staple of daytime TV, even growing more relevant and realistic during the late 1960s and throughout the 1970s to keep pace with its audience. The stage was thus set for its prime-time emergence with the 1978 debut of *Dallas*, which enjoyed both a serial narrative and "characters who were larger than life, based on the struggles for money and power," and lots of partner swapping, scandal, and sexual intrigue.[84] From 1980 through 1985, *Dallas* was either the no. 1- or no. 2-rated show in the country, averaging between forty-three and fifty-three million viewers a week for five straight seasons, and even setting the-then record 53.3 rating and 76 share (ninety million viewers) for the "Who Shot J. R.?" cliffhanger episode on November 21, 1980.[85]

Dallas was an "international phenomenon" throughout the 1980s, attracting viewers in over ninety countries with its "saga of power, rivalry, lust, and greed." Still, CBS nose-dived throughout the decade by failing to update its older, slumping, mass-appeal shows. Audi-

Dallas *was an international phenomenon throughout the 1980s, attracting viewers in over ninety countries. Left to right: Larry Hagman as J. R. Ewing, Linda Gray as Sue Ellen Ewing, Patrick Duffy as Bobby Ewing, and Charlene Tilton as Lucy Ewing Cooper. Courtesy of CBS/Landov.*

ence expectations rose in response to a new generation of quality dramas. *Dallas*, in turn, became "a symbol to some of what went wrong with television drama." Fans of *Dallas* and other prime-time soaps were "seduced into strong personal identification by a sequence of quick and slick emotional manipulations," contend David Marc and Robert Thomson, "only to be dragged through the muck of pathos and, once exhausted, left with little or nothing in the way of spiritual catharsis or even satisfying insight."[86] Ironically, "the 'quality dramas' of the 1980s were perhaps the greatest beneficiaries of *Dallas* and its imitators," adds Thompson in *Television's Second Golden Age*. "*Hill Street Blues, St. Elsewhere, thirtysomething*, and *L.A. Law* all employed continuing storylines," knitted plot structures, and large ensemble casts, just like *Dallas*.[87] They broke with traditional formulas, however, mixing and matching generic conventions, often grappling with complex contemporary issues (such as racism, sexism, and class conflict), while also demonstrating a knowing awareness about television as a medium and how it works.[88] In the end, these quality dramas brought a whole new level of emotional depth and sophistication to TV as a narrative art form, challenging viewers with their nakedly honest portrayals, which sometimes even reached moments of true epiphany, such as when "Dr. Morrison's [David Morse] young wife is killed in an accident" during the second season of *St. Elsewhere*:[89] "her heart is used in a transplant, and the episode ["Qui Transtulit Sustinet"] ends with the unbearably poignant scene of Morrison pressing his head to the chest of the transplant patient—listening to his wife's heart."[90] *Dallas*'s less gut-wrenching, more superficial and stereotypical style of serial melodrama paled in comparison.

The slow decline of CBS during the 1980s mirrored the waning fortunes of its one-time invincible blockbuster *Dallas*. When *Dallas* first made it into the top 10 at no. 6 in its second season (1979–1980), CBS was no. 1 with a 31 percent share of the prime-time audience as the three major broadcast networks combined for a 90 percent total of all viewers. Five seasons later (1984–1985), *Dallas* was no. 2, while CBS was still no. 1 with a 27 percent share, although the three-network hold on the American audience was already down to 77 percent. By the end of the decade (1988–1989), *Dallas* had fallen to no. 30 (soon to be no. 61 in 1990–1991), as CBS was deeply mired in third place for only the second time in its entire history, with a pallid 20 percent share of all prime-time viewers. NBC, ABC, and CBS were caught in a kind of freefall, sharing just 67 percent of the available audience, with no end in sight to their spiraling downward.[91]

By the early 1990s, the ascent of cable television and the descent of the traditional broadcast networks was an unmistakable and irreversible foregone conclusion. Cable penetration in the United States rose from 42.8 percent in 1985 to 60.6 percent in 1991.[92] By 1990–1991, basic cable attracted 20 percent of all domestic viewers, while premium channels such as HBO added another 6 percent to this total.[93] These figures would nearly double again over the next decade. The whole TV viewing experience, in fact, was changing for most Americans. The time-shifting capability of the videocassette recorder (VCR) was a welcome addition for most television watchers in the 1980s. Only 1.1 percent of TV households in the United States had VCRs in 1980; this number climbed to 20.8 percent in 1985 and then skyrocketed to 71.9 percent by 1991.[94] Along with the VCR (and other new media technologies such as videodisc players and video games) came remote control keypads. These small, handheld devices were first introduced in the mid 1950s, but they did not become commonplace in most American homes until the widespread adoption of cable and VCRs during the 1980s.

"There's no doubt that the remote control switch revolutionized the way we watched TV in the '80s," announced David Lachenbruch in *TV Guide* in January 1990. By 1991, at least 37 percent of all domestic viewers admitted that they preferred channel surfing (or quickly flipping through the 33.2 channels they now received on average) than just turning their television sets on to watch one specific program.[95] Consumers at home were slowly becoming more proactive in their TV viewing behavior, while their adoption of these new television-related

accessories aided in the industry's wholesale transition from broadcasting to narrowcasting. Nothing illustrated this transformation better than the arrival of people meters during the mid 1980s, providing
a new level of precision to the way TV audiences were measured.
Nielsen's audimeter was first introduced in 1973. It automatically calculated which channel was being watched but not much else. People
meters added a remote control keypad to the system. These remotes
were programmed ahead of time to correspond to the demographic
characteristics of individual household members (including their age,
sex, race, educational level, and annual income). Participants were
subsequently asked to punch in and out as they watched TV. This action recorded who exactly was viewing which programs and when.
Two companies—A. C. Nielsen and AGB (Audit of Great Britain)—
tested competing people meter systems in the United States between
1984 and 1988. They vied with each other for market share, while also
fine-tuning the technology by trial and error. Nielsen finally prevailed
in 1989, although critics still complained that people meters dispro-
portionally favored young, urban, professional viewers. They were the
segment of the population most comfortable with using these higher-
tech remotes on a regular basis. This particular people meter bias was
tolerated by the industry, however, since most sponsors were most interested in reaching this specific cohort anyway.

Yuppie audiences became the make-or-break commodity of the television industry during the late 1980s and early 1990s. If the new people
meter system captured them, then that was what mattered most. Steven
Bochco delivered another yuppie-friendly quality drama to NBC in October 1986 with *L.A. Law*. He and Terry Louise Fisher created this serial
hybrid, mixing the lawyer show with the soap opera and the sitcom. A
former Los Angeles deputy district attorney, Fisher had just served as
one of the head writers and producers on CBS's Emmy-award-winning
series, *Cagney & Lacey*, which debuted in 1982 and lasted six seasons.
Cagney & Lacey presented two no-nonsense, assertive female leads
(played by Tyne Daly and Sharon Gless), who succeeded against all odds
in a predominantly male profession (undercover police officers). *Cagney &
Lacey* was also the first prime-time program on television where most of
the behind-the-scenes creative personnel were women, including its cre-
ators Barbara Corday and Barbara Avedon: "Of the 125 episodes in the series, women were credited as producer on all episodes, as writer or
co-writer on 75, and as director on 21."[96] Having so many creative positions filled by women on *Cagney & Lacey* marked a major change in the
television industry, where, with increasing regularity, female producers
were finally entering the once-exclusive old-boy's enclave of prime time.

By the mid 1980s, for example, women producers almost single-handedly revived the nearly moribund situation comedy, beginning with Marcy Carsey and her partner Tom Werner's *The Cosby Show* in 1984 for NBC and later *Roseanne* in 1988 for ABC, Susan Harris's *The Golden Girls* in 1985 for NBC (after scoring a cult hit with *Soap* in the late 1970s for ABC), Linda Bloodworth-Thomason's *Designing Women* in 1986 for CBS, and Diane English's *Murphy Brown* in 1988 also for CBS.

The Cosby Show and *L.A. Law* popularized NBC's ten-year legacy of socially progressive quality programming from *Saturday Night Live* to *Hill Street Blues* and *St. Elsewhere* as never before, while moving far beyond the unmistakable "boy's club" atmosphere of *SNL*'s first generation (Belushi and Chase both adamantly claimed that "women were not funny") and the "predominantly male" orientation of MTM's hybrid dramas.[97] *The Cosby Show* was the most popular program of the 1980s bar none, sitting all by itself on top of the Nielsen rankings for four straight seasons from 1985 to 1988 before finally sharing the no. 1 spot with *Roseanne* in 1988–1989. At its peak, *The Cosby Show* averaged between fifty-eight and sixty-three million viewers a week from 1985 to 1987, attracting both high-end niche viewers and the older, less-affluent suburban segments of the mass audience. *The Cosby Show* had genuine crossover appeal, bridging yuppie (Cliff and Clair Huxtable were the ideal professional power couple) with more conservative family values (represented by four generations of happy, healthy, well-adjusted Huxtables). *The Cosby Show* was genuinely multicultural, politically correct, and conspicuous in its consumption for all. In fact, the generational shift from mass to niche programming was even evident in the changing iconography of wealth and living the good life as portrayed on prime time during the Reagan years from 1981 to 1989. The Ewing clan's hundred-thousand acre Southfork Ranch in *Dallas* eventually was replaced by the Huxtable family's fashionable Brooklyn brownstone in the imaginations of most Americans. Likewise, Blake's (John Forsythe), Krystle's (Linda Evans), and Alexis's (Joan Collins) haute couture evening wear on *Dynasty* was eclipsed by Sonny Crockett's (Don Johnson) and Rico Tubbs's (Philip Michael Thomas) hip-casual Armani ensembles on *Miami Vice*. Yuppie-targeted television no longer reserved its consumptive fantasies and desires to just the commercials in between the personal dramas and grim realities of everyday life at Hill Street Station and St. Eligius Hospital.

A prime example of this more aggressive style of conspicuous consumption was Arnie Becker's (Corbin Bernsen) Jaguar XJ6 with its "L.A. Law" vanity plate, which was the featured image in the opening title sequence of TV's newest quality drama. *L.A. Law* replaced *Hill Street Blues* in November 1986 in the 10 o'clock slot on NBC's high-appointment-profile Thursday night lineup. "Appointment television" was the "latest catch phrase buzzing through Hollywood," referring to the trend among young, urban, professional viewers who made a concerted effort to find time in their busy schedules to watch their favorite prime-time shows, rather than "just plopping themselves in front of the set and numbly enduring whatever's on."[98] As a top-15 show averaging twenty to twenty-five million viewers a week through the late 1980s and early 1990s, *L.A. Law* was the most successful quality drama on television at the time. Produced at Twentieth Century-Fox Television, Bochco, Fisher, and head writer David Kelley infused *L.A. Law* with the right mix of men and women protagonists (four each), along with a comfortable blend of for-profit and pro bono plotlines. Robert J. Thompson reports that "major stories usually concerned cases that addressed complex contemporary legal issues, ranging from date rape and child abuse to capital punishment and euthanasia of AIDS patients. This kind of material had been the province of Terry Louise Fisher when she was working on *Cagney & Lacey*, and as co-creator of *L.A. Law*, her influence was clearly showing here."[99] By 1986–1987, NBC was securely positioned as broadcast TV's no. 1 network, where it would stay ensconced through the 1991–1992 season. Grant Tinker left NBC in the wake of GE's takeover of RCA, being replaced as board chair and CEO of the network by Robert Wright in August 1986. From that point onward, NBC became less the quality network and more the reigning symbol of the television establishment. For a time, ABC and a number of cable channels filled the quality programming vacuum by becoming TV's latest networks to target younger upscale viewers above all others.

Brandon Stoddard was promoted to president of ABC Entertainment in November 1985 after a decade at ABC Circle Films, where he helped develop "some of the network's most distinguished programming" during that period, including miniseries such as *Roots*, *The Thorn Birds*, and *The Winds of War*, as well as Glenn Gordon Caron's stylish detective-romantic comedy hybrid, *Moonlighting*, which debuted in March 1985.[100] Over the next three and a half years, Stoddard transformed the lowest-brow schedule in broadcast television into prime time's newest quality lineup by assembling an in-house stable of creative producers and writers under long-term contract (most notably Steven Bochco in 1978), while simultaneously nurturing a steady stream of increasingly personal and innovative dramas and comedies such as Marshall Herskovitz and Edward Zwick's *thirtysomething*, Bochco and Fisher's *Hooperman*, and Andrew Adelson's *Max Headroom* in 1987; followed by William Broyles Jr. and John Sacret Young's *China Beach*, Carol Black and Neal Marlen's *The Wonder Years*, and

Carsey and Werner's *Roseanne* in 1988. The critical hit *thirtysomething* and the no. 1 blockbuster *Roseanne* formed the yin and yang of Stoddard's short but memorable tenure as head programmer (when ABC rose to no. 2 in 1987–1988 but never seriously challenged NBC for no. 1). Both attracted blue-chip demographics, although *Roseanne* cornered the pink-collar and blue-collar segments of the mass audience as well. Certainly, "*thirtysomething* was the very picture of the viewers that ABC wanted in its audience: 30-ish, upwardly mobile, preferably with children, and spending lots of money on consumer goods."[101] In contrast, Roseanne Barr was the wise-cracking down-to-earth un-yuppie. Her satiric view of men, marriage, children, and housework placed her firmly at the cutting edge of a new generation of women comics. *Roseanne* presented a boisterous and unrepentantly working-class family that was seemingly mired in an endless succession of no-win options, unlike the couples and singles on *thirtysomething*, who often struggled to make sense of too many choices.

Both of these programs struck responsive chords with American audiences for very different reasons. After their initial runs on ABC, *Roseanne* and *thirtysomething* also found their own separate niches in the thriving off-network syndication market of the late 1980s and early 1990s. *Roseanne* followed the path blazed by *M*A*S*H*, *Laverne & Shirley*, and *The Cosby Show*, among other popular sitcoms (along with a handful of one-hour dramas such as CBS's *Magnum, P.I.*; NBC's *The A-Team*; and ABC's *The Fall Guy*). All of these programs were being sold into both domestic and international syndication well before they had stockpiled the usual five years' worth of episodes. This standard inventory (5 years×26 annual episodes on average=130 episodes) was the typical backlog for any off-network series because it enabled a show to be stripped (or scheduled Monday through Friday) for at least a year in syndication (allowing for two plays per episode). Three factors changed this calculus in the Cable Era. First, the increasing number of new independent stations and cable networks drove up the subsequent demand for off-network product; second, this spike in demand caused an acute shortage in the number of suitable programs that actually totaled five years' worth of episodes; and, third, prime-time budgets skyrocketed throughout the Cable Era (stimulated primarily by the rise in quality productions). For example, the average cost of thirty minutes of prime-time programming climbed from $115,000 in 1975–1976, to $265,000 in 1980–1981, to $365,000 in 1985–1986, to $700,000 in 1991–1992.[102] Because studios and independent companies budgeted their programs at a deficit (meaning their up-front costs far exceeded the license fees paid to them by the networks), these producers were eager to syndi-

Roseanne presented a boisterous and unrepentantly working-class family headed by Roseanne Conner (Roseanne Barr) and her husband Dan (John Goodman). Courtesy of Paramount Pictures/Heldref.

cate their series as soon as possible in order to get out of debt and start making profits.

In this regard, "*M*A*S*H* was the watershed that changed the marketplace," being the first program to earn $100 million in domestic syndication. *The Cosby Show* subsequently broke the $1 billion barrier when it was sold into syndication across the United States for a second five-year cycle in 1990–1991. That same season, *Roseanne* was licensed domestically for $2 million per episode.[103] (The series would eventually total 221 half-hour episodes). In addition to these domestic revenues, overseas syndication was amounting to an average 40 percent of a show's backend earning potential by 1992: "the global television market was becoming more lucrative and complex in the 1990s, just as the domestic market had in the 1980s."[104] For its part, *thirtysomething*'s niche appeal limited its syndication opportunities in comparison to what was available to a former top-10 hit like *Roseanne*. Still, Herskovitz and Zwick's Emmy-award-winning paean to "yuppie angst" was a most comfortable fit on the cable network, Lifetime, as were a handful of other quality dramas, including *L.A. Law, Moonlighting,* and *China Beach.*[105] Lifetime resulted from "a merger between Viacom's Cable Health Channel and Hearst/ABC's Daytime" in

February 1984.[106] It took several years for a clear identity to emerge for Lifetime following this corporate transaction. As late as 1986, for instance, this new channel was still aiming for a "general audience (especially women)" with a somewhat indistinct and scattershot lineup "devoted to health, science, and better living: nutrition shows; shows on fitness, preventive medicine, sex, parenting; and weekday movies."[107] By 1988, though, "its print ads in the trades" described the network as a "unique environment designed to attract an elusive audience" made up of "high spending women" who were "highly selective about the programming they watch[ed]."[108] Overall, *thirtysomething* and the other upscale serial melodramas that Lifetime licensed through syndication were perfectly suited to this quality female audience.

"Melodrama, whether packaged as fiction or reality, clearly draws a strong female audience and remains the vital force in women's television," acknowledge Jackie Byars and Eileen Meehan. "Lifetime may conceptualize its working women as economically independent, but not as emotionally independent from men. The channel thus programmed its prime-time hours for upscale women *and* men who would spend their evening 'cocooning' in front of the television set."[109] Similarly, the male-centered *Hill Street Blues* and *St. Elsewhere* ended up on the newly reconfigured arts and culture channel Bravo. Bravo was originally founded as a pay-TV service in October 1984 by the Northeast cable operator, Cablevision Systems Corporation. Over the next four years, Bravo recruited a modest 500,000 subscribers with a schedule consisting of 70 percent international films and 30 percent performing arts specials. Then in December 1988, Cablevision sold 50 percent of its nine programming services (including American Movie Classics and Sportschannel, as well as Bravo) to NBC, whose CEO Robert Wright was eagerly looking for more opportunities in the cable sector. Such partnerships between broadcast and cable entities were becoming increasingly common in the Reagan-Bush era of deregulation. Two immediate effects of this merger in April 1989 were the joint launch of CNBC, a consumer-news and business channel, and the transitioning of Bravo from a premium to a basic cable network. By the early 1990s, Bravo was targeting affluent higher-brow men and women ages eighteen to fifty-four with a lineup that contained American independent and international films, performing arts programming, and select off-network series such as the recent NBC hybrids *Hill Street Blues* and *St. Elsewhere*. Bravo was the ideal niche for these two pioneering quality shows. Moreover, the cable sector of the television industry was already taking steps to supplement its licensing of older off-network programs with original productions tailor-made to the individual specifications of each channel's target audience.

HBO led the way in this regard by producing its first original series, *Not Necessarily the News*, and its first made-for-pay TV movie, *The
Terry Fox Story*, in 1983, followed by its first miniseries, *All the Rivers
Run*, in 1984. The cable sector next "eclipsed broadcasting's assets
and revenue values by the late 1980s." In its "short history, cable television [had already] redefined television," argues Sharon Strover. "It
spawned a huge variety of 'narrowcast' programming services as well
as new broad appeal services," such as the USA Network which was
the first cable channel to syndicate the popular MTV-influenced police drama *Miami Vice*. Cable "altered the structure of the programming industry by developing new markets for both very old and very
new program types."[110]

It also combined with an ever-growing number of independent stations to push the broadcast networks into more distinctive and custom-
ized programming by siphoning off more than 30 percent of their
one-time captive audience from 1976 through 1991. Cases in point were
the new quality shows that appeared during the 1980s. "Ironically or
not, as network television draws smaller and smaller percentages of the
total viewing audience, TV programming gets better," observed TV
critic Tom Shales in 1988; "network executives seem inclined to give
writers and producers more leeway to pursue a vision, and slowly, prime
time is becoming less smothered with standardization than it used to
be."[111] Beginning in the mid 1970s, therefore, a niche market model
supplanted the old way of doing business throughout the American
economy. In television, specifically, made-to-order series by a new generation of creative writer-producers replaced the two-decade-long dominance of Hollywood's cookie-cutter mode of telefilm production. The
best and most influential new programs defied easy classification while
attracting young, urban, professional audiences through their well-
targeted, quality appeals. The broader economic benefits of consumer
segmentation also rendered the increasingly outdated mass-market
model of the Network Era obsolete. In turn, branding became the standard way in which networks and production companies differentiated
their programming from the competition.

Like America itself, TV has always existed in a state of transformation, being continually reshaped by a wide assortment of technological,
commercial, and social factors. Television in the United States grew
from a local to a regional medium during the 1940s and 1950s, finally
becoming the centerpiece of national culture by the start of the 1960s.
Even though the first TV satellite, Telstar 1, was launched in July 1962,
American television never fully realized its international promise until
satellites and cable once again reinvented the medium after 1975. The
shift in television from broadcasting to narrowcasting also marked the

steep decline in the one-time invincible three-network oligopoly, which eroded in the face of seventy-four new cable channels, nearly three hundred independent stations, and a viable fourth broadcast network by 1991.[112]

More than anyone, Ted Turner emerged as the unofficial spokesperson for cable TV after his launch of WTBS in 1976 and his subsequent founding of five additional cable services—CNN, CNN Headline News, TNT (Turner Network Television in 1988), the Cartoon Channel (in 1992), and TCM (Turner Classic Movies in 1994). CNN, in particular, "ranks as perhaps the most important innovation in cable television during the final quarter of the 20th century."[113] Ridiculed at first as "Chicken Noodle News," CNN grew into the first place that people worldwide turned to for late-breaking stories only a decade later when it reached into more than sixty million American homes and 140 other countries. Nothing illustrated the arrival of cable television better than CNN's nonstop live coverage of the January 16, 1991, outbreak of the Persian Gulf War: "The network was the communications loop between Washington, Baghdad, and Kuwait."[114] Even President Bush reportedly watched CNN for twelve consecutive hours that night.[115] With his innovation of CNN, "Ted Turner had forever changed the history of television news."[116] His career at Turner Broadcasting System (TBS) is an apt object lesson into the changing nature of the television industry during the Cable Era.

THE CHANGING FACE OF TELEVISION
Turner Broadcasting System

9

Jimmie L. Reeves and
Michael M. Epstein

No one exemplifies the changing face of television during the closing decades of the twentieth century more than Robert Edward (Ted) Turner III. The mustachioed media mogul with chronic foot-in-mouth disease made Turner Broadcasting System (TBS) into one of the primary beneficiaries of the cable and satellite revolutions—revolutions that would transform the global television experience. Though the legend of Ted Turner does not exactly conform to Horatio Alger's rags-to-riches stories, Turner's personal journey from the obscurity of outdoor advertising to the prominence of *Time* Magazine's Man of the Year has consumed thousands of column inches of newsprint and inspired numerous biographies. Rather than document, yet again, the admittedly fascinating trysts and travesties, triumphs and tragedies of Turner's personal life, this particular exploration of TBS's place in the history of television will focus instead on Ted Turner as change agent. And as change agent, Turner's innovations would leave a profound imprint on television during the 1970s, 1980s, and 1990s.

Any exploration of the rise of the independent station, the strategic deployment of off-network syndicated series as counterprogramming, the forging of new synergies in sports programming, the exploitation of alternative forms of advertising, the diffusion of satellite delivery technology, the development of the superstation concept, the proliferation of niche cable networks, and the internationalization (then the globalization) of television news must take into account the contributions and achievements of Ted Turner. The early years of what would ultimately become TBS occurred during the last decade of the Network Era (1948–1975), a period in American media history when television broadcasting was dominated by a three-network oligopoly. Next, Turner's introduction of the superstation concept was a harbinger of the coming cable television explosion, a period when the broadcasting standard would be overshadowed and undermined by an emergent satellite-and-wire paradigm. The heyday of TBS, which roughly spans the same period as the Reagan and Bush administrations, coincided with the triumph of the Cable Era (1976–1994)—a period when the mass-marketing and mass-culture business models of the fading network system would be supplanted by the niche-marketing and cult-culture models of the booming cable-satellite system. Finally, the most recent changes at TBS and the progressively lowered profile of Ted Turner came after the advent of the Digital Era (1995–present), a time in television history marked by technological convergence, industrial consolidation, and brand marketing.

TURNER AND THE NETWORK ERA

In 1963, at age twenty-four, Ted Turner inherited Turner Advertising after his father, Robert Edward (Ed) Turner Jr., committed suicide with a .38-caliber pistol. Though holding his father's company together was a struggle early on, the young CEO weathered the adversity and quickly turned Turner Advertising into the largest firm of its kind in the South. Ranking fifth nationally in total number of billboards, Turner's company controlled ten key markets spread over eight states. And in the late 1960s, Turner used his outdoor advertising business as a springboard for diving into broadcasting. After he got his feet wet by acquiring Chattanooga radio station WAPO in 1968, he quickly purchased radio stations in Charlotte and Jacksonville. But perhaps the most important moment in the business career of Ted Turner was January 1, 1970, when he purchased WJRJ, an independent television station in Atlanta that broadcast on UHF Channel 17.[1]

Channel 17 had lost $900,000 the year before Turner acquired it— and virtually all of Turner's advisors were dead set against the purchase. But to understand why reversing the fortunes of Channel 17 was perhaps Ted Turner's greatest feat as an entrepreneur, it is necessary to first examine the operating rules of the inequitable system that Turner encountered when he set sail into the turbulent waters of broadcasting. The early 1970s was, after all, the peak moment of the Network Era, when CBS, NBC, and ABC had a more or less captive audience. Exercising a stranglehold on 90 percent of the prime-time audience at the height of their power, the major television networks found themselves in a comparable situation as that faced by the major Hollywood studios in 1946 when the motion picture industry experienced its most profitable year ever. There was not much room left for growth. Though ABC was still struggling to gain parity with CBS and NBC, almost every market in the nation was covered with network affiliates, and virtually every profitable minute of the weekly schedule had been mined for advertising revenues. In other words, the old network system, like the "Fordist" manufacturing economy it had helped sustain for so many years, had essentially run its course.[2]

Indeed, the most important thing to grasp about the Network Era and its ultimate decline is its relationship to Fordism. As manifested in the expansive manufacturing economy of assembly-line production and mass consumption that drove the general prosperity of the great postwar boom in the United States, Fordism was characterized by "rigidity": long-term and large-scale fixed capital investments, collective bargaining for long-term contracts, sustained federal regulatory oversight of key industries (including broadcasting), and long-term state commitment to entitlement programs. As chief products and major producers of the Fordist economic and political order, CBS, NBC, and ABC performed the absolutely crucial ideological function of promoting Fordism's ethic of consumption. In other words, Fordism and American commercial television were entangled in the shared pursuit of producing confident consumers. Since the Fordist manufacturing economy was based on mass consumption and mass marketing, popularity during the first two decades of the Network Era was defined in terms of brute ratings points. Consequently, all of the networks during this period, especially after set ownership penetrated deep into the working classes, would come to embrace the "lowest common denominator" or "least objectionable" programming philosophies.[3]

In the early 1970s, though, CBS made television history when it initiated a daring new programming philosophy that departed from the logic of Fordism. In prime-time television's first bold step down the road to niche marketing, CBS cancelled Mayberry R.F.D.; Hee Haw; The Jim Nabors Hour; and Green Acres—not because the programs failed to generate large ratings numbers, but because advertisers did not value the demographic skew of their audiences. In concert with this rural purge, CBS embarked on a quest for "quality demographics" that would, as Jane Feuer argues, result in the reinvention of the situation comedy. Most notably, CBS struck pay dirt by violating the "least-objectionable" doctrine with Norman Lear's All in the Family, a series that openly courted controversy. With Lear's caustic social comedies and MTM's character-driven "warmedies," CBS targeted its programming at the infamous yuppie (young, urban, upwardlymobile professional) so valued by advertisers. Of course, in the process, CBS also alienated a large number of middle Americans, especially those residing south of the Mason-Dixon Line.[4]

Ted Turner shared this alienation and saw it as an opportunity to lure audiences away from the networks. But Turner's quest for profitability would be complicated by a major historical disadvantage—UHF stations had been second-class citizens in the television industry since 1952 when the FCC issued its Sixth Report and Order. This FCC action ended the historic freeze on television station licensing that had been enforced since 1948 and, in addition, created an uneven playing field between the established VHF stations and the newly minted UHF broadcasting service. It is important to note that VHF broadcasters enjoyed a "natural" technological advantage over their UHF brethren. Because they were located in a lower frequency band (54 to 216 MHz) in the electromagnetic spectrum, very high frequency signals tended to behave like sound waves, bending not only around obstacles but also over the curvature of the earth. UHF transmitters operated at comparatively higher frequencies (470 to 890 MHz)—which meant that their signals behaved more like light than sound and tended to shoot off into outer space rather than cling to the bowed surface of the globe. For the UHF license holders, this technological disparity translated into economic disadvantages: if a UHF signal and a VHF signal were transmitted from the same tower with the same effective radiated power, the VHF station would have far greater range, larger populations would be able to tune in the signal, and advertisers on the station would potentially expose many more eyeballs to their commercial messages.

The technological disadvantages of owning a UHF station were compounded by another, less "natural" factor. For many years, consumers had to invest more money and expend extra effort to receive the underdog UHF stations available in any particular market. UHF reception required a special antenna, and TV set manufacturers were slow to make UHF tuners standard equipment on new receivers (until the FCC intervened in 1962). When Turner was initially trying to build an audience for Channel 17, consumers with older sets had to add on a UHF tuner at additional expense. In fact, Turner once boasted to advertisers about the intelligence of his viewers, claiming that "you have to be smart to figure out how to tune in a UHF antenna in the first place." "Dumb guys can't do it," Turner would say. "Can you get Channel 17? No? Well, neither can I. We aren't smart enough. But my viewers are."[5]

Although Turner claimed he knew nothing about the broadcasting business when he purchased WJRJ, he did understand the advertising business—and 90 percent of mastering commercial broadcasting was grasping the ins and outs of advertising. So, Turner did not exactly start from scratch when he embarked on a short, but intense, period of studying broadcast trade journals and ratings reports. Turner changed the call letters of the station to WTCG (which stood for "Turner Communication Group"), then developed a list of priorities that would guide his strategic moves. He called these priorities "the five Ps": programming, personnel, promotion, penetration, and profits.[6] It was Turner's first "P" that initially earned him a reputation as a so-called genius—but, technically, Turner's talent was not so much in programming as in counterprogramming. For example, at almost the same moment that CBS was purging its schedule of "hayseed comedies," Turner was acquiring such rural favorites as *Petticoat Junction, The Andy Griffith*

Show, and *Gomer Pyle, U.S.M.C.* In addition, Channel 17 also scheduled, in daily back-to-back "strip form," other classic off-network series like *The Lucy Show*, *Gilligan's Island*, *Leave It to Beaver*, and *Father Knows Best*. Thus, WTCG became a showcase for what Turner called "good old days" programming—off-network series from the 1950s and 1960s that were relics of the lowest common denominator philosophy. In addition to recycling "old-fashioned" network fare, Turner also filled out his schedule with cartoons, country music blocks, and such timeless Saturday morning kiddie fare as *The Three Stooges*, *The Little Rascals*, and *Abbott & Costello*. Classic Hollywood movies, too, would be a staple of WTCG. For several years, Turner even performed as the host of *Academy Award Theater*, a movie showcase scheduled on Sunday morning to counter the traditional religious fare appearing on competing stations. Clearly, Turner's "good old days" counterprogramming was meant to appeal to the Southern audience that was then being systematically abandoned by the networks.[7]

Given that Turner would one day achieve fame and recognition as the founder of the world's first twenty-four-hour news network, it is seems strange at first glance that news had virtually no place in his design for making WTCG a profitable enterprise. But, again, the key concept driving Turner's scheduling strategy was counterprogramming. Pouring resources into a news operation would essentially amount to attacking one of the major strengths of his competitors in the Atlanta television market. Even the weakest of the three, the ABC affiliate, had recently undertaken an extensive overhaul that included investing in a "crack experienced news team." Rather than try to compete head to head in the news game with Atlanta's established network affiliates, Turner decided to run what was then the FCC minimum of forty minutes a day of news and public affairs programming. But few would benefit from this mandatory "public service" because Turner scheduled the WTCG newscast at three o'clock in the morning after the "Late, Late Movie." In the early evening, Turner counterprogrammed by scheduling the original cult television show, *Star Trek*, while other Atlanta stations were airing national and local newscasts.[8]

Though old-fashioned programming consumed most of its schedule, it was in the area of sports programming that WTCG made the biggest splash. Turner's first venture into the world of sports was professional wrestling. With the help of a former girlfriend who was married to one of Atlanta's top wrestling promoters, Turner lured a popular wrestling show away from the local ABC affiliate. Outfitting WTCG's small studio with a full-sized ring, Turner aired wrestling three times a week—and the station's ratings started moving upward. Though deemphasized and undervalued in most accounts of the Turner success story, professional wrestling was a key weapon in TBS's programming arsenal for the next three decades. Like the good-old-days series, serials, and movies, professional wrestling invoked and capitalized on nostalgia for the early days of the medium when "Gorgeous George" Wagner was one of television's biggest stars and the faux-sports form appeared at one time or another on the prime-time schedules of all four national networks (especially DuMont). Although wrestling would be exiled from network prime time after 1955, this sport managed to survive as a regionalized entertainment spectacle in the highly undesirable time slots of local late-night and weekend schedules. Securing a permanent place in Channel 17's lineup would be the first step for wrestling to make a national comeback. But another intrepid entrepreneur, Vincent Kenneth McMahon Jr., then surpassed Turner by developing wrestling into one of the primary attractions of the cable fringe in the 1980s and 1990s.[9]

Of course, Turner's most celebrated achievements in the world of professional sports was in Major League Baseball (MLB). His MLB adventure began in 1973 when Turner outbid WSB (Atlanta's then-dominant NBC affiliate) for the right to broadcast Braves games. Turner told Tom Bradley of *Television/Radio Age* that he "knew that the Braves and WSB both weren't entirely happy with their situation":

> They [WSB] were only showing 20 games. We entered into lengthy negotiations with the Braves management and made commitments for 60 games. It cost us about $1.3 million but we needed a strong prime-time sports package to counterprogram against the network reruns during the spring and summer, and to go with a package of older, classic films we had purchased.[10]

Just three years later, on January 3, 1976, Turner bought the struggling franchise from the Atlanta-LaSalle Corporation for about $10 million. Like the purchase of Channel 17, Turner's acquisition of the Braves seemed ill-advised. Many believed he paid too much for one of the doormats of MLB, but Turner's detractors did not understand that for anyone else the price tag may have been exorbitant—but for Ted Turner, the Braves were a bargain. The move complemented the synergy of owning *both* a sports team that played 162 games every year and an independent television station that had a voracious appetite for regular programming. In this synergy, the whole of the Braves/WTCG collaboration would be greater than the sum of its parts as the station would become the primary vehicle for marketing and promoting the Braves, and vice versa. Once this synergy was set in motion, Turner plowed profits back into improving the team, which, in turn, resulted in elevating the ratings for

Braves games (as well as WTCG's other programming). Moreover, the elevated ratings resulted in more fans in the seats at home games, and higher attendance led to more profits, which was reinvested in the team—and so on. While this synergy was increasing the value of both properties, Turner did not have to worry about paying escalating costs for the broadcast rights to Braves games after the team actually started winning. By the mid 1990s, no one was laughing at Turner for paying too much for the Braves because—thanks to this synergy—the franchise had become a perennial powerhouse in the National League and was worth in the neighborhood of $200 million.[11]

At the end of Turner's first year as a television station owner, WTCG lost $900,000 and his company (which had never before been unprofitable) recorded a net after-tax loss of over $700,000. The situation, though still dire, improved somewhat in 1971 when WTCG "only" lost $500,000. The turning point for WTCG came in 1972. Not only did the station break even that year, but also Turner's destiny became forever tangled up in the fortunes of the cable television industry. Sixteen years later, Turner posed in cowboy garb for a poster that made reference to a country-western hit of the 1980s: the poster was inscribed with the words, "I was cable when cable wasn't cool." In 1972, the cable business definitely was not "cool"—but in the next decade, thanks to changes in the regulatory climate, the dawning of the age of the communication satellite, audience dissatisfaction with the limited viewing options of the existing commercial television system, and large-scale economic transformations that were increasingly global in scope, cable would become one of the hottest growth sectors in the U.S. communication industry. Turner, with his insignificant UHF station in Atlanta, was poised to ride the wave of the cable revolution—and ride it he did.[12]

TURNER AT THE DAWN OF THE CABLE ERA

Before 1972, cable television was basically a common carrier. Cable television was born in 1948 in isolated places like Astoria, Oregon, and Lansford, Pennsylvania. Local entrepreneurs like L. E. Parsons, a radio station manager, and Bob Tarlton, an appliance dealer, built community antennas to intercept broadcast signals and distribute them to populations who were aching to experience the magic of this exciting new communication medium. Although this community antenna television (CATV) only provided content that was freely available over the air in nearby metropolitan areas, the parasitic business enjoyed stable growth throughout the 1950s. But to protect copyright holders and local broadcasters, the

FCC enacted a number of rules in the mid 1960s that, for a time, stunted the continued growth of the cable industry. In 1972, after cable interests overcame the copyright obstacle by agreeing to pay fees determined by a federally appointed tribunal, the FCC issued a mandate that ultimately put Ted Turner on the road to becoming a billionaire. The FCC ruling opened the door for cable operators to use a series of microwave transmitters to import distant signals of struggling independent UHF stations like WTCG. With the help of Andy Goldman, a fellow sailing enthusiast, Turner quickly worked out an arrangement with TelePrompTer (which at that time was the largest cable operation in the country) to import WTCG's signal into Huntsville, Muscle Shoals, and Tuscaloosa, Alabama. He also worked out other partnerships to distribute his microwaved signal to cable operators in the rural hill country of southern Georgia and northern Florida, expanding the audience for WTCG into Macon, Columbus, and Tallahassee. As Porter Bibb put it, "Ted Turner had crossed the line from broadcaster to something else, but even he couldn't have foreseen how far this first step into the brave new world of cable television would take him":

> Turner knew that his real market was an ever-expanding market beyond Atlanta.... Through the good offices of the FCC, Ted Turner had taken a dog-eared independent UHF and turned it, in less than thirty-six months, into an invaluable regional franchise, the first "cable network" in television history. Perhaps more important, the signal he delivered proved uniquely popular with WTCG's newly expanded audience, which was in total sync with Turner's escapist programming.[13]

The turnaround in WTCG's fortunes was indeed startling. In 1972, the station broke even. The next year, it not only won the Braves contract but also recorded $1 million in profits. By 1974, the station ranked as the top independent UHF station in the country.[14]

In 1972, when Turner first used terrestrial microwave technology to export Channel 17's signal beyond the Atlanta market, the 2,841 cable systems in the United States provided essentially a common-carrier service to a total of six million subscribers. By the time Turner launched the Cable News Network (CNN) in 1980, the number of cable systems in operation had swelled to more than four thousand while the total number of cable subscribers had almost tripled to sixteen million. In 1990, the year CNN won a Peabody Award for coverage of the Tiananmen Square uprising, well over half the homes in the United States were wired into almost ten thousand cable systems as total subscribers now exceeded fifty million. Although the "cable boom" was also driven by economic and cultural factors, the timing of the boom was largely an outcome of an interrelated regulatory and technological development—the advent of the commercial communication satellite.

On June 18, 1973, the Annual Convention of the National Cable Television Association (NCTA) opened in Anaheim, California, with what Patrick Parsons and Robert Frieden identify as "the first coast-to-coast satellite retransmission of a domestic television signal designed specifically for use by cable television systems." Arranged by TelePrompTer (Turner's cable partner in Alabama), the demonstration relayed from Madison Square Garden to convention rooms in the Disneyland Hotel was the forgettable heavyweight championship match between boxers Jimmie Ellis and Ernie Shavers. The NCTA demonstration was hyped at the time as a historic event—but its significance was dwarfed by HBO's experimental satellite distribution of another heavyweight title fight between Muhammad Ali and Joe Frazier. The fight itself would go down in sports history as the "Thrilla in Manila," but the satellite transmission from the Philippines marks October 1, 1975, as a watershed moment that forever changed the economics of cable—and broadcast—television. Though only two cable systems (one in Jackson, Mississippi, and the other in Fort Pierce–Vero Beach, Florida) were equipped to receive the Thrilla in Manila live, the experiment was a success. The Cable Era had arrived, and the broadcast networks, like the once-glorious satellites now trapped in degenerating orbits, would begin a slow descent.[15]

The success of HBO laid the groundwork for other satellite cable networks—most notably, those associated with the Turner media empire. WTCG, though, had two major obstacles to overcome before joining HBO on RCA's Satcom 1. First, Turner did not have access to the deep pockets of Time, Inc., and had to come up with the money to build a transmitting Earth station. Second, he had to work through a regulatory maze that prevented him from holding a broadcast license and also owning a common carrier like a satellite-transmission company. So the superstation concept would not become a reality for almost two years, though Turner and his comrades had drawn up its blueprints in early 1975 (months before HBO's Thrilla in Manila triumph).[16]

During the agonizing wait, Turner appeared before the House Subcommittee on Communication, which was considering the future of cable television. Championing the cable industry as a public service, Turner's testimony defended the superstation concept by attacking the "broadcast monopoly": "I would love to become a superstation," Turner proclaimed; "I would love desperately to create a fourth network for cable television, producing our own programs, not just running *I Love*

Lucy and *Gilligan's Island* for the fifty-seventh time. And I intend to go that way, if we are allowed to." On December 17, 1976, the FCC approved Southern Satellite System's petition as a common carrier after taking almost a year to determine that the spin-off company was, indeed, independent of the Turner Communication Corporation. On that same day, WTCG's signal was beamed up to Satcom 1 and the world's first superstation had finally arrived. On August 21, 1979, Turner renamed both his company and its flagship superstation: Turner Communications Corporation would henceforth be known as Turner Broadcasting System, Inc., and WTCG was duly rechristened WTBS.[17]

TURNER AND THE TRIUMPH OF THE CABLE ERA

Just as commercial television during the Network Era had been one of the chief products and producers of Fordism, cable television in the 1980s exhibited a complicated product/producer relationship with the post-Fordist service economy. The Cable Era's combination satellite-and-wire distribution system, augmented by remote controls, personal computers, and video cassette recorders, was both source and outcome of what Mike Davis identifies as the "overconsumptionism" of post-Fordism. Unlike the mass-marketing model that dominated the Network Era, American television in the Cable Era would both conform to—and actively promote—the emergent logic of niche marketing that energized the service economy of post-Fordism. Though the broadcast networks would also shift from mass marketing to niche marketing in the 1970s and 1980s, it was the booming cable industry that became a veritable incubator for specialized programming services. In a five-year span beginning in 1979, cable's "foundation" services would exploit many profitable programming niches: all-sports programming (claimed by ESPN in 1979), children's programming (Nickelodeon in 1979), educational programming (the Learning Channel in 1980), popular music programming (MTV in 1981), weather reporting (the Weather Channel in 1982), and women's programming (Lifetime in 1984).[18]

Turner's superstation idea basically replicated the broadcast networks' strategy of scheduling a broad array of programming forms to build a demographically broad audience base (a strategy followed again on cable by the USA Network beginning in 1980). However, Turner's next—and most celebrated—venture in cablecasting *would* conform to post-Fordism's logic of niche marketing. And, clearly, market considerations were what sparked Turner's initial interest in launching an around-the-clock cable news service. As Turner reportedly told Maurice Wolfe (Reese) Schonfeld in November 1978, "There are only four things that television does. There's movies—and HBO has that. There's sports—and now ESPN's got that, unfortunately. There's the regular series kinda stuff—and the networks do that. All that's left is news." Therefore, Turner recognized that in the new cable environment he had to counterprogram the networks, and he had to "counterniche" other cable services in the post-Fordist media marketplace.[19]

Money was one gigantic reason that the news niche was still available for Turner to excavate in 1978. A twenty-four-hour news service would require years of profitability to recoup huge start-up costs—and long-term profitability was far from a sure thing. At the time, none of the major television networks believed that viewer demand could sustain even a one-hour national newscast every day (though each of the three major TV networks spent about $100 million every year to cover news for their daily, half-hour telecasts). Furthermore, Time, Inc., had already studied the risks and rewards of producing just eight hours of live news that would be repeated once a day—but the giant media company with decades of experience in the business of magazine journalism was not willing to shoulder the expense of starting up a worldwide television news-gathering organization. The fact that Ted Turner was eager to commit the resources of his relatively small company to a journalistic enterprise that was even more costly and ambitious than that envisioned by Time, Inc., sent shock waves through TBS. The prospect of financing the operation was apparently too daunting for Will Sanders, who stepped down as chief financial officer of TBS in June 1979. And at least one anonymous message appeared on Turner's desk begging him to steer clear of a risky endeavor of such a grand scale that it might "sink the whole company."[20]

Turner was essentially starting from scratch when he took on the challenge of constructing, outfitting, staffing, programming, and maintaining a nonstop news network. Just as he knew very little about television when he bought Channel 17, and next to nothing about baseball when he bought the Braves, Turner was not-so-blissfully ignorant of the news profession when he became obsessed with this new field of dreams. Though Turner could certainly be foolish in his arrogance, he also seemed to be strangely wise in his ignorance—that is, he had a knack for recognizing what he didn't know and acting accordingly. Where "programming" was the most decisive "P" in his turnaround strategy for WTCG, "personnel" would be his first order of business in claiming cable's news niche. Turner obviously needed to enlist the assistance of an experienced news professional who shared his passion for the concept of an all-news channel. In Reese Schonfeld he found such a seasoned journalist.

Schonfeld had amassed over twenty years of experience in the news business when he agreed to Turner's burning question: "Can it be done?" When Turner approached him about the opportunity to build CNN from the ground up, Schonfeld had just recently organized his own satellite-delivered news service, the Independent Television News Association (ITNA). According to Whittemore, at ITNA Schonfeld established a reputation as the "Electronic News Godfather, whose talent, experience and energy made him the prime candidate to challenge the networks headon." Turner accepted Schonfeld in a leadership role, at least for a while, because Schonfeld not only understood the woof-and-warp of news gathering and the nuts-and-bolts of satellite technology but also shared Turner's loathing of the broadcast networks—and organized labor.[21] In fact, Schonfeld was so powerful during the early development of the network that he even vetoed Turner's initial plan for programming CNN. Turner had originally envisioned a two-hour programming cycle broken down into four parts (news, sports, soft features, and financial features). Schonfeld preferred a much more "fluid" and open structure, one that could both involve viewers in the news-making process and also exploit the new network's ability to go live to breaking stories.[22]

Schonfeld was also instrumental in screening, signing, and orchestrating the talent who would lend their faces to the new network. The first big-name television journalist to sign on with CNN was Daniel Schorr. Schorr's television career stretched back to the Edward R. Murrow era at CBS in the 1950s. In the 1970s, as CBS's senior Watergate correspondent, Schorr gained membership in an exclusive club—President Nixon's "enemies" list. His reputation as a man of principle was further enhanced in 1976 when Schorr resigned from CBS News because he felt the network had failed to cover his back during a confrontation with Congress over freedom of the press. A tough reporter who embodied the highest standards of journalistic professionalism, Schorr gave CNN instant credibility. As brand equity for the new network, this credibility was immediately exploited in a news conference at the May 1979 NCTA convention when Turner and Schonfeld introduced Schorr as senior Washington correspondent for the news network of the future.[23]

Schorr's credibility also proved invaluable in Schonfeld's recruitment of other serious television journalists. Bernie Shaw, one of the few African Americans to break the color barrier in mainstream television news, left ABC to join CNN's Washington bureau. Mary Alice Williams, who had been recently fired as WNBC-TV's anchor of the *Morning News* in New York City, signed on as anchor and chief of

CNN's New York City bureau, located in offices of the World Trade Center. Sandi Freeman, who had been cohosting *AM Chicago* on WLS (a station owned and operated by ABC), was selected to host an evening call-in show. Kathleen Sullivan left KTVX-TV in Salt Lake City to become one of cable television's first media stars at the CNN anchor desk in Atlanta. Early morning anchor John Holliman; business reporters Stuart Varney, Lou Dobbs, and Myron Kandel; media critic Kevin Sanders; husband and wife anchor team Don Farmer and Chris Curle; sportscasters Nick Charles and Bob Kurtz; and Hollywood gossip-correspondent Lee Leonard—all appeared as part of the CNN ensemble on June 2, 1980, the network's first full day of coverage.[24]

In the personnel area, Schonfeld also took credit for "devising a so-far union-proof employment system." Early on, Schonfeld recognized that the chief advantage of locating CNN's headquarters in Atlanta rather than New York or Washington, D.C., was that Georgia was a right-to-work state. As a former hired gun of Joseph Coors (he once served as vice president of operations for Coors' Television News, Inc.), Schonfeld was rabidly antiunion—and nonunion labor had always been a key element of Schonfeld's formula for establishing CNN with Turner's limited resources. As Robert Goldman and Gerald Jay Goldman observe, "The dirty little secret about CNN was that they hired young people and paid them slave wages for interminable hours." An almost perfect example of how job markets in almost every American industry were being transformed by the new economic logics of post-Fordism, the labor force at CNN took on a split-level configuration with a bottom-heavy shape: some high-wage jobs, many low-wage jobs, and a "missing middle." Put another way, a crucial component of CNN's profitability involved paying unskilled service-economy wages for what had previously been treated at the television networks as skilled manufacturing-economy work.[25]

Although Schonfeld certainly left a lasting imprint on CNN, Turner did much more than borrow money from First National Bank of Chicago and deliver a speech at the 1979 NCTA convention in Las Vegas. Thanks to Turner's resolve and resourcefulness, CNN survived several early crisis moments that very well could have rendered all of Schonfeld's creative and managerial efforts meaningless. The most significant of these crises arrived in August 1981 when Westinghouse and ABC announced an agreement to join forces in a venture called Satellite News Channel (SNC). Turner's response to this aggressive invasion into his cable territory was to counterattack immediately by giving Schonfeld the go-ahead to develop a second news channel—one that would provide complete, updated newscasts every half hour. Less than six months later, on January 1, 1982, Headline News premiered as CNN2 in more than 800,000 cable homes. The ensuing battle between TBS and Westinghouse/ABC was costly to both sides—but Turner finally prevailed in the fall of 1983. Faced with predicted losses of $40 to $60 million, the Westinghouse/ABC alliance caved in to stockholder pressure and sold SNC to Turner for $25 million. As *Time* put it, "David conquered Goliath with his checkbook." At 6:00 P.M., October 27, 1983, Turner pulled the plug on SNC's high-tech news operation in Stamford, Connecticut.[26]

Schonfeld, though, was not at CNN headquarters to celebrate the end of SNC. In May 1982, the owner of TBS made it clear to the cocreator of CNN that every employee in a media organization is expendable. After clashing with Schonfeld over personnel decisions (including Schonfeld's firing of Sandi Freeman and hiring of Mike Douglas), Turner "decided to make a change." Schonfeld was summarily dismissed (though he agreed to serve for a while as a consultant to a newly formed CNN board of directors).[27] Turner's willingness to readily make changes is perhaps the only thread that links the professional and personal transformations that have distinguished his life in the decades following his entry into the news business. On the one hand, Turner's network would change forever the practice of electronic journalism, establishing once and for all the commodity value not only of the packaged news item but also of the news-making and news-gathering process itself. On the other hand, being associated with the news business would also lead to profound ideological and political changes in Turner himself. Ultimately, the interaction between Turner and the news business would result in CNN becoming a major force in the internationalization of both television and Ted Turner.

An early moment in the ideological transformation of Ted Turner occurred soon after the June 1, 1980, launching of CNN when Turner was profoundly disturbed by the contents of a federal study commissioned by fellow Georgian Jimmy Carter: *The Global 2000 Report to the President*. Published in the summer of 1980, the *Global 2000 Report* looked ahead twenty years to the new millennium and stated correctly that "if present trends continue" the world would be "more crowded, more polluted, less stable ecologically, and more vulnerable to disruption" than the world existing in the final months of the Carter administration.[28] In addition to Jimmy Carter, a strange and diverse cast of strange bedfellows began to influence Turner over the course of the 1980s. On a trip to Cuba in 1981, Turner bonded with Fidel Castro on a duck hunt along the south coast of Cuba. El Presidente had invited Turner to Havana because CNN's live and even-handed reporting of Cuba's 1981 May Day Parade impressed him. When Turner returned from the trip, he told conservative friends confused by his new hunting buddy that "Castro's not a communist. He's a dictator—like me." But Castro was not the only communist leader to rub elbows with Turner. Soviet Politburo member Georgi Arbitov and Chinese ambassador Zhou Boping joined former President Carter and the Aga Khan on the international board of directors of Turner's Better World Society (formed in 1985 to address global population and environmental problems). In 1986, moreover, when he was in Moscow to attend the first of his Goodwill Games, Turner met with Mikhail Gorbachev.[29] Still, Turner's environmental activism would not completely displace business at the top of his personal agenda. And buying CBS was near the top of Turner's business and personal priorities.

Though the CBS whale had at one time scoffed at the prospect of being swallowed by the TBS minnow, the Tiffany network's corporate brass suddenly started taking this upstart from Georgia seriously when someone figured out that Turner's plan was indeed viable. It was a daring scheme devised by E. F. Hutton's merger-and-acquisitions division to grab CBS for $5.41 billion with no money down. Unlike the synergistic TBS in the 1980s (where the whole was greater than the sum of its parts), CBS was ripe for a hostile takeover because the sum of its corporate parts diminished the whole. Turner hoped to finance the acquisition by selling off all the elements of the giant corporation that did not work synergistically with TBS. Turner's goal was to own one of the major broadcast networks—and he planned to auction off some of CBS's other properties (radio stations, a recording label, a magazine holding, and a toy division) to eliminate $3 billion in debt incurred by the transaction. Interest on the rest of the debt would then be serviced by cash flow from the network and its television stations.[30]

When CBC managed to fend off Turner by taking on nearly $1 billion in debt to buy back 21 percent of its own stock, Turner quickly moved to the next item on his business agenda—buying a Hollywood studio. CBS announced the buy-back plan on July 3, 1985, and only a little over a month later, Turner signed a purchase agreement with Kirk Kerkorian to buy MGM/United Artists (UA) for $1.5 billion on August 6, 1985. Soon after consummating the deal, it became clear that Turner had bitten off more debt than he could chew. By early June 1986, Turner was forced to sell off some of MGM/UA's assets. He sold the studio lot and film lab to Lorimar for $190 million. But the toughest transaction involved selling the studio and video business back to Kerkorian for a measly $300 million. After these transactions, Turner was left with the MGM/UA film library and more than $1 billion in debt.[31] To make matters worse, Turner's first attempt to exploit the resources of the film library resulted in his being treated like an unwelcome hillbilly in

Tinseltown. Such luminaries as Woody Allen, John Huston, Billy Wilder, Burt Lancaster, and Jimmy Stewart lined up to bash Turner after he announced plans to colorize a select group of classic movies (among them, *Yankee Doodle Dandy*, *Captain Blood*, *Father of the Bride*, *The Maltese Falcon*, *High Sierra*, and *Dark Victory*).[32]

Turner's financial situation continued to deteriorate—but Turner still had a "trump card," although he now "had a debt larger than some Central American countries." According to Goldberg and Goldberg, he still "understood how much his networks were worth across the country—to the Sammons and the TCIs, the Paragons, Coxes, and Jones Intercables. Without his programs—without CNN and WTBS—they only had HBO, ESPN, and a handful of rarely watched channels to offer their viewers." As an old and trusted friend, Turner asked some of his peers in the cable industry to bail him out. They agreed, though their actions were motivated less by altruism than by old-fashioned self-interest. On June 3, 1987, a consortium of thirty-one cable companies—mobilized and orchestrated by John Malone of Telecommunications Inc.—paid $562 million for 37 percent of TBS. The terms of the bailout left Turner the majority stockholder of TBS—but much of his power was now shared with a newly configured board dominated by representatives of the cable consortium. Most vexing of all to Turner was the provision that any expenditure of $2 million or more had to be approved by a "supermajority" of twelve of the fifteen directors.[33] Though inhibiting, the board took a decisive role in Turner's legendary financial turnaround in the late 1980s. Paradoxically, the key to this about-face was the MGM library. Unlike the colorization controversy (which had actually been an effective marketing strategy for TBS), Turner's next scheme for exploiting the 3,500 films in the MGM library (including 1,450 films from the old RKO and Warner studios) was an unqualified success. On October 3, 1988, the library became the primary programming reservoir for a new cable channel—Turner Network Television (TNT). TNT's launch was the most successful in cable television history, starting with seventeen million viewers and rising to fifty million within a year. The spectacular success of TNT, strangely enough, was directly attributable to the bailout of Turner by the cable consortium. With so many cable systems now financially entangled with equity holdings in TBS, selling the new cable channel was quite literally a done deal. With the success of TNT, Turner was at least partially exonerated for paying so much for MGM/UA.[34]

Despite the triumphant and redemptive launch of TNT, Turner's crowning achievement in the 1980s continued to be CNN and its spin-offs. In the early 1980s, millions of Americans discovered CNN as they watched live reports of fire sweeping through the MGM Grand and rockets boosting the space shuttle *Columbia* into space on its maiden voyage. In the mid 1980s, CNN International became the first transatlantic channel. Thanks to contracts negotiated by Bob Ross and Bob Wussler, CNN reached into many world capitals, even some located on the other side of the Iron Curtain.[35] The network's emerging international audience could watch coverage of a fascinating mixture of stories that CNN fan Frank Zappa lauded as "randomonium," which was perhaps best captured in the contrast between two of the most memorable news stories associated with CNN in the mid 1980s. The first news event occurred on January 28, 1986, when millions of students in classrooms across the nation gathered to watch the launch of the space shuttle *Challenger* with New Hampshire schoolteacher Christa McAuliffe aboard. Seventy-three seconds into the flight, jubilation turned to horror as a "major malfunction" blew the *Challenger* and its crew to smithereens in the cold blue sky over Florida. The second story, which unfolded on three days in October 1987, had a much happier ending. This news item began on October 14 when the world learned that an eighteen-month-old girl known simply as "baby Jessica" was trapped twenty-two feet down an abandoned well in the back yard of her aunt's home in Midland, Texas. In what became a worldwide human interest story, CNN carried round-the-clock images of frantic rescue attempts that culminated in a company from Tennessee flying in special equipment to bore a hole parallel to the well. After hours of nonstop drilling, the rescue cables began to finally rise from the parallel shaft—and Earl Maple, who was directing the coverage from CNN Center in Atlanta, instructed reporter Tony Clark to "let the pictures tell the story."[36]

Later, CNN continued the same strategy in May 1989, with coverage of pro-democracy demonstrations at Tiananmen Square and the joyous November 1989 destruction of the Berlin Wall. But many consider January 16, 1991, to be CNN's finest hour. Taking shelter under a table in their downtown hotel room as Baghdad came under U.S. air attack, Peter Arnett, Bernie Shaw, and John Holliman provided the first live pictures and descriptions of a war in progress from behind enemy lines. Attracting the largest TV audience in history for a nonsporting event, CNN's initial coverage of Operation Desert Storm was witnessed by an estimated one billion people worldwide. This moment, recently memorialized in the HBO production *Live from Baghdad*, secured CNN's reputation as the global network of record for live breaking news. CNN's coverage of the Persian Gulf War was also a decisive factor in Turner's selection as *Time* magazine's Man of the Year in 1991.

Nothing illustrated the arrival
of cable television better than
CNN's nonstop live coverage
of the January 16, 1991,
outbreak of the Persian Gulf
War with Bernard Shaw,
John Holliman, and Peter
Arnett. Courtesy of Library of
American Broadcasting at the
University of Maryland.

TURNER AND THE DIGITAL ERA

With his recognition as Man of the Year, Ted Turner had finally won the embrace of the media establishment he had set out to transform. Yet, despite *Time*'s assertion that Turner had been tamed by his success in cable, the years from 1992 onward proved to be his most volatile.[37] Like many visionaries, Turner did not have the foresight to remain in control of his vision once cable reached the promised land of corporate profitability. In many respects, Turner was a victim of his own successful efforts to marry popular content with cable distribution. With Turner Broadcasting in 1992, the cable industry had a content provider that offered programming that viewers wanted to watch, including twenty-four-hour news, classic MGM and RKO films, professional wrestling, and team sports. More than anyone else in the 1980s, Turner had given households a reason to subscribe to cable as an alternative to broadcasting. And subscribe they did. In the decade since he founded CNN, the number of cable subscriptions increased roughly threefold, from 17.6 million to 54 million.[38]

Ten months after Turner was named Man of the Year, the U.S. Congress passed the Cable Television Consumer Protection and Competition Act of 1992.[39] After letting the marketplace dictate the growth of cable for almost a decade, Congress began to see cable's penetration of the marketplace as anticompetitive to broadcasting. Under the 1992 Cable Act, the government introduced a number of regulations that would slow the growth of the cable industry and cut into its profits. The new law not only allowed the FCC to regulate subscriber rates, but broadcast stations were given the right to opt for free retransmission of their signals on local cable systems. This latter provision essentially resurrected the "must-carry rules" of the 1970s that Turner had successfully challenged in court in the mid 1980s. Both the old and new versions of must-carry were antithetical to Turner's business model of controlling the development of content channels for cable operators. By 1993, Turner was again challenging the must-carry rules on First Amendment grounds in federal court. For the government, requiring cable companies to carry broadcast stations for free was an appropriate means to keep broadcasting competitive and programming diverse. In turn, cable's rapid market penetration effectively allowed the industry to determine the flow of television content into a majority of American households. For Turner and TBS, the new rules were tantamount to government dictates on their private speech that required the cable operator to set aside a large number of channel slots that would otherwise be available to cable programmers. For example, TBS had acquired Hanna-Barbera's animation business in 1991, which gave it the rights to hit cartoons like *The Flintstones*, *Scooby Doo*, and *Yogi Bear*. As had been the case many times before in his career, Turner parleyed the popularity of this content into a new cable channel, the Cartoon Network, and made it available to system operators. With the must-carry rules in place, however, cable systems had fewer channel slots available for nonbroadcast channels. This would not only be a problem for the Cartoon Network, but for a variety of other TBS channels that were rolled out in the 1990s, including CNNfn, CNN/SI (Sports Illustrated), and Turner Classic Movies. After two trips to the U.S. Supreme Court in 1994 and 1997, Turner lost his free speech battle. Today, the decisions in *Turner Broadcasting System v. FCC* are considered landmarks in support of the government's authority to regulate cable as a competitive threat to broadcasting.

Despite the must-carry rules, Turner continued to develop and deliver new content channels in the 1990s, but now the focus was different. In concert with the changing regulatory climate in the United States, TBS moved aggressively to develop the CNN and Turner brands internationally. During this period, many cable content providers, including Turner's rival, Rupert Murdoch, had established or acquired operations in overseas markets that were both ripe for development and outside the regulatory reach of the U.S. government. In Europe, Asia, and Latin America, TBS packaged English and foreign-language versions of its popular Cartoon Network and TNT channels and inked deals with international hotel chains to increase carriage of its flagship

CNN International channel, which emerged in the 1990s to become the leading English-language television news service in the world after years of relatively slow growth. At a time when news divisions at the broadcast networks were closing overseas bureaus and laying off foreign correspondents, CNN was increasing its visibility in world capitals, opening new offices with locally trained producers, and hiring journalists with international credentials such as Wolf Blitzer, Octavia Nasr, Christiane Amanpour, and Nic Robertson. Although Ted Turner had realized as early as 1985 that exporting American content internationally would represent an opportunity for his company, TBS's operations imported internationally produced content into American homes by 1997, including Japanese *anime* on the Cartoon Network, in-depth coverage of Latin America on CNN en Español, and overseas reports from non-CNN journalists every weekend on the *CNN World Report*. Even today, CNN employees are not permitted to use the word "foreign" to describe international viewers, guests, or issues. Ted Turner learned early what cable content providers take for granted today—good content will attract viewers regardless of territorial boundaries or nationality.

As conglomerates such as the News Corporation, GE, Disney, and Viacom increased their stakes in cable, Turner realized that without a corporate partner TBS could not remain competitive in the Digital Era as an independent company. For Turner, the previous twenty years had been about bringing content to the cable wilderness. By 1995, however, the landscape had changed. The media giants who had largely ignored cable when it was a backwater were now producing their own cable content and developing their own channels as alternatives to those offered by TBS. Unlike Turner, all of these media giants owned studios that produced films and television programming, and all of them had a flagship presence on broadcast television. Because these companies owned broadcast networks, the same 1992 Cable Act that ushered in the new must-carry rules also provided broadcasters with a lucrative alternative. Networks and local stations were given the discretion to charge huge copyright licensing fees to cable operators seeking retransmission consent.

The News Corporation's Fox network, which in 1993 rattled the broadcast establishment by outbidding CBS for NFL football, pursued an aggressive strategy with cable operators, going so far as to remove its network from cable systems that would not meet Fox's price. Although a few local systems tried to call Fox's bluff, fan demand for the Fox network's sports and entertainment content ultimately brought cable to the table. Once in a bargaining position, it was clear that a cash payment for transmission would be out of the question. Cable operators, used to paying low fees for content provided by cable companies like TBS, simply could not generate the revenue necessary to pay Murdoch outright. Like Turner, Murdoch already realized that while content may be king, if you don't control the conduit, no one will see your content. In deals that must have been galling to a cable-reared maverick like Turner, Murdoch bartered retransmission consent for something that in the 1990s was more valuable than money—the slots on cable systems that were becoming more sought after despite the increase of band capacity. Murdoch effectively leveraged his popular broadcast content to gain entry into the cable marketplace for Fox-branded channels such as Fox Family, FX, Fox Sports Net, regional Fox Sports networks, Fox Movie Channel, and even his upstart competitor to CNN, the Fox News Channel. In just a few years, Murdoch was well on his way to establishing the type of channel presence on cable systems that had taken Turner nearly twenty years to build.

By 1995, Turner was faced with a choice. He could try to keep TBS independent—and risk losing ground to competitors who enjoyed the synergistic benefits of studio facilities and broadcast outlets. Or he could merge his operations with an ally who would provide synergy to TBS while at the same time respecting Turner's management of his cable operations. Ted Turner also feared that a politically conservative rival like Murdoch might attempt a hostile takeover of TBS, the management of which was no longer fully in Turner's control after the MGM library acquisition. On September, 22, 1995, Turner addressed both of these concerns by announcing that TBS would merge with Time Warner, Inc., one of the allies in the cable consortium that bailed Turner out in 1987. The marriage of TBS and Time Warner, consummated in October 1996, was part of the zeitgeist of consolidation that occurred in the late 1990s as media companies restructured their operations to remain competitive in the Digital Era. But for Turner, it was not enough to consolidate with sibling services in other media or complementary content; the key to growth of the Turner cable brands was the supply-chain logic of vertical integration. As Turner put it to Ken Auletta, "You want to be like Rockefeller was with Standard Oil. He had the oil fields, and he had the filling stations, and he had the pipelines and the trucks and everything to get the gas to the stations."[40] Time Warner, indeed, had the cable equivalent of these holdings, boasting a fledgling broadcast network, movie studios, music businesses, and magazines, as well as being the leading owner of local cable systems in the country where it could feature Turner's channels on its systems by providing scarce channel space, promoting TBS services to its subscribers, and denying TBS's competitors' access. And that was what made the Time Warner merger different from the other consolidations that occurred in the 1990s. Indeed, in this merger, Ted Turner sought to secure a competitive advantage for his TBS channels that had eluded virtually all his rivals, including Murdoch.

After the Time Warner merger, as Richard Hack suggests, Turner had little interest in the conglomerate's other properties, preferring instead to concentrate on expanding the company's cable business.[41] As Turner saw it, not only would TBS become a supplier of content to Time Warner's cable system division, but also his channels would provide branding opportunities and distribution windows for Time Warner's content-producing properties, such as *People*, *Sports Illustrated*, *Time*, and the motion picture studios. Emboldened by the synergy of content and conduit, Turner and Time Warner set out to use their supply-chain advantage anticompetitively in the late 1990s. Time Warner owned the largest number and best-positioned cable systems in the country, including franchises in most of New York City and Los Angeles's San Fernando Valley. In both of these markets, for example, Time Warner took steps to keep channels in direct competition with TBS's off the local cable dial. At least for a short time, Time Warner Cable in New York was able to keep the nascent Fox News Channel from competing with CNN in the no. 1 television market. Turner not only wanted to deny Fox access to audiences, but he also kept Fox from being seen by advertising industry executives based in Manhattan. Time Warner fought the issue in the courts and won.[42] The conglomerate even stood ready to challenge Mayor Rudolph Giuliani—Murdoch's friend and ally—when he offered to allow Fox News to transmit over a city-owned channel.[43] The situation was similar in the San Fernando Valley, when Time Warner Cable abruptly dropped the local ABC station from its system during negotiations with Disney over retransmission consent.[44] In this instance, the deal breaker was Disney's insistence that Time Warner provide a channel slot for the Disney Toon channel. Time Warner's refusal reflected its desire to protect its valuable Cartoon Network from direct competition. Only after a public outcry and reproach from the FCC did Time Warner go back to the bargaining table and thus open the door to this kind of competition.

Many histories chart the rise and fall of empires and great individuals. But the Turner narrative does not quite conform to this story arc. Instead, the final chapter of the saga of Ted Turner is not so much about a fall but a fade. At first, Turner's power and influence at Time Warner was considerable. In the long run, though, the merger with Time Warner turned out to be a Faustian bargain for Turner. He simply did not have the money to control everything in the cable industry. To realize his vision, Turner needed to integrate his supply chain into a consolidated company that he did not own. By doing that, however, he ultimately ceded control of the cable businesses he created. For several years, Time Warner's Gerry Levin allowed Turner to operate the TBS division with a measure of autonomy. Nevertheless, Time Warner's Balkanized management structure was such that Turner was dismayed that some of his own company's cable system operators were unwilling to carry emerging CNN-branded channels in the face of low subscriber demand, which eventually led to the demise of CNN/SI in 2002 and CNNfn in 2004. By the time Time Warner joined America Online (AOL) in 2001, Turner was the newly merged company's largest shareholder and a billionaire many times over. But even with all that wealth, Ted Turner was relegated to the sidelines of AOL Time Warner's management. Unable to protect TBS from the culture clash of computer executives bent on forcing uneasy synergies between his cable channels and AOL's flagship-turned-flagging Internet service provider (ISP), Turner resigned from what had become a largely ceremonial title of vice chairman of Time Warner in 2003 (AOL was dropped from the corporate title in early 2003 because of huge losses to the ISP). By 2006, moreover, Turner vacated his seat on the conglomerate's board of directors. The cable industry was no longer an undiscovered country ready to be exploited for profits by a swaggering free spirit with a penchant for self-aggrandizement and impulsive decision-making. In the age of consolidation, the cable industry was now just one of many sectors in the newly emerging world of digital television.

In *Citizen Turner*, Robert and Gerald Jay Goldberg employ *Citizen Kane* as a cinematic analogy for understanding the Turner story. A more apt metaphor, though, is probably John Ford's classic Western, *The Searchers*, which fades out with Ethan Edwards (John Wayne) walking away framed by a sunset. Edwards had restored order to this outpost on the frontier—but it was clear that there would be no place for a man like him in this newly civilized community. When Turner resigned as vice chairman in 2003, the Turner Broadcasting System website listed twenty-eight branded media properties and sports franchises as components of the TBS region of Time Warner: TBS Superstation, Turner Network Television, Cartoon Network, Turner Classic Movies, Turner South, Boomerang, TNT Europe, Cartoon Network Europe, TNT Latin America, Cartoon Network Latin America, TNT and Cartoon Network Asia/Pacific, Atlanta Braves, Atlanta Hawks, Atlanta Thrashers, Goodwill Games, Cartoon Network Japan, Cable News Network, CNN Headline News, CNN International, CNNfn, CNN/Sports Illustrated, CNN en Español, CNN Airport Network, CNN Radio Noticias, CNN Interactive, CNN Newsource, CNN+, and CNN Turk. These holdings are reminders of Turner's heyday as a change agent when he contributed much to the rise of cable beginning in 1972 and helped internationalize the face of television through the 1990s.

PART IV

BECOMING GLOBAL

I WANT MY NICHE TV

> The future of television program delivery is changing radically, and you will not be satisfied either with the selection offered to your neighbor or by the need to view anything at a specific time. For this reason, cable companies are thinking more and more like telephone companies . . . not only in the corporate sense but in terms of network architecture as well.
>
> NICHOLAS NEGROPONTE, *Being Digital*, 1995[1]

Just as cable penetration was reaching two-thirds of all TV households in the United States during the mid 1990s, this sector of the television industry was already outgrowing the top-down distribution model that it inherited from the three-network oligopoly in the mid 1970s. Besides the major broadcast networks, niche programming was the accepted norm in the rapidly expanding multichannel universe of the 1990s. When American viewers flipped through their channel line-ups, they began to see all sorts of networks based on traditional story forms (Biography Channel, Comedy Central, History Channel), narrative genres that were previously popular on radio and in the movies (SOAPnet, Westerns, Sci Fi Channel), formats that harked back to the earliest days of television (news, sports, children's programming), webs devoted to specific demographic groups (Lifetime, BET, Univision for Spanish-speaking audiences), and even services designed to offer helpful advice about a wide range of lifestyle choices and activities (HGTV [Home and Garden Television], Travel Channel, Food Network). Never before had TV networking been so intimately linked to the process of program development and genre formation, subject to the delicate negotiation that took place between the industry and its business and creative personnel, the shows they produced, and the consumptive and identity-building behavior of audiences that network executives targeted with increasing precision every year. The recent proliferation of television networks spiked from 79 in 1992, to 106 in 1994, to 145 in 1996, to 281 in 2000.[2] The identifiable turning point was the passage of the Telecommunications Act of 1996 that encouraged the trends toward a greater consolidation of ownership across the various mass media, as well as an accelerating convergence of technologies and content resulting from the emerging digital revolution.

The pivotal influence in this changeover from the Cable Era to the Digital Era in 1995 was the widespread adoption of the Internet by millions of pioneering consumers, beginning with the introduction of the first commercially available graphical browser, Netscape Navigator 1.0, on December 15, 1994, thus making web travel relatively easy for the vast majority of Americans beyond the exclusive domain of computer scientists and other high-tech specialists. Nielsen Media Research first started measuring Internet use in November 1995. These initial Nielsen numbers indicated that thirty-seven million, or 14 percent of the U.S. population over the age of sixteen, already had access to the Internet and that twenty-four million, or 11 percent, actively used the web multiple times a week.[3] In addition, cable and satellite TV continued to extend their reach and popularity throughout the decade, as 83 percent of the nation's 100.8 million households in 2000 subscribed to either cable (68 percent) or DBS (direct broadcast satellite TV) (15 percent).[4] DBS (which is also called DTH, direct-to-home satellite TV) languished far behind the industry's overly optimistic projections for its early adoption in the 1980s, garnering just 2.5 million subscribers, or 2.7 percent of all television households in the country by the end of 1989.[5] Five years later, however, DBS adopters were climbing steadily—from 4.5 million in 1995, to 8.4 million in 1997, to 12.3 million in 1999. This sudden upsurge in DBS subscriptions was the direct result of higher-powered satellite feeds that produced better and more reliable television reception, as well as an ever-greater selection of channels. DirecTV, owned by General Motors subsidiary Hughes Electronics, and the Dish Network, a division of EchoStar Communication, dominated this sector of the television industry, accounting for 99 percent (DirecTV 65 percent and the Dish Network 34 percent) of the 15.3 million DBS subscribers who were signed up by 2000.[6]

Three overlapping delivery systems—broadcasting, cable, and satellite TV—now distinguished networking in the United States as television entered the Digital Era. The backstory to this transition starts with a second, much longer wave of even larger corporate mergers than the three earlier consolidations (Capital Cities and ABC, GE with RCA and NBC, and Laurence Tisch's takeover of CBS) that reshaped the television industry in 1985–1986. This newest round of transactions started with the $15.2 billion merger of Time, Inc., and Warner Communication in 1989, creating Time Warner; leading to Viacom's $10 billion purchase of Paramount Communication in 1994; Westinghouse's $5.4 billion acquisition of CBS in 1995 (with Westinghouse changing its name to CBS in 1997); Microsoft's $220 million collaboration with NBC to launch MSNBC in 1995; Disney's $19 billion takeover of Capital Cities/ABC in 1996; Time Warner's $6.3 billion purchase of Turner Broadcasting in 1996; Viacom's $36 billion acquisition of CBS in 1999; online service provider AOL's $104 billion merger with Time Warner in 2001; and GE/NBC's $3.65 billion purchase of Vivendi Universal in 2004. In the wake of these mega-mergers, three brand-new part-time broadcast networks were eventually created, beginning with Time Warner's WB (Warner Bros. Network) and Viacom's UPN (United Paramount Network) in January 1995, as well as Paxson Communications' PAX TV in 1998. By 2000, six multimedia transnational corporations owned a majority of the most important network properties across all three industrial sectors—broadcasting, cable, and DBS. Six of the seven broadcast networks (ABC, CBS, NBC, Fox, WB, and UPN) were subsidiaries of only five mega-media conglomerates: Disney was the parent of ABC; Viacom, of CBS and UPN; General Electric, of NBC; News Corporation, of Fox; and Time Warner, of WB. In addition, GE/NBC owned a minority 32 percent interest in PAX TV.

By early 2003, moreover, seventeen of the top-20 basic cable networks were either completely owned or co-owned by four of the five aforementioned transnational corporations: Disney had ESPN, A&E (Arts and Entertainment), Lifetime, ABC Family Channel, ESPN2, and History Channel; Viacom had Nickelodeon, Spike TV, MTV, and VH1; General Electric had USA Network, A&E, CNBC, and History Channel; and Time Warner had TNT, CNN, TBS, and CNN Headline News. As far as the four leading pay-TV channels, Time Warner also owned HBO and Cinemax, while Viacom owned Showtime and the Movie Channel. The fifth mega-media conglomerate, Rupert Murdoch's News Corporation, purchased DirecTV in December 2003, thus taking over America's largest satellite TV company in one bold stroke. Corresponding with this unprecedented rise in consolidation and numbers (339 networks in 2003 to 531 by early 2006), the niche priorities of the Cable Era had now transitioned into the more-specialized personal-usage market model of the Digital Era.[7]

This new focus was built around one overriding design principle— synergy—which industry insiders recognized as the most efficient way of capitalizing on the growing tendency toward ever-greater audience fragmentation. As mega-media conglomerates became unprecedentedly large, their executive staffs attempted to maximize their presence across as many distribution channels as possible. Consequently, television networks in general evolved into being content providers, above all else, where their programming was adapted to as many platforms as possible (television, video, Internet, audio, and print) in order to generate multiple revenue streams for the umbrella corporation. Narrowcasting and audience segmentation were thus pushed to their logical extremes. In other words, they were given added precision with a bottom-up approach, in which targeted audience segments were grouped together by clustering them according to a sophisticated array of relevant demographic, psychological, and lifestyle characteristics.

Furthermore, television channels pursued these ever smaller niche audiences, programming and promoting their brand identities to viewers all year long, and catering twenty-four/seven to consumer needs across a wide array of programming choices that usually began on television but then extended quickly throughout a variety of related media platforms, usually publicized most aggressively on network websites. Branding—which refers to the defining and reinforcing of a network's identity—became an increasingly important strategy as the TV environment grew even more cluttered with literally dozens of marginal channels. Brand recognition emerged as the most valuable currency a channel could earn as television programming content was adapted to other in-house print, audio, video, and web-based media to be marketed to network consumers. Before 1995, "cable provided a single service—a clear video picture. Driven by competition and backed by billions of dollars of private capital, over the past decade [1996–2005], the industry has reinvented itself" and refashioned the way TV genres were employed as a networking strategy.[8] Television scholar Jason Mittell relates that "the classic network system used formulas, recombinant innovations and program cloning to try to appeal to viewers through a strategy of 'least objectionable programming'" during the Network Era.[9] TV production practices encouraged modest innovation in the execution of well-known programming formulas, leading to a recognizable rise-and-fall cycle of popular genres across all of the major broadcast networks at once. This pattern was widely evident beginning with the emergence of the three-network oligopoly in the 1950s and continued unabated through most of the Cable Era from the mid 1970s to the early 1990s.

Todd Gitlin refers to the 1980s as an "era of recombinatory excess" that found its most fundamental expression in the business of television, rather than what appears on the screen. In this way, he asserts, "recombinant style shapes not only the marketing of new toothpastes but the marketing of high as well as popular culture."[10] Gitlin made this prescient observation in the mid 1980s, which anticipated the accelerated convergence of advertising and entertainment that is now endemic to the Digital Era. More than anything else, this widespread move toward recombining, repositioning, and repurposing previously successful television formulas is what the current explosion in networking is all about. "There's nothing that delivers eyeballs like networks—nothing," notes reality programming mogul, Mark Burnett (CBS's *Survivor*, NBC's *The Apprentice*), "so one of the solutions [for the networks] is smarter marketing integration."[11] During the last two decades, genres have actually grown far more useful to the TV industry as marketing devices than as production strategies. They have become starting points on which to imagine whole new television services more so than innovative series (although any start-up network eventually needs to produce its own original programming as well, if it hopes to stay competitive after the initial novelty of a new channel wears off). TV genres are now an essential part of the brave new world of branded entertainment. Within the parlance of the television business, genres were first used as utility brands—for example, CNN was founded in 1980 as the all-news channel. The problem with utility branding is that this kind of marketing is literally too generic and therefore too easily copied. Turner Broadcasting and the entire industry soon learned that in 1983 when Westinghouse and ABC started the short-lived Satellite News Channel, followed in 1996 by MSNBC and Fox News.

"Utility brands offer a functional relationship to the viewer with the promise of providing useful information," explains Steven Schiffman, executive vice president of marketing for the Weather Channel; "the problem, though, is that a competitor can always come along who is even more useful."[12] Instead, TV genres are now employed as points of departure in fashioning a network's identity brand. Unlike utility branding, this more sophisticated type of branding is designed to tap into what a target audience really cares about, thus forging an emotional bond that reaches well beyond any content category. To take the case of news again, CNN has become the hard news cable network ("breaking news first" and "the most trusted name in news") from a decidedly middle-of-the-road perspective, while Fox News has clearly established itself as the conservative alternative (delivering the "fair and balanced" approach). In contrast, MSNBC has proven far less successful in crafting its own unique identity, with a lineup composed mostly of talk and softer news (shifting branding claims from "the whole picture" to "the best news on cable" to "America's news channel" in the hopes of eventually finding its special niche). "Identity brands have an 'emotive' relationship to the viewer," continues Schiffman: "They offer the 'promise of an experience' and a feeling, and they inspire loyalty in the face of competition."[13] Successful networking in the Digital Era aims at intensifying the connection between a channel and its target audience. High branding (which is a concept that is now an assumed part of television's popular discourse) does not just mean network logo, tag line, and program recognition but implies a strong relational bonding between a channel and its viewership. "Brands have begun taking the position that the viewer must really invite you in," asserts Jak Severson, CEO of Madison Road Entertainment (an independent television production studio), "which means it can't be about advertising as much as it has to be about entertaining."[14]

From the perspective of TV networking, then, branding operates much like the critical concept of a "supertext" once functioned for genre theorists a generation ago. As John Cawelti recounts, "the supertext (genre) claims to be an abstract of the most significant characteristics or family resemblances among many particular texts."[15] It functioned as an idealized focal point around which analysts envisioned the working parameters of a genre. Similarly, network executives strive to make their brands synonymous with the genre they are specializing in so that the "channel's spin" becomes the most influential determinant in television program development these days, more so than any aesthetic or narrative innovations. A TV genre in the Digital Era is therefore subject to the ongoing demands of branding a network. It is a shorthand tactic by which network programmers build a target audience; and since the endgame of networking is first and foremost attracting and holding a specific viewership, then the conventions of any television genre are readily stretched, recombined, and repurposed with that goal in mind. Genres have also become virtually interchangeable with the highest-profile network brands. For example, Keleman Associates of New York City won the 2000 Research Case Study Award by the Cable and Telecommunications Association for Marketing for its ESPN-funded study, "Television Network Branding in the Multichannel Universe." Among its findings, Keleman reported that viewers "identified powerful network brands within specific genres" for each of the eight programming categories under consideration: for survey respondents, ESPN meant television sports; Discovery, science and nature; HBO, TV movies; the History Channel, history documentaries; NBC, general entertainment; CNN, news and information; HGTV, how-to and do it yourself; and A&E, culture and the arts.[16]

Global branding emerged as the normative strategy for the most successful TV networks based in the United States during the late 1990s. The top 10 percent of all television channels were then busy establishing a reach that traveled well beyond America's borders. When viewers worldwide watched TV, they generally disregarded the distinctions between service promos, shows, and ads; consequently, successful branding was as dependent on network-defining promotional

tactics (logos, interstitials, vignettes) as it was on popular programming. Executives and producers alike used genres strategically to inspire every kind of content that went out through cable lines or over
the air. Accordingly, television genres were far more elastic, improvisational, and recombinant than they had ever been. Two cases in point
are the A&E Television Networks (AETN) and the Scripps Networks.
These examples are particularly instructive because they run the
gamut of corporate size and income in networking but still basically
reflect the same types of branding patterns that are now standard operating procedure in the Digital Era.

For its part, AETN is co-owned by two major mega-media conglomerates (Disney/ABC and General Electric/NBC Universal) and a mini-
major corporation (Hearst) with combined revenues of $57.3 billion in
2003, while the Scripps channels are held solely by one mini-major
(E. W. Scripps) with annual earnings totaling $1.5 billion in compari-
son.[17] AETN is a joint venture shared by Disney/ABC (37.5 percent),
the Hearst Corporation (37.5 percent), and General Electric/NBC Universal (25 percent). Founded in 1984, AETN is the parent corporation
of A&E (over eighty-nine million subscriber households in 2006), the
Biography Channel (thirty million), the History Channel (eighty-eight
million), the History Channel International (thirty-eight million), and
the recently created AETN International, the History Channel en Español, the Military History Channel, and the Crime and Investigation
Channel. In 2005, the combined reach of AETN stood at approximately 280 million homes telecasting in twenty languages across 120
countries.[18]

In addition, television services such as the eight networks comprising AETN typically identify their target audiences by demographic
makeup (with A&E, for instance, it's upscale women aged twenty-five
to fifty-four), lifestyle characteristics (AETN features viewers who are
interested in the arts and culture as a pastime), and what TV executives
call "passion or touch points" (where channels establish as close a relationship as possible with viewers, building brand loyalty over time). In
general, passion and touch points entail nurturing one or more signature programs (usually "original" series); extending the brand beyond
television into a number of transmedia ventures (such as related websites, home video/DVDs, print); expanding the reach of the original
brand—the foundational network—into one or more spin-off channels; and constantly working to keep the network brand in tune with
the needs and desires of its niche target audience. A&E's signature program is *Biography*, which debuted in 1987 and averaged a nightly viewership of three million throughout the 1990s, spawning videotapes,
CDs, a magazine called *Biography* with a two million readership, and

the Biography Channel (a spin-off network created in 1998). The *Biography* franchise celebrated its fifteenth anniversary with episode one thousand in 2002. AETN first employed A&E and the *Biography* series to establish its brand ("the art of biography, drama, and documentary") before attempting any other offshoot services. A&E is thus a prime example of a foundational network (which is loosely defined in 2006 as a channel with at least eighty million subscribers).

A&E next spawned the spin-off network the History Channel in 1995, specifically earmarking men aged twenty-five to fifty-four, who up until then were an untapped segment of AETN's target constituency. On both the domestic and international fronts, "the History Channel [soon became] the fastest growing cable network ever."[19] The reason for this record-setting rise was because history proved to be a reliable television genre for attracting male viewers on a regular basis (along with news and sports programming). As a result, the History Channel quickly transformed into a foundational network on its own, prompting the launch of History Channel International in 1998, History Channel en Español in 2004, and Military History Channel in 2005. Significantly, TV genres are stretched today to conform to their respective network brands. The History Channel and History Channel International provide an ideal case study into how this typically came to be in three important ways. First, genre content is localized to appeal to a rapidly increasing array of racial, ethnic, and international constituencies in the move to globalize a network brand. For instance, History Channel International "adapted programs to local needs, using dubbing or perhaps adding a new host" for any new affiliated region that chose to accept its signal. As the coverage of History Channel International grew dramatically after 1998, network executives made a concerted effort to enter into a series of "joint ventures . . . acquir[ing] locally produced programs" from participating nations to "fill out the rest" of its twenty-four-hour, seven-day-a-week schedule.[20] This careful attention to the expectations and desires of its rapidly expanding audience base also facilitated a quick and ready infusion of alternative styles and perspectives into the history genre from television producers on continents as widely diverse in cultural orientation as Europe, Australia, Latin America, Asia, and the Middle East.

Second, TV genres are typically subject to the same kind of stylistic influences that are affecting the rest of television at any given time (whether or not these content changes make sense in regard to the integrity or credibility of the form). For example, the History Channel has been as susceptible to the post-2000 "*Survivor* aftereffect" as any other network brand or genre. One recent instance of "reality history" is *Extreme History with Roger Daltry*, which debuted on the History

Channel in the fall of 2003. This half-hour series capitalized on the strategy of marketing history alongside rock 'n' roll by casting a well-known pop star as the show's featured host. A network press release even described "Roger Daltry, [the] lead singer of the legendary rock band The Who . . . [as] an avid history buff, [who] goes on location to demonstrate the challenge of surviving history's epic adventures, explorations, and battles."[21] Episodes include Daltry scaling the Montana Rockies like Lewis and Clark in 1805; driving steers through the Chisholm Trail of Texas and Oklahoma; and shooting the Colorado rapids in a wooden rowboat, much like John Wesley Powell did in 1869. Daltry's exploits as a celebrity surrogate reenacting a prefabricated historical narrative epitomized the History Channel's branding claim that it is the niche network—"where the past comes alive." Reality histories such as *Extreme History with Roger Daltry* also illustrated the ongoing negotiation between popular programming trends, branding imperatives, and generic change that remains a part of producing any kind of show for a niche network.

Third, network branding also sets in motion much of the transmedia and extratextual transformations that have occurred in television genres during the Digital Era. For instance, audiences of the History Channel and History Channel International, in particular, are provided with many interactive opportunities on the websites of these two networks (HistoryChannel.com and HistoryInternational.com), such as researching additional information about programs and the specific topics they raise, relaunching related video clips, checking out upcoming TV listings, playing history-related games, participating in online discussion groups about the network or specific series, downloading free classroom lesson plans, visiting the History Channel Store to purchase literally thousands of ancillary products (such as DVDs, videotapes, books, apparel, toys, posters, calendars, home décor, and unique gifts), and even taking tours (entitled "Lewis & Clark Trail," "Civil War Trail," "D-Day and the Battle of the Bulge") with other History Channel viewers.

The bottom line in identity branding is that it always aims to shift the emphasis in genre construction and reception from program viewing to some kind of consumptive activity. Nowhere is this trend toward generic transformation across multiple media more evident than on the task-oriented formats of four of the five Scripps Networks—HGTV (Home and Garden Television), Food Network, DIY (Do It Yourself Network), and Fine Living. Despite being the twenty-fifth largest media group in the United States, E. W. Scripps is modest in size and scope (twenty-one daily newspapers and ten TV stations, along with its cable networks) when compared with the combined holdings of AETN's co-owners (twenty-four broadcast and cable networks, ten television production studios and sixty-three TV stations, five radio networks and seventy-five radio stations, two movie studios and a theater chain, e-businesses and publications, newspapers, magazines, book publishing, music recording and publishing companies, sports teams, theme parks and resorts, restaurants, and retail outlets).[22]

E. W. Scripps's legacy is built solidly on the Cincinnati-based Scripps Howard newspaper chain, even though its five cable channels have recently emerged as the most profitable part of this mini-major's business portfolio. In a move designed to diversify into cable, E. W. Scripps purchased Cinetel Productions, an independent television studio in Knoxville, Tennessee, in early 1994.[23] On December 30 of that year, Scripps introduced HGTV into 6.5 million homes and forty-four markets, targeting an adult audience (which skewed female) aged twenty-five to fifty-four. HGTV found a ready niche by pioneering the lifestyle-oriented do-it-yourself home improvement genre with programming organized across five overlapping categories (decorating, gardening, remodeling, at home, and crafts). In 1997, Scripps bought a controlling interest in the Food Network from the A. H. Belo Corporation, another owner of newspaper and broadcast properties, while concurrently expanding the reach of HGTV into Europe, Japan, Australia, and the Philippines. Scripps then spun off DIY from HGTV in 1999 as a simultaneous on-air/online channel, providing more in-depth tips and step-by-step instructions for domestic repairs.[24] Fine Living soon followed in 2002 as an upscale extension of HGTV, specializing in adventure and travel advice, household upgrades, and consumer reports on higher-end products and luxury items. Scripps acquired the Nashville-based country music television network GAC (Great American Country, with a reach of forty million households) from Jones Media Networks in 2004. It also attempted to compete in the highly lucrative home-shopping genre with its short-lived Shop at Home Network between 2002 and 2006, which simply was unable to gain a foothold against its much larger, already established, and better-known rivals QVC (Quality, Value, Convenience) and the Home Shopping Network (HSN).

E. W. Scripps's foundational networks—HGTV (eighty-four million) and the Food Network (eighty-three million)—were two of the fastest growing channels in the television industry during the late 1990s and early 2000s, while DIY (twenty-three million) and Fine Living (nineteen million) held their own as up-and-coming spin-off networks. Programmers at HGTV and the Food Network, specifically, jump-started their respective services with signature programs (such as HGTV's *Room by Room* in 1994 and the Food Network's *How to*

Boil Water in 2000) that emphasized self-improvement lessons filtered through a traditional makeover story line. Moreover, the Beta Research Corporation's annually conducted "brand identity" survey ranked HGTV ninth and the Food Network tenth as most "family-oriented" among all broadcast, cable, and satellite TV networks in 2004, also listing the Food Network as first and HGTV as second "in terms of having well-liked hosts and personalities."[25] This last designation, in particular, underscores the host-driven relational nature of much of the programming produced by Scripps. Many of HGTV's original homegrown personalities are still popular and on the air, including Carol Duvall, Joe Ruggiero, and Kitty Bartholomew; and the Food Network has built its cooking shows around approximately three-dozen celebrity chefs starting in 1994 with its first breakout star, Emeril Lagasse. HGTV programming presently telecasts in twenty-three different countries (*The World's Most Beautiful Homes*), while the Food Network is similarly global in orientation with such series as the cult favorite *Iron Chef*, which was a recombinant cooking-comedy-game show originating in Japan in the 1990s. HGTV.com is also one of the online industry's fastest growing destinations, with over three million different visitors each month from around the world. Likewise, the international fan base of the Food Network includes four million unique users of foodnetwork.com on a yearly basis.

As is the case with the History Channel, the interactive posture taken by the target audiences of the Scripps Networks illustrates the sea change in TV reception patterns during the Digital Era. Today, TV fans are far more committed to their own networks of choice than ever before, and they are far more willing to extend their television watching into program-related activities on the websites of their favorite networks. The online communities now flourishing around HistoryChannel.com and HGTV.com provide two representative examples of how TV viewers market specific programs among themselves, participate in a whole host of old and new consumptive practices that are easily accessed on network websites, and, more specifically, contribute to the shaping of the History Channel and HGTV brands. Both the History Channel and HGTV, along with all of the other foundational networks in the television industry, regularly employ online discussion groups as a common "passion point" strategy for creating an even stronger and more long-lasting connection with their respective target audiences. Participants use these discussion boards to engage in interactive, text-based dialogues with other like-minded network devotees. Online chatting has emerged as the most direct way yet for website participants to express their preferences and negotiate an increasingly individualistic relationship with their networks of choice. All told, the television-viewing experience has now extended its reach into cyberspace where conversations swirl amid programming, advertisements, and the watchful eyes of network executives who work feverishly to keep their core fans satisfied while concurrently enticing as many new consumers as possible to sample their branded content. TV program development and genre formation thus came full circle as an institutional process (from networking to branding to consuming) during the first decade of the Digital Era.

UP CLOSE AND PERSONAL

> Television people are everywhere, watching everything, realizing (as only people with a solid grasp of American culture can) that the highbrow-lowbrow divisions so often imposed on television are nonsensical. It's not HBO; it's TV.
> CARYN JAMES, New York Times, 2000[26]

Mark Twain (né Samuel Clemens) famously wrote a short disclaimer to the New York Journal that "the report of my death was an exaggeration" when the press erroneously announced his passing in 1897; so, too, with the earliest postmortems about television a century later.[27] During the first decade of the Digital Era, American audiences were actually watching more TV than ever before. According to Nielsen Media Research, the typical television household in the United States had its set turned on for seven hours and fifteen minutes a day on average in 1995, seven hours and twenty-six minutes a day in 2000, and a whopping eight hours and eleven minutes a day by 2005.[28] Moreover, the average number of available channels per household shot up from 43 in 1997 to 96.4 in 2005, while individual viewers increased their favorite networks of choice from 10.3 in 1997 to 16.3 in 2005.[29] Even though the oldest baby boomers reached the half-century mark in 1996, the enormous size of this generation (seventy-six million) had the advertising and television industries reconsidering their once-sacrosanct obsession with the eighteen- to forty-nine-year-old cohort. By 2005, "more than half the nation's wealth [was] in the hands of people over 50, who [spent] an estimated two trillion dollars a year on products and services."[30] One magazine touted that "the massive post-war boomer generation that drove every significant cultural and marketing trend for 50 years—from Howdy Doody to the Beatles to the Ford Explorer—[was] defying marketers' expectations about how it want[ed] to live and shop." As baby boomers began turning sixty in

2006, this generation "which grew up with the mass market and witnessed the rise of network TV and then the Internet, [was] once again forcing marketers back to the drawing board, this time to rethink the rules of reaching graying customers."[31]

The aging of the big-four broadcast networks is a case in point. From 1995 to 2001, the median age of viewers for CBS went up from forty-eight to more than fifty-two; NBC, thirty-nine to more than forty-five; ABC, thirty-five to almost forty-seven; and Fox, twenty-nine to thirty-six.[32] During its short history, Fox had targeted teens, twenty-somethings, and minorities; these cohorts now became the main preoccupation of both the WB with a 29.1-year-old median age and, less successfully, the UPN with 34.1, as they struggled to establish themselves in the increasingly cluttered and competitive television environment. The prime-time share of broadcast network programming plummeted from 70 percent of all viewers in 1995–1996 (with ABC at 18 percent; NBC, 17 percent; CBS, 15 percent; Fox, 11 percent; UPN, 6 percent; and WB, 3 percent) to 61 percent in 1998–1999 (with CBS at 14.5 percent; NBC, 14 percent; ABC, 13 percent; Fox, 10 percent; WB, 5 percent; UPN, 3 percent; and PAX, 1.5 percent).[33] Furthermore, prime-time viewing of cable (48 percent of the audience) finally surpassed the numbers achieved by the big-four broadcast networks (46.6 percent) in 2002, as cable's comparative popularity increased even further (50.3 percent versus 44.8 percent) in 2003.[34]

PBS's story was similar. Back in the Network Era, public television had carved out a niche for itself as the quality alternative to CBS, NBC, and ABC, even though it remained a perennially underfunded enterprise that attracted only a small fraction of the audience that its commercial counterparts did. In addition, PBS's performance during the Cable Era was mixed. Public television doubled its day-long share (including prime time) from 2 percent of all viewers in 1976 to 4 percent by 1985, with a 58 percent cumulative rating of all U.S. TV households tuning into PBS at least once a week to watch one of its flagship series in the arts and culture (*Great Performances, Live from Lincoln Center*), drama (*Masterpiece Theater, Mystery!*), children's programming (*Sesame Street, The Electric Company*), news and documentary (*The MacNeil/Lehrer NewsHour, Frontline*), science (*NOVA, Nature*), or lifestyle programs (*Julia Child & Company, This Old House*).[35]

Nevertheless, public television was slow to react to the explosion in networking and the narrowcasting strategies of the Cable Era. Contrary to popular belief, "the demographics describing viewers of public TV more or less [matched] those of the nation as a whole," except for a negligible skew upward in terms of age, income, and education.[36]

Still, a whole host of new niche networks simply appropriated PBS's distinctive specialty areas one by one during the 1980s and into the mid 1990s, including A&E and Bravo with the performing arts, HBO and TNT with drama, Nickelodeon and the Disney Channel with children's programming, CNN and the Learning Channel with news and documentary, the Discovery Channel and Animal Planet with science, and HGTV and the Food Network with how-to and self-improvement shows, among many other cable channels. PBS was trapped in the inescapable dilemma of having to remain as broadly appealing as possible in order to justify public support, as well as to deflect the continuing accusations from its detractors in Congress that it was too highbrow, elitist, and liberal in orientation. As the most obvious way of distinguishing itself under the restriction of being more a broadcast service than a narrowcaster, public television responded by developing one-time blockbuster miniseries such as Carl Sagan's *Cosmos* (1980), Henry Hampton's *Eyes on the Prize: America's Civil Rights Years, 1954–1965* (1987), Bill Moyers's *The Power of Myth* with Joseph Campbell (1988), and especially Ken Burns's *The Civil War*, which amassed the largest audience of any program in the history of public television. The widespread reaction to *The Civil War*, in particular, was unprecedented. In the United States, 38.9 million Americans tuned into at least one episode of the five-night telecast, averaging 12 million viewers at any given moment.[37]

Several interlocking factors contributed to the extraordinary level of interest surrounding *The Civil War* during its U.S. debut, including the overall technical and dramatic quality of the miniseries, its accompanying promotional campaign, the momentum of scheduling Sunday through Thursday, the synergetic merchandising of all its ancillary products (a companion book published by Knopf, a nine-episode videotape version from Time-Life, and an accompanying Warner soundtrack), as well as addressing the war from the so-called bottom-up perspective, underscoring the role of African Americans, women, immigrants, workers, farmers, and common soldiers in the conflict, which added a more inclusive and human dimension to the traditional preoccupations with great men, transcendent ideals, and battle strategies and statistics. Most significant, though, was that *The Civil War's* premiere occurred in the wake of the first Persian Gulf war. Iraq had just invaded Kuwait on August 2, 1990, and an imminent escalation of hostilities was continually on the minds of most Americans. Corresponding TV coverage of a massive military buildup in the region provided the immediate backdrop for the series' opening episode on September 23, just seven and a half weeks later. Revisiting the country's quintessential war on television also meant reconsidering all of

Shelby Foote (seated, left), *author and principal onscreen commentator for PBS's* The Civil War, *with producer-director Ken Burns* (right). *Courtesy of General Motors/Owen Comora Associates.*

the Civil War's essential themes, including the ultimate costs of the conflict, the question of race and continuing discrimination, the changing roles of women and men in society, and the individual struggle for meaning and conviction in modern life. *The Civil War,* in many ways, reached across generational lines, bridging the world-views of the people who came of age during World War II along with Burns's own frame of reference as a baby boomer.

Overall, though, PBS relied almost exclusively on high-profile spe-cials throughout the remainder of 1990s instead of simultaneously updating its regularly scheduled programming. As a result, public television's share of the daily TV audience slowly faded to around 3 percent by 1995, while its core constituency grew progressively older to a median age of fifty-six by the time Pat Mitchell was hired away from CNN Productions to become PBS's first woman president and CEO in 2000. "Public television is going to do more original pro-gramming than ever before," she vowed at the time, noting that "there hasn't been a new series on the network in 15 years."[38]

In contrast, there was an unprecedented proliferation of original pro-gramming from the cable and satellite sector of the television industry because of the increased competition among so many new TV services at the start of the Digital Era. By the mid to late 1990s, the acknowledged leader in program quality and innovation was Home Box Office, Inc. (HBO). From an industrial viewpoint, HBO was a lot like the cat that was still living out its nine lives, nimbly landing on its feet time and again in an atmosphere of unparalleled change. Now into its third decade, HBO had parlayed its position among, between, and inside the various mass media to emerge as the prototypical entertainment corporation of the Digital Era. As media technologies converged in the 1980s and 1990s, HBO expanded its repertoire to take full advantage of this transformation. Home Box Office was the first pay–cable channel to scramble its signal to combat piracy in 1986; offer its service on DBS in 1994; adopt digital compression transmission enabling HBO to multiplex (or split its signal into two or more channels, thus expanding its service) in 1994; develop multiplexing further to the megabrand, "HBO the works," in 1998, which includes HBO2, HBO Signature, and HBO Family, later adding HBO Comedy and HBO Zone in 1999 and HBO Latino in 2000; as well as introduce HBO on Demand (VOD, video on demand) in 2001.

Likewise, the executive team that directed Home Box Office back in the late 1970s—Gerald Levin, Frank Biondi, and Michael Fuchs—realized even then that restricting their activities to merely being the wholesaler or intermediary between the movie studios and the nation's growing cable companies was a dead-end arrangement for HBO. Levin realized in tandem with Biondi and Fuchs that Home Box Office needed to situate itself squarely in the content development not the transmission business. The three of them understood that average American viewers really didn't care whether they saw their movies in theaters, broadcast over the air, by cable, or—beginning in the late 1970s—on videotape. Consumers just wanted convenient entertainment at affordable prices. Being both between and a part of the television, motion picture, and home video industries, Home Box Office was perfectly positioned to diversify into original TV and movie production, home video, and international distribution, even as these once separate entertainment sectors were beginning to converge into one globally expanding entertainment industry by the mid 1980s. Long before the term became fashionable, HBO was a brand that became indistinguishable with the notion of subscription television during the 1970s. More specifically, HBO's original image or utility brand was linked primarily to its function of providing Hollywood motion pictures to cable viewers in the comfort of their own homes, despite the fact that it also produced and telecast occasional stand-up comedy, sports, and music specials. The major problem with basing a company's brand loyalty on the most prominent product that it provided was that competitors invariably appeared who were willing and able to supply the public with the same service as the original seller.

In the particular case of Home Box Office, Viacom's Showtime was created soon after HBO in 1976 and began satellite transmission in 1978; Warner AMEX launched the Movie Channel in 1979; Time/HBO countered by creating Cinemax in 1980; and Times-Mirror began Spotlight in 1981. Also in 1981, the Justice Department prevented Twentieth Century-Fox, Universal, Paramount, Columbia, and Getty Oil from producing their own pay-movie channel, Premiere, as being monopolistic. HBO asserted its dominance as the channel that viewers most associated with movies, but by the 1990s it was similarly well known for its original series, miniseries, made-for-pay-TV movies, documentaries, stand-up comedy, and sports. HBO also transformed the creative landscape of television at the dawning of the Digital Era. It pursued the unusual and atypical strategy for TV of investing more money in program development (from $2 to $4 million per prime-time hour), limiting output (thirteen episodes per series each year instead of the usual twenty-two to twenty-six), and producing only the highest-quality series, miniseries, made-for-pay-TV movies, documentaries, and specials that it could. When HBO chairman and CEO Chris Albrecht was first promoted to programming chief in 1995, he called his executive staff together for a two-day meeting with the blessing of his boss, Jeffrey Bewkes, and asked them, "Do we really believe that we are who we say we are? This distinctive, high-quality, edgy, worth-paying-for service?" Albrecht remembers that the silence in the room was deafening. The executive team at HBO headed by Bewkes then began the slow and deliberate process of building "an outstanding one-of-a-kind programming service" because being an "occasional use" cable channel was "no longer sustainable" in the survival-of-the-fittest world of the Digital TV Era.[39]

Along with a handful of other channels, such as MTV, ESPN, CNN, Fox News, and a few others, HBO established as strong an identity brand as there was on television, spilling over into its overseas expansion (beginning with Latin America, Europe, and Asia), its DVD sales, its theatrical releases, its syndication of its own series on other channels (such as *Sex and the City* on TBS in 2004), and its production of original programs for other networks (such as *Everybody Loves Raymond* for CBS from 1996 to 2005). In 1997, Time Warner's then-chairman Gerald Levin remembered, "Twenty-five years ago, HBO invented a new form of television." Reflecting on the current state of the entertainment industry he added, "HBO, the brand, is so powerful and HBO, the concept, is so dynamic that it's entering the digital future with the creative edge qualitatively superior to our competition."[40]

In this way, HBO is also an idea or identity brand. Ever since 1996, Home Box Office has been marketed with the tag line, "it's not TV, it's HBO." What this branding slogan implies is that the series and specials produced by and presented on HBO are a qualitative cut above your usual run-of-the-mill television programming. By the late 1990s, HBO had emerged as the TV equivalent of a designer label. When Michael Fuchs assumed the top job at the network in 1985, his dual emphases were to increase the amount of HBO's original programming and to establish a growing presence for the network overseas. To his credit, he succeeded on both counts. Levin, Biondi, and Fuchs hired Sheila Nevins in 1979 to jump-start the network's documentary unit. She responded by executive producing a series of brash and gritty reality-based programs throughout the mid to late 1980s, including the network's first Oscar winner in 1987 (*Down and Out in America*) and first Emmy winner in 1988 (*Dear America: Letters Home from Vietnam*), culminating in the start of HBO's ongoing signature nonfiction series, *America Undercover*, in 1993.

Michael Fuchs also enjoyed a good working relationship with his talented finance VP and manager, Jeffrey Bewkes, and together they brought Chris Albrecht to Home Box Office in 1985. Albrecht immediately proved his value to the network by producing the first *Comic Relief* special the next year. Fuchs supported a significant increase in made-for-pay-TV movie productions under the banner HBO Films, as well as Robert Altman and Garry Trudeau's campaign mockumentary, *Tanner '88*, which won wide acclaim and another Emmy for the network. Fuchs also invested heavily in more original comedy programs, including a wide array of cutting-edge stand-up specials and a handful of thirty-minute series such as the one-of-a-kind talk parody, *The Larry Sanders Show*, which debuted in 1992, lasted six years, and eventually won a prestigious Peabody award. Of special note, Michael Fuchs made a concerted effort to enhance HBO's brand awareness by launching the company's first national image advertising campaign, "simply the best," in 1989. This initiative started the lengthy and expensive process of changing the overall impression of HBO from that of a first-run movie service to more of a premium network that produces and presents the best original programming on television. In the fiercely competitive environment of the Digital Era, networking aims to intensify the connection between a channel and its target audience. Hand in hand with Home Box Office's new commitment to producing original programming, Jeffrey Bewkes enlisted his executive vice president for marketing, Eric Kessler, to create an identity brand to complement HBO's new focus. Bewkes allocated "$25 million a year just to advertise the HBO brand," and Kessler and his team kicked off a new ad campaign on October 20, 1996, which was the beginning of "one of TV's all-time great tag lines—It's Not TV, It's HBO."[41]

Five years later, Home Box Office had become the hottest destination on television. From 1996 to 2001, HBO increased its percentage of original programming from 25 percent to 40 percent of its entire schedule.[42] In that way, the branding line, "it's not TV, it's HBO," marked a transitional moment in the industry when cable and satellite channels became the first place to look for breakout programming on all of television, no longer just the traditional broadcast networks. HBO had already established Sunday night as its own must-see TV evening of viewing with such innovative original series as *Sex and the City* in 1998 and *The Sopranos* in 1999. Those two series were simply the tip of an iceberg that, in hindsight, included such dramatic series as *Oz, Six Feet Under, The Wire,* and *Deadwood;* miniseries such as *From the Earth to the Moon, Band of Brothers,* and *Angels in America;* comedies such as *Curb Your Enthusiasm* and *Real Time with Bill Maher;* sports shows such as *Real Sports with Bryant Gumbel* and *On the Record with Bob Costas;* six Oscar-winning documentaries between 1999 and 2004 alone; and theatricals such as *Spellbound* (2002), *American Splendor* (2004), and *Maria Full of Grace* (2004), which eventually made their way on to HBO's prime-time lineup after their initial runs in movie theaters. Home Box Office epitomized appointment TV for its approximately thirty million subscriber households. During the 2005–2006 season, it was one of those networks of choice for more than 27 percent of the 110.2 million TV households in the United States. HBO subscribers were more than just viewers: they were paying customers, who shelled out approximately $15 a month to obtain this service. No longer were they settling for the least objectionable programming they could find; they were looking for something different, challenging, and more original on HBO, particularly since they were paying a monthly fee just to tune in. In this regard, the network won a record-setting thirty-two Emmys in 2004 after garnering an unprecedented 124 nominations.

Home Box Office, Inc., also posted nearly $1.1 billion in profits in 2004 for its parent conglomerate, Time Warner, up from its previous record-setting marks of $960 million in 2003 and $725 in 2002.[43] These dollar figures were the highest annual yields ever earned by any network in the history of television up to that time. Moreover, HBO's

HBO established Sunday night as its own must-see TV evening of viewing with such innovative original series as Sex and the City, *which premiered in 1998 with (left to right) Cynthia Nixon as Miranda Hobbes, Kim Cattrall as Samantha Jones, Kristin Davis as Charlotte York, and Sarah Jessica Parker as Carrie Bradshaw. Courtesy of HBO Production/Heldref.*

dramatic influence became evident on other cable and broadcast networks with the debut of such series as FX's *The Shield* in 2002, *Nip/Tuck* in 2003, and *Rescue Me* in 2004, all nurtured by then-network chief and former HBO executive Peter Liguori, as well as Fox's *24* in 2001 and *Arrested Development* in 2003. HBO was occasionally attracting audiences comparable to the broadcast networks as well, even though its subscriber base was less than 30 percent of the total number of TV households in America. For example, the most popular programs on all of television in 2001–2002 were NBC's *Friends*, averaging 24.5 million viewers each week; CBS's *CSI*, with 23.7 million; and NBC's *ER*, with 22.1 million. For its part, *The Sopranos* attracted fourteen million people per episode that season, which gave it an audience size equivalent to a top-10 to top-15 show in the broadcast universe rather than just the cable and satellite sector.[44] HBO was redefining what was possible in terms of both quality innovations on the small screen and how much money could be made by pursuing alternative business models for TV. Unlike HBO, the traditional broadcast networks were still captives to their old economic formula of relying on "a single revenue stream based entirely on advertising."[45]

Product placement was reintroduced on CBS with the unexpected success of Mark Burnett's Survivor *in 2000, when the audience for this reality-adventure soap opera game show mushroomed from an initially impressive 15.5 million viewers for the May 31 debut to an astonishing 51 million for its August 23 finale.* Left to right: *Contestants Richard Hatch and Rudy Boesch. Courtesy of CBS/Landov.*

Almost by accident, product placement was reintroduced on CBS with the unexpected success of Mark Burnett's *Survivor* in 2000, when the audience for this reality-adventure, soap opera, game show mushroomed from an initially impressive 15.5 million viewers for the May 31 debut to an astonishing 51 million for its August 23 finale.[46] *Survivor* turned out to be more than just a hit television show; it was a bona fide nationwide phenomenon that was featured on the covers of *Time* (June 26) and *Newsweek* (August 28). The show established reality programming as the hottest genre on all of TV, especially with audiences under age thirty-five, which made up 68 percent of its fan base.[47] Generation X (1965–1983) was weaned on MTV's annual reality favorite, *The Real World*, which premiered in 1992 and captured the high-and-low drama of seven strangers in their late teens and early twenties living for six months as roommates in a downtown Manhattan apartment. Every subsequent year, MTV changed the cast members and the locales (from Los Angeles to London and Honolulu, among other sites), populating each new installment with the usual array of recognizable "types: the Republican, the gay activist, the rapper, the Asian medical school student, the innocent suburban white girl, the liberal Jewish cartoonist."[48]

Burnett followed a similar strategy when he began developing what he called "nonscripted drama or dramality," rather than the catch-all label "reality TV," which he thought included too many "egregious rip-offs."[49] An English ex-patriot and former Red Devil (or alumnus of the elite Parachute Regiment of the British Army), Burnett found his niche producing physically demanding extreme sporting events such as the *Eco-Challenge* series of expedition-style races in British Columbia (1996) for MTV and ESPN; Morocco (1998), Australia (1998), and Argentina (1999) for The Discovery Channel; and Borneo (2001) for the USA Network, which is also the location where the first *Survivor* installment was staged. Burnett had originally purchased the U.S. rights to the "Survive" concept (described as "an adult version of *Lord of the Flies*") from British producer Charlie Parsons in 1998;[50] to be sure, "Europe was the original incubator for reality television in the late 1990s."[51] *Survivor* thus reflected a mixed pedigree of cable and European television.

Overall, then, cable and satellite–sector influences and programming innovations from Europe were becoming common sources of inspiration for broadcast programmers and producers during the mid to late 1990s. Parsons likewise licensed "Survive" to the Swedish TV production company, Strix, which turned it into the hit series *Expedition Robinson* (as in *Robinson Crusoe*), starting in 1997. He also franchised the concept to over thirty other countries, including Australia, Brazil, China, France, Germany, Italy, Japan, and Russia. For two years, Mark Burnett pitched the show to one American broadcast network after another—Fox, CBS, NBC, and ABC—before returning to CBS where entertainment president Les Moonves finally agreed to put *Survivor* on the air if the financial risk of $9.75 million, or $750,000 per episode for a thirteen-week run, could be mitigated. Burnett responded by lining up eight sponsors ahead of *Survivor*'s premiere with the promise of product placement, or what he called "associative marketing." Brands such as Reebok, Target, and Budweiser were therefore integrated into the story line so that the eight men and eight women who were allegedly marooned on a Malaysian Island in the South China Sea were seen wearing Reebok T-shirts and tennis shoes and occasionally brandishing a sixteen-ounce Bud. "I looked on *Survivor* as much as a marketing vehicle as a television show," admitted Burnett, as the first version of this long-running series, *Survivor: Borneo*, generated $52 million in profits, which he shared ($10 million to $42 million) with CBS.[52] *Survivor* soon replaced ABC's *Who Wants to Be a Millionaire?* as no. 1 in the ratings over the 2000–2001 season.

Who Wants to Be a Millionaire? was yet another international import (from Britain) with a highly adaptable format that by 2003 was franchised in an unprecedented seventy countries. In the United States, specifically, this prime-time quiz show hosted by Regis Philbin was first telecast on ABC in August 1999, where it became an instant sensation, attracting up to thirty million viewers a week during its first season, before the network ran the "Millionaire" concept into the ground by scheduling it for four nights a week in its second year on the air.[53] Still, *Who Wants to Be a Millionaire?* earned ABC over $300 million in profits from 1999 through 2002, signaling that the broadcast networks were then favoring reality-based series, including game shows (for example, NBC's *Fear Factor* in 2001—a Dutch import), makeover programs (ABC's *Extreme Makeover* in 2002), talent searches (Fox's *American Idol* in 2002—another British import), celebrity comedies (Fox's *The Simple Life* with Paris Hilton and Nicole Richie in 2003), job searches (NBC's *The Apprentice* with Donald Trump in 2004), and sports contests (NBC's *The Contender* with Sugar Ray Leonard and Sylvester Stallone in 2005). These relatively inexpensive offerings were at least temporarily taking the place of much higher priced, scripted, one-hour dramas (such as *ER* at $13 million per episode by 1998–1999) and thirty-minute comedies (*Friends* at $10 million per episode by 2003–2004).[54] The certifiable peak in the United States came in 2003–2004, when 39 percent of all new series, as well as six of the top ten shows in the country, were reality programs (with *American Idol* on Tuesdays at no. 1, *American Idol* on Wednesdays at no. 2, *Survivor: All-Stars* at no. 5, *Survivor: Pearl Islands* at no. 7, *The Apprentice* at no. 8, and *Monday Night Football* at no. 10).[55] Only four years after the debut of *Survivor*, "what Hollywood and Madison Avenue euphemistically [called] 'brand integration' was hard to miss" all over the television dial. For instance, the three judges on *American Idol* had their Coke beverage cups prominently displayed in front of them twice a week, while the wannabes on *The Apprentice* marketed products for such prominent sponsors as PepsiCo, Mattel, and Proctor and Gamble as the focus of their team assignments.

It was reported that "during the 2004–2005 television season, more than 100,000 product placements appeared on the six broadcast networks, an increase of nearly 28 percent from the previous season." The top ten shows for brand integration were all in the broadcast sector, led by *The Contender* with 7,521 product placements, *The Apprentice* with 3,659, and *American Idol* with 3,497.[56] Although pioneered through reality programming, "advertisers and their representatives [were also] increasingly working with writers and producers and the network's ad sales staff to incorporate products into the storylines of scripted shows."[57] The rapid adoption of digital video recorders (DVRs or PVRs, personal video recorders) beginning in 1999 also made it easy and routine for viewers to skip commercials on recorded material, thus ensuring an ever-greater move toward product placement on all kinds of broadcast and now cable and satellite television programming in the early to mid 2000s. By 2005, DVRs, or "ad zappers" as they were nicknamed, were "in 13% of American homes and 7% of European ones." Industry estimates predicted an 88 percent DVR saturation rate in the United States and 70 percent throughout Europe by 2010.[58]

In addition, all of Europe and English-speaking countries elsewhere were the largest international markets for TV syndicators from America during the 1980s and 1990s. The five "rich uncles" (France, Germany, the United Kingdom, Australia, and Canada) accounted for up to 75 percent of all foreign syndication revenues over those two decades. French Minister of Culture Jack Lang even went so far as to publicly single out *Dallas* in 1982 as an example of U.S. "cultural imperialism" and "a threat to the integrity of European culture." European audiences and their counterparts in North and South America, Australia, Asia, and Africa, however, favored American programming to such a degree that anywhere between 30 to 55 percent of Hollywood's "advertiser-supported TV revenues [depending on the year] came from outside the U.S." during the Cable Era.[59]

The Digital Era started the same way, as television "entertainment around the world [was largely] dominated by American-made products. It [was] *The Young and the Restless* in New Delhi, Bart Simpson in Seoul, and *Dr. Quinn, Medicine Woman* on Warsaw TV."[60] *Baywatch* emerged as the most-watched program on earth during the mid to late 1990s, attracting hundreds of millions of viewers in over 130 countries. Then a transition took hold with the adoption of the more-customized, personal-usage market model of the Digital Era, where local television industries in countries outside of the United States developed to a point that they began franchising TV formats rather than just importing more American programs. In this way, they adapted reality concepts such as "Survive" and "Millionaire," as well as previously scripted ideas, to their own indigenous cultures. Germany, for instance, had "a long-running hit called *Das Traumschiff* or *Dream Ship* [which was] a remake of *The Love Boat*."[61] MTV, too, had franchised "35 different channels worldwide [by 2002], 15 of them in Europe; some 80% of the content on MTV Italy, for example, is Italian-made." Similarly, there were then "22 different versions of CNN, including one in Turkish and two in German. As recently as

1996, 70% of the English-language version of CNN International was American; [five years later] that share had shrunk to 8%."[62] Global television sales still "totaled $2.5 billion" in revenues for American distributors in 2001, but that figure accounted for only 10 percent of all syndication income that year, with the rest of the earnings coming from the lucrative domestic market because of the escalating number of networks in the Digital Era.[63] By the turn of the new millennium, therefore, "local fare [glued] more eyeballs to TV screens than American programs. Although three-quarters of television dramas exported worldwide [in 2002 still came] from the United States, most countries' favorite shows [were] homegrown."[64] In fact, a "survey by Nielsen Media Research found that 71% of the top-ten programs in 60 countries were locally produced in 2001, representing a steady increase over previous years."[65]

The long-term popularity and growth potential of American television worldwide was still a given, but the United States was unlikely to ever dominate the global television market as it once did back in the 1980s and 1990s. Veteran producer-writer Norman Lear christened "the mid-1990s 'the third birth of television,'" as yet another generation came of age while the cable revolution seamlessly transitioned into the Digital Era.[66] "It's tempting to define Generation X as simply an age group, but that classification ignores the fact that Xers are all members of one TV generation," proclaims Rob Owen, author of *Gen X TV*: "Although not the first group of Americans to grow up on TV, Xers are the first group for whom TV served as a regulary-scheduled babysitter. Gen X was the first to experience MTV and the Fox Network, and they are an audience many advertisers are eager to reach." For the fifty million members of Generation X, moreover, "TV is the defining medium."[67] Their sense of irony, media sophistication, and omnivorous appetite for mixing and matching taste cultures were all clearly evident in the comedies (*The Simpsons, Friends*), dramas (*ER, The X-Files*), reruns (*The Brady Bunch, Happy Days*), and even guilty pleasures (*Beverly Hills 90210, Melrose Place*) they chose to watch en masse. All of America grew more jaded in the up-close-and-personal tabloid TV environment of the 1990s that featured one mismatched couple after another, beginning with the "ice follies" between rival skaters Nancy Kerrigan and Tonya Harding, leading to the murder involving husband and battered wife O. J. Simpson and Nicole Brown, and culminating with the affair between Bill Clinton and White House intern Monica Lewinsky that precipitated "the longest-running news miniseries of them all, 'Impeachment of the President.'"[68]

The X-Files was a cult favorite that advised its viewers to "trust no one." At its height, the series presented a powerful emotional storyline that was especially popular with members of Generation X. Courtesy of David Gray/Fox Broadcasting Company/Heldref.

With the emergence of the ever-present global news cycle, America reflexively aired its dirty laundry nonstop from coast to coast and then throughout the world. President Clinton eventually survived the Lewinsky scandal, presiding over the Millennium celebration in Washington, D.C., on January 1, 2000, as part of a global television event with an international audience exceeding 1 billion people. The daylong coverage followed the dual arrival of the New Year and the Millennium across all twenty-five time zones on earth. This transnational telecast was both lavish and skillfully choreographed, with a series of magnificent fireworks displays coming one after the other in quick succession from such illustrious sights as the Opera House in Sydney, to the Hong Kong skyline, to the Eiffel Tower in Paris, to the fabled crystal ball descending in Times Square. Two weeks earlier, al-Qaeda operative Ahmed Ressam had been arrested while trying to cross into the United States from Canada at Port Angeles, Washington. He later confessed and revealed to authorities the existence of a terrorist plot to blow up LAX (Los Angeles International Airport) on the eve of the Millennium. Instead, people of all ages, races, and ethnicities appeared on TV that night to celebrate the dream of one world and send out wishes for a peaceful and happy New Year. The next day, television critic Tom Shales described the coverage as "a head-spinning, globe-trotting day of don't-stop television. As it does too seldom, television showed us the world, made us feel part of the 'global village' envisioned by 20th-century philosopher Marshall McLuhan."[69] Unbeknownst to Shales and the vast number of viewers that night, the so-called Millennium bomber was a far more accurate harbinger of things to come—at least in the short term.

Televising 9/11 and Its Aftermath

The finality of toppling Saddam Hussein's statue. The thrill of that re-enactment of *Top Gun*. The sense of closure provided by the banner reading "Mission Accomplished." Like all wars of the TV age, the war in Iraq is not just a clash of armies, but a succession of iconic images. Those who control the images, and the narrative they encapsulate, control history. At least until a new reality crashes in.

FRANK RICH, *New York Times*, 2003[70]

In the years since the terrorist hijackings of September 11, 2001, Americans are still trying to grasp the full meaning of the events that left more than three thousand people from sixty-one countries dead at the World Trade Center's twin towers in lower Manhattan, the Pentagon in Washington, D.C., and a rural field in Pennsylvania. The initial shock of 9/11 sent stunning reverberations throughout the nation where most citizens simply sat glued to their television sets, struggling to make sense of the horrific imagery that was beaming back at them. To many, the 9/11 telecast and the first few days after the attacks resembled something akin to a summer disaster movie rather than an actual occurrence unfolding in real time. MSNBC reporter Ron Ansana spoke for many in his audience when he described lower Manhattan on September 11 as "a scene out of *Independence Day*."[71] The feeling of unreality that he effectively captured with his reporting was horrific and bewildering. "It honestly looked a bit like nuclear winter," Ansana later told Tom Brokaw in an afternoon NBC interview—"something you see in the movies with ash all over the ground, on top of cars, on police cars, on windows."[72] From Tuesday morning September 11, 2001, through Friday evening September 14, viewers around the world watched continuous TV coverage, mesmerized by the unthinkable images. Television brought home to Americans especially the polarizing effects of our post–Cold War world, including the backlash of Islamic fundamentalism and the catastrophic dangers inherent in terrorist attacks on targets within the United States.

Quickly, an understandable if formulaic narrative emerged: ordinary police and firefighters took the lead as America's unsung national heroes, while Osama bin Laden and the rest of al-Qaeda and the Taliban rose up as villains. Viewer attention was channeled into familiar plotlines featuring heroic public servants and villainous foreign terrorists. These rapidly emerging narrative patterns were further enhanced by the shocking repetitive power of seeing the two World Trade Center towers burning and finally collapsing time and again. "Early in the [twentieth] century, we thought history was something that happened temporally 'before' and was represented temporally 'after' us and our personal and immediate experience," recounts Vivian Sobchack; "today, history seems to happen right now—is transmitted, reflected upon, shown play-by-play, taken up as the stuff of multiple stories and significance, given all sorts of 'coverage' in the temporal dimension of the present as we live it."[73] TV transformed the events surrounding 9/11 into "instant history" by taking what were essentially localized New York City and Washington, D.C., catastrophes and turning them into a global media event with the whole world bearing witness.[74] Mimi White and James Schwoch believe that "in this sense, television acted as an agent of history and memory, recording and preserving representations to be referenced in the future."[75] In subsequent months and years, real-life footage from 9/11 has been regularly incorporated into numerous TV documentaries produced in America as well as internationally, while fictionalized scenes of domestic terrorism have appeared or were edited out of such widely diverse television programs as NBC's *Law & Order*, *The West Wing*, *Third Watch*, CBS's *The Agency*, and Fox's *24*, among many other series. This is because, "as historians who focus on popular memory have [long] insisted, we experience the present through the lens of the past—*and we shape our understanding of the past through the lens of the present*."[76]

Television's initial coverage of 9/11 masked a deeper reality grounded in the history, global politics, and competing Western and Middle Eastern socioreligious visions of the future. The terrorist acts committed on September 11, 2001, are the most striking examples to point to so far, revealing to anyone with a television set the darker impulses of globalization. The specter of Osama bin Laden materialized on numerous telecasts within hours of American Airlines Flight 11's first crashing into the north tower at 8:46 A.M., prompting CNN, Fox News, MSNBC, and the three morning news programs on NBC, CBS, and ABC to begin their 9/11 coverage. Fifteen minutes later, United Airlines Flight 175 flew directly into the south tower in full view of recording video cameras. Cohost Bryant Gumbel of CBS's *The Early Show* was conducting a cell phone interview with a nearby eyewitness at 9:03 A.M.:

Theresa Renaud: I am in Chelsea and we are at 8th and 16th. We're in the tallest building in the area, and my window faces south. Approximately ten minutes ago there was a major

explisión from about the 80th floor. . . . Oh there's another one—another plane just hit [gasps—yelling]. Oh my God! Another plane just hit—it hit another building, flew right into the middle of it.

Gumbel: This one into [Tower 2]?

Renaud: Yes, yes, right in the middle of the building . . . that was definitely on purpose.[77]

United Airlines Flight 175 flew directly into the south tower of the World Trade Center, in full view of recording TV and video cameras, at 9:03 A.M. on September 11, 2001. Courtesy of Reuters/Sean Adair/Landov.

Soon, "CNN was sporting a new graphic—'Attack on America'; the image of the jet penetrating the second WTC tower in heavy rotation; and a nation (and probably a good bit of the world) watched in horror as the towers collapsed."[78] The south tower fell at 9:59 A.M., and the north tower came crashing down a half-hour later, at 10:28 A.M.

By 10:50 A.M., NBC's Tom Brokaw was asking columnist and terrorism expert Brian Livingston, "How many groups could do this?" Livingston responded: "Very few. We have to be cautious, but we have to look to the Middle East. . . . We have to look at Osama bin Laden." By late morning, the name "bin Laden" was already surfacing on all the major national networks and the cable news channels. Soon stock footage of the tall, bearded Saudi exile and terrorist fused neatly with the continuing characterizations of 9/11 as a kind of present-day Pearl Harbor. TV coverage thus "invoked a familiar, even comforting narrative: a sleeping nation, a treacherous attack, and the need to rally patriotism and 'manly' virtues on behalf of retribution."[79] ABC, NBC, CBS, and Fox "largely scrapped commercial advertising" on the morning of September 11 and relied mainly on sustaining coverage for much of the next three and a half days in reaction to what was obviously "a national emergency."[80] The four major networks similarly took the unprecedented step of "putting rivalries aside" and sharing "all footage of [the] tragedies."[81] In turn, viewers nationwide found that watching TV helped them cope better with the collective trauma of 9/11: "Television channels that ran and reran horrific images of the planes, the crashes, the towers collapsing now also ran interviews with experts on how to talk to your children about the crisis, and how to manage stress."[82] "Religious invocation permeated the earliest breaking" telecasts as well, recalls video producer and scholar Marusya Bociurkiw, as "New York firefighters (the secular saints of the occasion)" stood "at attention as stretchers were carried out of the rubble."[83]

"After September 11 . . . coverage of [President George W.] Bush and his leadership [also became] more adulatory," observes investigative journalist Ken Auletta.[84] Most news, public affairs, and even entertainment shows became much more patriotic in their look, tone, and message. The "loose association between the authority of TV network news and political authority" grew increasingly closer over the next six months, as newscasts all over the dial sported redesigned "computer-generated logos, brass trumpetry, red-white-and-blue color schemes, and portentous newsreaders, not to mention [showing] deference to official spokespeople, marginalizing dissent, and adopting official news agendas." Television anchors, commentators, and reporters also took to wearing flag lapel pins "to express their solidarity not merely with the American government but with Americans feeling embattled and anxiety-ridden," recounts media critic Pat Aufderheide.[85]

The prevailing climate also exerted a chilling effect on the more freewheeling and irreverent political talk shows. On the Monday, September 17, episode of ABC's *Politically Incorrect*, for example, author Dinesha D'Souza sparked controversy by disagreeing with Bush's use of the word "coward" to describe the 9/11 terrorists. Host Bill Maher reacted quickly with characteristic brashness: "We have been the cowards, lobbing cruise missiles from 2,000 miles away. That's cowardly. Staying in the plane when it hits the building, say what you want about it, it's not cowardly."[86] As a result, Maher was forced to backtrack for the rest of the week. Sponsors Sears and Federal Express temporarily left the program because of a sharp surge in viewer complaints over the remark. General Motors and Schering-Plough pulled their ads for good. More strikingly, seventeen ABC affiliates refused to air *Politically Incorrect* any longer.[87] By Friday, September 21, a chastened Bill Maher felt compelled to appear on "the stage of *The Tonight Show with Jay Leno* . . . seeking forgiveness for what might have been a career ending gaffe."[88] Although *Politically Incorrect* survived through May 2002, and the professional fallout for Maher was only temporary, White House reaction was swift and unequivocal. On Wednesday, September 26, press secretary Ari Fleischer called Maher's comment "a terrible thing to say," chiding that "all Americans . . . need to watch what they say, watch what they do. This is not a time for remarks like that; there never is."[89]

For its part, network news was far more inclined to steer clear of controversy and support the Bush administration during the first six months after 9/11, and the president responded in kind by favoring his most sympathetic TV news advocates such as Brit Hume of Fox News. Bush also openly "cooperated with NBC's Tom Brokaw, CBS's Scott Pelley, and ABC's Diane Sawyer for lengthy interviews." He refused similar invitations from "television anchors Peter Jennings of ABC [and] Dan Rather of CBS," however. Jennings, in particular, remembers researching a story at the White House and being told by "a senior figure [that] 'it better be good.' " "I thought [that] was rather naked," recalls the veteran newscaster; "it wasn't a threat, but it didn't sound like a joke [either]."[90] "It's almost as if the media decided that critical analysis of the events leading to and from 9/11 [was] not only un-American, but potentially anti-American," asserts Australian communication scholar Leila Green, "and consistent with this more consensual approach to newsgathering [was] a ready willingness "to see a demonization of 'the enemy': bin Laden, the Taliban, al-Qaeda."[91]

Americans in general tuned into safe and reassuring television programming as a brief respite from the nerve-racking urgency of current events, especially as the war on terrorism heated up with the invasion of Afghanistan on October 7, 2001. President Bush addressed the nation that day at 1 P.M. (EST) to announce that "the United States military [had] begun strikes against al-Qaeda terrorist training camps and military installations of the Taliban regime in Afghanistan."[92] In addition, TV audiences received intermittent glimpses of Osama bin Laden through four separate videos telecast worldwide over the next three months. The first two tapes aired initially on the Al Jazeera Arabic-language network and showed a seemingly serene and determined bin Laden calling for Muslims everywhere to join in the struggle against the United States. As a response, the Bush administration released a third video on December 13 after it was "found by the CIA in a house in Jalalabad, Afghanistan." This tape showed "bin Laden boasting about the attacks," and demonstrated the U.S. Government's intention "to win the case against international terrorism in the court of public opinion." A fourth and final video appeared on Al Jazeera once again on December 27, showing a haggard though still defiant bin Laden. These four tapes changed few hearts and minds, in retrospect, as attitudes about 9/11 had congealed months before, "based to a certain extent on [each side's] need to believe one way or another."[93] President Bush specifically painted bin Laden as the latest in a long line of totalitarian tyrants, referring to him regularly during the waning months of 2001 while also invoking the memory of Pearl Harbor and urging "the younger generations of Americans to uphold the faith of their 'elders,' the World War II generation."[94]

From the earliest recorded images relayed back from the epicenter of the World Trade Center (later renamed "ground zero"), network and local TV were both firmly locked into a pro-American gaze. Patriotic expressions of all kinds were readily apparent throughout the

TV audiences worldwide received intermittent videotaped glimpses of Osama bin Laden that originated on the Al Jazeera Arabic-language network, showing a seemingly serene and determined bin Laden calling for Muslims everywhere to join in the struggle against the United States. Courtesy of Al Jazeera TV via Bloomberg News/Landov.

television environment after September 11. Many TV stations across the country simply keyed in the image of a tiny American flag at the bottom right-hand corner of their telecasts. The stars-and-stripes also became a familiar background fixture on the hit CBS sitcom *Everybody Loves Raymond*. Creator and executive producer Dick Wolf of NBC's *Law & Order* added the following voiceover as an introduction to the September 26th season premiere:

> On September 11th 2001, New York City was ruthlessly and criminally attacked. While no tribute can ever heal the pain of that day, the producers of *Law & Order* dedicate this season to the victims and their families, and to the firefighters and police officers, who remind us with their lives and courage what it truly means to be an American.[95]

Aaron Sorkin, creator and supervising producer of *The West Wing*, grappled with his own confusion concerning the nagging question of "why 9/11 occurred" by scripting a special episode entitled "Isaac and Ishmael," which aired on October 3, 2001, attracting "25.2 million viewers, the show's largest audience ever."[96] "Isaac and Ishmael" provides what one critic called "a smart, helpful civics lesson about America's relationship to the Middle East."[97] Sorkin addresses a number of highly relevant issues in the episode, including breakdowns in homeland security, unexpected and looming terrorist threats, and ethnic profiling.

Other prime-time programs dealt with the aftereffects of 9/11 in their own ways. On September 27, 2001, for instance, CBS postponed its debut of *The Agency*, a fictional series based on CIA counterterrorist investigations, because the pilot dealt with an anthrax scare in the United States (anticipating a rash of similar real-life episodes in Florida, New Jersey, New York, Washington, Missouri, and Indiana during October and November of 2001). On October 15, 2001, NBC's *Third Watch* next took the unusual step of having its regular starring cast members introduce ten-minute segments where actual police officers, firefighters, paramedics, emergency service personnel, and their families talked freely about their emotionally charged work experiences on September 11 and the days immediately after the terrorist acts. The producers and writers of *Third Watch* then incorporated the events of 9/11 into the series' fictional story line for the remainder of the season. In contrast, Fox executives ordered that a scene presenting a bomb exploding on a plane be edited out of the premiere episode of *24* later in November 2001. In these and other instances of self-restraint, network programmers erred on the side of caution, making sure that their prime-time dramas did not unduly disturb an already traumatized viewing public. Even humor was temporarily kept at bay. A study of late-night talk shows—"which examined [NBC's] *The Tonight Show with Jay Leno*, [CBS's] *The Late Show with David Letterman*, and [NBC's] *Late Night with Conan O'Brien*—also found twice as many 'serious' guests appearing" and the number of jokes "dropping by 54% in the month following the 9/11 terrorist attacks" compared with the previous four months.[98] Television additionally "made it a [regular] practice of airing long and patriotic half-time shows at [football games] and [playing] the 7th inning rendition of 'God Bless America' at baseball games instead of cutting away to commercials."[99]

The nation revealed a rising determination and expressed a renewed sense of purpose. Television "updates on blood drives, charities, and the celebrity telethon were tools to turn grief into action, to liberate the will, to do something."[100] The first major TV special produced in response to 9/11 was titled *America: A Tribute to Heroes*, "a telethon that aired ten days after the attacks on 30 different channels and was watched by 89 million viewers. The show raised $150 million, three times as much as any other television fundraiser in history."[101] Many other notable benefits followed, culminating with two TV extravaganzas six weeks later. *The Concert for New York City* originated from Madison Square Garden on Saturday, October 20, and lasted more than five hours—four of which were simulcast live on VH1. The star-studded lineup at this made-for-television event included classic rockers (Paul McCartney, Elton John, Mick Jagger), Hollywood and television stars (Harrison Ford, Jerry Seinfeld, Billy Crystal), filmmakers who each produced a short work celebrating the spirit of New York (Woody Allen, Spike Lee, Martin Scorsese), and a host of local and national politicians (Mayor Rudy Giuliani, Governor George Pataki, former President Bill Clinton). The honored guests of *The Concert for New York City* were the more than five thousand police and firefighters accompanied by their loved ones, as the program generated "over $30 million for the Robin Hood Relief Fund," which was created specifically to support the families of the 9/11 victims.[102] On the following evening, October 21, "CMT: Country Music Television achieved its highest rating ever," with its own "live three-hour telecast of *The Country Freedom Concert*" from Nashville, "a benefit which raised awareness and [$5.1 million] for the Salvation Army's wide-ranging disaster relief efforts."[103]

The most obvious change in prime-time viewing after 9/11 was the sudden loss of interest in quiz shows, especially ABC's once wildly popular *Who Wants to Be a Millionaire?* and the sudden rejection of most reality programs, save CBS's *Survivor* and a few other exceptions. "Reality shows," in particular, were "negatively affected," remembers advertising executive John Rash. "They "began to look remarkably self-indulgent [after September 11]." Instead, American audiences started consuming a tried-and-true diet of TV comfort food. NBC's *Friends*, for example, enjoyed its best ratings ever, ending no. 1 in prime time and no. 3 in national syndication behind such perennial favorites as Merv Griffin Productions' *Wheel of Fortune* and *Jeopardy!* Other evergreen hits, including ABC's *Monday Night Football* and CBS's *60 Minutes* performed as well in 2001–2002 as they had in years, as did cable channels specializing in nostalgic entertainment such as American Movie Classics, Nick-at-Nite, and TV Land. In one critic's opinion, "the most distressing post-Sept 11 trend" was "the exploitation of patriotism in ads. . . . Why is that Jeep driving up the face of the Statue of Liberty? And is Chevy really just trying to 'keep America rolling?' "[104] Overall, the widespread patriotic zeal expressed in fifteen-second and thirty-second spots, television news, and entertainment programming began to fade somewhat after the six-month commemoration of 9/11, as criticisms of the Bush administration's handling of the war on terrorism slowly grew louder, bolder, and more frequent. By July 2002, "the rally-'round-the-flag effect dissipated" slightly, leaving President Bush's poll numbers at a still noteworthy 70 percent, but clearly dropping.[105]

The public had grown deeply conflicted over the impending Iraqi crisis by February 2003. In a *New York Times*/CBS News poll, "three-quarters of Americans [saw] war as inevitable, and two-thirds [approved] of war as an option . . . [but] 59% of Americans said they believed the president should give the United Nations more time [and] 63% said Washington should not act without the support of its allies." More startling was that President Bush's "overall job approval rating [was then] down to 54% from 64% just a month [earlier, or at] the lowest level since the summer before the September 11, 2001 attacks."[106] Still, American-led forces invaded Iraq on March 19, 2003, complete with over six hundred "embedded" reporters relaying back jerky, real-time video images from the battlefield to an average audience of seven million on CNN, MSNBC, and the Fox News Channel combined, up from their usual joint total of two million.[107]

The "shock and awe" campaign unleashed on Iraq was also a made-for-TV spectacle designed as much to win audience approval as it was the war on the ground. During the first six months after 9/11, the Bush administration and the American people harmoniously embraced a "just war" scenario in Afghanistan. Television was the pivotal forum on which this tacit agreement between government policy and public consensus was reached. Now, a year and a half later, TV was again the most prominent medium on which to see a replay of the

American-led forces invaded Iraq on March 19, 2003. Exactly three weeks later, on April 9, CNN presented live coverage of a statue of Iraqi President Saddam Hussein being torn down in Firdos Square in downtown Baghdad. Courtesy of UPI/Landov.

"just war" story line—only this time there was far less agreement between the Bush administration and the American people, leading inevitably and inexorably to the highly contentious and controversial war in Iraq.

John Rossant, the European editor for *Business Week*, wrote on the one-year anniversary of 9/11 that "already that crystal-clear September morning is fast becoming an historical memory, the way some of us still remember a November day in 1963 when gunning down a young American president seemed to mark the end of one age and the beginning of another. We sense that history will divide into 'before September 11' and 'after.'"[108] Scholar Barbie Zelizer similarly pointed to the Kennedy assassination as a shared milestone for an earlier generation, reassessing how journalists had used that tragic event at the time to promote their own agendas and shape collective memory.[109] Many subsequent politicians, social commentators, authors, and artists have revisited the Kennedy shooting from a wide variety of perspectives over the past five decades. So, too, was the way in which 9/11 and its aftermath were already being used on television—and is likely to continue to be used by all sorts of vested interests in the future.

A case in point was the $10 million made-for-TV docudrama *DC 9/11: Time of Crisis*, which premiered on Sunday, September 7, 2003, and played in heavy rotation on Showtime throughout the remainder of the month. Produced by journeyman writer-director Lionel Chetwynd, *DC 9/11* re-creates the first nine days after the terrorist attacks from the perspective of being inside Bush's newly ordained war cabinet. Paul Fahri of the *Washington Post* notes that "Chetwynd is among the few outspokenly conservative producers in Hollywood, and one of the few with close ties to the White House." His depiction of President Bush was therefore unabashedly hagiographic in a script he wrote and later ran "past a group of conservative Washington pundits, including Fred Barnes, Charles Krauthammer, and Morton Kondracke."[110]

The climactic scene of *DC 9/11* involves actor Timothy Bottoms portraying George W. Bush as he presumably delivers his prime-time September 20th address to a joint session of Congress. Shots of Bottoms orating before a podium are intercut with emotionally stirring documentary footage of 9/11, culminating in a real shot of President Bush finishing this very same televised speech on the actual occasion. All told, Chetwynd and his production crew frame events in *DC 9/11* in order to authenticate and legitimize Bush as America's chief executive. They dramatize his performance as president—fully supported by an able and gifted cabinet of advisors—thus reenacting their shared handling of the unprecedented challenges surrounding September 11, 2001. If only 9/11 had unfolded as simply and heroically as this television depiction. In *Media Representations of September 11*, sociologists Steven Chermak, Frankie Y. Bailey, and Michelle Brown describe how 9/11 "has been narrativized by way of the media into a primary, recognizable discourse, one with a distinct logic—a clear beginning (September 11, 2001), forceful middle (war), and moral end (victory)."[111] During the first six months after 9/11, in particular, Americans mostly saw and heard only one side of the story transmitted through their TV sets. Problems eventually arose when developments on the ground did not seamlessly correspond with the official version of things as presented by the Bush administration spokespersons.

Probably the clearest example of this growing disconnect between the Bush team's framing of events and the ensuing media coverage is the president's carefully choreographed May 1, 2003, arrival on the deck of the U.S.S. *Abraham Lincoln* off the coast of San Diego, California, in an S-3B Viking aircraft to announce the allied victory in the war with Iraq. On that bright sunny day, the president was dressed in a green flight suit with a helmet tucked underneath his arm as he stood smartly before TV cameras with a giant "Mission Accomplished" banner in the background. Even at the time, the transparency of casting President Bush as the lead character in such an obvious made-for-television photo opportunity was criticized.

Within months, however, more direct press attacks surfaced on all of the major broadcast and cable news networks because of the continuing violence in Iraq and the failure to find any weapons of mass destruction. For instance, prominent CNN correspondent Christiane

Amanpour admitted on the Wednesday, September 10, 2003, edition of CNBC's *Topic A with Tina Brown* that "I'm sorry to say that, but certainly television—and perhaps to a certain extent my station—was intimidated by the administration and its foot soldiers at Fox News. And it did, in fact, put a climate of fear and self-censorship, in my view, in terms of the kinds of broadcast work we did."[112] The situation was further exacerbated on Thursday, October 23, when President Bush told reporters on camera that the "Mission Accomplished" sign was conceived by the Navy, not the White House. New press secretary Scott McClellan needed to qualify his boss's statement a week later when journalists found out otherwise.[113]

New incongruities soon surfaced in other entertainment and news programming. On Sunday, November 9, 2003, for example, NBC premiered an "unofficial dramatization" called *Saving Jessica Lynch*, a made-for-TV movie that was clearly titled in such a way as to echo Steven Spielberg's heroic World War II epic *Saving Private Ryan* (1998). Two days later, on Veteran's Day, the real Jessica Lynch spoke to Diane Sawyer in an exclusive ABC *Primetime Live* interview. She began by telling Sawyer: "I am not a hero. I'm just a survivor," referring to "when American forces were bogged down in the war's early days [and] she was the happy harbinger of an imminent turnaround: a 19-year-old female Rambo who tried to blast her way out of the enemy's clutches."[114] "They used me to symbolize all this stuff," Lynch confided to an audience of nearly sixteen million viewers, concluding with surprising frankness that "it's wrong."[115]

Then on April 28, 2004, CBS's *60 Minutes II* telecast a prime-time report featuring photographic evidence that documented Iraqi prisoner abuse by U.S. military personnel at Abu Ghraib prison, a facility previously run by Saddam Hussein's regime where dissidents were routinely tortured and executed. Correspondent Dan Rather interviewed Brigadier General Mark Kimmitt by satellite from Baghdad on the Army's three-month investigation, asking him to comment on a handful of pictures that CBS News had acquired, including the image of a hooded man standing scarecrow-like on a box with his arms extended as electrodes dangled from his fingers. "The first thing I'd say is we're appalled," admitted Kimmitt, who was chief military spokesperson for the Coalition Provisional Authority in Iraq: "This is wrong. This is reprehensible. But this is not representative of the 150,000 soldiers that are over here."[116] Despite Kimmitt's strong condemnation, though, there was no way to stop this photograph and other related pictures from being widely circulated on the Internet. Within twenty-four hours, these images were also seen on "the front page of newspapers and the lead story on television all over the world." More than a year later, cultural historian Melani McAlister concluded that "the damage done by the Abu Ghraib photographs to the reputation of the United States in the Arab world was incalculable."[117]

On the three-year anniversary of the 9/11 terrorist attacks, in fact, TV throughout the Middle East from Syria and Iran to Egypt, Saudi Arabia, and Jordan "showed programs that were very sympathetic to the American people, but very critical of the way President Bush's administration [was] handling the war on terrorism."[118] The relationship between the United States and the Arab world had always been complicated, but it grew even more so in the immediate wake of 9/11. Then-Secretary of State Colin Powell turned to Madison Avenue to blanket the region with "pro-American advertising," including "a series of TV spots featuring smiling Muslim Americans." Concerned with growing anti-Americanism throughout the Middle East, Powell said that "the goal . . . was nothing less than to 'rebrand American foreign policy.'" Characteristic of the transition from a niche to a personal-usage market mentality, nation-branding had become a common strategy in the Digital Era "to improve tourism, investment, or even foreign relations."[119]

After the rush to war in Iraq, the absence of any weapons of mass destruction, and the Abu Ghraib scandal, however, a perception gap deepened between the reality on the ground and the U.S. claims of spreading freedom and democracy all over the region. America's current image problems stemmed directly from its recent unilateralist policies, as well as the longer-standing, more systematic sociopolitical problems in the Middle East, such as widespread instability in Afghanistan after the Soviet war ended in 1989, the unresolved and chronic nature of the conflict between Israel and Palestine, the United States' steadfast support of Israel and its military presence in Saudi Arabia, the failure of most domestic economies in the Arab world to adequately provide job opportunities for their young adult male populations, and the profound economic, technological, and cultural changes wrought by globalization over the last generation.

Television programming from the United States still plays an essential part in how countries throughout the Middle East make sense of "brand America."[120] Besides Arabic, English-language networks and shows are widely available to over thirty million DBS-TV households in the region. Both free-to-air and pay-TV services have flourished since the mid 1990s, including the Orbit Satellite Television Network (with a package of thirty-nine channels) and Showtime Arabia (with Showtime, MTV Europe, MTV India, TV Land, Disney Channel Middle East, Cartoon Network Middle East, Nickelodeon Middle East, Discovery Channel Middle East, CNN International Europe, and Sportsnet

America, as well as thirty-three other channels). Television series such as *The Cosby Show*, *Friends*, *Oprah*, *Survivor*, and *Desperate Housewives* are among hundreds of U.S. programs that have been regularly telecast and consumed throughout the region over the past decade, reflecting "many of the appealing themes and myths of the United States itself: individuality, wealth, progress, tolerance, and optimism." For religious conservatives, though, American television programming "is still the noisy electronic spawn of the Great Satan, undermining traditional values and encouraging wickedness." When the Taliban took control of Afghanistan in 1996, for instance, they began by ending all local TV broadcasts, "but people continued to watch videotapes and foreign television channels on satellite dishes." In July 1998, the Taliban militia then ordered that the "nation's citizens get rid of their TVs, video players and satellite receivers. Such goods were deemed morally unacceptable by the Department for the Prevention of Vice and Promotion of Virtue."[121]

The war of ideas is also being waged on competing satellite news networks throughout the Middle East, including CNN International, BBC News, Euronews, and now three Arabic-language channels: the Qatar-based Al Jazeera (meaning "the island" or "the peninsula"), the Dubai-based Al Arabiya ("the Arab one"), and the U.S.-sponsored Al Hurra ("the free one"). According to Linda Tischler, "although it has been around since 1996, the original Arabic-language Al Jazeera first registered on most Americans' radar after September 11, when the station began beaming up images from inside Taliban-controlled Kabul." Al Jazeera is funded by the emir of Qatar, and the network presently reaches a worldwide audience of approximately fifty million people.[122] The Saudi-owned Al Arabiya was established as a more moderate alternative to Al Jazeera in 2003, while the Bush administration launched its own Al Hurra channel in 2004 as part of the government's all-out effort to rehabilitate its damaged image all over the region.

Only a decade and a half earlier, *The Cosby Show* was literally the "greatest show on earth," spreading its distinctly Western view of progressive family values, personal freedom, and racial and ethnic tolerance. Emerging hand in hand with the secular cosmopolitan culture that *The Cosby Show* epitomized was a fast-growing fundamentalist backlash from the guardians of tradition in virtually every region on earth, not just the Middle East. In a sense, the so-called culture wars that racked North America and Western Europe during the 1980s and early 1990s were now a global phenomenon, but with one significant difference—much of the current international fundamentalism was based above all else on religious orthodoxy. Moreover, these "culture wars" were proving far more violent worldwide than they ever were in the postindustrial West. September 11 and its aftermath were the clearest examples yet of America's increasing interdependence with the rest of the world and its subsequent vulnerability to the inevitable aftershocks that followed the arrival and spread of globalization.

11

Timothy J. Havens

THE GREATEST SHOW ON EARTH

The Cosby Show and the Ascent of U.S. Sitcoms in the Global Television Marketplace

The Cosby Show (1984–1992) was one of a rare, and probably now extinct, breed of American television series that captured and held the attention of vast audiences from nearly every walk of life for year after year of its prime-time run. The show attracted more viewers than any series in television history, reaching more than sixty-three million Americans in the 1986–1987 season and posting Nielsen ratings that had not been seen since *Bonanza*'s 1964–1965 season. *The Cosby Show* also made more money than any previous series, netting over $1 billion in domestic syndication sales and close to $1 billion in ad revenues for NBC during its eight years in prime time. Most observers agree that, in today's multichannel universe, with audience segments breaking up into smaller and smaller niches served by specialized programming, the days of blockbuster hits like *The Cosby Show, All in the Family* (1971–1979), *The Beverly Hillbillies* (1962–1971), and *Laverne & Shirley* (1976–1983) are gone forever. Nevertheless, the influence of *The Cosby Show* on the culture and the business of American television has long outlived the series itself.[1]

The story behind the creation of *The Cosby Show* is one of those quintessentially Hollywood tales of a creative person who overcomes hardships in the pursuit of a dream and whose perseverance is finally rewarded with success. Bill Cosby's initial idea for a television situation comedy about an intact African American family featured him as a janitor and his wife as a construction worker. But after a visit with television producers Marcy Carsey and Tom Werner, everyone agreed that the show should be set in upper-middle-class surroundings. Cosby shopped his idea to CBS and ABC, the top two networks at the time, but both passed on the series because of Cosby's poor track record in prime-time series and the fact that situation comedies had all but disappeared from the network schedules of the early 1980s. While Cosby's first prime-time series, *I Spy* (1965–1968), had been successful and his Saturday morning cartoon *Fat Albert and the Cosby Kids* (1972–1979) drew strong audiences, he had had several prime-time flops in a row, including *The Bill Cosby Show* (1969–1971), *The New Bill Cosby Show* (1972–1973), and *Cos* (1976). Eventually, the NBC network, which had spent nine years at the bottom of the network ratings, agreed to gamble on the show. The first episode, starring Bill

Cosby as obstetrician Heathcliff Huxtable and Phylicia (Allen) Rashad as his attorney wife Clair, aired on September 20, 1984, and the show almost immediately shot to the top of the ratings.[2]

The accomplishments of *The Cosby Show* are almost too numerous to list. The show rewrote the manual on how African Americans could and should be represented on television. Along with its perennial partner *Family Ties* (1982–1989), *The Cosby Show* helped lift NBC from last place in the network ratings to the top position for six straight years. It also single-handedly put an unknown production company, Carsey-Werner, on the Hollywood map, where it immediately became one of the most respected producers of ensemble situation comedies. Industry insiders credit the series with resurrecting the situation comedy genre, which had all but disappeared in a flood of prime-time soap operas in the early 1980s. And, the show's distributor, Viacom, made television history when it required local television stations around the country to bid for the privilege of rerunning the series.[3]

While *The Cosby Show*'s importance in American television history has been well documented, critics and scholars have paid little attention to the series' international success. Still, it became as popular with international viewers as it was with American viewers and was exported to more than seventy countries. Throughout the 1980s, *The Cosby Show* consistently topped the ratings in Canada, Australia, and New Zealand, and it was the most popular American import in nations across Europe, beating out previous international favorites like *Dallas* (1978–1991), *Dynasty* (1981–1989), and *The A-Team* (1983–1987). This series was a certifiable international hit, and its success changed the business of international television trade. Ironically, though *The Cosby Show* is remembered in the United States for demonstrating that a sitcom featuring a nuclear, upper-middle-class African American family could be popular, in international circles the show primarily paved the way for an increased exportation of white American sitcoms.

THE CHANGING ROLE OF INTERNATIONAL SALES

Before recounting *The Cosby Show*'s international success, it is helpful to understand the connections between domestic and international television distribution that existed in the United States in the mid 1980s and early 1990s, the prime years of *The Cosby Show*'s international success. American television producers and distributors became more and more dependent on international sales revenues during this time period due to changes in the domestic television industry and the explosion in commercial channels across Europe. Throughout the 1980s, the American broadcast networks—ABC, NBC, and CBS—saw a steady drop in their audience shares, as new cable networks sprang up, cable spread into more and more homes, and Twentieth Century-Fox cobbled together several formerly independent television stations into a fledgling new network—Fox. Consequently, the networks became more and more sensitive about operating costs, including the license fees that they paid to production companies for the rights to broadcast prime-time series.

Since 1970, the major networks had been prohibited from owning most of the television programs they broadcast during prime time by the Federal Communications Commission's (FCC) Financial Interest and Syndication Rules (Fin-Syn). As a result, Hollywood studios and independent production companies unaffiliated with the networks produced almost all prime-time television. For example, Viacom International held both the domestic and international distribution rights to *The Cosby Show* from 1984 through 1995, when Carsey-Werner repurchased the rights. In essence, the Fin-Syn rules forbade the networks from profiting from domestic syndication, which are sales made to local television stations across the country that then rerun popular networks series outside of prime time.[4]

Domestic syndication has long been the "Holy Grail" of television program sales, offering profits that dwarf the license fees paid by the networks. This fact led to the still common practice of "deficit financing," where networks pay only a portion of the costs of production in return for rights to air a series during prime time, after which producers sell the series in syndication, securing their profits over the long term. However, getting a series into domestic syndication can be difficult because local stations typically want at least three years' worth of episodes so that they can "strip" schedule the series Monday through Friday at the same time. By the mid 1980s, fears about diminishing audiences and the loss of advertising revenues led the networks to pull series off their prime-time schedules quicker than ever, thus threatening producers' syndication revenues. Meanwhile, producers' costs were skyrocketing, leading many to seek out international sales revenues to help recoup costs in the years before domestic syndication.[5]

Although American companies had been distributing programming internationally since the 1960s, it was only in the mid to late 1980s that these markets became crucial sources of revenue. One of the main reasons behind this change in production financing owed to the worldwide explosion of channels and broadcast hours due to new satellite and cable delivery systems, broadcast deregulation, and the privatization of public broadcasting channels worldwide. Very often, these start-up channels relied on cheap imported programming in their first few years, often increasing their use of more costly local productions only after they had gathered an audience and turned a profit. In Europe, the largest market for American television exports, the number of television channels grew nearly twentyfold between 1984 and 1996.[6]

The deregulation of broadcasting throughout the 1980s, particularly in Europe and Asia, also helped usher in this wave of new channels, as countries where one or two public channels had previously dominated the airwaves opened to commercial broadcast competition. In response, many public channels were sold to commercial interests, while some others that remained in public hands had to compete for viewers with the commercial channels, leading to their increased use of imported American programming for reasons of economics and viewer popularity. By the late 1980s, then, American producers had come to rely on international sales to help defray production deficits associated with network series. In 1987, William Saunders, an executive vice president at Twentieth Century-Fox, commented on the rapidly changing importance of international revenues: "Three or four years ago, any money that came in from international, we'd say, 'Oh, that's nice.' Now it's a very important part of the budget process."[7]

VIACOM AND THE SELLING OF *THE COSBY SHOW*

The Cosby Show's international popularity coincided with the changing importance of international sales for American companies. A close examination of Viacom's international marketing strategies reflects both this change and the growing recognition that, against conventional industry wisdom at the time, situation comedies could achieve popularity on the international markets.

Viacom was created in the wake of the FCC's Fin-Syn rules, when CBS spun off its syndication wing into a separate company. By the mid 1980s, however, Viacom's library of earlier CBS hits such as *The Mary Tyler Moore Show* (1970–1977) was aging, and the company was on the lookout for new programming. Before finding *The Cosby Show*, its previous efforts had netted only such forgettable shows as *Dear Detective* (1979) and *The Lazarus Syndrome* (1979), though the company also held the rights to some B-movies and *Perry Mason* specials. Therefore, when Carsey-Werner ran into trouble financing *The Cosby Show*'s high budgets, Viacom agreed to pump in extra funds in return for the right to distribute the show worldwide.[8]

Observers estimate that *The Cosby Show* never earned more than $100 million in international revenues. While this figure pales in comparison with the more than $1 billion the series brought in from domestic syndication, it still represents wide international appeal, given that international buyers paid significantly less than their domestic counterparts for the rights to air the series. In addition, when *The Cosby Show* soared to the no. 1 spot in the United States, Viacom was unable to recoup its investment until 1987, when enough episodes had been produced for domestic syndication. For three years, then, international sales offered the only revenues from the series while the company awaited domestic syndication profits. In fact, in 1987 Viacom reported $770 million in unfulfilled domestic distribution contracts, owing chiefly to revenues from *The Cosby Show* that it was unable to collect because the show had not yet reached a sufficient number of episodes.[9]

It is difficult to say with certainty the precise revenues that Viacom received from selling rights to *The Cosby Show* internationally, but a close examination of the company's financial reports from the time give us a good sense of how profitable the show was. In the first two years of the show's run, revenues from foreign exports remained steady or fell slightly, but from 1986 until 1989, exports grew between 12.2 percent and 29.3 percent, totaling more than $20 million by decade's end. Of course, not all of these revenues can be attributed to sales of *The Cosby Show*, but the series was certainly the most popular international property owned by Viacom at the time.[10] *The Cosby Show* far outperformed any of its domestic competitors in international sales. *Family Ties*, for instance, occasionally challenged *The Cosby Show* for the top-rated position in the U.S. market and was also sold internationally by Paramount Pictures. While the quality of the writing and acting in *Family Ties* rivaled that of *The Cosby Show*, and many remember the series as *The Cosby Show*'s "white obverse,"[11] *Family Ties* achieved only lackluster international sales.

Viacom's international distribution strategy for *The Cosby Show* is likewise difficult to reconstruct. In all likelihood, the strategy was mostly opportunistic and haphazard, rather than carefully planned, due to low expectations for the series in international markets. We can see these low expectations reflected in the way Viacom advertised its programming in *TV World*, one of the main international television trade journals at the time. In 1984 and 1985, the company's slogan, "the world turns to Viacom for great drama," was repeated in several advertisements for drama programming, especially the miniseries *Peter the Great* (1986). The first mention of *The Cosby Show* came in a February 1985 advertisement promoting four series—*Me and Mom*

(1985), *Star Games* (1985), *Peter the Great*, and *The Cosby Show*—in which mention of *The Cosby Show* is buried at the end of the second paragraph of copy.[12] Obviously, Viacom did not view the show as a lucrative international commodity at the time.

Most of the international sales in 1984 and 1985 were to either Scandinavian or non-European general entertainment television networks. These markets were still dominated by one or two public broadcast networks that had low revenues and, consequently, paid low license fees for imported programs. In Denmark and the Netherlands, the state broadcasters reported that *The Cosby Show* was the top-rated import in 1986. In South Africa, where the show consistently ranked no. 1, the state broadcasting authority began airing the show in 1985 on a newly introduced channel that targeted a broad audience, unlike the existing channels that served specific ethnic or racial groups. The monopoly socialist television network in Poland reported that the show was popular in the fall of 1986. State-run channels in Israel and Lebanon likewise reported in 1988 that the series had been an unqualified success for more than a year.[13] Because these were not primary international markets for American distributors, it would have been easy for Viacom's executives not to notice the show's popularity in these territories, or to write off the popularity as little more than a curiosity.

Slowly, the growing success of *The Cosby Show* in international markets began to sink in at Viacom, particularly as a handful of larger European territories started broadcasting the show. In these increasingly lucrative and competitive territories, the show performed best in newly commercializing markets at small television stations. The show flopped in Belgium in 1985, where it was carried on the state broadcast system before commercial television was introduced. In Italy, which had had pervasive, if illegal, private television since the mid 1970s, the show performed well on private station Canale 5 from 1985 onward. The public television network in Spain broadcast the show in 1988, but no information identifies how long the series ran or how popular it was.

France's M6, a theme channel dedicated to popular entertainment, began programming the show in 1988, soon after private television broadcasting became legal, and continued with good ratings for at least six years. In the United Kingdom, meanwhile, the series began airing in 1985 on Channel 4, a commercial broadcaster aimed at affluent viewers. While the series achieved only a "cult following" of between two and three million viewers per episode, it was one of the top-rated shows on Channel 4 and received high Appreciation Scores, which measure viewers' levels of enjoyment. Finally, in Germany, the public broadcaster ZDF began broadcasting the series in 1987, but it did not develop much of a following until it moved to the commercial broadcaster Pro7 in 1989.[14]

Viacom's growing awareness of *The Cosby Show*'s European popularity, combined with the promise of new, private channels across the continent that would require cheap American imports to fill out their broadcast schedules, led the company to take a more aggressive approach to promoting the show. By 1986, Viacom reported sales of *The Cosby Show* in more than sixty countries. In February 1986, the company felt it financially worthwhile to take out a full-page ad for the show in *TV World* announcing that the domestically renowned series was available for international distribution. By November 1986, we find a full-page ad announcing that *The Cosby Show* is "the world's newest superpower" and claiming that the show "has transcended language and culture." Although the show had overcome non-European languages and cultures before this ad was published, sales to Western European markets provided the catalyst for Viacom's revised international marketing strategy and somewhat hyperbolic claims. However, international sales revenues remained tiny in comparison with domestic sales, even in the largest foreign markets, in part because many of the channels that bought the show had selective audiences rather than general audiences that can fetch higher advertising revenues. U.K.'s Channel 4 reportedly paid between £10,000 and £15,000 per episode ($16,000–$23,000 in 1990 dollars), while France's M6 paid between 20,000 and 30,000 French francs per episode ($3,000–$4,500 in 1990 dollars). Domestic sales, meanwhile, amounted to more than $4 million per episode.[15]

Why did Viacom have such low expectations for a series that had smashed so many domestic television records, especially considering that other top-rated American series such as *Dallas* and *Dynasty* had recently performed remarkably well abroad? The answer lies in *The Cosby Show*'s programming genre and the generally low opinion of the international marketability of situation comedies at the time.

Despite the importance of international sales revenues for domestic production funding, considerable uncertainty exists among executives about which kinds of programming will appeal to which audience in which territories. Up to the mid 1990s, these uncertainties were exacerbated by a virtual absence of international ratings data. Uncertain sales revenues profoundly influence the pricing of international programs, distributors' efforts to promote those programs, buyers' attitudes toward them, and the sales revenues that specific programs generate from international markets. Consequently, a good deal of industry lore circulates among international executives about the kinds of programming that can and cannot "travel," based on past experiences, conjecture, and efforts to identify similarities among international hits.

One of the most pervasive ways of thinking about television programs, among industry executives, critics, and audiences alike, is in terms of genre. Genres are program types—such as game shows, police dramas, and soap operas—that help identify prominent characteristics shared by different television shows and the audiences that are likely to be attracted to those shows. In international television trade, it is generally accepted that some genres have a broader international appeal than others. Michael Solomon, formerly president of International Television at Warner Bros., explains that "soft pictures, cute romantic comedies are very hard to sell outside the United States. But if you have a suspense drama, an action-adventure-type drama, that sells abroad." Broadly speaking, action-adventure is considered the most universally appealing genre. As Dirk Zimmerman, former president of Group W Productions, puts it, "Car goes down the street, car makes the wrong turn, car blows up . . . everybody understands that."[16]

In the 1980s, conventional industry wisdom held that American situation comedies could not sell internationally, due to the culturally specific nature of comedy and the difficulties of translating verbal comedy into other languages. As a result, American sitcoms suffered from perceptions that they were "quintessentially American." Such American sitcom mega-hits as *All in the Family* and *Three's Company* (1977–1984), for instance, posted meager international sales, despite the fact that they were based on imported British series and consequently had a certain level of international cachet. While *M*A*S*H* (1972–1983) and *I Love Lucy* (1951–1957) had achieved international success before *The Cosby Show* arrived, they were seen as exceptions that proved the rule. As one trade journal article from the period begins, "Comedy doesn't travel, according to the experts."[17] Jim McNamara, a former president of worldwide television for MCA (currently Universal Pictures), estimated that, in the early 1980s, only about 5 percent of American situation comedies found international buyers.[18]

Regardless of the challenge of selling sitcoms internationally, the genre became increasingly popular in domestic syndication from the mid 1980s to the mid 1990s. Again, *The Cosby Show* had a central role in this trend, because its popularity spawned a number of imitators. In the domestic market, sitcoms attract desirable, young demographics; are easy for television stations to schedule because they last only thirty minutes; and retain more of their audience in reruns than any other genre. Therefore, American distributors found their libraries stocked with sitcoms in need of international buyers.[19]

By the mid 1990s, negative attitudes about the international marketability of situation comedies had been revised. As one commentator writes, "the old paradigm against the international appeal of sitcoms has changed. It's not that sitcoms don't work, it's that some kinds of sitcoms don't work."[20] Virtually every account credits *The Cosby Show* with a pivotal role in changing the one-time conventional wisdom that sitcoms didn't travel well in foreign markets.

The Global Appeal of *The Cosby Show*

Why did *The Cosby Show* draw international viewers like no sitcom in recent memory? Of course, the changes in the television industries across the globe outlined above help explain why the show might have appealed to the raft of upstart channels that began in the mid 1980s. But how did *The Cosby Show* achieve high levels of audience satisfaction in so many of the nations where it was telecast? The answer lies with the international viewers themselves.[21]

Although no comprehensive research into international viewers' reasons for watching *The Cosby Show* took place at the time, a number of newspaper articles did report viewers' attitudes in various parts of the world. A scholarly article about the show's reception in the Caribbean and a book that includes some written comments alongside numerical reports on viewers' satisfaction levels also give us glimpses into the kinds of pleasures that viewers may have gotten from watching the show.[22]

Unlike most shows before it, *The Cosby Show* presents a picture of a comfortably well off, upper-class African American family that faces few problems from the world outside its living room walls. Based on their discussions with numerous black and white American focus groups from across the socioeconomic spectrum, Sut Jhally and Justin Lewis in *Enlightened Racism* argue that the show strikes a politically conservative chord by failing to portray the economic and social hardships that so often constitute part of what it means to be black in the United States. The authors criticize the show for ignoring these thorny issues and leaving white viewers with the impression that African Americans no longer face economic barriers in American society, at the same time that it flatters African American viewers by avoiding traditional buffoon characters.[23] Whatever the reader may think of these arguments, the fact that *The Cosby Show* avoids most overt references to American economic hardships may have made the show more accessible to international viewers, who might have found such allusions unfamiliar and confusing.

The Cosby Show *presents a picture of a comfortably well off, upper-class African American family composed of* (left to right, bottom row) *Lisa Bonet as Denise, Bill Cosby as Dr. Heathcliff "Cliff" Huxtable, Keshia Knight Pulliam as Rudy, Phylicia Rashad as Clair Hanks Huxtable and* (left to right, top row) *Sabrina Le Beauf as Sondra, Tempestt Bledsoe as Vanessa, and Malcolm Jamal-Warner as Theodore "Theo." Courtesy of Library of American Broadcasting at the University of Maryland.*

When politics did surface on *The Cosby Show*, it mostly involved issues with long histories and international currency, such as civil rights, anti-apartheid, and education movements. In one episode, for instance, the family watched a rebroadcast of Martin Luther King Jr.'s illustrious "I Have a Dream" speech. Huxtable son Theo displayed an anti-apartheid poster on his bedroom door in the first several seasons. And the importance of education for personal and racial uplift, especially the role of historically black colleges and universities in educating African Americans, became a recurring theme in the series. Due to the long history of these political issues and their international visibility, international viewers would have found them much easier to understand than the kinds of flash-in-the-pan political issues that dominate series such as *Murphy Brown* (1988–1998) and *West Wing* (1999–2006).

The Huxtable family's economic status was also reflected in the allusions that the show made to high-class African American culture, rather than the hip-hop references that filled most African American sitcoms in the late 1990s and early 2000s. Episodes of the show often featured jazz, blues, and rhythm and blues music. Work by African American painters, many with black figures and scenes, decorated the living room walls. As Herman Gray points out, the series made accessible to viewers an African American upper-class lifestyle that had been around for centuries but rarely got noticed by popular culture. In fact, the main political work of the show was this effort to uncouple portrayals of African Americans from their prior connections with poverty and popular youth culture. In this way, the series was able to achieve a comparatively dignified depiction of African Americans, shorn of conventional reliance on black stereotypes, inner-city settings, and youth culture. Moreover, as Gray points out, through the use of African American high culture, it was impossible to treat the characters' race as "an object of derision and fascination."[24] Much like their African American counterparts, nonwhite viewers abroad appreciated and enjoyed the fact that show portrayed nonwhites with dignity rather than derision.

Despite the show's break with conventional popular images of African Americans, it nevertheless retained a good deal of physical humor, which has been prevalent in African American culture since the days of slavery.[25] For instance, in one episode, all of the family members perform a lip-synch pantomime of Ray Charles and the Raylettes' "Night Time Is the Right Time" to the delight of the Huxtable grandparents. Much of the humor derives from Bill Cosby's exaggerated facial expressions and reaction shots. In international markets, The Cosby Show's physical forms of comedy retained their humor because they were not based in verbal expressions that often lose their subtlety and effect in translation.

Finally, The Cosby Show tried to include something for every viewer in order to gather the entire family in front of the set at a time when cable channels were focused on fragmenting the family into demographic niches. Episodes frequently featured multiple story lines that highlighted family life, the romance between Cliff and Clair, the travails of teenage life with Denise and later Theo and Vanessa, and childhood with Rudy and later Olivia. Thus, viewers from a wide range of circumstances could find characters and plots that intersected with their own lives and interests. This kind of diversity extends beyond the borders of the United States as well, as we frequently see international characters and plots. Theo's math teacher Mrs. Westlake, for instance, is Portuguese. In the final episode, we discover that Denise is living in Singapore. As John Downing has written, these "aspects of international culture are part of the Huxtables' taken-for-granted world."[26] As such, we might expect the show to appeal more to international viewers than a series focused solely on a single slice of American life.

Black viewers from around the world responded well to the show's unique depiction of black dignity through the show's humor and the trope of African American high culture. Consider these comments from international black viewers:

> I like this show because it depicts black people in a positive way. I think [Cosby] is good. It's good to see that black people can be professionals.—United States[27]

> Black people in this show are not isolated, no fun is made of Blackness, and the characters are shown leading wholesome normal lives.—Barbados[28]

> The show makes me proud of being Black.—South Africa[29]

Obviously, in order to feel the racial pride that these viewers express, they need to share a belief that blacks have been historically ridiculed in white popular culture and that *The Cosby Show* is breaking with those traditions. In fact, these comments offer a good reminder that the international circulation of culture has been happening for centuries and is not a new feature of the electronic media age. Furthermore, the ridicule of blacks—and nonwhites in general—has been a part of that trade since the sixteenth century. Apparently, this fact has not escaped the attention of blacks worldwide.[30]

Black viewers also derived solace from the show's depiction of well-to-do African Americans. A black South African viewer says:

> *The Cosby Show* . . . is saying, "Come on you White guys [in South Africa], the Blacks are not so bad as you make them out to be. Look at us, we are having a good life and normal problems here in America. Give those guys down there a chance. Let's change for the better and live together, not apart."[31]

For this viewer, the show imagined a world free of racial violence, economic hardship, and political disenfranchisement. As John Downing has noted regarding domestic viewership, the setting of the show "is not simply a matter of blanking out the ugly realities of continuing oppression, but also offers some sense of resolution to the grinding realities of racial tension and mistrust in the United States."[32] It would seem the show offered similar solace to black viewers abroad.

Other nonwhite viewers expressed similar feelings of pride and hope watching *The Cosby Show*. Some Lebanese viewers thought that the Huxtables "came across as successful and smart, without having sold out to white culture." Another Lebanese viewer commented that, "American blacks are a little like us. They have big families."[33] Obviously, the first statement demonstrates that these viewers consider the maintenance of one's cultural identity a respectable goal, and the dignified portrayals of black high culture in the series signaled for them the family's refusal to "sell out." Furthermore, we see again the show's ability to create an idyllic world for these viewers, where cultural integrity and material plenty can go hand in hand. In fact, this comment reflects a recognition that material success for nonwhites worldwide is a dangerous proposition that has the potential to destroy local cultures. Certainly, we see evidence in both comments that the presence of African American actors and the ways in which blackness was linked with high culture and material success had an important role in these viewers' enjoyment of the show.

For some white viewers abroad, the race of the characters was also a part of *The Cosby Show*'s appeal. A Swedish journalist wrote, "the fact that [the Huxtables] are Black also plays into [the appeal of the show]. They are so much more attractive than White people."[34] While this comment is complimentary, it also reflects hundreds of years of libidinal preoccupation with black culture among whites. Black culture has long aroused fear and rebuke in white society, at the same time that whites have been intrigued by the perceived energy, sexuality, and naturalness of black culture. Most writers agree that this perception of black culture has more to do with what is repressed in white culture than what is actually present in black culture, and the fascination typically works to exacerbate differences and stereotype blacks as primitive.[35]

In a similar vein, a white South African viewer commented, "You'd be surprised what [Cosby] has meant to the Afrikaner. The Afrikaner doesn't mix with Black men. The television brings the Black man's quality right into his living room."[36] Again, while this viewer remarks positively about blacks, he still demonstrates a desire to experience black "difference" vicariously in the form of a nonthreatening sitcom. At least for some white viewers, the fact that *The Cosby Show* featured black actors was integral to their enjoyment of the show because it gave them a glimpse into the lifestyle of a group that has historically been defined as fundamentally different from them.

Not all viewers abroad considered race an important feature of *The Cosby Show*. For example, two very different reactions illustrate that, for some, the national origins of the show trumped the show's racial content. First, a pro-apartheid viewer in South African claimed:

> The greatest divide between Black and White in this country is
> not the color of one's skin but the First- and Third-World values
> and attitudes displayed by the different race groups. . . . Therefore,

we do not see *The Cosby Show* as being about Black people, but we
see it as a very entertaining sitcom displaying beliefs and values
we can associate with.[37]

For this viewer, *The Cosby Show* is primarily a Western show that ex-
tols American values, and the race of the characters is of lesser importance. In a similar vein, several of the Bahamian viewers that Monica
Payne interviewed for an article titled "The 'Ideal' Black Family? A Caribbean View of *The Cosby Show*" disliked the show because of its
American-ness. "The North American influence coming from the
show I believe to be detrimental on the whole," said one viewer. "Especially the norms of the children's behavior and their fashions I believe
have a negative effect on [Bahamian] youth."[38] Each of these comments is perhaps somewhat surprising and becomes comprehensible
only when we realize that the show was simultaneously black and
American.

As the foregoing overview of international audience responses to
The Cosby Show demonstrates, foreign viewers found a variety of pleasures in the series. The upper-middle-class domestic setting offered
admirable values for some and idyllic goals for others, while emptying
the series of controversial and parochial political issues. This setting
also provided the series with a transnational urban sensibility that international viewers could identify with. The dignified portrayals of
blackness, especially the series' allusions to African American high
culture and the absence of traditional stereotypes, appealed to nonwhite viewers worldwide, who share a history of stereotyping and ridicule at the hands of white Europeans. At the same time, some white
viewers around the world found the portrayal of a slice of black life different enough to be titillating, yet similar enough to be comforting.

In summary, perhaps the most masterful thing about the series
was its ability to please so many viewers in such different ways, without alienating others. Of course, not every viewer enjoyed the series,
but even the comments from those who disliked it are useful in helping us understand what kinds of messages international viewers saw
in the show. While we have no way to determine how widespread any
of these attitudes were at the time of the series' international broadcasts, or whether other kinds of responses were more common, the
similarities of some of these responses from different parts of the
world is striking. To what degree, then, did international television executives recognize these dimensions of the show's popularity abroad,
and how did the show's performance influence industry attitudes toward the situation comedy in general and African American sitcoms
in particular?

Television Executives Learn from *The Cosby Show*

By 1996, Jim McNamara at MCA (Music Corporation of America) estimated that the major U.S. studios (MGM, Twentieth Century-Fox, Paramount Pictures, Sony Pictures, Universal Pictures, Walt Disney, Warner Bros.) found international buyers for about 70 percent of their situation comedies, up from only 5 percent in the early 1980s. McNamara wasn't alone in his assessment. Lisa Gregorian, former vice president of marketing and research for Warner Bros. International Television, commented, "I think, in general, comedies have a much more significant place on the international (broadcaster's) schedules than they once did 10 years ago." Tony Lynn, a former executive vice president of international television at MGM/UA, also agreed that "American comedies [became] accepted in international broadcast during the eighties."[39]

The main international trade journals carried several feature articles in the early and mid 1990s addressing the revised notions in the industry about the international popularity of American sitcoms, almost all of which cite *The Cosby Show* as pivotal in turning around executives' opinions. The primary change that the series helped usher in was a belief that family-based situation comedies could be successful internationally. While other series—including *Full House* (1987–1995), *Fresh Prince of Bel-Air* (1990–1996), *Family Matters* (1989–1998),

The Cosby Show's "universal" family themes allowed the show to overcome cultural barriers of nation, race, and language to become the "greatest show on earth." Courtesy of Carsey-Werner Productions/Heldref.

and *Golden Girls*—also contributed to the rethinking of the genre, *The Cosby Show* was the earliest and most successful example of the trend.[40]

Virtually every international television executive seems to agree that *The Cosby Show*'s "universal" family themes allowed the show to overcome cultural barriers of nation, race, and language. For instance, the following are strikingly similar explanations for the success of the series:

> *The Cosby Show* was a universal hit. It was conveying universal values of family and generosity. One might think that this guy was typically American, but he was not thought of as such around the world.—Arthur Dela, former chair of Paris-based Arathos, owner of satellite systems in Eastern and Central Europe[41]

> *The Cosby Show* . . . is such a universal experience of a man trying to raise children. . . . These are like universal issues of family.— Vice president of international television at a major Hollywood distributor

> [*The*] *Cosby* [*Show*] is universal. . . . It's not just purely a black comedy with black actors. It's a comedy that reaches out to all cultures and generations because the problems they face are general problems that everyone faces every single day.—Jeff Ford, controller of acquisitions at U.K. Channel 5

> What travels is [*The*] *Cosby* [*Show*]. It's universal, I mean, it has nothing to do with America. Things that happen in every household, it happens in *Cosby* as well.—Frank Mulder, director of program acquisitions and sales, NOS, a Dutch public broadcasting consortium[42]

While these comments may be accurate, international audience research is underdeveloped in many territories, and even the most advanced ratings data do not tell us why viewers watch a particular series—only that they watch. Furthermore, the investigations that have been conducted into why viewers around the world enjoyed the show almost uniformly identified racial and national identities as important.

One striking element of executives' comments about *The Cosby Show* is how similar they are to many white American viewers' comments that the Huxtable family didn't come across as black.[43] There were two reasons for this. First, as discussed here, the show did not depict African American culture in the same way as its predecessors, but through allusions to African American high culture. Second, because the show extolled strong middle-class values in an upper-middle-class setting, many middle-class white viewers could easily identify. In many ways, the interpretation of *The Cosby Show* among white television executives from the United States and Europe mirrored those of white American viewers. For example, several executives referred to the show as either "white" or "not black":

> The black sitcoms we've been involved in have been the Cosbys. And that's not a black sitcom.—Herb Lazarus, president of Carsey-Werner International

> The reason [for the success of] shows like . . . *Cosby* . . . is the fact that a lot of them are very white.—Director of international research at a major Hollywood distributor

> The black sitcom works best if it's, let's say, as white as possible, which is surely the case with *The Cosby Show*.—European television buyer[44]

In each of these comments, executives are misinterpreting the absence of allusions to popular youth culture and poverty as an absence of African American culture in the series. By calling the series "white," these executives deny the presence and importance of African American elements in the show, at the same time that they implicitly suggest that truly "black" shows lack the appropriate focus on family themes and settings that situation comedies need in international trade. Moreover, this category of experience is explicitly defined as "white."

The Cosby Show, in retrospect, seems to have done more to facilitate the export of white American sitcoms than it did for black American sitcoms. First, industry executives misinterpreted the show's depiction of an upper-middle-class African American lifestyle as a depiction of white American culture. Second, most African American series are targeted at teenagers and young adults, because it is thought that viewers of all races in this age group readily "cross over" racial lines in their consumption of television and popular culture. Consequently, most African American situation comedies produced today target this demographic with youth-oriented settings, themes, plots, and characters rather than the kinds of domestic themes and plots that executives consider suited for international sales.

The point of these observations is not to criticize television executives for their inherent racial biases. All human beings carry with them a complex web of cultural assumptions, experiences, and blind spots that color the way they understand various phenomena. International television executives are no different. The difference is that their cultural worldviews shape the flow of popular culture around the globe.

THE COSBY SHOW'S CONTINUING INFLUENCE IN THE GLOBAL TELEVISION Marketplace

The Cosby Show helped establish the belief among international television executives that some American situation comedies focused on middle-class family issues can overcome worldwide cultural differences and become successful. Even more impressive is the fact that the show seemed to accomplish this feat without a great deal of promotion on the part of its distributor, Viacom, which, instead, considered the series' international sales prospects to be marginal due to prevalent attitudes at the time about situation comedies. Published audience comments suggest that, much as in the domestic market, The Cosby Show's abilities to bring together different segments of the audience by refusing to alienate anyone were central to its appeal abroad. This capacity allowed the show to draw viewers from various national, racial, religious, and economic backgrounds as few television shows ever had.

What truly made The Cosby Show the greatest show on earth, however, was the combination of its capacity to speak to a broad cross section of viewers worldwide, along with its ability to serve the economic needs of a quickly internationalizing American television industry during the 1980s and 1990s. Between 1988 and 1998, revenues from sales to foreign television channels at the Hollywood majors nearly quadrupled, from less than $1 billion to nearly $4 billion.[45] Although conventional estimates suggest that perhaps as many as one billion people worldwide have seen an episode of I Love Lucy, making it perhaps the most watched series in American television history, it was distributed at a time when international sales meant very little to the domestic television industry. Consequently, the series had little influence on how international television operates.

The Cosby Show, meanwhile, aired during the most rapid period of television internationalization in history. Not only was the series key in revising prevailing attitudes toward the situation comedy genre among international television professionals at a time when sitcoms were becoming more numerous in the domestic market, it also gave rise to the now common practice of figuring international sales revenues into domestic production budgets for situation comedies from the outset.

Today, television executives must consider a sitcom's international sales potential before they are willing to sink a great deal of money into a project. *The Cosby Show* also demonstrated that probably every top-rated American network series can find wide international appeal, regardless of its programming genre. Reasoning from the global popularity of *Dallas* and *Dynasty* before *The Cosby Show*, most television professionals believed that drama was the only television genre with strong international appeal. Nowadays, however, due to *The Cosby Show*'s clear demonstration that sitcoms, too, can be popular internationally, American distributors and international buyers alike assume that just about any top-rated American series will perform well with viewers abroad.

Although *The Cosby Show* revolutionized the financing and thinking of international television distribution, more profound insights about the global circulation of television programming went unnoticed by executives, specifically the fact that the national and racial origins of the characters were central to international viewers' enjoyment of the series. In the wake of *The Cosby Show*'s success, a handful of African American situation comedies began to achieve some notable international success. *Family Matters*, *Moesha* (1996–2001), and especially *The Fresh Prince of Bel-Air* achieved respectable—even impressive—sales within and beyond Europe. Lisa Gregorian of Warner Bros. International Television also identified the growing popularity of African American sitcoms in international television sales as a significant new trend, owing mainly to the success of *The Fresh Prince of Bel-Air*. "People say Cosby started this," she commented in 1997, "and he undoubtedly had a hand in it. But *Fresh Prince of Bel Air* broke the barriers of many territories that previously wouldn't have touched comedy like this."[46] In spite of Gregorian's observations, other executives have not echoed her words before or since. Instead, the main benefactors of the revised attitude that family-oriented sitcoms can sell well abroad have been such white series as *Roseanne* (1988–1997), *Home Improvement* (1991–1999), and *Sabrina, the Teenage Witch* (1996–2003), all of which performed strongly in European and Latin American markets. As a senior executive at one of the major Hollywood studios explained, "I think there is a general sense that if [a show] is too tied to the African American experience, then it won't work internationally."[47]

Why did television professionals discount race and national origin when discussing the reasons behind the series' global success? While this is a complex question, the fact that the United States is a predominantly white market that exports primarily to other mostly white markets is an important piece of the puzzle. In the mid to late 1980s, the two main industry organizations for American television and film exports—the Motion Picture Export Association and the American

Film Marketing Association—reported that more than 60 percent of their revenues came from European sales. Also among the "elite eight" nations that account for nearly three-quarters of U.S. audiovisual exports are the predominantly white nations of Canada and Australia. Because the primary U.S. network audience shares racial and class identities with the principal audiences in their most lucrative foreign markets, American television distributors have a strong incentive not to consider how *The Cosby Show*'s portrayals of blackness may have contributed to its international success, given that most of the programming they produce and sell addresses white characters and themes. Instead, it might be expected that distributors will vociferously deny that race was central to the popularity of *The Cosby Show* abroad, which in fact they did.[48]

While the idea that "universal family themes" underwrote *The Cosby Show*'s international success may seem plausible, it is based on liberal-humanist assumptions about cross-cultural trade that are, at the very least, debatable. "Classic humanism postulates that, in scratching the surface of the history of men a little . . . one very quickly reaches the solid rock of human nature," writes the French semiotician Roland Barthes; "progressive humanism, on the contrary, must always . . . scour nature, its 'laws' and its 'limits' in order to discover History there."[49] In other words, while it may be natural to assume that universal human experiences explain the global popularity of television series such as *The Cosby Show*, it is equally likely that viewers in different parts of the world find relevance in different aspects of imported series, depending on their society's relationship to imperialism, racism, capitalism, and so forth. However, as the assumption that all cultures have universal similarities is one of the dominant fictions of Western modernity, it is not surprising to find it running through the comments of Western television professionals. Moreover, because these professionals are in the business of selling their programming as widely as possible, they have good reason to promote the idea that all the world's cultures are basically the same.

Nevertheless, as the American television industry confronts an increasingly multicultural world, both at home and abroad, television professionals will have to rethink some of their most basic assumptions about the universal appeal of white, middle-class American values. As the greatest television show on earth to date, *The Cosby Show*'s international success offered television professionals a unique opportunity to learn about how worldwide differences in race and ethnicity are related to the circulation of popular television programming and the enjoyment that viewers derive from these imported television products. Too often, these lessons go largely unlearned.

12

TUNE IN LOCALLY, WATCH GLOBALLY
The Future of Television in the Age of the Internet

Through a Lens, Dimly

> We are the first generation to live in a global cosmopolitan society, whose contours we can as yet only dimly see.
> Anthony Giddens, *Runaway World*, 2000[1]

Globalization and the new media technologies that support it are relatively new phenomena. Anthony Giddens observes in *Runaway World: How Globalization Is Reshaping Our Lives* that "in the late 1980s the term [globalization] was hardly used, either in the academic literature or in everyday language. It has come from nowhere to be almost everywhere."[2] Globalization, in this regard, refers to a set of circumstances that have developed since the end of the Cold War. These conditions include the influence of electronic money on the global economy; the rise of multinational corporations (including the ascendancy of a relatively small number of mega-media conglomerates); and the shrinking of the earth through international commerce, travel, and the expansion of worldwide communication systems. Most contemporary analysts, such as Giddens, generally acknowledge that globalization was fueled first and foremost by economics. Still, he and other social commentators also recognize that globalization has profound cultural implications, influenced in large part by the same new media technologies, especially the Internet, that have redefined global markets and the world economy. "Globalization is political, technological and cultural, as well as economic," he continues; "it has been influenced above all by developments in systems of communication, dating back only to the 1960s."[3] Giddens is specifically referring to the more than two hundred orbital satellites currently carrying several television signals and tens of thousands of phone calls each, along with the unprecedented spread of the Internet since 1995 when travel over the World Wide Web (a hypertext-based information retrieval system) became a taken-for-granted part of everyday life for most Americans, as well as hundreds of millions of people around the world who were able to find and afford access.

Unlike any other medium before it, the Internet was global from the outset. Even though the roots of the Internet date back to the late

1960s, it wasn't until 1995 that it actually caught on with the general public in the United States when the World Wide Web became widely accessible through Netscape's graphical browser. From that point on, the Internet grew faster than any other communication medium in human history. As a comparison, radio took fifty years to be adopted by fifty million American households; television took twenty years; the personal computer, fifteen years; and the Internet, four years. By 1998, there were 175 million Internet hosts (networked computers) worldwide, and 67 percent of them were located in the United States (divided between both work sites and homes); by September 11, 2001, this number had risen to 430 million hosts, with 40 percent still in America, although this global imbalance was dropping annually.[4] Even though the United States remained the most connected country on earth in 2005 (with a 69 percent penetration rate), 35.6 percent of the hosts were then found in Asia; 28.5 percent in Europe; and only 22.2 percent in all of North America. The rest of the world was catching up to the Americans in this regard. By 2006, moreover, 1.22 billion people, or 15.7 percent of the global population (of 6.5 billion), were regular Internet users.[5] Twice that total were everyday television watchers as well. In 1962, the year that the first communication satellite Telstar 1 began transmitting TV and phone signals around the world, there was one television for every twenty human beings on earth; by 2000, there was one set for every four people with no foreseeable slowdown to the worldwide spread of TV in sight.[6] In addition, there were one billion television households worldwide in 2006, with just a little over 11 percent of these TV homes situated within the United States.[7]

Way back before the Network Era even began in 1945, science fiction writer and inventor Arthur C. Clarke first proposed in a *Wireless World* article that "television services in different parts of the world" could be linked by "extra-terrestrial relays." Clarke acknowledged that his suggestion may be "too far fetched to be taken seriously," but only thirty years later, at the dawn of the Cable Era, forty geosynchronous satellites were then orbiting the earth with another 160 DBSs (direct broadcast satellites) soon to be launched between 1976 and 1994.[8] In the interim, Congress had periodically flirted with rewriting the nearly obsolete Communication Act of 1934, and it finally got down to business during the early years of the Clinton administration. Al Gore became the president's chief spokesperson on the initiative, and he was prominently featured in a star-studded signing ceremony in the grand rotunda of the Library of Congress on February 8, 1996, that included media moguls Ted Turner of TBS and soon-to-be-partner Gerald Levin of Time Warner; various Democratic and Republican politicians; and a wide array of lobbyists, lawyers, and FCC regulators. Gore chatted amiably with comedian Lily Tomlin, who appeared via a video-and-voice Internet hookup as one of her signature characters, Ernestine, the wisecracking, gum-chewing telephone operator. Tomlin played Ernestine to the hilt, assuring the vice president that "he wasn't as stiff as he seemed. 'You're just a techno-nerd,' she snorted, as Mr. Gore politely thanked her."[9] To underscore the enormous technical, commercial, and sociocultural potential of the information superhighway—a nickname first given to the Internet by denizens of California's Silicon Valley during the late 1980s—"President Bill Clinton signed the Telecommunication Act of 1996 into law using the very pen President Dwight D. Eisenhower used in 1957 to authorize the interstate highways."[10]

This legislation, coupled with a robust economy, fueled a "television boom" throughout America and the rest of the world. The "dot-com frenzy" ushered in a wholesale transformation of TV in which the medium was reinvented yet again in the wake of the tsunami-like arrival and impact of the Internet.[11] In a nutshell, the Telecommunication Act of 1996 "unleash[ed] a 'digital free-for-all,' in the words of Representative Edward J. Markey, the Massachusetts Democrat who had been one of the lawmakers pushing for a communications overhaul since the late 1980s."[12] This legislation continued the deregulatory swing of the pendulum that had begun in the early 1980s at the start of the Reagan administration. Barriers between various telecommunication sectors—broadcasting, cable, local and long-distance telephone, and high-speed data transmission—were removed, allowing each segment of the industry to cross over commercially into the other (for example, a cable company could now provide TV, phone, and Internet service all by itself, and vice versa). The legislators intended to spur competition in order to increase the number of consumer choices (which occurred) while lowering prices (which didn't). Proprietary limits were also relaxed on the local level (allowing cross-ownership of television and radio stations along with newspapers), as well as on the national level (by upping the total coverage for TV group owners to 35 percent of the U.S. population instead of the previous 25 percent cap). Furthermore, all ownership restrictions on radio were lifted (resulting in the formation of mega-chains such as Clear Channel Communications, which grew from forty-three to twelve hundred radio stations in less than a decade).

Finally, the Telecommunication Act of 1996 mandated that the television industry develop its own program-rating system within a year (or the FCC would step in and create one for it); it required that all thirteen-inch and larger TV sets manufactured in the United States after 2000 be outfitted with a V-chip (a viewer-controlled computer chip that allows parents to block unwanted violent or sexually explicit content); and it outlawed all indecent Internet materials directed toward minors (a provision that was quickly struck down as unconstitutional by the U.S. Supreme Court in 1997).[13] In retrospect, the longer-term effect of the Telecommunication Act of 1996 had more to do with advancing the interests of the mega-media conglomerates and paving the way for the transition to digital television than it did in stimulating industry competition, lowering consumer costs, and cleaning up objectionable content of all kinds on the nation's TV and computer screens. The rush to industry consolidation had begun long before the passage of this legislation, but the mergers between Disney and Capital Cities/ABC and between Time Warner and Turner Broadcasting were literally being reviewed by a friendly FCC at the time of the signing ceremony, with approval of each a foregone conclusion. The government was essentially creating the conditions for big media in America to grow even bigger nationally, as well as globally. The year before, the FCC had also rescinded the twenty-three-year-old Financial Interest and Syndication (Fin-Syn) Rule, "thus allowing networks to own all or part of the programs they air and allowing studios to own TV networks." Almost simultaneously, Viacom "started UPN, Time Warner WB, Walt Disney bought Capital Cities/ABC, and Twentieth Century-Fox turned Fox Broadcasting into a full-fledged network."[14] Despite premature forecasts of television's ultimate demise, TV proved more resilient than ever during the Digital Era.[15]

The "traditional media" such as television are "not dead," asserted News Corporation president and CEO Peter Chernin in a 2006 *Wall Street Journal* editorial; "in fact, our companies [including Fox Broadcasting which he presided over in the late 1980s and early 1990s] are leading the charge into the networked digital future."[16] The climate that once encouraged independently owned TV production companies such as TAT Communications and MTM Enterprises was now an age-old vestige of a bygone era. Norman Lear had cashed out of TAT in 1985, and MTM Enterprises was acquired by religious broadcaster Pat Robertson's International Family Entertainment in 1993. After 1995, the traditional broadcast networks were back producing "more of their own shows," while the movie "studios [wanted] to guarantee distribution of their shows by buying and founding their own networks."[17] For the first time in a generation, the major broadcast networks in the United States were again vertically integrating, meaning they were producing their own shows, telecasting them on prime time, and then syndicating them at home and internationally with virtually no restrictions whatsoever. By 1998, for example, 30 percent of ABC's prime-time programming was now being created inside the Disney conglomerate, while 45 percent of Fox's series were originating within the News Corporation. By 2001, ABC was up to 50 percent in-house, and Fox was up to 62 percent. Before Viacom's acquisition of CBS in 1999, this network was already producing a comparatively high 60 percent of its own prime-time programming. Once the merger between these two corporations took place, however, that figure skyrocketed to 81 percent by 2001.[18] The Digital Era was both reinventing and reinvigorating the TV industry: "Movies may still have [had] the edge for glamour, but as a business television [dwarfed] feature films, even in America: with a total turnover of $100 billion [in 2002], it [was] around six times bigger."[19]

Seven General Tendencies of TV in the Digital Era

> The key to the future of television is to stop thinking about television as television. TV benefits most from thinking of it in terms of bits.
> Nicholas Negroponte, *Being Digital*, 1995[20]

Television was reinvented for the third time as a technology, an industry, and an institutional force with the coming of the Digital Era. The TV signal was now better, cheaper, faster, and more efficient than ever before because of its conversion into 1s and 0s (the binary code). No longer did it travel on analog radio waves over the air or through wires as it originally had during the Network and Cable Eras. Instead, TV's new digital reincarnation evolved at the speed of light into something akin to "anything, anytime, anywhere television."[21] This description implies that TV had grown more personal, adaptable, available, portable, and widespread than at any time in its history. Seven general tendencies emerged after 1995 to distinguish TV's extreme makeover in the Digital Era.

First, *television (like the Internet) was now global in context and cultural reach.* The development of a truly global television culture since the mid 1990s was profoundly affecting societies all over the world. Media sociologist Todd Gitlin and Norwegian communication scholars Helge Rønning and Knut Lundby suggested that the one-time dominance of U.S.-made popular culture—especially television—had resulted in a kind of "cultural bilingualism" where TV from the United States doesn't so much replace "indigenous cultures, but American products are [usually the] favorite second choice" of most people worldwide.[22] TV flourished in metropolitan centers in the Digital Era as cities grew faster than ever before, accounting for up to 50 percent of the global population by 2005.[23] In this way, people from New York to Buenos Aires to Tokyo to Johannesburg to Paris switched easily among franchised versions of MTV and *Sesame Street*, to reruns of *The Cosby Show* and *Friends*, to downloads of *CSI* and *Desperate Housewives*, to literally thousands of easily accessible and globally popular television-related websites and blogs. Such routine patterns of transnational reception are now taken for granted as part of global television culture in the 2000s, binding together (however tenuously) "the urban classes of most nations into a federated cultural zone."[24] *Sesame Street*, for instance, is now a global phenomenon, having been adapted into more than twenty international versions that are televised regularly in over 120 countries.

Second, *television and the Internet are highly compatible media.* The usual historical narrative that accompanies the arrival of any new mass medium is that the young upstart technology wages an all-out Darwinian assault on its predecessors for, first, survival and, then, outright supremacy in the communication marketplace. According to an earlier version of this scenario, TV was supposedly going to replace radio in the United States during the Network Era. Domestic radio did switch its emphasis from being more a local than a national medium in response to television's fast-growing rise from coast to coast throughout the 1950s. Nevertheless, radio in America was still thriving as a $21 billion industry in 2005 (although this capital valuation was admittedly less than 20 percent the size of TV at the time). That same year, though, radio also attracted 200 million listeners a week on average (or almost 69 percent of the population).[25] Likewise, many pundits have recently claimed that the Internet is destined to supplant television in households nationwide. For example, a 2004 survey conducted by the Pew Internet and American Life Project of 1,286 media experts found that 53 percent of those polled believed that the Internet would "replace television's central place in the home," resulting in TV's inevitable decline by 2014. "Predictions [about] the Internet are no more likely to come to pass than similar predictions made in the early years of television," cautions Jorge Reina Schement, director of the Institute for Information Policy at Penn State University.[26] Because of digital convergence, there is currently far more commingling than competition occurring between TV and the Internet. They share center stage as far and away the most popular media in the United States. In 2005, U.S. Census Bureau statistics reported that the average American spent seventy-seven full days watching television and an additional nine full days using the Internet.[27]

"Television is still the 800-pound gorilla because of how much the average person is exposed to it. However, that is quickly evolving," contends Robert Papper of Ball State University's Center for Media Design; "the day is coming when most TV will arrive over the Internet. We're going to stop looking at them as different media."[28]

Third, *the overriding experiential effect of television and the Internet together is environmental.* Today the notion that there is such a thing as a media environment—and that TV, in particular, acts on people environmentally, socially constructing a large part of the reality that they take for granted—is no longer a radical idea. Marshall McLuhan first suggested this in lectures during the 1950s and then wrote about it in a series of books throughout the 1960s. His envisioning of the electronic media as a new kind of environment was far from commonsensical at the time. In hindsight, McLuhan was presciently ahead of his peers in both his observations and the way he conveyed them. His unusual prose style might be described as digital, involving the discontinuous juxtaposition of witty aphoristic "probes" (a word he used to describe the sense of exploration in his writings rather than just following the nearly universally accepted approach of logically engaging in argument—one thought after another—in a rigorously linear fashion). McLuhan was the first media critic to describe TV as something much more than just a medium, an industry, or an institution. He believed that the sweep and impact of television was even larger and more subtle than any of these three characteristics separately. In 1964, he claimed in *Understanding Media* that "TV is environmental and imperceptible, like all environments." For him, television was the pivotal medium up until that time, declaring "in terms of the electronic age, a totally new environment has been created."[29]

Four years later in *War and Peace in the Global Village* (1968), McLuhan further noted that "the television environment is total and therefore invisible. Along with the computer, it has altered every phase of American vision and identity."[30] Coupled with his inclusion of cyberspace, he frequently argued that "the western world [was] imploding" as a result of these new electronic media.[31] Soon the eastern half of the world was bursting inward on itself as well. McLuhan died in 1980, so he was only able to sense the vague outlines of the future, never seeing the full transformative impact of how the media would converge during the Digital Era. He famously suggested, though, that "the electronic media, television in particular, were turning the world into a 'global village.' "[32] As early as 1967, he hypothesized that "the next medium, whatever it is—it may be the extension of consciousness—will include television as its content."[33] In this way, "the Internet helps complete his [global village] metaphor to the point of making it a reality," concludes Paul Levinson in *Digital McLuhan*; for "online villagers . . . the Internet shattered the barrier that kept them bottled up with no input on the living room side of their television screens."[34] Instead, TV in the 2000s is increasingly personalized, mobile, and interactive.

Fourth, *digital convergence has enhanced and extended television's relevancy, influence, and profitability across multiple platforms, including traditional TV sets, DVDs, the Internet, MP3 video players, stand-alone and portable DVRs, and mobile phones.* The key to thinking about television in the Digital Era is to reenvision it in terms of screens (of all shapes and sizes) rather than merely households (which no longer captures a complete and accurate picture of TV penetration).

By 2002, the price for one thirty-minute episode of an originally scripted prime-time series ranged from $1 to $2 million, depending on the network. Thus, the mega-media conglomerates looked "to spread the cost of programming across as wide a footprint as possible."[35] "Repurposing" emerged as the watchword in American TV throughout the early 2000s, referring to the process by which television content was adapted across as many in-house platforms as possible. By mid decade, the United States was on the threshold of being converted into an "on-demand nation" where one-on-one distribution of TV programming via the Internet or cable had arrived, providing yet another alternative (along with pay television and retailing DVDs) to the advertiser-supported model. In this way, the technical infrastructure underpinning the personal-usage market structure was securely in place by the mid 2000s. The wire-and-wireless grid that encircled the United States was well on its way to becoming fully digitized, with a complete shutdown of all analog signals scheduled for New Years Day 2009. By November 2005, thirty-eight million American households already had high-speed broadband access; twenty-four million had cable video on demand; and ten million had digital video recorders, with these numbers projected to at least double by the analog cutoff date of December 31, 2008.[36] More important, mobile phones with video capability had two million subscribers in the United States by March 2006.[37] Worldwide, too, there were "two billion mobile phone users [or] twice the number of TV households," who, in the aggregate, represented a future market that could receive "news updates, sports scores, and entertainment delivered directly to their handsets."[38] For the youngest generation of Americans, christened Millennials (or the net generation) by sociologists and the popular press, "cell phones served as a third screen along with televisions and computers."[39] The new Digital Era of "on-demand entertainment" was signaling the beginning of "the end of TV" as most people once knew it before 1995.[40]

Fifth, *millennials were at the forefront of television's transition from a niche to a personal-usage market model, although Generation Xers and baby boomers also embraced the Digital Era changeover.* Frank N. Magid

Associates, "one of the most successful and influential television and entertainment consulting companies" for more than half a century, published a study on September 21, 2004, comparing generational media preferences in the United States.[41] This white paper found that Millennials (born between 1984 and 2002), Gen Xers, and boomers (Magid didn't include the silent and G.I. generations in this survey), all selected TV and the Internet as their top two media choices, although Millennials were the most committed to the Internet while baby boomers most preferred television.[42] All in all, Millennials are the first generation to grow up during the digital revolution. Consequently, "they carry an arsenal of electronic devices—the more portable the better. Raised amid a barrage of information, they are able to juggle a conversation on Instant Messenger, a Web-surfing session, and an iTunes playlist," of which an increasing percentage contains TV episodes from such series as ABC's *Desperate Housewives*, Comedy Central's *The Daily Show with Jon Stewart*, and the Sci Fi Channel's *Battlestar Galactica*, along with choosing among thousands of media files available for video podcasting.[43] For instance, "ABC's broadband efforts—which include selling $1.99 shows through iTunes, streaming ad-supported programs on ABC.com, and the $4.95-per-month subscription service ABC News Now [for mobile phones, DVRs, PCs and laptops]—are aimed squarely at Millennials." In addition, ABC sold five million program downloads through iTunes in the first six months of 2006.[44]

As far as mobile phones are concerned, they "aren't going to replace TVs or computers, but they will become a complementary source of media," declares business scholar Dan Steinbock: "It's likely that cellphone video may be used to deliver short bursts of information, which in turn will cause people to seek out a TV or computer screen for more extended viewing."[45] Similarly, the aforementioned 2004 Magid Associates study found that viewers from each of the last three American generations preferred watching programs of thirty minutes or longer on televisions rather than on computer or cell-phone screens. Millennials, though, enjoyed "watching video clips on the Internet" the most.[46] In response to this growing consumer demand, ABC, CBS, NBC, Fox, and "at least 34 cable networks [were] offering broadband video channels" by June 2006. "Network websites [were] no longer [just] repositories for facts, figures, and features promoting programming to be watched on a TV set." They also featured "constantly expanding amounts of video programming" targeted at Millennials, above all, as well as Gen Xers and baby boomers. "Today's young people started off using personal computers very early in their lives," explains ESPN360 broadband channel general manager Tanya VanCourt; "now it's become a way of life for those currently coming of age."[47]

In October 2005, ABC's
Desperate Housewives
became one of the first
television series whose
episodes were made available
for downloading through
iTunes at $1.99 apiece.
Courtesy of Reuters/Landov.

Globally, moreover, there exists a "critical mass of teenagers—800 million in the world, the most there have ever been—with time and money to spend, [making them] one of the most powerful engines" behind the continued spread of television and the Internet during the Digital Era.[48] Millennials are the ultimate "placeshifters," consuming TV and other "media on the go" wherever they happen to be living out their lives. Gen Xers and baby boomers additionally join Millennials as avid "timeshifters." DVRs, in particular, give "consumers a new degree of control: instead of being at the mercy of the broadcast schedule or VCRs, they [can] now be their own television programmers, scheduling shows at their own convenience, pausing live television and skipping easily past commercials."[49]

In an "age of instant media gratification," "content is still king," affirms Doug Herzog president of Comedy Central and Spike TV (both subsidiaries of Viacom).[50] Similarly, hit programming is even more important than ever before in the Digital Era. As the one-time sacrosanct business model of television splinters into several alternative options beyond just advertiser-supported programming—including product placement, subscription services (ranging from twenty-four-hour networks such as HBO to part-time content-providers such as ABC News Now), DVD sales, and program downloads—breakout signature shows are the most essential ingredient that enables this newly emerging multidimensional, personal-usage market structure to flourish. Viewers, for example, are not going to pay money to download mediocre run-of-the-mill programs. Hit series help to brand networks, generate word of mouth, and ultimately create multiple revenue streams. More than anything, broadcast, cable, satellite, and now online networks in the Digital Era are content providers, launching programs and thus priming the public to watch them in their initial runs, before consumers pay directly for these shows as they migrate to other distribution windows within and outside the conglomerate. Joel Surnow and Robert Cochran's 24, for instance, debuted on Fox on November 6, 2001. A year later, the series (which was produced by Imagine Entertainment for Twentieth Century-Fox Television) was already being syndicated worldwide, and its first season was also available on DVD in North America and Europe. By 2006, 24 (which cost $300 million to produce, with 120 episodes so far budgeted at an average $2.5 million each) had earned $156 million in license fees from the Fox network, $120 million in international syndication, and $200 million in DVD sales for seasons one through four; it was also among the most popular new programs being downloaded on iTunes and myspace.com/24onmyspace.[51]

After 1995, moreover, hit series in the broadcast sector such as NBC's *The West Wing* and *The Apprentice*, CBS's *Survivor* and *CSI*, ABC's *Who Wants to Be a Millionaire?* and *Desperate Housewives*, Fox's *24* and *American Idol*, UPN's *Star Trek: Voyager* and *Everybody Hates Chris*, and WB's *Buffy the Vampire Slayer* and *Gilmore Girls*, all played major parts in re-creating and reinforcing the brand identities of their respective networks. PAX TV came close to bankruptcy and was finally restructured and rebranded as i (Independent Television) in 2005 and then ION in early 2007 because it never produced any hit programs of note and thus spent most of its seven-year history hemorrhaging money.[52] Likewise, UPN and WB were merged in 2006 as the CW (a fifty-fifty joint venture between the CBS Corporation and Warner Bros. Entertainment, a subsidiary of Time Warner) after losing a combined $1 billion over the previous decade because these part-time networks lacked the sheer number and variety of popular shows necessary to compete head-on with NBC, CBS, ABC, and Fox.[53]

In fact, consolidation without content innovation proved to be a limited business strategy in the Digital Era. A case in point is the 1999 Viacom/CBS marriage that ended in a kind of divorcement on January 3, 2006, despite the fact that Sumner Redstone remained the

Content is still king in the Digital Era, and no series better illustrates this tendency than Fox's American Idol, *with its trio of celebrity judges* (seated, left to right) *Simon Cowell, Paula Abdul, and Randy Jackson, and its aspiring contestants, such as* (standing) *third-season winner, Fantasia Barrino. Courtesy of Reuters/Fred Prouser/Landov.*

executive chairman of both conglomerates. The promise of synergy between Viacom and CBS with its supposed "cradle-to-grave one-stop shopping for advertisers" was never fully realized.[54] Instead, a new Viacom was created to shelter the younger higher-growth subsidiaries, such as the MTV network division (including MTV, Comedy Central, Nickelodeon, Spike TV, and VH1) and the movie studios (Paramount Pictures and Dreamworks), while CBS Corporation maintained control over the older, slower-growing properties such as CBS-TV, UPN (soon to be 50 percent of the CW), CBS Radio, Simon and Schuster, and CBS Outdoor Advertising.[55]

In a similar vein, the 1996 Disney/ABC and 2001 AOL/Time Warner mergers also experienced early growing pains, although both alliances eventually held together (with Time Warner even dropping "AOL" from its corporate title in early 2003 when the value of this Internet service provider plummeted $35 billion after the dotcom bubble completely burst during 2001 and into 2002).[56] In 2004–2005, ABC actually became the first broadcast network in over a decade to have two breakout hits in the same season with Marc Cherry's *Desperate Housewives* and J. J. Abrams, Damon Lindelof, and Jeffrey Lieber's *Lost*. Not since NBC premiered its one-two punch of David Crane and Marta Kauffman's *Friends* and Michael Crichton and John Wells's *ER* in 1994–1995 had one of the big-four networks had this degree of success during a single fall launch (although having multiple hits in any particular season was a fairly common occurrence throughout the

Network and Cable Eras). The fact was, though, that breakout programming was more likely to originate in the cable and satellite sector of the industry after 1995. The fight among so many TV services to not only survive but distinguish themselves in such an increasingly competitive environment had resulted in an unprecedented proliferation of original programming, with HBO leading the way as the most innovative and lucrative bright spot inside the Time Warner conglomerate. At the time, "HBO's achievements had a dramatic impact on the entire media culture; creatively it put its rivals to shame," proclaimed Peter Bart, editor of *Variety*, in 2002. This pay television channel owed its success "to a potent mix: stable management; savvy blanket promotion of its shows; and a business model that relies on subscriptions rather than advertising."[57] Significantly, "the traditional business model of television production [was] being rewritten," and the network that initially set this whole transitional process into motion with its distinctive breakthrough programming during the mid to late 1990s was HBO.[58]

For the first time in television history, the quality alternative was not CBS (as it was in the early 1970s), NBC (in the early to mid 1980s), ABC (in the late 1980s), or even PBS. "HBO is perhaps the greatest single producer of quality television drama and comedy in the English-speaking world," admitted British TV critic David Herman in 2004. "American television is on a roll," he continued, "[and] most of these programs, especially the most recent ones [citing *The Larry Sanders Show, Sex and the City, The Sopranos, Curb Your Enthusiasm, Six Feet Under*, and *Deadwood*], have been made by one company, Home Box Office."[59] Freed from direct ratings pressure, HBO invested its considerable cache of subscription dollars into hiring the best available talent, allowing them more time to produce their series, and requiring fewer episodes per season in order to differentiate its product from its competitors in an evolving made-to-order television market. The network also reached deeply into the creative community. Its talent pool included writer-producers such as Tom Fontana (*St. Elsewhere, Homicide: Life on the Street, Oz*), Darren Star (*Beverly Hills 90210, Melrose Place, Sex and the City*), David Chase (*Northern Exposure, I'll Fly Away, The Sopranos*), Alan Ball (*Cybil, American Beauty, Six Feet Under*), and David Milch (*Hill Street Blues, NYPD Blue, Deadwood*). HBO's ability to attract the entertainment industry's top creative people was unmatched by any other broadcast, cable, or pay television network. For example, *Seinfeld*'s creator, Larry David, the producer and star of *Curb Your Enthusiasm*, "brought the project to HBO." All told, "the network's tendency to permit creative freedom made it a magnet for experienced producers, directors and

Hailed by the New York Times *as possibly "the greatest work of American popular culture of the last quarter century," HBO's* The Sopranos *emerged as perhaps the best example of quality television drama in the English-speaking world during the 2000s. Courtesy of HBO Production/Heldref.*

writers looking for an outlet for projects to which they [were] deeply committed."[60]

By the mid 2000s, HBO engendered a certain backlash from its competitors and some television critics for not being able to produce more breakout hits fast enough, but the aftereffect of the network's shows was clearly evident in the programming and branding strategies of many other networks such as Fox (with *24*, to mention just one of its relevant series in this regard), FX (with *The Shield*), the USA Network (with *Monk*), TNT (with *The Closer*), Showtime (with *Weeds*) and even ABC. When Marc Cherry created *Desperate Housewives*, for example, "he decided to 'write an HBO show'—something like the ones [he] himself loved, maybe 'a *Sex and the City* meets *Six Feet Under.*' "[61] *Desperate Housewives* at its best was the kind of custom-tailored program that defied easy categorization. Audiences at first weren't sure whether it was a darkly dramatic sitcom or a hip, ironic soap opera. From a business point of view, *Desperate Housewives* was more edgy and idiosyncratic than the standard-grade product that usually succeeded in the advertiser-supported environment of the broadcast sector. The series became an immediate buzzworthy hit for ABC that both elevated the profile of the network and prepared the general public for the program's eventual release across a variety of subsequent platforms, including syndication, DVD, and the fast-growing on-demand window. According to Cherin, "the mass digital conversion of the past ten years" placed "consumers at the very heart" of an increasingly personalized TV business environment.[62] Although, according to a 2005 tracking study conducted by the Cable and Telecommunications Association for Marketing, "more than three-quarters (77%)" still tuned into programs at "their scheduled date and time,"[63] a growing segment of the national audience (23 percent) was already timeshifting and placeshifting, "liberated from the constraints of the old analog world."[64]

Surprisingly, too, they were watching more TV than ever before in the history of the medium. As of 2005, "viewers [in the United States] averaged 30.6 hours of television a week [or] 10% more than five years ago."[65] They were thus spending four hours and thirty-seven minutes a day watching TV.[66] Individual daily usage of the Internet also amounted to an additional one hour and thirty-three minutes, not counting all the "e-mail and software interactions."[67]

Seventh and finally, therefore, *both television and the Internet have expanded the boundaries of what it means to be a literate person in the twenty-first century.* Now that the highly touted and long-awaited five hundred-plus-channel universe has finally arrived, watching TV is "the number three activity" for the average person in America "after sleep and work."[68] The percentage of the U.S. population "18 and older who used television" in any given day during 2005 was 90.6 percent, while the figure for the Internet was 68 percent.[69] Almost without exception, Americans are mediacentric, and, interestingly, they are largely unaware of how much TV they actually consume. The no. 1 finding in the 2004 Middletown Media Report conducted by researchers at Ball State University's Center for Media Design is that "people spend more than double the time with the media than they think they do (11.7 hours a day)." When multitasking (or consuming two media at once) is factored into the equation, that total rises to 15.4 hours of media usage each and every day. "TV is not only the 800 pound primary gorilla," writes director Robert Papper and his Ball State colleagues, "it's also the 800 pound secondary gorilla, and so it's commonly on when other media are in use."[70] Overall, then, 96 percent of the U.S. population multitasks "about a third of the time they are using media."[71] In addition, "most multitasking involves television plus another activity" such as (in descending order) surfing the Web, checking e-mail, or talking on the telephone.[72] Consequently, the superabundance of electronic media in the Digital Era is unprecedented, and so, too, is the intimate role that television and the Internet together have in the lives of most Americans.

Living in what Microsoft founder Bill Gates has christened the "digital decade" means adjusting to the lightning-fast changes in direction that have been brought about by TV and cyberspace, as well as being able to negotiate these transitions with the widest possible repertoire of literacy skills.[73] The introduction of personal computers

(PCs) into most professional workplaces during the 1980s greatly expanded the media consumption of the majority of Americans beyond just leisure-time activities. Bringing PCs home to surf the Internet, along with sending and receiving e-mails, in the 1990s triggered what forecasters called the "twenty-four/seven" effect where there is little to no downtime whatsoever in America's current juiced-up life cycle. The rise of multitasking during the 2000s further hastened the full flowering of the present twenty-four/seven world. As far back as 1935, author and perceptual psychologist Rudolf Arnheim predicted that "television is a new hard test of our wisdom. If we succeed in mastering the new medium it will enrich us. But it also can put our minds to sleep."[74] Twenty years later during the Network Era, a great deal of ink and airwaves was spent worrying about why Johnny couldn't read.

The children and adults of today live in the quick-time environment of digital TV and cyberspace, having been brought up with an entirely new set of mass-mediated perceptions. Thus, today's literacy needs go well beyond the ability to just read, write, and speak competently. Media (including television) literacy is a matter of personal initiative and public interest, but it's not something that can be legislated. Research indicates that only 52 percent of the public is even aware of the TV ratings system, while a paltry 5 percent incorporate the V-chip into their family's viewing habits.[75] Each of us needs to take steps to recognize and think about the implications of the ongoing communication revolution. We also have to deepen our historical understanding of television and the Internet, as well as refine our critical viewing and listening skills.[76] Becoming increasingly media literate is a continuing developmental process; it is also a longer term commitment to improving the ecology of the electronic media environment in which we all live.

Introduction

1. Caryn James, "To Get the Best View of Television, Try Using a Wide Lens," *New York Times*, 1 October 2000, sec. 2, p. 39.

2. Erik Barnouw, *A History of Broadcasting in the United States*, Volume 1: *A Tower of Babel: To 1933* (New York: Oxford University Press, 1966); Erik Barnouw, *A History of Broadcasting in the United States*, Volume 2: *The Golden Web: 1933–1953* (New York: Oxford University Press, 1968); Erik Barnouw, *A History of Broadcasting in the United States*, Volume 3: *The Image Empire: From 1953* (New York: Oxford University Press, 1970).

3. Christopher H. Sterling, "An Appreciation of Erik Barnouw's *A History of American Broadcasting in the United States*," *Film and History* 21.2–3 (May/September 1991), p. 45.

4. For example, Gleason L. Archer Jr., *History of Radio to 1926* (New York: American Historical Society, 1938); Gleason L. Archer Jr., *Big Business and Radio* (New York: American Historical Society, 1939); Orrin E. Dunlap, *The Story of Radio* (New York: Dial Press, 1935).

5. Asa Briggs, *The History of Broadcasting in the United Kingdom*, Volume 1: *The Birth of Broadcasting: To 1926* (London: Oxford University Press, 1961); Asa Briggs, *The History of Broadcasting in the United Kingdom*, Volume 2: *The Golden Age of Wireless: 1926–1939* (London: Oxford University Press, 1965). See also Asa Briggs, *The History of Broadcasting in the United Kingdom*, Volume 3: *The War of Words: 1939–1945* (London: Oxford University Press, 1995).

6. Edwin Emery and Henry L. Smith, *The Press in America: An Interpretive History of the Mass Media* (Englewood, N.J.: Prentice Hall, 1954); Lewis Jacobs, *The Rise of the American Film* (New York: Harcourt Brace, 1939); Arthur Knight, *The Liveliest Art* (New York: Macmillan, 1957); Kenneth MacGowan, *Behind the Screen* (New York: Delacorte, 1965); Frank Luther Mott, *American Journalism* (New York: Macmillan, 1965); Terry Ramsaye, *A Million and One Nights* (New York: Simon and Schuster, 1926).

7. Erik Barnouw, *Tube of Plenty: The Evolution of American Television*, 2nd Revised Edition (New York: Oxford University Press, 1990).

8. Christopher H. Sterling and John M. Kittross, *Stay Tuned: A History of American Broadcasting*, 3rd Edition (Mahwah, N.J.: Lawrence Erlbaum, 2002).

9. Erik Barnouw, *Media Marathon: A Twentieth-Century Memoir* (Durham, N.C.: Duke University Press, 1996).

10. Sterling and Kittross, *Stay Tuned*, p. 16.

11. Ibid., p. xx.

12. For broadcasting, see Robert C. Hilliard and Michael C. Keith, *The Broadcast Century and Beyond: A Biography of American Broadcasting*, 4th Edition (Boston: Focal Press, 2004). For radio, see Michele Hilmes, *Radio Voices: American Broadcasting 1922–1952* (Minneapolis: University of Minnesota Press, 1997); J. Fred MacDonald, *Don't Touch That Dial! Radio Programming in American Life from 1920 to 1960* (Chicago: Nelson-Hall, 1979). For television, see Barnouw, *Tube of Plenty*; J. Fred MacDonald, *One Nation under Television: The Rise and Decline of Network TV* (Chicago: Nelson-Hall, 1994); Mary Ann Watson, *Defining Visions: Television and the American Experience since 1945* (New York; Harcourt Brace, 1998); Michele Hilmes, *Only Connect: A Cultural History of Broadcasting in the United States* (Belmont, Calif.: Wadsworth, 2002); David Marc and Robert J. Thompson, *Television in the Antenna Age: A Concise History* (Malden, Mass.: Blackwell, 2005).

13. Hilmes, *Only Connect*, pp. xvi–xvii.

14. For aesthetic, see Jane Feuer, Paul Kerr, and Tise Vahimagi, eds., *MTM: "Quality Television"* (London: British Film Institute, 1984). For biographical, see David Marc and Robert J. Thompson, *Prime Time, Prime Movers: From I Love Lucy to L.A. Law—America's Greatest TV Shows and the People Who Created Them* (Boston: Little, Brown, 1992). For cultural, see Cecelia Tichi, *Electronic Hearth: Creating an American Television Culture* (New York: Oxford University Press, 1991). For industrial, see William Boddy, *Fifties Television: The Industry and Its Critics* (Urbana: University of Illinois Press, 1993). For intellectual, see Daniel J. Czitrom, *Media and the American Mind: From Morse to McLuhan* (Chapel Hill: University of North Carolina Press, 1982). For international, see Anthony Smith, ed., *Television: An International History*, 2nd Edition (New York: Oxford University Press, 1998). For political, see Craig Allen, *Eisenhower and the Mass Media: Peace, Prosperity, and Prime-Time TV* (Chapel Hill: University of North Carolina Press, 1993). For social, see Lynn Spigel, *Make Room for TV: Television and the Family Ideal in Postwar America* (Chicago: University of Chicago Press, 1992). For technological, see Brian Winston, *Media Technology and Society: A History from the Telegraph to the Internet* (New York: Routledge, 1998).

15. Hilmes, *Only Connect*, p. 2.

16. Susan Douglas, Listening In: Radio and the American Imagination from Amos 'n' Andy and Edward R. Murrow to Wolfman Jack and Howard Stern (New York: Times Books, 1999); Robert Sklar, Movie-Made America: A Cultural History of American Movies, Revised and Updated (New York: Vintage, 1994).

1. An Idea Whose Time Had Come

1. David Sarnoff, "The Birth of an Industry," in *Pioneering in Television: Prophecy and Fulfillment* (excerpts from speeches and statements), 3rd Edition (New York: National Broadcasting Company, 1947), p. 40.

2. Sarnoff, "The Promise of Intercity Networks," in *Pioneering in Television*, p. 38.

3. Jeff Kisseloff, *The Box: An Oral History of Television, 1920–1961* (New York: Penguin, 1995), p. 6.

4. Louise Benjamin, "David Sarnoff," in Horace Newcomb, ed., *Encyclopedia of Television*, Volume 3 (Chicago: Fitzroy Dearborn, 1997), p. 1434.

5. Sarnoff, "Progress Here and Abroad," in *Pioneering in Television*, p. 31.

6. Kenneth Bilby, *The General: David Sarnoff and the Rise of the Communication Industry* (New York: Harper and Row, 1986), p. 133.

7. Erik Barnouw, *A History of Broadcasting in the United States*, Volume 1: *The Golden Web: 1933–1953* (New York: Oxford University Press, 1968), p. 125.

8. Michael Ritchie, *Please Stand By: A Prehistory of Television* (Woodstock, N.Y.: Overlook Press, 1994), p. 48.

9. John Western, "Television Girds for Battle," *Public Opinion Quarterly* 3 (October 1939), p. 552.

10. Christopher H. Sterling and John M. Kittross, *Stay Tuned: A History of American Broadcasting*, 3rd Edition (Mahwah, N.J.: Lawrence Erlbaum, 2002), p. 164.

11. Sarnoff, "Program Service to the Public," in *Pioneering in Television*, pp. 35–36.

12. Bilby, *The General*, pp. 132–133.

13. Norman Siegel, "Television Near, But It's Still a Problem Child," *New York World-Telegram*, 1 January 1938, p. 1.

14. Western, "Television Girds for Battle," pp. 547–548.

15. Kisseloff, *The Box*, p. 52.

16. "Television II: 'Fade in Camera One!'" *Forbes*, May 1939, p. 69.

17. David E. Fisher and Marshall Jon Fisher, *Tube: The Invention of Television* (San Diego: Harvest, 1996), p. 278.

18. Erik Barnouw, *Tube of Plenty: The Evolution of American Television*, 2nd Revised Edition (New York: Oxford University Press, 1990), p. 89.

19. Eugene Lyons, *David Sarnoff* (New York: Pyramid Books, 1966), p. 255.

20. Sarnoff, "The Birth of an Industry," in *Pioneering in Television*, p. 41.

21. Barnouw, *Tube of Plenty*, p. 89.

22. Orrin E. Dunlap, "Ceremony Is Carried by Television as Industry Makes Its Formal Bow," *New York Times*, 1 May 1939, p. 1.

23. Ritchie, *Please Stand By*, p. 60.

24. Dunlap, "Ceremony Is Carried by Television," p. 1.

25. Quoted in "One Family in Eight Eager for Television," *New York Times*, 30 April 1939, p. 36.

26. National Broadcasting Company, "NBC Television Schedule Begins with Variety Show," 4 May 1939, Press Release, Library of American Broadcasting, University of Maryland, College Park.

27. "April 1939 Television Is Introduced at the New York Worlds Fair by RCA and NBC," *TV History through Visual Images*, at http://framemaster.tripod.com/1939wf.html.

28. "Quick Facts—1939," *Television History—The First 75 Years*, at http://www.tvhistory.tv/1939%20QF.htm.

29. Iain Baird, "Television in the World of Tomorrow," *Echoes*, Winter 1997, at http://members.attcanada.ca/~antenna1/Baird/RCA.html.

30. Kisseloff, *The Box*, p. 52.

31. Dunlap, "Ceremony Is Carried by Television," p. 1.

32. Ritchie, *Please Stand By*, p. 59.

33. Charles H. Sewall, "The Future of Long-Distance Communication," *Harper's Weekly*, 29 December 1900, p. 1263.

34. Ibid.; Judy Wajcman, *Feminism Confronts Technology* (University Park: Pennsylvania State University Press, 1991), p. 43.

35. Daniel J. Czitrom, *Media and the American Mind: From Morse to McLuhan* (Chapel Hill: University of North Carolina Press, 1982), p. 3.

36. Ibid., pp. 4–5.

37. Albert Abramson, "The Invention of Television," in Anthony Smith, ed., *Television: An International History*, 2nd Edition (New York: Oxford University Press, 1998), p. 9.

38. Ibid. See also Albert Abramson, *The History of Television, 1880–1941* (Jefferson, N.C.: McFarland, 1987).

39. Leo Marx, *The Machine in the Garden: Technology and the Pastoral Ideal in America* (New York: Oxford University Press, 1964), p. 197.

40. Henry David Thoreau, "*Walden, 1854,*" in Carl Bode, ed., *The Portable Thoreau*, Revised Edition (New York: Viking, 1964), p. 306.

41. Lee de Forest, "Doubts about Television," *Literary Digest*, 6 November 1926, pp. 73–74. See also Lee de Forest, *Father of Radio: The Autobiography of Lee de Forest* (Chicago: Wilcox and Foller, 1950). De Forest's 1906–1907 discovery of the audion, or three-element vacuum tube, made radio-wave detection, rudimentary amplification, and reception possible, thus auguring the birth of modern electronics.

42. Bilby, *The General*, p. 8.

43. Henry James, *The American Scene* (London: Penguin, 1991), p. 151.

44. Mark Twain and Charles Dudley Warner, *The Gilded Age: A Tale of Today* (New York: Penguin, 2001).

45. James W. Carey, with John J. Quirk, "The Mythos of the Electronic Revolution," in James W. Carey, *Communication as Culture: Essays on Media and Culture* (Boston: Unwin Hyman, 1989), p. 121.

46. Gerald Mast, revised by Bruce F. Kawin, *A Short History of the Movies*, 5th Edition (New York: Macmillan, 1992), p. 22.

47. Carolyn Marvin, *When Old Technologies Were New: Thinking about Electric Communication in the Late Nineteenth Century* (New York: Oxford University Press, 1988), p. 3.

48. Quoted in Fisher and Fisher, *Tube*, p. 13–14.

49. Remy Chevalier, "Robida, The Future Man!" *World Explorer Magazine* 2.4 (1995), pp. 24–29, at http://www.remyc.com/robida.html.

50. Albert Abramson, *The History of Television, 1880 to 1941* (Jefferson, N.C.: McFarland, 1987, pp. 5–20; Fisher and Fisher, *Tube*, pp. 16–20.

51. Abramson, "The Invention of Television," p. 11; Fisher and Fisher, *Tube*, p. 29.

52. The telephone business was formally established with the creation of the Bell Telephone Company in 1877.

53. James Gleick, *What Just Happened: A Chronicle from the Information Frontier* (New York: Pantheon, 2002), p. 6.

54. C. Fred Post, "Television: Will It Be the Century's Wonder Industry?" *Printer's Ink Monthly*, May 1939, p. 4.

55. Marvin, *When Old Technologies Were New*, p. 154.

56. Ibid., p. 175.

57. Ibid., p. 157.

58. Marshall McLuhan, *Understanding Media: The Extensions of Man* (Cambridge, Mass.: MIT Press, 1994), pp. 8–9.

59. "The Problem of Television," *Scientific American Supplement* 63.1641 (15 June 1907), p. 26292.

60. Fisher and Fisher, *Tube*, p. 120.

61. Evan I. Schwartz, *The Last Lone Inventor: A Tale of Genius, Deceit, and the Birth of Television* (New York: HarperCollins, 2002), p. 20.

62. "Hugo Gernsback Is Dead at 83: Author, Publisher and Inventor," *New York Times*, 20 August 1967, p. 88.

63. Hugo Gernsback, "Editorial," *Radio-Craft* 19.4 (January 1948), p. 7.

64. "Hugo Gernsback Is Dead at 83," p. 88.

65. Daniel Stashower, *The Boy Genius and the Mogul: The Untold Story of Television* (New York: Broadway Books, 2002), pp. 17, 60.

66. *Answering Your Questions Regarding Radiovision* (Jersey City, N.J.: Jenkins Television Corporation, 1930), p. 3.

67. Stashower, *The Boy Genius and the Mogul*, p. 60.

68. Quoted in Fisher and Fisher, *Tube*, p. 41.

69. Donald G. Godfrey, "Radio Finds Its Eyes," *Television Quarterly* 35.2 (2005), p. 51.

70. Steve Runyon, "Charles Francis Jenkins," in Horace Newcomb, ed., *Encyclopedia of Television*, Volume 2 (Chicago: Fitzroy Dearborn, 1997), p. 857.

71. " 'Radio Vision' Shown First Time in History by Capital Inventor," *Washington Sunday Star*, 14 June 1925, p. 1.

72. Stashower, *The Boy Genius and the Mogul*, p. 61; Fisher and Fisher, *Tube*, p. 41.

73. Ritchie, *Please Stand By*, p. 23.

74. A. Dinsdale, "And Now, We See by Radio!" *Radio Broadcast* 10.2 (1926), p. 140.

75. "John Logie Baird: 1888–1946," *Adventures in Cybersound*, at http://www.acmi.net.au/AIC/BAIRD_BIO.html.

76. Dinsdale, "And Now, We See by Radio!" p. 140.

77. "John Logie Baird: 1888–1946"; John Baird, "Television To-day and To-morrow," *Baird Television News Letter*, August 1939, p. 1.

78. Christopher H. Sterling, "John Logie Baird," in Horace Newcomb, ed., *Encyclopedia of Television*, Volume 1 (Chicago: Fitzroy Dearborn, 1997), p. 137.

79. Godfrey, "Radio Finds Its Eyes," p. 52.

80. "Home Televisor Will Entertain Ten Persons: Latest Jenkins Invention Will Prove Practical, Declare Sponsors," *New York Evening World*, 15 December 1929, p. 26.

81. Fisher and Fisher, *Tube*, p. 91.

82. James Von Schilling, *The Magic Window: American Television, 1939–1953* (New York: Haworth, 2003), p. 4.

83. "Far-Off Speakers Seen as Well as Heard Here in a Test of Television," *New York Times*, 8 April 1927, p. 1.

84. Ibid.

85. Erik Barnouw, *A History of Broadcasting in the United States*, Volume 1: *A Tower in Babel: To 1933* (New York: Oxford University Press, 1966), p. 185.

86. Ibid., pp. 161–162.

87. Quoted in Kisseloff, *The Box*, p. 24.

88. Russell B. Porter, "Play Is Broadcast by Voice and Acting in Radio-Television," *New York Times*, 12 September 1928, p. 1.

89. Orrin E. Dunlap Jr., *The Outlook for Television* (New York: Harper and Row, 1932; reprint, New York: Arno Press, 1971), p. 88.

90. Quoted in "Radio-Movies in the Home," *Literary Digest* 98.9 (1 September 1928), pp. 18–19.

91. Quoted in Porter, "Play Is Broadcast by Voice and Acting in Radio-Television," p. 1.

92. C. E. Huffman (Chief Engineer of the Jenkins Television Corporation), "Visit to GE Television Demonstration and Laboratories," Report, 24 May 1930, pp. 2–3. File 142-473A, National Museum of American History, Smithsonian Institution Archives.

93. "Tips to Televisionaries," *Outlook and Independent* 155.5 (4 June 1930), p. 179.

94. Fisher and Fisher, *Tube*, pp. 197, 360.

95. Ibid., p. 36.

96. Quoted in Kisseloff, *The Box*, p. 29.

97. Ibid., p. 31.

98. Nathan Miller, *New World Coming: The 1920s and the Making of Modern America* (New York: Scribner, 2003), p. 150.

99. Quoted in Stashower, *The Boy Genius and the Mogul*, pp. 15–16.

100. Fisher and Fisher, *Tube*, pp. 126–127.

101. Donald G. Godfrey, *Philo T. Farnsworth: The Father of Television* (Salt Lake City: University of Utah Press, 2001), p. 11.

102. Claire Noall, "From Utah Farm Boy to Inventor of Television: Fascinating Story," *Deseret News* (Salt Lake City), 14 November 1948, p. F3.

103. Fisher and Fisher, *Tube*, p. 127.

104. Neil Postman, "Electrical Engineer: Philo Farnsworth," *Time* 100 153.12 (1999 Special Issue), p. 92.

105. Noall, "From Utah Farm Boy to Inventor of Television," p. F3.

106. Quoted in Mitchell Wilson, "Strange Story of Birth of Farnsworth Television," *Rigby Star* (Idaho), 29 January 1953, p. 1.

107. Quoted in Stashower, *The Boy Genius and the Mogul*, p. 22.

108. Noall, "From Utah Farm Boy to Inventor of Television," p. F3.

109. Godfrey, *Philo T. Farnsworth*, p. 31.

110. Evan I Schwartz, *The Last Lone Inventor: A Tale of Genius, Deceit, and the Birth of Television* (New York: HarperCollins, 2002), p. 127.

111. Godfrey, *Philo T. Farnsworth*, pp. 34, 36.

112. "S.F. Man's Invention to Revolutionize Television," *San Francisco Chronicle*, 3 September 1928, sec. 2, p. 11.

113. Godfrey, *Philo T. Farnsworth*, p. 36.

114. Daniel J. Kevles, "SciTech: The Forces Are with Us," *Chronicle of Higher Education*, 1 August 2003, p. B11.

115. Jack Nachbar, "Introduction," in Jack Nachbar, ed., *Focus on the Western* (Englewood Cliffs, N.J.: Prentice Hall, 1974), p. 3.

116. Kevles, "SciTech," p. B11.

117. Donald G. Godfrey, "Philo Farnsworth," in Horace Newcomb, ed., *Encyclopedia of Television*, Volume 1 (Chicago: Fitzroy Dearborn, 1997), p. 596.

118. Stashower, *The Boy Genius and the Mogul*, p. 16.

119. Albert Abramson, *Zworykin, Pioneer of Television* (Urbana: University of Illinois Press, 1995), p. 16.

120. Fisher and Fisher, *Tube*, p. 123.

121. Abramson, *Zworykin*, pp. 42, 50–51.

122. "Radio-Movies in the Home," p. 18.

123. Fisher and Fisher, *Tube*, p. 137.

124. Abramson, *Zworykin*, pp. 76–77.

125. Bilby, *The General*, pp. 121–122.

126. Ibid., p. 121.

127. Fisher and Fisher, *Tube*, p. 198; Kisseloff, *The Box*, p. 24.

128. Kisseloff, *The Box*, p. 24.

129. Fisher and Fisher, *Tube*, pp. 197–198.

130. Barnouw, *A Tower in Babel*, p. 252.

131. Bilby, *The General*, p. 105.

132. Erik Barnouw, *Tube of Plenty: The Evolution of American Television*, 2nd Revised Edition (New York: Oxford University Press, 1990), p. 72.

133. Fisher and Fisher, *Tube*, p. 220.

134. Bilby, *The General*, p. 122.

135. George Everson, *The Story of Television: The Life of Philo T. Farnsworth* (New York: W.W. Norton, 1949; reprint, New York: Arno Press, 1974), p. 125.

136. Thomas Ropp, "The Real Father of Television," *Arizona Republic Magazine*, 6 May 1984, p. 6.

137. Abramson, *Zworykin*, pp. 90–91.

138. Godfrey, *Philo T. Farnsworth*, p. 46.

139. Quoted in Donald G. Godfrey and Michael D. Murray, "Introduction: Origins of Innovation," in Michael D. Murray and Donald G. Godfrey, eds., *Television in America: Local Station History from Across the Nation* (Ames: Iowa State University Press, 1997), p. xvi.

140. Kisseloff, *The Box*, p. 31.

141. Ibid., p. 33.

142. Abramson, *Zworykin*, p. 118.

143. Gleick, *What Just Happened*, p. 264.

144. Quoted in Kisseloff, *The Box*, p. 33, 37.

145. Schwartz, *The Last Lone Inventor*, p. 196.

146. Godfrey, *Philo T. Farnsworth*, p. 61.

147. "Moon Makes Television Debut in Pose for Radio Snapshot," *Christian Science Monitor*, 25 August 1934, p. 1.

148. "Tennis Stars Act in New Television; Instrument Demonstrated at Franklin Institute Said to Be Most Sensitive Build," *New York Times*, 25 August 1934, p. 14.

149. National Broadcasting Company, "The Birth of an Industry," 1939, Press Pamphlet, Library of American Broadcasting, University of Maryland, College Park, pp. 6–7.

150. Orrin E. Dunlap, "First Field Test in Television, Costing $1,000,000, to Begin Here," *New York Times*, 8 May 1935, p. 1.

151. Elmer W. Engstrom, *Television: An Experimental Television System* (New York: RCA Institutes Technical Press, 1936), pp. 253–254.

152. National Broadcasting Company, "The Birth of an Industry," p. 9.

153. Fisher and Fisher, *Tube*, p. 220.

154. Abramson, *Zworykin*, p. 105.

155. Godfrey, *Philo T. Farnsworth*, p. 75.

156. Ibid., p. 85.

157. Quoted in Kisseloff, *The Box*, pp. 40–41.

158. Godfrey, *Philo T. Farnsworth*, p. 141.

159. "New Television Station Planned for Philadelphia," *New York Times*, 13 December 1936, p. X14.

160. Quoted in Kisseloff, *The Box*, p. 41.

161. Ibid., pp. 35, 39.

162. Stashower, *The Boy Genius and the Mogul*, p. 243.

163. Everson, *The Story of Television*, p. 245.

164. Quoted in Kisseloff, *The Box*, p. 39.

165. Stashower, *The Boy Genius and the Mogul*, p. 244.

166. Fisher and Fisher, *Tube*, p. 229.

167. Sarnoff, "The Birth of an Industry," in *Pioneering in Television*, p. 41.

168. Godfrey, *Philo T. Farnsworth*, p. 128.

169. "Communications," *Time*, 20 February 1939, p. 62.

170. Godfrey, *Philo T. Farnsworth*, p. 128.

171. Abramson, *Zworykin*, p. xiv.

172. For example, ibid.; Godfrey, *Philo T. Farnsworth*; Stephen F. Hofer, "Philo Farnsworth: Television's Pioneer," *Journal of Broadcasting* 23.2 (Spring 1979), pp. 153–165; Frank Lovece, "Zworykin v. Farnsworth," *Video* 9.9 (September 1985), pp. 96–98; Thomas Ropp, "Philo Farnsworth: Forgotten Father of Television," *Media History Digest* 5.2 (Summer 1985), pp. 42–58; Schwartz, *The Last Lone Inventor*; Stashower, *The Boy Genius and the Mogul*. The documentary is titled *Big Dream, Small Screen: The Story behind Television* (Public Broadcasting System, 1997), produced by Windfall Films for *The American Experience* at WGBH in Boston, 60 minutes.

173. Quoted in Kisseloff, *The Box*, p. 40.

174. Abramson, *Zworykin*, p. xiv.

175. Sterling and Kittross, *Stay Tuned*, p. 165.

2. Not Going According to Plan

1. "Home Televisor Will Entertain Ten Persons: Latest Jenkins Invention Will Prove Practical, Declare Sponsors," *New York Evening World*, 15 December 1929, p. 26.

2. Alva Johnston, "Television's Here," *Saturday Evening Post*, 6 May 1939, p. 8.

3. "TELEVISION: Only Expense Keeps It 'Just around the Corner," *Newsweek*, 16 February 1935, p. 28.

4. "Television in the Home Is Brought Closer to Reality by Marketable Set," *Newsweek*, 23 May 1938, p. 21.

5. Market Research Corporation of America, "Television-Receiving-Set-Market Survey," February 1935, Report, Library of American Broadcasting, University of Maryland, College Park, pp. 6, 9.

6. Owen P. White, "What's Delaying Television?" *Collier's*, 30 November 1935, p. 10.

7. "Movies by Air," *New York World-Telegram*, 9 January 1936, p. 1; "Television," *Variety*, 15 January 1936, p. 1.

8. Norman Siegel, "Television Near, but It's Still a Problem Child," *New York World-Telegram*, 31 January 1938, p. 1.

9. Don Wharton, "Television in America," *Scribner's Magazine*, February 1937, p. 64; "Will Television Be with Us This Year, Next Year, or When?" *Radio Jobber News*, March 1937, pp. 1–2.

10. Wharton, "Television in America," p. 64; "Will Television Be with Us?" pp. 1–2.

11. Wharton, "Television in America," p. 62.

12. William S. Paley, *As It Happened: A Memoir* (New York: Doubleday, 1979), pp. 200–201.

13. "Hatching Television Eggs," *Broadcasting* 12.8 (15 April 1937), p. 44.

14. James Von Schilling, *The Magic Window: American Television, 1939–1953* (New York: Haworth, 2003), p. 36.

15. Quoted in Jeff Kisseloff, *The Box: An Oral History of Television, 1920–1961* (New York: Penguin, 1995), p. 72.

16. Quoted in David E. Fisher and Marshall Jon Fisher, *Tube: The Invention of Television* (San Diego: Harvest, 1996), pp. 305–306.

17. Joseph H. Udelson, *The Great Television Race: A History of the American Television Industry, 1925–1941* (University: University of Alabama Press, 1982), p. 148.

18. "New Television Service; Supplementary Sound Program Offered by NBC," *New York Times*, 20 March 1940, p. 20.

19. Kenneth Bilby, *The General: David Sarnoff and the Rise of the Communication Industry* (New York: Harper and Row, 1986), p. 135.

20. Roy Norr, "Confidential Memorandum on the Public Relations Aspects of the Television Problem," 1 May 1940, Report for Ames and Norr, New York, Library of American Broadcasting, University of Maryland, College Park, p. 5.

21. James Lawrence Fly, "Regulation of Radio Broadcasting in the Public Interest," *Annals of the American Academy of Political and Social Science* 213 (January 1941), p. 102.

22. "FCC Stays Start in Television, Rebukes R.C.A. for Sales Drive," *New York Times*, 24 March 1940, p. 1.

23. Norr, "Confidential Memorandum," p. 6; "FCC Head Explains Television Delay; Order Suspending Large-Scale Output of Receivers in Public Interest, J. L. Fly Says," *New York Times*, 3 April 1940, p. 21.

24. U.S. Senate Committee on Interstate Commerce, Development of Television, 76th Congress, 3rd Session, *Congressional Quarterly*, April 10–11, 1940, pp. 59–61.

25. Bilby, *The General*, p. 135.

26. Norr, "Confidential Memorandum," p. 6.

27. Fisher and Fisher, *Tube*, p. 291.

28. Ibid., p. 295.

29. Bilby, *The General*, p. 135; Christopher H. Sterling and John M. Kittross, *Stay Tuned: A History of American Broadcasting*, 3rd Edition (Mahwah, N.J.: Lawrence Erlbaum, 2002), pp. 210–211.

30. J. Fred MacDonald, *One Nation under Television: The Rise and Decline of Network TV* (Chicago: Nelson-Hall, 1994), p. 25.

31. Harry Castleman and Walter J. Podrazik, *Watching TV: Six Decades of American Television*, 2nd Edition (Syracuse, N.Y.: Syracuse University Press, 2003), pp. 12–13.

32. Quoted in Kisseloff, *The Box*, pp. 62, 558.

33. Fisher and Fisher, *Tube*, p. 295; David Weinstein, *The Forgotten Network: DuMont and the Birth of American Television* (Philadelphia: Temple University Press, 2003), p. 14.

34. Weinstein, *The Forgotten Network*, p. 14.

35. Castleman and Podrazik, *Watching TV*, p. 13; Johnston, "Television's Here," p. 42.

36. Castleman and Podrazik, *Watching TV*, p. 42.

37. Ted Nielsen, "A History of Network Television News," in Lawrence W. Lichty and Malachi C. Topping, eds., *American Broadcasting: A Source Book on the History of Radio and Television* (New York: Hastings House, 1975), p. 421.

38. Bilby, *The General*, p. 138.

39. *The Story of Television* (Clifton, N.J.: Allen B. Du Mont Laboratories, 1953), p. 31.

40. Kisseloff, *The Box*, p. 93.

41. Quoted in Bilby, *The General*, p. 138.

42. Sterling and Kittross, *Stay Tuned*, p. 827.

43. MacDonald, *One Nation under Television*, p. 31.

44. "Re Television," *Broadcasting* 8.10 (15 May 1935), p. 30.

45. "Television Tasks," *Business Week*, 8 June 1935, p. 20.

46. Hugo Gernsbeck, "Is Television Here?" *Radio-Craft* 7.2 (2 August 1935), p. 69.

47. William Schrage, "Television in Foreign Lands," *New York Sun*, 18 February 1939, p. 1; Sterling and Kittross, *Stay Tuned*, p. 864; Weinstein, *The Forgotten Network*, p. 14.

48. Von Schilling, *The Magic Window*, p. 44.

49. National Broadcasting Company, "NBC's Major Role in Television," December 1956, Press Release, Library of American Broadcasting, University of Maryland, College Park, p. 4.

50. *The Story of Television*, p. 31.

51. Quoted in Kisseloff, *The Box*, pp. 93, 557.

52. Ibid., p. 93; Von Schilling, *The Magic Window*, p. 49.

53. Quoted in Kisseloff, *The Box*, p. 96.

54. Fisher and Fisher, *Tube*, pp. 281–283.

55. Quoted in Kisseloff, *The Box*, p. 97.

56. Von Schilling, *The Magic Window*, pp. 48–49.

57. Robert Dallek, *An Unfinished Life: John F. Kennedy, 1917–1963* (Boston: Little, Brown, 2003), pp. 106–107.

58. Bilby, *The General*, p. 143.

59. Louise Benjamin, "David Sarnoff," in Horace Newcomb, ed., *Encyclopedia of Television*, Volume 3 (Chicago: Fitzroy Dearborn, 1997), p. 1435.

60. Bilby, *The General*, p. 138.

61. Von Schilling, *The Magic Window*, p. 48.

62. Bilby, *The General*, pp. 141, 151.

63. Von Schilling, *The Magic Window*, p. 48.

64. Robert Sobel, *RCA* (New York: Stein and Day, 1986), p. 139.

65. Donald G. Godfrey, *Philo T. Farnsworth: The Father of Television* (Salt Lake City: University of Utah Press, 2001), pp. 139, 153–155.

66. Paley, *As It Happened*, pp. 154–158.

67. Kisseloff, *The Box*, p. 94.

68. Sterling and Kittross, *Stay Tuned*, p. 253.

69. Ibid., p. 255.

70. MacDonald, *One Nation under Television*, p. 36.

71. Robert Pepper, "The Pre-Freeze Television Stations," in Lawrence W. Lichty and Malachi C. Topping, eds., *American Broadcasting: A Source Book on the History of Radio and Television* (New York: Hastings House, 1975), p. 140.

72. Sterling and Kittross, *Stay Tuned*, p. 255.

73. Ibid., p. 256; MacDonald, *One Nation under Television*, p. 37.

74. Erik Barnouw, *Tube of Plenty: The Evolution of American Television*, 2nd Revised Edition (New York: Oxford University Press, 1990), p. 99.

75. Bilby, *The General*, p. 172.

76. Fisher and Fisher, *Tube*, pp. 309, 312.

77. Von Schilling, *The Magic Window*, p. 48.

78. Barnouw, *Tube of Plenty*, p. 100.

79. Garth Jowett and Laura Ashley, "Frank Stanton," in Horace Newcomb, ed., *Encyclopedia of Television*, Volume 3 (Chicago: Fitzroy Dearborn, 1997), p. 1569.

80. Sterling and Kittross, *Stay Tuned*, p. 303.

81. Henry R. Luce, "The American Century," *Life* 10.7 (17 February 1941), p. 64.

82. Barnouw, *Tube of Plenty*, p. 103.

83. Gilbert Seldes, "The 'Errors' of Television," *Atlantic Monthly* 176.6 (May 1937), p. 541.

84. Michael Kammen, *The Lively Arts: Gilbert Seldes and the Transformation of Cultural Criticism in the United States* (New York: Oxford University Press, 1996), p. 446; Gilbert Seldes, *The Seven Lively Arts* (New York: Harper and Brothers, 1924).

85. Quoted in Kisseloff, *The Box*, pp. 73, 75, 77, 558.

86. Kammen, *The Lively Arts*, p. 251.

87. Kevin Dowler, "Worthington Minor," in Horace Newcomb, ed., *Encyclopedia of Television*, Volume 3 (Chicago: Fitzroy Dearborn, 1997), p. 1054.

88. Kammen, *The Lively Arts*, p. 274.

89. Amy Henderson, *On the Air: Pioneers of American Broadcasting* (Washington, D.C.: Smithsonian Institution Press, 1988), p. 133.

90. MacDonald, *One Nation under Television*, p. 16.

91. I am following the lead of David Weinstein in *The Forgotten Network: DuMont and the Birth of American Television* (Philadelphia: Temple University Press, 2003), who explains that "Allen B. Du Mont spelled his name 'Du Mont.' I have retained this 'Du Mont' spelling when referring to Allen Du Mont. . . . Allen B. Du Mont's company was generally spelled 'DuMont' in the contemporary press, and historians have continued to use the 'DuMont' spelling for DuMont Laboratories and the DuMont Television Network" (p. vi).

92. Kisseloff, *The Box*, pp. 63, 68, 556.

93. Weinstein, *The Forgotten Network*, p. 15.

94. Castleman and Podrazik, *Watching TV*, pp. 15–16.

95. "Bust by Television," *Newsweek*, 29 April 1946, p. 61.

96. Castleman and Podrazik, *Watching TV*, p. 29.

97. Ibid., p. 15.

98. Von Schilling, *The Magic Window*, p. 73.

99. Castleman and Podrazik, *Watching TV*, p. 20.

100. Tim Brooks and Earle Marsh, *The Complete Directory to Prime Time Network and Cable Shows, 1946–Present*, 7th Edition (New York: Ballantine, 1999), pp. 122–123.

101. "First Television of Baseball Seen," *New York Times*, 19 May 1939, p. 29.

102. "Collegians Play Ball as Television Mirrors the Game," *New York Times*, 21 May 1939, p. 10.

103. Quoted in Kisseloff, *The Box*, pp. 135–137, 560–561.

104. Quoted in "Sports Coverage, Then and Now: A Far Cry from the Flatbush Safari," *TV Guide*, 28 November 1959, p. 19.

105. National Broadcasting Company, "Milestones NBC Television, 1928–1956," December 1956, Press Release, Library of American Broadcasting, University of Maryland, College Park, p. 7.

106. "Short Stops on Video," *Variety*, 8 October 1947, p. 1.

107. Castleman and Podrazik, *Watching TV*, p. 30.

108. Von Schilling, *The Magic Window*, pp. 94, 95.

109. Castleman and Podrazik, *Watching TV*, p. 35.

110. Brooks and Marsh, *The Complete Directory to Prime Time Network and Cable Shows*, p. 469.

111. Timothy Scheurer, "The Variety Show," in Brian G. Rose, ed., *TV Genres: A Handbook and Reference Guide* (Westport, Conn.: Greenwood, 1985), p. 308.

112. Jack Gould, "The Paradoxical State of Television," *New York Times Magazine*, 30 March 1947, p. 14.

113. Scheurer, "The Variety Show," p. 308.

114. Quoted in Kisseloff, *The Box*, p. 112.

115. Von Schilling, *The Magic Window*, p. 80.

116. Quoted in Kisseloff, *The Box*, p. 112.

117. Brooks and Marsh, *The Complete Directory to Prime Time Network and Cable Shows*, p. 550.

118. Ned E. Hoopes, "Introduction," in William I. Kaufman, ed., *Great Television Plays* (New York: Dell, 1969), p. 9.

119. Douglas Gomery, "Finding TV's Pioneering Audiences," *Journal of Popular Film and Television* 29.3 (Fall 2001), p. 127.

120. Donald G. Godfrey and Michael D. Murray, "Introduction: Origins of Innovation," in Michael D. Murray and Donald G. Godfrey, eds., *Television in America: Local Station History from Across the Nation* (Ames: Iowa State University Press, 1997), p. xxvii.

121. Gomery, "Finding TV's Pioneering Audiences," p. 125.

122. Von Schilling, *The Magic Window*, p. 103.

123. Philip Hamburger, "Television: The World of Milton Berle," *New Yorker*, 29 October 1949, p. 91.

124. Arthur Frank Wertheim, "The Rise and Fall of Milton Berle," in John E. O'Connor, ed., *American History/American Television: Interpreting the Video Past* (New York: Frederick Ungar, 1983), p. 69.

125. Jack Gould, "Family Life, 1948 A.T. (After Television)," *New York Times Magazine*, 1 August 1948, p. 12.

126. Sterling and Kittross, *Stay Tuned*, pp. 864, 867.

127. Gomery, "Finding TV's Pioneering Audiences," p. 122.

3. LEARNING TO LIVE WITH TELEVISION

1. M. C. Faught, "Television: An Interim Summing Up," *Saturday Review of Literature*, 26 August 1950, quoted in Gary A. Steiner, *The People Look at Television: A Study of Audience Attitudes* (New York: Alfred A. Knopf, 1963), p. 4.

2. Dorothy Barclay, "A Decade since 'Howdy Doody,'" *New York Times Magazine*, 21 September 1958, p. 63.

3. Henrietta Battle, "Television and Your Child," *Parents*, November 1949, pp. 45, 56–58.

4. Bianca Bradbury, "Is Television Mama's Friend or Foe?" *Good Housekeeping*, November 1950, pp. 58, 263–264.

5. Karen E. Altman, "Television as Gendered Technology: Advertising the American Television Set," *Journal of Popular Film and Television* 17.2 (1989), pp. 46–56; Richard Butsch, *The Making of American Audiences: From Stage to Television, 1750–1990* (New York: Cambridge University Press, 2000).

6. Lynn Spigel, *Make Room for TV: Television and the Family Ideal in Postwar America* (Chicago: University of Chicago Press, 1992), p. 1.

7. Ibid., pp. 2, 44; Carolyn Marvin, *When Old Technologies Were New: Thinking about Electric Communication in the Late Nineteenth Century* (New York: Oxford University Press, 1988); Brian Winston, *Media Technology and Society, a History: From the Telegraph to the Internet*, Revised Edition (New York: Routledge, 1998).

8. Spigel, *Make Room for TV*; Douglas Gomery, *Shared Pleasures: A History of Movie Presentation in the United States* (Madison: University of Wisconsin Press, 1992).

9. Spigel, *Make Room for TV*, p. 3.

10. Barclay, "A Decade since 'Howdy Doody,' " p. 63.

11. Florence Brumbaugh, "What Effect Does Advertising Have on Children," in Erna Christiansen, ed., *Children and TV: Making the Most of It*, Bulletin 93 (Washington, D.C.: Association for Childhood Education International, 1954), pp. 22, 20.

12. *Christian Century*, 26 December 1951, p. 499.

13. James Miller, "TV and the Children," *Nation*, 22 July 1950, p. 87.

14. Josette Frank, "On the Air: And Now—Television," *Child Study*, Winter 1948, p. 19.

15. Dorothy Diamond and Frances Tenenbaum, "Should You Tear'em away from TV?" *Better Homes and Gardens*, September 1950, p. 56.

16. Spigel, *Make Room for TV*, p. 280.

17. Paul Witty, "Children and TV: A Fifth Report," *Elementary English*, October 1954, p. 349; Paul Witty, "Children and TV," in Erna Christiansen, ed., *Children and TV: Making the Most of It*, Bulletin 93 (Washington, D.C.: Association for Childhood Education International, 1954), p. 7 See also Lynn Spigel, "Seducing the Innocent: Childhood and Television in Postwar America," in William S. Solomon and Robert W. McChesney, eds., *Ruthless Criticism: New Perspectives in U.S. Communication History* (Minneapolis: University of Minnesota Press, 1993), pp. 259–290; James Gilbert, *A Cycle of Outrage: America's Reaction to the Juvenile Delinquent in the 1950s* (New York: Oxford University Press, 1986); Ellen Wartella and Sharon Mazzarella, "A Historical Comparison of Children's Use of Leisure Time," in Richard Butsch, ed., *For Fun and Profit: The Transformation of Leisure into Consumption* (Philadelphia: Temple University Press, 1990).

18. Mary Ann Watson, *The Expanding Vista: American Television in the Kennedy Years* (New York: Oxford University Press, 1990), p. 9; Anna McCarthy, *Ambient Television: Visual Culture and Public Space* (Durham, N.C.: Duke University Press, 2001).

19. Russell A. Jenisch and Wasue Kuwahara, "The Nation's Station: WLW-TV, Cincinnati," in Michael D. Murray and Donald G. Godfrey, eds., *Television in America: Local Station History from Across the Nation* (Ames: Iowa State University Press, 1997), p. 160.

20. Jenisch and Kuwahara, "The Nation's Station: WLW-TV," p. 160; Watson, *The Expanding Vista*, p. 9; Tom Genova, "Television History: The First 75 Years—1947 Quick Facts," 9 April 2001, at http://www.tvhistory.tv/1947%20QF.htm (accessed 26 December 2006).

21. Frank, "On the Air," p. 19.

22. A 1950 survey claimed that twenty million people who did not yet own a set nevertheless still viewed TV in public places such as stores, bars, or someone else's home. Craig Allen, "Tackling the TV Titans in Their Own Backyard: WABC-TV, New York City," in Michael D. Murray and Donald G. Godfrey, eds., *Television in America: Local Station History from Across the Nation* (Ames: Iowa State University Press, 1997), p. 10.

23. Jack Alicoate, ed., *1957 Film Daily Yearbook of Motion Pictures* (New York: Film Daily, 1957), p. 923.

24. Susan Douglas, *Listening In: Radio and the American Imagination, from Amos 'n' Andy and Edward R. Murrow to Wolfman Jack and Howard Stern* (New York: Times Books, 1999).

25. Lynn Spigel and Denise Mann, eds., introduction to *Private Screenings: Television and the Female Consumer* (Minneapolis: University of Minnesota Press, 1992), p. vii.

26. Michael D. Murray and Donald G. Godfrey, eds., introduction to *Television in America: Local Station History from Across the Nation* (Ames: Iowa State University Press, 1997), pp. xxiv, xxii. Stations padded out the afternoons with inexpensive, old Hollywood products from the early 1930s, such as old black and white westerns, serials, "Our Gang" comedy shorts, ancient cartoons, and even silent films.

27. Spigel, *Make Room for TV*, pp. 78, 81. Audience reception studies have made important differentiations between the way that viewers watch movies in a theater and television at home in their living rooms, noting the small size of the screen; the greater use of real-life-size heads in close-ups; and how "active" viewers watch in a distracted manner while playing, talking, or doing other things; and talking back to the set. See also Will Booker and Deborah Jermyn, eds., *The Audience Studies Reader* (New York: Routledge, 2003); David Morley, *TV, Audiences and Cultural Studies* (New York: Routledge, 1992).

28. Spigel, *Make Room for TV*, 38; Jim Heimann, *All-American Ads of the 40s* (Berlin: Taschen, 2002), pp. 228–229, 235.

29. Arthur Asa Berger, *The TV-Guided American* (New York: Walker, 1976), p. 2.

30. Watson, *The Expanding Vista*, p. 11.

31. Spigel, *Make Room for TV*, p. 73.

32. Jeff Miller, "US Television Chronology 1875–1970," 2004, at http://members.aol.com/jeff560/chronotv.html (accessed 26 December 2006); Lisa Parks, "Cracking Open the Set: Television Repair and Tinkering with Gender, 1949–1955," in Janet Thumim, ed., *Small Screens, Big Ideas: Television in the 1950s* (London: IB Tauris, 2001), p. 224. Radio had grown from being in 0.2 percent of U.S. homes in 1922 to 46 percent in 1930 to 81 percent in 1940 and 95 percent in 1950, while television's adoption was twice as fast, over merely a ten-year period (Spigel, *Make Room for TV*, p. 29; Steiner, *The People Look at Television*, p. 25).

33. Jack Alicoate, ed., *1951 Film Daily Yearbook of Motion Pictures* (New York: Film Daily, 1951) pp. 764–765; Roland Marchand, *Advertising the American Dream:*

Making Way for Modernity, 1920–1940 (Berkeley: University of California Press, 1986).

34. Douglas Gomery, "Finding TV's Pioneering Audiences," *Journal of Popular Film and Television* 29.3 (2001), p. 123; Ginger Rudeseal Carter, "WSB-TV, Atlanta: The "Eyes of the South," in Michael D. Murray and Donald G. Godfrey, eds., *Television in America: Local Station History from Across the Nation* (Ames: Iowa State University Press, 1997), p. 89; Tom Genova, "Television History: The First 75 Years—1948 Quick Facts," 9 April 2001, at http://www.tvhistory.tv/1948%20QF.htm (accessed 26 December 2006).

35. Alicoate, *1951 Film Daily Yearbook*, pp. 764–765; Spigel, *Make Room for TV*, p. 32.

36. Figures calculated from data at Genova, "Television History—1948 Quick Facts."

37. Gomery, "Finding TV's Pioneering Audiences," pp. 122–123; Alicoate, *1951 Film Daily Yearbook*," pp. 764–765.

38. Even while TV reception was limited to urban audiences, movie attendance across the nation plummeted, from a weekly high of ninety million viewers in 1947 to only fifty-one million in 1952. Nighttime radio listening fell as well; for example, the Bob Hope show's ratings dropped in half from 1949 to 1951 (Alicoate, *1957 Film Daily Yearbook*, pp. 111–112; Gomery, *Shared Pleasures*).

39. Quoted in Michael Woal and Linda Kowall Woal, "Forgotten Pioneer: Philco's WPTZ in Philadelphia," in Michael D. Murray and Donald G. Godfrey, eds., *Television in America: Local Station History from Across the Nation* (Ames: Iowa State University Press, 1997), p. 48.

40. Allen, "Tackling the TV Titans," pp. 6–7; Douglas Gomery, "Rethinking Television Historiography," *Film and History* 30.2 (2000), pp. 17–28; Genova, "Television History—1948 Quick Facts."

41. Douglas Gomery, "Rethinking TV History," *Journalism and Mass Communication Quarterly* 74.3 (1997), p. 511; Margot Hardenbergh, "The Hustler: WTNH-TV, New Haven," in Michael D. Murray and Donald G. Godfrey, eds., *Television in America: Local Station History from Across the Nation* (Ames: Iowa State University Press, 1997), p. 21.

42. Carter, "WSB-TV Atlanta," pp. 79, 89; Fran Matera, "WTVJ-TV, Miami: Wolfson, Renick, and 'May the Good News Be Yours,'" in Michael D. Murray and Donald G. Godfrey, eds., *Television in America: Local Station History from Across the Nation* (Ames: Iowa State University Press, 1997), p. 110.

43. Jenisch and Kuwahara, "The Nation's Station: WLW-TV," pp. 160–163; Mary E. Beadle, "In the Public Interest: WEWS-TV, Cleveland," in Michael D. Murray and Donald G. Godfrey, eds., *Television in America: Local Station History from Across the Nation* (Ames: Iowa State University Press, 1997), pp. 273–274.

44. Murray and Godfrey, introduction to *Television in America*, p. xxiv; David Weinstein, "Capitalizing on the Capital: WMAL-TV," in Michael D. Murray and Donald G. Godfrey, eds., *Television in America: Local Station History from Across the Nation* (Ames: Iowa State University Press, 1997), pp. 69–70.

45. Gomery, "Finding TV's Pioneering Audiences," pp. 122–123.

46. Don Caristi, "First in Education: WOI-TV, Ames, Iowa," in Michael D. Murray and Donald G. Godfrey, eds., *Television in America: Local Station History from Across the Nation* (Ames: Iowa State University Press, 1997), p. 201.

47. Miller, "US Television Chronology 1875–1970."

48. Interview with W. D. Rogers, April 1992, quoted in Jay A. R. Warren, "A West Texan Fulfills His Dream: KDUB-TV, Lubbock," in Michael D. Murray and Donald G. Godfrey, eds., *Television in America: Local Station History from Across the Nation* (Ames: Iowa State University Press, 1997), pp. 172–174, 185; also, pp. 273–274.

49. Data calculated from the number of TVs shipped to local dealers from 1945 to 1953 as a percentage of households in each state, October 1953. Jack Alicoate, ed., *1954 Radio and Television Yearbook* (New York: Radio Daily Corporation, 1954), pp. 296, 828.

50. Ibid. Radio ownership in the Deep South lagged 15 percent behind the rest of the nation, as well.

51. Lynn Spigel, "Installing the Television Set," in Lynn Spigel and Denise Mann, eds., *Private Screenings: Television and the Female Consumer* (Minneapolis: University of Minnesota Press, 1992), p. 3.

52. Steiner, *The People Look at Television*, p. 4; Michael Curtin, "From Network to Neo-Network Audiences," and Justin Lewis, "From Mass to Meanings," both in Michelle Hilmes, ed., *The Television History Book* (London: British Film Institute, 2003), pp. 122–125 and 126–129.

53. Steiner, *The People Look at Television*, p. 17.

54. Ibid., p. 228.

55. Ibid., p. 25.

56. Paul Lazarsfeld, "Afterword: Some Reflections on Past and Future Research on Broadcasting," in Gary A. Steiner, *The People Look at Television: A Study of Audience Attitudes* (New York: Alfred A. Knopf, 1963), p. 411–412.

57. Horace Newcomb, "The Opening of America: Meaningful Difference in 1950s Television," in Joel Foreman, ed., *The Other Fifties: Interrogating Mid-Century American Icons* (Urbana: University of Illinois Press, 1997), pp. 103–104.

58. Battle, "Television and Your Child."

4. HERE COMES TELEVISION

1. Quoted in John Lahr, "The C.E.O. of Comedy," *New Yorker*, 21 December 1998, p. 76.

2. "The Child Wonder," *Time*, 16 May 1949, p. 70.

3. Harry Castleman and Walter J. Podrazik, *Watching TV: Six Decades of American Television*, 2nd Edition (Syracuse, N.Y.: Syracuse University Press, 2003), p. 36.

4. Frank Rich, "TV Guy: Born in Vaudeville, He Lived in Television," *New York Times Magazine*, 29 December 2002, pp. 22, 24.

5. "The Child Wonder," p. 70.

6. Joe Cohen, "Vaude's 'Comeback' Via Vaudeo: Talent Agents Hopping on TV," *Variety*, 26 May 1948, p. 1.

7. Richard Corliss, "Tuesdays with Uncle Miltie: Mr. Television, the Pioneer of a New Medium, Says Goodnight," *Time*, 8 April 2002, p. 71.

8. Franklin J. Schaffner, *Worthington Minor* (Lanham, Md.: Scarecrow Press, 1985), p. 185.

9. William S. Paley, *As It Happened: A Memoir* (New York: Doubleday, 1979), pp. 238–239.

10. Quoted in Ron Simon, "The Ed Sullivan Show," in Horace Newcomb, ed., *Encyclopedia of Television*, Volume 3 (Chicago: Fitzroy Dearborn, 1997), p. 547.

11. Tim Brooks and Earle Marsh, *The Complete Directory to Prime Time Network and Cable Shows, 1946–Present*, 7th Edition (New York: Ballantine, 1999), p. 299.

12. Jack Gould, "Television Review," *New York Times*, 4 July 1948, p. X7.

13. Quoted in Amy Henderson, *On the Air: Pioneers of American Broadcasting* (Washington, D.C.: Smithsonian Institution Press, 1988), p. 137.

14. Brooks and Marsh, *The Complete Directory to Prime Time Network and Cable Shows*, p. 847.

15. Ibid.

16. Paley, *As It Happened*, p. 200.

17. Christopher H. Sterling and John M. Kittross, *Stay Tuned: A History of American Broadcasting*, 3rd Edition (Mahwah, N.J.: Lawrence Erlbaum, 2002), p. 297.

18. James Von Schilling, *The Magic Window: American Television, 1939–1953* (New York: Haworth, 2003), p. 115.

19. Erik Barnouw, *Tube of Plenty: The Evolution of American Television*, 2nd Revised Edition (New York: Oxford University Press, 1990), p. 104.

20. James L. Baughman, "Nice Guys Last Fifteen Seasons: Jack Benny on Television, 1950–1965," in Gary R. Edgerton and Peter C. Rollins, eds., *Television Histories: Shaping Collective Memory in the Media Age* (Lexington: University Press of Kentucky, 2001), p. 314.

21. Sterling and Kittross, *Stay Tuned*, p. 298.

22. Ed Weiner and the Editors of *TV Guide*, "Milton Berle," *The TV Guide TV Book* (New York: HarperPerennial, 1992), p. 130.

23. Brooks and Marsh, *The Complete Directory to Prime Time Network and Cable Shows*, p. 11.

24. Lawrence W. Lichty and Malachi C. Topping, eds., *American Broadcasting: A Source Book on the History of Radio and Television* (New York: Hastings House, 1975), p. 440.

25. Henderson, *On the Air*, p. 78.

26. Ted Sennett, *Your Show of Shows*, Revised Edition (New York: Applause Theatre and Cinema Books, 2002), pp. 11–12.

27. Castleman and Podrazik, *Watching TV*, p. 39.

28. Sennett, *Your Show of Shows*, p. 18.

29. Brooks and Marsh, *The Complete Directory to Prime Time Network and Cable Shows*, p. 1145.

30. Quoted in Max Wilk, *The Golden Age of Television: Notes from the Survivors* (Chicago: Silver Spring Press, 1999), pp. 167–168.

31. Von Schilling, *The Magic Window*, p. 146.

32. Brooks and Marsh, *The Complete Directory to Prime Time Network and Cable Shows*, p. 1145.

33. Lichty and Topping, *American Broadcasting*, p. 440.

34. Erik Barnouw, *The Sponsor: Notes on a Modern Potentate* (New York: Oxford University Press, 1978), p. 47.

35. Pat Weaver, with Thomas M. Coffey, *The Best Seat in the House: The Golden Years of Radio and Television* (New York: Knopf, 1994), pp. 197–198.

36. Barnouw, *The Sponsor*, p. 47.

37. Brooks and Marsh, *The Complete Directory to Prime Time Network and Cable Shows*, p. 665.

38. Sterling and Kittross, *Stay Tuned*, pp. 827, 864.

39. Henderson, *On the Air*, p. 136.

40. Arthur Frank Wertheim, "The Rise and Fall of Milton Berle," in John E. O'Connor, ed., *American History/American Television: Interpreting the Video Past* (New York: Frederick Ungar, 1983), pp. 70, 75.

41. Rich, "TV Guy," p. 24.

42. Mary Ann Watson, "And They Say Uncle Fultie Didn't Have a Prayer," *Television Quarterly* 30.2 (Fall 1999), pp. 84–85.

43. Jack Gould, "TV Transforming U.S. Social Scene; Challenges Films," *New York Times*, 24 June 1951, p. 1.

44. Mortimer W. Loewi, "New York TV Will Pass A.M. by Fall," *Television*, July 1949, p. 9; Jack Gould, "TV Makes Inroads on Big Radio Chains," *New York Times*, 27 June 1951, p. 20.

45. "This Week's Cover," *Saturday Evening Post*, 5 November 1949, p. 3.

46. "The Younger Generation," *Time*, 5 November 1951, pp. 45, 50.

47. William Manchester, *The Glory and the Dream: A Narrative History of America, 1932–1972* (Boston: Little, Brown, 1973), pp. 576, 580.

48. Douglas Tallack, *Twentieth-Century America: The Intellectual and Cultural Context* (New York: Longman, 1991), p. 221.

49. Charles McGrath, "Big Thinker: His Book Crowned an Age When Eggheads Had the Answers," *New York Times Magazine*, 29 December 2002, p. 34.

50. David Riesman with Nathan Glazer and Reuel Denney, *The Lonely Crowd: A Study of the Changing American Character* (New Haven, Conn.: Yale University Press, 1989), pp. 20–21, 25.

51. Stephanie Coontz, *The Way We Were: American Families and the Nostalgia Trap* (New York: Basic Books, 1992), p. 24.

52. Elaine Tyler May, *Homeward Bound: American Families in the Cold War Era*, Revised and Updated Edition (New York: Basic Books, 1999), p. 166.

53. Coontz, *The Way We Were*, p. 24.

54. Daniel J. Boorstin, *The Americans: The Democratic Experience* (New York: Vintage, 1973), pp. 1, 290, 370–393.

55. Lynn Spigel, *Make Room for TV: Television and the Family Ideal in Postwar America* (Chicago: University of Chicago Press, 1992), p. 101.

56. David Halberstam, *The Fifties* (New York: Fawcett, 1993), p. 195.

57. George Lipsitz, *Time Passages: Collective Memory and American Popular Culture* (Minneapolis: University of Minnesota Press, 1990), pp. 41–42.

58. Ibid.

59. Kathleen Brady, *Lucille: The Life of Lucille Ball* (New York: Billboard Books, 2001), p. 226.

60. Ibid., p. 213.

61. Jack Gould, "TV's Top Comediennes," *New York Times Magazine*, 27 December 1953, pp. 16–17.

62. Michele Hilmes, *Radio Voices: American Broadcasting, 1922–1952* (Minneapolis: University of Minnesota Press, 1997), pp. 131, 146–147, 271–272.

63. William Boddy, *Fifties Television: The Industry and Its Critics* (Urbana: University of Illinois Press, 1993), p. 51.

64. J. Fred MacDonald, *One Nation under Television: The Rise and Decline of Network TV* (Chicago: Nelson-Hall, 1994), p. 59.

65. *Broadcasting Yearbook 1963* (Washington, D.C.: Broadcasting Publications, 1963), p. 20.

66. Thomas Doherty, *Cold War, Cool Medium: Television, McCarthyism, and American Culture* (New York: Columbia University Press, 2003), p. 2.

67. Barnouw, *Tube of Plenty*, pp. 102–103.

68. Kristine Brunovska Karnick, "NBC and the Innovation of Television News, 1945–1953," *Journalism History* 15.1 (Spring 1988), p. 26.

69. Ann M. Sperber, *Murrow: His Life and Times* (New York: Freundlich Books, 1986), p. 314.

70. Quoted in Don Hewitt, *Tell Me a Story: Fifty Years and Sixty Minutes in Television* (New York: Public Affairs, 2001), p. 105.

71. David Halberstam, *The Powers That Be* (New York: Knopf, 1979), p. 38.

72. Quoted in Alexander Kendrick, *Prime Time: The Life of Edward R. Murrow* (Boston: Little, Brown, 1969), p. 86.

73. Jack Gould, "Murrow's 'This Is Korea' Film over CBS Captures Poignancy and Frustration of Life in Battle," *New York Times*, 29 December 1952, p. 25.

74. J. Fred MacDonald, *Television and the Red Menace: The Video Road to Vietnam* (New York: Praeger, 1985), p. 22.

75. Daniel J. Leab, "*See It Now*: A Legend Reassessed," in John E. O'Connor, ed., *American History/American Television: Interpreting the Video Past* (New York: Frederick Ungar, 1983), p. 13.

76. Quoted in *American Masters: Edward R. Murrow—This Reporter*, Part 1 (PBS, 30 July 1990), 58 minutes.

77. Jack Gould, "Murrow vs. McCarthy: 'See It Now' on CBS Examines Senator and His Methods," *New York Times*, 11 March 1954, p. 38.

78. Quoted in "Report on Senator Joseph R. McCarthy," *See It Now*, 9 March 1954.

79. Jack Gould, "TV and McCarthy," *New York Times*, 14 March 1954, p. 2.

80. Quoted in Fred W. Friendly, *Due to Circumstances beyond Our Control* (New York: Vintage, 1968), p. 43.

81. Joseph E. Persico, *Edward R. Murrow: An American Original* (New York: McGraw-Hill, 1988), p. 380.

82. Quoted in *American Masters: Edward R. Murrow—This Reporter*, Part 2 (PBS, 6 August 1990), 58 minutes.

83. Quoted in "Reply by Senator Joseph R. McCarthy," *See It Now*, 6 April 1954.

84. Helen Dudar, "A Post Portrait: Ed Murrow," *New York Post*, 1 March 1959, p. 23.

85. Barnouw, *Tube of Plenty*, p. 182.

86. R. D. Heldenfels, *Television's Greatest Year: 1954* (New York: Continuum, 1999), p. 132.

87. Ronald Garay, "Army-McCarthy Hearings," in Michael D. Murray, ed., *Encyclopedia of Television News* (Phoenix: Oryx Press, 1999), p. 11.

88. Doherty, *Cold War, Cool Medium*, p. 260.

89. Erik Barnouw, *A History of Broadcasting in the United States* Volume 3: *The Image Empire: From 1953* (New York: Oxford University Press, 1970), p. 54.

90. Friendly, *Due to Circumstances beyond Our Control*, p. 77.

91. Manchester, *The Glory and the Dream*, p. 516.

92. Sperber, *Murrow*, pp. xvii–xviii; Persico, *Edward R. Murrow*, p. 434.

93. Friendly, *Due to Circumstances beyond Our Control*, p. 69.

5. THE HALCYON YEARS

1. Pat Weaver, with Thomas M. Coffey, *The Best Seat in the House: The Golden Years of Radio and Television* (New York: Knopf, 1994), pp. 210–211.

2. Russell Lynes, "Highbrow, Middlebrow, Lowbrow," *Harper's Magazine*, February 1949, p. 19; Russell Lynes, "The Taste-Makers," *Harper's Magazine*, June 1947, pp. 481–491.

3. Michael Kammen, *American Culture, American Tastes: Social Change and the 20th Century* (New York: Basic Books, 1999), p. 95.

4. "High-brow, Middle-brow, Low-brow," *Life*, 11 April 1949, pp. 99–102.

5. E. B. White, "One Man's Meat," *Harper's Magazine*, October 1938, p. 553.

6. James L. Baughman, "The Promise of American Television, 1929–1952," *Prospects: An Annual of American Cultural Studies* 11.1 (1987), p. 129.

7. Lynes, "Highbrow, Middlebrow, Lowbrow," p. 26.

8. Thomas Whiteside, "Profiles: The Communicator (Part I)," *New Yorker*, 16 October 1954, pp. 40, 55.

9. Quoted in ibid., p. 36.

10. Quoted in William Boddy, "Operation Frontal Lobes versus the Living Room Toy: The Battle over Program Control in Early Television," *Media, Culture, and Society* 9.3 (July 1987), p. 348.

11. Whiteside, "Profiles (Part I)," p. 40.

12. Pamela Wilson, "NBC Television's 'Operation Frontal Lobes': Cultural Hegemony and Fifties' Program Planning," *Historical Journal of Film, Radio and Television* 15.1 (March 1995), p. 90.

13. Whiteside, "Profiles (Part I)," pp. 40, 50–51.

14. Weaver, *The Best Seat in the House*, pp. 4, 6.

15. "The Chicago School," *Time*, 11 September 1950, p. 73.

16. Ted Nielsen, "Television: Chicago Style," *Journal of Broadcasting* 9.4 (Fall 1965), p. 306.

17. Ibid., pp. 311–312.

18. Michael Curtin, "Organizing Difference on Global TV: Television History and Cultural Geography," in Gary R. Edgerton and Peter C. Rollins, eds., *Television Histories: Shaping Collective Memory in the Media Age* (Lexington: University Press of Kentucky, 2001), p. 346.

19. Robert Lewis Shayon, "Chicago's Local TV Corpse," *Saturday Review*, 11 October 1958, p. 32.

20. Vance Kepley Jr., "From 'Frontal Lobes' to the 'Bob-and-Bob' Show: NBC Management and Programming Strategies, 1949–65," in Tino Balio, ed., *Hollywood in the Television Age* (Boston: Unwin Hyman, 1990), p. 47.

21. Quoted in Vance Kepley Jr., "The Weaver Years at NBC," *Wide Angle* 12.2 (April 1990), pp. 53–54.

22. Bernard M. Timberg, with "A Guide to Television Talk" by Robert J. Erler and Foreword by Horace Newcomb, *Television Talk: A History of the TV Talk Show* (Austin: University of Texas Press, 2002), p. 35.

23. Harry Castleman and Walter J. Podrazik, *Watching TV: Six Decades of American Television*, 2nd Edition (Syracuse, N.Y.: Syracuse University Press, 2003), p. 48.

24. Thomas Whiteside, "Profiles: The Communicator (Part II)," *New Yorker*, 23 October 1954, p. 70.

25. Bernard M. Timberg, "Why NBC Killed Arlene Francis's *Home* Show," *Television Quarterly* 30.3 (Winter 2000), p. 81.

26. Castleman and Podrazik, *Watching TV*, p. 86.

27. Timberg, "Why NBC Killed Arlene Francis's *Home* Show," p. 82.

28. Amy Henderson, *On the Air: Pioneers of American Broadcasting* (Washington, D.C.: Smithsonian Institution Press, 1988), p. 54; Vance Kepley Jr., "Sylvester (Pat) Weaver," in Horace Newcomb, ed., *Encyclopedia of Television*, Volume 3 (Chicago: Fitzroy Dearborn, 1997), p. 1814.

29. Kepley, "The Weaver Years at NBC," p. 59.

30. Weaver, *The Best Seat in the House*, pp. 259–260.

31. Kenneth Bilby, *The General: David Sarnoff and the Rise of the Communication Industry* (New York: Harper and Row, 1986), pp. 255–256.

32. Weaver, *The Best Seat in the House*, p. 209.

33. Richard A. Peterson and Roger M. Kern, "Changing Highbrow Taste: From Snob to Omnivore," *American Sociological Review* 61.5 (October 1996), pp. 900–907; Herbert J. Gans, *Popular Culture and High Culture: An Analysis and Evaluation of Taste*, Revised and Updated Edition (New York: Basic Books, 1999), p. 12.

34. Whiteside, "Profiles (Part I)," p. 38.

35. Steve Allen, *Hi-Ho, Steverino! My Adventures in the Wonderful Wacky World of TV* (Fort Lee, N.J.: Barricade Books, 1992), p. 96.

36. For example, Erik Barnouw, *A History of Broadcasting in the United States*, Volume 3: *The Image Empire: From 1953* (New York: Oxford University Press, 1970), p. 60; Erik Barnouw, *Tube of Plenty: The Evolution of American Television*, 2nd Revised Edition (New York: Oxford University Press, 1990), p. 190; Les Brown, *Les Brown's Encyclopedia of Television*, 3rd Edition (Detroit: Gale Research, 1992), p. 308; Kepley, "Sylvester (Pat) Weaver," p. 1814; Robert Metz, *The Tonight Show* (New York: Playboy Press, 1980), p. 26; Bilby, *The General*, p. 254; Christopher H. Sterling and John M. Kittross, *Stay Tuned: A History of American Broadcasting*, 3rd Edition (Mahwah, N. J.: Lawrence Erlbaum, 2002), p. 308; Timberg, *Television Talk*, pp. 45, 213.

37. Quoted in Ben Alba, *Inventing Late Night: Steve Allen and the Original Tonight Show* (Amherst, N.Y.: Prometheus Books, 2005), pp. 56–57.

38. Allen, *Hi-Ho Steverino!* p. 67.

39. Tom Shales, "Steve Allen, Television's Font of Wit," *Washington Post*, 1 November 2000, p. C1.

40. "'Big Town' Press Set to Roll on TV," *New York Times*, 27 September 1954, p. 29.

41. Jack Gould, "Television in Review: Allen's 'Tonight' Goes Well on Network," *New York Times*, 3 November 1954, p. 41.

42. Gilbert Millstein, "Portrait of an M.A.L. (Master of Ad Lib)," *New York Times Magazine*, 9 January 1955, p. SM17.

43. "Steve Allen," in *Current Biography Yearbook* (New York: H.W. Wilson, 1982), p. 1.

44. Val Adams, "News of TV and Radio: NBC Seeking Show to Rival Sullivan—Items," *New York Times*, 9 January 1955, p. X13.

45. Val Adams, "New 3-Year Pact for Steve Allen; NBC Signs TV Performer as Show's Revenue Rises—Coast Move Still in Air," *New York Times*, 26 September 1955, p. 42.

46. Richard F. Shepard, "'Tonight' Weighs Adding Saturday; Steve Allen Show on NBC May Expand TV Week—Kovacs Sought to Fill In," *New York Times*, 15 October 1955, p. 33.

47. Metz, *The Tonight Show*, pp. 82–93.

48. Ibid., p. 124.

49. Ed Papazian, *Medium Rare: The Evolution, Workings and Impact of Commercial Television*, Completely Revised and Updated (New York: Media Dynamics, 1991), p. 382.

50. Ed McMahon, *Here's Johnny!* (Nashville: Rutledge Hill Press, 2005), p. 40.

51. Tim Brooks and Earle Marsh, *The Complete Directory to Prime Time Network and Cable Shows, 1946–Present*, 7th Edition (New York: Ballantine, 1999), p. 502.

52. Papazian, *Medium Rare*, p. 383.

53. Barnouw, *Tube of Plenty*, p. 350.

54. McMahon, *Here's Johnny!* pp. 34–35.

55. *Broadcasting Yearbook 1963*, p. 20; *Broadcasting Yearbook 1966* (Washington, D.C.: Broadcasting Publications, 1966), p. D37.

56. Christopher Anderson, *Hollywood TV: The Studio System in the Fifties* (Austin: University of Texas Press, 1994), p. 5.

57. John Sharnik, "It's Go Western for Young Men," *New York Times Magazine*, 24 September 1950, pp. SM9, SM16.

58. Leo Bogart, *The Age of Television*, 2nd Edition (New York: Frederick Ungar, 1958), p. 253.

59. Howard L. Davis, "The Rise and Demise of Howdy Doody: A Backstage Story by a Real Insider," *Television Quarterly* 30.3 (Winter 2000), pp. 71–73, 78.

60. Suzanne Hurst Williams, "The Howdy Doody Show," in Horace Newcomb, ed., *Encyclopedia of Television*, Volume 2 (Chicago: Fitzroy Dearborn, 1997), p. 803.

61. "Mr. Crockett Is Dead, Shot as Salesman," *New York Times*, 1 June 1955, p. 38; Peter T. White, "Ex-King of the Wild Frontier," *New York Times Magazine*, 11 December 1955, p. SM27.

62. Douglas Gomery, "Leonard Goldenson," in Horace Newcomb, ed., *Encyclopedia of Television*, Volume 2 (Chicago: Fitzroy Dearborn, 1997), p. 704.

63. Barnouw, *Tube of Plenty*, p. 116.

64. Anderson, *Hollywood TV*, p. 138.

65. Castleman and Podrazik, *Watching TV*, p. 94.

66. "Leonard Goldenson, Force behind ABC, Is Dead at 94," *New York Times*, 28 December 1999, p. B10.

67. "The abc of ABC," *Forbes*, 15 June 1959, p. 17.

68. J. P. Telotte, *Disney TV* (Detroit: Wayne State University Press, 2004), p. 8.

69. Quoted in Janet Wasko, *Understanding Disney: The Manufacture of Fantasy* (Malden, Mass.: Blackwell, 2001), p. 21.

70. Jack Gould, "Television in Review: Disney Brings His Band to the Home Screen," *New York Times*, 29 October 1954, p. 34.

71. Telotte, *Disney TV*, p. 9.

72. Kathy Merlock Jackson, *Walt Disney: A Bio-Bibliography* (Westport, Conn.: Greenwood, 1993), pp. 88, 302.

73. Margaret J. King, "The Recycled Hero: Walt Disney's Davy Crockett," in Michael A. Lofaro, ed., *Davy Crockett: The Man, the Legend, the Legacy, 1786–1986* (Knoxville: University of Tennessee Press, 1985), p. 143.

74. Quoted in Leonard Maltin, *The Disney Films*, Updated Edition (New York: Crown, 1984), p. 122.

75. Bill Cotter, *The Wonderful World of Disney Television: A Complete History* (New York: Hyperion, 1997), p. 64; Castleman and Podrazik, *Watching TV*, p. 95.

76. "The Wild Frontier," *Time*, 23 May 1955, p. 92.

77. Jackson, *Walt Disney*, p. 56; King, "The Recycled Hero," p. 148; Enid LaMonte Meadowcroft, *The Story of Davy Crockett* (New York: Grosset and Dunlap, 1952).

78. John Lardner, "Devitalizing Elvis," *Newsweek*, 16 July 1956, p. 59.

79. David Halberstam, *The Fifties* (New York: Fawcett Books, 1993), p. 475.

80. Karal Ann Marling, *As Seen on TV: The Visual Culture of Everyday Life in the 1950s* (Cambridge: Harvard University Press, 1994), p. 180.

81. Castleman and Podrazik, *Watching TV*, p. 110.

82. Elliot E. Cohen, "A 'Teen-Age' Bill of Rights," *New York Times Magazine*, 7 January 1945, p. SM9.

83. "Presley Termed a Passing Fancy," *New York Times*, 17 December 1956, p. 28.

84. Halberstam, *The Fifties*, p. 473.

85. John P. Shanley, "Dick Clark: New Rage of the Teenagers," *New York Times*, 16 March 1958, p. X13.

86. William Boddy, *Fifties Television: The Industry and Its Critics* (Urbana: University of Illinois Press, 1993), p. 147.

87. Anderson, *Hollywood TV*, p. 141.

88. Ibid., p. 255; Boddy, *Fifties Television*, p. 148.

89. Anderson, *Hollywood TV*, p. 223.

90. Boddy, *Fifties Television*, pp. 149, 155.

91. *2000 Report on Television: The First 50 Years* (New York: Nielsen Media Research, 2000), p. 18.

92. Barnouw, *Tube of Plenty*, p. 262.

93. David Gunzerath, "James T. Aubrey," in Horace Newcomb, ed., *Encyclopedia of Television*, Volume 1 (Chicago: Fitzroy Dearborn, 1997), pp. 103–104; Boddy, *Fifties Television*, p. 155; "The abc of ABC," p. 17.

94. Anderson, *Hollywood TV*, p. 138.

95. Ibid., p. 309.

96. Castleman and Podrazik, *Watching TV*, p. 121.

97. Quoted in "Topside TV Talk," *Newsweek*, 22 April 1957, p. 72.

98. Kepley, "From 'Frontal Lobes' to the 'Bob-and-Bob' Show," p. 41.

99. Quoted in Castleman and Podrazik, *Watching TV*, p. 121.

100. Anna Everett, "'Golden Age' of Television Drama," in Horace Newcomb, ed., *Encyclopedia of Television*, Volume 2 (Chicago: Fitzroy Dearborn, 1997), p. 699.

101. Brooks and Marsh, *The Complete Directory to Prime Time Network and Cable Shows*, p. 980.

102. Quoted in Ned E. Hoopes, "Introduction," in William I. Kaufman, ed., *Great Television Plays* (New York: Dell, 1969), p. 10.

103. Castleman and Podrazik, *Watching TV*, p. 129.

104. Thomas Leitch, *Perry Mason* (Detroit: Wayne State University Press, 2005), p. 5.

105. J. Fred MacDonald, *Who Shot the Sheriff? The Rise and Fall of the Television Western* (New York: Praeger, 1987), p. 58.

106. Brooks and Marsh, *The Complete Directory to Prime Time Network and Cable Shows*, pp. 1245–1246.

107. John G. Cawelti, *The Six-Gun Mystique*, 2nd Edition (Bowling Green, Ohio: Bowling Green State University Press, 1984), p. 2.

108. MacDonald, *Who Shot the Sheriff?* pp. 49–50.

109. Barnouw, *Tube of Plenty*, pp. 262, 264.

110. Brooks and Marsh, *The Complete Directory to Prime Time Network and Cable Shows*, p. 811.

111. *2000 Report on Television*, p. 18.

112. Castleman and Podrazik, *Watching TV*, p. 136.

113. Boddy, *Fifties Television*, p. 149.

114. Sally Bedell Smith, *In All His Glory: The Life of William S. Paley* (New York: Simon and Schuster, 1990), pp. 377–378.

115. Sterling and Kittross, *Stay Tuned*, p. 377.

116. Halberstam, *The Fifties*, p. 664.

117. Thomas Doherty, "Quiz Show Scandals," in Horace Newcomb, ed., *Encyclopedia of Television*, Volume 3 (Chicago: Fitzroy Dearborn, 1997), p. 1331.

118. Halberstam, *The Fifties*, p. 663.

119. Ibid., p. 665.

120. Sterling and Kittross, *Stay Tuned*, p. 861.

121. Newton N. Minow, "Television and the Public Interest," text of speech delivered at the National Association of Broadcasters Convention in Washington, D.C., 9 May 1961, p. 2.

122. Mary Ann Watson, *The Expanding Vista: American Television in the Kennedy Years* (New York: Oxford University Press, 1990), p. 23.

123. Minow, "Television and the Public Interest," p. 2.

124. Jack Gould, "TV Spectacular: The Minow Debate," *New York Times Magazine*, 28 May 1961, pp. SM14–SM15.

125. Wilson, "NBC Television's 'Operation Frontal Lobes'," p. 101.

126. Jack Gould, "Millions of Viewers See Oswald Killing on 2 TV Networks," *New York Times*, 25 November 1963, p. 10.

127. For example, Michael Curtin, *Redeeming the Wasteland: Television Documentary and Cold War Politics* (New Brunswick, N.J.: Rutgers University Press, 1995); Watson, *The Expanding Vista*, pp. 43–45.

128. Thomas Doherty, "Assassination and Funeral of President John F. Kennedy," in Horace Newcomb, ed., *Encyclopedia of Television*, Volume 2 (Chicago: Fitzroy Dearborn, 1997), pp. 880–883.

6. Television and the Presidency

1. Joseph E. Persico, *Edward R. Murrow: An American Original* (New York: McGraw-Hill, 1988), p. 315.

2. Quoted in David Schoenbrun, *America Inside Out: At Home and Abroad from Roosevelt to Reagan* (New York: McGraw-Hill, 1984), p. 265.

3. Ibid., p. 266.

4. Kathleen Hall Jamieson, *Packaging the Presidency: A History and Criticism of Presidential Campaign Advertising* (New York: Oxford University Press, 1996), p. 41.

5. Earl Shorris, *A Nation of Salesmen: The Tyranny of the Market and the Subversion of Culture* (New York: Avon Books, 1994), p. 11.

6. Schoenbrun, *America Inside Out*, p. 271.

7. Quoted in A. M. Sperber, *Murrow: His Life and Times* (New York: Freundlich Books, 1986), p. 384.

8. Steve Neal, *Harry and Ike: The Partnership That Remade the Postwar World* (New York: Touchstone, 2001), p. 247.

9. Ibid., p. 248, 249.

10. Reuven Frank, *Out of Thin Air: The Brief Wonderful Life of Network News* (New York: Simon and Schuster, 1991), p. 53.

11. Quoted in Robert L. Hilliard and Michael C. Keith, *The Broadcast Century: A Biography of American Broadcasting* (Boston: Focal Press, 1992), p. 143.

12. Quoted in Jeff Kisseloff, *The Box: An Oral History of Television, 1920–1961* (New York: Viking, 1995), p. 399.

13. Quoted in ibid., p. 399. See also Jamieson, *Packaging the Presidency*, pp. 58–68 and pp. 82–89.

14. Quoted in *The First 50 Years of Broadcasting* (Washington, D.C.: Broadcasting Publications, 1982), p. 109.

15. Quoted in Edwin Diamond and Stephen Bates, *The Spot: The Rise of Political Advertising on Television* (Cambridge, Mass.: MIT Press, 1984), p. 52.

16. Ibid., p. 47.

17. Erik Barnouw, *Tube of Plenty: The Evolution of American Television* (New York: Oxford University Press), p. 210.

18. Quoted in Jamieson, *Packaging the Presidency*, p. 85.

19. Barnouw, *Tube of Plenty*, p. 136.

20. Shorris, *A Nation of Salesmen*, p. 175.

21. Joseph Laffan Morse, ed., *The Unicorn Book of 1953* (New York: Unicorn Books, 1954), p. 370.

22. Robert Donovan, *Eisenhower: The Inside Story* (New York: Harper and Brothers, 1956), p.146.

23. Critique of President Eisenhower's Telecast of June 3, 1953, sent to Gabriel Hauge, Dwight D. Eisenhower Library Files, Abilene, Kansas.

24. Michael Emery and Edwin Emery, *The Press and America: An Interpretive History of the Mass Media* (Englewood Cliffs, N.J.: Prentice Hall, 1992), p. 366.

25. Lewis L. Gould, *The Modern American Presidency* (Lawrence: University Press of Kansas, 2003), p. 116.

26. Clarence G. Lasby, *Eisenhower's Heart Attack: How Ike Beat Heart Disease and Held on to the Presidency* (Lawrence: University Press of Kansas, 1997), p. 191.

27. Quoted in Michael R. Beschloss, *Eisenhower: A Centennial Life* (New York: HarperCollins, 1990), p. 140.

28. For example, Sharon Jarvis, "Presidential Nominating Conventions," in Horace Newcomb, ed., *Encyclopedia of Television* (Chicago: Fitzroy Dearborn, 1997), p. 1284.

29. Diamond and Bates, *The Spot*, p. 79.

30. Barnouw, *Tube of Plenty*, p. 210.

31. Craig Allen, *Eisenhower and the Mass Media: Peace, Prosperity, and Prime-Time TV* (Chapel Hill: University of North Carolina Press, 1993), p. 148.

32. Stephen E. Ambrose, *Eisenhower: The President* (New York: Simon and Schuster, 1984), p. 421.

33. Vance Packard, "Resurvey of '*Hidden Persuaders,*'" *New York Times Magazine*, 11 May 1958, p. 10.

34. Discussed in Allen J. Matusow, *The Unraveling of America: A History of Liberalism in the 1960s* (New York: Harper and Row, 1984), p. 9.

35. Some passages on the history of the television and the Kennedy presidency originally appeared in somewhat different form in Mary Ann Watson, *The Expanding Vista: American Television in the Kennedy Years* (New York: Oxford University Press, 1990).

36. Theodore C. Sorensen, *Kennedy* (New York: Bantam Books, 1965), p. 102.

37. Quoted in Joe Garner, *Stay Tuned: Television's Unforgettable Moments* (Kansas City: Andrews McMeel, 2002), p. 65.

38. Robert E. Sanders, *The Great Debates*, Freedom of Information Center Publication No. 67 (Columbia: University of Missouri, 1961), p. 11.

39. Quoted in Garner, *Stay Tuned*, p. 65.

40. Quoted in Kisseloff, *The Box*, p. 401.

41. Quoted in Ambrose, *Eisenhower*, p. 604.

42. Diamond and Bates, *The Spot*, p. 102.

43. Gene Wyckoff, *The Image Candidates: American Politics in the Age of Television* (New York: Macmillan, 1968), pp. 44–45.

44. Quoted in "Television: The Vigil on the Screen," *Time*, 16 November 1960, p. 15.

45. Earl Mazo, *The Great Debates*, Occasional Paper (Santa Barbara, Calif.: Center for the Study of Democratic Institutions, 1962), pp. 4–5.

46. "The President and TV," *Television Magazine*, May 1961, p. 48.

47. George Herman, Oral History Collection, John F. Kennedy Library, Boston, Massachusetts.

48. Ray Scherer, "What You Can't See: How Three Presidents Came to Grips with Television in the White House," *TV Guide*, 13–19 January 1962.

49. George E. Reedy, *The Twilight of the Presidency* (New York: New American Library, 1970), p. 104.

50. George Herman, Press Panel Oral History, John F. Kennedy Library, Boston, Massachusetts.

51. Quoted in Carl M. Brauer, *John F. Kennedy and the Second Reconstruction* (New York: Columbia University Press, 1977), p. 260.

52. Brauer, *John F. Kennedy and the Second Reconstruction*, p. 263.

53. The CBS Evening News with Walter Cronkite, videotape, 2 September 1963, available for viewing at the John F. Kennedy Library, Boston, Massachusetts.

54. Charles A. H. Thomson, *Television and Presidential Politics: The Experience in 1952 and the Problems Ahead* (Washington, D.C.: Brookings Institution, 1956), p. 158.

55. Quoted in Ralph G. Martin, *A Hero for Our Times: An Intimate Story of the Kennedy Years* (New York: Ballantine, 1983), p. 288.

7. A Great Awakening

1. Allen Ginsberg, *Howl and Other Poems* (San Francisco: City Lights Books, 1956), p. 34.

2. Daniel J. Boorstin, "The Luxury of Retrospect," *Life, Special Issue: The 80s*, Fall 1989, p. 37.

3. Taylor Branch, *Parting the Waters: America in the King Years, 1954–1963* (New York: Touchstone, 1988), p. 203.

4. Anna Everett, "Civil Rights Movement and Television," in Horace Newcomb, ed., *Encyclopedia of Television*, Volume 1 (Chicago: Fitzroy Dearborn, 1997), p. 370.

5. Tom Mascaro, "Documentary," in Horace Newcomb, ed., *Encyclopedia of Television*, Volume 1 (Chicago: Fitzroy Dearborn, 1997), p. 519.

6. Linda M. Perry, "Civil Rights Coverage," in Michael D. Murray, ed., *Encyclopedia of Television News* (Phoenix: Oryx Press, 1999), p. 45.

7. Marshall Frady, *Martin Luther King, Jr.* (New York: Viking, 2002), p. 100.

8. Branch, *Parting the Waters*, p. 881.

9. Christopher H. Sterling and Timothy R. Haight, eds., *The Mass Media: Aspen Institute Guide to Communication Industry Trends* (New York: Praeger, 1978), pp. 273–274.

10. Everett, "Civil Rights Movement and Television," p. 372.

11. Ibid.

12. Jannette L. Dates and William Barlow, eds., *Split Image: African Americans in the Mass Media*, 2nd Edition (Washington, D.C.: Howard University Press, 1993), p. 284.

13. Thomas Cripps, "*Amos 'n' Andy* and the Debate over American Racial Integration," in John E. O'Connor, ed., *American History/American Television: Interpreting the Video Past* (New York: Frederick Ungar, 1983), p. 39.

14. Christopher D. Geist, "From the Plantation to the Police Station: A Brief History of Black Stereotypes," in Christopher D. Geist and Jack Nachbar, eds., *The Popular Culture Reader*, 3rd Edition (Bowling Green, Ohio: Bowling Green State University Press, 1983), p. 157.

15. Cripps, "*Amos 'n' Andy* and the Debate over American Racial Integration," p. 50.

16. Quoted in Donald Bogle, *Primetime Blues: African Americans on Network Television* (New York: Farrar, Straus and Giroux, 2001), pp. 6, 115, 125.

17. Leonard Wallace Robinson, "After the Yankees What? A TV Drama," *New York Times Magazine*, 15 November 1964, p. SM44.

18. Christopher H. Sterling and John M. Kittross, *Stay Tuned: A History of American Broadcasting*, 3rd Edition (Mahwah, N.J.: Lawrence Erlbaum, 2002), p. 834.

19. Ed Papazian, *Medium Rare: The Evolution, Workings and Impact of Commercial Television*, Completely Revised and Updated (New York: Media Dynamics, 1991), p. 49.

20. Robinson, "After the Yankees What?," p. SM44.

21. Richard Oulahan and William Lambert, "The Tyrants Fall That Rocked the TV World: Until He Was Suddenly Brought Low, Jim Aubrey Ruled the Air," *Life*, 10 September 1965, p. 90.

22. Jack Gould, "TV: In the Wake of Aubrey's Dismissal at C.B.S.," *New York Times*, 2 March 1965, p. 71.

23. Discussed in Les Brown, *Les Brown's Encyclopedia of Television*, 3rd Edition (Detroit: Gale Research, 1992), p. 300.

24. Quoted in "Networks Offer Definition of Sex," *New York Times*, 12 May 1962, p. 51.

25. David Halberstam, *The Powers That Be* (New York: Knopf, 1979), p. 252.

26. Gould, "TV: In the Wake of Aubrey's Dismissal at C.B.S.," p. 71.

27. Harry Castleman and Walter J. Podrazik, *Watching TV: Six Decades of American Television*, 2nd Edition (Syracuse, N.Y.: Syracuse University Press, 2003), p. 156.

28. David Marc, *Demographic Vistas: Television in American Culture* (Philadelphia: University of Pennsylvania Press, 1984), p. 56.

29. "'Vast Wasteland' Speech Holds True after All These Years," Chicago Tribune, 24 April 2001, p. 17.

30. Erik Barnouw, *Tube of Plenty: The Evolution of American Television*, 2nd Revised Edition (New York: Oxford University Press, 1990), p. 403.

31. Sterling and Kittross, *Stay Tuned*, pp. 864, 867.

32. Marc, *Demographic Vistas*, p. 40.

33. David Thorburn, "Television as an Aesthetic Medium," *Critical Studies in Mass Communication* 4.2 (June 1987), pp. 167–168.

34. Val Adams, "Benny to Return to N.B.C. Network," *New York Times*, 26 September 1963, p. 71.

35. Andrew Grossman, "The Smiling Cobra," *Variety*, 7 June 2004, p. 68.

36. Halberstam, *The Powers That Be*, p. 253.

37. Val Adams, "Unexplained Move Stuns Industry: Post Goes to John A. Schneider," *New York Times*, 1 March 1965, p. 1.

38. Charles Champlin, "Can TV Save the Films?" *Saturday Review*, 7 October 1967, p. 11.

39. "Table 36: Network TV Programming Summary," in Lawrence W. Lichty and Malachi C. Topping, eds., *American Broadcasting: A Source Book on the History of Radio and Television* (New York: Hastings House, 1975), p. 440.

40. Judith Crist, "Tailored for Television," *TV Guide*, 30 August 1969, p. 6.

41. "Specials, Specials," *Hollywood Reporter: Television's Fall Issue*, September 1978, pp. 29–30.

42. Bill Davidson, "Every Night at the Movies," *Saturday Evening Post*, 7 October 1967, p. 32.

43. Henry Ehrlich, "Every Night at the Movies," *Look*, 7 September 1971, p. 62.

44. "Johnny North," *TV Guide*, 2 May 1964, p. 8.

45. Henry Harding, "First Attempts at Making Movies for TV," *TV Guide*, 4 July 1964, p. 14.

46. Quoted in "Johnny North," p. 9.

47. Davidson, "Every Night at the Movies," p. 32.

48. Crist, "Tailored for Television," p. 7.

49. Thomas Guback, "Theatrical Film," in Benjamin M. Compaine, ed., *Anatomy of the Communication Industry: Who Owns the Media?* (White Plains, N.Y.: Knowledge Industry, 1982), p. 247.

50. Sterling and Haight, *The Mass Media*, pp. 297–298.

51. Richard Levinson and William Link, *Stay Tuned* (New York: Ace, 1981), pp. 4, 28.

52. Cobbett Steinberg, *TV Facts*, Revised and Updated (New York: Facts on File, 1985), pp. 79–81.

53. Quoted in Patrick Milligan, "Movies Are Better Than Ever—On Television," *American Film*, March 1980, p. 52.

54. "Movies on the Tube," *Newsweek*, 10 April 1972, p. 87.

55. Milligan, "Movies Are Better Than Ever," p. 52.

56. "Man of the Year: The Inheritor," *Time*, 6 January 1967, p. 18.

57. Sterling and Haight, *The Mass Media*, p. 377.

58. Bob Spitz, *The Beatles: The Biography* (New York: Little, Brown, 2005), p. 473.

59. Tim Brooks and Earle Marsh, *The Complete Directory to Prime Time Network and Cable Shows, 1946-Present*, 7th Edition (New York: Ballantine Books, 1999), p. 679.

60. Aaron Spelling and Jefferson Graham, *Aaron Spelling: A Prime Time Life* (New York: St. Martin's Press, 1996), pp. 66–67.

61. Brooks and Marsh, *The Complete Directory to Prime Time Network and Cable Shows*, p. 675.

62. Castleman and Podrazik, *Watching TV*, p. 202.

63. Quoted in "Mothers' Brothers," *Time*, 30 June 1967, p. 41; "Man of the Year: The Inheritor," p. 18.

64. Chester J. Pach Jr., "And That's the Way It Was: The Vietnam War on the Network Nightly News," in Michele Hilmes, ed., *Connections: A Broadcast History Reader* (Belmont, Calif.: Wadsworth, 2003), p. 189.

65. Michael J. Arlen, *Living-Room War* (New York: Penguin, 1982), pp. 6, 83.

66. Daniel C. Hallin, "Vietnam on Television," in Horace Newcomb, ed., *Encyclopedia of Television*, Volume 3 (Chicago: Fitzroy Dearborn, 1997), p. 1767.

67. Quoted in Don Oberdorfer, *Tet!* (New York: Da Capo, 1984), p. 158.

68. George Gallup, *The Gallup Poll: Public Opinion, 1935–1971* (New York: Random House, 1972), pp. 1967, 2074, 2099, 2105.

69. Pach, "And That's the Way It Was," pp. 187–188.

70. Walter Cronkite, "We Are Mired in Stalemate," in *Reporting Vietnam: Part One. American Journalism 1959–1969* (New York: Library of America, 1998), p. 582.

71. Quoted in Halberstam, *The Powers That Be*, p. 514.

72. Josh Ozersky, *Archie Bunker's America: TV in an Era of Change, 1968–1978* (Carbondale: Southern Illinois University Press, 2003), p. 1.

73. Bert Spector, "A Clash of Cultures: The Smothers Brothers vs. CBS Television," in John E. O'Connor, ed., *American History/American Television: Interpreting the Video Past* (New York: Frederick Ungar, 1983), p. 181.

74. Aniko Bodroghkozy, *Groove Tube: Sixties Television and the Youth Rebellion* (Durham, N.C.: Duke University Press, 2001), p. 140.

75. Ibid., p. 145.

76. Brooks and Marsh, *The Complete Directory to Prime Time Network and Cable Shows*, p. 875.

77. Ozersky, *Archie Bunker's America*, p. 41.

78. Brooks and Marsh, *The Complete Directory to Prime Time Network and Cable Shows*, p. 437.

79. Ed Papazian, *Medium Rare: The Evolution, Workings and Impact of Commercial Television*, Completely Revised and Updated (New York: Media Dynamics, 1991), p. 169.

80. "Awe, Hope and Skepticism on Planet Earth," *Time*, 25 July 1969, p. 16.

81. "Man Walks on Another World: Historic Words and Photographs by Neil A. Armstrong, Edwin E. Aldrin, Jr., and Michael Collins," *National Geographic* 136.6 (December 1969), p. 738.

82. Andrew Chaikin, *A Man on the Moon: The Voyages of the Apollo Astronauts* (New York: Viking, 1994), p. 2.

83. Barnouw, *Tube of Plenty*, p. 424.

84. Bruce J. Evensen, "Moon Landing," in Michael D. Murray, ed., *Encyclopedia of Television News* (Phoenix: Oryx Press, 1999), p. 153.

85. Barnouw, *Tube of Plenty*, p. 425.

86. "The Moonshoot: Watching It All at Home, the Astronauts' Families Coaxed Them On," *Life*, 1 August 1969, p. 29.

87. "Threshold of a New Age," *U.S. News and World Report*, 28 July 1969, p. 21.

88. William E. Farrell, "The World's Cheers for American Technology Are Mixed with Pleas for Peace," *New York Times*, 21 July 1969, p. 10.

89. Walter Rugaber, "Nixon Makes Most Historic Telephone Call Ever," *New York Times*, 21 July 1969, p. 2.

90. Barnouw, *Tube of Plenty*, p. 427.

91. Evensen, "Moon Landing," p. 154; "The Moon: A Giant Leap for Mankind," *Time*, 25 July 1969, p. 12b.

92. Quoted in Evensen, "Moon Landing," p. 153.

93. "Awe, Hope and Skepticism on Planet Earth," *Time*, 25 July 1969, p. 16.

94. "The Moon: A Giant Leap for Mankind," p. 13.

95. Quoted in "The Watchers," *Newsweek*, 28 July 1969, p. 28.

96. Barnouw, *Tube of Plenty*, pp. 427–428.

97. "Awe, Hope and Skepticism on Planet Earth," p. 16.

98. "What's Next in Space: 9 More Flights to the Moon," *U.S. News and World Report*, 4 August 1969, p. 28.

99. Quoted in "Men Walk on the Moon," *New York Times*, 21 July 1969, p. 1.

100. Quoted in Seth Schiesel, "Paul L. Klein, 69, a Developer of Pay-Per-View TV Channels," *New York Times*, 13 July 1998, p. B9.

101. *2000 Report on Television: The First 50 Years* (New York: Nielsen Media Research, 2000), p. 18.

102. Ibid.

103. Leonard Sloane, "ABC on Its Way out of the Cellar," *New York Times*, 9 November 1975, p. F1.

104. Les Brown, "Fred Silverman Will Leave CBS-TV to Head ABC Program Division," *New York Times*, 19 May 1975, p. 46.

105. Patricia Aufderheide, "Public Television," in Horace Newcomb, ed., *Encyclopedia of Television*, Volume 2 (Chicago: Fitzroy Dearborn, 1997), p. 1316.

106. *FCC Report and Order on Network Television Broadcasting*, adopted 4 May 1970, 23 FCC 2d, pp. 382, 384, 389.

107. Brown, *Les Brown's Encyclopedia of Television*, p. 434.

108. David J. Londoner, "The Changing Economics of Entertainment," Report for Wertheim and Co., Toronto, 1978, p. 11.

109. "Justice vs. the Networks," *Newsweek*, 24 April 1972, p. 55.

110. For example, William B. Blankenburg, "Nixon vs. the Networks: Madison Avenue and Wall Street," *Journal of Broadcasting* 21.2 (Spring 1977), pp. 163–175; Edith Efron, *The News Twisters* (Los Angeles: Nash, 1971); Erwin G. Krasnow and Lawrence D. Longley, *The Politics of Broadcast Regulation*, 2nd Edition (New York: St. Martin's Press, 1979).

111. Quoted in Paul Laskin, "Television Antitrust: Shadowboxing with the Networks," *Nation*, 14 June 1975, p. 715.

112. Gary Edgerton and Cathy Pratt, "The Influence of the Paramount Decision on Network Television in America," *Quarterly Review of Film Studies* 8.3 (Summer 1983), pp. 9–23.

113. *United States v. National Broadcasting Company*, No. 74–3601-RJK (C.D. Col. 17 November, 1976); *United States v. CBS, Inc.*, No. 74–3599-RJK (C.D. Col. 31 July 1980); *United States v. American Broadcasting Company*, No. 74–3600-RJK (C.D. Col. 14 November, 1980).

114. Hallin, "Vietnam on Television," p. 1768.

115. Brown, *Les Brown's Encyclopedia of Television*, p. 605.

116. Ronald Garay, "Watergate," in Horace Newcomb, ed., *Encyclopedia of Television*, Volume 3 (Chicago: Fitzroy Dearborn, 1997), p. 1803.

117. Brown, *Les Brown's Encyclopedia of Television*, p. 605.

118. "Man of the Year: The Inheritor," p. 20.

119. Sloane, "ABC on Its Way out of the Cellar," p. F2.

8. THE SKY'S THE LIMIT

1. "The Man with the Golden Gut: Programmer Fred Silverman Has Made ABC No. 1," *Time*, 5 September 1977, p. 46.

2. Donald Parente, "A History of Television and Sports," Ph.D. diss., University of Illinois at Urbana-Champaign, 1974, pp. 65–67; Christopher H. Sterling and John M. Kittross, *Stay Tuned: A History of American Broadcasting*, 3rd Edition (Mahwah, N.J.: Lawrence Erlbaum, 2002), p. 355.

3. Christopher H. Sterling and Timothy R. Haight, eds., *The Mass Media: Aspen Institute Guide to Communication Industry Trends* (New York: Praeger, 1978), p. 375.

4. Quoted in Bruce Berman, "TV Sports Auteurs," *Film Comment* (March–April 1976), p. 35.

5. Marc Gunther and Bill Carter, *Monday Night Mayhem: The Inside Story of ABC's Monday Night Football* (New York: Beech Tree Books, 1988).

6. Quoted in Bill Carter, "Roone Arledge, 71, a Force in TV Sports and News, Dies," *New York Times*, 6 December 2002, p. A1.

7. Joe Garner, *Stay Tuned: Television's Unforgettable Moments* (Kansas City, Mo.: Andrews McMeel, 2002), p. 127.

8. John C. Tedesco, "Roone Arledge," in Horace Newcomb, ed., *Encyclopedia of Television*, Volume 1 (Chicago: Fitzroy Dearborn, 1997), p. 81.

9. Quoted in Carter, "Roone Arledge, 71, Dies," p. A1.

10. Garner, *Stay Tuned*, p. 128.

11. Simon Reeve, *One Day in September: The Full Story of the 1972 Munich Olympics Massacre and the Israeli Revenge Operation "Wrath of God"* (New York: Arcade Publishing, 2000), p. ix.

12. "News of Olympic Drama: 22 Hours of Uncertainty," *New York Times*, 7 September 1972, p. 18; John J. O'Connor, "TV: 'Real World' Proves to Be Curiously Elusive; McKay quoted in "A.B.C. Munich Report Raises New Questions," *New York Times*, 7 September 1972, p. 87.

13. Harry Castleman and Walter J. Podrazik, *Watching TV: Six Decades of American Television*, 2nd Edition (Syracuse, N.Y.: Syracuse University Press, 2003), pp. 230, 259.

14. Quoted in Julian Rubinstein, "The Lives They Lived; The Emperor of the Air," *New York Times*, 29 December 2002, sec. 6, p. 36.

15. *2000 Report on Television: The First 50 Years* (New York: Nielsen Media Research, 2000), p. 18.

16. "The Hot Network," *Time*, 15 March 1976, p. 82.

17. Jennifer Moreland, "Olympics and Television," in Horace Newcomb, ed., *Encyclopedia of Television*, Volume 2 (Chicago: Fitzroy Dearborn, 1997), p. 1197.

18. "Brought to You by . . ." *Time*, 19 July 1976, p. 62.

19. Castleman and Podrazik, *Watching TV*, p. 259.

20. "ABC's Wider World of News," *Time*, 16 May 1977, p. 79.

21. Carter, "Roone Arledge, 71, Dies," p. A1.

22. "ABC's Wider World of News," p. 80.

23. Carter, "Roone Arledge, 71, Dies," p. A1.

24. *2000 Report on Television*, p. 18.

25. Quoted in Les Brown, "Fred Silverman Will Leave CBS-TV to Head ABC Program Division," *New York Times*, 19 May 1975, p. 46.

26. "The Man with the Golden Gut," p. 51.

27. Lawrence Van Gelder, "TV's Man for All Networks," *New York Times*, 21 January 1978, p. 38.

28. Les Brown, "Silverman, Who Led ABC to Top, Will Leave to Head Rival NBC," *New York Times*, 19 May 1975, p. A1.

29. *2000 Report on Television*, p. 18.

30. Van Gelder, "TV's Man for All Networks," p. 38.

31. Stephen Zito, "Out of Africa," *American Film*, October 1976, pp. 8–17.

32. Dwight Whitney, "When Miniseries Become Megaflops," *TV Guide*, 19 July 1980, p. 3.

33. "The Effects of 'Roots' Will Be with TV for a Long Time," *Broadcasting*, 7 February 1977, p. 52.

34. Douglas Gomery, "The Television Industries," in Benjamin M. Compaine and Douglas Gomery, eds., *Who Owns the Media? Competition and Concentration in the Mass Media Industry*, 3rd Edition (Mahwah, N.J.: Lawrence Erlbaum, 2000), p. 208.

35. Robert Campbell, *The Golden Years of Broadcasting: A Celebration of the First 50 Years of Radio and TV on NBC* (New York: Scribner's, 1976), p. 84.

36. Mark Kriegel, *Namath: A Biography* (New York: Viking, 2004), p. xii.

37. Erik Barnouw, *Tube of Plenty: The Evolution of American Television*, 2nd Revised Edition (New York: Oxford University Press, 1990), p. 509.

38. Les Brown, "The Networks Cry Havoc," *New York Times*, 12 February 1978, pp. F1, F7.

39. Sterling and Kittross, *Stay Tuned*, p. 511.

40. Jeri Baker, "Can the Cost-Cutters Beat the System?" *Channels: '87 Field Guide to the Electronic Environment* 6.11 (December 1986), p. 41.

41. Les Brown, *Les Brown's Encyclopedia of Television*, 3rd Edition (Detroit: Gale Research, 1992), p. 229.

42. Quoted in N. R. Kleinfield, "ABC Is Being Sold for $3.5 Billion; 1st Network Sale," *New York Times*, 19 March 1985, p. A1.

43. Sally Bedwell Smith, "Turner Makes Offer for CBS; Wall St. Skeptical on Success," *New York Times*, 19 April 1985, p. A1; "At CBS News, a Feeling of Relief; 19 Months of Upheaval," *New York Times*, 11 September 1986, p. D6.

44. Alex S. Jones, "And Now, The Media Mega-Merger," *New York Times*, 24 March 1985, sec. 3, p. 1.

45. John Crudele, "GE Will Purchase RCA in a Cash Deal Worth $6.3 Billion," *New York Times*, 12 December 1985, p. A1.

46. Quoted in Geraldine Fabrikant, "Company News; Head of CBS Quits under Pressure; Paley in Key Role," *New York Times*, 11 September 1986, p. A1.

47. Les Brown, "Looking Back: Five Tumultuous Years," *Channels: '87 Field Guide to the Electronic Environment* 6.11 (December 1986), p. 9.

48. Sterling and Kittross, *Stay Tuned*, p. 864; George Gilder, *Life after Television: The Coming Transformation of Media and American Life* (New York: W.W. Norton, 1990), p. 22.

49. Ed Papazian, *TV Dimensions '97* (New York: Media Dynamics, 1991), p. 21.

50. Brown, "Looking Back," p. 9.

51. Janet Wasko, *Hollywood in the Information Age: Beyond the Silver Screen* (Austin: University of Texas Press, 1994), p. 75.

52. David Gunzerath, "'Darn That Pay TV!': STV's Challenge to American Television's Dominant Economic Model," *Journal of Broadcasting and Electronic Media* 44.4 (2000), p. 670.

53. George Mair, *Inside HBO: The Billion Dollar War between HBO, Hollywood, and the Home Video Revolution* (New York: Dodd, Mead, 1988), pp. 26, 30–31, 53.

54. Brown, *Les Brown's Encyclopedia of Television*, p. 316.

55. Craig Leddy, "Cable TV: The Tough Get Going," *Channels of Communications: The Essential 1985 Field Guide to the Electronic Media* 4.11 (December 1984), p. 35.

56. Brown, *Les Brown's Encyclopedia of Television*, p. 316.

57. Sterling and Kittross, *Stay Tuned*, pp. 454, 834.

58. Ben Brown, "Broadcast TV: Making Money the Old-Fashioned Way," *Channels of Communications: The Essential 1985 Field Guide to the Electronic Media* 4.11 (December 1984), p. 26.

59. Jeri Baker, "Target Practice: The Networks under the Gun," *Channels: The 1988 Field Guide to the Electronic Environment* 7.11 (December 1987), p. 66.

60. *2000 Report on Television*, p. 18.

61. Tom Shales and James Andrew Miller, *Live from New York: An Uncensored History of* Saturday Night Live (Boston: Little, Brown, 2002), p. 3.

62. Ibid., pp. 19–20, 27.

63. George Plasketes, "The Rise and Fall of *Saturday Night Live*: Lorne Michaels as a Television Writer-Producer," in Gary R. Edgerton, Michael T. Marsden, and Jack Nachbar, eds., *In the Eye of the Beholder: Critical Perspectives in Popular Film and Television* (Bowling Green, Ohio: Bowling Green State University Press, 1997), pp. 27–33.

64. Shales and Miller, *Live from New York*, pp. 52–53.

65. Ibid., p. 69.

66. R. C. Longworth, "Chicago: City on the Brink," *Chicago Tribune*, 13 May 1981, p. A1.

67. Joseph Epstein, "Why John Irving Is So Popular," *Commentary* 73.6 (June 1982), p. 61.

68. Grant Tinker and Bud Rukeyser, *Tinker in Television: From General Sarnoff to General Electric* (New York: Simon and Schuster, 1994), p. 96.

69. "All-Time Best Cop Show: *Hill Street Blues*," *TV Guide*, 17 April 1993, p. 38.

70. Tim Brooks and Earle Marsh, *The Complete Directory to Prime Time Network and Cable Shows, 1946–Present*, 7th Edition (New York: Ballantine, 1999), p. 451.

71. Jane Feuer, "MTM Enterprises: An Overview," in Jane Feuer, Paul Kerr, and Tise Vahimagi, eds., *MTM: "Quality Television"* (London: British Film Institute, 1984), p. 25.

72. Tinker and Rukeyser, *Tinker in Television*, pp. 135–136.

73. Todd Gitlin, *Inside Prime Time* (New York, Pantheon, 1983), pp. 75, 279–295, 307–310.

74. Robin Nelson, "*Hill Street Blues*," in Glen Creeber, ed., *Fifty Key Television Programmes* (London: Arnold, 2004), p. 104.

75. Castleman and Podrazik, *Watching TV*, p. 299.

76. Jane Feuer, "The MTM Style," in Horace Newcomb, ed., *Television: The Critical View*, 4th Edition (New York: Oxford, 1987), pp. 52, 54.

77. Susan McLeland, "Grant Tinker," in Horace Newcomb, ed., *Encyclopedia of Television*, Volume 3 (Chicago: Fitzroy Dearborn, 1997), p. 1679.

78. Michael B. Kassel, "Brandon Tartikoff," in Horace Newcomb, ed., *Encyclopedia of Television*, Volume 3 (Chicago: Fitzroy Dearborn, 1997), p. 1625.

79. Tinker and Rukeyser, *Tinker in Television*, p. 177.

80. Kassel, "Brandon Tartikoff," p. 1626.

81. Jane Feuer, *Seeing through the Eighties: Television and Reaganism* (Durham, N.C.: Duke University Press, 1995), p. 62.

82. Tinker and Rukeyser, *Tinker in Television*, p. 171.

83. McLeland, "Grant Tinker," p. 1679.

84. Brooks and Marsh, *The Complete Directory to Prime Time Network and Cable Shows*, p. 228.

85. *2000 Report on Television*, pp. 19–20.

86. David Marc and Robert F. Thompson, Prime Time, Prime Movers: From I Love Lucy to L.A. Law—America's Greatest TV Shows and the People Who Created Them (Boston: Little, Brown, 1992), p. 202.

87. Robert J. Thompson, *Television's Second Golden Age: From* Hill Street Blues *to* ER (Syracuse, N.Y.: Syracuse University Press, 1996), p. 35.

88. Robert J. Thompson, "Television's Second Golden Age: The Quality Shows," *Television Quarterly* 27.3 (Winter 1996), pp. 75–81.

89. Thomas Schatz, "*St. Elsewhere* and the Evolution of the Ensemble Series," in Horace Newcomb, ed., *Television: The Critical View*, 4th Edition (New York: Oxford, 1987), p. 98.

90. "All-Time Best Drama: *St. Elsewhere*," *TV Guide*, 17 April 1993, pp. 11–12.

91. J. Max Robins, "The Four Networks: Bang the Drum Slowly," *Channels: 1990 Field Guide to the Electronic Environment* 9.11 (December 1989), p. 73.

92. Sterling and Kittross, *Stay Tuned*, p. 871.

93. *2000 Report on Television*, p. 17.

94. Sterling and Kittross, *Stay Tuned*, p. 866.

95. David Lachenbruch, "Television in the '90s: The Shape of Things to Come," *TV Guide*, 20 January 1990, p. 13.

96. Thompson, *Television's Second Golden Age*, p. 108; Julie D'Acci, *Defining Women: Television and the Case of* Cagney & Lacey (Chapel Hill: University of North Carolina Press, 1994), p. 207.

97. Shales and Miller, *Live from New York*, pp. 144–146; Schatz, "*St. Elsewhere* and the Evolution of the Ensemble Series," p. 92.

98. Tom Shales, "ABC's Triple Threat; *Life Goes On, Chicken Soup, Roseanne*: Hot Shows, Hot Fun," *Washington Post*, 12 September 1989, p. E1.

99. Thompson, *Television's Second Golden Age*, p. 108.

100. Brown, *Les Brown's Encyclopedia of Television*, p. 537.

101. Brooks and Marsh, *The Complete Directory to Prime Time Network and Cable Shows*, p. 1020.

102. "Prime-Time Programming Costs: A Three-Decade Analysis," *Media Matters: The Newsletter for the Media and Advertising Industries*, August 1986, pp. 8–9; "The Returning Shows," *Channels*, September 1986, pp. 58–59; "Can the Major Networks Curb Prime-Time Program Costs over the Long Haul?" *Media Matters: The Newsletter for the Media and Advertising Industries*, November 1989, pp. 8–9; "The Rise and Rise of Program Prices," *Broadcasting*, 23 September 1991, p. 44.

103. Tinker and Rukeyser, *Tinker in Television*, pp. 175–177.

104. Timothy Havens, *Global Television Marketplace* (London: British Film Institute, 2006), p. 28.

105. Patricia Hersch, "thirtysomethingtherapy: The Hit TV Show May Be Filled with 'Yuppie Angst,' but Therapists Are Using It to Help People," *Psychology Today* 22.10 (October 1988), p. 62.

106. Jackie Byars and Eileen R. Meehan, "Once in a Lifetime: Constructing 'The Working Woman' through Cable Narrowcasting," in Horace Newcomb, ed., *Television: The Critical View*, 6th Edition (New York: Oxford, 2000), p. 154.

107. "A Guide: Satellite Channels—Basic Channels," *Channels of Communications: The Essential 1985 Field Guide to the Electronic Environment* 5.11 (December 1985), p. 57.

108. Byars and Meehan, "Once in a Lifetime," p. 154.

109. Ibid., pp. 148, 155.

110. Sharon Strover, "United States: Cable Television," in Horace Newcomb, ed., *Encyclopedia of Television*, Volume 3 (Chicago: Fitzroy Dearborn, 1997), p. 1721.

111. Tom Shales, "Dark, Potent *China Beach*: On ABC, A Drama Series about Women in Vietnam," *Washington Post*, 26 April 1988, p. B1.

112. Sterling and Kittross, *Stay Tuned*, p. 502.

113. Douglas Gomery, "Cable News Network," in Horace Newcomb, ed., *Encyclopedia of Television*, Volume 1 (Chicago: Fitzroy Dearborn, 1997), p. 271.

114. "The Best of the Rest: Cable Television—CNN," *TV Guide*, 17 April 1993, p. 92.

115. Bruce J. Evensen, "Persian Gulf War," in Michael D. Murray, ed., *Encyclopedia of Television News* (Phoenix: Oryx Press, 1999), p. 188.

116. Gomery, "Cable News Network," p. 272.

9. THE CHANGING FACE OF TELEVISION

1. Robert Goldberg and Gerald Jay Goldberg, *Citizen Turner: The Wild Rise of an American Tycoon* (New York: Harcourt Brace, 1995), pp. 100–101, 116–117; Eric Guthey, "Ted Turner's Media Legend and the Transformation of Corporate Liberalism," *Business and Economic History* 26.1 (Fall 1997), p. 185; Eric Guthey, "Of Business Biography, Media Romance, and Corporate Family Drama," *Business and Economic History* 26.2 (January 1997), p. 290.

2. Goldberg and Goldberg, *Citizen Turner*, pp. 121–125.

3. Jimmie L. Reeves, Mark C. Rogers, and Michael M. Epstein, "Rewriting Popularity: The Cult Files," in David Lavery, Angela Hague, and Marla Cartwright, eds., *"Deny All Knowledge": Reading* The X Files (Syracuse, N.Y.: Syracuse University Press, 1996), pp. 24–26.

4. Jane Feuer, "Genre Study and Television," in Robert C. Allen, ed., *Channels of Discourse, Reassembled: Television and Contemporary Criticism* (Chapel Hill: University of North Carolina Press, 1992), p. 152.

5. Quoted in Goldberg and Goldberg, *Citizen Turner*, p. 131.

6. Tom Bradshaw, "How an Indie 'U' Made It Big with 'Good Old Days' Programming," *Television/Radio Age*, 24 June 1974, p. 26.

7. Ibid., p. 51.

8. Goldberg and Goldberg, *Citizen Turner*, p. 133; Bradshaw, "How an Indie 'U' Made It Big," pp. 50–51. The quasi-newscast featured the eccentric performances of Bill Tush, a weatherman inherited from WRJR who Turner transformed into a news director/anchor and a local cult figure. See Porter Bibb, *It Ain't as Easy as It Looks: Ted Turner's Amazing Story* (New York: Crown, 1993), pp. 84–85.

9. Bibb, *It Ain't as Easy as It Looks*, p. 79.

10. Quoted in Bradshaw, "How an Indie 'U' Made It Big," p. 51.

11. Goldberg and Goldberg, *Citizen Turner*, pp. 175–177.

12. Bibb, *It Ain't as Easy as It Looks*, pp. 85–87; Bradshaw, "How an Indie 'U' Made It Big," pp. 25–26.

13. Bibb, *It Ain't as Easy as It Looks*, pp. 87–88.

14. Bradshaw, "How an Indie 'U' Made It Big," p. 25.

15. Patrick R. Parsons and Robert M. Frieden, *The Cable and Satellite Television Industries* (Boston: Allyn and Bacon, 1998), pp. 53–54.

16. Goldberg and Goldberg, *Citizen Turner*, pp. 158–173.

17. Ibid.

18. Mike Davis, *Prisoners of the American Dream: Politics and Economy in the History of the U.S. Working Class* (London: Verso, 1986), p. 156; Reeves, Rogers and Epstein, "Rewriting Popularity," p. 29.

19. Hank Whittemore, *CNN: The Inside Story* (Boston: Little, Brown, 1990), p. 34.

20. Bibb, *It Ain't as Easy as It Looks*, pp. 151–153; Goldberg and Goldberg, *Citizen Turner*, p. 242; Whittemore, *CNN*, pp. 29–31.

21. Whittemore., *CNN*, p. 28.

22. Reese Schonfeld, *Me and Ted against the World: The Unauthorized Story of the Founding of CNN* (New York: Cliff Street, 2001), p. 5.

23. Whittemore, *CNN*, pp. 46–49; Goldberg and Goldberg, *Citizen Turner*, pp. 235–237; Bibb, *It Ain't as Easy as It Looks*, pp. 162–165.

24. Schonfeld, *Me and Ted against the World*, p. 84; Whittemore, *CNN*, pp. 142–164.

25. Schonfeld, *Me and Ted against the World*, p. 382; Goldberg and Goldberg, *Citizen Turner*, pp. 285–286; Davis, *Prisoners of the American Dream*, p. 220; Barry Bluestone and Bennett Harrison, *The Deindustrialization of America: Plant Closings, Community Abandonment, and the Dismantling of Basic Industry* (New York: Basic Books, 1982), p. 95.

26. Goldberg and Goldberg, *Citizen Turner*, pp. 295–296; Whittemore., *CNN*, pp. 254–256.

27. Schonfeld, *Me and Ted against the World*, p. 291.

28. Gerald O. Barney, ed., *The Global 2000 Report to the President: Entering the 21st Century* (Washington, D.C.: Seven Locks Press, 1988), pp. 2–3.

29. Goldberg and Goldberg, *Citizen Turner*, pp. 284–285, 327–331, 367–368.

30. Ibid., p. 345.

31. Ibid., pp. 352–360, 363.

32. Richard Hack, *Clash of the Titans: How the Unbridled Ambition of Ted Turner and Rupert Murdoch Has Created Global Empires That Control What We Read and Watch* (Beverly Hills: New Millennium Press, 2003), pp. 242–243.

33. Goldberg and Goldberg, *Citizen Turner*, pp. 378, 379.

34. Bibb, *It Ain't as Easy as It Looks*, pp. 319–320; Goldberg and Goldberg, *Citizen Turner*, pp. 396–398.

35. David Kohler and Steve Korn, former TBS lawyers, personal interview by the author, Los Angeles, 22 February 2006.

36. Quoted in Joe Garner, *Stay Tuned: Television's Most Unforgettable Moments* (Kansas City: Andrews McMeel, 2003), pp. 96–99.

37. Priscilla Painton, "The Taming of Ted Turner," *Time*, 6 January 1992, pp. 35–37.

38. National Cable and Telecommunications Association, citing Nielsen Media Research, at http://www.ncta.com/industry_overview/indStats,cfm?statID=1 (accessed 24 February 2006).

39. Cable Television Consumer Protection and Competition Act of 1992 (1992 Cable Act), codified at U.S. Code 47 (1992), §§ 521–573.

40. Quoted in Ken Auletta, *Media Man* (New York: W. W. Norton, 2004), p. 63.

41. Hack, *Clash of the Titans*, p. 348.

42. *Fox News Network, L.L.C. v. Time Warner Inc.*, 962 F.Supp. 339 (E.D.N.Y., 1997); Hack, *Clash of the Titans*, pp. 349–356.

43. *Time Warner Cable of New York City v. City of New York*, 943 F.Supp. 1357 (S.D.N.Y., 1996).

44. "Time Warner Cable Violated Communications Act and FCC Rules by Deleting ABC Television Stations during Nielson Audience Rating Sweeps Period,

FCC Cable Services Bureau Rules," *Entertainment Law Reporter* 21.12 (May 2000), at http://web.lexis-nexis.com.proxy.lib.odu.edu/universe/document?_m=5e0502d3 604a1cc94a9627402477b992&_docnum=1&wchp=dGLbVlz-zSkVA&_md5=202 d36ob44e7b42e8ob96a81e2bf8463 (accessed 20 April 2006).

10. The Business of America Is Show Business

1. Nicholas Negroponte, *Being Digital* (New York: Vintage, 1995), p. 34.

2. Mavis Scanlon, *2006 Industry Overview* (Washington, D.C.: National Cable and Telecommunications Association, 2006), p. 14.

3. Julian Dibbell, "Nielsen Rates the Net," *Newsweek*, 13 November 1995, p. 121; *1998 Report on Television* (New York: Nielsen Media Research, 1998), p. 46.

4. Christopher H. Sterling and John M. Kittross, *Stay Tuned: A History of American Broadcasting*, 3rd Edition (Mahwah, N.J.: Lawrence Erlbaum, 2002), p. 871; Scanlon, *2006 Industry Overview*, p. 8.

5. Scott Chase, "The FCC Sends DBS Flying," *Channels: 1990 Field Guide to the Electronic Environment* 9.11 (December 1989), p. 97.

6. Sterling and Kittross, *Stay Tuned*, p. 874.

7. Scanlon, *2006 Industry Overview*, p. 14.

8. Ibid., p. 5.

9. Jason Mittell, "Genre Cycles: Innovation, Imitation, Saturation," in Michele Hilmes, ed., *The Television History Book* (London: British Film Institute, 2003), p. 48.

10. Todd Gitlin, *Inside Prime Time* (New York: Pantheon, 1983), p. 79.

11. Quoted in Sara Jacobs, "Branded Entertainment," *Hollywood Reporter*, 4 May 2004, at http://209.11.49.186/thr/television/feature_display.jsp?vnu_content_Id= 1000502256 (accessed 4 May 2004).

12. Quoted in Louis Chunovic, "Topic of Branding Is Red-Hot at CTAM," *Television Week*, 30 July 2001, at http://www.tvweek.com/advertise/073001ctam.html (accessed 21 February 2004).

13. Ibid.

14. Quoted in Jacobs, "Branded Entertainment."

15. John G. Cawelti, "The Question of Popular Genres Revisited," in Gary R. Edgerton, Michael T. Marsden, and Jack Nachbar, eds., *In the Eye of the Beholder: Critical Perspectives of Popular Film and Television* (Bowling Green, Ohio: Bowling Green State University Press, 1997), p. 68.

16. ESPN Press Release, "ESPN Research Study Honored by CTAM: Network Branding Survey Singled out as Top Case Study of the Year," 14 March 2000, at http://www.sportsticker.com/ESPNtoday/2000/mar_00/CTAMAward.htm (accessed 21 February 2004).

17. Kim McAvoy, "Special Report: The B&C 25 Media Groups," *Broadcasting and Cable*, 12 May 2003, p. 12.

18. "A&E Television Network," 31 December 2005, at http://www.answers.com/ topic/a-e-television-network (accessed 22 May 2006).

19. "Making History with History," *Reveries*, March 2001, at http://www.reveries .com/reverb/media/scheff (accessed 23 March 2004).

20. "The History Channel: Making the Past Come Alive," *Video Age International* 17.4 (March-April 1997), pp. 22–23.

21. *"Extreme History with Roger Daltry*: Surviving History's Epic Challenges . . . One Day at a Time," Press Release, History Channel, 14 July 2003, at http://www.prnewswire.com/cgi-bin/stories.pL?acct=104&story=/www/story/07-14-2003/0001918305&edate (accessed 6 May 2004).

22. McAvoy, "Special Report," pp. 12, 14.

23. E. W. Scripps Corporation, "Our History," 2003, at http://www.scripps.com/corporateoverview/history/index.shtml.

24. Home and Garden Television, "Background Information on HGTV," Press Release, 16 September 2002, at http://www.hgtv.com/hgtv/about_us/article/0,1783, HGTV_3080_1420294,00.html.

25. Mike Reynolds, "Study: Several Cable Nets Are 'Family-Oriented,' " *Multichannel News*, 14 April 2004, p. 16; Jim Forkan, "Fox News Scores Branding Points," *Multichannel News*, 22 April 2002, p. 12.

26. Caryn James, "To Get the Best View of Television, Try Using a Wide Lens," *New York Times*, 1 October 2000, sec. 2, p. 39.

27. For example, most notably, George Gilder, *Life after Television: The Coming Transformation of Media and American Life* (New York: W. W. Norton, 1992).

28. *2000 Report on Television: The First 50 Years* (New York: Nielsen Media Research, 2000), p. 14; Sterling and Kittross, *Stay Tuned*, p. 867; Scanlon, *2006 Industry Overview*, p. 15.

29. Ed Papazian, *TV Dimensions '97* (New York: Media Dynamics, 1991), p. 21; "Nielsen Report: Americans Have More TV Channels, Watch Less of Them," *Media Buyer Planner*, 14 March 2006, at http://www.mediabuyerplanner.com/2006/03/14/nielsen_report_americans_have_m/index.php.

30. Meg James, "Over 50 and Out of Favor: Advertisers and Thus Networks Are Fixated on 18-to-49-Year-Olds, but Aging Baby Boomers Say They Shouldn't Be Taken for Granted," *L.A. Times*, 10 May 2005, at http://www.latimes.com/business/la-fi-fifty10may10,0,1745275.story?coll=la-home-headlines.

31. Louise Lee, with David Kelly, "Love Those Boomers: Their New Attitudes and Lifestyles Are a Marketers Dream," *Business Week*, 24 October 2005, p. 94.

32. Rob Owen, *Gen X TV: The Brady Bunch to Melrose Place* (Syracuse, N.Y.: Syracuse University Press, 1997), p. 58; Steve McClellan, "The Graying of the Networks," *Broadcasting and Cable*, 18 June 2001, p. 32.

33. Morrie Gelman, "ABC Picked to Repeat in Prime Time," *Broadcasting and Cable*, 31 July 1995, p. 25; *1998 Report on Television*, p. 25; *2000 Report on Television*, p. 18.

34. Allison Romano, "Cable's Big Piece of the Pie," *Broadcasting and Cable*, 30 December 2002, p. 8; Michael McCarthy, "TV Watchers Can Tune in to Wider Selection of Channels," *USA Today*, 12 April 2004, p. 2B.

35. J. J. Yore, "Public Television: An Institution on Hold Recalls Its Great Hopes," *Channels: The 1988 Field Guide to the Electronic Environment* 7.11 (December 1987), p. 85; *1998 Report on Television*, p. 20.

36. Patricia Aufderheide, "Public Television," in Horace Newcomb, ed., *Encyclopedia of Television*, Volume 1 (Chicago: Fitzroy Dearborn, 1997), p. 1316.

37. Statistical Research Incorporated (Westfield, New Jersey), "1990 Public Television National Image Survey," commissioned by the PBS Station Independence Program, 28 September 1990, pp. 2.1–2.8.

38. *1998 Report on Television*, p. 20; quoted in Marilyn S. Mason, "PBS Faces up to the Competition," *Christian Science Monitor*, 4 May 2001, p. 13.

39. Bill Carter, "He Lit up HBO: Now He Must Run It," *New York Times*, 29 December 2002, sec. 3, p. 1; quoted in Carla Power, "Art of the Tube; Market This: HBO Has Put America ahead of Britain as the Leader in Quality TV, and It's Rolling in Profits to Boot," *Newsweek International*, 1 December 2004, p. 77.

40. Quoted in Cynthia Littleton, "Net Still Growing Strong," *Variety*, 3 November 1997, p. 35.

41. Elizabeth Lesly Stevens, "Call It Home Buzz Office: HBO's Challenge—To Keep the High-Profile Programs Coming," *Business Week*, 8 December 1997, p. 77; Verne Gay, "What Makes HBO Tick?" *Cable World*, 4 November 2002, p. 2.

42. "Jeffrey L. Bewkes: Home Box Office," *Business Week*, 14 January 2002, p. 62.

43. John Dempsey, "Billion Dollar Baby: Cable Fees, DVDs Drive HBO's Profits," *Daily Variety*, 23 December 2004, p. 1; Thane Peterson, "The Secrets of HBO's Success," *Business Week*, 20 August 2002, at http://www.businessweek.com/bwdaily/dnflash/aug2002/nf20020820_2495.htm.

44. Polly LaBarre, "Hit Man: Chris Albrecht (Part 1)," *Fast Company*, September 2002, p. 90.

45. Bill Carter, *Desperate Networks* (New York: Doubleday, 2006), p. 1.

46. Bill Carter, "And Then There Were 16," *New York Times*, 28 January 2001, sec. 13, p. 4.

47. James Poniewozik, "We Like to Watch: Led by the Hit *Survivor*, Voyeurism Has Become TV's Hottest Genre," *Time*, 26 June 2000, pp. 56–62.

48. Owen, *Gen X TV*, p. 126.

49. Bill Carter, "Survival of the Pushiest," *New York Times*, 28 January 2001, sec. 6, p. 22.

50. Carter, *Desperate Networks*, pp. 74, 79.

51. Doreen Carvajal, "In Europe, Reality TV Turns Grimmer," *New York Times*, 27 December 2004, p. C6.

52. Quoted in Carter, "Survival of the Pushiest," p. 22.

53. Joel Stein, "Going *Millionaire* Crazy?" *Time*, 17 January 2000, pp. 80–85.

54. Gloria Goodale, "TV Feeds Hunger for Real Stories," *Christian Science Monitor*, 11 September 1998, p. 1; Carter, *Desperate Networks*, pp. 198, 334.

55. Carvajal, "In Europe, Reality TV Turns Grimmer," p. C6; Marc Peyser, "Family TV Goes down the Tube," *Newsweek*, 23 February 2004, p. 54.

56. Lorne Manly, "On Television, Brands Go from Props to Stars," *New York Times*, 2 October 2005, sec. 3, p. 6; Brooks Barnes, "Product Placement Big Business for 'Apprentice,'" *Wall Street Journal*, 5 September 2004, at http://vh10066vi.mocgbahn.net/apps/pbcs.dll/article?AID=/20040905/BUSINESS/409050308/1014.

57. Manly, "On Television, Brands Go from Props to Stars," p. 1.

58. "Big Brother Is You, Watching," *Economist*, 11 April 2002, at http://www.economist.com/printedition/displayStory.cfm?Story_ID=1066250; Daren Fonda, "The Ad Zappers," *Time*, 10 June 2002, Inside Business Section, pp. Y25–Y26; David Kiley and Tom Lowry, "The End of TV (As You Know It)," *Business Week*, 21 November 2005, p. 44; Brad Stone, "The War for Your TV," *Newsweek*, 29 July 2002, pp. 46–47.

59. Todd Gitlin, "The Adorable Monsters of American Culture: Mickey Mouse, Bruce Willis, and the Unification of the World," *Sources* 6.1 (Spring 1999), pp. 75–76.

60. Paul Farhi and Megan Rosenfeld, "American Pop Penetrates Worldwide," *Washington Post*, 25 October 1998, p. A1.

61. Suzanne Kapner, "U.S. TV Shows Losing Potency around the World," *New York Times*, 2 January 2003, p. A8.

62. "Think Local: Cultural Imperialism Doesn't Sell," *Economist*, 11 April 2002, at http://www.economist.com/printedition/displayStory.cfm?Story_ID= 1066620.

63. Kapner, "U.S. TV Shows Losing Potency around the World," p. A8.

64. Philippe Legrain, "Cultural Globalization Is Not Americanization," *Chronicle of Higher Education*, 9 May 2003, p. B9.

65. Kapner, "U.S. TV Shows Losing Potency around the World," p. A8.

66. Quoted in Daniel B. Wood, "At Dawn of Television's 'Third Era,' Networks Already Feel the Heat," *Christian Science Monitor*, 22 May 1995, p. 10.

67. Owen, *Gen X TV*, pp. xii, 5.

68. The headline on the January 24, 1994, cover of *Time* magazine was "Ice Follies: The Strange Plot to Cripple Nancy Kerrigan; Frank Rich, "What O. J. Passed to the Gipper," *New York Times*, 20 June 2004, sec. 2, p. 1; the Clinton quote is also from Rich.

69. Tom Shales, "As the Century Turns: Technicolor Wonders Linking the World," *Washington Post*, 1 January 2000, p. C1.

70. Frank Rich, "Pfc. Jessica Lynch Isn't Rambo Anymore," *New York Times*, 9 November 2003, sec. 2, p. 1.

71. Ron Ansana, *MSNBC News* Broadcast, 11 September 2001.

72. Ron Ansana, *NBC News* Broadcast, 11 September 2001.

73. Vivian Sobchack, ed., *The Persistence of History: Cinema, Television, and the Modern Event* (New York: Routledge, 1996), p. 5.

74. Daniel Dayan and Elihu Katz, "Political Ceremony and Instant History," in Anthony Smith and Richard Paterson, eds., *Television: An International History*, 2nd Edition (New York: Oxford University Press, 1998), pp. 97–106.

75. Mimi White and James Schwoch, "History and Television," in Horace Newcomb, ed., *Encyclopedia of Television*, Volume 2 (Chicago: Fitzroy Dearborn, 1997), p. 771.

76. Emily S. Rosenberg, "September 11, through the Prism of Pearl Harbor," *Chronicle of Higher Education*, 5 December 2003, p. B13.

77. Transcript of Bryant Gumbel, CBS News, *What We Saw: The Events of September 11, 2001—In Words, Pictures, and Video* (New York: Simon and Schuster, 2002), p. 18.

78. William Uricchio, "Television Conventions," *Television Archive: A Library of World Perspectives Concerning September 11th, 2001*, at http://tvnews3.televisionarchive .org/tvarchive/html/article_wu1.html.

79. Rosenberg, "September 11," p. B13.

80. Felicity Barringer and Geraldine Fabrikant, "As an Attack Unfolds, a Struggle to Provide Vivid Images to Homes," *New York Times*, 12 September 2001, p. A25.

81. Lisa de Moraes, "Putting Rivalries Aside, TV Networks Share All Footage of Tragedies," *Washington Post*, 12 September 2001, p. C7.

82. Pat Aufderheide, "Therapeutic Patriotism and Beyond," *Television Archive: A Library of World Perspectives Concerning September 11th, 2001*, at http://tvnews3 .televisionarchive.org/tvarchive/html/article_pa1.html.

83. Marusya Bociurkiw, "Homeland (in)Security: Roots and Displacement, from New York, to Toronto, to Salt Lake City," *Reconstruction* 3.3 (Summer 2003), at http://www.reconstruction.ws/033/bociurkiw.htm.

84. Ken Auletta, "Fortress Bush: How the White House Keeps the Press under Control," *New Yorker*, 19 January 2004, p. 61.

85. Aufderheide, "Therapeutic Patriotism and Beyond."

86. Bill Maher, *Politically Incorrect*, 17 September 2001.

87. Matthew Nisbet, "Economically Incorrect: The Real Reason Bill Maher Got Canned," *American Prospect*, 3 June 2002, at http://www.prospect.org/ webfeatures/ 2002/06/nisbet-m-06–03.html.

88. Ciro Scotti, "Politically Incorrect Is Downright American," *Business Week*, 26 September 2001, at http://www.businessweek.com/bwdaily/dnflash/sep2001/ nf20010926_1917.htm.

89. Office of the Press Secretary, "Press Briefing by Ari Fleischer," White House, Washington, D.C., 26 September 2001, at http://www.whitehouse.gov/news/ releases/2001/09 /20010926–5.html#BillMaher-Comments.

90. Quoted in Auletta, "Fortress Bush," p. 64.

91. Lelia Green, "Did the World Really Change on 9/11," *Australian Journal of Communication* 29.2 (2002), p. 3.

92. President George W. Bush, "Presidential Address to the Nation," Treaty Room, White House, Washington, D.C., 7 October 2001, at http://www.whitehouse .gov/news/releases/2001/10/print/20011007–8.html.

93. Howard LaFranchi, "US Strengthens Its Case against bin Laden," *Christian Science Monitor*, 13 December 2001, p. 3.

94. Denise M. Bostdorff, "George W. Bush's Post-September 11 Rhetoric of Covenant Renewal: Upholding the Faith of the Greatest Generation," *Quarterly Journal of Speech* 89.4 (November 2003), p. 294.

95. *Law & Order*, "Who Let the Dogs Out?," 26 September 2001.

96. Mark Armstrong, "Viewers Flock to Preachy 'West Wing,'" *E! Online News*, 4 October 2001, at http://www.eonline.com/News/Items/0,1,8920,00.html.

97. Marilyn S. Mason, "TV's Changing Landscape," *Christian Science Monitor*, 7 December 2001, p. 13.

98. Matthew T. Felling, "Late Night Humor Bounces back from September 11th," *Center for Media and Public Affairs*, 20 February 2002, at http://politicalhumor .about.com/gi/dynamic/offsite.htm?site=http%3A%2F%2Fwww.cmpa.com%2Fpr essrel%2F2001latenightjoke.htm.

99. Citizens Union Foundation, *Gotham Gazette: NYC News and Policy*, 11 September 2002, at http://www.gothamgazette.com/rebuilding_nyc/topics/culture/ television.shtml.

100. Aufderheide, "Therapeutic Patriotism and Beyond."

101. Citizens Union Foundation, *Gotham Gazette*.

102. Jon Wiederhorn, "Concert for New York City Raises over $30 Million," *VH1 Music News*, 2 November 2001, at http://www.vh1.com/news/articles/1450485/ 11022001/mccartney_paul.jhtml.

103. CMT: Country Music Television, "Six Million Viewers Watch 'The Country Freedom Concert' on CMT to Set a Network Ratings Record," 25 October, 2001, at http://www.findarticles.com/cf_dls/m4PRN/2001_Oct_25/79441943/p1/article .jhtml.

104. Mason, "TV's Changing Landscape," p. 13.

105. Peter Grier and Abraham McLaughlin, "America Anxious on Many Fronts," *Christian Science Monitor*, 12 July 2002, p. 1.

106. Patrick E. Tyler and Janet Elder, "Threats and Responses: The Poll; Poll Finds Most in U.S. Support Delaying a War," *New York Times*, 14 February 2003, p. A1.

107. Project for Excellence in Journalism, "Embedded Reporters: What Are Americans Getting?" *Journalism*, 3 April 2003, at http://www.journalism.org/resources/research/reports/war/embed/default.asp; Associated Press, "Study: TV Viewers Experience Combat Fatigue," *Salon*, 28 March 2003, at http://www.salon.com/ent/wire/2003/03/28/TV/; Brian Lowry and Elizabeth Jensen, "The 'Gee Whiz' War," *Los Angeles Times*, 28 March 2003, p. E1. Embedded reporters are newspeople attached to a military unit that is involved in an armed conflict.

108. John Rossant, "Special Report: A Fragile World—September 11 Shattered the Old Certainties. What Will Arise in Their Place?" *Business Week*, 11 February 2002, p. 24.

109. Barbie Zelizer, *Covering the Body: The Kennedy Assassination, the Media, and the Shaping of Collective Memory* (Chicago: University of Chicago Press, 1992).

110. Paul Farhi, "'D.C. 9/11' Spins Tale of President on Tragic Day: Showtime Docudrama Depicts a Defiant, Decisive Bush," *Washington Post*, 19 June 2003, p. C1.

111. Steven Chermak, Frankie Y. Bailey, and Michelle Brown, eds., *Media Representations of September 11* (Westport, Conn.: Praeger, 2003), p. 5.

112. Christiane Amanpour, CNBC's *Topic A with Tina Brown*, 10 September 2003.

113. Office of the Press Secretary, "Press Briefing by Scott McClellan," White House, Washington, D.C., 29 October 2003, at http://www.whitehouse.gov/news/releases/2003/10/20031029–2.html#6.

114. Rich, "Pfc. Jessica Lynch Isn't Rambo Anymore."

115. Jessica Lynch, *Prime Time Live*, 11 November 2003.

116. Brigadier General Mark Kimmitt, *60 Minutes II*, 28 April 2004.

117. Melani McAlister, *Epic Encounters: Culture, Media, and U.S. Interests in the Middle East since 1945*, Updated Edition with a Post-9/11 Chapter (Berkeley: University of California Press, 2005), pp. 297–299.

118. Jalal Ghazi, "How Arab TV Covered the Third Anniversary of 9/11," *NCM* (New California Media—a Project of the Pacific News Service and WorldLink TV), athttp://news.ncmonline.com/news/view_article.html?article_id=ac411c66ac4ebb7498f66cf20489a585.

119. Clay Risen, "Re-branding America: Marketing Gurus Think They Can Help 'Reposition' the United States—and Save American Foreign Policy," *Boston Globe*, 13 March 2005, p. D1.

120. Simon Anholt with Jeremy Hildreth, *Brand America: The Mother of All Brands* (London: Cyan Books, 2004).

121. Farhi and Rosenfeld, "American Pop Penetrates Worldwide," p. A1.

122. Linda Tischler, "Al Jazeera's (Global) Mission," *Fast Company*, April 2006, p. 42.

11. The Greatest Show on Earth

1. Janet Staiger, *Blockbuster TV: Must-See Sitcoms in the Network Era* (New York: New York University Press, 2001).

2. Brian Lowrey, "'Cosby' Finale End of an Era for Television," *Variety*, 30 April 1992, p. 1; Virginia Mann, "Cosby Exits Laughing," *Record*, 30 April 1992, p. D1; Wayne Walley, "Carsey-Warner: Cosby's Co-Pilots Stay Small and Lean," *Advertising Age*, 16 June 1986, p. 38.

3. Michael Eric Dyson, *Reflecting Black: African American Cultural Criticism* (Minneapolis: University of Minnesota Press, 1993); Herman Gray, *Watching Race: Television and the Struggle for "Blackness"* (Minneapolis: University of Minnesota Press, 1995); Lowrey, "'Cosby' Finale End of an Era for Television."

4. Lawrence Barns, "TV's Drive on Spiraling Costs," *Business Week*, 26 October 1981, p. 199; Peter J. Boyer, "Production Cost Dispute Perils Hour TV Dramas," *New York Times*, 6 March 1986, p. C26; "FCC Repeals Remaining Financial Interest and Syndication Rules," *Entertainment Law Reporter* 17.5 (1995), at http://web.lexis-nexis .com (accessed 4 January 2007); Paul Richter, "Networks Get the Picture of Cost-Cutting," *New York Times*, 26 October 1986, sec. 5, p. 1.

5. Bruce M. Owen and Steven S. Wildman, *Video Economics* (Cambridge: Harvard University Press, 1992); Richter, "Networks Get the Picture of Cost Cutting."

6. "Europe's 'Other' Channels: Numbers Double Every Three Years," *Screen Digest*, 1 March 1997, pp. 57–64.

7. Quoted in Richard W. Stevenson, "TV Boom in Europe Is Aiding Hollywood," *New York Times*, 28 December 1987, p. D1.

8. Paul Richter, "Viacom Quietly Becomes a Major Force in TV," *Los Angeles Times*, 22 September 1985, sec. 5, p. 1.

9. James Flanigan, "The American Dream Is Best Export U.S. Has," *Los Angeles Times*, 9 September 1987, sec. 4, p. 1; John Lippman, "Banking on the Huxtables," *Los Angeles Times*, 30 April 1992, p. D1; Richter, "Viacom Quietly Becomes Major Force in TV"; Viacom, *Securities and Exchange Commission Form 10-K*, 1987, at http://web.lexis-nexis.com (accessed 4 January 2007).

10. Viacom, *National Automated Accounting Research System Annual Report*, 1985, at http://web.lexis-nexis.com (accessed 4 January 2007); Viacom, *Securities and Exchange Commission Form 10-K*, 1987; Viacom, *Securities and Exchange Commission Form 10-K*, 1991, at http://web.lexis-nexis.com (accessed 4 January 2007).

11. Ella Taylor, *Prime-Time Families in Post-War America* (Berkeley: University of California Press, 1989), p. 163.

12. Viacom advertisement, *TV World*, February 1985, p. 116.

13. Linda Fuller, The Cosby Show: *Audiences, Impact, and Implications* (Westport, Conn.: Greenwood, 1992); "What's Hot on TV Worldwide," *Advertising Age*, 1 December 1986, Global Media section, p. 60; Carla Hall, Victoria Dawson, Jacqueline Trescott, Desson Howe, and Megan Rosenfeld, "Thursday Night at the Huxtables," *Washington Post*, 6 November 1986, p. D1; Steve Mufson, "The 'Cosby Plan' for South Africa," *Wall Street Journal*, 30 July 1986, sec. 1, p. 17; Marilyn Raschka, "Hold Your Fire, It's 'Cosby' Time: TV Show's Popularity Cuts across All Factions in Beirut," *Chicago Tribune*, 19 June 1988, sec. 5, p. 1.

14. "Belgian Parliament Adopts TV Law as Flanders Socialists Withdraw Ban," *New Media Markets*, 26 November 1986, at http://web.lexis-nexis.com (accessed 4 January 2007); James Buxton, "Italy's Private Television Networks Become Legal," *Financial Times*, 6 February 1985, p. I2; Fuller, *The Cosby Show*; Greg Henry, "Why Is It That a Show Which Pulls a Massive 51 Per Cent Following in Its Home Country Can Only Muster a Measly Three Million Viewers Here?" *Televisuality*, 21 April

1986, pp. 33–34; "La Cinq and M6 Still Not Meeting Obligations," *New Media Markets*, 24 May 1989, at http://www.lexis-nexis.com (accessed 4 January 2007).

15. Henry, "Why Is It?"; "La Cinq and M6 Not Meeting Obligations"; Viacom advertisement, *TV World*, February 1986, p. 25.

16. Both quoted in Mark Schapiro, "Lust-Greed-Sex-Power: Translatable Anywhere," *New York Times*, 2 June 1991, p. B29.

17. Betsy Tobin, "The Language of Laughs," *TV World*, October 1990, pp. 29.

18. Richard Huff, "Sharing the Joke," *Television Business International*, October 1996, p. 52.

19. Cheryl Heuton, "An Enviable Situation: The Format Once Declared Dead Now Rules Syndication," *Channels*, 17 December 1990, pp. 36–38.

20. Greg Spring, "Why Some U.S. Sitcoms Can Conquer Europe," *Electronic Media*, 5 October 1998, p. 6.

21. Fuller, *The Cosby Show*, reports on audience surveys in thirty countries that verify that the show was an audience favorite in virtually every market.

22. Monica Payne, "The 'Ideal' Black Family? A Caribbean View of *The Cosby Show*," *Journal of Black Studies* 25 (1994), pp. 231–249; Fuller, *The Cosby Show*.

23. Sut Jhally and Justin Lewis, *Enlightened Racism* (San Francisco: Westview, 1992).

24. Gray, *Watching Race*, p. 81. The political consequences of *The Cosby Show*'s efforts to connect racial dignity with upper-class life and culture have been widely debated in the books and articles cited earlier in this chapter.

25. Mel Watkins, *On the Real Side: Laughing, Lying, and Signifying—The Underground Tradition of African American Humor That Transformed American Culture from Slavery to Richard Pryor* (New York: Simon and Shuster, 1994); Shane White and Graham White, *Stylin': African American Expressive Culture from its Beginnings to the Zoot Suit* (Ithaca, N.Y.: Cornell University Press, 1998).

26. John Downing, "'The Cosby Show' and American Racial Discourse," in G. Smitherman-Donaldson and T.A. Van Dijk, eds., *Discourse and Discrimination* (Detroit: Wayne State University Press, 1988), p. 62.

27. Quoted in Jhally and Lewis, *Enlightened Racism*, p. 81.

28. Quoted in Payne, "The 'Ideal' Black Family?" p. 235.

29. Quoted in Fuller, *The Cosby Show*, p. 111.

30. For an overview of the history of ridiculous black stereotypes in white Western culture, see, in particular, Jan Nederveen Pieterse, *White on Black: Images of Africa and Blacks in Western Popular Culture* (New Haven, Conn.: Yale University Press, 1992).

31. Quoted in Fuller, *The Cosby Show*, p. 114.

32. Downing, "'The Cosby Show' and American Racial Discourse," p. 70.

33. Quoted in Raschka, "Hold Your Fire," p. 16.

34. Quoted in Fuller, *The Cosby Show*, p. 107.

35. For good discussions of the history of white portrayals of black culture in the Western Hemisphere, see Pieterse, *White on Black*, and Eric Lott, *Love and Theft: Blackface Minstrelsy and the American Working Class* (New York: Oxford University Press, 1993).

36. Quoted in Mufson, "The 'Cosby' Plan," p. 17.

37. Quoted in Fuller, *The Cosby Show*, p. 114.

38. Quoted in Payne, "The 'Ideal' Black Family?" p. 284.

39. Gregorian quoted in Huff, "Sharing the Joke," p. 52; Lynn quoted in Richard Mahler, "What Sells Best Overseas," *Electronic Media*, 15 January 1990, p. 82.

40. Hillary Curtis, "Have Comedy, Will Travel?" *TV World*, August/September, 1997, pp. 31–36; Huff, "Sharing the Joke;" Spring, "Why Some U.S. Sitcoms Can Conquer Europe;" Tobin, "The Language of Laughs."

41. Quoted in Mahler, "What Sells Best Overseas," p. 82.

42. The preceding three quotations are taken from personal interviews that I conducted with international television executives in 1999; some of these interviews were granted on condition of anonymity.

43. Jhally and Lewis, *Enlightened Racism*, pp. 36–48.

44. Herb Lazarus, president, Casey-Werner International, personal communication, 11 May 1999; anonymous director of international research at a major Hollywood distributor, personal communication, 11 May 1999; anonymous European television buyer, personal communication, 11 May 1999.

45. Ann S. Dinerman and Dom Serafini, "The World's 95 Power TV Buyers," *Video Age International*, June 16, 1997, p. 1; William Dawkins, "US Film Makers Step up Attack on EC Television Proposals," *Financial Times*, August 1, 1989, p. I2.

46. Quoted in Curtis, "Have Comedy, Will Travel?" p. 36.

47. Anonymous vice president of international sales at a major Hollywood distributor, personal communication, 28 June 1999.

48. Dinerman and Serafini, "The World's 95 Power TV Buyers," p. 1.

49. Roland Barthes, "The Great Family of Man," in *Mythologies*, trans. Annette Lavers (New York: Hill and Wang, 1972), p. 101.

12. Tune in Locally, Watch Globally

1. Anthony Giddens, *Runaway World: How Globalization Is Shaping Our Lives* (New York: Routledge, 2000), p. 37.

2. Giddens, *Runaway World*, p. 25.

3. Ibid., p. 28.

4. "Millennium in Maps: Cultures," *National Geographic* 196.2 (August 1999), p. 140; A. C. Nielsen, "429 Million People Worldwide Have Internet Access, According to Nielsen/NetRatings," Press Release, 11 June 2001.

5. Miniwatts Marketing Group, "World Internet Users and Population Statistics," *Internet World Stats*, June 2006, at http://www.internetworldstats.com/stats.htm.

6. "2000: Globalization Realized?—A Small World after All," *National Geographic* 196.2 (August 1999), p. 140.

7. Peter Chernin, "Golden Oldies," *Wall Street Journal*, 9 February 2006, p. A12.

8. Arthur C. Clarke, "Extra-Terrestrial Relays: Can Rocket Stations Give Worldwide Radio Coverage?" *Wireless World*, October 1945, p. 305.

9. Edmund L. Andrews, "Communication Bill Signed, and the Battles Begin Anew," *New York Times*, 9 February 1996, p. A1.

10. Steve Rosenbush and Peter Elstrom, "8 Lessons from the Telecom Mess," *Business Week*, 13 August 2001, at http://www.businessweek.com/magazine/content/01_33/b3745001.htm.

11. "Power in Your Hand," *Economist*, 11 April 2002, at http://www.economist.com/printedition/displayStory.cfm?Story_ID=1066262.

12. Edmund L. Andrews, "Communication Reshaped: A 'Digital Free-for-All'; A Measure's Long Reach," *New York Times*, 2 February 1996, p. A1.

13. Fritz J. Messere, "Telecommunication Act of 1996: U.S. Communications Policy Legislation," in Horace Newcomb, ed., *Encyclopedia of Television*, Volume 3 (Chicago: Fitzroy Dearborn, 1997), pp. 1740–1744.

14. Elizabeth Lesly, with Ronald Grover and I. Jeanne Dugan, "*Seinfeld*: The Economics of a TV Supershow and What It Means for NBC and the Industry," *Business Week*, 2 June 1997, p. 120.

15. Especially, George Gilder, *Life after Television: The Coming Transformation of Media and American Life* (New York: W. W. Norton, 1992); George Gilder, *Telecosm: How Infinite Bandwidth Will Revolutionize Our World* (New York: Free Press, 2000).

16. Chernin, "Golden Oldies," p. A12.

17. Lesly, with Grover and Dugan, "*Seinfeld*," p. 121.

18. "All in the Family: In Television, It's Best to Be Big," *Economist*, 11 April 2002, at http://www.economist.com/printedition/displayStory.cfm?Story_ID=1066632.

19. "Power in Your Hand," at http://www.economist.com/printedition/displayStory .cfm?Story_ID=1066262.

20. Nicholas Negroponte, *Being Digital* (New York: Vintage, 1995), pp. 48–49.

21. Ibid., p. 174.

22. Todd Gitlin, "The Adorable Monsters of American Culture: Mickey Mouse, Bruce Willis, and the Unification of the World," *Sources* 6.1 (Spring 1999), p. 76; Helge Rønning and Knut Lundby, *Human Communication in Media and Communication* (Oslo: Norwegian University Press, 1991).

23. "A More Urban World: The Ascent of Cities," *National Geographic* 196.2 (August 1999), p. 140.

24. Todd Gitlin, "Who Are the World?" paper presented at the American Enterprise Institute Conference: The New Global Popular Culture—Is It American? Is It Good for America? Is It Good for the World? in Washington, D.C., 10 March 1992, p. 1.

25. Heather Green, Tom Lowry, and Catherine Yang, "The New Radio Revolution," *Business Week*, 3 March 2005, p. 32.

26. Quoted in Susannah Fox, Janna Quitney Anderson, and Lee Rainie, *The Future of the Internet: Technology Experts and Scholars Evaluate Where the Network Is Headed in the Next Ten Years* (Washington, D.C.: Pew Internet and American Life Project, 2005), pp. 37–39.

27. U.S. Census Bureau, *Statistical Abstract of the United States* (Washington, D.C.: U.S. Government Printing Office, 2006), pp. 845–847.

28. Quoted in Howard Wolinsky, "Breaking Down Our Wired World," *Chicago Sun-Times*, 15 January 2006, p. A26.

29. Marshall McLuhan, *Understanding Media: The Extensions of Man* (New York: Signet Books, 1964), p. ix.

30. Marshall McLuhan and Quentin Fore, with coordination by Jerome Agel, *War and Peace in the Global Village* (New York: Bantam Books, 1968), p. 134.

31. McLuhan, *Understanding Media*, p. 19.

32. Paul Levinson, *Digital McLuhan: A Guide to the Information Millennium* (New York: Routledge, 1999), pp. 6–7.

33. Eric McLuhan and Frank Zingrone, eds., *Essential McLuhan* (New York: Basic Books, 1995), p. 296.

34. Levinson, *Digital McLuhan*, p. 7.

35. "All in the Family: In Television, It's Best to Be Big."

36. David Kiley and Tom Lowry, "The End of TV (As You Know It)," *Business Week*, 21 November 2005, p. 44; Alex Pham and Claire Hoffman, "Broadcasters Agree to Go All Digital: After Resisting for Years, TV Stations Agree to Stop Transmitting Analog Signals in 2009," *L.A. Times*, 13 July 2005, at http://www.latimes.com/business/la-fi-dtv13jul13,0,7634224.story?track=tottext; Barry Fox, "Television's Big Switch," *The Economist: Intelligent Life*, Summer 2005, at http://www.economist.com/intelligentlife/leisure/displayStory.cfm?Story_ID=3930878.

37. Glen Dickson, "ABC: Millennials and Mobile Key for New Media," *Broadcasting and Cable*, 24 May 2006, at http://www.broadcastingcable.com/index.asp?layout=articlePrint&articleID=CA6337518.

38. Chernin, "Golden Oldies," p. A12.

39. Gregory M. Lamb, "It Rings, It Plays, It Has TV," *Christian Science Monitor*, 21 July 2005, p. 14.

40. Kiley and Lowry, "The End of TV (As You Know It)," p. 40.

41. Eric Rothenbuhler, "Frank N. Magid Associates," in Horace Newcomb, ed., *Encyclopedia of Television*, Volume 2 (Chicago: Fitzroy Dearborn, 1997), p. 982.

42. Frank N. Magid Associates, Inc., "Generational Media Study," 21 September 2004, at http://www.online-publishers.org/pdf/opa_generational_study_sep04.pdf.

43. Scott Carlson, "The Net Generation in the Classroom," *Chronicle of Higher Education*, 7 October 2005, p. A34.

44. Dickson, "ABC: Millennials and Mobile Key for New Media," at http://www.broadcastingcable.com/index.asp?layout=articlePrint&articleID=CA6337518.

45. Quoted in Lamb, "It Rings, It Plays, It Has TV," p. 14. See also Dan Steinbock, *The Mobile Revolution: The Making of Worldwide Mobile Markets* (London: Kogan Page, 2005).

46. Frank N. Magid Associates, "Generational Media Study."

47. Quoted in R. Thomas Umstead, "Broadband Channels: Ready for Primetime," *Multichannel News*, 5 June 2006, at http://www.multichannel.com/index.asp?layout=articlePrint&articleid=CA6340644.

48. Erla Zwingle, "Goods Move. People Move. Ideas Move. And Cultures Change," *National Geographic* 196.2 (August 1999), p. 17.

49. Maureen Ryan, "6 Ways TV Is Changing Your Life," *Chicago Tribune*, 1 May 2005, at http://www.chicagotribune.com/news/local/chi-0505010466may01,0,926375.story?page=1&coll=chi-news-hed.

50. Quoted in Lorne Manly and John Markoff, "Steal This Show," *New York Times*, 30 January 2005, sec. 2, p. 1; Ryan, "6 Ways TV Is Changing Your Life."

51. Jacques Steinberg, "Digital Media Brings Profits (and Tensions) to TV Studios," *New York Times*, 14 May 2006, sec. 3, p. 1.

52. Bill Carter, "Deal Brings an End to NBC-Paxson Feud," *New York Times*, 8 November 2005, p. C7.

53. John Eggerton, "WB, UPN Fold Shocks NATPE in Vegas," *Broadcasting and Cable*, 24 January 2006, at http://www.broadcastingcable.com/article/CA6301540.html?display=Breaking+News; Allison Romano, "The Mating Game: Orphaned Stations Consider a New Option," *Broadcasting and Cable*, 27 February 2006, at http://www.broadcastingcable.com/article/CA6310996.html?display=Feature.

54. Karl Taro Greenfeld, "A Media Giant," *Time*, 20 September 1999, p. 53.

55. "Viacom Completes Split into 2 Companies," *New York Times*, 2 January 2006, p. C2.

56. David D. Kirkpatrick and Jim Rutenberg, "AOL Reporting Further Losses; Turner Resigns," *New York Times*, 30 January 2003, p. A1.

57. Quoted in "Up the Tube," *Economist*, 11 April 2002, at http://www.economist .com/printedition/displayStory.cfm?Story_ID=1066319.

58. Steinberg, "Digital Media Brings Profits (and Tensions) to TV Studios," p. 1.

59. David Herman, "Thank God for HBO," *Prospect*, November 2004, at http:// www.prospect-magazine.co.uk/article_details.php?Id=6510.

60. "The Way of Success: A Bent toward Counterprogramming Informs Much of the Original Programming on HBO," *Multichannel News*, 4 November 2002, p. 6.

61. Bill Carter, *Desperate Networks* (New York: Doubleday, 2006), p. 162.

62. Chernin, "Golden Oldies," p. A12.

63. Linda Haugsted, "Making Sense of New Tech," *Multichannel News*, 15 May 2006, at http://www.multichannel.com/index.asp?layout=articlePrint&articleid= CA6334322.

64. Chernin, "Golden Oldies," p. A12.

65. R. Thomas Umstead, "Cable Follows Script for Summer Success," *Multichannel News*, 22 May 2006, at http://www.multichannel.com/index.asp?layout= articlePrint&articleid=CA6336344.

66. Shelly Freierman, "Drilling Down: We're Spending More Time Watching TV," *New York Times*, 9 January 2006, p. C3.

67. Howard I. Finberg, "Our Complex Media Day," *Poynteronline* (Poynter Institute), 26 September 2005, at http://www.poynter.org/content/content_view.asp?Id= 89510.

68. Bradley Johnson, "How U.S. Consumers Spend Their Time: A U.S. Government Study of a Day in the Life of America," *Advertising Age*, 2 May 2005, at http:// www.adage.com/news.cms?newsid=44895.

69. Wolinsky, "Breaking Down Our Wired World," p. A26.

70. Robert A. Papper, Michael E. Holmes, and Mark N. Popovich, "Middletown Media Studies: Media Multitasking and How Much People Really Use the Media," *International Digital Media and Arts Association Journal* 1.1 (Spring 2004), pp. 5, 29, 37.

71. Sharon Waxman, "Hot on the Trail of Consumers: At an Industry Media Lab, Close Views of Multitasking," *New York Times*, 15 May 2006, p. C1.

72. Finberg, "Our Complex Media Day."

73. Edward C. Baig, "Gates Foresees Digital Decade," *U.S.A. Today*, 8 January 2002, at http://www.usatoday.com/tech/news/2002/01/08/gates-interview.htm.

74. Rudolf Arnheim, *Film as Art* (Berkeley: University of California Press, 1957), p. 195. Originally published 1935.

75. Kathy Roeder, "Technology Is Changing How Americans Watch TV, Says TV Watch," TV Watch Press Release, 8 March 2006, at http://releases.usnewswire. com/GetRelease.asp?Id=62036.

76. For example, Patricia Aufderheide, *Media Literacy: A Report of the National Leadership Conference on Media Literacy* (Washington, D.C.: Aspen Institute, 1993); David Bianculli, *Teleliteracy: Taking Television Seriously* (New York: Continuum, 1992); David Buckingham, *Media Education: Literacy, Learning and Contemporary Culture* (Cambridge, U.K.: Polity Press, 2003); James A. Brown, *Television "Critical*

Viewing Skill" Education: Major Media Literacy Projects in the United States and Selected Countries (Hillsdale, N.J.: Lawrence Erlbaum, 1991); Peggy Charren and Martin W. Sandler, *Changing Channels: Living (Sensibly) with Television* (Reading, Mass.: Addison-Wesley, 1983); Robert Kubey, ed., *Media Literacy in the Information Age: Current Perspectives* (Somerset, N.J.: Transaction Publishers, 2001); Janette K. Muir, *Introduction to Media Literacy* (Dubuque, Iowa: Kendall/Hunt, 1998); W. James Potter, *Media Literacy*, 3rd Edition (Thousand Oaks, Calif.: Sage, 2005); W. James Potter, *Theory of Media Literacy: A Cognitive Approach* (Thousand Oaks, Calif.: Sage, 2004); Art Silverblatt, *Media Literacy: Keys to Interpreting Media Messages* (Westport, Conn.: Praeger, 1995); Kathleen Tyner, *Literacy in a Digital World: Teaching and Learning in the Age of Information* (Hillsdale, N.J.: Lawrence Erlbaum, 1998).

GENERAL INDEX

TELEVISION PROGRAMMING INDEX